ENGLISH RECUSANT LITERATURE
1558–1640

Selected and Edited by
D. M. ROGERS

Volume 299

ORAZIO TORSELLINO
The Admirable Life of S. Francis Xavier
1632

ORAZIO TORSELLINO

The Admirable Life of S. Francis Xavier

1632

The Scolar Press

1976

ISBN 0 85967 300 6

Published and printed in Great Britain by
The Scolar Press Limited, 59-61 East Parade,
Ilkley, Yorkshire and
39 Great Russell Street,
London WC1

NOTE

IHS

SOCIETATIS IESV · OBIIT A. M.D.LII.

VERA EFFIGIES S. FRANCISCI XAVERII

THE ADMIRABLE LIFE
OF S. FRANCIS
XAVIER.

Deuided into VI. Bookes

Written in Latin by Fa.
Horatius Turſellinus
of the Society of IESVS
And tranſlated into Engliſh
by T. F.

PRINTED
AT PARIS.
Anno Dom. M.DC.XXXII.

F. W. delin.

M. Baes. f.

TO THE RIGHT
HONOVRABLE
THE LADY
DOROTHY SHIRLEY.

*IGHT HONOV-
RABLE,*

   HAVING tranſlated
the R. Father *Horatius Turſellinus* Hiſtory of *S. Francis Xauiers* life, out of Latin
into Engliſh; I am emboldned, ſetting
     A   all

THE EPISTLE

all former defignes afide, to dedicate the fame vnto your Honour.

The times vvill not permit me to expreffe to the World, the Reafons and Grounds I haue in my Hart, for fo bold a refolution. The Almighty Spectator fees and beholds them, in vvhofe diuine applaufe I reft fully comforted, and content. Yet thus much I neyther can, nor vvill conceale: Your Noble Lineage, farre more ennobled vvith the rare difpofitions of your Mind, hath made me not to reft, vntill I refolued to leaue behind me to the vvorld, this firft, perpetuall Monument of the deferued Refpect, and Regard, I ovve vnto Your Honour.

Hearing alfo, vvhich is famous ouer all our Land, vvith hovv great *Refolution* and *Conftancy*, your Honour had ftood firme, and immoueable in the Profeffiõ of the Catholike Roman Faith,

and

and this euen in the middſt of ſtrongeſt
Reaſons, Tryalls, & Prouocations to the
contrary ; I could not but deſigne the
Worthieſt Champion of the ſame Fayth,
to be held vp, & imbraced in the chaſt,
and conſtant armes, of ſo Worthy and
Renovvned a Perſonage , as your Honour.

This ſelf-ſame Faith vvhich hath byn
by You ſo Heroically maintayned , did
this Holy and Religious Man *S. Francis
Xauier*, carry on alõg in theſe our daies,
not only into *India*, and the vtmoſt O-
rient; but firſt of all did bring it alſo, into
that ſtout, and Warlike *Iapony*, novv
much more ennobled, vvith the purpled
Bloud of ſo many Glorious Martyrs that
haue layd dovvne their deareſt liues, in
teſtimony, & defence thereof. And therfore , as he vvent before in *Latin* vnder
the Protection of the Vicar of Chriſt,
Pope *Clement* the eight; ſo novv it vvill

A 2   not

not feeme amiffe, that he appeare in *English* vnder the Patronage of your Honourable Fauour : And by your Meanes brought, as it vvere, out of *India* in to *England* , there made knovvne and vievved of all.

You , MADAME , shall be a Patroneffe to your Patron , and a Mother to your holy Father *S . Francis Xauier* , attired in this English Habit, vvhich I haue made for him . If I haue leffened him vvith my Tranflation , You may comfort your felfe vvith the incomparable vvorth of fo renovvned a Patron . If I make him leffe , yet the King of *Trauancoris* , together vvith his fubiects, ftiled him GREAT FATHER , and by his Royall Edict cõmanded, that all should obey the GREAT FATHER as himfelfe. The King of *Amangucium* in *Iapony*, ioyfully receiued Prefents from him, and heaped Royall fauours vpon his

perſon. The King of *Bungo* ſent for him by letters, honourably entertayned, prote-cted, reuerenced, and admired him. *Iohn* the third King of *Portugall*, vvho firſt moued and cauſed his going into *India*, gaue into his hands the Popes letters Patents, vvhereby he vvas made Apoſtolicall Legat in the *Eaſt*, ſeconded him vvith his Royall Fauour, commaunded his Acts to be ſought out, iuridically examined, and proued. When they came to his hands, he ſent them to ROME, and by his Embaſſadours, laboured to haue him a Canonized Saint; vvhich thē being hindred by the Kings death, hath byn of late performed by Pope *Gregory* the XV. ſo as novv all Catholique Princes, and Kings bend their Royall knees, and are humbly proſtrate to *S. Francis Xauier*, yea the Popes triple Crovvne lyeth dovvne at his glorious feete.

Beſides, that vvhich I dedicate to your

Ho-

Honour , is not so much a Saints Lyfe,
as a complete History , artificially cōpi-
led vvith much pleasing variety , and e-
legancy ; vvherein diuers , and sundry
courses are traced forth . for all to fol-
lovv. Bishops & Priests, Ecclesiasticall &
Laymen, Kings and subiects , Souldiers
by Sea and Land , Rich and Poore , all
shall find that vvhich belōgs vnto them.
For this holy Saint, though he vvere so
far gone in contemplation , that force of
Celestiall ioyes made him often cry out,
It is inough, O Lord , It is inough : yet vvas
he for all that , neuer out of *Action* , but
dealing vvith al sorts of people vvrought
himselfe out , euen *All to all.*

Moreouer, so various is this History,
as it cannot be but delightfull and pleasant , by reason of so many Countryes
briefly & liuely described ; so many different dispositions and strange manners;
so many Rites and Ceremonyes of false
Re-

DEDICATORY.

Religions, togeather vvith fundry fuper-
ftitions of Idolatrous Priefts; The ignorant *Brachmans* in *India*; The fuperftitious *Caciz̧es* in *Socotora*; The arrogant
Bongi in *Iapony*, muft needs yield a pleafing, and attractiue delight to all attentiue Readers.

Finally (vvhich is moft to be efteemed) there vvilbe foũd shining throughout this vvhole Hiftory, all kind of heauenly vvonders & miracles; not as Tongues only from Heauē, ãnouncing Gods
Glory, Goodneffe, Prouidence, and Mu-
nificence; but as certaine diuine Markes
alfo, of *S. Francis Xauiers* moft eminent
Sanctity.

Wherefore, as I confider his glorious
VVorth, vpõ my knees I pray vnto him
that hevvould vouchfafe to be a fingular
and fpeciall Patron to your *Honour*; but
as he he goes vefted in this English attire
vvhich I haue made him, I humbly requeft

THE EPISTLE

queſt, your *Honour* vvould be pleaſed to
be a Patroneſſe vnto him. Wherein I reſt
confident, and

Your Honours ;

*Humble Seruant , and
Beadſman ,*

T. F.

THE AVTHOR

TO THE READER.

TRVE it is, Nothing is begun and ended at one, and the selfe same tyme; nor are after-thoughts only, better then the workes themselues. Some yeares past, I wrote the like of Francis Xauier, with as much exactnes and fidelity, as possibly I could: but the very shape thereof, when I saw it (being diuulged in my absence) could I hardly know, it was so defiled & distayned with faults. Nor came it forth, indeed, more faulty, then mayned. For when as formerly the King of Portugall had commanded Xauerius famous Deedes to be sought out by his Viceroy of India; those things only of note, which he had wrought within the Portugheses dominions, were then collected, and set downe: nor yet those entierely neither, but only such, as could be knowne, and testified by sufficient Witnesses that were present. As for his other acts, especially those which he perfourmed among the Chineses and Iaponians (although very memorable and illustrious) they were for the most part, as yet, detayned in silence, and obscurity.

Those

Those therfore in like manner comming at last vnto my hands; & being written by such persons as at that tyme conuersed with the Iaponians *and* Chineses *; I was not vnwillingly induced to set my selfe to worke againe, by translating them into Latin, and inserting them in their due place amongst the rest. And although I was heerein to vndertake the compiling of almost a new worke, and thereby driuen at the first into some feare from the enterprize : yet my loue, as well to* Xauerius, *as my desire of the publicke vtility, ouercame all the difficultyes with were presented to my fancy. For so great was the copiousnesse and worth of his new exploytes, that of foure Bookes (least they might grow ouer-great) it was necessary to make six. Besides, I haue in this, done my best also, to procure, that, as our* Xauerius *hath heereby gotten a new Make; so he may appeare in publicke, more corrected and exact, although humane frailty can neuer be wary inough against errours. So as, he may well be said a most wise and iust Esteemer of things, who iudgeth that to haue bin corrected best, which in this kind may seeme to haue fewest faults.*

THE

THE
TABLE OF
CHAPTERS AND
CONTENTS.

THE FIRST BOOKE.

ã 2   Chap.

THE TABLE

THE SECOND BOOKE.

ã 3   THE

THE TABLE

THE THIRD BOOKE.

THE FOVRTH BOOKE.

THE FIFTH BOOKE.

ly

THE SIXT BOOKE.

ē

Chap.

THE TABLE.

THE

THE PREFACE.

COURTEOUS READER.

I purpose heere to set downe the admirable & renowned Lyfe of S. Francis Xauier : a man specially borne for the saluation of India, and the furthest Easterne world. Of all the nine first Disciples of our Holy Father S. Ignatius of Loyola, he most resembled his Mayster : and of the Society was the first who laboured in India, Iaponia, & those barbarous Countries, opening the way both for the Indians vnto heauen, & for the Society into India; wherby he brought no lesse renowne, then left example to his Order. For which cause, the whole Society not without good reason, desired long since to haue so fayre a Pourtraicte, beautified with such admirable vertue, liuely drawne in colours for Ours to behold; seeing the glorious exploits of Predecessours, do cōmonly inflame the harts of generous spirits, with a

cer-

certaine kind of heauenly fire, which hardly can be quenched, vntill by imitation they become true patternes of their noble Vertues.

Now, as on the one side I perceaued, that other Authors in their Histories, had with great honour, touched Xauerius chiefest acts : so was I on the other side not a little grieued, that for the space of aboue 35. yeares, there had bin none who thought vpon the setting forth his life (then shining with so many and so illustrious vertues) in a proper volume by it selfe, either by giuing that charge, to some other, or by vndertaking it themselues. VVherfore being moued of late, as well through perswasion of some dearest friends, as (which is more) by the command of Superiours to vndertake the same, I was put in some hope to performe, what others had conceaued of my ability therin; & for my deuotion to Xauerius, I was not only not vnwilling, but very willing also, as tyme should afford, to set vpon this taske, to th'end the memory of a man so worthy, yea euen of immortality it self, & who triumpheth now in heauen, might be renewed, not only to the minds of our owne Religious, but to Posterity also.

Moreouer, it seemeth vnto me, this falleth out, not so much by humane, as diuine prouidence, that euen

at

at this tyme his moſt induſtrious and laborious man-
ner of life , should be layd open to the view of Ours,
when as we behould ſuch a glorious harueſt of ſoules
brought in from thoſe far countries, which by him
were firſt cultiuated & manured. For now the newes
is brought unto vs, of the conuerſion of many great
Princes & Kings of Iaponia, *with almoſt all their*
people, to the Chriſtian faith ; and of a paſſage alſo,
through Gods aſſiſtance , made into China *for the*
preaching of the Ghoſpell there, which was hertofore
by the Diuels craft wholy ſtopped , & euen rāpier'd
up aſwel with walles, as lawes. Both which certainly
next after God, we muſt attribute to holy Xauerius
who not only lead the way to our Society for the cō-
uerſion of thoſe Nations , but left that enterprize
alſo fully ready , and eaſy to be compaſſed .

VVherfore my intention is to ſet downe heere in
writing the life of this moſt Bleſſed man , being full
of all variety of matter . And though my VVill and
Deſire be more ready to obey , then either Ability or
Hope to ſatisfy ; yet confiding in Xauerius *praiers*
for whoſe ſake I undertooke the worke, and alſo in
the diuine power of Obedience, I truſt my Forces wil
in ſome ſort be anſwerable to my VVill, & my En-
deauours to Expectation. The which, if through my

ſlen-

slendernes I be not able to bring to passe; yet shall I gaine this much at least, that my endeauours, how poore soeuer, may serue to stirre vp others, more studious & industrious, to vndertake the same. And howsoeuer it falleth out, I will neuerthelesse reserue this comfort to my selfe, that I haue bin obedient to my cheifest Father, and (as much as in me lay) endeauoured to preserue the memory of so great, and holy seruant of God. For peraduentnre I may giue future Ages to vnderstand from what seed so plentifull a haruest of new Christians, in those desert places, hath sprunge, whereof that most industrious and skilfull Husbandman, who sowed in teares, hath *with* aboundant ioy, *brought his handfulls home. And albeit our Predecessours haue studied more how to expresse the worthy acts of* Francis *in their deeds, then put them downe in writing; yet will I gather only that which is either extant in approued Authors, or els is come vnto my hands frõ those who haue byn present, or haue had them from eye witnesses of the same.*

First then, concerning his infancy and childhood I shall set downe some few things, which my selfe came to know by Martin Azpilqueta of Nauar *(some few months before his death) a man for ver-*

tue

tue and learning famous, who was both kinſman, &
in former times companion alſo to Xauerius. For
the reſt of his life, thoſe who conuerſed with him,
when his vertue did not ſo greatly appeare, negle-
ɛted to obſerue; but when as afterward it began to
ſhew it ſelfe vnto the world, the King of Portugal
cõmanded his aɛts to be more carefully obſerued, &
put downe in writing; & for this reaſon we haue not
all the parts of his life furniſhed alike with vertues
and worthy deeds. Nor do I thinke that thoſe who
knew the life of our Father Ignatius, will take any
great delight in reading the beginnings of Xauerius, or thoſe firſt aɛtes of his feruẽt vertue, as known
for the moſt part vnto thẽ already, but will rather
make haſt to thoſe other of his notable Aɛts in India: yet muſt they remember, that ſeing from thoſe
firſt beginnings Xauerius became ſo noble a ſouldiar of Chriſt (although for iuſt cauſes his deeds haue
byn related otherwhere) they ought not therfore
to be paſſed ouer with ſilence in their proper place.
But now let vs come vnto his life it ſelfe, where
we will firſt ſpeake of his parentage, which was
very Noble, on either ſide.

TO S. FRANCIS XAVIER
the Apoſtle of *India,* and *Iaponia,*
vpon his *Motto,*

{ *Satis eſt, Domine, ſatis eſt.* }

Inough, O Lord, *Inough,* are thy loude thankes,
When drops of Heauens dew harts boūdleſſe bankes
All-ouerflowing are, like Ocean mayne :
Thy Breſt's too narrow for ſo large a ſtrayne,
Enlarge, O Saint, thy ſoules moſt inward roomes,
Emboſome all that Power, which ſtreaming comes :
Children of thine ſtand vnder, who are bleſt
In taking in their fill, thy Ouer-feaſt.

T. F.

O F

OF THE LIFE
S. FRANCIS XAVIER.
The I. Booke.

Of the Linage, diſpoſition, & education
of S. Francis Xauier.

CHAP. I.

IN that part of *Nauarre*, which lyeth towards *Spayne*, at the foote of the *Pyrenæan* mountaines, not far from *Pamplona* the head Citty of that Kingdome, there is ſcituate a Caſtle called *Xauerium*, fortifyed both by nature and art, the ancient & proper manſion of the family of the *Xauiers*, where vntil this day is to be ſeen the place where *S. Francis Xauier* was borne; for the Nobility (according to the cuſtome of that Country) dwelleth for the moſt part in Caſtles out of Townes. His Anceſtours, for their warlike proweſſe, and

approued

approued loyalty to their Kings, haue purchafed to
themfelues and their pofterity, many great Honours
and Dignities, and haue byn no leffe renowned for
their owne vertue, then their Soueraignes fauours. towards them.

His kindred by the mothers-fide, was very Illuftrious and Noble; The antiquity wherof may for almoft a thoufand yeares togeather, draw a very fayre
His No- pedigree of famous Warriours, teftifyed by approued
bility of monuments. His Grandfather by the fame lyne was
birth. named *Martin Azpilqueta*, a man no leffe noble for
his owne vertue, then for the greatnes of his Ance-
ftors, who was now almoft the only branch left of
that moft renowned family. He tooke to wife *Ioane
Xaueria*, a Virgin in honour equall to himfelfe. By her
he had iffue an only daughter called *Mary*, the ftemme
& hope of both families; fo that, two of the nobleft
families of *Nauar* depended vpon the life of this yong
Maydé; who was no leffe eminét for beauty thé vertue
as being anfwerable therin to her moft excellét Name.

She was ioyned in marriage to *Iohn Iaffus*, a man
His Pa- Noble both for antiquity of his family & wealth, but
rents. efpecially for his learning & prudence, as being the
chiefe Priuy-Coufellour to King *Iohn* of *Nauarre*. He
now hauing through the perfuafion of his Father-in-
law, remoued his dwelling from the Caftle *Iaffo* the
aunciét Seat of his Anceftours, to *Xauerium* his wiues
Ioynter, & hauing more fortunate fucceffe in marriage then his fayd Father-in-law had, prouided better
for the family of the *Xauiers* then his owne. For hauing
by *Mary* many children (wherof this our *Francis* was
one.)

one) he began to take great care how he might keepe vp, two of the moſt ancient families of *Nauar*, which were now ſomewhat in declining. Whereupon he re-ſolued to leaue the Name of his own Family, although it were neither meane nor obſcure, and to giue his children, and poſterity the name of his wiues kindred; ſo as ſome of them were called *Azpilqueta's*, others *Xauiers*. Theſe therfore were the Parents and Aunce-ſtours of *Francis Xauier*, borne in the yeare of our Lord 1497. and raigne of King *Iohn* of *Nauarre*, & of Pope *Innocentius* the VIII. He was the leaſt of all his bro-thers, yet as another Dauid the greateſt by Gods holy Prouidéce deſigned to that perfeſtió of ſanſtity wher-unto he arriued, by aſſiſtance both diuine & humane.

From his cradle he was brought vp in the boſome of his moſt vertuous Parents, and by them inſtruſted **His Edu-** in all Piety during his childhood. He was alſo in his **cation.** yong and tender youth trayned vp by careful Tutors, in thoſe artes, wherby the vnderſtanding of man is moſt of all adorned. He was moreouer of a very ver-tuous diſpoſition, of an excellent conſtitution, and comlines of perſon, of a great and ſharpe wit, giuen more to his booke, thē vſually childré are. None more innocét, none more pleaſant, none more affable then he ; which made him beloued of all both at home and **His vir-** abroad. Yet he was not more gracious in the eye of **ginall** the world, then of heauen ; whereof this is an eui- **chaſtity.** dent argument, that notwithſtanding ſuch abounding fortunes, & youthly liberty, ioyned to a Perſonage ſo beautifull and comely, he was alwayes maiſter ouer himſelfe, his Chaſtity ſtill hauing predominancy o-

uer

ouer all difordinate appetites. And by Gods particular affiftance he euer preferued the flower of virginall Integrity, without fpot or ftayne; fo that, the Heauenly fpoufe, *who feeds among the Lillies*, may feeme euen then to haue haue taken vp his habitation in his breft.

His Chaftity (as is the nature therof) fharpened his wit, and prepared his mind as a moft pure foile, to receiue the feeds of wifedome. Therefore making no account of his brothers words who went about by warlike difcourfes to draw him to be a man of armes (the ancient ornament of their Anceftours) he ftucke clofe to his refolutiō, & whether ftirred vp by the late example of his Father, or drawne by the delight of knowledge, or moued by diuine inftinct, he preferred the glory of learning, before warlike prayfes. Yet the defire of Honour, a deepe rooted Euill by fucceffion from his anceftours, intermingled it felfe with his beft intentions. For, as great Nobility ordinarily afpireth to excellency; fo he by reafon of his liberall Education, became of an high, and lofty fpirit. And relying much vpon his wit began to looke after great and high matters, therby to augment the Honour of his Noble Family. For this caufe therefore he refolued, to furnifh himfelfe with the greateft knowledge and learning he could, the only way, as he thought, to increafe in himfelfe both dignity and wealth; a refolution more glorious to the fhew, then found in fubftance.

CHAP.

CHAP. II.

At Paris, by Ignatius *of* Loyola, *he is con-*
uerted to a vertuous Life.

THE Vniuerſity of *Paris* was at that time famous both for antiquity, and learning, & alſo very much frequented, in reſpect of her excellent Profeſſours and Maiſters, by the long continuance of peace, the beſt wits of Enrope reſorting thither to furniſh themſelues with all kind of eminent knowledge. *Francis* therfore being not more deſirous of learning then glory, as ſoone as he thought himſelfe ſcholler good inough, went alſo to *Paris*; where, as ſoone as he came, being admitted into the Colledge of *S. Barbara*, the chiefe reſidence of the whole Vniuerſity both for Readers and Schollers, he betoke himſelfe wholy to the ſtudy of Philoſophy, that he might afterwards with more facility and eaſe apply himſelfe to Diuinity. *The Colledge of S. Barbara.*

This generous reſolution he ſecondeth with Cō-ſtancy, a Vertue able to effect the greateſt matters. He was not tyred out with cōtinuall labours; nor drawne by any diſordered paſtimes, or pleaſures (the greateſt plagues of inconſtant youth) frō his intended courſe. But contrary wiſe in a Schoole ſo much frequented, Emulation of choice wits (the greateſt incitement to ſtudy) drew on more eagerly his deſires, bent wholy to the attainiug of excellency. And the ſucceſſe was *He ſtudieth Philoſophy at Paris.*

not vnanfwerable to his endeauour . So as hauing no
leffe profperoufly then conftantly ended his courfe of
Philofophy , he purchafed to himfelfe , not only learning , but alfo honour due thereunto . For as foone as
he had giuen worthy teftimony of his labours to the
moderatours of the Vniuerfity, he tooke (as the cuftome is) degree of Maifter : and being alfo preferred
to read Philofophy , he did for fometyme explicate
Ariftotle there publickly , not without prayfe . Then
from Philofophy he paffeth to Diuinity, & followeth
it with the fame feruour of fpirit , and temper of life .
In this meane tyme, *Francis* defirous (as is vfuall) to
maintaine his Nobility & Eftimation amongft his E-
quals , fell into extraordinary expences , for which
caufe, *Iaffus* his Father began to thinke of calling him
home.

*He inter-
preteth
Ariftot-
le at Pa-
ris publi-
kely .*

   Xauierius had at *Gandia* (a noble Citty of *Spaine*)
an elder fifter that was there Abbeffe of religious vir-
gins , called, by reafon of their aufterity of life , *Dif-
calceats*, a woman of eminent fanctity . She vnderftã-
ding her fathers intention , & learning alfo by diuine
reuelation , what a great man *Francis* would one day
proue, intreated him by her letters very ferioufly , to
furnifh *Francis* (who was yet at *Paris* , in his chiefeft
ftudies) with all things abundantly , and to fpare no
coft,though he fhould fpéd al he had vpõ him;for that
God had ordayned him to be the Apoftle of the new
World , and the further Eafterne parts . Thefe letters
are yet extant in the Caftle of *Xaueriũ*, as witneffes of
this Prophefy,the euent wherof afterward proued to
be true. *Iaffus* therfore taking courage by the predictiõ

*A Pro-
phecy
concer-
ning his
Apoftle-
fhip in
the new
world.*

                                                          of

of his daughter, of whose eminent Sanctity he had certain proofe, from thenceforth allowed *Francis* all necessary expences in abundant manner. But whilst *Xauierius*, attending more to Honour, then his owne saluation, directeth his study of Diuinity to humane ends, Gods powerfull hand intercepted his vaine endeauours, & turned the same to a more glorious pursuit of a pious and holy life.

    Francis (as we said before) remained still in *S. Barbara's Colledge*, and had for his chamberfellow one *Peter Faber*, a *Sauoyard* by Nation, a man of a greater wit, then descent. At the same time *Ignatius Loyola* (who afterward was the Institutour and Founder of the Society of Iesus) coming to *Paris*, gaue himself also to the study first of Philosophy, & afterwards of Diuinity. As soone therfore as he met with *Faber* and *Xauerius*, their like dispositions and studies, as many times it hapneth, brought them presently acquainted; And at last *Ignatius*, being by them courteously recei- *His ac-* ued for companion and chamber-fellow, requited *quainta-* this their friendship most aboundantly. For percei- *ce with* uing in them both notable forward wits, and hauing *S. igna-* perfectly found out their natures, he began to draw *tius.* them by friendly offices, to giue them wholsome cofell (as occasion serued) & by sweet meanes to allure *S. Igna-* them to the perfection of a Christian life: insinuating *tius his* vnto them that they should seriously thinke with the- *aduises.* selues, that man endowed with an immortall Soule was not borne for this short and miserable life, but for « euerlasting blessednes; and to remēber that whatsoe- « uer they saw heere, was not so much giuen to mortall « men. «

» men to vfe and enioy , as to bring them to know and
» loue God; that they fhould preferre thofe goods which
» were eternall and properly their owne , before that
» which was temporall, and only lent vnto them . For
» what would it auaile a man to gaine the whole world,
» and loofe his owne foule ? If the fonne of God himfelf
» had now left men moft certaine meanes for faluation, what difcretion were it to remaine among their
» deadly enemies dartes without thofe helps , to defend
» them ? Wherfore they fhould fometimes , and that e-
» uery eight day , if they would follow his aduife, arme
» themfelues with the Sacraments of Confeffion & the
» holy Eucharift : for being armed with thefe heauely
» weapons, they might eafily withftand their enemy ;
» wheras being naked without them , they fhould as it
» were giue him their throates to cut &c.

　　Thefe admonitions were not alike gratefull , &
acceptable to them both. *Faber*, who had no great defire to any thing of this world , embraced them with
great affection . But *Francis* hauing his mind fet fully
vpon defire of greatnes, wholy reiected them. For he
was of a very liuely, yet tractable nature , if euill cuftome had not corrupted it . Being therfore a yonge
man of a great fpirit, with froward and ouer-thwart
anfwers, oftentimes of fet purpofe carped at *Ignatius*
and his words , yea, and fometimes alfo in very re-
proachful maner fcoffed at his excellent piety : but he
on the other fide vfed al the fweet meanes he could to
reclaime him from his infolency . And not in vaine ;
for Patience at laft ouercame Pertinacy . And *Xauerius* being by little and little made tractable, by that fo
gentle

gentle & courteous vſage began to beare ſome reſpect towards to him , and at laſt touched by Gods diuine ſpirit , left himſelfe to be wholy ruled, and guided by him. Ignatius gently handleth *Francis* his wild-neſſe.

But it is a great matter to go to God with a free mind wholy diſcharged of all other affections. For *Fa-ber* indeed contemning all things of this world , and hauing now for the ſpace of foure yeares, frequen-ted the holy Sacraments, according to *Ignatius* his ad-uiſe, it was eaſy to perſwade him to caſt off all other cares , and make himſelfe a ſouldiar in that battaile wherein Chriſt himſelfe carrieth the prime Banner. But *Xauerius* ſtill feeding his mind with vaine hopes & imaginations of Honours , although he imbraced the ſame courſe of life , yet ſtifly reſiſted the holy Ghoſt, & would not follow his Captaine Chriſt , *going forth vnto him out of the Campe, carrying his reproach .* He was for other things pious and tractable , but in this one thing hard to be dealt with all . For which cauſe *Igna-tius* begged him of God more earneſtly with teares ; which were not loſt. Heb. 13.

For *Francis* his hart being thereby very much mollified , commeth at laſt to bend , and receauing a a ſtroke from heauen concerning the ſaluation of his ſoule , vpon a time entred into himſelfe , and began ſilently to thinke & examine what Nature on the one ſide, and what Vertue on the other could ſay for thé-ſelues . Shall I , ſaith he, giue eare to God who cals, & nakedly follow my naked Sauiour ? But then I muſt vndertake an hard, and abiect courſe of life . Shall I neglect Gods call , and ſtill retaine my Reputation, & *Francis* his deli-beration about chãging his cour-ſe of life.

man-

» manner of life, which I haue begun ? But then I am
» in great danger , that if I draw backe when God cal-
» leth, he wil with indignation laugh at my destruction.
» But how shall I be able to beare the bitternes, & igno-
» miny of the crosse ? What then ? shall I rather choose
» to take part with the enemies of Christ his Crosse ,

Phil. 3 .   *whose end is destruction, and glory in their confusion?* with
» what face shall I looke vpon myne aquaintance? How
» shal I endure to heare what my companions will say?
» But to be drawen from a vertuous and blessed course
» of life by mens speaches, is an argument not only of
» extreme lightnesse, but of meere madnes also . What
» exceeding great sorrow will this vnexpected newes
» bring to my friends, and kinsfolke? But, shal the loue
» eyther of Parents , or any mortall creature whatsoe-
» uer touch me neerer then myne owne saluatió? neerer
» then the loue of God, and Christ himselfe?

With these, and such like contrary cares he
stood wauering with a perplexed & doubtfull mind,
and hauing spent some dayes in these kind of cogitations, at last, this cóbat was ouercome, & he yielded
himselfe to God who had vrged him so hard; and vpon
a suddain changed into another man he began to *looke*

Heb. 12.   *vpon the author and consummatour of Faith Christ Iesus,*
who (ioy being proposed vnto him) susteined the Crosse, con-
temning confusion . And first , as by *Ignatius* help he
was raysed vp , so by *Ignatius* help he remained constant in his resolution. And from that time being as it
were borne a new , more ioyfully & happily then before , he yielded very rare , and goodly fruit of Christian perfection, being now more like *Ignatius* then
himselfe.   CHAP.

CHAP. III.

*His Feruour in the mortification of his bo-
dy, and study of Perfection.*

OR within a little while he sought with
greater desire after mortifications & contempt of himselfe, then he had before after dignities and honours: such (for the
most part) is the property of excellent dispositions,
to apply themselues wholly to whatsoeuer they take
vpon them. *Francis* therfore ayming at the highest Mortifi-
toppe of Sanctity, began first (as the custome is) to cation.
combat with his owne body. For knowing the flesh
to haue contrary desires to the spirit, he resolued to
bring it vnder, that the vntamednes therof might be
no hindrance to him in the way of Christian perfection. Wherfore both in his yonger dayes, & all his life
after, he did no lesse often the zealously vse the ordinary austerity of fasting, disciplines and hayrecloth,
as fit meanes to tame & moderate disordinate affections, and to make satisfaction for sinnes. And euen at
his very entrance into this new war-fare, he gaue
manifest tokens of his noble disposition and courage.

For being in his yonger yeares accustomed often
to leap amongst his Equals & companions in a field His agi-
neere to the Citty, (that being then the only sport lity of
wherin he tooke delight) vpon a certaine tyme he body.
tooke ouermuch content in his owne agility of body,
wherin he far outwet all the rest in leaping; wherfore

as foone as he had altered his courfe of life, although
that offence had byn but light, yet he mortifyed himfelfe for it very feuerely. For binding his body very
hard with a fmall cord which caufed him intollerable
paine, he went fome dayes together in that manner;
and to purge his mynd of the pride he had taken therin, he exercifed himfelfe all that while meditating v-
pon deuout matters, that the greatnes of the paine
might reftraine both his mind and body from the like
exceffes heerafter. And this hard hand he kept ouer
his youthfull motions, as well to excite and ftirre vp
his mynd, as to make fatisfaction for his finnes. As
he was once imployed in thofe pious confiderations,
which we call fpirituall Exercifes, and therin endeauouring by abftinence to bring vnder & make fubiect
the vnruly motions of his body, out of a defire he
had to obtaine a cóplete victory ouer himfelf, he was
carryed fomething to farre, abftayning foure whole
dayes from eating any thing. A rafh attempt indeed,
but yet faultleffe, being excufed by the feruour of his
new beginning, and youthfull yeares. For nothing
is more hard, or a greater ftep to vertue, then the mai-
ftry ouer ones felfe : but for Nouices and new beginners neuer to exceed, whilft they follow the battaile
in their feruour, is a thing rather to be wifhed, then
hoped for.

Wherfore *Xauerius* continually ftriuing & with
diligent care ouercomming himfelfe, became euery
day to grow ftronger therein. That which moft of all
helped him, was his often and deuout meditation vpõ
the life and death of our Sauiour Iefus Chrift, and his
vnfpeakeable

Margin notes:
He tyeth about parts of his body a litle rope

Foure dayes he abftaines from ea-ting any thing.

Coqueft of him-felfe.

vnſpeakeable Charity, the greateſt incitements to the
loue of God, and chriſtian perfection. And the more
thoſe pious meditations increaſed in him the loue of
God, ſo the more his hart was ſet on fire with a defire of ſauing ſoules, and ſuffering of martyrdome.
Which thing went ſo farre at laſt, that as the ſonne of
God had deliuered himſelfe to death for his ſaluation;
ſo he againe, vowed himſelfe wholy and entierly for
euer, to employ himſelfe for his glory, & the ſaluatiõ
of ſoules. And to the end that nothing might ſeparate
him from this Charity of Chriſt, by the aduiſe of
S. Ignatius he determined, togeather with the other
companions (who were then nine in nũber) to bind
himſelfe to God by certaine vowes, which might be
a meanes to bring him to the crowne of Martyrdome.

    In the yeare therfore 1534. they for that pur-
poſe aſſigned the feaſt of the Aſſumption of the *B. V.
Mary*, intending therby to haue her both witneſſe &
patroneſſe of their vowes. When that day was come
they, hauing their minds ſet on fire by continual meditation, met all togeather in a Church neere *Paris*
called *Mons Martyrum,* that the place might adde
flames to their earneſt deſire of martyrdome. Where
after they had heard maſſe and fortified themſelues
with the ſacred Euchariſt, repleniſhed with ſpirituall
ioy they make their vowes, and dedicate themſelues
to God. The ſumme of their vowes was this, that hauing finiſhed their courſe of Diuinity, diſpoſſeſſing
themſelues of all things, they would in perpetuall pouerty employ their ſeruice for the glory of God, and
the ſaluation of ſoules; and that vpon a ſet day they

*Medita-
tion vpõ
the life
& death
ofChriſt*

*His deſir
of Mar-
tyrdom.*

*He binds
himſelfe
to God
by vow.*

would

would go to *Hierufalem,* there to labour for the conuerfion of the *Turkes* , with eminent hazard of their
liues. And if by chance this determination of theirs
fhould be hindred by any accident, at the yeares end
they would go to *Rome,* and offer their endeauours to
his Holines towards the faluation & helpe of foules,
without exception either of time, place, or mention
of prouifion, or allowance for their iourney.

Vpon the making of thefe vowes, there follo-
Yeerly re wed a new, but yet pious cuftome of often renewing
newing the fame, thereby to keep them frefh in memory, and
of vowes increafe a religious deuotion towards thē. They made
thefe vowes not only that yeare, but alfo renewed thē
euery yeare vpon the fame day, and place, with the
fame folemnity, alacrity, and fruite as long as they
ftudied at Paris. But *Xauerius* vfed this cuftome often-
Frequēt times by himfelfe with great feruour, finding by ex-
renoua- perience that by often renewing his vowes, he found
tion of his vigour and ftrength of mind againe renewed, like
vowes. the youth of an Eagle. And this great defire of perfection in vertue was no hindrance at all to his ftudies;
but there was a tyme when he manifeftly fhewed, that
he tooke more delight in being a fouldiar of Chrift thē
in his ftudies, for whofe only fake, he now employed
himfelfe therein,

CHAP.

CHAP. IIII.

He goeth to Venice *vvith extreme payne of body.*

HE had now almoſt finiſhed his courſe of Diuinity, when preſently he was to depart for *Italy*. For the Fathers had agreed among themſelues, that vpon a ſet day, to wit the 24. of Ianuary 1537. they would meete al together at *Venice*, with *S. Ignatius*, who was gone thither before vpon certayne occaſiõs. In the meane tyme before the appointed day of their iourney came, *France* was all vp in armes, by reaſon of *Charles* the fifth his warre made vpon the Frenchmen : which accident made them haſten their determined iorney, by ſetting aſide all care of ending their courſe of ſtudies. *Xauerius* was indeed much grieued for this hindrance, but yet carried it diſcreetly, eſteeming it as good to leaue his ſtudies for Gods ſake, as to follow them.

He breaketh of his courſe of Diuinity not farre from the end.

Therfore vpon the 13. day of Nouember, a moſt vnſeaſonable tyme of the yeare, hauing, according to their vowes, giuen all they had to the poore, except only their writings, and ſome litle thing to help them in their iorney, he togeather with his other company ſetteth forth on the way. Their manner of trauailing was this. They were cloathed in courſe and old habits, euery one with a ſtaffe in his hand, and a ſhort leather mantle vpon his ſhouldiers, like poore pilgrimes; about.

Their manner of trauaile.

bout.

bout their neckes they hunge their beades, therby to
be knowne for Catholikes as they trauayled amongſt
heretiques, and their writings they carryed at their
backe in a little bagge.

They vſed euery day to cōmunicate, being the only
comfort of all their labours, therby both to renew
their forces, & reuiue their ſpirits being wearyed with
paynfull trauayle. When they departed from their lodging they allwayes commended themſelues to God,&
when they came into it they gaue him thankes. Being
vpon the way they firſt ſpent ſome time in meditating
vpon heauenly matters; then they vſed ſome pious diſcourſe together, and now and then they lightned the
labour and weariſomneſſe of their iorney with ſinging
of hymnes, Pſalmes, and ſpirituall Canticles.

In this manner for the moſt part taking his way
into *Italy* through *Loraine* and *Germany*, to auoyd the
troubles of the warre, he endured the Autumne ſhowres of *France*, and the winter coldes of *Germany*. And
although he were not accuſtomed to trauaile on foote
yet he cheerfully vndertooke, and performed this ſo
longe & tedious iorney, being loaden with his writings; and this in the dead of winter, and through
moſt fowle wayes many times euē couered ouer with
ſnow, and frozen vp with ice, eſpecially as he paſſed
the Alpes. And beſides the weight of his bagge, and
badnes of the way, he voluntarily vſed another mortification which put him to intolerable paine, ſo great
was his courage to indure all incommodities and labours for the loue of God. For before he began his
iorney he had for a good while togeather, (either to
exerciſe

*Volun-
tary mor
tificati-
on in his
iorney.*

exercife himfelfe in patience, or elfe to mortify his body ; tyed about his armes and thighes little cordes, which through continual ftirring about neceffary bufines of the houfe, had caufed the flefh to fwell, and therby gauled him moft pitifully. Yet fo great was his defire and courage to fuffer, that albeit the iorney he was to go on foote was fo long and hard , he would not for al that take of thofe cordes which did fo much afflict him .

When therfore this torment being of itfelfe very paynfull was now feconded with fo hard a iorney on foot, the extreme griefe which the cords did put him to, was alfo very much increafed . But he being no leffe couragious in enduring torments, then in vndertaking them, kept on his way, and did not only cóceale, but alfo conténe all the paine he felt therby . For he hoped that, that might by vfe & cuftome be affwaged as well as other corporal moleftations, which he had made triall of . But when the vehemency *Through* thereof daily encreafed, his confidence being turned *anguifh* into care, he began to faint not through want of cou- *of body* rage but of ftrength . At laft therfore when he could *in the* no longer neither diffemble nor endure the violence *way .* of the payne, being through neceffity conftrained to yield, he fweetly intreated his companions to pardon him, for he was indeed fo weary, that he could not go one ftep further . They at firft wondred to fee him who before was all feruour, vpó the fodain to faint, and languifh in that manner ; but when the paleneffe of his countenance difcouered the greatnes of his interiour paine, they held him vp as he fainted, and a-

sked

ked him what new accident was befallen him. Then
he taking breath awhile, which was before stopped
through griefe, was enforced to open vnto them the
whole matter. They all condoling his case, but secretly admiring his vertue, intreated him to rest awhile
vntil the violence of the paine were a little assvaged;
then as soone as they thought he had rested inough,
& recouered a little strengh, they brought him fayre
and softly to the next Inne, and presently sent for a
Physitian, who hauing diligently viewed, and consi-
dered of the soare, resolutely answereth that the cords
could not be seene, much lesse cut. And although the
ends of the cords did appeare, yet they had made such
vlcers, that they could neither be vnloosed, or cut,
without most extreme paine. Therfore (because the
disease surpassed art, & the cause therof went beyond
all custome) he stood awhile in a maze like one that
knew not what to say. At last fearing the successe he
could not be persuaded eyther by *Francis* or his com-
paniōs to medle with it, there was such danger in the
Cure; And so departed without so much as making
the least triall.

His ma-
lady be-
ing held
despe-
rate, the
Physitiā
giues
him o-
uer

The Fathers his companions then were in great
solicitude and anxiety, not only for what would become of the Patient, but also for their owne iorney,
which was hindred by this vnexpected chance to the
great hindrance of them all. And *Francis* grieued no
lesse that his companions were enforced to stay for
him, then for his owne infirmity. Despayring therefore of humane, they had recourse to diuine help,
ech one humbly imploring assistance from Heauen.

Their

Their prayers were not in vayne, for God himſelfe
played the Phiſitian, and preſently applyed a remedy
to that deſperate Cure. A ſtrange thing, the next morning *Francis* riſing out of his bed found all the cordes
broken aſunder & fallen of, all the ſwelling gone, &
nothing to remaine of the ſoares but certaine markes,
where the ropes had byn. Then being ſtroken into admiration & reioycing not ſo much for himſelfe as for
his companions ſake, with a lowde voyce gaue thankes to Almighty God; wherat his companions came
running to him, asking him the cauſe of that new
ioy? Which hauing vnderſtood, and being aſtoniſhed at the euident miracle, gaue (as reaſon was)
all due praiſe and thankes to God; and lifting vp their
handes to heauen & weeping for ioy began preſently
to extoll the heauenly Fathers prouidence, and ſingular bounty towards them.

He is cu-
red from
heauen

Then they preſently ſet on againe to their trauaile, moſt ioyfull for that good ſucceſſe, inciting one
another to employ al their labours in the ſeruice of ſo
ſweet a Lord; And *Francis* throughout the whole iorney (as he was alwayes before wont to do) applied
himſelfe with ſuch diligence & alacrity in helping &
ſeruing his companions as was wonderfull. For as they
all ſtroue to the vttermoſt (this only being the emulation among them) to excell one another in courteſy, he either out of feruour of ſpirit, or naturall ciuility farre outwent the reſt. And this care and deſire
of his was no greater to helpe his companions, then
to procure the ſaluation of others. Wherſoeuer occaſion was giuen him of helping his neighbours, either

In the
way he
ſerueth
his có-
panions.

with

Vpon
the way
he hel-
peth his
neigh-
bours.
with counſel , aduiſe or example , he with great zeale made his commodity therof , and imbraced the ſame as opportunity ſerued. And herein his labour was not in vaine ; for many Catholiques were therby reclaimed to a good life , and ſome Heretiques alſo reduced to the wholſom way of truth. Which way ſoeuer they paſſed , they left behind them tokens of ſanctity for all to behould, and Catholiques to imitate. And ſo it hapned oftentimes , that euen Hereticks themſelues taken with admiration at their ſanctity , would courteouſly ſhew them their way , tell them what difficulties they were to paſſe , and when need was , would themſelues freely conduct them in their iorney . Thus true and kindly vertue ſheweth it ſelfe , and putteth euen ſauage people in mind of humanity .

Francis therfore by the aide both of heauen and earth, hauing waded through all the incōmodities & dangers of the way, vpon the tenth day of *Ianuary* the yeare following , arriued ſafe with his companions at *Venice.* There he foūd *Ignatius* of *Loyola* with the greateſt deſire expecting his deereſt ſonnes & cōpanions. Then according to the cuſtome of the ſociety they ſalute and imbrace one another moſt ioyfully , with the greateſt demonſtration of loue that might be imagined . And this their ioy made them forgetfull of all their toylſome paſſed labours .

CHAP.

CHAP. V.

At Venice *he serueth in the Hospitall of the* Incurable, *and from thence goeth to* Rome *to the Pope.*

THE Fathers had already agreed al togeather to go to *Rome* there to aske leaue of the
Pope to go to *Hierusalem* to preach theGos-
pell, and there to remayne at their owne
liberty. It seemed therfore good vnto thē, that vntill
the extremity of the winter were ouer past, that they
should begin to practise theselues at *Venice* in that kind
of spiritual warfarre, which afterward they were to
vndertake, Wherfore deuiding themselues to the publike seruice of the Hospitals of that Citty, as into so
many Prouinces, *Francis* requested that he might haue
the care of the *Incurable*, a fit meanes to gayne, as he
desired, a most noble conquest ouer himselfe ; the
which office he performed with no lesse feruour of
spirit, then he had desire thereunto .

As soone therfore as he came thither, he begā to go
about the beds & couches of those poore soules , speaking comfortably and sweetly to the afflicted; encouraging them that were giuen ouer by the surgeons,
with hope of life euerlasting; hartening them that lay
a-dying, & mouing all most affectionatly to patience,
modesty, & vertuous life, endeauouring by all meanes
possible to cure their minds, whose diseases were in-

curable

curable. And confidering moreouer, that if he ferued
them in things belonging to their bodies, he might the
more eafily helpe them in their foules : He therefore
would himfelfe fweep the hofpitall, make the beds,
rid away the filth, performe euen the moft bafe and
abiect offices of the place (thofe being the firft grouds
of Chriftian humility) & finally as the cuftome is,
wafh the bodies of the dead, & bury the as they ought
to be. And in the midft of all thefe imployments there
appeared in his countenance and lookes fuch, and
fo eminent a Piety, that you would haue thought he
had feene Chrift with his eyes in thofe poore ficke
perfons, and employed all his labours in feruing of
him. Thefe things were done, in the fight of a moft
frequented Hofpitall, in the view of a moft noble Citty, with fuch vnufuall cheerfulnes and ioy, that many flocking thither through the reporte of fo new a
thing, *Francis* became a fpectacle not only to God &
his Angels, but to men alfo. In fo much that his care &
charity towards the ficke, renewed agayne the moft
comfortable memory of *S. Rocke* (whofe Name is moft
famous at *Venice*) for his fingular benignity in that
kind.

In the meane time his vertue breathed forth a
moft delightful odour in the Celeftial Court. For hauing gotten the care of one that was fick of a confup-
tion and the Pox, the more horrour he had of him (as
being delicate both by nature and cuftome) the more
diligence he vfed in tending and feruing him. Vpo this
occafion he fought many noble combats & got moft
glorious victories ouer himfelfe. For though Reafon
did

With
fpeciall
care he
ferueth a
fick man
full of
foares.

did withhold the vnbridled contradiction of nature ; and diuine grace ouercome the horrour of that pestilent diseafe : yet for all that, the loathfomneffe of the vlcers, and the intollerable ftench therof, did fometimes, fo ouercharge his ftomacke (as it often falleth out)that he had euen an auerfion from his faid Patient. But neither could the Deuils nor Natures affront beguile *Xauerius.* For as foone as he perceiued his charity to waxe fomewhat cold, fharpely rebuking himfelf of cowardize & want of courage in this kind he refolued by way of reuenge to rid himfelfe of that dainty difpofition. And without further delay armed with the loue of Chrift his Sauiour, after the example of *S. Catherine* of *Sienna,* he nobly ouercommeth himfelfe, and fucketh out once, & againe with his mouth the putrified matter out of his Patients loathfome vlcers.

He fucketh out the filthy matter.

This extraordinary vertue was recompenfed by God with an extraordinary reward. For he did not only giue him conqueft ouer himfelfe for that prefent, but euer after gaue him ftrength and courage to beare all annoyances euen of the moft vlcerous & leaprous. In fo much as from thenceforward, he would not only without difficulty , but with a kind of delight alfo hadle & dreffe fuch loathfome difeafes as others durft not without horrour once looke vpon, fo important a thing it is for the obtaining of true freedome of fpirit, but once nobly to ouercome ones felfe. Wherfore throughout the whole courfe of *Francis* his life there appeared a perpetuall victory ouer himfelfe in all things, and an extraordinary charity towards poore

Conqueft of himfelf.

ficke

ficke and needy perfons. Hauing layd this foundation he bent all his cares for his intended voyage.

Now therfore the fpring comming on , the Fathers thought good to make no delay , but according to their vow, as fpeedily as they could haften towards *Rome* . But there fell at that time fo extraordinary great raynes , that the wayes became very foule; and Lent was alfo at hand, a very incommodious time for religious men to trauaile in. Yet for feare delay fhould make that leffe grateful in the fight of almighty God , which was of it felfe moft acceptable vnto him , they all had fo religious a care of performing their vow , that they thought it by no meanes fitting to expect any longer , but prefently to fet forwards . Thus did they accommodate, not their vowes to themfelues , but themfelues to their vowes.

Religious regard towards vowes.

At the beginning therfore of Lent they all togeather make haft to *Rome* ; by thus much now more poore then in their former iorney , in that without any penny of Viaticum for their expences they put thefelues on the way, depeding only vpon Gods providence . In their iorney they dayly obferued their former practife of Piety, and the rather becaufe of the holy time of Lent; & although by reafon of their trauailing on foote they endured great difficulties what by the painfulnes of the iorney, and their very poore diet , which they alfo begged as they went , yet euery day did they ftrictly obferue their faft, fo that it is hard to fay , whether they obferued with more deuotion , the Precept of Fafting , or the Euangelicall Counfell of Pouerty . Yet through Gods prouidece their religious

Iorney-ing on foot in Lent and begging he truly fafteth.

ous

ous confidence was not any way fruftrated . For although they were much combred with raine and ill
weather , yet kept they on their iourney , paffing on
foote through *Lombardy* where the wayes efpecially
at that time of yeare were very fowle & troublefome.
And fometimes alfo they were forced , with all patience and cheerfulnes bare-footed to trauayle thirty
miles a day, refreshing themfelues only with a piece of
browne bread and water , in moft rayny weather ,
when the fields were fo fwelled & ouer flowen with
flouds of water , that in fome places they waded euen
vp to the neeke . At laft by the fpeciall prouidence of God, who gaue them fufficient forces, and deliuered them from all dangers in this their iourney , he
brought them fafe vnto the place they defired.

Taking but a lit-le piece of bread they go on foot a good dayes iorney.

As foone as they came to *Rome* , the firft thing
they did was to vifit the Churches of *S. Peter,* and *S.
Paul,* and to humbly befeech thofe moft holy Patrones
both of the Citty and whole world , that God would
through their interceffion giue profperous fucceffe to
their Intentions . Then confiding in the patronage
and fauour of fo mighty Protectours , they fought
meanes to haue acceffe vnto his Holines (who at that
time was *Paul* the third of the noble family of the *Far-
nefi,* a man right eminent both for grauity, and prudence) and to defire his approbation of that which
they had at firft determined . There was at the fame
time in *Rome,* Embaffadour for the Emperour , *Peter
Ortizius* a Spaniard, a man of no leffe authority , then
courtefy. He hauing brought them to the Pope, and
earneftly commended them vnto him , his Holynes

E   as

as the custome is, benignely and courteously admitteth them to the kissing of his feet . Then to make triall of their learning he caused them to dispute, sometimes in Philosophy, and sometymes in Diuinity in tyme of dinner, as that most worthy Princes custome was . Wherin when all of them, but especially *Xauerius*, had giuen great demonstratiõ both of their ability & vertue, presenting their petition concerning their iorney to *Hierusalem*, the Pope without any difficulty, yea with great approbation granteth them what they demaund, and out of his Fatherly charity to all Nations , tooke such affection to their vertuous desires, although meere strangers to him, that for his singular bounty & liberality, he dismissed them not only with his benediction, but also with a large Viaticum to beare their charges in that long and tedious iourney. But they not forgetfull of pouerty euen amidst such pléty, put that money giuen thē for their vowed pilgrimage into a Bankers hands to be kept, vntill they were ready to go. And in the meane time they liued by begging publickly vp & downe the Citty, more knowne now for their Religious modesty then their learning, by reason that abandoning of their owne accord the familiarity of great and noble Personages , they had vndertaken that abiect and humble course of life.

CHAP.

CHAP. VI.

At Vincenza he saith his first Masse , ha-
uing first prepared himselfe thereto .

W H E N they had dispatched all things at
Rome with fortunate and speedy successe ,
in the same manner almost as they came
thither, they returne againe to *Venice* intending with the first occasion to imbarke themselues for
Hierusalem. There, inflamed with a longing desire of
an heauenly life , to vnite and tye themselues more
firmely to God , they resolue to consecrate their liues
wholy to Christ , as they had long since done their
goods . Therfore hauing for that end prepared themselues by interiour recollection , at a solemne Masse
they vow perpetuall Pouerty and Chastity in the hāds
of *Hierome Verallus* who was then Legate for the Sea
Apostolique . *Francis* was neuer before seene to be
more replenished with heauenly ioy then at this time.
For being very cheerfull , as might be discerned by
his lookes , he gaue his whole hart to God, being euen
ouerwhelned in his soule with his diuine grace ; and
calling to mind his former practise , he frō that time ,
all his life, euery day renewed the vowes which once
he had made.

But whilst he expecteth an opportunity for his
intended nauigation he againe applieth himselfe with
greater feruour then before , to his exercises of Cha-

He vow-
eth per-
petuall
pouerty
and Cha-
stity.

rity,

rity, which he neuer forgot, although they had been intermitted by reafon of his iorney. And the *Venetians* fo much the more admired & efteemed this great charity of *Francis* towards the ficke, by how much longer, this his labour continued with them then before. For it fell fo out, that the Turkes and Venetians beginning that yeare to make warre vpon one another, the paifidge into *Palestine* was ftopt, which before was alwayes open for Pilgrims. And the feas were fo befet with the Turkifh fhips that none could paffe out of *Italy* to the Eafterne coafts without manifeft daunger of death or captiuity. Which accident, as it firft delayed the good Fathers iorney to *Hierufalem*, fo it afterwards brake it cleane of, God referuing their labours for better vfes. For he fent thefe his hyred feruants in fuch fort into his vineyard, that leauing the Turkifh foyle, as barren, and euen paft bearing fruite, they might employ thefelues, fome in pruning the ouergrowne vineyardes of Chriftians, & others in cultiuating the defertes of *India*, & *Iaponia*, which before that were neuer fo much as touched. So whilft *Francis* (not knowing Gods defignement) betweene hope and feare expected euery day fome opportunity for his long defired nauigation, many monthes paffed away in his forefayd labours of the Hofpitall, in all which time he neuer became flacke in his indeauours nor any whit remiffe in his charitable exercifes.

But feing at laft all hope of going to *Hierufalē*, vtterly to fayle, he tooke it very heauily, and was much grieued, that he was fo depriued of all meanes to fee thofe holy places of *Palestine*, and alfo of the occafion

cafion of fuffering martyrdome for Chrift : notwithftanding beholding therin the prouidēce of God (the
only cōfort of all humane accidents) he bare the fame
with courage and conftancy, although it gaue him o-
therwife no fmall refentment . Then they confulted
among thēfelues what was beft to be done, & turning
all their cares another way , it feemed good vnto them
that they fhould all take holy Orders , that fo they
might attend with more profit to their owne perfection , and faluation of others.

In the moneth of Iune therfore , vpon the Natiuity of *S. Iohn Baptift* hauing vfed great preparatiō therunto , they were made Priefts by the Bifhop of *Arbe*
(for the other holy Orders they had receyued a litle
before.) And it is reported of them, that al the time of
confecration they were fo ouercome with ioy that the
good Bifhop himfelfe participated thereof. For he af-
nrmed afterwards, that whilft he did the ceremonies,
he felt a new kind of heauenly ioy and delight, the like
whereof he neuer had before experienced By this
tyme all hope of paffing into *Paleftine* was fo wholy
taken away , that they feemed almoft freed frō their
vow : yet that there might not remayne the leaft
fcruple in their mynds , they thought good ftill to
watch if there might be any occafion offered of performing the fame vntill the yeare were fully come a-
bout, for fo it was expreffed in their vow.

In this meane fpace being forthwith to offer to
God the firft fruites of their Priefthood , they withdrew themfelues out of the great concourfe of that
moft populous Citty , & the better to attend to recollection

He is made Prieft.

Prepara-tion for his firft Maffe.

lection they separated themselues into diuers places
neere by, some one way, some another. *Francis*, together with *Alphonsus Salmeron*, betooke himselfe to
Mont Celsus, a village distant some fifteene miles
from *Padua*: there desirous to be solitary he withdrew
himselfe farre from all men, that he might vnite himselfe neerer to God: And hauing found in a priuate
place, a desolate and ruinated cottage, he thatched the
roofe therof with straw, and so made himselfe a litle
sorry habitation, wherein he tooke so much the more
delight, because it represented to him the manger of
Christ his Sauiour, and his great pouerty. Then, that
experiéce might make a deeper impressió in his mind
of the pouerty of IESVS whilst he was a child, and of
his solitude when he was a man, he tasked himselfe to
this kind of life: he eats very sparingly of such meate
only as he got by begging, he lay vpon the bare groūd
with straw vnder him in the forsayd houell exposed
to rayne, wind, and weather; and to stirre vp his
mynd with more then ordinary feruour to the conté-
plation of heauenly things he euery day imposed vpon
himselfe certaine voluntary pennances; and remembring that God leadeth a soule into solitude, and there

Gse 2.

Psal. 84. speaketh to her hart, he gaue more attentiue eare to
what his Lord God should speak within him. He prayed therefore very much & often, & whatsoeuer spare
tyme he had, he imployed it in reading of holy bookes, and deuout meditation of heauenly things. What
discommodities, and paynfull labours he endured in
that place, and what true and perfect consolation he
receiued, through conuersation with the heauenly

spouse

ſpouſe we may eaſier imagine, then by words expreſſe. This is certaine, that the litle which he begged would hardly find him bread , to which if perchance he got a litle oyle, or other meate , he thought he had then made a dainty meale indeed.

In this ſolitary kind of life he paſſed fourty dayes with exceeding great comfort , according to the exãple of his heauenly Maiſter, who remained ſo many dayes in the wildernes. And no doubt but by his conuerſation with God , through his exceeding feruour of ſpirit and inflamed loue to his Creatour , he receiued as many heauély graces, as he did ioyes. Somtimes therfore going forth into publicke, he began according to Chriſt his example to teach the people, and to make them partakers of that which he had receiued from heauen . This was his manner of preaching : remẽbring that Chriſt was wont to preach in the fields vpon mountaines , and by the ſea ſhores, wherſoeuer he ſaw any hope of doing good , there would he put himſelfe amongſt aſſembles of people to preach, and eſpecially would he teach thoſe, who moſt of all wanted inſtruction , and ſuch as neuer vſed to come to ſermons , that ſo God might alſo be found of them that did not ſeeke him. Therfore gathering togeather the people in croſſe wayes and ſtreets, and borrowing a ſtoole out of ſome ſhoppe, ſtanding theron he would ſpeake of vertuous and godly life with more feruour of ſpirit then flouriſh of words, to ſuch as either ſtood there idle , or elſe were in their playes and paſtimes: in ſo much as ſome who came to his ſermon only , to get ſomething to laugh at, being moued by the weight

After his ſolitary life he beginneth to teach the peple .

of

of his fpeach, & the diuine force wherwith he fpake, in fteed of laughing, went away weeping. Nothing caufed him to be more admired, or helped on his butrnes better, then refufing to take money, a token of fanctity moft pleafing to all men. For when all faw that he neyther asked any thing of the people about him, nor would take any thing which was offered him, they could not but think that he fought the faluation of others, more then his owne commodity.

Hauing thus employed his labours and indeauours in *Mont Celfus*, with no leffe good fucceffe in helping of others, then in the perfection of himfelfe, he went to *Vincenza* fent thither by *Ignatius*. Where hauing agayne recollected himfelfe in moft diligent mann r, and thinking it now time to performe that for which he had long prepared himfelf, this our new Prieft, with plentifull teares of ioy, offereth his firft, heauenly & wholfome facrifice to the diuine Maiefty. Yow would fay that he did not fo much belieue that which is conteyned vnder thofe facred myfteries, as he faw, and beheld it with his eyes. And fuch indeed was the ardent fire which inflamed both his foule and body, that they who beheld the teares ftreaming fo fweetly from his eyes, could not themfelues abfteine from weeping. And this fingular feeling of deuotion he frō thence forward reteined throughout his whole life, in fuch fort, as if comming euery day likè a new Prieft to the Aultar, he had tafted that firft fweetnes of thofe facred myfteries.

CHAP.

CHAP. VII.

He asſiſteth the Cittyes of Bononia, *and* Rome, *vvith his Sermons*.

HE day appointed for their Pilgrimage to *Hieruſalem* was now paſt, & yet there was no hope of paſſage, the Enemies nauy ſtill keping the ſeas. Therfore they were, according to the tenour of their vowes, to leaue themſelues to the diſpoſition of the Pope ; And for this cauſe the Fathers agreed among themſelues that *Ignatius Loyola Peter Faber*, & *Iames Laynes*, ſhould go to *Rome* in name of the reſt, & offer to his Holines their endeauours & labours for the help of ſoules. In the meane time the others diſperſing themſelues throughout the moſt famous Academies of *Italy*, ſhould inſtruct the ſtudents in vertue, & draw more to be of their Company, if it ſhould ſo pleaſe God. In this diuiſion the vniuerſity of *Bononia* fell to *Xauier* his lot, with no ſmall benefit to that Citty. For as ſoone as he came thither, he went to ſay Maſſe at the Sepulcher of *S. Dominick*, to whome he was euer eſpecially deuout. And it hapned that there was preſent at his Maſſe *Elizabeth Caſiline* of *Bononia*, a religious woman of the moſt holy Order of *S. Dominick*, who perceauing Francis his great deuotion, deſired ſo ſpeake with him. Their diſcourſe was ſuch that ſhe was wholy poſſeſſed with an opinion of his ſanctity.

F
This

This *Elizabeth* had an Vncle called *Hierome Caſiline*, a man both learned and noble, who was alſo Chanon of *S. Petronius*, & Rectour of *S. Lucies* Colledge where he then dwelt. *Francis*, at her requeſt, went vnto him, and by his courteous ſpeach, and candide behauiour got his affection ſo, that he moſt willingly and freely inuited him to his houſe. *Xauier* humbly accepted of ſo worthy a mans courteſy for his lodging, but to eate there he abſolutely refuſed, becauſe he begged his meate, as he was accuſtomed. In the meane time *Caſiline* obſerued him, greatly admiring his vertues, wherof he gaue alſo publicke teſtimony. *Francis* therfore, although his courage was greater then his forces, becauſe he was at that time ſickly and weake, yet his admirable feruour of ſpirit abundantly ſupplied what he wanted in ſtrength. For ſuch was his great deſire of doing good to all, that there was almoſt no worke of Chriſtian charity, wherin he had not a ſweet and louing hand, no otherwiſe then if he had enioyed the greateſt health that could be.

He lodged with Hierome Caſiline.

His diligence in helping his neighbours euen whē he was il himſelf.

Hauing ſaid Maſſe euery day, as his cuſtome was, he afterwards employed himſelfe in ſeruing the ſick in the Hoſpitals, and the poore that were in priſon, in teaching children, and ignorant perſons the principles of Chriſtian doctrine, & in hearing Confeſſions. He moreouer preached to the people in the ſtreets and publicke high wayes, and that not more frequently then profitably. For he vſed not the then new flouriſhing and Rhetoricall kind of ſpeach, but followed altogeather that old, feruent, and Apoſtolicall manner

His manner of preaching.

of

of preaching. There was in him no curious fetting
forth of arguments, nor ornament of words, but all
feruour of mynd and fpirit, intermixed with moſt
pithy and graue fentences, wherto his plaineſſe, and
as it were negleⅆ of ſpeach (an euiⅆt marke of truth)
gaue great luſtre and force. The modeſt and humble
compoſition both of his countenance, & whole body
breathed out that faⅆity which lay hiddē in his foule.
The piety which ſhined forth from his face & lookes
euidently demonſtrated, that whatſoeuer he ſaid,
came from the bottome of his hart, and from the fire
of Charity, which inflamed his breſt. Wherupon his
words carrying more feruour with them then eloquence, were like burning torches to the vnderſtanding of thoſe that heard him, and like a flame of fire
to their affeⅆions : fo as therby might manifeſtly appeare how fiery the diuine word is, when men ſpeake
fo, as God alwayes ſupplieth them with matter. For
Xauiers drift was not to haunt after fauour and vulgar applauſe of the people, but to cauſe in his auditours affeⅆions, a feare and loue of God, and indeed
to feeke truly the ſaluation of foules, not his owne
eſteeme.

In fine the ſubſtance of his fermons was to lay before the people the moſt bitter & euerlaſting tormēts
which are ordained for the reprobate in hell, and the
moſt ſweet & neuer-ending rewards layd vp for the
iuſt in heauen; as alfo to ſhew the deformity of finne,
and the beauty, and louelyneſſe of vertue, not in curious, but in weighty and ſubſtantiall words. And
Gods word being caſt and fowen in this manner, was

The ſu-
bſtance
& fruit
of his
fermons.

recei-

receiued by the hearers, with prōpt & willing minds, & yielded that fruite which *Francis* defired. For many were by the grace of God drawne out of the finke of finne, many alfo brought to frequent the Sacraments, great ftore of money was likewife giuen in Almes, wherof notwithftanding he touched not a farthing, but caufing it to be diftributed amongft the needy, himfelfe begged from dore to dore, prouiding therby both for the neceffity of the poore, & mantaining the dignity of a Preacher. Whēce it came to paffe (which he chiefly aymed at) that, not only very many being penitent for their finnes, lead afterwards a pious and Chriftian life, but alfo (which he cared not for) that his name was made famous by the fpeach and good report of all : Yet he was not more admirable in his fermons, then in his priuate difcourfes and exercifes.

Caſiline his Hoft, who as before we faid, diligently obferued him, gaue this teftimony : That *Xauier* was fparing in his words, but wōderfully efficacious. For he was wont to difcourfe with fuch feruour of fpirit of diuine matters, that he inflamed the harts of his Auditours. When he faid maffe, efpecially that of the Paffion, it was ordinary with him to fhed abundāce of teares, with great inward feeling. In offering of which facrifice he faw him once at the time of his firft *Memento* fo abftracted from his fenfes, that although his minifter pulled him oftentimes by the veftment, yet he did not in any wife perceiue him, but remained fo a whole houre before he came to himfelfe again. For he was indeed (as is faid of *Daniel*) a man of *defires, and much prayer*. Thefe things therfore drew many

(marginal notes:)
Loue of Pouerty

Xauier fparing in his words but wōderfully efficacious.

Saying Maffe of the Paffion he is abftracted from his fenfes.

many of that Citty, but especially his Hoft to the loue of his singular piety, and made his memory also gratefull and famous amongst them after his departure.

And thus he left behind him at *Bononia*, footsheps of long continuance as well of his sanctity, as of his industrious labours. For *Casiline* from thence forward bare great respect to that lodging and chamber of *Xauerius*, and made thereof a place for those of the Society to lodge in, as they trauayled to and fro that way. But in processe of time when the Society of I E S V S made meanes for a house at *Bononia*, by the speciall prouidence of God, there fell vnto them, the next howse to *Xauiers* forsaid lodging, and the Church of *S. Lucia* wherin he had oftentimes said masse; at what time the said lodging was, through the memory of that holy man, and deuotion of the place, turned into a Chappel, that it might be a monument both of *Xauiers* lodging, & sanctity of life. But when afterward the Church of *S. Lucia* was repayred, it was thought good to take in that Chappell to the same, & dedicate it to the Circumcision of our Sauiour, so that you would thinke *Xauier* being inspired from heauen, ordained that place for the Society to inhabite.

The place where he lodged turned into a Chappell.

Francis, hauing performed all things wel at *Bononia* came to *Rome* (as was agreed) about the midst of Lent in the yeare of our Lord 1539. The fathers at that time, had begged a lodging at the foote of an hil of certaine litle Gardēs (now called *Mons Trinitatis*) in a place there which *Quirinus Garzoni*, an honest and vertuous Cittizen of Rome had lent vnto them. There they all liued by begging; and being no lesse desirous

F 3   of

of their neighbours faluation, then of their owne perfection in vertue, they agreed amongft themfelues to
imploy all their endeauours in aduancing Chriftian
Religion, and to labour what they could in Chrifts
vineyard, hoping that, that Citty being the feat of
Religion, and made fertile by the bloud of fo many
Martyrs, would yield moft plentifull fruit of piety.

Taking therfore a right courfe in the execution
of this their vertuous determination, they firft prefét
themfelues to the Vicegerent of the Pope, and to the
Paftours of Parifhes. And hauing obtained leaue to
preach wherfoeuer they would, they deuide themfelues throughout the principall Churches of the Citty.
And *S. Laurence* in *Damafus,* a very famous & remar-

He prea-
cheth in
*S. Lau-
rence* of
Damafus.

keable Church, fell vnto *Xauerius,* and *Fabers* lot,
to preach therin by turnes. In this Church therfore
preaching oftentimes before a frequent and fauourable audience, not of pleafing but profitable and neceffary matters, he reaped a harueft proportionable
to his feed, and caufed in his auditours not fo much
admiration as profit, which is the chiefe thing in a
Preacher. For by his often preaching he endeauoured
to allure the people to an honeft & téperate life, & to
frequent the holy Sacraments. And his other companions béding all their forces likewife to the fame end,
deuotion feemed now againe to be fet on fire in the
harts of the *Romans,* and old *Rome* by little & little to
appeare agayne in her former luftre and renowne.
Yet *Xauier* was not fo imploied in helping the people
by his Sermons, as that he forgot the yonger fort
therof, but with very diligent care inftructed them,

euen

euen ſtreet by ſtreet, in the precepts and myſteries of
the Chriſtian faith ; knowing for certaine that the
chiefe good of the whole Citty depended principally
vpon the inſtruction and vertuous education of children. In the meane time theſe good Fathers, through
their induſtry and labours, brought the Society of
Ieſus to a forme of Religion, which then began, not
only to be eſtabliſhed at home, but alſo to be in great
eſteeme abroad, by reaſon of the vertuous and induſtrious labours therof : In ſo much that *Ignatius* & his
côpaniôs were famous throughout the whole world,
God intending to ſpread this his new flocke ouer all
Nations.

CHAP. VIII.

The Prouince of India, *is by God aſſigned
to* Xauerius.

THE Society of Ieſus was not as yet confirmed by the Popes authority, when the
fame of *Ignatius* and his companions moued *Iohn* the 3. King of Portugall to demand ſome of them of his Holines, and of *S. Ignatius*,
by *Peter Maſcarenas* his Embaſſadour, reſident at that
time in the Citty. The reaſon of this his demaund
was, becauſe the Portugheſes at that time furniſhed
with the kings ſhippes, had with no leſſe fortunate
ſucceſſe, then valorous attempt by vnknowne ſeas,
found out new wayes and Countries, neuer before
heard

The King of Portu-
gall de-
manded
ſome of
the Soci-
ety.

heard off, and hauing subdued many sauage and barbarous prople, had penetrated, euen beyond the Riuers of *Indus* and *Ganges*, into the vtermost East.

The most pious King therfore knowing of what
importāce it was to introduce Christianity into those
Nations, resolued with himselfe to send thither some
vertuous and approued Preachers of the holy Gospel;
thinking himselfe not worthy the name of a Christian King, vnlesse he procured to bring that sauage
people, now vnder his power, to the faith of Christ,
He had heard, by many letters, of *Ignatius* and his
Companions singular guifts, and great paines in helping their neighbours. Wherfore desirous of such mē,
he gaue in charge to *Mascarenas* his Embassadour a-
foresaid, to procure in his name as many of them as he
cold, both of his Holines (at whose disposition he
vnderstood them to be) and of *Ignatius* their founder
and Superiour. *Mascarenas* failed not to performe
with all diligence what his King had commanded, &
so dealt with the Pope and *Ignatius*; but could obtayne only two of them out of so small a number.

The enterprise was indeed no iesse dangerous,
then laborious, because they were by continuall nauigation for many monthes togeather to passe through
the vast Ocean, & horrible raging seas as it were into
another world, where also they should be hourely in
as great danger in labouring amongst those barbarous and wild people, as they were in comming to
them. But those things which vse to affright, & keepe
backe others, drew on these men of God, and louers
of the Crosse, to whome it would be *Christ to liue, and*
gaine

Phil. f. 1.

gaine to dye. Therfore when it was knowne that two were to go into *India* they being all in good hope, and euery one wiſhing it might be himſelfe, did with ſiléce expect the euent of that great buſineſſe.

At that time *Ignatius* a man venerable both for his admirable ſanctity, and inſtitution of the Society, gouerned his companions more by authority, then by any command he had ouer them. He therfore at the firſt allotted out for India *Simon Rodrigues*, & *Nicolas Bobadilla*, not without the pious emulation of their other companions : but indeed God reſerued it for *Francis. Rodrigues* was already paſſed into Portugal, although he were there ſick of a quartan ague; & *Bobadilla* was ſtill ſo ſicke at Rome, that he could not go with the kings Embaſſadour, who then made haſt a-way. Wherfore *Ignatius* hauing very ſeriouſly con-ſulted with God by prayer, calleth vnto him *Francis*, who had now ſome little ſuſpicion of the matter. Then with a cheerfull countenance as his ordinary cuſtome was : Francis, quoth he, God himſelfe hath certainly aſſigned *India* for you. *Bobadilla*, whome I had appointed for it, being as you ſee, detained with a long ſicknes, cannot vndertake it. The reſt of our Companions, for the moſt part, by command of his Holines, are employed heere in Italy in charitable ex-erciſes. You I thought to haue kept with my ſelfe for other occaſions; but God, who hath choſen you out for his Ghoſpell, hath otherwiſe ordained. Shew your ſelfe therfore a man; follow God your Capitaine who by infallible ſignes calleth you into *India* : let that heauenly flame wherwith we haue alwayes ſeene

Ignatius his ſpe-ach.

G you

» you set on fire, stirre you vp now to this worthy en-
» terprize. Take courage answerable to your nobility of
» mynd, to the greatnes of the employment which you
» are to vndertake, and to the expectation which both
» heauen and earth hath of you . Your knowne vertue,
» and especially that prompt obedience of yours,
» which is wont to be ready not only at euery com-
» mand, but also at the least becke, maketh me say no
» more to you about this matter, seeing, what I haue
» sayd, may seeme more then inough to him, whome
» this had byn sufficient, *Go, follow God who calleth you into*
» *India.*

    At these words *Francis*, with a virginall blush in
his countenance, after he had sayd that he was ready
to vndertake all things for Christ his sake, with teares
of ioy trickling from his eyes, gaue *Ignatius* next vnto
God great thankes, because he had accomplished his
desire. For he had felt himselfe indeed long since moued by God to procure the saluation of the *Indians*,
and now by diuine instinct he saw the same approued
by his authority, whome he tooke to be the Interpreter of Gods will. Therfore he would without fayle vndertake it how paynefull or dangerous soeuer it were.
For although all other, both humane and diuine helps,
should fayle him for Gods seruice, yet certaynly his
promptitude of will to obey him should neuer be wāting, & his obedience & life should end both together.

Francis
his obe-
dience
and gre-
atnes of
mynd.

    There appeared hereby in *Francis* not only an ad-
mirable promptitude in obedience, but also a singular
courage. For the Society at that tyme had not any o-
ther place, but only at *Rome*, where he might haue en-
tertayne-

tertaynement or lodging : And in *Portugall* and *India*
he was to find such condition as he could best procure
for himselfe. Moreouer his iorney into *India*, and trauailing there among those barbarous people , carried
with it no lesse danger then misery . But he thirsting
after martyrdome , began to hope for that in *India*,
which *Hierusalem* had denied him . Wherfore through
courage of mynd, and confidence in God contemning
all difficulties and dangers, he as readily resigned himselfe to *Ignatius*, & with as great obedience, as though
God himselfe had commaunded him . And so departing from his chamber he prepared himself for his iorney, reioycing much that the employment which he
desired, was thus now put into his hands euen by God
himselfe .

   There was not any one of the whole howse who
did not affirme for certayne , that it was Gods particular prouidence , that *Xauier* should be chosen before
all others , to take the essay of that new Prouince of
India. For they then called to mind his frequent speaches , wherein he was accustomed to extoll the great
fruite and haruest in *India*, and to bewayle the misery
of so many *Indians* who perished through ignorance.
Therfore they thought him most fit to remedy their
calamity, who had greatest feeling and compassion of
it. They also remembred a certayne vision, which *Iames Laynes* affirmed was tould him in tymes past by
Francis himselfe , when they were chamber-fellowes.
For *Xauier* oftentymes in his sleep thought he carryed
for a good while an *Indian* vpō his shoulder, who seemed so heauy , that being weary with the weight, he

was awaked out of his sleepe: which at last the euent shewed to haue byn rather a presage of a future verity, then only a dream. *Francis* therfore carying with him these hopes & cogitations into *India*, and being ready the next day to set forward on so long a iourney, was an argument how little he affected worldly things, who depended wholly vpon God.

CHAP. IX.

Hauing byn with his Holynesse, he goeth into Portugal, *and giueth arguments of of great vertue in the way.*

BVT before he began his iorney thinking al all things would succeed prosperously and happily with him, if by the authority of Chrifts Vicar he vndertooke so hard an enterprize, he went vnto the Pope, who then was *Paul* the third, and hauing, as the custome is, kissed his feete, he demaunded his benediction, and graunt of certayne Indulgences, being ready to go into *India*, without making any mention of his command. Wherevpon the Pope reioycing for this expedition, receyued him courteously and giuing him his benediction with most cordiall affection spake vnto him, almost in manner following.

I truly, render infinite thankes vnto the diuine Goodnes, that in my Popedome, the fayth is agayne to be brought into *India*, which hauing byn first plan-

ted

ted there by the Apoftles, was by litle and litle extin- «
guifhed by the barbarous carriage of thofe Nations. As «
for your felfe, do you (being rayfed therunto not on- «
ly by our authority, but alfo by the impulfe of God «
himfelfe, whofe perfon we beare) vndertake this fo «
great charge with like greatnes of mynd, remembring «
that God by men calleth you into *India* ; Thinke with «
your felfe who calleth, not who you are. Remember «
that you are called by him, who calleth afwell *thofe* Rom. c. 4.
things which be not, as thofe things which be. Nor doeth «
he fo much feeke men that are fit for his worke, as «
that he maketh men fit by choofing them. Whomefo- «
uer he chofeth, to him he giueth fufficient courage & «
ftrength. For who knoweth not, that the Apoftles «
were of themfelues vnprouided of all things : and yet «
they being poore fifhermen without eyther learning «
or experience in other affaires, what did not they do, «
being fent, and guided by God? What Kingdomes, «
what Nations, what people did not they make fubiect «
to the Croffe? «

And to fay nothing of others, how wel did *S. Thomas* «
the Apoftle carry the matter for the Chriftian caufe in «
India, whither you now goe vnder the conduct of the «
fame God? How many barbarous nations did he win «
to ciuility? How many Aultars of falfe Gods did he «
ouerthrow? How many kingdoms did he bring vnder «
the fweet yoke of Chrift? Neyther ought the terrour «
of miferies, or death it felfe make you flacke in ad- «
uenturing. For to one that thinketh vpon life euer- «
lafting, this life is vile; and to a mortall man nothing «
is more to be defired, then a good and happy death. «

,, To one therfore who contemneth, nay defireth death,
,, what can feeme hard, bitter, or horrible? Go one ther-
,, fore, and by Gods holy conduct, and *S. Thomas* his e-
,, xample, extend farre and wide in the eaft, the bounds
,, of Chriftian Religion. The hand of God is not abbre-
,, uiated. He that in times paft founded the Church by
,, Apoftles, increafed and adorned it afterward by A-
,, poftolicall men.

Then *Francis* fhewing by his countenance, his fubmiffion of mind, anfwered almoft in this manner. For
,, my part (moft holy Father) I do not know what I can
,, do in this kind, why I aboue al others fhould be chofen
,, for this great worke. This I leaue to them to iudge
,, of, who haue chofen me. For it belongeth not to
,, him that obeyth, to iudge what he can do, but to
,, them that command. But I, by how much I diftruft
,, in my owne forces, by fo much I confide in the affi-
,, ftance and prouidence of God, *who chofeth weake things*
1. Cor. 2. *of the world, to confound the ftronge, that all flefh may not*
,, *glory in his fight*. Therfore I affuredly hope, that he
,, who hath layd this charge vpon me, wil alfo giue me
,, forces for the performance therof, according to his
,, pleafure.

The Pope when he perceiued in his countenance,
and by this fpeach a token of great worth in *Xauerius*,
iudging that he who was to propagate the faith a-
Francis mong the *Indians*, had need of greater authority; of
made le- his owne accord, gaue vnto him his owne power, as
gate Apo farre as fhould be needfull. For he made *Francis* his
ftolicall
of *India*, legate Apoftolicall in *India*: And therof gaue letters
patents to the King of Portugals Embaffadour to be
deliuered

deliuered to his King, wherewith, if he thought it good, he might honour *Francis* at his departure into *India. Francis* therfore, who thought himselfe, not sufficient to vndergo so great a burthen, returned home more glad that that Honour was differred, then if it had presently been giuen vnto him. Thence he tooke leaue of his friends not without many teares on both sides, all being very sory for his departure: and with him he carryed nothing at all, but his ordinary habit, & a Breuiary. He went from *Rome* to Portugall in company of *Mascarenas* the Kings Embassadour in the yeare of our Lord 1540. hauing for his companion *Paul Camertes*, who about that tyme had byn by *Ignatius* receaued into the Society.

In his iourney he gaue no lesse signes of modesty, then of sanctity. For although he were giuen to the contemplation of heauenly things, yet being not altogether vnmindfull of humane, he shewed himselfe so courteous vnto all, that when he came to the Inne, he would leaue the best chambers & beds to other of his company, contenting himselfe with the worst things. And when the seruants neglected to looke vnto their maisters horses, or discharge other inferiour seruile offices, he would himselfe do them all, shewing himfelf therin rather a seruant indeed, then a companion. Yet none was more pleasant in couersation then himfelfe, none more ready in all kind of courtesies. He sought by all meanes to deserue well of all, he spake to euery one louingly and friendly, he would himself visit others in a courteous manner, and alwayes bid them welcome with a cheerfull countenance, who came

He loo
kes to o-
thers
horses.

came vnto him; he did eafily and willingly yield vnto
others; his difcourfe was feafoned with a fweete and
pleafing affability. But (which is hardeft of all) he
kept fuch a meane in all thefe things, that tempering
courtefy with grauity, both his actions and wordes
fauoured all of fanctity. It was his proper and continuall cuftome to difcourfe of matters which were eyther pious in themfelues, or els feafoned with piety,
and to incite all with whome he conuerfed, by occafion eyther of fpeach or otherwife, to the hatred of
vice, & amendment of life; fhewing them that it was
harder to endure vices, then the remedies thereof.
And the wholfome bitternes of thefe difcourfes he alwayes allayed, with the fweet fawce of many courteous offices.

Diuers accidents alfo made *Xauerius* his paynefull
care no leffe admirable for his deeds, then for his
words. Vpon a tyme the Embaffadour being angry
with his Harbinger, becaufe he had byn negligent
in preparing his lodging, reprehended him fharpely
for it; but being gotten from his Maifter (as he was
intemperate both in his paffion and fpeach) he inueighed vehemently agaynft him to his companions in
Francis his hearing; who thinking it beft to diffemble
the matter for the prefent whileft he was yet in choller, forbare to fpeake vnto him, that his mind being
pacifyed he might the eafier be cured. The next day
therfore he obferued the man, watching an occafion
to reprehend him: and when it grew towards night,
the Harbinger, as the cuftome was, began to ride on
before to prouide lodging: whereupon *Francis* getting

He ex-
pects a
fit time
to repre-
hend.

prefently

prefently on horfe-backe (for moft commonly he
went on foote for pouerty fake, although he might
haue had a horfe) fet fpurres to his fide, and made haft
after him. When he had almoft ouertaken him , the
Harbingers horfe by chance(yet very fitly for his purpofe) falling downe, lay vpon the man with all his
weight , by which misfortune he was in daunger to
haue byn flayne, but that *Xauerius* came at the very
point , and faued his life. Then taking that as an occafion to tell him of his former fault : What, quoth he,
would haue byn come of thee , if fuddaine death ,
which was not farre of, had furprized thee, being out
of the ftate of grace by reafon of thy anger yefterday,
and intemperancy of thy tongue, for which thou haft
not yet fatisfyed? Thefe wordes fo ftroke the Harbinger (who now faw manifeftly the dáger which he had
efcaped) to the hart, that he was fory for his fault ,
and being put in mynd of his fury the day before , acknowledged his vnbridled paffion , and intemperance of tongue, and then by *Xauerius* perfuafion gaue fa-
tisfaƈion to his companions whome he had fcandali-
zed.

    Francis alfo did not only comfort and affift with
all courtefy his companions when they were weary
with trauayling , but alfo in their daungers gaue them
fuccour , with his prayers , when he could not with
his hands. One of the Embaffadours chiefe pages , although diffuaded by the reft, aduenturing to ride o-
uer a fwift riuer, was brought euen to the point to be
caft away ; for being now carryed into the violent
ftreame, and not able to guide his horfe , whereby
H he

he became inuolued in the turnings of the waters, was by force thereof carryed away without any hope to escape drowning; whereat when others were greatly affrighted, *Francis* his vertue ouercame the dã ger. For encouraging others to pray with him to God, he himselfe began with all attention. And his prayers wanted not their desired effect, for vpon a suddaine the page getting out of the maine streame with his horse, to a shallow place where the water ranne with lesse force, and so taking courage, by Gods assistance, and his companions who called out vpon him, he got at last vnto the banke, on the further side of the riuer, being as all acknowledged, by *Francis* his prayers deliuered from present death.

By his prayers he saueth one from drowning.

Afterwards as they trauayled ouer the Alpes, where being not able to take sure footing by reason of the driuing of the snow, and the craggy rockes & pathes, their horses being tyred with no small daunger to their maisters, the Embassadours Secretary fell by chance from his horse, and was suddainly swallowed vp in a huge masse of snow. The place was vpõ a slippery and steepy rocke, vnder which ran a swift torrent. The greatnes of the danger stroke all his companions into such a feare, that none durst vndertake to assist him, least he should rather pull them after him who should go to help him, then himselfe be pulled vp agayne; so they being all amazed stood still looking one vpon another. As they thus stood, on commeth *Xauerius*, and regarding anothers life more then his owne, leapt presently from his horse, and by mayne strength drew him vp out of the snow, & deliue-

He draweth the Embassadours Secretary out of the snow

liuered him from manifeſt danger, with no ſmall perill of his owne life ; whereupon the Secretary being
obliged to *Francis* for ſo great a fauour, honoured him
euer after as the author of his life, and ſaluation. The
Embaſſadour alſo himſelfe moued by theſe wonderfull acts, and alſo by the ſweetnes of his moſt holy behauiour, bare great affection vnto him.

Francis moreouer did not content himſelfe with
helping his companions, but beſides, he helped all he
met, in as much as he was able, eſpecially at the lod-
gings, and Innes, taking all occaſions both by inſtruction, and admonition to incite them to an honeſt &
Chriſtian life. From that tyme alſo his ſingular piety
hath left behind it an example of Euangelicall perfection, both for religious to imitate, and others to
admire.

Hauing paſt the *Pyrenæan* mountaynes they were
come to the borders of *Pamplona,* where his iorney lay
not farre from his owne territory; his mother, kinsfolkes, and friends were not farre out of the way ; if
he ſhould let ſlippe that occaſion, he knew wel inough
that by reaſon of the great diſtance from *India* thither
he ſhould morally neuer after haue opportunity to ſee
them. He knew alſo, that there could not come any
hindrance of his iourney eyther by his mother, ſhe being a vertuous woman (for his good Father was now
dead) or by his kniſfolkes. His companions importuned him ; the Embaſſadour himſelfe vrged him to viſit and ſalute them by the way. But *Xauerius* fearing
leaſt ſome of the company, through want of conſideration, might be afterwards deceiued by his exam-

He paſ-
ſeth by
his owne
country
without
ſaluting
his kin-
dred.

ple,

ple, he could by no meanes be drawen thereunto.
Thus he shewing an holy hate to his friends, both proued himselfe to be the true disciple of Christ, and also
gaue a document to Religious persons, that they
should with far greater reason hould their friends for
enemies, if they went about to hinder them in the seruice of God.

But least this vnusuall thing should offend eyther
the Embassadour, or any other of the company who
were not acquainted with this kind of heauenly Philosophy, he endeauoured by his mild speach and solid
arguments to make good to them what he had done.
Hauing therfore passed *Spaine* with speed, he made like
hast with the Embassadour vnto *Lisbone*, where the
King of *Portugall* resided. But the Embassadour throgh
long and inward friendship, and familiarity with *Xauier* had now gotté such an opinion of his vertue, that
he could not withhould himself from sending an expresse messenger with letters before vnto the King, to
certify him of *Francis* his comming, and prayse-wor-
thy qualities, which caused in the King a great desire
to see and honour him; which soone after he did ari-
uing at *Lisbone*, where he was already knowne, and
much desired, through report of his vertues.

CHAP.

CHAP. X.

Beeing louingly entertayned by the King of Portugall *, he exciteth them of Lisbone to deuotion.*

LISBONE is a Citty, wherin the Court is kept, not farre from the Ocean sea , the greatest without comparison, of all *Portugall* ; and by reason of an excellent Hauen in the mouth of the riuer *Tagus*, which runneth by that Citty , it is a place very populous for the comming thither of *Indian* merchandise. As soone therefore as he was come thither , being glad of his ariuall at the place from whence he was to embarke himselfe for *India* , he found *Simon Rodriguez* his companion (who as we sayd, was come thither before, for this iourney into *India*) still sicke of a quartane ague, and it hapned that that was his sick day. A strang thing: he comming to him vpon a suddain, & imbracing the sicke man, caused in him such ioy , that his ague neuer after came agayne, and so whether through the greatnes of the ioy, or rather by *Xauiers* vertue, he was quite ridde of his sicknes. When he had a litle rested himselfe after his trauaile, being sent for to the Court, he went thither, togeather with *Simon* who was now recouered , offering both himselfe, and all he was able to do for the help of the *Indians*. The King hauing vnderstood much by his Embassadour of *Francis* his great vertue, after he had courteously receyued

Description of Lisbone.

He cureth Simon Rodriquez of a quartane.

H 3   the

thē both in a great assembly of the Nobility, spake vnto them in this manner. Fathers, quoth he, I am very

glad of your ariuall in *Portugall* for the good of *India*.
And I do not doubt but you, are as glad of it, as my
selfe. For there is opened vnto you, to shew your vertue, the great and vast Countries of *India*, which as I
hope, being carefully and faythfully manured, giueth great promises of a most plentifull haruest of
soules, so great an inclination the people euery where
seeme to haue to the Christian fayth. I for my part, as
long as I carry this Crowne, will preferre Religion
before my Kingdome, and then, shall I account my
selfe King of those Nations, when I shall heare that
they are obedient to the King of Heauen. Wherefore
you cannot doe any thing which willbe more gratefull to mee, and to God also as I hope, then to ioyne
all your forces with me for reducing of the East to the
faith of Christ, our cōmon Lord and Father. If I were
to deale with other kind of men then you, I would
exhort you not to feare the difficulties which nature
may obiect, or the threates of the raging Ocean, or
the miseries of so tedious, yea almost infinite iorney,
or the encountring with barbarous nations; or that
your feruour of piety should not be slacke in going
thither, whither others out of desire of gayne runne
with alacrity. But why do I by wordes endeauour to
inflame your Vertue, knowing well inough, by the
warre you haue vndertaken for Christ, and his Gos-
pels sake, that out of dangers you bring glory to God,
and euerlasting saluation to men; and that you desire
nothing more in this life then to dye a worthy death
for

for Gods fake? It is certaine that nature hath locked vp «
nothing fo clofe, to the which true vertue is not able «
to penetrate. By Gods affiftance you will open a way «
for the Gofpell, not only into *India,* but alfo into the «
furtheft Eaftern parts of the world. There remayneth «
for you eyther a life of eminent merit, or a glorious «
death. Therfore whileft the Nauy is in prouiding a- «
gainft the fpring, do you alfo prepare what fhall be «
neceffary for your iourney. We will take care that «
you want nothing, eyther in *Portugall,* or *India.* «

Then they giuing moft humble thankes vnto the «
King, anfwered in this manner. That they had long *Xauiers*
fince manifeftly feene the great defire he had of adua- *and Ro-*
cing Gods honour, and had not only heard at *Rome* by *driquez*
the report of many, of his liberality anfwerable to his *anfwere*
religious defire: but had themfelues alfo experienced «
it of late in their iorney by many proofes; fo that they «
ought rather to endeauour to correfpond to his Maie- «
fties worthy merits, then to make any queftion whe- "
ther he would be like himfelfe, or no. And becaufe "
their greateft defire was to bring the light of the Gof- "
pell into *India,* & other barbarous nations, he fhould "
therefore without delay vfe them in whatfoeuer they "
could do, for the help of thofe countries. For albeyt "
they well knew both themfelues and his Maiefty, & "
found themfelues to haue neyther ability nor forces "
anfwerable to fo weighty a charge, or to his fo great "
feruour: yet their confidence was that God who layd "
vpon them that burthen would fupply what was wa- "
ting on their behalfe. What danger fhould be refufed "
for Gods fake, and where God leadeth the way? As "

for

,, for themselues, their chiefest care ought to be of Gods
,, glory, and to preferre a worthy death before any life
,, whatsoeuer.

　　Heerupon there arose a strife betweene the Kings
liberality, and *Francis* and *Simons* modesty. The King
promising them all things in aboundance, performed
more in deeds, then he spake in words; and they on
the other side through the strict obseruance of the pouerty which they had vowed, would not vse the
commodities the King offered them. At last the seruants of God remayning constant in their resolution, ouercame the Kings, bountifull nature, and so
he yielded vnto them, drawne therto not through
the equity of their cause, but through admiration of
their vertue. Departing from the King and refusing
a fayre lodging which was freely offered them, they
presently went to the publicke Hospitall of the sicke,
with great commendation both of their humility
and piety. For it was knowne well inough, that
they desired to lodge there before all other places,
that they might more freely serue the sicke for Christs
sake. And herein their charity, and diligent labours
were answerable to that, which the Citty expected
from them.

Refusing
a fayre
lodging
they go
to the
Hospital
of the
sicke.

　　Their manner of life in the Hospitall was this.
In the morning before day, they spent an houre in
prayer and meditation, and hauing read their diuine
office they sayd Masse at breake of day. The rest of
their tyme they imployed both seriously and cheerfully in helping and instructing the sicke, sometymes
comforting those that were sad and afflicted, other-
whiles

Their
manner
of life in
the Hos-
pitall.

whiles encouraging thofe that were ready to dye, to
that laft battayle and encounter ; fometymes agayne
hearing their Confeffions , and at others tymes re-
foluing thofe who asked their aduife in matters concerning their confcience. Which labour of theirs paffed not away eyther in obfcurity or without fruit, feing moft of the Citty drawne by the reporte of their *Many of*
fanctity , came thither flocking vnto them. And they *the Citty*
by continually difcourfing of pious matters , & things *are recal-*
concerning euerlafting faluation , with great feeling *led to a*
and feruour of fpirit., drew many to the hatred of vice *good life*
and loue of vertue, and efpecially to the frequent vfe
of the holy Sacraments. Which pious cuftome of frequenting the fame being then, after a long tyme , firft
renewed in *Lisbone*, was afterward fpread ouer al *Por-* *The fre-*
tugall, both to the great good of the Cittizens themfel- *quent*
ues and commodity of all their Citties . For innume- *vfe of the*
rable people euery where (as the *Portughefes* are very *Sacra-*
much inclined to piety) renewing that moft pious *ments is*
& holy cuftome, and taken with the comfort of lea- *brought*
ding a godly life, by diuine inftinct, intred into fundry *into Por-*
religious Orders : fome alfo defired to be of their So- *tugall.*
ciety , which was at that tyme confirmed by Pope
Paul the III.

   And thus through fo great a reformation of behauiour in the people, the Citty began to appeare of
another forme then before. So as now, not only the
meaner fort , but the Nobility alfo frequented their
lodging for the Sacraméts fake, and to aske their confayle in other matters ; the pouerty of the place & the
men, making the fame more remarkable, by reafon

that the chiefe of the Citty reforted often to the lodging of poore ftrangers; and laftly their contempt of all worldly things ftroke all men into admiration For it was now reported among the people, that twelue Priefts (for two more had ioyned themfelues to the other ten) had at *Rome* made a certaine Society among themfelues; of which number they feemed to behould in thefe two, who were prefent with them, I know not what refemblance of an Apoftolicall life. And fo the people, whether in regard of the number of twelue or for a certayne likeneffe to them in their lyfe, began to call them Apoftles (too great a Title indeed) although the good Fathers withftood, and wholy difclaymed the fame what poffibly they could, but in vaine for the *Portughefes* being a nation no leffe conftant in what they once haue begun, then pious in their refolutions, could not be brought by any means to reuoke that, which once they had giuen to truth, as they verily belieued. Yea this matter went fo farre, that the fame name was afterward deriued to others of the Society, almoft throughout all *Portugall.*

In Portugall he is called an Apoftle.

CHAP. XI.

His Iourney into India *is hindred, but all in vaine.*

V T the *Portughefes* fingular deuotion, by rather burdenning, than gracing the Fathers with fuch a Title, was afterwards
                                                some

fome hindrance to their *Indian* voyage, yet fo, that
although men were diuerfly inclined, ftill Gods will
ftood firme concerning *Francis*. For fome of the principall of the Citty who were much affected to *Xauerius*
and *Rodriguez*, valewing the profit of the Citty, not
only by the prefent fruit, but alfo for the hope of future commodity, contriued among themfelues how
they might ftay thefe men in *Portugall*, efteeming their
owne good to be preferred before others. Firft therefore this matter was treated off by the chiefe of the
Kingdome, and afterwards when it had gotten many graue abettors and furtherers, at laft is brought
vnto the King. Then the Noblemen euery one of
them fhewed how much benefit that Royall Citty had
reaped by *Ignatius* his companions in fo fhort a fpace,
and what great help all *Portugall* might hope from
them, if it could enioy them, not as ftrangers for a
tyme, but as perpetuall inhabitants thereof. And that
the good of *Portugall*, and of that Princely Citty, as
being his chiefe and Royall feate, ought to be dearer
vnto his Maiefty then *India* : Why therefore for the
fuccour of barbarous Nations fhould he depriue his
owne natiue Country of fo excellent helps ? Why
fhould *India* abroad, rather then *Portugall* at home, be
more deare vnto him? Wherfore if it feemed good vnto his Maiefty as it did to them, he fhould plant thofe
worthy men, as feeds of that generation, in *Portugall*,
and fo erect a Seminary at hand which might fupply
them, with fit Priefts to fend into *India*.

The King approuing his Nobles opinion, & iudging it meet to prouide firft for thē who were neereft

to

to him, leauing off for the present his determination
of helping *India*, resolued to detaine them both in *Portugall* to begin a Seminary of the same Institute. Which
as soone as *Rodriguez* & *Xauerius* vnderstood by their
friends, being indeed moued at the vnexpected newes,
they presently certify *Ignatius* by letters of the Kings
new determination, asking him what they should do.
Who hauing acquainted his Holines with the busines,
thought it good to leaue it wholly to the Kings arbi-
trement, nothing doubting but the treating thereof
before him, would make him thinke better of it. Letters are at the same tyme dispatched from his Holines
to the King, and from *Ignatius* to his companions,
wherin the matter was left wholly to his maiesty. But
if he would know, what *Ignatius* his opinion was
therin, it seemetd to him most conuenient that a se-
paration should be made, so as *Rodriguez* might stay in
Portugall, & *Francis* go forward into *India*.

The King therfore following *Ignatius* his Coun-
saile, sendeth for them both, who being vncertayne
what would be resolued off, depended wholy vpon
the diuine prouidence. Then the King in a courteous
manner, as his custome was, shewing them first what
was granted to him from *Rome* concerning their dis-
posall, declareth what he had now resolued : to wit,
That *Simon* should stay in *Portugall* to begin a Colledg
at *Conimbria* which might be a Seminary for members
to be sent into *India*, and that *Francis* should go into
his designed Prouince of the East. Wherefore they
should both, with all speed, prepare themselues with
like diligence to their offices, although they were
diffe-

different, knowing that many times equall rewards are aſſigned for vnequall ſeruices, God not reſpecting ſo much the worke, as the good will wherwith it is done.

Heereupon *Xauerius*, being preſently changed from his great feare, into great ioy, gaue the King many thankes, that he had granted his deſire, and had ſo prudently tempered the want of his companion, with the ioy he gaue him of the diuiſion, that he promiſed not only to be gratefull, but alſo to vſe all care and diligence to be anſwerable for ſo great a benefit. But *Rodriguez* being fruſtrated of his hope and deſire, and at the firſt ſtroken with ſuch an vnexpected declaration, ſhewed by his lookes, and countenance to be ſomewhat troubled: but preſently recollecting himſelfe he anſwered grauely and quietly, almoſt to this effect: That the taking of *India* from him had ſtroke him with ſuch griefe to the hart, that he was not able to coceale it; yet ſince *Ignatius*, the King, and his Holineſſe agreeing all in one thing, ſufficiently declared it to be Gods holy will, he would moſt willingly, at his Maieſties commaund, leaue off that employment for whoſe ſake he had vndertaken it. Wherfore he remained wholly at the Kings diſpoſall, and was glad that by beginning a Seminary, he might alſo in ſome ſort labour for *India*, ſince he might hope to help them by his ſchollers, whome he could not by himſelfe. Thus departing from the King, each of them addreſſed their cares, for the performance of their charge.

CHAP.

CHAP. XII.

Being ready to take shipping for India *, he receiueth from the King the Popes Letters patents of Legate Apostolicall & refuseth to take any thing for the charges of his iourney.*

RANCIS therfore seeing his iorney to be approued by such euident signes both from God and men, began to furnish himselfe for it, not with prouision of victualls and other things necessary and conuenient, but with pious meditations and profitable considerations. For he would not vndertake so weighty a charge rawly & vnprouidedly, but with serious ponderation & preparation, and by thinking with himselfe now whilst he was at leasure, of what he was afterwards to make vse, that so he might not spend his tyme in speculation of that, wherein he was to employ himselfe in the practise.

When the tyme drew neere for his iourney into *India,* the King calling him, is sayd to haue spoken vnto him particularly to his effect. *Francis Xauier,* our ships are ready, the tyme that you haue so earnestly desired of going into *India,* is now come. For my part **I** haue hitherto had so many, and so great arguments both of your vertue & prudence, that I hould it needlesse

The Kings speach.

Ieſſe to vſe any exhortation vnto you, preſaging what "
will follow by that which is already paſt. Yet that we "
may not ſeeme to be wanting in our duty , we will as "
the ſaying is, *ſpurre on him, who runneth already*. Fuſt "
therfore , I commend vnto you the Ethincke Nations "
which are vnder our ſubiection , endeauouring to v- "
nite them to the Church, that my dominions may not "
be further extended then Gods Religion . Then out of "
our fatherly affection towards them, I deliuer & com "
mit the Portugheſes that remaine in thoſe places to "
your truſt, in ſuch ſort that I would haue you ſupply "
the place of our beneuolence towards them. You are "
not ignorant, I know, that Kirgs haue need of many "
hands and eyes, for the gouernment of their king- "
domes. Wherfore I pray, & beſeech you by that very "
God, who is your guide and companion in this iorney "
that (as farre as you may with conueniency) you "
would diligently viſit our garriſons there , and after- "
wards certify vs of all things appertaining to Religi- "
on; that ſo, all impediments, if there be any , being "
ſpeedily remoued , the Chriſtian Religion by your ad- "
uiſe and labour , and by our aſſiſtance and authority, "
may ſpread it ſelfe ouer *India* and the Eaſt. As for my "
ſelfe I will looſe my kingdome, before I will leaue off "
my deſire to aduance Religion . For I am reſolued to "
employ all the meanes and forces I am able for the "
propagation therof. It is your part to be anſwerable "
both to the charge you haue vndertaken , and to our "
deſire. What ayde or help ſoeuer, either the honour "
of God , or the Chriſtian cauſe ſhall ſeeme to require, "
demaund it confidently, and it ſhall be granted, and I "

ſhall

,, ſhall thinke my expences a gayne for Religion ſake.
,, Wherfore proceed cheerfully, and ſeeing that you go,
,, (no doubt, by diuine inſtinct, and conduct,) vpon
,, an enterprize which of al others is hardeſt, maintayne
,, ſtill that couragious mynd, which hitherto you haue
,, borne, and carry with you into *India* that vertue and
,, ſanctity of which all *Portugall* ſpeaketh to be in you.

Then the King taking out of his boſome the Popes Breue ſaid further. And that you may know what
,, moſt ample power is granted you, towards the effec-
,, ting of what you take in hand, not only by mee, but
,, alſo by Chriſt his Vicar vpon earth, behold heer his
,, Holines Breue, wherin he maketh you his Legate A-
,, poſtolical in *India*, which may be both a teſtimony of
,, your power, and an incitement to your vertue.

Then *Xauier*, who had all this while bluſhed to
to heare his owne prayſes, receiuing the Breue with
no leſſe reuerence, then modeſt baſhfulneſſe, replyed.
,, If I (moſt excellent Prince) could find that your e-
,, ſteeme of me were as true, as it is good, I ſhould very
,, much reioyce for the opinion of ſo noble a Perſon as
,, your Maieſty is, & giue great thakes to God the giuer
,, of all good things. But aſſuredly, your ſingular Good-
,, nes is much deceyued, the by opinion of anothers ver-
,, tue. I knowing mine owne weakenes and imperfecti-
,, ons, ſhould I not be thought a mad man, if concerning
,, my ſelfe, I ſhould belieue others before my ſelf? Verily
,, Syr, I being a ſinnefull man, and wholly vnfit for
,, this godly enterprize (which I ſay becauſe it is true,
,, and not for humilities ſake) both your Maieſty, and
,, his Holines do impoſe a farre greater burden vpon

mee,

mee, then my feeblenes is able to fufteine; yet had I ra- «
ther be oppreffed with the weight of the burden, then «
eyther refufe, or caft off that charge, through pufil- «
lanimity, which by Gods will is layd vpon mee. For «
God when impofeth a burden, he affoardeth alfo for- «
ces to beare it, & with power giueth alfo ability for the «
execution therof. Wherfore by the helpe of his hea- «
uenly affiftance, I will do my beft to make it appeare «
that I remember, what perfon I prefent in this weak- «
neffe of myne, fince the charge is impofed vpon me by «
God, his Holines, & your maiefty. And my life fhall «
leaue mee fooner, then I will violate my fidelity, eyther in word in deed.

Hauing fayd thus, the King aduifeth him in a moft
courteous manner to thinke well with himfelfe, what
he might ftand in need off in *Portugall* or *India*, for he
had giuen charge to his officers in ech kingdome that
they fhould carefully procure him, whatfoeuer he
defired. And withall he giueth him his Letters Royall, conteyning no leffe authority then commendations. *Francis* then hauing giuen thankes to the King
and kiffed his hand, as the cuftome is, went home to
bid his friends farewell, that he might embarke himfelfe. And the King was no leffe liberall in deeds then
he had byn in words: for he gaue very ftrayte command to his Captaynes and Officers, and that they
fhould furnifh *Francis* and his companions both in
Portugall and *India* with all things needfull for their
owne maintenance, and for the increafe of Gods honour and glory. So as *Xauerius*, and others of the Society from that tyme forward, dilated the fayth of

K   Chrift

Xauier & others of the Society of Iesus are mantayned in *India* by the libe- rality of the King of Portu- gall.

Chrift in *India* , *Malaca* , the *Moluca's* , and *Iaponia* , maintayned by the Kings liberality . But albeyt all things were plentifully afforded vnto them , yet their modefty fo contended with the kings bounty , that they would take nothing but what was merely need- full , iudging it good , to draw fparingly of another mans liberality , that it might the longer continue.

Wherfore in procuring their owne commodities they in all places fpared the Kings treafure , but efpe- cially vpon their iorney into *India*. And when *Francis* more for the loue of pouerty , then for bafhfulnes ab- ftained wholy from asking any thing at all , the Offi- cers of their owne accord , fhewed him what a ftraite charge the King their maifter had layd vpon them , to furnifh him abundantly with whatfoeuer he fhould want , or defire for his iorney . And withall intreated him to giue them as foone as might be , a note of what things he required , that they might be procured in time. *Francis* hartily thanked both the King for his li- berality , and them for their diligent care : but indeed for his part he required or defired nothing at all. Whē the Officers had often done thus , & receaued alwayes the fame anfwere from *Francis*, they preffed him by in-

Loue of pouerty in his iourney.

treaties , & were very earneft with him that he would at leaft take fome prouifion. At laft to fatisfy their im - portunity(leaft his too much ftáding out might make him feeme obftinate) he fo yielded vnto thē, that with all he ftill kept his former refolution . Then he asked to haue a courfe rugge , or mantle , to keepe him from the extreme cold which he knew they were to endure when the fayled about the *Promontorium bonæ Spei* , &

a

a few litle bookes, whereof he fhould haue great need in *India.* And befides this, he could not be brought by any intreatie to permit any thing els to be prouided for him. Therfore Count *Caſtānerius* Generall of the Nauy feeing *Francis* in the Admirall-fhip, as the King had commaunded, without any prouifion for his iourney, taking compaffion on him, tould him that the King had fent a Page vnto him with great charge to fee him aboundantly prouided of all things fitting for his voyage. But *Francis* earneftly intreated the Generall that nothing might be giuen vnto any, for his prouifion. Notwithftanding the Count was earneft with him to take at leaft a feruant to affift him vpon neceffary occafions. Nay, quoth *Francis*, as long as I haue the vfe of thefe hands, I hope I fhall not need of any other feruant. At which anfwere of *Xauerius* the Count had no more to fay, as he himfelfe affirmed afterward when he related this paffage to others, and withall highly extolled him for his fingular abftinence. Thus furnifhed with no other prouifion then his confidence in God, at the beginning of the fpring he fetteth forth for *India*.

K 2   CHAP.

CHAP. XIII.

In his iourney to India *he giueth admirable tokens of his vertue.*

Wayes into India.

IN tymes past when the Romane Empire stood entire, and Christian Religion flourished in *Asia* (for *India* is a part of *Asia*) there were most commonly two beaten rodes into *India*, the one through *Syria* by the riuers *Euphates* & *Tigris*, & the *Persian* gulf; the other through *Ægypt* by the gulfe of *Arabia* and the *Red sea*. But now those countries being possessed by the forces and superstitiō of the *Saracens*, the passage is not so secure, as it is short, for the Christians of Europe through places annoyed with their enemies. Wherfore the *Portugheses* coasting about by *Affricke*, which lyeth vpon the *Mediterranean* Ocean, and from *Affricke* (as vast as it

A league of Portugall.

is winding about by *Arabia* and *Persia*, sayle into *India*, fetching thereby a mighty circuit. For by these turnings of the sea, *India* in distant from *Portugal* more then foure thousand leagues; I meane those leagues which vsually amongst the *Portughese* marriners conteyne euery one three miles. And in this circuite the Equinoctiall line, which through the heat of the sunne is extreme scorching, cutting of *Affricke* almost in the midst, must necessarily be twice passed.

Prince Henry openeth a new way into India.

The first who with as great courage as skil aduētured vpon this so long, & hard a way, was Prince *Henry* sonne to *Iohn* King of *Portugall* the first of that name,

a man

a man very well experiéced in the Mathematicks. The caufe of this his attempt was, that he might by laying open a new way, haue for himfelfe and the *Portughe-fes* friendly trafficque with the King of *Æthiopia*, commonly called *Preftre-Iohn*, whome he knew raygned in the furtheft part almoft of *Affricke*, not farre from the gulfe of *Arabia*. This defignement hauing prof-perous fucceffe, three Kings of *Portugall* following, to wit *Alphonfus* the V. *Iohn* the II. and *Emanuel* the I. profecuting the fame by litle and litle, brauely & for-tunately opened, and fortifyed a way euen into *India* it felfe. For they tooke the ilands, which lye vpon the coft of *Affricke*, and many other commodious pla-ces, where the *Portughefes* haue their garrifons euen to this day. *Xauerius* therfore making this circuit into *India* put to fea from *Portugall* vpon the eight day of of April in the yeare of our Lord 1541. He went in the fame fhip with *Martin Alphonfus Sofa* newly made Gouernour of *India*. He had of the Society two com-panions only *F. Paul Camertes* a Prieft of fingular ver-tue (who being affigned by *Ignatius*, had accompa-nyed him from *Rome*) and *Francis Manfilla* a Portu-ghefe, who had in *Lisbone* ioyned himfelfe companion to him. They met by the way in this their iourney with many things worthy to be obferued, they being indeed learned men, and very skilfull in Geometry, Philofophy, and Aftrology. In the mediterranean fea they difcouered many Ilands of note, lying vpon the Promontory of *Affricke* fome leffe, fome more diftant both from one another, and alfo from the continent. Amongft thefe are the *Fortunate Ilands* (commonly

called

The Gardens of the Hesperides.

called the *Canaries*) and the Ilands of *Promontorij viridis*, which some are of opinion were the gardens of the *Hesperides*, the three daughters of *Atlas*, so much spoken of in the Fables of Poets. And by these remarkeable places the Nauy passed so neere, that most of them were within sight. Besids this, the sky being very cleere and the sea calme they saw many vnusuall & strange kind of fishes, to the great admiration, and delight of the passengers.

But *Xauerius* although he did not indeed contemne the knowledge of such things, yet thinking with himselfe that he went not to fetch learning or pleasure out of *India*, but for the glory of God, and saluation of soules, began himself within the ship to set forth sights more gratefull to God, & more profitable to men. The chiefe Admirall-ship was rather like a Towne then otherwise, being full not only of marriners, but also of souldiers, the Gouernours retinew, merchants, & seruants, to the number of a thousand persons or therabout. *Francis* therfore as soone as he was entred into his iourney, began togeather with his companions to employ himselfe in the most diligent manner he could in procuring the saluation of his neighbours, by instructing the marriners, and passengers, and soldiers in the Christian doctrine, partly by reprehending their ill behauiour, and partly by exhorting them to cleanse their soules from all filth of sinne. And not in vaine. For thereby the custome of swearing was taken away, many of deadly enemies became friends, many confessed their sinnes with sorrow of hart and many were reclaymed from a bad, to an honest life. *Xauerius*

rius carried alwayes a cheerfull countenance, winning the affections of all by the sweetnes of his behauiour. And for this cause some who were euen drowned in most abominable vices & villanies, & who comonly could not endure the sight of a religious man, were much delighted with *Francis* his most pleasing conuersation. And he knowing well how to deale with such kind of dispositions, drew them at first, by sweet meanes, and by litle & little, from their bad courses; and when at length he found them tractable, then he incited & spurred them on in the way of piety & vertue.

He winneth by his sociable behauiour greatsinners.

In the meane tyme God afforded him matter answerable to his generous and vertuous mind. This tedious and laborious nauigation (as commonly it hapneth) had so extremely worne out the marriners, and other passengers, that now very many fell sicke in the ships, and their victuals greatly increased the same. For they fed continually vpon salt meates, & oftentimes vpon musty bisket: besides, they had for the most parte, no other drink but stinking & corrupted water, which by reason of the nature of the liquour, and small quantity thereof, did rather increase then allay the extreme thirst which the salt meates caused in them. So as the bad humours of such vnwholsome diet being disperced through their veines, ingendred in them diseases no lesse grieuous then deadly. For their gummes swelling after a loathsome manner, and breaking out into horrible vlcers, did not only put the sick men to great torment, but also (which was most miserable) made them that they could not eate. And this contagion by litle and litle increasing through their griefe of mynd,

The difficulties of the *Indian* nauigation

and

and want of neceſſary commodities, began to ſpread
it ſelfe ouer the whole multitude, who were much
thronged vp in ſtraite places for want of roome. For
though the King had, beſides neceſſary prouiſion of
victuals appointed for euery ſhip an Apothecary-ſhop
of excellent drugs, which is no ſmall comfort for ſicke
perſons, yet the ſame could not ſuffice the great number of the diſeaſed. The great feare alſo of the infecti-
on (as it hapneth) made euen friends themſelues to
leaue off the care of one another, & euery man to prouide as well as he could for his owne ſafety. So as the
ſicke being deſtitute both of phiſicke, and attendance
dyed not more through the cōtagious diſeaſe, then for
hungar, which was a worſe plague. Beſides the filth of
the ſhip did ſo extremly annoy theſe poore wretches,
that it was farre more troubleſome and loathſome vnto them, then vnto the others who were in health.

Xauier therfore when he ſaw the ſhip, wherin he
ſayled full of ſick perſons, calling to mind what he had
accuſtomed himſelfe vnto, at the beginning of his cō-
uerſion gaue an euident proofe of his benignity and
vertue. That which hartned him on, would haue
made another afrayd. He ſaw the hatches of the ſhip
ſtrowed not only with ſicke bodyes, but alſo with
halfe dead; he knew the diſeaſe to be very infectious;
he ſaw deaths griſly lookes before his eyes. Yet for all
this, turning feare into charity, and knowing it was
a kind of Martyrdome, to hazard ones life by ſuch
contagion, for the ſauing of ſoules, he reſolued to
help the ſayd ſicke the beſt he could. And ſo he preſently began to heare the confeſſions of thoſe who lay

**His in-
credible
courage
of mind.**

a

a dying; he cleanſed the ſick mens bodies of their filth; he waſhed their linnen, dreſſed their meate, minced it ſmal, and fed them with his owne hands. He miniſtred phiſicke to the weake; he moſt louingly cheered vp thoſe that were ſad; and put them, that were out of hart, in hope of recouery both of body, and ſoule. And thus by ſeruing all indifferently, without regard of perſons, & that with diligence & alacrity, he made euen thoſe that were in health to beare him great reſpect and reuerence.

CHAP. XIIII.

Seruing the ſicke, he arriueth at Mozambicum.

A L L did indeed admire the ſingular ſanctity of life which they ſaw in *Xauerius* his côtinuall diligence, his feruent prayer, & meditating at ſet tymes, and his fatherly loue and Charity to all, without exception. By which meanes he gained both the loue and reſpect of all the reſt, but eſpecially of *Soſa* the Generall. For although the King had vpon his ſetting forth very ſeriouſly cômended *Francis* to *Soſa*, yet his owne vertue (a moſt efficacious kind of commendations) commended him dayly more, and more vnto him. For which reſpect *Soſa* both to fulfill his Kings commaud, and out of his owne accord gaue him all things largely and bountifully. Yet *Xauerius* himſelfe liued alwayes by begging

In the ſhip he liueth by begging.

L   what

what he wanted of the paſſengers for Gods ſakes, and through zeale of pouerty in himſelfe ſtirred vp others to charity and bounty. Which practiſe he with ſuch conſtancy reteyned, that neyther the Generall himſelf nor any of his Honourable retinew could at any tyme draw him from the obſeruance of higheſt pouerty. But this one thing got *Xauerius* much more loue & eſteeme in the ſight both of God and men, to wit, that ſparing from his owne belly, he would moſt freely deuide amongſt the ſicke all what he begged of the paſſengers, and what was aſſigned him by the Generall. For being reſolute in keeping his purpoſe, he eate very ſparingly, and of ſuch meate as required no great labour to make it ready; not ſo much to ſatisfy nature, as to ſuſtayne it.

His conſtancy in keeping of pouerty.

Yet in this meane tyme, his new care of helping the ſick did not interrupt his old cuſtome of teaching the Catechiſme. For euery day he both inſtructed the ignorant ſlaues, marriners, ſouldiers, and other paſſengers in the myſteryes and precepts of our fayth, & alſo exhorted them by pious ſermons to liue Chriſtianlike. And in all theſe labours you would haue thought him not to be tyred out, but to grow ſtronger thereby. Which was neuer more apparently ſeene, then in this *Indian* voyage. For beſides his extreme labour, this alſo was, as it were, added thereto, that whilſt he did all theſe things, he paſſed the Torrid Zone, and the Equinoctiall line not long after the tyme of the Equinoctium. At which tyme there is commonly in that tract of the ſea, eyther through the ſcorching of the ſunne which hägeth ouer their heads,

His enduring of labour.

The diſcommodities of the torrid Zone

or

or by the reflexion thereof vpon the ftill fea , fuch an
intollerable heate , that the ftrongeft men being almoft burnt vp, and confumed with heat and fweat,
do euen faint away, and languifh . And no meruayle,
feeing the paffengers being thruft vp togeather in
clofe roomes of the fhip, can hardly draw their breath,
or at thofe tymes fcarfely take any comfort, eyther in
meate or drinke . For all their drinke , and victualls
being vfually corrupted by the vapors of the fcalding
funne, do for the moft part loofe their force and goodnes for a tyme, vntil they be paft the forfayd line. Many times alfo the winds wholy ceafing, there followeth
for many dayes, & fometymes weekes together, fuch a
calme, that the fhips are not able to moue, to the great
irkefomneffe and griefe of the paffengers . And as the
intollerable heate of the funne , continuing almoft
throughout the whole Torrid Zone, caufeth vehemet
feuers amongft them that paffe vnder it, fo doth it alfo
bereaue many of their liues.

At this time when ficknes came vpon them fo
faft, in fo great a mortality of marriners & paffengers,
as euen they who were well, and had nothing to do
could fcarfe breath, *Francis* forgetfull of him felfe vnderwent the burden of all thefe inconueniences with
courage anfwerable thereunto , iudging it meet as he
faw the fick mens incumbrances to grow greater , fo
alfo to increafe his diligence in helping them. And albeit he was ready to languifh away alfo , through intollerable heate , yet fuch was his courage of mind
fuch the force of the holy Ghoft (who is euer a moft
fweet refrefhment in heat) that he applied himfelfe no

leffe

leſſe carefully then before, both in the ſeruice of thoſe
that were ſick and ready to dy, as alſo already dead.

Hauing thus ſayled through the exceſſiue difficulties of the Equinoctiall line, and being now paſſed a-
bout two thouſand leagues, a greater feare came vpon
them then before, ſince they were to vndergo a greater
danger. For the Promontory of *Good Hope*, a very vnfortunate place by reaſon of moſt cruell tempeſts and
ſhipwrackes, threatned to them no leſſe peſtilence &
mortality then they had already endured. This Promontory taketh its name of *Bonæ ſpei*, or *Good Hope*, for
this reaſon, that hauing once paſſed the difficulties &
dangers therof, you then may hope for a proſperous
nauigation. For the the African coaſt growing ſharpe
in the forme of a wedge, runneth an huge way into
the ſouthern Ocean towards the frozen climate: ſo as
two moſt vaſt ſeas meeting from both ſides of Africk
and continually toſſed with contrary windes, make
a moſt hydeous conflict with themſelues. And this
hapneth eſpecially in the monthes of Iune and Iuly, at
which time in thoſe parts it is the midſt of winter
wholy contrary to Europe, and in which moneth ordinarily, they muſt paſſe that Promontory, who go
from *Portugall* into *India*. And although the ſhippes to
auoid that raging fury & violence of the ſea, as much
as they can, vſe to keep off a great way from land, yet
do they ſeeme to fly the danger more then the domage.
For whilſt they fetch a great compaſſe about, the further they go from the Promontory, the neerer they
come to the frozen Zone, & ſo do neither auoid the
cruell ſtormes, nor yet eſcape the intollerable cold.

Wherfore

The Pro
monto-
ry of
Good
Hope.

Wherfore although they be more secure from danger of shipwracke, yet by reason of the vnusuall and vehement tossing of the shippes, the passengers become extremely sea-sick, and vomit. And as the same could not but augment their disease who were already sick; so also *Francis* his labour was of necessity increased therby: especially when he himselfe being all frozen with cold, sea-sick, and full of loathsomenesse in his stomack, did at the same time performe all those heroicall exercises of Charity. But the diuine vertue which was in him ouercame the weakenes of his nature, and his noble and constant courage, held in the troublesome vomiting of his stomake. And so when he was not able to help himself, he failed not to help those that were sick, euen in the most dangerous time of all. Moreouer, he did not only affoard all the help and assistance he could for the present, to those that accompanied him in this Indian nauigation; but left also an example for others of the society who were to go thither afterwards, how they should carry themselues in that iorney; which they at this day diligently obserue, & are a great help and comfort to the shippes wherin they sayle.

Sofa therfore the Vice-Roy & the other *Portughefes* hauing now passed the Promontory of *Good Hope*, and the dangers therof, by fetching the aforsaid cōpasse, & greatly reioycing by giuing thankes to God, & congratulating one another as the custome is, they sailed amayne along the other side of Africk, which lyeth towardes the South and the East. And hauing gotten beyond the Promontory, almost 600. leagues,

after

after they had spent fiue whole months in continuall
nauigation, and *Francis* in perpetuall labour, they arriued at *Mozambicum* in the latter end of Auguſt, eſcaping, through a more ſafe then proſperous nauigation, many & great dangers. For it is ordinarily but
halfe a yeares ſayle into *India* from *Portugall*: ſo as ſetting out in March, they come for the moſt part to *Goa*
in the beginning of September. But if through ill
weather, cótrary wind, or calmes their courſe be hindred (as now it hapned) they are cóſtrayned to winter at *Mozambicum*.

CHAP. XV.

In the Hoſpitall of Mozambicum *he hel-peth the ſick, being himſelfe at the ſame time ſicke.*

MOZAMBICVM (called *Praſus* in former
times) is a little Iland in the Eaſtern coaſt
of *Africk*, commodious and conuenient
rather for the hauen, then for the tempera-
ture of the ayre (for it lyeth vnder the *Torrid Zone*.)
There be in this Iland but two Townes, one belonging to the *Portugheſes*, the other to the *Saracens*, their
friends. It is diſtant from *Portugall*, if we take our
meaſure not ſtraight on, but by the windings which
ſhippes make thither, aboue 3000. leagues, and from
India about 900. The farre greateſt part of the iorney

The Iláḍ
Mozam-
bicum.

was

was now paſt, and ſcarſe the fourth part remained. But the nauy came later to *Mozambicum* then it ſhould haue done, becauſe both conuenient tyme, and wind had fayled them: So as they were conſtrained to ſtay there al the following winter. At *Mozambicum* therfore when the reſt refreſhed themſelues after the toſſing of ſo long a iorney, only *Francis* who loued labour better then eaſe, tooke almoſt no reſt at all, through the inflamed deſire he had to inſtruct the ignorant, and help the ſicke. I do not doubt, but they who ſhall read this often repetition of *Francis* his laborious endeauours, in inſtructing the ignorant, and ſeruing the ſick, will beſides their ſatisfaction therein, reflect vpon that alſo which my ſelfe in more ſerious thoughts, haue often wondred at, to wit, from whēce he had thoſe wonderfull forces, by which he was ſo often able to vndergoe at once ſo many, & ſuch great labours. But the worthy man being indowed with an incredible courage both of body and mind, and Diuine Grace miniſtring ſtrength to his able nature, was of ſuch force and vigour, that he alone would, and could do in a manner all things for Gods ſake. And wheras he applied himſelfe continually in the ſame workes of Chriſtian charity without any weariſome tedioſneſſe, he neuer omitted any thing, which he ſaw was either good for men, or gratefull to God.

His ſtrength of body & mind.

Therfore as though he had come thither with his forces intire, & no whit weakened, he preſently tooke vp his lodging in the Hoſpitall at *Mozambicum*, erected there by the King, as in other places alſo where the *Portugheſes* haue fortes. His labour was now no leſſe

at

at land, in the hofpitall, then it had bin at fea in the
fhip. For there was, at that time, in Towne both very
great fickneffe, and a multitude of difeafed perfons.
And that which greatly augmented this contagion in
time of Autumne was this, that all the fhippes which
had fet out from *Portugal* that yeare for *India*, lighting
alike vpon ill weather, and peftered with the fame
ficknes, were forced to ftay all winter in that place.
This occafion gaue an new edge vnto *Xauiers* induftry
to vndertake the care of that great multitude of fick
mē. For thinking it fitting for him to beftow his charity alfo vpon the other fhippes, in as much as he was
able, by labouring continually both day and night, he
applied himfelfe to help the afflicted, to adminifter
the Sacraments to the ficke, to comfort the fad, and to
rayfe them vp that lay a dying to hope and confidence in God. All therfore that were fick efteemed *Francis*
to be fent them by God almighty, as the onely remedy
which the afflicted Nauy had. Yet he did not giue
himfelf fo wholy to the fick, as to become vnmyndfull of the reft. For at the fame time vpon holy dayes
he preached before the Viceroy & others, in prefence
of a very great audience, that he might thereby helpe
the foules alfo of thofe who were in health.

　　　Whilft he was thus bufied, and wholly imployed
in helping both ficke, and healhfull in all he could, he
vnderftandeth that a boy, who came in the fame fhip
with him, was fallen fuddainly dead. Whereupon he
prefently asked euery one (whome he met) whether
that boy had learned the principles of the Chriftian
fayth? And when he found that he dyed wholy ignorant

rant therof, he was prefently ftroken to the hart with
fuch griefe, that he fhewed exceeding fadnes in his
countenance, although otherwife he was alwayes
wont to looke cheerfully. Wherefore *Sofa* the Vice-
Roy demanding of him the caufe of his heauines, whē
he vnderftood what it was by his own relation, asked
him, whether he knew that boy to be ignorant in his
Chriftian fayth? No quoth *Francis*, for if I had certainly known that, I would not be fad, for I would without doubt haue taught him with the reft. Then *Sofa*
vrging him agayne, why therefore would he afflict
himfelfe fo much, feeing it was not his fault? Becaufe
(quoth he) there was one in the fame fhip with me,
who knew not his Chriftian fayth, & I knew it not:
Such a care he had of the good of mens foules, and
of the inftruction of children. But how much profit
and benefit arofe from his great Charity, the ficke
found rather by wāting the fame then by inioying it.
For within a few dayes after *Xauerius* fell ficke himfelf
whilft he was helping others with the greateft feruour
he could, wherin indeed, his fortitude wanted not
matter to worke vpon. So great and dangerous a feuer
inuaded him, that he was let bloud feauen tymes within few dayes; whereof, for all that, he did not only
make light account, but imbraced it willingly, as
though it had bin fent from God. But to the end his
generous vertue might be the more euidently feene,
this corporall ficknes was feconded with a greater of
the mind; for he fell alfo into a Phrenfy. This held
him three whole dayes, during which time the Phyfitians who had care of him, tooke their folemne

M   oathes,

He fal-
leth ficke.

oathes, that in things blonging to the body, and his health (as the nature of the difease was) he feemed to be out of his wits : but in matters diuine, and things belonging to the foule (wherin phrenfy vfeth chiefly to fhew it felfe) he was to their great aftonifhment fo well in his fenfes, that he fpake not one word which might feeme to fwarue frō reafon; of fuch force is the vfe and cuftome of vertue. And in this ficknes *Francis* was not more obferuant of piety, then of pouerty. He lay in the publicke Hofpitall amongft the reft, hauing his bed & all other things like vnto them. There wanted not men of Nobility and Efteeme, who whē he fell firft fick ftroue to take him into their houfes, & there to haue care of him, and this as earneftly they intreated of him, as poffibly they could. But all in vayne. For being a true louer of holy Pouerty, in few wordes, he thanked them for their courtefy, but would not accept of their liberality. As long as he was ficke, he lay amongft the common multitude without any difference at all. But the violence of his ficknes was more dangerous then long, which being foone mitigated, he began to be better. This fuddain châce did not any whit diminifh his alacrity in his refolution, but rather increafed his diligence; and no wonder, for now he had learnt by his own experience how much ficke mē ftood in need of other mens help. Therfore as foone as his feuer began to decline, forgetting himfelf, he would with neuer the leffe diligēce goe about the Hofpitall, comfort the afflicted, heare confeffions, & endeauour what he could to help the ficke, though himfelf were fick, euen at that tyme.

He refufeth to be carried outof the hofpitallinto priuat houfes.

Being fick he helpeth the fick.

Neuer

Neuer did *Francis* his benignity fhew it felfe with more fplédour & admiration then at this time. For the Phifitian vifiting (as his cuftome was) the ficke that kept their beds, light by chance vpon *Xauerius*, who hauing a great feuer vpon himfelfe, ftood notwith-ftanding by them that lay fick, and did his beft indea-auour to ferue them, no otherwife then if he had byn perfectly well. The Phifitiã being amazed at that ftrãg accident, ftood ftill a while, then feeling his pulfe, and finding him certainly to haue more need of atten-dance then they whome he ferued, intreated and ear-neftly befought him to go to bed, and reft himfelfe at leaft, vntill his feuer had remitted of its heate, and then he might, if he would, rife agayne, to help the ficke. Whereupon *Francis* thinking he was bound to obey the Phifitian, & yet not to leaue thofe that were in danger, anfwered, That this next night he fhould haue fome occafion with a certaine ficke perfon, who was not well prepared for death, and was in immi-nent danger, and hauing fecured his faluation then he would take his reft. He whome he meant, was one of the pooreft marriners of the fhip, who falling mad through a burning feuer, had not yet made his con-feffion. The next day therefore the Phifitian found *Francis* talking with the fayd marriner, who lay in *Xauerius* bed, and he fate by hearing his confeffion; for hauing foũd him vpon a fuddain lying on the hatches he was fo moued with compaffion towards him, that he prefently layd him in his owne bed. And it feemeth this ftrãge charity of his was honoured with as ftran-ge a miracle. For as foone as this frantick man was

A marri-ner be-ing mad feemeth to be re-ftored to his fen-fes by *F.* his bed.

M 2   layd

layd in *Xauiers* bed, he returned agayne to his senses.
And *Francis* prophecy of his death was not without
ground. For the very same day towards night he
dyed, after he had receyued the Sacraments, full of
great confidence in God. And then it was manifestly
seene that *Xauerius* tooke such paines with him, because he forsaw him to be in imminent danger, both
of lyfe and saluation.

　　Now *Francis* being very glad for this marriners
safety, went presently to bed, for his owne health,
obeying the Phisitian in al things, leauing behind him
an example of no lesse obedience then Christian charity: but as soone as he was recouered of his feuer, he
againe with no lesse diligence then before, set himselfe
to his former labours of helping the sick. And to per-
seuer constantly in that which he had begun well, &
happily, he still kept on the very same course of these
his industrious exercises to the last day of his iourney.
And in this halfe yeares space (for they wintred so long
at *Mozambicum*) he gaue such proofs of his eminent
sanctity, that all, both inhabitants, and they of the
nauy held him generally for a Saint. Wherefore they
doubted not to hold themselues bound to *Xauerius* for
many things which succeeded with them prosperously at the same tyme; ascribing also to his vertue and
merits, that in so great a sicknes, & amongst such a
number of sick persons, so few had dyed at *Mozam-*
bicum that winter, thinking for certayne, that his
diligent Care lightned their diseases, and his Sanctity
tooke them away.

　　Now the tyme was come that they were to depart,

and

The opi-
nion of
Francis
his san-
ctity.

and yet very many of the ficke were not recouered.
Moreouer the Vice-Roy himfelfe began to feele fome
grudgings of an ague; wherfore making all haft, he
thought it beft to leaue them who for want of health
cold not follow him(wch was almoft the whole nauy)
in the wintering places, vntill they hauing recouered
their forces, might be able to paffe into *India*. And fo
hauing eafily perfuaded Father *Paul*, & Fa. *Manfilla* to
ftay at *Mozambicum* with the ficke, he determined
to take *Xauerius* with him, who might be to all both
a comfort in this iourney, and an affured help alfo, if
any thing fhould fall out amiffe.

CHAP. XVI.

Hauing ftayed avvhile at Melinda, *and
in the Iland of* Socotora, *to the great
benefit to the inhabitants, he arriueth at
length in* India.

THE next yeare therfore in the month of
April, *Sofa* the Vice-Roy preparing a great
Galeon for his *Indian* iourney, putteth to
fea with a ftrong band of Souldiars, commanding the Nauy to follow him, as foone as their
health would permit. With him *Francis* alfo departed,
both the *Portughefes* and the inhabitants bidding him
farewell with many teares, and great tokens of beneuolence. *Sofa* hauing a profperous gale, had fai-

led

led in few dayes 700. miles , or thereabout , beyond

The Citty *Melinda.*

Mozambicum, & comming to *Melinda* (a fayre towne of the Saracens , yet friend to the *Portughefes*) he ftaied there a while. In this Citty there be very many *Portughefe* merchants , of whome if any chance to dye there, they are buryed with croffes vpon their graues.

The Croffe in honour amongft the *Saracens*.

Alfo neere vnto the Citty there is a goodly, and fayre Croffe of marble guilded , erected by the *Portughefes* ; which when *Xauerius* beheld, he exceedingly reioyced and gaue thankes to God for that great vertue & glory of the Croffe, becaufe like a conquerer it triumphed in the middeft of the Saracens , and in the Diuels Dominion. This ioy of his was afterward increafed by a memorable accident.

A principall *Saracen* of that Citty, complayning to *Francis* that the Religion of the *Saracens* grew to decay, demaded of him whether it were fo among Chriftians . For of 17. Temples which were in *Melinda* , he wondred to fee but three only frequented , and thofe but of a very few , not knowing the reafon why their deuotion fayled. And all that mifery, fayd he, procee-

Mahomets Religion going to decay.

ded certainly from fome great finne of theirs . But *Xauerius* reioycing that the prefence of the Croffe had fo weakened the Deuils force , tould him , that it was not fo much to be admired that *Mahomets* fuperftitio did now fayle, as that it had held vp fo long. For God being the Author of true Religio could not endure the prayers of the fuperftitious *Saracens* : and that indeed was the caufe why he would haue their Religion alfo ouerthrowne. Thefe things comming to the hearing of a chiefe man of the *Saracens* fuperftition (called in their

their language *Caciz*) a great Doctour in the Maho-
metā law, he protested openly, that vnlesse *Mahomet*
came to them agayne within two yeares, he would
quite forsake him, so decayed was all reuerence to his
Deity in their perplexed minds. But *Francis* being not
able for want of tyme to free them, for the present,
whose mynds were wholy led away with superstitiō,
nor could endure any wholsome counsayle; all that
he could do, was to enkindle in them a desire of Christian liberty, very seriously aduising them to cry oftentymes to God the Creator of man, that he would
vouchsafe to bestow his grace and light vpon them.

After a small space, he set to sea againe, & with new
feruour of spirit held on his old custome to help the
passengers, but especially the sicke (who were not
wanting in the ship) in whatsoeuer he was able. In
which kind he went as farre, as Charity could possibly extend it selfe. He was austere and hard vnto himselfe, that he might be bountifull to others. For a
great part of that iorney he lay aboue hatches among
the cōmon mariners & soldiers, that he might lend his
cabbin and bed to the sick: for his repose he had a hard
Cable rope to lye on, and an Anchor for his pillow.
From hence forward *Francis* had new matter of merit
giuen him both in respect of men, and religion. The
Viceroy hauing sayled roūd about the cost of *Affricke*,
arriued at the Iland of *Socotora*, 1730. miles almost frō
Mozambicum. This Iland lyeth vpon the furthest promontory of *Africke*, which now they call *Guardafu*,
in tyme past *Aromata*, and it is opposite to the *Arabian*
Gulfe, and to the *Mecaan* sea, so called of the Citty
Meca

He lends his chamber and bed to the sick.

A cable rope is his bed.

Meca, a place notorious for the Sepulcher of *Mahomet*.

Socotora is about 100. miles compaſſe. It is a land
waſt, very craggy, and ſtony, without any ſigne almoſt of tillage. It beareth neyther wheate, rize, wine
nor apples, being wholy barren ; yet it aboundeth
with catle, and Dates, whereof the inhabitants make
their bread. Morouer it is a very intemperate ayre being burnt vp with the extreme heat of the ſunne. The
people are wholy rude and ignorant, there being no
ſigne of learning among them, nor a man that can
read. They dwell in Villages, and euery village hath
his *Caciz*, in maner of a Curate. And theſe *Cacizes* haue
no more learning then the reſt, only they do recite by
hart certayne prayers in a ſtrange language, which
they themſelues do not vnderſtand. But the inhabitants glorying that they are Chriſtiãs, beare great deuotion to *S. Thomas* the Apoſtle, and deriue their pedigree from them who were in ancient tymes baptized
by the Apoſtle in that Iland. And although Chriſtianity is at this day extinguiſhed among them, yet they
haue many ſignes of Chriſtian Religion. Their Churches or Temples are built, and adorned magnificently
and deuoutly. They haue Croſſes vpon their Aultars
with lampes before them : and becauſe their pouerty
will not affoard them bells, they call the people together with woodden ratles (as the cuſtome is with vs
in holy Weeke.) Their *Cacizes* although they be marryed, are notwithſtanding notorious for their abſtinence ; as often as they faſt, they abſteyne not only from fleſh, and whitmeates, but alſo from fiſh,
which they haue in great aboundance ; ſo that they
will

The Iſlãd Socotora.

Cacizes like Curates.

Cacizes famous for abſtinence.

they will rather dye then taſt any ſuch thing. Beſides they haue alſo euery yeare two Lents, wherof one laſteth two moneths, and if any be ſo prophane as to eate fleſh at theſe times, they are forbidden to come within the Temple. But it is very euident that the *Cacizes* being themſelues ignorant, there hath byn none for a long tyme, eyther inſtructed in the Chriſtian fayth or baptized. And that which increaſed their miſery was the cruell impiety of a *Saracen* Prince, who had by force ſubdued the inhabitants. For he did not only keepe them in miſerable ſubiection, but taking alſo their litle children out of their armes, endeauoured to trayne them vp in the execrable ſuperſtition of *Mahomet*.

The miſerable conditiō of the Socotoreans.

Xauerius therfore by beholding theſe inhabitants & conuerſing with them, was ſurprized with no leſſe griefe, then ioy, much lamenting, that degenerating from their anceſtours, ignorāt of the Religion which they profeſſed, and deſtitute of Catholicke Prieſts, they ſhould be ſubiect to the *Saracens*, like ſheepe to wolues. Wherefore allthough he hauing a great deſire to inſtruct them (as much as tyme would giue him leaue) yet was he a ſtranger, and wanted their language anſwerable to his will and deſire. But nothing is hard where charity aboundeth. Wherfore leauing ſuch ſignes, as be proper to particular nations, he vſed ſuch as be common to all; and ſo the little while he ſtayed there, he inſtructed thoſe ignorant people in the Chriſtian fayth by noddes, and beckes, and all other ſignes he could inuent. He baptized alſo many children, with the free conſent of their parents.

He endeauours to inſtruct the Socotoreans by ſignes

He baptizeth a greatnūber of children

N   Pre-

Prefently they began euery one to bring their childrē
vnto him, earneſtly entreating him, that he would
be pleaſed to ſtay with them, aſſurng him that there
was not one in the whole Iland who would not be
baptized.

Xauerius therfore although be well ſaw the rude-
neſſe of the people and diſcommodities of the place,
yet thinking of nothing but their ſaluation, went to
the Viceroy, and ſhewing him what a forward harueſt
he had now found, intreated him, that he might with
his good liking remain there ſome time. But the Viceroy knowing that that Iland was ſubieſt to the pillage
of the Turkes, thought it not good to put ſuch a man
in hazard to be taken captiue by them. Therfore cō-
mending him for his ſingular charity towards thoſe
poore ſoules, he aduiſed him, not to ſuffer himſelf to
be deceiued with the ſhew of the preſent good. Be not
quoth he, ouer greedy to ſet vpon the firſt, for feare
you looſe that which is better. Why do you ſo much
deſire to labour heer, where the labour is greater then
the fruit, and where the hopes are leſſe then the dangers? Another country, another people, other Chriſtians expeſt you, with whome you may employ your
labours, both with more ſafety, and fruite.

He deſi-
res to
ſtay in
Soçotora.

Then *Francis*, ſeeing him of a different opinion, &
well conſidering that he knew more then himſelf, anſwered, that he was wholy at his diſpoſe. Then con-
forting the inhabitants, he promiſed them that he
would alwayes, wherſoeuer he was, haue a great care
of their ſaluation. And exhorting them to keep, in
the meane time, the true religion in the midſt of a corrupted

rupted generation, he gaue them assured hope of speedy help. In which promise he did not fayle. For after he was departed from them, by the first occasiō which was offered him, he directed letters to *Iohn* King of *Portugall* wherin he earnestly commended to his kingly prouidence the Christians of *Socotora*, who straying like sheep without a pastour, & abandoned of al, were greatly oppressed by tyranny. For in that Iland there was a *Saracen* Prince who cōtrary to al right & equity tyrannizeth ouer the inhabitants, who be eyther Christians, or affected to the Christian fayth, hauing had their first beginning from the disciples of *S. Thomas* the Apostle, vexing & oppressing them in a miserable manner; yea taking the children by violence out of their parents bosomes he endeauoureth to make them slaues to *Mahomet*, & the Deuill. He therefore intreated his maiesty, as a most religious King, not to permit them by litle & litle to fall away from the grounds of Christianity, to the customes, and rites of the *Saracens*; and that they might not willingly giue their soules to him, who had by force gotten dominion ouer their bodyes. They were in danger vtterly to be vndone, vnlesse his Maiesty from *Portugall* would help them. And there was no doubt, but God, who had giuen him such ability, that he alone of all the Kings in Christendome was able to performe it, would also giue him the will and desire to protect & defend those miserable and afflicted soules. Wherefore he should with all speed endeauour by his Royall assistance, to maintayne them in the faith of their Sauiour who had redeemed both them, and vs with his most pretious

N 2   bloud

bloud : Efpecially feeing that all this, might be done
without any danger or charges at all . For he needed
only to command his Royal Nauy which was yearly
to paffe that way , to deliuer the *Socotoreans* by force
from the moft barbarous Tyranny of that Saracene
Lord .

They So-
cotoreans
*at Fran_*
*cis his in_*
treaty
are deli-
uered
from the
Saracens
tyranny.
    Thefe letters and requefts of *Francis* loft not their
defired effect . For the caufe feemed no leffe worthy
of confideration to the King, then it had done vnto
him, neither did he take it leffe to the hart . Wherfore
with that fpeed , which befeemed his religious Piety,
he fent thither a nauy ; and the warre was as fortunate
as pious . For they taking *Socotora* by force , beate out
the Saracens, and freed the inhabitants from the fub-
iection of their Tyrannicall Lord ; and moreouer placed a ftrong garrifon in the Iland, that their liberty
might be no leffe gratefull then fecure. But *Xauier* not
content with this , beftowed vpon them afterward a
benefit greater then their liberty . For he fent fome of
the Society into that Iland, who might againe cultiuate that ouergrowne vineyard of our Lord, and deliuer them alfo from the Tyranny of the Deuill , who
were already freed from the Saracens .

    As foone as the fhip departed from *Socotora*, *Fran-*
cis fetled himfelfe agayne to his former taske of helping the fick; and at laft with the fame laborious and
charitable exercifes, as he began his Indian voyage,
hauing paffed the coaftes of *Arabia* and *Perfia* , he arriued at *Goa* a famous Citty of *India* vpon the VI.
of May 1542. which day being the feaft of *Saint*
Iohn ante portam Latinam, is very memorable among
the

the *Indians.* For vpon that very day *Xauerius,* who by the fpeciall benefit & fauour of God, was borne for the good of thofe nations, brought with him great light and faluation into *India,* togeather with the light of the Gofpel, and by himfelfe reuiued thofe loft coun-tries, & opened a way to others of the Society for the conuerfion of other nations; the which fhalbe plainly feene by that which followeth in this Hiftory. For heerafter I well fet downe *Xauiers* actes more at large then hitherto I haue done. Becaufe thofe things which I haue already fpoken of, are, although not doubtfull, yet a litle obfcure, becaufe for the moft part they want the cleere teftimony of letters. But henceforward I will fpeake of fuch things, which were left written partly by himfelfe, and partly by thofe, who through long and familiar conuerfation with him in *India,* did not only obferue them whilft he liued, but had alfo particular knowledge of them after his death.

N 3   OF

OF THE LIFE OF
S. FRANCIS XAVIER.

The II. Booke.

In vvhat ſtate be found India.

CHAP. I.

The deſcription of India.

INDIA, being a place much ſpoken of by Poets, and Hiſtoriographers, is a Country of Aſia, almoſt twice as long, as broad, ſomwhat like in proportion to a mans tongue. Towards the North it butteth vpon the Mount Caucaſus; in the Weſt it is inuironed with the Riuer Indus, from whence it taketh its name; as the Eaſt in like manner, is with the riuer Ganges; and from the temperate Zone it ſtretcheth it ſelf out, euen vnto the Southern Ocean. The forſaid riuers iſſuing from the mountaines of Scythia, and deuiding

uiding themselues into two mayne Torrents, the further they runne, the broader they leaue the land betweene them; and hauing run almost a thousand miles (that is, very neere halfe the length of *India*) they fall finally into the sea. Betwixt the mouths of these riuers (where *India* is broadest) it hath 800. miles, or there about in breadth. From thence by litle & little it groweth narrower, vntill it commeth vnto the Promontory of *Commorinum*, where in forme of a wedge it shooteth out a mighty way towards *Asia*.

India, in the inward partes of the land, is inhabited by Pagans of the same Country. Towards the coast which lyeth vpon the riuer *Indus*, they haue for the most part Kings of their own nation; but towards *Ganges* they be *Saracens*. For the *Saracens* hauing now long since gotten thither out of *Arabia* & *Persia*, by litle and litle, partly by policy, and partly by force haue brought many of the *Indians* vnder their subiection. The *Portughefes* also hauing free passage thither by sea, and by occasion of their often going to those Countries, vnknowne to others, haue in ech Coast therof taken the possession of many Townes of good note, for which cause they are very famous throughout *India*, & the whole East. The sea coast of *India*, which for a great part lyeth vnder the Torrid Zone, is continually almost so beaten vpon with the sunne, that it remaineth, euen parched & withered vp all the yeare long. Yet the heat is so tempered by seasonable raynes and Eastern windes, that it is inhabited without any great incommodity; although in summer (which they haue twice a yeare, by reason the sunne passeth

yearely

yearely the Equinoctiall line twice) all things are
burnt vp with the forfayd fcorching heates.

The Country is fertile, efpecially of Rize which
they vfe infteed of wheat: next to Rize, they haue a
certayne Palme-tree, whereof they gather not only
greene, and dry fruite, but alfo (which may feeme incredible) furnifheth them with wine, vineger, and
oyle; yea and befides this, with matter likewife for
houfes, fhips, ropes, and bookes; Nature in this manner making one tree a ftorehoufe almoft of all things.
They haue alfo aboundance of fifh and cattle, & very
great ftore of Pearles, which lying inclofed in fhell-
fifhes, the inhabitants fearch after with great diligéce
in the holes of rockes. And this is the greateft caufe
why ancient writers fpeake fo much of the wealth of
India, fince Riot hath fet a price vpon the Sea's excre-
ments.

The Natiue people of the Country being blacke
of complexion, couer themfelues from the nauell to
the knee with fine linnen, leauing all the reft of their
body naked. They are ordinarily of a feruile, and deceiptfull nature: yet in fo rich a country the people
are moft commonly poore, their riches being ordinarily engroffed in a few mens hands, by reafon of their
Kings, & Princes tyranny ouer them. Yet want doth
not with-hould them from exceffe in their attire: For
all, both men and women, haue commonly gold, or
copper iewells hanging at their eares, which by art
they drawe downe to their fhoulders, as a thing they
much glory in. Moft of them alfo weare for an ornament bracelets vpon their armes, fo effeminate they

are

are become in their attire. Many other things besides
are recounted of their customes, which I hould not
worth the speaking of, with further hindrance to this
history.

The head Citty of *India* is *Goa*, scituate in an I-
land of the same name, almost right against the *Persian*
gulfe, distant from the mouth of the riuer *Indus* some
300. miles, or thereabout. This Citty being fortifyed
by art and nature (for the Iland wherin it standeth is
diuided from the cōtinent by a strait arme of the sea)
for the multitude and fayrenesse of buildings, for traffique, wealth, and number of Cittizens, and inhabitants, may not vnworthily be compared with the
chiefe Citties of *Europe*. And therfore both the Arch-
bishop, & the Viceroy of *India* haue therin their seates,
and is very much frequented by the *Portughcses*. There
be very certayne proofes, not only of *S. Thomas* the
Apostles being in *India*, but also that he watered the
same with his bloud, bringing very many therein to
the fayth of Christ : but their posterity liuing mixt
with *Ethnickes* and *Saracens*, are now by litle and litle
fallen into abominable superstitions, so as for a very
long tyme (excepting a few villages, the inhabitants
whereof take their name from *S. Thomas*) there was
almost no signe of Christianity left in *India*, but only a bare report thereof, vntill the *Portughcses* obtayning *Goa*, and other Townes of *India*, deliuered the
Indians from the seruitude of the *Saracens* & other Ty-
rants, and restored them agayne to the light of the
Gospell. For by liuing amongst them they gayned the
inhabitants to become members of Christ.

O   At

At this tyme *Iohn Alboquercius* of the Order of
S. Francis, a man famous both for his learning and religious feruour, was Bishop of *Goa* (hauing likewise
authority ouer all *India*, by reason that there was neuer a Bishop therein but only himselfe.)He with a few
others of his owne Order, although he laboured more
for the Christian cause, then from so small a number
could haue byn expeded, yet through want of Priests,
could not do so much good, as necessity required.
There were then no religious men in all *India*, but
the *Franciscans*, who were so imployed in assisting the
Portugheses, that they had no time to attend to the Eth-
The *Fra-*   nickes. Of these, Friar *Iames Borban* was most emi-
ciscans   nent, both for his learning, vertue, and zeale of pro-
zeale of   pagating the Christan fayth. For he hauing conuerted
Religion   and baptized certayne *Indian* children, after he had
instruded them in the mystertes of the Christian faith,
and taught them the *Portughese* language,he vsed them
as his interpreters in the conuersion of Ethnickes;
which inuention had good suuesse, answerable to the
witty contriuing therof. He therfore assisted by pious
and worthy persons, began to thinke vpon greater
matters; and instituting a Seminary for the *Indians*,
he imployed himselfe wholy in teaching the students
therof. Wherfore albeyt the Bishop, and the *Francis-*
The be-   *cans* out of their singular piety, desired to spread the
ginning   Christian fayth ouer *India*, yet they being but few in
of a Col-   number were not able to supply so many places. Ther-
ledge in   fore the superstition of the *Ethnickes* and *Saracens* bare
Goa.   great sway not only in other townes of the *Portugheses*
but also in the Citty of *Goa* it selfe. For the Pagans &
Saracens

Saracens being wealthy , and liuing euery where a-mongst the *Portughefes*, practifed their execrable rites publikely euen at noone day , the Gouernours of the Fortes winking therat , eyther becaufe the forces of their new commaund were not as yet fufficiently efta-blifhed , or elfe becaufe their was no body to couince them of their errour , and bring them to the true wor-fhip of Chrift .

Moreouer , if any inferiour *Ethnickes* chanced to become Chriftians , they were fo tormented by the richer fort , that they durft fcarfe profeffe themfelues Chriftians . For the *Ethnicke* and *Saracen* merchants , who dealt with the Kings wares, and cuftomes , were fo rich euen in *Goa* , that through fauour, & power they could do much both with the *Portughefes*, & the Chriftian Magiftrates . So as the new Chriftians be-ing oppreffed, the conuerfion of the *Ethnickes* grew ve-ry cold. The ftate of the *Portughefes* themfelues was not much better. In many places there was very fel-dome vfe of Sacraments , and of fermons almoft none at all. Becaufe in all *India* there were but two or three Preachers at the moft , and not many more Priefts . Wherfore moft of the *Portughefe* garrifons were ma-ny tymes for whole yeares togeather , without eyther fermon or Maffe . And befides this , the beaftly and wicked conuerfation of the *Saracens* and *Ethnickes*, drew them on to much lewdnes. For none were more corrupted in their behauiour then they, nor more forcible to fet fenfuall luft on fire ; & ech one giuing himfelfe to vncleane pleafures , efteemed nothing lighter almoft, then his owne wiues honefty .

The miferable conditiõ of the Neophi-tes.

The loofe be-hauiour of the Portughe-fes in In-dia.

Wher-

Wherfore the *Portughefes*, although naturally they be inclined to temperance and frugality, yet giuing themfelues amidft fo corrupt a nation, to ouermuch banquetting, & to other things which follow therof, kept commonly with them in their houfes, many harlotts, which they had bought, as flaues. And hauing none to reprehend their vices, their luft was growne to fuch a height, that they counted it a point of honour, to liue lewdly, & efteemed no gaine vniuft or difgracefull; fo much had couetoufneffe, fortifyed by bad cuftome, changed all things. It was ordinary amongft them to paffe diuers yeares, without eyther Confeffion or Communion; and if any did confeffe more then once in a yeare, they were commonly held for hypocrites. In fo much that if any one would perchance, out of remorfe of confcience, go oftener to confeffion, he muft do it priuatly to auoyd the note & fpeach of others, like *Nicodemus* who came to Chrift by night. Moreouer the *Portughefes* wiues, and harlots being natiue of that Country, although they were Chriftians, yet through ignorance of the myfteries of the Chriftian fayth, were entangled with the fuperftition of the Pagans and *Saracens*. And their children were like their parents, or rather worfe. This was the ftate of matters in *India* when *Xauerius* came thither; who being very ioyfull that he was at laft (according to his hartes defire) arriued there, & vnderftanding of the forefayd things, bent all his endeauours for the remedying of fo many and great euils. And which is to be much admired, in fo great feruour of fpirit, he carrried himfelfe no leffe warily then diligently.

CHAP.

CHAP. II.

Hauing gotten the good vvil of the Bishop,
he beginneth to labour in India.

H E was not ignorant that many Contro-
uersies and contentions, with no lesse dō-
mage then scandall to the people, might
easily arise betweene Bishops, and other
Ecclesiasticall Pastours if ech of them should stand to
defend the vttermost of their right, without yielding
any thing at all therein. First of all therefore thinking
it good to cut of all occasion of debate and strife, and
That he might prouide good things, not only before God, but
also before all men, he resolued by all meanes to gayne
the good will & liking of the Bishop. Calling therfore
vpon God, and the Archangell Patron of *India*, as his
custome was, he goeth to the Bishop, and hauing saluted him in an humble and most reuerend manner, he
sheweth that he was come into *India* sent by Pope *Paul*
the III. and *Iohn* III. King of *Portugall* to conuert the
Ethnickes to the Fayth of Christ, and to instruct the
Neophites (or yong beginners) and the *Portugheses* in
matters of Christian piety. But being accustomed
more to obey then to command, he had rather follow
anothers mans iudgement then his owne: and for that
his Grace being the chiefe Prelate, he desired to be
wholy at his command, & to attempt nothing, but
with his Lordships aduice & good liking. Then shew-

Hegoeth
to the Bis
shop of
India.

O 3   ing

By great
humility
he wyn-
neth the
Bishop
of *Goas*
good
will.

ing the Popes, and the Kings Letters, which teſtifyed him to be Legate Apoſtolicall, he caſt himſelfe at the Biſhops feete, giuing vp all into his Lordſhips hands, and deſiring to make no other vſe of them, then he ſhould thinke conuenient.

Neuer, peraduenture, was it more euidently ſeene how ſoone true Humility winneth mens affections. *Alboquercius* admiring to ſee ſo great humility, & mo-deſt behauiour in ſuch a man, anſwered to his gentle ſubmiſſion with the like courteſy; for preſently he ta-keth him vp in a friendly māner, & giueth him againe both the Patents and the Letters, telling him, that it would be very gratefull to him, that he, being Legate Apoſtolicall, ſhould vſe the authority which was gi-uen him, according to the Popes and the Kings plea-ſure : neyther did he doubt but he would make ſuch vſe of it, as might make good the opinion which ſuch worthy perſonages had conceyued of him. And from that time forward there was engendred betweene the Biſhop, & *Xauerius* ſo great a loue and reſpect towards one another, that in moſt friendly manner they im-parted to ech other their moſt priuate counſayles. *Francis* therfore being glad that the Biſſhop would aſ-ſiſt him in the aduancement of the Chriſtian cauſe, began more cheerfully to employ all his forces in hel-ping the ſicke at *Goa*, as being the taske which he had vndertaken.

Wherfore out of hand taking vp his aboad in the Kings Hoſpitall, he neuer gaue ouer ſeruing them who were extreme ſicke, with all the diligence he poſſibly could, ſometimes ſpeaking to them a part, ſometymes
exhorting

exhorting them all togeather, and fometymes adminiftring to them the Sacraments of pennauce and thholy Euchariſt, vntill their change of behauiour gaue
him hope of amendment in their liues. His chiefe labour was to help thē, that were grieuouſly ſicke, vpon
whome he attended very diligently, not only in the
day, but alſo in the night, which made all to admire
his ſingular charity, and more then fatherly loue towards them, who were meer ſtrangers vnto him. For
Francis his bed was commonly ſayd to be at his feete
who was ſickeſt in the Hoſpitall; chooſing to lye
there all night that he might be preſently ready to help
if any occaſion of ſuddaine death ſhould chance to
happen. And among all theſe employments he had no
leſſe care in the obſeruance of holy pouerty, then in
exerciſing actes of charity.

Francis lyeth hard by thē that are dangeroufly ficke.

   Xauerius had yet the ſame apparell which he brought
vpon his backe out of *Portugall*, much like to that
which the poorer ſort of Prieſts vſe to weare in *Portugall*. But fearing leaſt his difference in apparel might
auert the *Indians* affections from him, he reſolued to
cloath himſelfe according to the cuſtome of the Prieſts
in thoſe countries. Wherfore knowing that the Society of IESvs hath no particular and proper habit, but
ſuch as the Prieſts where they liue are wont to weare,
out of the familiarity which he had with the ſteward
of the Hoſpitall, he friendly intreateth him to get him
an ordinary Caſſocke ſuch as the poore Prieſts of that
Country were wont to weare. But he not attending ſo
much to what was requeſted him, as what he thought
conuenient, hauing regard of *Francis* his dignity and

His loue of pouerty in his apparell.

                                                          au-

authority, bringeth him an habit of Water-chamlet; and this liberality of his he secondeth with a more liberall speach, telling him that the Priests do there vse such kind of habits, by reason of the extreme heates of *India*, and that although it were Chamlet, yet it was a playne and homely weare amongst them. But *Xauerus* not liking such curious apparell, You may, quoth he, then if you pleale giue this Chamlet habit to some of the Priests you speake of; as for me, one of course black linnen, if you thinke good, will be sufficient, for it is meet for him who hath vowed pouerty, to haue such an habit, as may be a token & signe therof.

He vseth a coate of black linnen without either girdle or cloake. The Steward being ouercome with the verity of this answere, caused presently an habit to be made for him of course hempe linnen downe to the ankles, such a one as he desired. *Francis* euer after wore this habit, according to the fashion of those coutry Priests, without either girdle or cloake, choosing rather to abate of his apparel, then any whit of his pouerty. And in this, his moderation was not more apparent then his constancy. For the same kind of habit he vsed alwayes afterwards in *India*, which practise of his, bare such authority amongst others of the Society, that according to his example, they kept the same kind of habit a great while. But now adayes they vse both girdle and cloake, as the *Portugheses* do accustome; which fashion many of the Priests in *India* do also follow. Afterwards the Maister of the Hospitall perceiuing *Francis* his shoes to be worne out and broken, & the vpper-leather, and soales to be clowterly sowen togeather,

He refuseth to change his old and ill-fauoured shoos for new.

ther, brought him a new prayre. But he being euery
where like vnto himfelfe, could by no meanes be intreated to change his old fhoes for new, faying that
his owne would ftill ferue him well inough, fo immoueable he was in his obferuance of Pouerty.

He refu-
feth to
change
his torne
& ill fa-
uoured
fhoosfor
new.

   Xauerius was then about 45. yeares old, which
age moft cõmonly excelleth more in grauity of iudgment, then ftrength of body. Yet he being of a couragious fpirit, fhrucke not at any labour. For although
at that time his principall care was to helpe the fick,
yet he was no way wanting to them that were in health when any neceffity either fpirituall are corporall
occured. After he had done his endeauours with all
diligence about the fick, in the morning he was ready
to heare the Cõfeffions of them that came vnto him,
for which caufe he was alfo oftétimes fent for by the
principall men of the Citty. And fuch a multitude defired to confeffe vnto him, that his diligence though it
were extraordinary, was not for al that able to fatisfy
the tenth part of them. In the afternoone his cuftome
was commonly to vifit thofe that were in prifon, and
to relieue them with almes which himfelfe begged
for them; where alfo teaching them how to make a
good Confeffion, he by that meanes heard many of
their whol life paft. This example alfo of *Xauerius* was
not without force with others. For the new Viceroy
tooke this courfe once euery weeke, both in a louing
manner to vifit the fick, & to comfort them that were
in prifon, by examining and difpatching their caufes;
which cuftome he continued as long as he ftayed in
India.

He hel-
peth pri-
foners
with al-
mes.

P   Vpon

Vpon Sundayes alſo *Xauierius* aſſiſted the leapers (who haue an Hoſpitall in the ſuburbes) ſeruing thē as well in other things, as in hearing their Confeſſiōs and miniſtring vnto them the holy Sacrament of the Aultar; wherin he ſo wiſely behaued himſelfe, that there was not one of thē who did not receiue the holy Sacraments at his hands. When he thought he had ſufficiently holpen the ſick, he went into a Church of

our B. Lady hard by the Hoſpitall to make them alſo who were in health partakers of his labours. There on Sundayes & holy dayes in the fore-noone he preached to the Portugheſes, in the after-noone he very diligē-tly explicated to the people of that country the chiefe principles of our beliefe, whereunto reſorted more to heare him then the Church wherin he taught was able to conteine. Then he reconciled & made friends ſuch as were at diſcord and debate among themſelues. And

in his priuate conferences he omitted no meanes that might be good for the Cittizens ſpirituall profit. Ha-uing wonne the Portugheſes by his affability of ſpeach he admoniſhed thē in a frindly manner of their vices: and as for other lewd perſons he deterred them from their wickedneſſe, by laying the feare of death & the terrour of hell-fire before their eyes, whome as ſoone as he perceiued to be any thing moued, then he endea-uoured ſometimes by intreaties, ſometimes by perſwa-ſion to drawe them to make a good confeſſion for ſa-

tisfaction of their ſinnes & amendment of their liues: wherupon, as it is well knowne, many were ſo mo-ued and encouraged, that after they had made their cōfeſſions, they began a new life, putting away their
Concubines

Concubines , & making reſtitution of what they had
vnlawfully gotten.

CHAP. III.

He very dexterouſly cauſeth thoſe vvho
kept Concubins, either to marry them, or
to put them avvay: and inſtructeth chil-
dren, and ignorant perſons in the Ca-
thechiſme.

VT he found farre greater difficulty and
trouble among them concerning their Cō-
cubines, then about other mens goods. For
at that time the Portugheſes of *Goa,* were
through want of wiues of their owne nation, greatly intangled with the loue of women-ſtrangers ,
wherof many were of the country of *Sion,* or *Pegu,* &
ſome others of *Iaponia,* and *China,* ſince theſe do farre
excell the *Indian* women both in beauty of body and
comelines of perſon. Wherefore the Portugheſes diſ-
daining to marry with them, kept them as their Concubines. *Xauerius* thinking with himſelf that he ought
to apply ſome remedy to this great euill , began to diſpoſe thē with al the endeauours he could vſe. And firſt
he went about to winne thē by all courteous meanes ;
then as he met them in the ſtreets , he would merily
requeſt them to inuite a poore Prieſt to their ordinary
fare , which they willingly accepted of.

P 2   He

He now fitting at table, would before, or at their repaſt, intreat his hoſt to cauſe his children to be called : whereupon the litle children comming preſently at their fathers cal, *Francis* would take them vp in his armes, & hug them in his boſome, thanking God who had giuen the Father ſuch children for the hope of his family, & withall would pray God to grant thē a good & holy life. Then would he deſire that their mother might be called (a thing which in another would haue bin temerity, but his Sanctity eaſily excuſed it:) when ſhe was come he would ſpeake ſweetly vnto her, and commend her beauty to his hoſt, therby to draw him to take her to his wife, ſaying, that doubtleſſe ſhe was of an excellent diſpoſition and louely countenance, ſo that ſhe might well be accounted a Portugheſe, that the children which he had by her were certainly worthy of a Portugheſe to their father. Why therfore did not he marry her? What wife could he haue better? And he ſhould do well to prouide with al ſpeed for his childrens credit, and the womans honeſty.

He cauſeth ſom to marry their concubines, & others to put them away.

Which wholſome counſail of his proued not vnprofitable. For by his words and authority, without great difficulty he perſwaded many of them to marry their Concubines being himſelfe witnes therof. But if by chance he lighted vpon any one who had, by ſome ill fauoured *Indian*-woman, children like vnto her ſelfe, then as conceiuing great indignation therat he would cry out: Good God! what a monſter haue we here? Do you keep a Diuel in your howſe? Can you keep cōpany with this vgly beaſt? Can you haue children by her? Follow my counſail, driue this monſter,

this

this prodigious creature prefently out of your howfe, &feeke you a wife worthy of your felfe: fo as putting away his concubine, he maried a wife. Moreouer he would not by any meanes (as much as lay in him)fuffer the Portughefes to marry black, or tawny Mores, but fuch as were faire and well-fauoured, to the end they might abfteine from adultery, and ech one content himfelfe with his owne wife.

He wold not haue the Portugefes to marry ilfauoured wiues thereby to keep them frō adultery and concubines.

In this meane time he left not off to inftruct, and drawe all men to the loue of piety, and of a Chriftian life: which labour of his was not in vaine. For this heauenly kind of difcipline did fo worke in the Cittizens, and in habitants behauiours, that *Goa* feemed to be quite changed, from what it had bin a litle before: fo as by reafon of thefe his pious exercyfes in the day, and continuall prayer in the night, he became to be of great credit and efteeme both with the Portughefes and the Indians. But being a man truly vertuous he vfed this their efteeme which was had of him, not as an incitement to pride, but as a fpurre to further vertue. For he thirfting more after the faluation of foules then his owne prayfe, was alwayes thinking of fome new wayes, how to helpe them, for the performāce wherof there was nothing which he would not do. And amongft the reft he had one inuention which in fuch a man as he, gaue an admirable example of Chriftian fimplicity, & was alfo more profitable in effect, then fayre to the fhew.

He being a man of graue yeares and authority, went vp & downe the high wayes, & ftreetes with a litle bell in his hand (fo far was he from thinking any

P 3   thing

He cal-
leth chil-
dren and
seruants
together
with a
litle bell
and tea-
cheth
them the
Christiã
doctrine.

thing disgracefull to him, that might be gratefull to God, and profitable for mans saluations) to call the children and seruants together to Christian doctrine, at the corners of streets and Crosse wayes, sometymes stirring vp the inhabitãts to piety with these, or such like wordes : *Faythfull Christians, for the loue which you beare to Christ, send your Children and seruants to the Christian doctrine* ; which new inuention made infinite of children, slaues, and others to runne flocking vnto him from all places ; all whome, himselfe marching before, he would leade into our B. Ladyes Church, singing aloud the Cathechisme vnto them, and teaching them the same, thereby to cause them more willingly to come to heare him, and so more easily to remember what was taught them in the manner of singing : both which proued afterwards to be so. And herein he vsed no lesse prudence then diligence. For knowing very well, that his labour would then be profitably imployed, if those things which ought to be learned, were well vnderstood, all that he sunge he would explicate briefly and cleerly, according to the capacity of his auditours.

He spea-
keth ho-
mely of
set pur-
pose.

The fruit
of Cate-
chizing.

To the ruder sort, and to slaues he would purposely speake after a rude and homely manner, that their owne fashion of speach might keep them more attentiue, and make deeper impression in their mynds : which endeauour of his was neyther fruitlesse, not in vayne. For from hence arose that so worthy a custome of teaching, and learning the Christian doctrine, which is at this day practised in *India*. And because men reaped more fruit by it, then was expected, the

Bishop

Bishop caused the same to be practised by others, in the other Church: so as aduācing himself in this new piety, those of the Society following *Francis* his institution, others stirred vp therunto partly by the Bishops command, and partly by the example of the Society, it came at last, to be a custome, throughout all *India*, to the great aduancement of the Christian cause. For this practise so spred it selfe abroad both in *Goa* and other places, that euery where, in the schooles, high wayes, streetes, howses, fieldes, and shippes, there were, in steed of vaine & idle songes, sung and heard the principles of Christian faith, with great delight Wherupon it grew to a custome, that children who could scarse speake, did striue to sing most of those verses by hart. And in this exercise *Xauerius* gaue no lesse noble proofe of his temperance and moderation then of his industrious labour. For of all that was giuen him vnder the title of Almes, he reserued nothing to himselfe, but gaue all to the sicke, and poore, in the most priuate manner he could, to the end humane prayse might not depriue him of any reward in the sight of God.

Moreouer he detested from his hart not only vaine glory, but also all honours, wherein few are found firme and constant. For when they vsed to giue him that honour which was due to his vertue, he would not only in his wordes & countenance, but also by the gesture and carriage of his whole body, shew a dislike not only of the honour, but also of those who gaue it him, deeming it an vnworthy thing for a Christiã, who should alwayes haue in mind the reproaches of Christ

Flying of honour.

his

his mayſter, to take delight in honours. Let therefore
thoſe who hunt after titles of honors, hearken what I
am heere to ſay. *Xauerius* being a true contemner of
all worldly things, and eſpecially of himſelfe, did no
leſſe deſpiſe popular applauſe and honour, then others
commonly ſeeke after it: So as now all might ſee, that
nothing could happen more heauy, or croſſely vnto
him, then to ſee his actions prayſed, or himſelfe honoured. But as honour followeth them moſt of all
that fly from it, this his flying from honour, as ordinarily it hapneth, made him more honoured and admired. All were ſtroken with admiration that a Prieſt
of ſingular learning and vertue, comming as a ſtranger out of another world, ſhould do ſo many and ſuch
excellent things, for no reward at all, no not ſo much
as for prayſe or glory.

He is cal-
led the
Apoſtle
in *India.*

    Therfore as before it had hapned in *Portugall*, ſo
alſo now it fell out in *India,* that he began to be comonly called an *Apoſtle*, but indeed with no ſmall
griefe of mynd vnto him: yet the rude multitude preuayled through their conſtancy or rather pertinacy
therein; For that tytle of *Apoſtle* was ſo ſetled vpon
him, that he could by no meanes ſhake it of; & from
him was it afterwards deriued alſo to his other Companions: but they aſſuming a new Name, whereof
we will preſently ſpeake, cauſed that Title, too glorious and vnfit for them, to be at laſt forgotten.

CHAP.

CHAP. IIII.

He procureth a Colledge at Goa *, for the Society.*

ERTAINE deuout men of *Goa* hauing through the perſwaſion of *Fr. Iames Borban* the Franciſcan contracted a league amongeſt themſelues, for the increaſe of the Chriſtian faith, as we haue before declared, had begun a Seminary there of *Indians*, a few months before *Xauerius* arriuall. And hauing found by experience the great want therof, they agreed that it was beſt to haue many children and youthes of moſt of the coūtries of *India* to be inſtructed in the rites of the Chriſtian faith, & to be brought vp in learning, who might be ſent afterward ech one to his owne coūtry, wherof ſome might be made Prieſts, others interpreters. This their pious determination by common conſent they bring vnto *Ferdinand Rodrigues* the Kings Treaſurer, (who at that tyme, in the abſence of *Steuen Gama* the Viceroy of *India*, was Gouernour of *Goa*) deſiring his aduiſe, & aſſiſtance therin. Wherupon by his authority a Seminary was inſtituted at *Goa*, and children of moſt of the Prouinces of *India* (eſpecially thoſe of the *Canarines*, to whome *Goa* it ſelfe appertaineth,) of *Cingala, Malauara, Cellano, Bengala, Pegu, Malaca, China* and the *Abiſsines.* placed therein, & inſtructed in the

Q   precepts

precepts of the Christian faith, who might afterwards become Priests or Interpreters ; and if any of them should not proue fit for eyther of both, they should notwithstanding be there maintained vntill they had learned some trade. And for the better managing of the temporall state of this Seminary, it was thought conuenient, that there should be certaine Procurators chosen by the said Company: but for the education & bringing vp of the children, it was to be committed to the *Franciscans*.

Thefe things being thus difpofed, the Kings *Treafurer* in name of the viceroy of *India*, and of the King of *Portugal* affigned to this Seminary of *Goa* out of the publick treafury a ftipend of 800. crownes, which had belonged to the Pagan Priefts, God by his diuine prouidence turning, in this manner, the Diuels treafure to his owne feruice. This penfion being afterward doubled by the Treafurer, was confirmed by the Viceroy, and the Kings authority. They began alfo to build howfes for that end with a Church therunto adioyning. And becaufe the faid Seminary was founded for the propagatiō of the Chriftian faith, it was intituled *A fancta Fide*, of the Holy Faith ; the reuenewes, and almes whereof were fuch, that an hundred fchollers might well be maintained therwith, but as yet there were not aboue threefcore. *Friar Iames Borban* who was the firft beginner, was Rectour thereof. But it feemes this Seminary was ordayned by God for a Colledge of the Society of Iefus, as *Borban* himfelfe, after he began to be acquainted with them, more then once foretould, being very glad that it fo fell out. Hauing
therfore

therfore taken an exact view of *Xauerius* eminent maner of life, and greatly approuing his induſtry in the
bringing vp of children, he of his owne accord offred him the gouerment of the Seminary: But he hauing reſolued to trauaile all *India* ouer, to preach the
Ghoſpell of Chriſt, would not take vpon him that
burden. *Borban* was very earneſt with him, laying be
fore his eyes what an important buſines it was, and
ſhewing what great fruit might enſue therof, ſince it
being a Seminary of Prieſts, and Interpreters, a ſupply might be continually raiſed therout, for the helpe
of Ethinke nations, a matter of the greateſt moment
that could be deuiſed for the aduancement of Religiō.

He refu-
ſeth the
gouerne-
ment of
the Semi
nary.

But when he perceiued that he could not preuaile,
he began both by himſelfe, & by *Soſa* the new Viceroy
to deale with *Xauerius*, that in caſe he neither could,
nor would take vpon him the charge & Gouerment,
yet that he would at leaſt cōmit the ſame to ſome one
of his Companions. Now *Francis* euery day expected
F. Paul and *F. Manſilla* from *Mozambicum*, & others
alſo out of *Portugall*. And therfore conſidering with
himſelf of what vſe ſuch a Colledge might proue, at
laſt he accepted of the offer, & made *F. Paul Camertes*
Rector therof in his place; and with the good liking
both of the Viceroy and *Borban*, he ſent to *Rome* for
ſome others of the Society, to be maiſters to the fore-
ſaid ſchollers.

Afterwards the reuenewes being by the Kings liberality increaſed, when they thought of enlarging
their houſe to receiue more ſchollers, *Soſa* the Viceroy furthered them therin, both with his authority &

bounty.

bounty. Wherupon both a new Church, and other buildings were begunne, and in short tyme finished, principally by his help and assistance. The Church was dedicated to *S. Paul,* whence also the Colledge was called *S. Pauls* Colledge. And from this time forward the Fathers were called by the Name of the *Society*. For when afterwards that Colledge (excepting the Seminary of the *Indians*) was by the King of *Portugall* giuen to the Society of Iesus, for the instituting of such as were appointed for *India*, and the East, the Fathers tooke their Name from the place.

It is now enlarged by the Kings liberality, and furnished with buildings, being indeed a worthy monument of the King of *Portugall* his bounty, and a most ample Seminary of Preachers and Priests for the help of *India* and the East; the Seminary at *Conimbria* being by his Maiesties order turned into that of *Goa.* For besides many students of the *Indian* Nation, who liue in separate houses, there be to the number of an hundred of the Society, wherof some are there receiued, and others sent thither out of *Portugall*, to be brought vp in learning and vertue, vntill they be able to helpe the *Indians*, and the people of those Eastern partes by their preaching and example. This place the diuine Prouidence ordained first of all for the Society in *India*, before their Name was so much as heard of in those parts, and it is the mother and head Seate of many other Colledges which were afterward founded in the East. But now to come againe to the order of our History, (which hath bin by vs a little interrupted, through the fit occasion we

had

had to fpeake of this Colledge which *Xauerius* procured at *Goa)* this Seminary , as we haue fayd, being affigned to the Society , God gaue vnto *Xauerius* a new
and fertile harueft in *India* to manure .

CHAP. V.

He goeth to help the Neophytes, or nevv
Chriftians of Comorinum.

O fooner had *Xauerius* reftored Chriftian
difcipline at *Goa* which was fallen to decay
but prefently with great care he began to
think vpon the inhabitants of the Promó-
tory of *Comorinū*, & the Coaft of *Pifcaria*, who had bin
lately conuerted to the Chriftian faith , but were left
without Priefts. This Country of *Pifcaria* confifting   Pifcaria.
more of villages then townes , is inhabited by Fifher-
men (whom they call *Paraua's*) & aboundeth greatly
with Pearles, from the fifhing wherof it is commonly
called *Pifcaria* . But the habitantes not knowing their
owne Country Treafures, employ themfelues wholy
in fifhing of pearles for the Saracēs. In this coaft there
is a Town of no fmal note called *Tutuchurinum*, wherin, vpon a very fleight accident, was rayfed a deadly   A deadly
warre, and imminent deftruction to that nation , and   warre v-
was alfo the occafion of their receyuing the Chriftian   pon a
fayth . A *Saracen* wrangling with a *Paraua* (as by na-   fleight oc-
ture they are paffionate and apt to offer difgrace) pul-   cafion.
led contumeliously a ring out of the *Paraua's* eare ,

Q 3   which

which he had hanging therat, as that country fashion is, and withall tore out the hole in the flesh, which with them is the greatest disgrace that can be imagined. Wherupon the *Paraua*, to reuenge the iniury, killed the Saracen.

But (as in hoate bloud there often follow murders and massacres, whereof there is no end vnlesse peace be made) the quarrel wch first began by wrangling of two persons vpon so slight occasion, through desire of reuenge, did afterwards breed a deadly war throughout the whole nation. For the *Paraua's* hauing had many of their side slayne, for one Saracen whome they had killed, resolued to wash away that disgrace with their enemies bloud; & priuatly gathering great troopes out of all the villages, make a suddain assault vpō the Saracens, & massacred a great number of thē. The Saracēs againe being mad with rage raised al their forces against the *Paraua's*, resoluing to destroy and vtterly extinguish the whole nation. Whereupon they presently make ready as great a Nauy as they could, and with great summes of mony corrupt and stirre vp the *Paraua* Kings, against their owne subiects; persuading themselues, that thus enuironing their enemies both by sea and land, they might more easily destroy them.

The *Paraua's* now, when they saw themselues thus beset, enuironed by their enemyes, and betrayed by their owne Kings, not knowing what to do in this case, they beganne to thinke of forraine ayde, so to help themselues in this extremity. There chanced at the same tyme to be present among them a Christian

Knight

Knight (called *Iohn de Cruz*) a man of good account in
his own Country, a *Malabar* by birth, yet more resem-
bling a Portughese then his owne Nation; who for
his valour hauing byn made a Christiã Knight by the
King of *Portugall*, had brought at that very tyme certayne horses for a present to the Kings of the *Paraua's*.
The chiefe therfore of the *Paraua's* by reason of their
former familiarity go vnto him, & lay open the whole
matter before him, asking his counsayle, and aduise
what they should do? *Cruz* being a man both graue
and pious, and hoping this feare of theirs might be
an occasion to bring in the Gospell of Christ among
them, so as at once, they might be set free from the
misery, both of their warre, and their superstition,
tould them his opinion was, that in this extremity of
danger, they were to fly to extreme remedyes : and
seeing, contrary to all iustice and equity, they were
betrayed by their owne Kings, and hardly charged on
all sides by their enemies forces, they should implore
ayde of the Almighty King of Heauē, & of the Portugheses their friends, who were his deuoted and religious seruants; that so, protected by the Portugheses
and the diuine assistance, they might not only defend
themselues, but also triumph ouer their enemies. For
if they would yield themselues subiect to the Christiã
Religion, & to the Portugheses, they certainly would
fight with all their forces for them, both in regard of
religion, and becaufe they were now become their su-
iects, and would also by the help of God, carry the
whole businesse with as good successe, as valour. And
hauing conquered, & ouerthrowne the Saracens, the
deadly

deadly enemyes of Chriſtians, they might alſo perhaps, giue vp the fiſhing of pearles (as taken from the
Saracens by right of warre) vnto the *Paraua's*, in reſpect they were become Chriſtians, as a pledge of their
Religion.

To this counſaile they gaue willing eare. And the
Paraua's were neyther deceyued by the Knight, nor
the Knight by them: for all things came to paſſe as he
had fortold. Now, when the feare of their enemies, &
the authority of that vertuous knight had driuen them
to enter league with the Portugheſes, preſently their
chiefe Magiſtrates (whome they call *Pantagarines*) diſpatch an Embaſſage of certayne principall men amóg
them, to the Portugheſes at *Cocinum*. to whome they
gaue in charge, that as ſoon as they came thither, with
the firſt occaſion, they ſhould become Chriſtians; &
then, putting the *Paraua's* vnder the protection of the
Portugheſes, they ſhould demaund ſuccour of them a-
gaynſt the imminent fury of the Saracens, and withall, Prieſts to inſtruct, and make the reſt Chriſtians.

Cocinū. *Cocinum* is a goodly Citty belonging to the Portugheſes, ſcituated on the ſea betweene the Promontory
of *Comorinum* and *Goa*, the chiefe of all *India* both for
extent and worth, next vnto *Goa*. As ſoone therfore
as the *Paraua's* Embaſſadours arriued at *Cocinum*, after
almoſt two hundred myles iourney, they very fortunately find there preſent *Michael Vaſæus* the Suffragan, or Biſhops Vicar-generall, a man very zealous for
the propagation of Religion: who courteouſly receiuing them, led them to the Gouernour, and commended them and their buſines no leſſe ſeriouſly then effe-
ctual-

fectually vnto him. The Gouernor hauing in a friendly måner heard the *Paraua's* embaffage, he both fhewed
them all courteſy for the preſent, and promiſed them
alſo to deale their matter with the Viceroy of *India*.
And what he ſayd, he performed in a more example
manner, after that the Embaſſadours had deſired to be
baptized. The Viceroy being certifyed of the whole
buſineſſe by the Gouernour of *Cocinum*, as he was a
man of extraordinary zeale, was very glad of that occaſion, and commaunded forthwith that ayde ſhould
be ſent to the *Paraua's*. In the meane tyme the *Paraua's*
Embaſſadours being all baptized, were called *de Cruz*
(of the Croſſe) for *Iohn de Cruz* his ſake, who had
giuen them that counſaile. And ſo great is the reward
which good counſaile deſerueth, that the other chiefe
men alſo of that nation did afterwards take the ſame
name.

*The Co-
morines
are bap-
tized.*

The Gouernor therfore by commaund from the Viceroy prepareth out of hand a ſtróg nauy, haſtneth to
the coaſt of *Piſcaria*, ioyneth battayle with the enemy;
where the matter ſeemed to ſurpaſſe all humane forces. For the *Saracens* were ouerthrowen at the firſt
onſet, and entirely conquered by one battaile. Then
the *Paraua's* being deliuered from all feare of warre,
the Gouernour turned his care to procure the ſaluation of their ſoules; and ſending thither Prieſts, there
were baptized to the number of 20000. Now the Portugheſes returning Conquerours, were not content
with the protection & ſafegard of their ſubiects, but
gaue them moreouer (as *Cruz* had foretould) the fiſhing of pearles, for congratulation of their becom-

R   ming

ming Chriſtians. Wherby the caſe was now ſo altered, that the Saracens might not fiſh, without the *Paraua's* gaue them leaue. Thus, God drawing good out
of euill, by the tearing of one eare, was an occaſion of
the ſaluation of a whole Nation.

But humane frailty was not anſwerable to the
will and ordinance of God. For the Prieſts (I ſpake
of) when they had baptized a great number of the
Paraua's, being diſmayed through the intemperatneſſe
of the ayre, and want of victualls, returned home a-
gayne. And ſo thoſe poore new Chriſtians, who perchance had not byn conuerted to the fayth of Chriſt
ſo much for the loue of true Religion, as for the
feare of daunger they were lately in, being left deſtitute of Paſtours and wholly ignorant, fell agayne
into their old ſuperſtitions and cuſtomes. *Xauerius* being certifyed hereof by *Michael Vaſaus* the Suffragan,
his mynd was poſſeſſed with various affections; for as
he much reioyced at ſo great an aduancement of the
Chriſtian cauſe, ſo was he extremly grieued for their
ſuccourleſſe eſtate; yet was he agayne comforted
through firme hope, that himſelfe might be able
ſhortly to help & comfort thē. For now the Ethnicks
and Neophites that were about the Citty of *Goa*, and
who at that tyme vſed his help, were very well prouided through the endeauours of *F. Borban* & others,
and therfore he much deſired to ſuccour theſe, who
were left deſtitute of all aſſiſtance.

Whereupon forthwith he reſolued to go to *Piſcaria*, to fiſh for the ſoules of the fiſher-men themſelues
which were farre more precious then their pearles.

And

The Co-
morines
are for-
ſaken by
the Prieſts.

And prefently he goeth to the Bifhop, as his cuftome
was, to whome he declareth what determination he
had made, but withall leaueth the whole matter to his
difcretion . Who approuing of what he had determined, wifhed him a happy iorney, & with al courtefy
difmiffed him . At whofe departure the teares which
ftood in *Alboquercius* eyes fhewed euidently how much
he loued *Xauerius* for his humility. The *Francis* hauing
gotten the Bifhops approbation , goeth to *Sofa* the
Viceroy , and opening the matter vnto him, earneftly
requefteth his furtherance for the accomplifhment
therof, if he thought it fitting. The viceroy the tooke
God to witneffe , that he was very fory for his departure , but for as much as he doubted not but that his
going would be for the *Paraua's* foules good , the grief
which his abfece would caufe, would be therby made
more tolerable ; and withall commaunded him to be
boutifully & freely prouided of whatfoeuer his iorney
fhould require. *Xauerius* thanked him for his fo great
courtefy, telling him that he wanted nothing but only
conueniency of tranfporting thither; for feeing it was
dangerous to go by land , in refpect of the many enemies , he intreated with all fpeed to go by fea. *Sofa* prefently granteth his requeft , giueth him a fhippe , and
alfo comandeth his officers to furnifh him of al things
neceffary .

But *Xauerius* was ftill like himfelfe, in refolutely
and conftantly refufing al commodities, either for his
fuftenance , or iorney . So as when the officers offred
yea euen thruft vpon him neceffary prouifions, he
thanked them kindly, and returned them all back

The Bi-
fhops lo-
ue to *Xa-
uerius.*

The Vi-
ceroyes
refpect
to him.

His loue
of pouer
ty.

R 2   again̄e

agayne. But when they preffed him earneftly, and would haue no deniall, he condefcended fomwhat to their importunities(with no leffe commendations for his courtefy in yielding, then for his parfimony in taking) and accepted of a Iacket of leather, & a payre of bootes to defend him from the heate of the funne, which in thofe places, being neere to the Equinoctiall line, he knew to be exceeding great. Thefe things being known, his friends began euery one to bring him other neceffaries for his iourney, but he corteoufly returned all backe agayne, becaufe as he fayd, they were rather hindrances then helps vnto him. And fo he departed, together with the Gouernor of the Coaft of *Pifcaria*, who went thither alfo in the month of October, of this prefent yeare 1 5 4 3.

CHAP. VI.

He laboureth in the Promontory of Co-morinum.

The Co-morine Promō-tory.

T H E Promontory of *Comorinum* being almoft of equall diftance from the Riuers *Indus* and *Ganges*, ftretcheth forth to the Equinoctiall line 400. miles almoft from the City of *Goa*. Hence *India* bending it felfe elbow-wife from the fame place, & the coaft of *Pifcaria* lying betweene the Eaft and the Weft, runneth out almoft 200. myles towards *Ganges*. The whole country is as poore in victuals, as it is rich in pearles. For the inhabitants

bitãts liue vpon rice, milke, fifh, & fome flefh, but they
want bread, wine, fruites, and fuch like things ; and
commonly there is among them no vfe of Phifitians,
or medicins. The people (according to the capacity
of Barbarians) are of reafonable temperate and quiet
difpofitions, but very rude. There is not any country Intolle-
in *India* more fcorched with the funne then this. For rable
when the funne beateth vpon the plaine fands, there is heate of
fuch an intollerable heate that it burneth vp all things the fun.
like a fire. Yet, all this great intéperatenes both of the
ayre & place, together with the like want of victualls
and phifick, *Xauerius* with an vndaunted courage vnderwent of his owne accord, thirfting more after
foules, then others did after pearles.

    Now fome, who hauing paffed a few labours,
and incommodities, and may perhaps, pleafe and *Xauiers*
footh vp themfelues, as though they had fuffered all labours.
the inconueniences that could be, for Chrifts fake,
fhall do well to obferue what we fhall heerafter fet
downe of *Xauerius* extreme and infinite labours, vn-
fpeakable miferies, and want of all things in the Promontory of *Comorinum*. For we may be very much
afhamed of our felues, if we cópare our labours with
his toyles in this new vineyard of Chrift. This long
and vncoth Tract was inhabited by fifhermen, who
dwelt partly in Villages, and partly in Townes to
the number of thirty, whereof twenty belonged to
the Chriftians, in which, befides the forfayd 20000.
newly chriftned, who were yet to be inftructed in the
precéps of their fayth, there were very many others,
both yong and old, to be baptized. He was alfo often-

tymes

tymes to combat both with the heat of the funne, and
with the fand, which in that parching fhore did not
only finke vnder him, but forely fcorched his feete as
he trauayled. But he difcouraged at nothing, went
through with that fo hard an enterprife with as great
a fortitude as he had vndertaken it. For he alone, as if
he had had the courage & forces of many Priefts, nothing regarding the heate of the fun, imploied himfelf
continually in trauerfing the villages and townes of
that Coaft, going oftentimes euen barefoot through
thofe fcorching fands (after his bootes were worne
out) and daily baptizing of infants, children, and o-
thers whome he found willing to become Chriftians;
inuenting many ftrange meanes to hinder them from
facrificing vnto Idols, in ioyning men and women
together with the lawfull bands of marriage, cathe-
chizing euery one according to their capacity, and
making friends thofe who were at variance, being almoft confumed and burnt vp with intollerable heat
and fweat, without any compaffion of himfelfe, or
care of his owne body.

His vfuall cuftome was to fleepe vpon the bare
ground, to liue vpon a little Rice, according to the
He dref- country fafhion, & that but ill dreffed alfo by himfelf
feth rice among fo many great employments. Sometimes alfo
for him- although very feldome, he vfed a little fifh with his
felfe. Rice, or a little fower milke which the Neophytes or
new Chriftians of themfelues brought vnto him. Befides this, he encountred with many great difficulties,
which the want of things neceffary, and the incommodity of thofe places could not but caufe in him, being

ing a ftranger: yet aboue all other difficulties the want
of language did moft trouble him. For when he que-
ftioned the inhabitãts of matters belonging to Religiõ,
they anfwered they were Chriftians, but being wholy ignorant of the Portughefe language, they had not
learned the inftructions and precepts of the Chriftian
fayth. *Xauerius* had brought with him two fchollers
from the Colledge of *Goa*, who were of ripe yeares, &
skillfull both in the Portughefe, & the *Malauarian* tongue which thofe country people vfed. But finding by
experiéce that to inftruct children & ignorant people
by an interpreter, to be a thing both very tedious, and
of fmall profit, he choofe rather to learne himfelfe
their language, then to vfe interpreters ; fo great defire
he had of their conuerfion.

 Therefore he caufed his fayd Interpreters to turne
the principles of the Chriftian doctrine into the *Mala-*
uarian tongue. Then he (although he were now grown
into good yeares) becomming agayne, as it were, a
child for Chrift, getting the fame by hart, went vp &
downe the ftreetes with a litle bell in his hand calling
the children and people together, in fome conuenient
place, and there taught them thofe principles he had
learned in their owne language. His feruour in teaching made the people learne with more alacrity. And
in the fpace of a month the childré which before were
rude and knew nothing, had gotten almoft by hart all
what he had taught thé; fo that *Francis* neither repented himfelfe of his labour in teaching them, nor they
of their diligence in learning. Nay they were fo fet v-
pon learning, that they neuer ceafed to folicite him to
giue

The Co-
morenfi-
ans igno-
rance.

Their
forward-
nes in le-
arning.

giue them set prayers one after another to learne by hart, & heerin they would so presse him, that he could scarce haue leasure to recite his diuine office in quiet, they neuer making an end of begging of him, vntill he had performed their desire.

He vseth children for the instructi on of their Pa_ rents and others.

Xauerius therfore as soone as he perceiued all things to succeed well in these first beginnings, not conten- ting himselfe with the good of a few, bethought how he might help a greater number. And to the end his in- struction might the more dilate it selfe, he caused the children by litle and litle to teach their parents, kins- folkes, seruants, and neighbours those things which they themselues had learned of him. So as these chil- dren, of schollers becomming in a short time maisters, were no small furtherance to the Christian cause. Yet *Xauerius* although he vsed these helpes, did not for al that take any lesse paynes himselfe. For vpon sundaies before a great company, of children, men, and wo- men beginning with the Creed, he briefly explicated vnto them the twelue articles of the Christian fayth & the ten Commandements, some at one time, some at another. He was heard attentiuely and diligently,

The Christiã law in the iudgmẽt of the ve ry Eth- nikes thẽ selues is confor- mable to reason.

with the astonishment not only of the Christians, but also of the Ethnickes, who came in great troopes to heare him, admiring that the Christian Law, was so agreable and conformable to Reason.

But *Xauerius* well knowing, that to explicate diuine matters as they ought, the diuine assistace was more necessary then humane industry, before euery article of the Creed and ech Commaundement he caused the people to recite certayne versicles made for
the

the purpose, wherein Chrift, and the B. Virgin Mary were pioufly inuoked, to affift them particularly both to belieue, and practife thofe things with they heard taught. Sometymes alfo he would tell them confidetly, that if they could obtayne thofe things of God, which they defired of him, concerning the obferuance of the Chriftian Fayth, and his diuine Law, they would afterwards receiue more good, and aboundant benefits from heauen, then yet they durft in their harts prefume to wifh for. He inftructed the *Neophites* and the *Cathecumens* altogeather with, whome indeed he tooke more paynes and labour, becaufe they were in more danger of perditió. But the number was fo great of fuch as became Chriftians (for oftentimes he baptized whole villages in one day) that euen his hands & armes were fo weary with baptizing, that he could not poffibly lift them vp. And oftentimes alfo he was fofpent with repeating fuch things vnto them as appertayned to the Chriftian myfteries, that both his voice and forces fayled him.

He baptizeth whole villages.

Yet for all this his noble vertue and courage fought for no releafement of his labour, but rather how he might gaine new matter of merit : fo that you would haue thought his body could not be tyred out, nor his courage ouercome by any labour whatfoeuer. He fought out dayly many infants heere and there, and baptized them : yet his chiefe endeauour was to inftruct litle children, knowing very well that the bringing vp of tender youth was a matter of great impor tance, as forfeeing that they being inftructed in their infancy, might be more profitable to the aduance-

His vertue ouercome by labour.

His teaching of yong children.

S   ment

cement of the Christian fayth, then their parents; whereof he had many euident tokens. For he had obserued, that these Neophite-children being very apt to learne their Christian doctrine, were greatly desirous to teach the same vnto others ; and that they did so detest the worshipping of Idols, and all kind of superstition, that if their parents did offend therin, they would not only reprehend them themselues, but presently tell *Francis* of it. And to this forwardnes of the children, his helping hand was not wanting. For if at any tyme they tould him of any such thing, he would presently take the children by the hand, & go with them to the house, where that heynous offence was committed, and as though an alarum had byn giuen to battaile, he would set vpon the place where the Idols were, and together with the children rush vpon them, breake them to pieces, spit and tread vpon the, & lastly vtterly destroy them, making in this manner the worship of the Deuill, a laughing-stock to children.

CHAP.

CHAP. VII.

Hauing vvrought many miracles by him-
selfe, and the nevv Christians, he is for
his extraordinary Humility,commonly
called the Holy Father.

FTER he had sufficiently instructed in
the Catechisme, the places which first occured to him, going to the Towne of *Tu-*
tuchurinum, he lodged by the way in an
obscure village of Ethinckes, who contemning their
neighbours examples would not heare of the Christiã
faith. Wherupon *Francis* vrging them with the authority of all the coast of *Piscaria*, they all togeather answered, that they could not do it, by reason of their
Kings auersion; which was not so indeed, but a pre-
tense only to set a glosse vpon their obstinate Superstition. In which case *Xauerius* being vncertaine
what to do, God out of his prouidence gaue him an
admirable occasion of bringing his designes about.
There was a certaine womã of good worth, who had
now bin very dangerously in trauaile of Child-birth
three whole dayes; & her life was desperate. Her husband & kinsfolkes were also weary with praying to
their deafe Gods for her safe deliuery, & al in vaine
the which *Francis* vnderstanding, & putting his trust
in God, went thither in all hast with an Interpreter

A womã
is by ba-
ptisme
deliue-
red from
the dan-
ger in
child-
birth.

S 2   and

and gaue them some hope of help. Forthwith, hauing gotten the consent of the family , he began to deale with her , that seing there was no hope of her reco-uery , she would prouide for her soule , and withall he began briefly to explicate vnto her the chief points of the Christian fayth. Wherwith she being touched from heauen , and giuing credit thereto , *Xauerius* de-maunded , whether she would be a Christian ? Very willingly ,quoth she. Then *Francis* reading ouer her the Ghospell , baptized her , being euen ready to dye. A wonderfull thing . The baptisme caused her so easy a deliuery , that presently she brough forth her child without any paine or difficulty. For which prosperous euent he being exceedingly glad , presently baptizeth the infant newly borne , and then all the other of the house,who were both astonished at the miracle , and not a little replenished with ioy.

  This fact being so admirable, and wrought in presence of so many witnesses , was instantly diuul-ged: wherupon *Xauerius* iudging it a fit occasio to vrge the people whilest they were thus amazed , began to be instat with the chiefe men of the Village, that they should not doubt to imbrace that Religion , wherof they had lately seene so euident a testimony . But they tould him first , they would not do it without their Kings licence ; yet afterwards , hauing obtayned the same of his Lieutenant, they were almost all bapti-zed,together with many whole familes,so as that Vil-lage presently became Christian.

He bap-
zeth a
whole
village.

  Frō thence *Francis* going to(*Punical* (a Town of great resort)was there louingly receiued by the Neophytes

where

where prefently hauing, according to his cuftom, bap-
zed many infats, he began to inftruct the people & the
childrē in the Catechifme. There was at the fame time
in that Towne a great mortality, and ficknes among
the people, fo as very many came daily vnto him frō
all places, requefting him to vifit their houfes, & fay
fome prayers ouer the ficke. And many alfo who had
none to follicite for them, being extremely fick, crept
vnto him as well as they could for the fame caufe. *Xa-*
uerius being moued as well out of his owne compaffio-
nate nature, as by that pittyful fpectacle, had a fcruple
to deny thofe poore foules fo iuft requefts, fearing left
if he fhould be flacke therin, the Chriftian Religion
might receiue fome detriment therby. Therfore he
fpent much time, and tooke great paines, in vifiting
them & reading the holy Gofpell ouer the fick : & not
in vayne. For it is well knowne, that very many fick
in that fea coaft were by him cured, & many poffeffed
perfons deliuered. And it is certainly reported that he
there reftored three dead men to life, befides a yong
maide of *Cangoxima,* of whome I will fpeake in her
proper place.

He hea-
leth the
ficke, de-
liuereth
poffeffed
perfons.

Punicall, as we faid, is a towne of good note in the
coaft of *Comorinum.* In this towne there dyed a certaine
yong man of a good family, who being by his frinds
brought to *Francis,* and layd at his feete with great lamentation, the good Father tooke him by the hand,
and commanded him in the name of Chrift to aryfe ;
wherupō he prefently rofe vp aliue. This act *Xauerius*
out of his true humility, fuppreffed as much as poffibly he could, by diffembling the matter, but all in

A youth
is rayfed
from
death.

He fup-
preffeth
his mira-
cles.

S 3

vaine.

vaine. For there wanted not witnesses therof, nor men
to spread it abroad, although it were a matter of great
moment wherof they were to be the authors. And this
miracle was afterward confirmed by another the like.

In the same towne a Christian woman went to
Francis, and with teares bewayling her misfortune of
being left desolate, most humbly besought him, that
he would be pleased to go to her little sonne who had
bin lately drowned in a well. He bad the woman
be of good courage, for her child was not dead, and
presently goeth along with her, as she desired. As
soone as he came to the house he fell downe vpon his
knees, and hauing prayed a while he made the signe of
the crosse vpon the dead body ; wherupon the child
presently start vp from the beere wheron he lay, not
only aliue, but also found, and in perfect health. At
which miraculous accident the Christians who stood
about were all astonished, and cryed out for ioy. But
Xauerius earnestly intreated them by al meanes possible
to make no words therof, & so secretly retyred himselfe from thence. They people could not ouercome
theselues as he requested, to keep silent so miraculous
an euent ; and besides that, *Xauerius* his dissembling
the matter, made his sanctity the more to appeare.

Moreouer (to speake nothing of others) *Iohn
Triaga* a Portughese, a deuout and graue man, & very
familiar with *Xauerius*, being demanded iuridically by
the Bishop of *Goa* his Vicar, after the Fathers death,
testified, that himselfe was present at *Punicall* when
Francis raysed to life a certaine boy, and also a little
girle. And withall testified, that he had vnderstood
by

A boy drowned in a well is rayſed agayne to lyfe.

Two reſtored to life.

by many, that *Xauerius* had reftored another to life in
a village called *Bembari*; wherof himíelfe had fometymes asked *Xauerius*, & although, out of humility, he
feemed fo fuppreffe the matter, yet he might eafily
perceaue it was true, which he went about to côceale.
And all this, is very fufficiently teftified, vnder the
depofition and feale of the Viceroy of *India*, by the
King of Portugals command.

   Now, whileft *Xauerius* thus laboureth about the
fick, and the dead, there wanted not other many and
dayly imployments, to inftruct children, conuert the
Ethnickes, baptize thofe that were conuerted, bury
the dead, and fatisfy thofe who asked his aduice. But
the cumberfomnes of the fick, by reafon of their great
number, and the bruit which was now fpread abro;d
of thofe that were cured, did fo greatly increafe daily,
that it was not poffible for one to fatisfy all. Moreouer, as many times it hapneth, there arofe contentions among the people, whilft euery one did ftriue to
get *Francis* firft to their houfe. Therfore to condefcend
to their iuft demaunds without any breach of peace,
he found out an inuention, which was as profitable
as neceffary, to fend in his place certaine Chriftian
childrê fit for that purpofe. Thefe children by *Xauiers*
appointment going about to the houfes, firft called togeather thofe of the family and their neighbours, then
hauing recited the Creed all togeather, they exhorted
the fick to haue an affured hope and confidence in God
by whofe help they were to recouer their health; &
all laft when they had ftirred vp all that were prefent
to deuotion, then they added certaine pious and godly
prayers.   This

He cu-
reth the
ficke by
children.

This inuention of his was not in vayne. For what by the fayth of the children, & of the standers by and the sicke, and of *Francis* Author thereof, it caused in the diseased health both of body and soule. In so much that very many Neophites were therby confirmed in their beliefe, & many Ethnickes brought to the faith of Christ : the force whereof they had experienced by the recouery of their health. But if any of the said children could get *Xauerius* Beades, he thought himselfe highly honoured, for that infallibly they cured all the sick who were touched therwith; wherfore, as iewels famous for the wonders wrought by thē, euery one did striue to get them ; so as being carryed about continually to the sicke, they seldome brought them backe to *Francis*, seruing rather to worke miracles thē to pray vpon. And by the meanes of these children he did not only help those who were sicke, but assisted also possessed, and obsessed persons.

There was one, who being possest, was wonderfully tormented by the Deuill, to whome *Francis* being requested to go, but could not by reason of other employments, sent in his place certayne Children **He deli-** (who assisted him in teaching the Christian doctrine) **uereth a** with a crosse, and tould them what they should do. **possessed** The children went to the possest man, and, as *Xaue-* **person** *rius* had instructed them, gaue him the crosse to kisse, **by the** **children** and they themselues recited certayne prayers which they knew by hart. Whereupon presently, to the astonishment of all that were present the possest man was deliuered, not so much by the fayth, and sanctity of the children, as of *Francis* himselfe. The report

report heereof being fpread far and neere with great
applaufe to *Xauerius*, his fame became more remarkable by his humility. For thefe miracles which he *Xauiers*
wrought by diuine power, by fending children vp & humili-
downe, he would not acknowledge as done by him- ty.
felfe, but afcribed them to the faith of the children, &
of the fick perfons: fo as endeauouring by all meanes
to debafe himfelfe, and to hide his owne vertue, he He is
made the fplendour of his fanctity the more appeare. called
Wherfore fhining, as he did, not only with that emi- Holy
nency of vertue, but alfo with Chriftian humility, he Father.
was now commonly called the *Holy Father.* Thus hidden Vertue becometh more glorious.

CHAP. VIII.

*He fubftituteth Deputies in his place to
teach the Chriftian doctrine, and procureth for them a certaine ftipend of the
King of Portugall.*

THIS approued fidelity and induftry of the
neophytes in curing difeafes made *Xauerius* He ta-
defirous to make thē his fellow-labourers keth
in inftructing the people. Wherfore making children
choice of fuch as were no leffe diligent then vertuous, the cate-
he fent them abroad, bidding them teach the Cathe chifme
chifme to the rude and ignorant in houfes, wayes, with him
and ftreetes, in manner as he had inftructed thē. When

T   he

he faw this courfe which he had inuented , was able
to go on by it felfe, he with the children went to another Village , intending in the fame manner to inftruct the reft of the townes. All which when he had
once gone ouer , neuer thinking of reft , but as it
were dallying with his labours , he againe returned to
the firft village , there to amend what he fhould find
amiffe ; and in the fame manner went ouer all the reft
which before he had vifited .

In the meane time alfo, thinking it neceffary to
eftablifh the Chriftian faith, not only for the prefent
but alfo for the time to come, he left in euery towne &
village a Copy of the Chriftian do rine, willing thofe
that could write , to copy it out, and the reft to learne
it by hart, and to repeate it ouer euery day. He ordayned alfo in all the forfaid villages , that vpon all holydayes , the Neophytes fhould affemble themfelues into one place, and there all togeather fing the Chriftian
doctrine . And that thefe things might be well and
duely obferued, thinking it expedient to leaue fome
in his place , he appointed in euery Towne and Village, one to haue a care of matters concerning Chriftian religion , whome in their language they called the
Canacaple . And that this order which was fo neceffary, might neuer ceafe, or decay, he procured of the
Viceroy of *India* an yearly ftipend for the *Canacaples* .
The reafon of this was, that in tyme of neceffity there
might alwayes be fome to baptize the infants newly
borne when they fhould be in any danger of death ,
and to fupply in other things that which could not
be well differred , and withall to affift the Neophytes,
                                                    when

when *Francis* was farre of, and could not so speedily come vnto them. So as, in euery place he appointed one or two who excelled the rest in the vnderstanding of the Christian doctrine, graue carriage, feruour of piety, and integrity of life, teaching them the manner and forme of baptisme, and giuing them in charge, that if at any tyme necessity should require, they should with all speed baptize litle infants; and if any matter of importance besids, chanced to happen, they should presently certify him thereof.

These, euery one in his Village, for want of Priests, being as it were the Curats or Pastours, had the care of the Church, and twice euery day they taught the Catechisme both in Latin, and in their owne countrey language: in the morning to the men, and in the afternoone to the women. They also, as the Christian custome is, denounced the Banes of Matrimony, making enquiry what impediments there might be to hinder any from lawfull marriage; but their principall charge was to baptize litle infants, who through weakenes might be in danger of death. And when *Xauerius* made his visit in the sayd Villages, these his substitutes presently deliuered vp vnto him the number of childrē which were borne that yeare, of those who kept concubines in their houses, and of such as had any emnity or discord amongst themselues, that therby he might with all speed apply remedy therto. And by this meanes he knew, & composed all difficulties euery where; so that making very litle stay any where he might passe on to other places.

To these *Canacaples* at *Xauerius* request were assigned

400 crownes yearely, out of the publicke Treasury, by the viceroy of *India*, and afterward confirmed by the King of *Portugal.* This said mony was accustomed to be payd to Queene Catherin of *Portugal*, to buy her shoes, and Pantofles . Wherfore *Francis* wrote vnto her maiesty very pleasantly and piously, that she could haue no fitter shoes or Pantofles, to climbe to heauen then the Christian children of the *Piscarian* coast, and their instructions . Wherefore he humbly intreated her to bestow her shoes and Pantofles, as a Tribute, vnto their teachers and instructors, therby to make her selfe a ladder to heauen, for she might be glad of such an occasion, then the which she could not perhaps haue wished a better . The Queene, as a woman of notable piety, approued of his request, and very willingly, and freely assigned the same to the *Canacaples*, and maisters of the Neophytes. And thus, by *Xauerius* meanes, by the *Queenes* liberality, & the Kings authority, this order was instituted and established, with no lesse merit of the benefactors, then profit to the Christian cause.

His letter to the Queene of Portugall.

The liberality & piety of the Queene of Portugall

CHAP. IX.

He conuinceth the Brachmans, and conuerteth some of them.

The Brachmans & their religion.

IN this meane while, *Francis* had no small ado with the *Brachmans*. These *Brachmans* descending fro the race of Kings & Priests,

are

are amongſt all the nations of *India* the chiefe, both
for Nobility and Wiſedome. They worſhip one God
(whome they call *Parabram*) the begining of al things,
and perfect in euery reſpect, as being Creatour of heaueſ & earth. But togeather with this truth they mingle
innumerable fables to deceiue the common people.
They ſay, he hath three ſonnes, who gouern the world,
and yet haue all the ſame nature, and diuinity. This
forſooth, is ſignified by the girdle the *Brachmans* theſelues weare, at the end wherof there be three little
cords hanging from one knot: hauing in this manner,
either through the malice of men, or craft of the Diuel
corrupted the miſtery of the *B. Trinity*, which was anciétly receiued among them. They haue alſo goodly
Temples dedicated to theſe Gods, with three Towres,
which being ſeparated at the baſis, by little & little do
ioyne altogeather in the toppe. They haue their images drawen out in diuers ſhapes, which in times paſt
they tooke vpon them, which they call *Pagods*.

These *Brachmans*, whome among the *Indians* are
indeed famous for their learning and abſtinence, are
in the Promontory of *Comorinum* moſt notorious for
their ignorance, and lewdnes. For not enduring the
pouerty which that part of *India* ſuſtayneth, they couer their naturall lewdnes with abhominable deceipt, and whilſt themſelues in priuate, ſit at their banquets with ſolemne muſick of tabers and pipes, they
perſwade the ſimple people that their Gods are a feaſting; and withall demaund of them, in their Gods
name, whatſoeuer they want for the maintenance
of themſelues and their families, denouncing the ven-

The Brachmans wickednes and lewdneſſe.

T 3   geance

geance of the Gods againſt them, vnleſſe they preſently performe what they be commanded.

Xauerius therfore conuincing them openly of deceipt, began to accuſe them to the people, and to manifeſt their falſe dealing : which occaſion cauſed the
ſaluation of many, who giuing ouer Idolatry became
Chriſtians. And the *Brachmans* being aſtoniſhed as wel
at his great learning, as at the miracles wrought by
him, turning their hate into reuerence, endeauoured
to gaine his fauour and friendſhip, both by guiftes, &
all other meanes they could deuiſe. But his loue of
pouerty was not ouercome by any ſuch fauours, and
though he reiected their guiftes, to keep his owne liberty free, yet notwithſtanding he conſerued good
correſpondence, and friendſhip with them. And as he
went his circuit about the townes of the Chriſtians,
oftentimes he lodged in their abiding places (which
are alſo called *Pagods*, as their Gods are) hoping that
ſome of them might be conuerted, with the ſaluation
of many ſoules.

Vpon a tyme he came to a certaine Pagod, where
were aſſembled almoſt two hundred *Brachmans*, who
had vnderſtood of his comming thither. Hauing ſaluted one another, and many wordes paſſed to and
fro, *Francis* demaunded of them in ful aſſembly, what
their Gods commaunded thoſe to do, who were to
come into heauen to them ? After long ſtrife amongſt
them who ſhould giue the anſwere, it fell at laſt, by
common conſent, to the lot of an ancient man of 80.
yeares of age, the eldeſt amongſt them; who craftily
ſhifting off the Queſtion, asked *Xauerius* agayne,
what

The
Brach-
mans de-
ſire Fran-
cis his
friēdſhip

Pagods.

Francis
his con-
ference
with the
Brach-
mans.

what the Chriftians God commaunded them to do?
But he perceyuing the old mans euafion, tould him
he would not fpeake a word of any Chriftian affayres, vntill he had anfwered his queftion, as good
reafon he fhould. Then the old man being driuen
to it by neceffity, with open manifeftation of his ignorance, fayd: That their Gods commaunded them two
things: The one was, that they fhould not kill any
Cow, becaufe with kine the Gods were worfhipped:
The other was, that they fhould beftow liberall guifts
vpon the *Brachmans*, the chiefe Priefts & Minifters of
the fayd Gods.

Then *Xauerius*, moued at the ignorance and impudency both of the man, and the thing, prefently
rofe vp, and intreated them, that they would alfo now
heare him. And with a lowd voice reciting the Creed
and the ten Commandements, he briefly explicateth
the fame in their country language: and then he de- The
clareth the ioyes of the bleffed in heauen, and the tor- Brach-
ments of the damned in hell: and finally who they mans
were that fhould go to the one, and other place. As approue
foone as they heard this, on a fuddain they all rofe vp, ofthe
and euery one imbracing him, wonderfully extolled Religiõ.
the Chriftian Religion, containing fuch agreable myfteryes and precepts as thofe were: fuch is the force of
truth, euen with peruerfe minds, if light from heauen
fhine vpon them. Then they asked him many other The ri-
things very ridiculous, and fuch as we who by Gods diculous
goodnes vnderftãd the Truth, do abhorre to heare; to queftiõs
wit, whether the Soule of man dyeth togeather with Brach-
the body, as other liuing creatures do? What fhould mans.

be

be the caufe, why we feeme in our fleepe to be with
our friends, although they be far of? Is it not bicaufe
our foule, the body being afleep, leaueth its manfion,
and flyeth abroad? Whether God be white or black?

The
Brach-
mans
thinke
God to
be black. for they themfelues being blackifh by nature, out of
the efteeme they beare to their owne colour, thinke
that God is black, and do oftentimes befmeare their
Idols with oile in fuch manner, that they be not only
black, but euen vgly alfo, and horrible to behould, in
fo much that you would thinke you faw the Diuels
themfelues, and not their images.

Xauerius when thefe queftions were asked him,
knowing well how to accommodate his fpeech to his
Auditours, anfwered not fo learnedly, as futably to
their capacities, fo that not one of all the company
durft open his mouth to contradict him. But when
he preffed them to imbrace the Chriftian Religion,
which they faw fo manifeftly proued vnto them, they
anfwered, that indeed they were afraid of what the
people would fay, and that they fhould want meanes
to liue, if they fhould change their courfe of life. And
fo thefe wretches making more account of what the
people would fay, then of their owne faluation, contemned the light which began to fhine vpon them, &
remained obftinate in their darknes.

Now although, as we fayd, the *Brachmans* carry
away the bell for wifedome among the *Indians* : yet
there was only one found among them all, worthy of
that name, a Schoole-man of a famous Academy of
India, who out of the familiarity which he had with
Xauerius, declared to him certaine myfteries of that

Academy

Academy, wch held: that there was one God maker of
the world, who raigning in heaue ought to be worshi-
ped of mortal me : that euery eight day (which we cal
Sunday) ought to be kept holy : & that a time would
come when all fhould profeffe one Religion. Moreouer he defired to know the myfteryes of the Chriftian
fayth, which at length *Francis* declared vnto him, and
withall fpake thefe wholfome words of our Sauiour, *Marc.16.*
Qui crediderit & baptizatus fuerit, faluus erit, He that be- *Math.*
lieueth & is baptized fhal be faued. The Brachman no-
ted downe in a litle booke thefe words with their explication, and intreated *Xauerius* to baptize him vpon
certayne conditions . But *Xauerius* reiecting his conditions being neyther iuft nor honeft, thought it good
to differre his requeft for a tyme, & fo difmiffed him ;
bidding him to publifh that myftery of one God to the
people, hoping that he would indeed becom a perfect
Chriftian, & be occafion of no fmall aduancement to
the Chriftian caufe. But yet there was another yong
Brachman who gaue not only greater hopes, but alfo A Brach
proued better indeed. He being of an excellent wit & man ba-
behauiour, was inftructed, and baptized by *Francis*, & ptized
by his appointement vndertooke to teach children teacheth
their Catechifme; Chrift thus choofing to himfelfe the Ca-
maysters of his doctrine, out of the Diuels fchoole. techifme

At this time now, God would fhew manifeftly
how pleafing *Xauerius* labours were vnto him. He wet An iniu-
vpon fome occafions to an Ethincke noble-man, who ry done
being a barbarous & vnciuil fellow, contemning the to *Fran-*
vertuous and holy man, fhut him out of his houfe, in a *cis* is re-
rude & difgracefull manner; & fcoffing at him, faid : uenged
by God.

V   Serue

Serue me in the fame fort, if euer I come to the Chriftians Church. This iniury offred to *Francis* being publifhed abroad by thofe who were prefent, no body had leffe feeling of it, then he to whome it was done. It feemed doubtleffe, both to the *Portughefes*, and the Neophites an vnworthy fact, as deferuing indeed to be reuenged by God himfelfe. Therfore he who taketh vengeance vpon iniuries done vnto his feruants, fent fpedily a due punifhmet vpon that contumelious man.

A few dayes after, the fame Noble man being vnarmed, chanced to meet with his armed enemies not far from the Chriftians Church : wherefore being not able to refift he thought to defend himfelf by running away. Now as he fled, they followed him clofe with their deadly weapons, & were euen come to the Chriftians Church, wherin that wretch (not thinking the of the contumelious words which formerly he had vtteed againft *Xauerius*) thought to faue himfelfe. But the Neophites comming forth in haft at the clamour and tumult which they heard, fo ftopped vp the entrance to the Church, and, as it ordinarily hapneth, the laft came fo hard preffing vpon the firft, that he could not poffibly haue way to enter, fo to faue himfelfe. They feing this, & knowing the man, cryed out that God the reuenger of *Xauerius* his iniury had by diuine iudgment debarred him of the refuge he defired. And fo he who before had contumelioufly fhut *Xauerius* out of doores, being purfued by his enemies, and endeauouring to faue his life by flying to the Chriftias Church, was himfelfe fhut out : God permitting him to be ferued in the like manner, as he ferued *Xauerius*.

CHAP.

CHAP. X.

Liuing in the coaſt of Piſcaria *vvith great ioy, and fruit of his labours, he comforteth the Neophites, vvho vvere much afflicted.*

VT, it is incredible to thinke, what aboū-dance of diuine conſolation *Xauerius* foūd in theſe extreme labours of his. Himſelfe ſignified it in a letter which he wrote to the Society at *Rome*. To which they ſhall do well to hearken, who preferring earthly commodities before diuine, thinke that the life of holy perſons is without all comfort & delight, as though there were no place for pleaſure, where riches & delicacies do not abound. In a clauſe therfore of his epiſtle inuiting others of the Society to the ſame labours, he writeth thus : *So great is the aboundance of the heauenly ioyes, which God beſtoweth* **Aboun-** *vpon them, who labour in this vineyard, for the conuerſion* **dance of** *of the Indians to Chriſt, that if there be any ioy in this life, I* **heauenly** *thinke it only to be heere.* Neither did he auouch this **ioyes.** without a true ground, and of what he had not expe-rienced in himſelfe. For being oftentimes in the midſt of thoſe labours, ouerwhelmed with heauenly conſo-lations, he hath bin ſecretly heard to breake forth into theſe words : *I beſeech thee, O Lord, do not ouerwhelme me with ſuch aboundance of ioyes in this life ; or if it pleaſe thee*

of

of thy infinite bounty, that still I flow with these flouds of delights, remoue me hence into heauen among the blessed; for he that hath once had an inward tast of thy sweetnesse, must needes liue a bitter life without thee.

The multitude of those that were baptized Xauerius therfore liued a whole yeare in the coast of *Piscaria* with infinite labour, and the like comfort; and that which much increased his ioy, was the great augmentation of the Christian faith. For as it appeareth by his owne letters, he baptized aboue a 1000.infants, who presently after their Baptisme went to heauen. Wherby we may gather what a multitude there were, either of infants that liued, or else of elder people whome he made members of Chrifts Church. And it is well knowen, that in that coast many villages, & some whole Townes, were by him conuerted to the Christian faith.

When he had thus carryed, and set in order the affayres of Christian Religion in the coast of *Comorinum*, about the latter end of the yeare 1543. he returneth to *Goa*, to deale in person with the viceroy of *India*, concerning certaine important busines about Christian Religion. Vpon this occasion he tooke with him some youths of the chiefe nobility of that Country, both as pledges, & supplies for the Christian faith to be broght vp in learning in the Seminary of *Goa*; for that by this tyme the Colledge there was for the most part built & furnished. Wherfore *Borban*, not suffering *Xauerius* to lodge in the Hospitall of the sick as he was accustomed, brought him home, and of his owne accord gaue ouer to him the whole gouernment therof, which he, with the consent of the said *Borban*, committed

mitted to *Fa. Paul Camertes*, who was lately come from
Mozambicum.

The fame of the admirable things which *Xauerius*
had wrought in the coast of *Piscaria* was come to *Goa*
before himselfe aried thither, and had much increafed his esteeme, aswell with others as with the viceroy
of *India*, who affected him exceedingly; and therfore
without difficulty he obteined of him whatfoeuer he
defired. Amongft other things, the report being
brought to *Goa* of thofe who were rayfed to life in the
coaft of *Comorinum*, made *Xauerius* name to be fpread
far and neere. Wherfore *Iames Borban* by reafon of his
ancient familiarity, taketh him afide, and earneftly
intreateth him, that for the honour of God he would
tell him the particulers of thofe, who were reported
to be rayfed to life by his prayers in the Country of
Comorinum. At which words *Xauerius* his countenáce
was all dyed ouer with a virginall crimfon-blufh, bewraying both his modefty & the truth of the matter.
Endeauouring therfore, as much as he could with
truth, to couer any matter which tended to his owne
glory, he imbraceth *Borban* in a friendly manner, and
fmiling fayth. Good Iefu, I rayfe dead men to life! O
wicked wretch that I am! Certaine mé indeed brought
to me a youth feeming to be dead, who being by me
commanded in the name of Chrift to aryfe, prefently
rofe vp: this indeed, and other fuch like things, they
who were prefent publifhed abroad for miracles. Yet
this his couering of thofe miracles (though his countenance fufficiently difcouered the truth) diminifhed
nothing at all the credit of what was reported of him,

his

V 2

Paul Camerts the
firft Rector of
the Colledge of
Goa.

His notable
fhamefaftnes at
his owne
prayfes.

His concealing
of miracles.

his humility therein being almost as admirable, as the miracles themselues.

    Xauerius hauing now dispatched the businesse for which he came, and taking *Francis Mansilla* for his cō-panion, returned againe into the coast of *Piscaria* vpon the 24. of March the next yeare following, & setleth himself to his old exercises of Charity. He had now be-sides *Mansilla* 3. assistants, *Iohn Lesian* a Spanish Priest, & two other Priests also of that coūtry, who at *Xaue-rius* request wēt thither for the same cause, partly frō *Goa*, & partly from *Cocinum*. Hauing made these men partners of his charge, he neuer ceased going about, baptizing infants, & exhorting others to do the same. His labour was as much, if not more, then before, and his difficultyes greater. For being a stranger, & wholy ignorant of the *Malauarian* language (in so much be-sides the Cathechisme he scarce knew one word ther-of) yet liued he, and conuersed amongst the *Malaua-rian* Neophytes without an interpreter; which thing did notwithstanding rather stirre vp, then hinder his endeauours. To baptize infants he had no need of an interpreter; & the poore and wretched people did of themselues open vnto him their miseries in such sort, that he might easily vnderstand them. He also by his study, and endeauours came to be his owne interpre-ter: for albeyt he were vnskillfull in the country ton-gue, yet made he good shift to preach vnto the people, expressing oftentimes by his contenance and gesture, what he could not do in words.

    But to keep an order and *decorum* in all things, he called them not al together, but caused the men & the

women

He brin-geth some to help him in the coast of *Piscaria*.

women to come by turnes, euery other day to the Catechifme. His chiefe care was to baptize infants and inftruct children, becaufe he knew certaynely, that fuch as dyed before they loft their innocency, being baptized, were made partakers of the kingdom of heauen, the which many that were of riper yeares loft by returning agayne to their former bad life. And he did not only himfelfe imploy his chiefeft endeauours in helping that tender age, but alfo gaue moft diligent charge to F. *Marfilla* his companion to do the fame. Moreouer as occafion & place required, he helped the Neophytes, not only fpiritually but corporally alfo.

He teacheth mē and womē their Catechifme apart.

What a care he had of baptizing infantes.

Vpō the Eaft of the coaft of *Pifcaria* there lieth bordering a wild & fauage kind of people, whome they cal *Badages*. Thefe gathering together a great army, either out of hatred to Religion, or through defire of pillage, had inuaded the borders of the Chriftians of *Comorinum*, fpoyling & wafting all before them. The Chriftians being affrighted at this fuddain incurfion abandoning their villages, had gotten ouer a little arme of the fea, and there hid themfelues amongft the rockes, a fit place for fuch a purpofe: where abiding in the open ayre and the funne (the heate wherof, as we fayd, is moft extreme in thofe partes) they were miferably burnt vp, and brought to fuch want of neceffary meanes to liue vpon, that fome dyed for meere hunger. This fearefull newes did not only moue *Xauerius* to piety towards them, but alfo ftirred vp his carefull endeauours to affoard new fuccour, in this new accident. He therfore prefently bringeth vnto thefe poore foules, twenty fmall veffels loaden with prouifion.

The Badages a fauage nation.

The calamity of the Comorinenfians.

Francis his fuccour to relieue the neophyts in their mifery.

prouifion. And withall writeth to the *Pantagarines*, &
magiftrates of the Coaft thereabout, to make a col-
lectiõ among the richer fort, for the reliefe of their
miferies. So as he prouided for them, not only for the
prefent, but alfo for the time to come. But as foone as
that ftorme was ouerpaft, by retyrement of the enemy, gathering togeather his difperfed fheep, he omitted nothing belonging to the duty of a good Paftour.
He rayfed vp thofe that were caft downe, and comforted them that were afflicted, both by cõpaffionate
words, & all other fweet means. But, behould a new
tempeft aryfeth, fo much the heauier, by how much
lõger it endured. They who were officers in the Coaft
of *Pifcaria* being couetous and intemperate men, began after a proud and auaricious manner to dominier
ouer the neophytes. Wherupon *Xauerius* being no leffe
moued at the vnworthineffe of the fact then it deferued, firft oppofed himfelfe ftoutly againft their couetoufneffe; & at laft, when he faw he was not able to
withftand them himfelfe, he thought to requeft the
viceroy of *India* (remaining then at *Cocinum*) to ayde
him, and for that purpofe refolued to go vnto him.
But new occafions occurring, hindred both his determination, and iorney which now he had begun.

CHAP.

CHAP. XI.

He conuerteth the Kingdome of Trauancoris *to the Christian Faith, and defendeth the Neophytes from the Barbarians.*

HAVING now spent in the Coast of *Pifcaria* halfe a yeare in the forsaid labours;
and by his endeauours and diligent care
so greatly profited therein, that finding
at his comming thither but twenty, both villages and
townes in al, & those very rude; he left now to his cōpanions thirty, all of them well instructed & ordered.
Wherfore composing all things as well as he could, he
leaueth the charge of the Neophytes to *Fa. Mansilla*,
taking his iorney towards *Cocinum* through the coast
of *Trauancoris* which lyeth next to *Pifcaria*.

Trauancoris *is a sea coast, on that side of *India* where The cost
Goa standeth, bending towards the West, and lyeth *Trauan-
betweene the Promōtory of *Comorinum* & the Towne coris.
Colanum, almost 30. miles from *Cocinum*, and is said
to be in length about 80. miles. There were in that
Coast, of sea villages to the number of 30. inhabited
partly by Ethnicke fisher-men whome they call *Machoa's*, and partly by Saracens. *Francis* therfore, what
for want of shipping, and to try their dispositions had
a desire to passe through their Country to *Cocinum*.

X   He

He wanted not friends who endeauored to diſſuade him from that iourney, ſhewing him that the *Machoa's* & *Saracens* hated him extremely, taking it very ill that the *Paraua's* their neighbours were become Chriſtiãs. Yet for all this he being driuen on more by God, thē by any other neceſſity, as afterwards the euent plainly demōſtrated, made no doubt of paſſing through their country. Depending therefore vpon the diuine Prouidence, and thinking alſo that he ſhould gayne by the bargayne if he chanced to dye for Chriſt, he beginneth his iorney through the midle of the Country about the midſt of the yeare of our Lord 1544. As he trauayled he viſited the villages which lay in his way, and (as the goodnes of God farre exceedeth all that pious men can expect) he experienced his diuine bouty no leſſe fauourable to his enemies, then to himſelfe, ſo peaceable he found all things, and the people greatly diſpoſed to receiue the ſeed of the holy Ghoſpell.

First therfore hauing gotten friendſhip with their King, and working vpon the Barbarians harts as well with hope as with feare, ſometimes propounding to them the amity of the Portugheſes, & thē againe denouncing againſt them threats from heauen, he without any great difficulty brought them to imbrace the faith of Chriſt ; eſpecially when, being wonne by offices of Chriſtian Charity, they had obtayned leaue by an Edict from their King, to change their Religions. Wherfore *Xauerius* reioicing at this ſo fortunate ſucceſſe imployed himſelfe inceſſantly in going about from towne to town, to baptize & inſtruct the people

in

Hisnotable courage of mind.

Gods prouidence.

in the myſteries of the Chriſtian faith . What an infinite nũber were by his meanes made Chriſtians, may
be coniectured by this, that he baptized at one time
aboue ten thouſand . His manner of inſtructing and
baptizing was this. When he came to any village to
baptize , calling all the men, women, and children togeather into one place, after he had taught them, that
there was one God, the Father, the Sonne, & the holy
Ghoſt , he commanded them euery one to make vpon
themſelues thrice the ſigne of the Croſſe in honour of
the moſt B. Trinity, according as he had befoɾe inſtructed them . Then putting on a Surpliſe , with a cleare
voice he pronounced the myſteries, & precepts of the
Chriſtian Religion, & explicated the ſame briefly (as
well as he could) in their owne language. And when
they ſeemed to be ſufficiently inſtructed, he bad them
aske God pardon publickly for the ſinnes of their life
paſt, and demanded whether they did really and truly
belieue all and euery point of the Chriſtian Religion ?
Thẽ they, by putting their armes a croſſe gaue a ſigne
that they did belieue, and ſo he baptized them, putting downe euery ones name in writing, as his cuſtome was.

 When all were baptized, *Xauerius* cauſed the Temples of the Gods to be preſently throwne downe, and
their Idols to be broken in pieces. One could not haue
beheld a more gratefull or pleaſant ſpectacle, then to
ſee them now trample thoſe Idols vnder their feete,
which a litle before they had with ſo great reuerence
adored. Which great iniury the Diuel certainly would
not haue left vnreuenged, if *Francis* had not had as

X 2   great

Margin notes: The nũber of thoſe he baptized · His mãner of baptizing. · He ouerthroweth the temples & Idols.

great courage to withstand the danger, as to offer him that affront . For he stirred vp the *Badages* agayne (of whome we spake before) who are no lesse cruell enemies to Christian Religion , then brutish & sauage by nature, against the flock of Christ , which as yet was but yong and tender. Wherfore a mighty army of thefe barbarians made a suddaine incursion vpon the borders of *Trauancoris*, & began to spoile the villages of the Christians. The inhabitants making a dolefull outcry , togeather with the lamentation of women and children , being all in vproue , betooke themselues to flight, yet with little hope to escape , being round beset by their enemies .

Atumult amongst the Trauancore-sians.

Xauerius (for it happened he was then present) being stirred vp by the tumult, wrought a memorable act . For, wholy forgetting himselfe , by reason of the eminent danger he saw before his eyes , he flyeth in a-mongst them , like a Lion , and with an vndaunted courage, both of spirit and countenance , rebuketh thofe barbarous people; who were wonderfully ama-zed to behold his courage and boldnes , since being slaues to the Deuill and forgetfull of their owne free-dome and saluation , they came so violently to offend others . Then as a good Paftour he putteth himselfe into the formest presse of the Christians, either to rule his flocke by authority , or if he could not do that , to dy togeather with them . But the *Badages*, although most barbarous & cruell, could not indure thofe fiery flames which seemed to shine forth of *Francis* his coūtenance and face, and so for feare, and reuerence to his person, they spared the rest. Yet all this while he

A me-morable deed of his.

was

was not free from danger of death . For the Ethnickes out of hatred to Chriſtian Religion, lay oftentimes in waite for him , whome notwithſtanding he defeated partly by his prudence, and partly by diuine aſſiſtāce, as then it happened .

Vpon a tyme ſome of them ſeeking after him to kill him , he ranne into a wood , where climbing vp into a tree he ſate there all night, and ſo eſcaped their hands, being ſheltred more by Gods aſſiſtāce, then eyther by the tree, or night. And his enemies plots againſt him were ſo frequent , that ſome of the Neophytes who were moſt pious and faithfull vnto him, kept alwayes of their owne accord , watch in the night before his lodging , to defend him. Notwithſtanding the continuall treacheries of theſe barbarous people , he omitted neyther his nightly prayer , which ſcarcely permitted him two houres reſt , nor ceaſed from his dayly iourneys of the day, euē in the heat of the ſunne; for that going about the Townes, he went barefoote, in a ragged coate , and with an ordinary Hat on his head. Yet this careleſnes of his corporall habit did no way obſcure the ſanctity of his ſoule, but made it more eminent. He was now commonly called the *Great Father* , and the King of *Trauancoris* commanded by publicke Edict throughout his whole kingdom, that all ſhould obey the *Great Father* , no otherwiſe then himſelfe.

The Chriſtians had not at that tyme any Church in that Coaſt , wherfore he was conſtrained to ſay maſſe either vnder ſome tree, or ſome ſayle of a ſhippe. But now, it is reported, there be built aboue twenty

By the goodnes of God he eſcapeth death .

He is called great Father.

The mul titude of thofe who followed him whē he preached.

Churches and Chappels in that Country. And when he was to preach, for want of a pulpit, he would frō fome commodious tree, fpeake vnto the multitude, which was fomtimes infinite. For when he went out into the fieldes to preach, there followed him many times fiue or fix thoufand perfons. His care alfo was not leffe in augmenting the flocke of Chrift, then in maintaining what he had gotten. That the Neophytes might alfo, after his departure, retaine what they had learned, vpon his going away, he did not only leaue a copy of the Chriftian doctrine in euery Towne, but alfo taught them the manner how to exercyfe it euery morning and euening, and for that end appointed a Moderatout ouer them. Yet all this time he refrained from too much dealing with thofe who dwelt vp higher in the hart of the coūtry, knowing very well that the fea coafts, where the Portughefes commaunded, were farre more fit to receiue and maintaine the Chriftian faith, then the vpland Coun-

The vpland coū-try of *India* not fit to re-ceiue the fayth of Chrift.

try of *India*, where the *Brachmans*, deadly enemies to our Religion, had the poffeffion. He therfore trauailed all ouer that country lying by the fea fide, going from village to village, euery where baptizing & inftructing as many as he could in the Chriftian faith: fo as now almoft all the townes of the *Machoa's* & *Paraua's* had, by Francis his meanes, put themfelues vnder the fweet yoke of Chrift; when the report therof comming to the bordering Ilands, fet on fire the *Manarians* a neighbouring people, to emulate their piety.

CHAP.

CHAP. XII.

Neophytes slayne for Religion , become an ornament to the Christian Fayth.

Anaria is a litle Iland, lying ouer against the coast of *Piscaria,* distant from the continent an 150. miles. There was therein a village called *Patinus,* at that tyme of litle note, but now greatly enobled by the death of many Martyrs. The inhabitants of this place had a great desire to receaue the Christian Religion , wherof they had heard many notable things reported, as well of *Xauerius,* as of the *Comorines.* Wherefore they earnestly inuited *Francis* to come thither and baptize them. But he being imployed about other most important affaires cōcerning Religion, and not able to go himselfe , sent a certayne Priest in his place to instruct them in the Catechisme , and to baptize them. Wherupon followed a great storme of persecution , which notwithstanding proued very profitable vnto them. For the King of *Iafanapatana ,* vnder whose dominion that Iland is, out of a Barbarous cruelty, being also incensed with the hatred he bare vnto Christians , was so enraged , that sending thither an army of men , what by fyre & sword destroyed, and wasted the whole Towne. There are sayd to haue byn slayne at that tyme for Religion more then 600. persons. Thus , that vast solitude , brought forth fresh and fragrant flowers of Martyrs,

for

for heauens ornament. Since which tyme, that place hath reteyned the name of the *Towne of Martyrs*.

About the fame tyme, it fell out fortunately, that the fayd King of *Iafanapatana* his owne brother, and heire to the fame kingdome, fearing his brothers fury had fled to the Viceroy of *India*, promifing that if he could by the Portughefes forces be reftored to his Fa-

The towne of Nagapatana.

thers kingdome, he with his nobles and greateft part of his fubiects would become Chriftians. The Viceroy greatly defirous as well to aduance Religion, as to reuenge the flaughter of the Innocents, was much incenfed agaynft the Tyrant. Whereupon he prefently fendeth a very ftrong Nauy to *Nagapatana* (which is a fea Towne fcituated in the continent, ouer againft the Iland of *Manaria*, about 200. miles from the Promontory of *Comorinum*) and withal commandeth them to make warre vpon the King of *Iafanapatana*, and eyther to put him to death, or elfe to handle him in fuch måner as *Xauerius* fhould iudge expedient, and to reftore the Kingdome to his brother.

The Ilåd of Macazaria.

In the meane tyme whileft *Xauerius* remayned at *Cocinum*, there was brought thither ioyfull newes, of many Ethnikes in the moft remote Kingdome of *Macazaria* conuerted to the Fayth of Chrift. This *Macazaria* is a great Iland, about a 1000. miles beyond *India* and the Riuer *Ganges*, and diftant from the *Moluca's* towards the eaft about 130. In this Kingdom three Noble and principall men, befids many others of the people, were lately conuerted to the Chriftian fayth, and baptized by a Portughefe Merchant called *Antony Payua*: God in that manner bringing in thither his

Ghofpell

Ghofpel euen by the meanes of good & vertuous merchants. They had therfore fent certayne men to the
Citty of *Malaca*, to requeft of the Portughefes there,
fome Priefts who might better inftruct them in the
Chriftian Religion; for that which the merchant had
commanded them, was only this: that fince they had
liued like bruite beafts, now hauing by baptifme receaued the fayth of Chrift, they fhould endeauour heerafter to liue like men, and withall to ferue one God
with purity and fanctity of life. The Gouernour of
Malaca approuing their demands, granted them certayne Priefts. And although *Francis* made no doubt
but they would worthily behaue themfelues for the
aduancement of Chriftian Religion; yet had he alfo
a great defire to be partaker of that labour, thinking
that in fo large a Kingdome there would be great occafion of worke, and need of many induftrious labourers, to plant and cultiuate the holy Ghofpell.

At the very fame tyme almoft, there came newes
alfo from the Iland of *Ceilanus*, which at the firft feemed heauy and fad, but afterwards proued ioyfull.
The eldeft fonne of the King of that Iland being moued by conference with the Portughefes (for they en- **The**
deauoured to bring in the Gofpel, as well as merchan- **Kings**
dize into *India*) had together with many others refol- **fonne**
ued to become a Chriftian. As foone as the barbarous **with 600**
King his Father had notice therof, all-mad with rage **more are**
and fury, commanded his fonne, with others of his **flaine for**
confayle (to the number of 600. as was reported) to be **Religion**
publikely flaughtered. But the enemy of Baptifme,
baptized them in their owne bloud: and whileft he
Y endea-

endeauoured to depreſſe Chriſtian Religion, he exalted it.

 For at the very ſame tyme , the Inhabitants ſaw
a great Croſſe of Fire in the ayre; and in the place
where the ſayd ſlaughter was committed , the ground
opening, made a great and plaine ſigne of the Croſſe,
which remaineth vnto this day, although the Ethnikes
haue endeauoured oftentymes to ſtoppe it vp, by caſting earth into it. So as many of the inhabitants , and
amongſt the reſt the Kings yonger ſonne, togeather
with his Couſin-german, & ſome of the Kings guard,
moued by theſe prodigious ſignes intended to become
Chriſtians. *Xauerius* being glad of this newes, albeyt
he had already reſolued to go vnto the *Macazarians*; yet
he iudged it not expedient to preferre this buſines before the other with which he was then in hand. In the
yeare therefore 1545 . in the month of Aprill, taking
Fa. Manſilla for his companion , he embarked at *Cocinum* with intention to go to the Iland of *Ceilanus*,
to try the diſpoſition of the Inhabitants , and from
thence with the firſt occaſion to paſſe ouer to *Nagapatana,* where the Nauy was ſaid to be ready prepared
for the foreſayd expedition .

(marginal note:) **Prodigious ſi-
gnes of
the
Croſſe.**

CHAP.

CHAP. XIII.

Being transported into the Iland of Ceilanus, *he reclaymeth the maister of the
shippe from a bad life.*

Eilanus is an Iland right ouer agaynst the They I-
land *Cei-*
lanus. coast of *Piscaria*, of great note both for pearles and other merchandize, but especially for the aboundance of *Cinnamon* which it beareth. It is extended in length an 150. miles, and in breadth 40. or thereabout. Vpon the furthest point thereof butteth the Iland of *Manaria* where the Neophytes, as we sayd, were slayne by the King of *Iafanapatana*. *Ceilanus* is indeed inhabited by the *Malauarians*, whome they call *Cingales*, but by reason of traffique it is much frequented by the Portughese Merchants. The Portugheses haue therin a fayre Towne, and by the shore are to be seene certaine Chappells built by them in tymes past for the exercise of Christian Religion. *Xauerius* being thither arriued, there hapned a memorable accident.

The Gouernour of the ship, being moued by the familiarity which he had gotten with *Francis*, had vpon the way freely opened his mind vnto him, and told him, how for a long tyme he had byn giuen to a certayne notorious sinne, from which he could not be absolued by the Priest. But *Xauerius* being a expert Physitian of the soule, laying before his eyes the

cle-

clemency, and mercy of Almighty God , that paſſeth all malice (which was an ordinary cuſtome in
him, therby to draw men to Confeſſion) made the
buſineſſe light and eaſy ; and promiſed him withall ,
that as ſoone as they were arriued (for then there was
neyther tyme nor meanes) he would vnty thoſe heauy bands of his . Hauing thus agreed betweene themſelues of the buſineſſe, the mayſter of the ſhip as ſoone
as he came to *Ceilanus*, as though he had byn certaine
of his ſaluation, caſt of all thought of making his confeſſion; & began to find excuſes, and withall to auoid
the ſight and company of *Francis*, that he might not
be challenged by him of his promiſe. But *Xauerius*, or
rather Gods Prouidence (*Which*, as holy *Iob* ſayth, *taketh the wiſe in their crafty plots*) deceyued the mayſter,
with all his ſleights. For on a ſuddaine , and vnawares
he findeth *Francis* walking by the ſhore ſyde, with his
eyes fixed towards heauen , as his cuſtome was ; and
now becauſe he could not auoyd meeting with him ,
hauing byn already eſpyed , & that he might not ſhew
himſelfe light or vnconſtant, he reſolued to ſet a good
face vpon the matter , and by ſome ſleight to delude
the others carefulneſſe.

Iob. 5.

He therfore firſt ſaluted him, and of his owne accord , asketh him; How long it would be, before he
would heare his Confeſſion ? As ſoone as he had ſpoken theſe words , faltring as it were in his ſpeech, and
ſhewing himſelf much troubled in mind, *Xauerius* foūd
preſently by his countenance, and trembling of body
that he had a great horrour of that which he required:
yet did he not let ſlip the occaſion offered him what-
                                                   ſoeuer

foeuer it were. Therfore, to free him from that vaine
feare, merrily and fweetly, as he was wont, Good Iefu, quoth he, will you go then to confeffion? I will
moft willingly heare you, & if you pleafe, euen heere
as we walk vpon this fhore. Wherupō the other being
ouercome not fo much by the irkefomnes of his foule
finnes, as by *Francis* his exceeding mildnes, but indeed
by Gods diuine impulfe, refolued to make a confeffion
of his whole life. *Xauerius* feeing him to begin with
feare and bafhfulnes, hearkened carefully vnto him
firft, as they walked vpon the fhore: But afterwards
when he perceiued him to go on with more courage
and freedome, taking him gently by the hand, he led
him into a chappell neere by. The other out of reuerence to the holy place, began to kneele downe, as the
cuftome is, therby to make an end of the Confeffion
which he had begun. But *Francis* perceauing he had
fome difficulty therin, forbad him to kneele for the
prefent; and to induce him to confeffe the more willingly he fpread a mat vpon a banke, that they might
there fit more commodioufly. They had not fate
long when God fo touched his hart, that rifing vpon a
fuddain, he fell downe at the Fathers feete, and with
aboundance of teares and fighes layd open all the fins
of his whole lyfe. And hauing thus waded out of
the pudle of finne, & disburdened his foule of all filth,
he began with great feeling to frequent the holy Sacrament of Confeffion (of the fruit and wholefom-
neffe whereof he had now gotten a taft) and ferioufly
to prouide for the faluation of his foule.

In the meane tyme *Xauerius* hauing infinuated

marginal note: Prudēce in taking away horrour in Con-feffion.

himfelfe

himlelfe into the *Ceilanians* friendſhip, got acceſſe to the Kings ſonne, whome he found perplexed, as well by his brothers example, as by thoſe prodigious ſignes whereof we ſpake before, & priuately baptized him, together with his Couſin-German ; whereupon he reſolued to fly, together with ſome chiefe men of the Kindgdome, to the Viceroy of *India*, and to craue his ayde agaynſt the ſauage cruelty of his Father, who had already imbrued his hands in the innocent bloud of his brother & kinſmen, & now thirſted after his alſo. *Xauerius* was likewiſe by him informed, that moſt of the *Ceilanians* being moued by thoſe miraculous ſignes of the Croſſe in the ayre, and vpon the ground, did already much incline to the Chriſtian fayth, but that their good deſires were hindred, through feare of the Tyrant his Father.

Francis being very glad of this newes, ſendeth preſently letters to *Fa. Paul*, who remayned at *Goa*, willing him to ſend two of the Fathers, who were euery day expected from Portugall, to *Ceilanus*, with thoſe noblemen, who where to be reſtored to their Kingdome, to haue a care of the Chriſtian cauſe in that Iland. And ſending backe *Fa. Manſilla* immediatly into the Promontory of *Comorinum*, he himſelfe croſſeth ouer to *Nagapatana*, for the occaſion which we haue already mentioned. But all that preparation, & *Francis* his expectation, when it ſeemed now to be vpon the point of ioyning battayle and obtayning victory, vpon a ſuddaine falleth to nothing. For at the ſame time a ſhip of the K. of *Portugall* (which being fraught with rich merchandize was bound back agayne from

the

the Kingdome of *Pegu* into *India*) being by force of
tempeſt driuen into *Iaſanapatana,* was preſently ſet v-
pon by that barbarous King . Wherefore the Viceroy
imploying his ſeruice for the Kings affayres , ſurcea-
ſed from battaile, vntil the Kings goods were recouered . And ſo by making this delay, the warre, as many
tymes it happeneth, was by differring , broken cleane
off . Yet God afterwards gaue to *Xauerius* what he deſired . For not long after that Tyrant being diſconfi-
ted by many ouerthrowes which *Conſtantine* the Viceroy of *India* gaue him , the Iland of *Manaria* was taken from him, & all the inhabitants became Chriſtiãs.
Thus the death of a few for Chriſt his ſake , was the
cauſe of liberty and ſaluation to many . *Francis* therefore not to looſe the labour which he had taken in that
iourney, and alſo ſeruing himſelfe of the wynd, which
though contrary for his returne , lay yet right for his
going forward, reſolued to make vſe of that occaſion.

CHAP. XIV.

He viſiteth the Sepulcher of S . Thomas
the Apoſtle *.*

HE Church of *S. Thomas* the Apoſtle was
not diſtant from this place aboue 150. miles
which was very famous both in regard of
his ſacred reliques , and of the great reſort
of *Indians,* who came to viſit it from remote places. He
therefore determined to go thither in the guize of a
poore

poore Pilgrime, that hauing done his deuotion to the Apoſtle, he might go on forward to *Malaca*, & from thence (vnleſſe God ſhould otherwiſe diſpoſe) to *Macazaria*, whither he had byn called by moſt ioyfull tidings . For he had lately vnderſtood that the Inhabitants of thoſe places were greatly diſpoſed to receaue the Chriſtian Religion, and that nothing hindred the conuerſion, and baptizing of many , but want of Prieſts .

  About the latter end therfore of Lent, he put to ſea from *Nagapatana* , with a better wind then good ſpeed . He had now ſayled about 40. miles when a contrary tempeſt conſtrayned the ſhip to remaine 7. daies in a certayne hauen which they chanced vpon by the way . There *Xauerius* minding more the pilgrimage which he had vndertaken, then humane imbecillity , left behind him a worthy example of abſtinence. For al that time (as he that had the care of him teſtified afterwards vpon his oath) he paſſed without taking any ſuſtenance at all , as though, being indeed inflamed with a deſire to viſit the holy Apoſtle, he had byn fed with heauenly food. Afterwards when the marriners hoiſed ſayle to be gone, he asked of the Maiſter, whether the ſhip were ſound & ſtrong inough? He replyed that it was an old, & weake ſhip. Then, quoth he, we muſt needs backe agayne to *Nagapatana*, for we ſhall haue a cruell ſtorme. Although little credit was giuen to this propheſy , yet it proued moſt true . But the Mayſter of the ſhip being deceaued by the weather & the ſea , went neuertheleſſe forward: and behould vpon the ſudain a terrible tempeſt riſing, droue the ſhip

He paſſeth 7. dayes without eating any thing

He fortelleth the marriners a tempeſt neere at hand.

back

backe againe to *Nagapatana* (as he had fortould them)
and not without great danger. Then the marriners &
paſſengers tooke notice of what he had ſayd, and held
it for a prophecy. And although *Francis* being thus
beaten backe with a contrary wind, could not arriue
where he intended, yet ſtill he perſeuered conſtantly
in his purpoſe, and came thither at laſt on foote, with
greater labour , and more merit.

There is a towne belonging to the Portugheſes
called *Meliapora,* rich , and much frequented, ſcituated in the ſea coaſt of *India* , almoſt in equall diſtance
(if you conſider the turnings of the ſea) about two
hundred leagues from the Promontory of *Comorinum*
& the riuer *Ganges* , built perhaps of the ruines of the
auncient , and famous Citty of *Calamina*. In this
Towne there is a Church of *Saint Thomas* the Apoſtle,
where the inhabitants , and other *Indians* ſay , he was
buried ; wherof euen to this day there be extant many remarkable ſignes. There is alſo to be ſeene the place where the Apoſtle is ſayd to haue byn martyred, &
a Chappell wherin he ſayd maſſe. Which chappell the
Portugheſes out of deuotion haue adorned, and made
thereof a ſumptuous Church, giuing the Towne the
name of *S. Thomas*. In this Chappell not long ſince, as
they digged very deep to lay the fondation of the new
Church, there was, as they ſay , the body of the Apoſtle found, with the ſword wherewith he was martyred, and a litle veſſell full of bloudy earth, which was
agayne with reuerence layd in the ſame place . Neyther is the conſtant report hereof vayne or doubtfull .
This auncient opinion which both they of that Coun-

*Meliapo-
ra* the
towne of
S. Thomas

The bo-
dy of *S.
Thomas*
the Apo-
ſtle.

Z   try

try and ſtrangers haue of the Body and Martyrdome
of the Apoſtle *S. Thomas*, is by God confirmed by an
yearely and perpetuall miracle. For they haue a ſtone
ſprinkled with the bloud of the Apoſtle, which retai-
neth the prints, as it were, of freſh bloud, and three
dayes before the feaſt day of *S. Thomas* (on which day

they ſay he was martyred) whilſt Maſſe is ſayd there,
the ſayd ſtone, being naturally white, by litle & litle
waxeth red, and ſweateth as though droppes of bloud
diſtilled from it on all ſides ; and at laſt when Maſſe is
ended, it returneth agayne to the former colour. For
which reſpect the Apoſtles Sepulcher is had in great
veneration, as wel of the Ethnickes as the Chriſtiãs.
For that there come vnto this place from all parts, a
great cõcourſe of Pilgrimes euen Ethnickes themſelues, who beare great eſteeme to the Martyrdome &
Sepulcher of the ſayd Apoſtle.

Hither therefore *Xauerius*, out of deuotion to *S.*
Thomas the Patron of *India*, came in the guize and habit of a Pilgrime, therby both to honour the Apoſtles
Sepulcher, and to aſſiſt the bordering neighbours in
matters concerning their ſaluation. He found in that
towne, beſides many inhabitants about 100. families
of Portugheſes, who had there ſetled themſelues, and
their meanes. *Xauerius* therefore, preſently vpon his
arriuall to this place, viſited no leſſe religiouſly then
affectionately the Apoſtle of the Indians ; admiring
his ſingular glory, whoſe vertue he emulated, as farre
as a mortall man was able. And firſt he earneſtly beſought God, that ſince he being a poore wretch was
called from heauen to imitate, though neuer ſo wea-
kely,

kely, so great an Apostle in conuerting of the *Indians*
to the faith of Christ, he would inspire him with some
of his Apostolicall vertues. Thē he instantly requested
S. Thomas, for the care and patronage which he had
ouer the *Indians*, that through his intercession, he
might neither want courage to vndergoe the dāgers,
nor forces to endure the labours in trauailing ouer, &
manuring *India*, & other barbarous Countryes : and
that neither his owne, nor others sinnes might be any
hindrance of his following the Mowers steppes, as
Ruth the *Moabitesse* did, in gathering vp the gleanings
of that our Lords field, and (to his poore ability)re-
posing the same in Christs sacred granary.

When he had satisfied his deuotion to the Apostle
he lodged with the Bishops Vicar (which he was accustomed to do, where there was no publicke Hospitall for the sicke, nor place of abode for Religious mē)
who was much edified with the great respect he saw
him beare to Ecclesiastical persons, & with his natural affability of speech & true simplicity. So as making
himselfe wholly knowne vnto the Prelate, by laying
open his hart before him, he easily wonne his fauour
and good will. This manner of courtesy, as I sayd before, *Xauerius* vsed, not so much to gayne friends, as to
help those whome he iudged worthy of friendship
For when he had once found out their dipositions, he
would by litle and litle draw them to whatsoeuer was
requisite, both for their owne saluation, and the diuine
seruice. This good Prelate therfore of *Meliapora* re-
quited *Xauerius* courtesy by returning him the like, &
imbracing him as a worthy person, whome he vsed

A man-
ner how
to gayne
& help
friends.

Z 2   thence

thence forwards with much affection and respect, especialy after he perceaued in him most euident markes of sanctity. For by the conference which he had with *Xauerius*, and by hearing his Confessions, he playnely found (as he afterward testified vpon his oath, which testimony we haue now in our hands, iuridically signed) that he had kept vnspotted the flower of Virginall Chastity, wherwith he was borne.

Xauiers Virginal chastity.

He remained in the Vicars house three or foure months, to the great profit both of the townes men, and himselfe. For he drew many out of the sinck of grieuous sinnes: & many dishonest louers, whome he could not well separate, he ioyned togeather in wedlock. He reconciled also to friendship, such as before were at deadly hatred one with another. He freed many who had bin long entangled with heinous offeces and abominations. Yet for all this, whilst he so much profited others, he neglected not his owne, giuing himselfe very much to contemplation of heauenly things, especially in the night, when he was free from other employments. And it hapned very often, that when he was sought for by his companions, he was found praying in some corner of the Apostles Church. For being at that time doubtfull what to do, and very vncertaine whether he should go forward to the *Macazarians*, or returne back into *India*, he consulted with God in the holy Apostles Church; so as there spending almost whole nights in cotinuall watching with great feruour of spirit, he craued the intercession, one while of the most B. Virgin mother of God, and another while of *S. Thomas*, & other Saints.

And

And at laſt being repleniſhed with incredible ioy from heauen, he perceiued it to be Gods will that he ſhould go forward to the *Macazarians*, not ſo much to inſtruct them (as afterwards he vnderſtood) as to help ſome others, who were in the way, vnknowne to him, and ſtanding more in need of his aſſiſtance. Wherfore being very deſirous to performe the will of God, he began to caſt about for ſome opportunity to paſſe ouer to *Malaca* as ſoone as might be, intending to make vſe of a Saracen, or Ethincke ſhip, if no *Portugheſe* could be gotten; nay, he ſaid morouer that he had ſuch confidence in God, that if no ſhip of burthen cold be had, and there were but any little boat to go to *Malaca*, he would make no doubt, by Gods helpe, to paſſe well ouer therin : ſuch a firme and conſtant reſolution he had, preſently to performe what he had by Gods inſtinct vndertaken.

By diuine inſtinct he determineth to go to the furtheſt part of the Eaſt.

His confidence in God.

CHAP. XV.

Being beaten by Diuels, he notvvithſtanding ſpendeth a vvhole night in Prayer.

WHILEST he thus remained, as we haue ſaid, in the Vicars houſe, there hapned one thing very worthy to be noted in that kind This howſe ioyned cloſe to the Apoſtles Church, into which was made a little dore, for the vicar to enter priuatly. Now *Xauerius* had a cuſtome, when he perceiued the vicar to be aſleepe (for he lay

alſo

alfo in his chamber) to fteale fecretly, and without noife, from of his bed, and to creepe along with great warines into the Apoftles church: yet did he not wholy deceaue the vicar, who often awaking on a fuddain perceiued him to be abfent. Wherfore he firft diffebled the matter, but afterwards, out of the friendly confidence which was betweene them, aduifed him not to go into the Church in the night time, nor to hazard himfelfe by going that way which was knowne to be haunted with bad fpirits, for he might perhaps meete with them in their vgly fhapes, when he leaft thought of them. At this *Xauerius* fmiled, thinking he had faid it to make him afrayd, and fo putting the Prelate off with a ieft, ftoole notwithftading the next night priuately into the Church when he perceiued him to be faft afleepe.

At this deuotion of Francis the enemies of mankind, were mad with rage and hatred, intending to driue him by terrour from that cuftome: & fo at midnight as he was praying before the Aultar of our B. Lady, they furioufly fet vpon him on a fuddaine, filling the Church with horrible roarings, confufed cryes, and hydeous noyfes. But finding him nothing afraid at thefe their threates, they fal vpon him altogeather, and beate him moft cruelly with fcourges, exercifing their malice vpon him, both in railings, & blowes. Amidft all thefe their violent ftrokes he hauing more care how to remaine conftant, then how to defend his owne backe, called vpon the mother of God who beheld this combat; and fo with vndaunted courage deluded at laft the Diuells vaine affaults, and continued

His conftancy whileft the Deuils whip him.

nued

nued on his prayer , not only without feare , but alſo with greater conſtancy. So as by this his manly & inuincible perſeuerance (a moſt deadly weapon againſt all diuelliſh incurſiõs)he eaſily droue away theſe troubleſome & outragious ſpirits. And moſt certaine it is that he by this victory , ſo brake their forces, that they neuer afterward durſt attempt any thing in that kind againſt him .

There lay a certaine yong man in a chamber ioyning to the Church, who being waked out of his ſleep with that noiſe, heard *Xauerius* crying out (as the Deuils tormented him) and oftentimes calling vpon the B. Virgin for help . And he obſerued, that he very often repeated theſe words : *Helpe me, O Lady . Wilt not thou helpe me, O Lady?* This yong man recounted what he had heard vnto the Vicar , & others of the houſe ; wherat , as often it hapneth, they all fell into a laugh He is ter; and the tale was ieſted on ouer all the houſe vn- ſicke of knowne to Francis ; who the next day , finding him- the ſtri- ſelfe very ſore with thoſe cruell ſtrypes , & deſiring pes. to riſe was not able to get out of his bed, &ſo lay there three dayes, all wearyed & tyred out, feigning himſelf His pa- to be ſicke, ſo therby to hyde what had hapned. The vi- tience in car hearing this came to viſit him , & asked him whe- ſuffering ther he were ſicke ? *Xauerius* anſwered that he was . ſcoffes Then demanding what his ſicknes was; he anſwered from wholy from the purpoſe, turning his ſpeach another thoſe of way. The Vicar knowing well the matter indeed, be- the houſe gan to ieſt with him, and repeated the ſame words , which he had vttered whilſt the Diuells beate him , *Helpe me O Lady . Wilt not thou helpe me, O Lady?* *Francis* when

when he perceiued that all was knowne, began to blush indeed; but yet with a smiling countenance, was no lesse couragious in enduring the speaches of men, then the blowes of the Deuils.

His cou-rage in comba-ting with the De-uill. As soone as he was recouered knowing very wel that the Deuills terrour is greater then his forces, and that like a cowardly Curre he barketh fiercely at those who giue backe, but runneth straight away when one resi-steth, he resolueth, like a Conquerour, voluntarily to returne agayne to his old place of combat, with more alacrity then before. Trusting therefore in Gods as-sistance, who especially restraineth the Deuils forces, he went oftentimes most couragiously & alone, euen in the dead night, to pray in the same Church, and place; & did so contemne those hellish mosters & their deuises, as well shewed that nothing is more shameful and weake then the Deuils, if one haue the courage to contemne them. For being thus stoutly vanquished, and perceiuing their open assaults had ill successe, they vsed other deceiptfull tricks, & endeauoured at least to distract him in his prayer, if they could not breake it of.

The De-uills make a noise in tyme of Xauiers prayer. Whilest therfore he was at his praier in the Church at midnight, as his custome was, they in hatred a-gainst him, come together in troupes, & make a horri-ble noise, & in a scoffing manner imitating the Clergy men, sing as it were Mattins in the Quire, thereby at least to distract him whome they could not otherwise afright. But how litle they profited heerin did euident-ly appeare. For *Xauerius* not regarding who they were, nor what they sung, thought they had byn the

Church

Church men comming to fing their mattins. The next
day therefore he demaunded of the Vicar, who thofe
Clergy men were who laft night fung their Mattins
with the doores fhut? He at firft wondring what Clergy men, and what mattins he meant, perceiued afterwards that they were Diuels, and fcoffers of Clergy-
men. Which thing after *Francis* his death he often declared to many.

CHAP. XVI.

He deliuereth a poffeffed perfon: and ta-
keth Iohn Durus *for his companion.*

IN the meane tyme *Xaucrius*, that he might
not leaue *Meliapora* without fome monument of his labours taken therin, he employed himfelfe, as his cuftome was, to
help the people of riper yeares both by priuate & publike exhortations, and to inftruct children in their
Catechifme. Neyther was there matter wanting for
him to worke vpon. In which kind this accident happened worthy of memory. There was a Cittizen of
great wealth who was poffeffed, and moft miferably
vexed by the Diuell. To whome *Francis* being called
for ayde, he fent in his place one of the children that
helped him in teaching the Catechifme with a Cru-
cifixe, who reading the holy Ghofpell ouer the poffeffed man, as the Father had inftructed him to do, caft
out immediately the infernall monfter, who was the

He deli-
uered a
poffeffed
man by
a child.

more

more enraged, becaufe he was driuen out by a child, & that a Neophyte.

There is alfo recounted another thing in a different kind, yet perhaps no leffe admirable then the former. There was a certayne yong man, a merchant called *Iohn Durus,* who came to *Francis* to confeffion, and hearing him difcourfe of diuine matters, found there were certaine other merchandize farre richer then thofe with which he traffiked, and of which he neuer heard before. Wherfore giuing ouer his former trading, and defirous to become a merchant of more pretious wares, intreateth *Francis* to receiue him for his cópanion. He at firft refufed him abfolutely (becaufe perhaps he faw in him a fecret inconftancy, & intractable difpofition) yet at laft, by much intreaty he obteined his defire ; and fo fetling his affayres, began to diftribute his goods among the poore. But in executing of this his good purpofe, he was more forward, then conftant. For whilft he was bufied about felling of his wares, he was vehemently follicited by the common Enemy of mankind, who did fo worke him vpon that hauing fet his hãd to the plough, on a fuddaine be began to looke backe, and fought againe moft greedily after thofe things which a little before he had contemned. Being thus wholy changed in mind, he packed vp his merchandyze in the moft priuat manner he could, and conueied them into a fhip intending to be gone. But although he deceiued others, yet he could not deceiue *Francis,* the which he moft of all fought to do.

Now hauing gotten al things togeather which he
thought

*He hard-
ly admit
teth Iohn
Durus in-
to the So
cty.*

Luc. 9.

thought requifite , as he was about to take fhipping,
Xauerius vpon a fuddaine caufeth him to be called vnto him . He the more to diffemble the matter , made
fhew of ready Obedience, and came vnto him prefently. *Francis* taking him afyde , with great forrow and
griefe in his countenance fayd : Thou haft finned *Durus*, thou haft finned . At which words he being ftroken to the hart, ftood like one diftracted and amazed,
wondring with himfelfe how *Xauerius* came to know
that which no mortal creature but himfelf could haue
fufpected . Then being filled with fhame , and teares ,
his confcience alfo accufing him, he cryed, I haue finned Father , I haue finned. Then *Francis* againe with
a ioyfull countenance replyed : Confeffion therefore
Child, Confeffion is requifite. Wherupō *Durus* hauing
his hart foftned by *Xauerius* words, and by the dew of
diuine grace , taking againe courage , and fome ref-
pite to examine himfelf, maketh his cōfeffion. Which
remedy he found no leffe expedient then wholfome .
For by the benefit of that holy Sacrament he was not
only pardoned his offence , but alfo conftantly reftored to his former good refolution. Wherfore without
delay, faithfully diftributing his goods amongft the
poore, he conftantly adhered to *Xauerius*,as before he
had promifed , fortifying this his refolution with the
remembrance of his former lightnes and inconftancy.

   At the fame time alfo came vnto *Xauerius* a new,
though fmall fupply of Companions. For that F. *Antony Criminalis* of *Parma* , & F. *Iohn Beira* of *Galliaco*, of
the Society of Iefus , being fent out of *Portugall* , were
very fitly arriued in *India* : of whofe cōming *Xauerius*
                                          being

His de-
termina-
tion of
flying a-
way fe-
cretly is
opened
to *Xaue-
rius* from
heauen.

A a 2

being certified by letters, greatly reioyed (as being the
firſt ſupply which had come vnto him out of Europe)
determining to ſet them preſently a worke, by reaſon
of ſo great want of Prieſts. And he himſelf, that his labours might not be reſtrained within the bounds of
India, intended with the firſt occaſion of ſhipping, to
viſit the furtheſt parts of the Eaſt.

CHAP. XVII.

He reformeth the bad liues of the people of Malaca.

HE departed from *Meliapora* the Citty of *S.
Thomas*, towards *Malaca* by ſea in the yeare
of our Lord 1545. The cauſe of this his iorney was, that hauing now holpen the Portugheſes, who dwelt in that Citty, he might paſſe on
to inſtruct the *Macazariãs* in the precepts of the Chriſtian faith. *Malaca* is a country compaſſed almoſt roũd
with the ſea, beyond *India* and the riuer *Ganges*, called in times paſt (as ſome thinke) the *Golden Cherſoneſus*. For being ioyned to the continent by a ſmall part
of land ſtretching out into the ſea, runneth forth in
length towards the Iland of *Somatra* (formerly named *Taprobana*) famous for Gold mines.

    In this Country right ouer againſt *Somatra* ſtan-
Malaca. deth the citty of *Malaca* belóging to the Portugheſes,
a place very rich, and of great note, from whome that
country hath its name, diſtant from the citty of *Goa*
neere

neere 600. leagues. It lyeth almoſt vnder the Equinoctiall Line, yet by reaſon of the frequent ſhowres
of raine which fall commonly euery day, there is as it
were almoſt a perpetuall ſpring, which doth greatly
allay the heates. For they haue alwayes two ſummers
and as many harueſts, both of corne & fruit. But the
Country is more pleaſant and fertill then wholſome,
for that the fruitfulnes of the place, and the vnwhol-
ſomnes of the ayre proceed from the ſame cauſes. And
beſides this, they haue another inconuenience which
doth more encumber them, to wit, the Saracens, and
Ethnickes who border vpon them. None of theſe difficulties did any wayes affright *Xauerius* to go on with
his reſolution. Nay rather the latter ſet him forward
to help them with more feruour, ſeeing them in danger by reaſon of their bad neighbours.

As ſoone as he arriued at *Malaca*, he goeth to the
Gouernour of the Citty, and certifieth him of his determination of paſſing to *Macazaria*. Wherupon he a-
gaine told *Xauerius*, how he had lately ſent thither a
ſtronge band of Portugheſes, togeather with a Prieſt
of eminent vertue to aſſiſt and guard the Chriſtians,
if any commotion ſhould by chance, be rayſed there
againſt thē. And therfore he wiſheth him if he thought
good, to abide a while at *Malaca*, vntill the ſhip were
returned, and ſhould bring newes how matters went
in *Macazaria*. *Francis* followed the Gouernours coun
ſaile, and in the meane time taking no reſt himſelfe,
begā to employ his endeauours for the ſpirituall good
of the Portugheſes. The *Malacenſians* were at this time
wholy corrupted with the bad cuſtomes of their bor

Conuerſation of Ethnickes pernicious to Chriſtians.

dering

dering neighbours, liuing indeed more like to *Saracens* and Ethnickes, then to Chriftians . For that through their owne carelefneffe rather then want of Priefts, al good order by little & little was fallen to decay; and their behauiours alfo growing daily worfe, they began to runne headlong vnto ruine . For hauing now loft all memory either of faluation or honefty, they for the moft part thought, that they might do whatfoeuer feemed pleafing or profitable to their fenfuality : So forcible is the contagion of bad company, to infect others with the fame vice .

 Francis therfore perceiuing them to be fo extremely corrupted, that now they had neither any feeling of their finnes, nor could endure any remedy to be ap-

A won-
derfull
art to
gaine
loft fou-
les.plyed thereto, fetteth vpon their loft foules, after a ftrange, and artificiall manner . Firft, as his cu-ftome was, he infinuateth himfelfe fweetly into their familiarity, winketh at their finnes, and hideth his defire of curing them. Then hauing wonne them by cuftome & friendly vfage, he by litle and litle pre-pareth the way to cure their inueterate difeafes ; fom-tymes laying before them their heinous finnes and of-fences, by propoūding vnto them Gods diuine lawes; at other tymes ftriking into them a terrour of Gods fearefull iudgements, by vrging of the variable ca-fualities of mans life. And at laft hauing difpofed their minds, he fetteth his hand to worke; he cutteth off a-uarice, taketh away the occafions of luft, mollifyeth and healeth their fore & wounded confciences (wher-of then they began to haue fome feeling) with the fweet oyle of Gods mercies. The fruite which he rea-

ped

ped therby well fhewed that his labours were not imployed in vayne . For it is certaynly knowne, that by
his meanes many made reftitution of goods vnlawfully gotten ; many put away their Concubines , and
thofe that made difficulty to put them away , were
perfuaded to marry them: a great number alfo cleafed
their guilty confciences by frequenting the holy Sacrament of Confeffion , and were brought to leade
a good and vertuous life .

Neyther did *Xauerius* profit the people more by the
fweetnes of his priuate difcourfe , then by the grauity of his publicke Exhortations . Vpon Sundayes he
preached in the greatChurch with no leffe fruite, then
applaufe of his Auditors. And to moue thē the more ,
and better to imprint wholefome feare in their minds
he with great feruour of fpirit foretould what heauen
threatned agaynft that Citty . It was obferued by
many, that he was wont oftentimes, when in his fermons he reprehended with greateft vehemency, the
loofe and wicked liues of the *Malacenfians* , to befeech
God to turne from them the wrath which hung ouer
their heads from heauen , and the punifhments which
a little after fell vpon them. For the yeare following
Malaca was greatly afflicted by a ftronge fiege of the
Saracens of *Iaua,* who alfo wafted the country round
about. And befides the calamity into which that cruell warre had brought them , there followed a contagious peftilence , which fpreading it felfe throughout
the whole Citty, caufed a great mortality both of the
Cittizens and ftrangers , in fo much as the fame became half defolate, whilft God reuenging the former
finnes

His Pro-
phecyes.

sins of the people , rayfed vp, as it were, a new Citty.

Xauerius therfore forefeing thefe euils to hang o-
uer their heads from heauen , and to appeafe, in fome
fort, the wrath of Gods diuine iuftice, fo to difpofe the
inhabitäts minds to indure thofe miferyes which were
neere at hand , after many threats agaynft them, warned them often to looke ferioufly about them. And not
in vayne ; for many being ftroken with the horrour
of Gods diuine indignation, & moued to compunctiõ,
arofe out of their deadly fleepe, and came againe vnto
themfelues . Amongft many paffages of this kind, a
certaine wonderful act which *Francis* there wrought,
did not a little moue the whole Citty.

There was a yong man of that Country called
Antony Fernandez, who by the Deuils cruell tormenting him had loft the vfe of his tongue, and was withal fallen into a moft dangerous difeafe, wherof he had
layne now three whole dayes in defpaire, giuen ouer
by the Phifitians . Wherfore his friends and kins-men
being fuperftitious and wicked people bring vnto him
certaine Sorcerers , a kind of diuellifh Phyfitians, for
remedy . But when their Witchcrafts did no good ,
Xauerius is fent for , who was no foeuer come into the
chamber where the fick man lay, but prefently he beginneth to rage , cry out, and writhe about his face,
eyes and mouth, after a foule and vgly manner ; you
would haue thought the Deuill were now roufing
himfelfe for the combat which he faw to be at hand .
There you might haue feene *Francis*, moued both out
of compaffion towards the yong man , and hatred a-
gainft the Deuill , to fetch many a deepe figh . Then
prefently

*A poffef-
fed fick-
man is
freed frõ
the De-
uill and
cured of
his dif-
eafes .*

prefently falling vpon his knees, he firſt offereth himfelfe by earneſt prayer vnto God, and then began to
exercife the raging yong man, after the accuſtomed
manner; wherein he continued, vntill comming to
himſelf he remained ſomewhat quiet without ſo great
vexation as before. The next day *Xauerius* hauing ſaid
Maſſe for the yongman, commeth agayne with courage and alacrity to the battayle. A wonderfull thing:
that obſtinate and importune foule Spirit which tormented him, being ſuddainly vanquiſhed, and driuen
out, the ſickman preſently recouered both his ſpeech
and ſenſes, and remayned free from any corporall infirmity. There was nothing which euer made *Xauerius* ſanctity of life, more remarkable both to the Chriſtians and Barbarians then this. For heerupon he began to be ordinarily called the *Holy Father*, hauing his
old name now renewed at *Malaca,* which he had left
behind him in *India.*

His name grew alſo famous, and much renowned A Prophefy.
by reaſon of a certaine prophecy which he afterwards
vttered in this manner. Vpon a tyme demaunding of
a Portugheſe Merchant who was to go into *India,* in
what ſhip he meant to go. The merchant pointed to
a certayne ſhip that lay there in the road. I would not
haue you (quoth *Francis*) go in that ſhip. But when
the merchant anſwered, that he had already put his
merchandize therinto, yet if he thought there were a-
ny daunger, he had rather haue his goods caſt away,
then himſelfe; *Xauerius* recollecting himſelfe a litle, as
though he had taken aduiſe of God, vttered this Ora-
cle: ſince, quoth he, you haue put your merchādiſe into

this

this ship, you may also venture your life therein. But if any tempeſt, or other accident happen; beware you do not caſt your goods ouer board, but haue a firme confidence that God will ſend you help, which will free both you and your goods from danger. The euent afterward ſhewed him to be no falſe prophet. For the ſhip in the mideſt of her courſe being driuen by a violent tempeſt was caſt vpon the ſands. Now the marriners being affrighted at the ſuddayne danger went about the lighten the ſhip of her burden, by caſting ouer board her loading, when as the merchant remembring what *Xauerius* had commaunded him, forbad them ſo to do in any caſe, telling them what the holy man had fore tould, and withall promiſing them, by that which he had ſayd, that God would aſſuredly ſuccour them. Which preſently proued true. For the ſea comming vpon a ſuddayne ouer thoſe ſands, the ſhip was ſtraight afloate, and ſo eſcaping that danger arriued ſafely at the hauen, by Gods & *Xauerius* aſſiſtance. The newes heereof being afterwards brought to *Malaca*, it is wonderfull to ſay, how much it increaſed his credit, and eſteeme of ſanctity.

In the meane ſpace *Francis* did not only omit any thing of his former old exerciſes of Chriſtian Charity, but alſo inuented new. For after the ſunne was ſet, he going vp and downe the Citty with a litle Bell, by ſome graue ſentéce or ſpeach admoniſhed the people to call vpon Gods diuine clemency, for the ſoules which were tormented in Purgatory, and for them that were in deadly ſinne. Which new inuention being no leſſe profitable for the liuing then for the dead,

He commédeth in the night tyme to the peoples prayers the ſoules in Purgatory and men in deadly ſinne.

did

did not a litle set on fire the *Malacensians* harts. These
labours of his, wherby he reftored the Chriftian difcipline wholy decayed in the Citty of *Malaca*, were
much increafed, by no fmall employment, which he
tooke in tranflating, with the help of an Interpreter,
the Chriftian doctrine into that language, which the
Macazarians did alfo vnderftand, to whome he greatly
defired to go, moued therto by the often good tydings
which came from thence. For that about the fame time newes was brought, that the people of that country were greatly inclined to receiue the feed of the
Chriftian Fayth, becaufe there were no Temples of
Idols amongft them, nor Idolatrous Priefts to draw
the to the worfhip of falfe Gods: They only adored
the Sunne when it rofe, and befids that, they had no
other God at all.

The pre-
paration
of the
Macaza-
rians to
receiue
the
Ghofpel.

Nothing now feemed longer to *Xauerius* then that
day, when as hauing turned the Catechifme into their
language, and vnderftood the ftate of the Iland, he
might go to inftruct them: yet in the meane tyme he
furnifhed himfelfe with contemplation of diuine
things, but fpecially with heauenly prouifion, for the
vndertaking of fo great a charge. For after he had
fpent whole dayes in offices of charity, he would in
the night defraud himfelfe of his fleepe, and fit vp
watching in prayer and meditation, that fo he might
come vnto the *Macazarians* wholy inflamed with heauenly fyre; and burning loue, both to God and men.
He had now fpent fome moneths at *Malaca*, yet there
came no newes of the fhip which he expected to returne. Wherefore with the Gouernours good leaue he

refol-

reſolued to go to *Macazaria*, haſtning to inſtruct that
nation in the Chriſtian fayth.

CHAP. XVIII.

In Amboynum he giueth many ſignes of his propheticall ſpirit, and charity.

A Propheſy.

A
S ſoone as he found opportunity of paſſage
whither he intended, he put to ſea at *Malaca*,
hauing *Durus* aforeſaid for his companion,
vpon the 10. day of Ianuay in the yeare of
our Lord 1546. & hauing had a proſperous nauigation
he arriued at laſt at his deſired hauen, but not without
many incommodities. For the maiſter of the ſhip caſting about, to come to the Iland of *Amboynum*, and
now thinking he had gone paſt the Hauen, was exceedingly troubled, being out of hope to get to his
intended place, becauſe the wind was ful againſt him.
But *Francis* bad him be of good courage, for the ſhip
was not yet paſt the place as he imagined, and that
the next day in the morning he ſhould arriue ſafe at
the port which he deſired. And ſo it fell out, although
they had very ill weather. At breake of day the next
morning they were in ſight of the Hauen. But the
wind was all that while ſo boyſterous and great, that
it ſeemed vnpoſſible by any meanes to caſt ancker,
therby to ſet *Xauerius* a land, which was the only cauſe
of their comming to that Iland.

As ſoone therfore as they were come to the mouth,

or

or entrance of the Hauen, vpon a suddaine that blu-
string wind, as though it obeyed *Xauerius*, ceased in
such sort, that the ship came very commodiously into
the hauen. But now behould, a second danger euen
in the very Hauen it selfe. *Xauerius* with a few others
had gotten into a litle boate to row to land, when as
on a suddayne they fell vpon two Pyratical ships. The
Portugheses who were in the boate with *Francis* made
away with al speed, therby to auoyd meeting with the
Pyrats. And so putting suddainly into the mayne for
feare, they were carryed a great way from land. But
now, hauing auoyded the danger, & making towards
the land agayne, they were put into a new feare, least
they might perchance meete with the same Pyrates
againe. *Francis* therfore fortelling what would happē,
bad them be of good comfort, & row without feare
to shore, for by Gods goodnesse they should come safe
to land. And the euent proued true as he had pro
phecyed. When *Xauerius* was landed, he was very
courteously receyued by the inhabitants, being also
before sufficiently recommended vnto them by fame
of his sanctity.

The wind o-beyeth Xauerius.

Another Prophe-sy.

    Amboynum is about some 80. miles in compasse,
and is an Iland of speciall note vnder the Portugheses
dominion, much frequented both by merchants, and
the people of that country. It is distant from *Malaca*
aboue 900 miles. There were then in this Iland, besides the garrison of Portugheses, seauen other townes
of Christians, without any one Priest among them
all, for he, who only had bin there, was lately dead.
Francis therfore going about to those desolate townes

Amboy-num.

baptized

baptized many infants and children . His manner of
going was this: Hauing a boy carrying a croſſe before
him , he himſelfe asked at euery dore, if they had any
ſick, any children to baptize , or any dead to bury ? If
he found any ſick , lifting vp his eyes , and hands to
heauen , he recited ouer them the Creed,& the Ghoſpell. And oftentimes with one and the ſame labour he
cured the ſick both body , and ſoule. He alſo ſolemnly
buried them that were dead,ſaying firſt the vſuall funerall prayers, & afterwards maſſe for their ſoules; ſo
that a queſtion might be made , whether he more aſſiſted the liuing, or the dead. But whilſt he ſought to
deſerue well of men , God out of his prouidence gaue
him a very ſpeciall ſubiect to worke vpon .

Of his
manner
of going
about.

About the ſame time *Ferdinand Soza* Captaine o-
uer certaine Spaniards , comming from *New Spaine* ,
(which is a Country in the other world, not further
diſtant from *Amboynum* then from Spaine)and going
to the *Moluca's*, arriued with his whole nauy at *Am-*
boynum. There were many ſhips, a very great number
of marriners & ſouldiers , an incredible multitude of
ſick , beſides a cruell peſtilence that had taken away
many Spaniards : whereupon it manifeſtly appeared
that God out of his ſingular bounty, had ſent *Xauerius*
before to be ready to aſſiſt & help them. For preſently
his inflamed charity began to ſet vpon the violence of
that peſtiferous diſeaſe, aſſiſting ſome by ſeruing thē,
and reconcyling others by the Sacrament of Confeſſion . One while he comforted the ſick, another while
he aſſiſted ſuch as lay at the point of death, and buried
thoſe that died with funerall obſequies. Thus he being
but

Ferdinãd
Soza a
Captai-
ne of the
Spani-
ards.

He relie-
ueth the
calamity
of the
Spaniſh
nauy.

but one man, performed the office of many.

But his greateſt labour of al was, to procure of thoſe
that had meanes, things neceſſary for the poore and
ſicke, and to ſeeke about with vnſpeakable labour &
paynes medicines for their diſeaſes, whereof in that
place there was great ſcarcity. Therefore hauing oftentymes begged ſuch thinges of one *Iohn Arauſius* He fore-
a Portugheſe merchant, who had great ſtore of ſuch tels that
like wares, he at laſt tooke it ill, & was very angry to *Arauſius*
ſee that he made no end of begging. So as when vpon will
a tyme, one asked him ſome ſuch drugs in *Francis* his ſhortly
name, he with much grudging gaue at length what dye.
he demaunded, but tould him therewithall, that he
ſhould aske him no more. Which thing comming
to *Xauerius* hearing, preſently by diuine inſtinĉt, What
quoth he, doth *Arauſius* thinke that he ſhall long inioy
thoſe things which he hath? He is ſurely deceiued;
Go tell him from me, that he need not be ſo ſparing
of his wares which death wil ſhortly take from him, &
that he himſelfe will dye ere it be long, in this very
Iland, and that his goods will fall to the ſhare of the
poore: therfore if he be wiſe, let him largely beſtow
what he hath vpon the ſicke poore people, for Gods
ſake, and make his benefit of that which may help
him after he is dead. The euent was anſwerable
to what he foretould. For not long after *Arauſius* dyed
in the ſame Iland, leauing no heyre behind him, & his
goods were diſtributed amongſt the poore, according
as the cuſtome is there, when one dyeth without hey-
res: and *Arauſius* being ſtroken with the terrour of death which was declared to him to be at hand, became
more

more wary of his owne carriage , and more liberall
also of his drugs to the poore.

He spent three monthes (for so long the Spanish
nauy remayned at *Amboynum*) in seruing the sicke, to
their exceeding great good , both of body and soule.
Yet *Xauerius* his diligent endeauours were no lesse
profitable to the whole, then to the sicke. For he neuer
gaue ouer to drawe out the corruption of their minds
both by the medicines of the Sacraments , and by priuate and publike exhortations . Which labour of his
was not in vayne . For he reaped indeed plentifull
fruite of peace, from those warlike people : many priuate grudges were taken away , many were reduced
to see their owne errours , & to betake themselues to
a vertuous life . Amongst whome *Cosmas Turrianus*
(who came in the Spanish Nauy) being moued by
Francis his eminent sanctity , resolued to imbrace his
course of life, & to enter into the Society. Then *Francis* hauing had good successe concerning the affayres
of the Christian fayth at *Amboynum*, after the nauy
was departed, going to *Macazaria* , tooke the Iland
of *Ternate* in his way, lying about 200. miles from *Amboynum*.

*The
fruite
which
the Spa-
nish na-
uy yiel-
led.*

OF

OF THE LIFE OF

S. FRANCIS XAVIER.

THE III. BOOKE.

He reformeth the Inhabitants corrupted behauiour, in the Moluca's.

CHAP. I.

MOLVCA is a Country diuided into many small Ilands (which they call the *Moluca's*) very famous by reason of the fertility, and traffique of spices especially Cloues, distāt from *Malaca* 1100. miles or therabout . It is full of Country townes , inhabited partly by *Ethnickes* and partly by *Saracens*; the fertility of the soile being such, that it doth not only keepe at home those that be there borne, from seeking commodities else where,

Moluca. Ilands.

where, but inuiteth alſo ſtrangers vnto it. The *Moluca's* are very many in number, moſt of them little in
in extent, and the greateſt thereof is but ſmall : for
there is none aboue 18. miles in compaſſe. They lye
vnder the Equinoctiall line, and runne out from the
north into the ſouth, diuided from one another almoſt
threeſcore miles. There are amongſt them other I-
lands of leſſer extent : but almoſt all the *Moluca's* be
ſubiect to one Saracen King, who is tributary to the
King of Portugall. *Ternate*, which without compariſon is the fayreſt of all theſe Ilands, hath in it a Citty
of the ſame name, ſubiect to the Portugheſes, which
Citty is inhabited chiefly by them, and other Chriſtians of that country.

Ternate the chiefe of the Moluca Ilands.

When *Xauerius* therfore was come thither, he lodged in the ſuburbs, at a Church of our B. Lady, called the *Barres*. There, hauing inuoked that mighty
Protectreſſe of the place, his moſt aſſured Patroneſſe,
he beginneth preſently to imploy himſelfe in his accuſtomed workes of Charity. The people of *Ternate*
had now openly let looſe their raynes, ſo much beyond thoſe of *Malaca*, to wickednes, by how much
further they were diſtant from *India*. For that throgh
dayly commercement, and conuerſation with the
Ethnickes and Saracens, they were growen ſo ſtupide
and blind, euen in matters of ordinary humanity, that
in making their bargaines concerning trafficque, they
eſteemed nothing vnlawfull, or vniuſt, whereſoeuer
there ſeemed any hope of gayne. This Citty therefore, being almoſt paſt recouery, *Xauerius* ſetteth vpon
for cure, with the ſame art which he had formerly
done

done at *Malaca*. For hauing gotten the Inhabitants good will, partly by winking at their manners, and partly by the sweetnes of his conuersation, he began by litle and litle to discouer their sores, and to apply remedies thereunto. Wherein his singular prudence manifestly shewed it selfe. For if he foūd any one intangled in the snares of dishonest loue, if he were a person of authority and esteeme, he vsed most commonly to deale with him in this sort.

Pruden-
ce in re-
calling
wicked
men.

First, he would discourse after a sweete familiar manner, & if he did not inuite him to his house, he would gently offer himselfe to be is guest. Sitting at table he would discourse pleasantly, thereby to open a way for good and wholesome counsayle. Then as soone as he had gotten to be inward and familiar with him, he would begin to speake of the foulenes of sin, and so by litle and litle come to the loathsomnesse of carnall concupiscence, & the inconueniences which ensue thereon; to which he would often also adde threats and vengeance from heauen. At last when he perceiued him to be moued, he would take him, in a gentle manner by the hand, and induce him to make his confession. And so in fine without much difficulty he eyther made him put away his Concubine, or else to take her in lawfull wedlocke. It is well knowne that in this kind he brought many to marry their Concubines, that the lawfulnes of wedlocke might extinguish the flames of dishonest lust.

The like course he tooke to draw from the the money which they had gotten by vsury or deceipt; the summe wherof was such, that the *Sodality*, called *of*

Mercy

Mercy there erected, being but meanly foūded, became therby rich & wealthy. This was not a litle furthered by his often exhorting and inſtructing of the ignorant people and children . Whereby the behauiour of the Citty was amended, vniuſt Contracts diſſolued, and the childrens eares and tongues ſo filled with the Catechiſme, that al places round about ſounded with the pleaſant tunes of the Chriſtian doctrine.

But the chiefe thing which moued the *Ternatians* was a certayne Prophecy that *Francis* vttered. He being now at *Ternate* ſo far off from *Amboynum*, ſaw by diuine reuelation *Iohn Arauſius* the merchant a dying, as he had foretould it would ſhortly happen. Therfore ſaying maſſe before a great aſſembly, when after the Offertory he turned about, as the cuſtome is, to the people, ſaying *Orate fratres*, Pray for (quoth he) & commend to God the ſoule of *Iohn Arauſius* who is now dead at *Amboynum*; yeſterday I ſaid maſſe for him and ſo do now againe to day. Wherat they that were preſent were ſtroken into an amazement, looking one vpon another , and asking how he could come to know that, ſeeing *Amboynum* was aboue 200. miles from that place, and it was knowen that no man had come from thence at that time. Then their admiration being turned into expectation of what would be the euent therof, they who had bin preſent, noted downe his words, and the time; and a few dayes after there cōmeth a ſhip from *Amboynum*, and bringeth newes of *Arauſius* his death. Wherupon comparing the things and times togeather, they found all to be iuſt as *Francis* had foretould. Then they made no doubt but

Xauerius

Xauerius aſſuredly knew the ſame by diuine reuelation : and therefore euery one did reuerence him, as a Prophet .

Now *Xauerius* began to prepare himſelfe for *Macazaria,* which was diſtant from that place only two dayes iorney . But it ſeemes it was not Gods holy will that he ſhould help them, who were already ſufficiently prouided for. At the ſame time he was informed by perſons of credit , that in *Maurica (* commonly called the Country of the *Mauri)* there were very many Chriſtians , who through want of Prieſts were brought into extreme danger of their ſaluation. Therfore iudging it beſt to aſſiſt thoſe who ſtood moſt in need , leauing of his iourney to the *Macazarians* who wanted not other helpes, he ſetleth himſelfe, and his whole endeauours thereunto .

CHAP. II.

He reſolueth to helpe the Inhabitants of Maurica, euen vvith the hazard of his life.

T HE Country of *Maurica* lieth diſtant frō *Ternate* well neere 200. miles. The land is rough and craggy , and exceeding barren of all things . As for corne and wine the inhabitants know not what they meane . They haue neither Cattle nor ſheepe , only a few ſwine, which ſerue them rather to wonder at, then to eate . There is

much

much want of frefh water, but ryce inough, & a great multitude of wild Bores. There be trees of an huge biggeneffe, from whence they get their bread & wine, fuch as it is. Other trees alfo they haue, of whofe barke being finely combed, fpun, and wouen after their fafhion, they commonly make themfelues garments.

The barbarousnes of the Mauri.

The people are altogether barbarous, & without any humanity; for they haue no figne at all of learning among them. But in cruelty they furpaffe all other nations; and fo farre are their Natures made fierce by cuftome from fparing of ftrangers, as they vfe to murder and poyfon euen one another, after a moft barbarous manner. There was but one Prieft among them who had care of their foules, and him they had alfo killed: fo as they had bin long without a paftour.

The incommodities of the coutry of *Maurica.*

The Country for the moft part is often fhaken with terrible earthquakes, cafting forth fyre & afhes beaten vpon with huge waues of the raging fea; fo as you would thinke that God did punifh the heerby for their abominable finnes Wherefore, thefe manifold feares kept all ftrangers from coming vnto them But *Francis* armed with an vndaunted courage againft all dangers, omitting (as we haue fayd) his iorney to *Macazaria*, which was the caufe of his comming thither, refolued with himfelf, to free them from eternall perdition, although it were with euident hazard of his owne life. Wherof writing to his friends in Portugall, he fayth, that to help thefe wretches with his owne manifeft danger, he was encouraged by thofe words of our Sauiour: *Qui voluerit animan fuam faluam*

Zeale of foules.

Matt. 10. *facere, perdet eam; qui autem perdiderit propter me, inueniet eam.*

eam. He that will faue his life, fhall loofe it, and he that fhall loofe it for me, fhall find it. Which fentence, he faid, feemeth very eafy and playne, in fpeculation, but not in practice, vnleffe God himfelfe interprete it interiourly in our foule.

Neuer did his fingular courage, and confidence in God fhew it felfe more then now. For when newes was brought to *Amboynum* that *Xauerius* meant to go to *Maurica*, the inhabitants were ftroken into admiration, as well at his vndaunted courage, as alfo with commiferation, by reafon of the great dangers he was to vndergo. And when they vnderftood, that he was vpon the point to depart, they prefently flocke vnto him, & tell him that, that place is rather a receptacle of wild beafts, then of men : That moft of the Inhabitants haue their hands imbrued in the bloud of their Wiues, Children, Parents, and Priefts. Therfore by Gods manifeft wrath they are continually fcourged with all kind of plagues, both from the land, fea, and heauen it felfe; and for this caufe ftrangers are much more to be kept farre from their fury. They moreouer declare vnto him, that euery moment almoft, he was to be in euident danger of his life amongft thofe people, who make but a paftime & ieft of murdring, & poyfoning one another, & thirft after nothing more then humane bloud. What prudence therfore could it be, to preferre fuch dangerous places, before thofe that were quiet? What reafon had he, being a ftranger to truft his life in their hands, who, as all wel knew, tooke no other delight, but in killing, and murdering one another?

They go aboue to terrify him frō his refolution of going to that barbarous nation.

Whileft

Whileſt his friends ſtood beating theſe things into his head, the dangers which they obiected touched no man leſſe, then himſelf who was to vndergo them. But

then they began with teares to intreate him, not to make ſo litle eſteeme of his owne life; and ſeeming withall diſpleaſed they adde lamentations to their in-treaties, ſaying: what Portugheſe is there in the world yea what ſtanger or Barbarian who knoweth *Xauerius*, will endure, that the inſtruction of a baſe Country ſhould be bought with the hazard of his life? Who can now hope, that the chiefe ſtay of the Eaſt, which ought to be perpetuall, will continue long, if ſo wil-lingly he put his life into manifeſt danger, forgetting that he draweth with him the ſoules of ſo many na-tions into the ſame ruine? He ſhould remember how the ſaluation of all *India*, & innumerable other Coun-tries dependeth on his life. If he, out of incredible for-titude, and courage of mind, contemned all dangers, yet at leſt he ſhould not draw with him, the ſoules of ſo many people, into hazard. The deſire of the com-mon good, ſhould ouerſway the particular; eſpeci-ally ſeeing it is manifeſt, that it was not worth the la-bour to inſtruct ſo ſauage a Nation, which had byn forſaken by their Prieſts, not ſo much for feare of dan-ger, as out of deſpayre to do any good among them. Wherfore they beſought him for Chriſt I E S V S ſake, the redeemer of mankind, that he would not, out of an vncertayne hope to ſaue a few, caſt both his owne life, and the ſaluation of innumerable nations into certaine danger, but would, as well beſeemed his prudence and vertue, preſerue himſelfe for the Ea-

ſterne

sterne Church, or at least reserue himselfe for dangers
answerable to the greatnes of his mind.

This piety of friends was more gratefull, then
pleasant vnto *Xauerius*. Imbracing therfore ech of thē
in a friendly manner, & bedewed with ech others teares, he replyed almost to this effect : *Quid facitis flen-
tes, & affligentes cor meum &c.* What do you, weeping *Act.21.*
and afflicting my hart? I acknowledge your fidelity ""
and good will, and thanke you, becaufe you haue o- ""
mitted no figne of loue towards me. But none of thefe ""
dangers moue me, confidering what God commaun- ""
deth. Let God prouide for thefe things, who vndoub- ""
tedly is the author of this determination ; vnder the ""
wings of whofe protection I feare nothing at all. For ""
to whome may I better commit my perfon and life ""
then to him, who hath the difpofing of the liues of ""
all moralls? A man that muft once dye, ought not to ""
feare death, which layeth hould on euery one, though ""
they feare neuer fo much. But a good death (which ""
is the entrance to immortality) is to be defired. And if ""
I dye, God certainly will not dye, who hath both a ""
farre greater defire of the faluation of Nations, then ""
I haue; & can alfo eafily fend labourers into his vine- ""
yard. Neither is the fruite little which fhall be reaped ""
in *Maurica*: for that is not to be eftemed little, where ""
there is occafion of great merit. I for my part, if there ""
be nothing elfe to hinder me, refufe no perill or dāger ""
for their faluation; which being in hazard, I am of du- ""
ty bound to prouide for. *Vt fuerit voluntas in cælo, fic* *Machab.*
fiat: what is iudged fitting in heauen, let that be done. *lib.1.*

Then they, out of the vehemency of their loue,

paſſing from intreaties to plaine force, wonne the
keeper of the Caſtle, not to permit him to haue any
ſhip to ſaile thence. The keper therfore indeauouring
although in vaine, to draw *Francis* frō that enterprize
aſwell by alledging the ſame dangers, as by the terrour
alſo of preſent death, when at laſt he ſaw he could not
preuayle with him, tould him flattly, that he would
ſuffer no ſhip to carry him thence. To whome *Xauerius*
replied, that he feared neither dangers, nor death
where the honour of God & ſaluation of ſoules was to
be ſought, and that he eſteemed none for his enemies,
but thoſe that hindred Gods diuine ſeruice. He was
certainly determined and reſolued to follow God who
called him into *Maurica*, neither was it want of ſhipping which ſhould ſtay him; for if he could not get a
ſhip, he would aſſuredly rely vpon God, and ſwimme
ouer.

*He pro-
teſteth
that if
he cānot
get a ſhip
he will
ſwimme
ouer.*

When therfore his friends perceiued him to be ſecure of Gods aſſiſtance, and to remayne immoueable
in his determination, not inuenting what more to do,
they came all weeping vnto him, & brought him all
kind of preſeruatiues agaynſt poyſon. But *Francis* fearing leaſt by conceauing, through anxiety of mind,
ſome vaine imaginations of dangers, he might caſt
vpon himſelfe too much ſolicitude and care, and out
of hope of humane helpe diminiſh his confidence in
Gods prouidence, gaue them thankes for their good
will, and withall tould them, that thoſe things would
be rather a burden then any help vnto him. And therfore intreated them that they would not loade him
with ſo much diffidence in God. But if they deſired to
baue

*He gi-
ueth to
his friēds
backe a-
gayne
their me-
dicines a-
gainſt
poyſon.*

haue him preserued from all plagues and poisons, they should dayly pray to God for him . For that was the most infallible, and most present remedy which could be found . And so taking leaue of his friends, he prepared himselfe for his iourney, with all alacrity .

Whilest he was thus vpon the point to depart, and venture vpon so great danger, there came good newes out of *India*, which added more flames to his zealous confidence: which was, that nine more of the Society of Iesvs were come from Portugal to *Goa*, fiue of them Priests, to wit *Francis Perez*, *Alphonsus Cyprian*, *Henry Henriquez*, *Francis Henry*, and *Nonnius Ribera* : the others who had not yet taken holy orders, were *Baltazar Nonnius*, *Adam Francis*, *Nicolas Nonnius*, and *Emanuel Morales*. *Xauerius* therfore hauing vnderstood of their arriuall before his departure from *Amboynum*, being very glad that such assistance was come so happily, appointed to euery one of them their employment, & presently dispatched letters to *Goa* to those of the Society, wherein he gaue order that *Francis Perez* should remaine in *Goa* to teach the schollers there, and that *Cyprian* and *Henry* should go to *Comorinum* for the help of the Neophites in that place: and the two Fathers who were already in *Comorinum*, with the rest of the nyne, he ordeined to repayre vnto the *Moluca's*, intending with this smal supply to visit all those Ilads, & assist euery one as farre as he was able . Then with Gods speciall fauour he began his iourney towards *Maurica*, taking ship at *Ternate* in the Month of May 1546. whither he soone after safely arriued .

CHAP.

CHAP. III.

He bringeth the sauage people of Maurica to ciuill behauiour, and instructeth them in the Christian Faith.

Maurica.

AVRICA (as we haue bin informed)is diuided into two Prouinces : the one is scituated in the Continent, and is called *Maurotia,* the other consisteth of two Ilands which they call *Maurotides.* Of these two Ilands one of them is horrible to behould, by reason of certayne burning rockes, out of which there oftentimes burst forth mighty stones of fyre, as bigge as trees, and *Burning rockes.* with such a noyse and violence, as no peece of Ordinance, though neuer so great, sendeth forth its bullets with a greater report : and sometimes also where the stone breaketh out in that vehemency aforesaid, there is cast forth from the same place such an huge quantity of ashes, that both men and women labou-*Ashes are cast out of the rockes.* ring a great way off in the fieldes, are so besmered, & euen couered with the same, that you would thinke them rather Deuils then men. Many wild Bores also are stifled & ouerwhelmed therwith in the woods: yea and fishes found euery where cast vp dead, vpon the shore.

The same Iland, that no inconuenience may be wanting, is so skaken with almost perpetuall earthquakes, that they who sayling by chance in the sea

neere

neere vnto it, are oftentymes greatly affrighted, thinking they be caſt vpon ſome rocke that lyeth in their way. Moreouer the winds being at continuall warres with one another, within the hollow caues of the earth, make ſuch a diſmall noiſe, & ſtrike ſuch an incredible horrour into the eares, that one would thinke he heard the roring of hel it ſelf: vpon which occaſion *Francis* was often wont to put them in mynd of the paines of hell fire, wherin Idolaters and bad Chriſtians are tormented for al eternity. There inhabit theſe places alſo, a kind of people called *Iauari*, who are without any knowledge of Chriſtianity, extremely wild and ſauage, and delight only in murder. And when they haue no ſtrangers to ſlaughter, they turne their fury vpon their owne wiues and children, and oftentimes do make no ſmall hauocke amongſt the Chriſtians. There be alſo ſome among them who account mans fleſh for dainties, eſpecially when they are killed in battaile.

Horribly earth quakes.

People wonderfully ſauage.

O eternall God! how ſtrongely is he guarded who truſteth in his diuine aſſiſtance, and is protected by him! How ſecure is one in the midſt of the greateſt dagers where God ſtandeth for him! Nothing ſurely is to be feared, nothing to be doubted when God as the Guide leadeth the way. Among theſe people then, more truely ſauage then bruite beaſtes, did *Xauerius* through help of the Higheſt, remaine for the ſpace of three monethes, beyond all mens expectation, with more profit to the inhabitants, then danger to himſelfe. For in this time he brought thoſe ſauage people to milder diſpoſitions, and reclaimed them to that ci-

Pſal. 90.

uill

uill carriage , which becommeth Chriſtians . They were at that time wholy ignorant, all alike, in matters of Chriſtianity , retayning only the meere Name of Chriſtians.

Francis therfore preſently went about to all the Chriſtian villages being neere thirty in number , baptizing infantes , inſtructing the elder ſort, hindring ſacrifices to Idols , and helping the neophytes in their miſeryes both ſpirituall and corporall . In his publick and priuate exhortations, he terrified that barbarous people with threatnings both from heauen & earth, ſhewing them, that they were not far from Hell , as they might well ſee by the fire and aſhes which were oftentimes caſt vp, and vomited forth in ſuch abundance, that many lewd and wicked men among them were throwne downe headlong, & deuoured therein. The ſame alſo was ſignified by thoſe huge earthquakes, wherwith the ground being ready to open threatned to ſwallow vp ſuch as for their deteſtable wickednes were hatefull in the ſight of almighty God. Therfore they ſhould by all meanes beware , that they fell not headlong into thoſe euerlaſting flames , wherof they had a continuall repreſentation before their eyes.

He terrifieth the barbarouspeople with the repreſentation of hell.

By theſe kind of exhortations, and other precepts of Chriſtian doctrine he wonderfully qualified their ſauage natures : ſo as within a ſhort ſpace all that Nation, then the which (as we ſayd) there had bin none worſe, or more inhumane vntill that day, began from that tyme to be not only mild and tractable , but willing to be inſtructed alſo in the myſteries of our faith; ſuch force hath Chriſtian diſcipline to drawe men to humanity .

Chriſtiā diſcipline qualifieth barbarous nature .

Here

Here in this place the vndaunted courage of *Francis* his mind manifeftly fhewed it felfe. It hapned that as he was in the Church at Maffe, vpon the feaft of *S. Michael* the Archangell, before a great number of the inhabitants, the whole Iland was vpon a fuddaine fo fhaken with an earthquake, that the Aultar it felfe feemed ready to be ouerturned. Wherupon moft of the people ranne away, ech one whither their feare caryed them; but *Xauerius* either as though he perceiued nothing, or rather contemning the feare, went on conftantly with his Maffe, faying the caufe therof to be, that *S. Michael* the Archangell did then with many torments throw downe all the Deuills of that coūtry into Hel who withftood Gods diuine honour: fo as he had more ado with men, then with the deuils themfelues. For there wanted not fome Idolaters both obftinate and potent who went about by threates & feares to hinder the going forward of the Gofpel. But in vaine. For *Xauerius* inuincible vertue and courage vpheld by diuine aide, ouercame all things.

His courage in the time of an earthquake.

In a few monthes therfore he ranne ouer all the Chriftian Villages, inftructed an innumerable multitude of the inhabitants in the Chriftian precepts, & brought many to imbrace the faith of Chrift. How much fruit he heaped togeather may be hereby gathered, in that, it is faid, he made in one towne called *Tolum,* 25000. Chriftians. And furely his labour was no leffe then the fruit. For running to and fro fo troublefome a country, he fuffered almoft all the difcommodities which could be imagined, as penury & want, heate, hungar, thirft, wearyfomneffe, and dangers.

The fruit of foules.

gers . But as commonly the pleasure is proportionable to the paine, so according to the multitude of his troubles he had côfortes to recreate his soule, which how great they were, may be coniectured, by the clause of a letter of his, to some of the same Society, where hauing spoken of the barrennes of those parts, & of the want of all things: *These things,* saith he, *I haue for this* **Psal. 94.** *end layd open vnto you, that you may know what abundáce of heauenly ioyes there be in these places. For such labours &* **Heauely cōforts in la bours & afflicti-ons.** *dangers vndertaken wholy and willingly for Gods sake, are treasuries filled with diuine, and vnspeakeable consolations: so that these Ilands may seeme most conuenient, and apt to make one loose his eyes, by shedding aboundance of most sweet teares. I for my part do not remember, that euer I was ouerflowed with so many, so great, and so continuall comfortes of mind, in such sort, as they wholy take from me all feeling of labours and miseries. So Francis.* Who out of his endeauouring to bring this sauage Nation to lead a Christian life, reaped no lesse fruite and comfort, then labour and merit.

CHAP. IIII.

He laboureth the second tyme, amongst the Ternatians.

 ETVRNING back from *Maurica* to the *Moluca'*, he came againe to *Ternate*, where being most ioyfully receaued by the *Ternatians*, he stirreth vp the slouthfull to the pursuite

purfuite of vertue , and confirmeth thofe that were
wauering. But the ordinary courfe he kept was this .
Vpon holy dayes he preached twice a day; in the morning to the Portughefes, in the after-noone to the people of that Couutry : exhorting the one to liue a good
and vertuous life , and inftructing the other in the
myfteries of the Chriftian faith , and auerting them
from worfhipping of Idols . Befides this, euery day
both before & after noone, he heard the Confellions
as well of men, as of women . Vpon euery Wenfday
and Fryday he made an exhortation a part to the wiues of the Portughefes (who for the moft part were
of that country borne) explicating the articles of the
Creed, of the ten Commandments, and of the Sacraments of Confeffion and Communion . It was then
the tyme of Lent: wherfore very many of them did
pioufly & religioufly folemnize the Feaft of Eafter, by
receauing the facred Eucharift , from which they had
vntill that time abfteined .

But now *Xauerius* hauing bin long abroad, was
by the domefticall care of the Society at *Goa* , called
home againe. Therfore he determined with all fpeed
to paffe ouer to *Amboynum* , there to expect paffage
backe into *India*. But the Gouernour of the Caftle of
Ternate , the Sodality of *Mercy* , and the other Portughefes by their earneft intreaty , inforced him to ftay
yet a while at *Ternate,* although it were not much a-
gainft his will, becaufe he did not repent himfelf of the
paines he tooke amongft thé. In the meane time *Francis*
had a great defire to try what good he could do vpon
the barbarous King of *Moluca,* who being tributary to

the

the King of Portugall, was in Religion a Saracen, not
so much by profession as in life. For he was not held
from becomming a Christian through any deuotion
to Mahomet, but through his owne exorbitant and
licentious lust. For besides whole troupes of Concubines, he had 100. wiues dwelling with him in his
Court.

This King therfore being moued aswell by *Xauerius*
courtesy, as by his sanctity of life, vsed him with all
honourable respect, notwithstanding that his Nobility openly repined thereat; and he much desired his
friendship, giuing some hope that he would one day
become a Christian; as when he sayd, that the Saracens and the Christians adore one God, and a time
would come when they should both professe one Religion. But although he seemed to take delight in *Frãcis* his company and discourse, yet his immoderate
sensuality of life kept him backe from being a Christian. This thing only could at last be got of him, that
he promised, one of his children (wherof he had very
many) should be baptized, vpon this condition,
that afterwards being a Christian, he might be made
King of the Iland of *Maurica*. *Xauerius* therfore, although the matter was not yet ripe, being glad of
that hope, did so keep friendship with the King, that
he laboured neuerthelesse in instructing the Country
people. For trying the disposition of the Ethnickes,
he found them to be farre lesse auerted from Christ,
then from *Mahomet*, although they were by the Saracens compelled to the mahometicall superstitions;
and that the Saracens themselues, being also ignorant

of

of their owne profeſſion, were not found obſtinate therin. Suppoſing therfore that it would be eaſy to conuert them both, if there were an houſe of the Society erected in *Moluca*, he reſolued by all meanes to do his beſt therein, and at laſt by helpe of the King of Portugall, who was a very great aduācer of the Chriſtian cauſe, he fully accompliſhed the ſame.

The Ethnickes of Moluca miſlike not Chriſt ſo much as Mahomet.

In the meane time his chiefe care was to inſtruct the Portugheſes and the neophytes: which labour indeed proued not vnprofitable. For within the ſpace of ſix months all his paines were recōpenſed with a moſt plentifull harueſt of the *Ternatians*. And he ſo applyed the townes-men with godly Exhortations, frequenting of Sacraments, & other holy exerciſes, that in all mens iudgement they ſeemed to be another people, then they had formerly byn: and it is well knowen, that the Chriſtian Inhabitants thereof, of an infinite number of Concubines which they kept, had put thē all away, except only two. Neither was there any thing which did the people more good, then the opinion of his ſanctity; a very forcible argument to perſwade, eſpecially when it is confirmed by ſignes from God. For as he was once in the middeſt of a Sermon vpon a ſuddain he deſired his Auditors to ſay deuoutly a *Pater* and *Aue*, for *Iames Ægidius* Admirall of the Portugheſe Nauy, who was then a dying at *Amboynum*, which was afterwards found to be true by aſſured teſtimonies. This thing then much increaſed the peoples eſteeme of *Francis* for the preſent, and afterwards their deſire to keep him.

A Colledge of the Society in Moluca.

A prophecy.

Hauing remayned there now ſix months, he prepared

pared

pared for his departure with intention to visit *Amboynum* agayne. Wherefore out of the extraordinary loue
which they bare vnto him, the whole Citty came flocking with him to the Hauen. And when he was ready
to depart, they brake forth into such a weeping, and
crying out, calling him, with their confused voyces,
Maister, Guardian, & *Father*, that euen pitty made him,
as though he had forgotten his iourney, remayne a
while in imbracing euery one of them, for that his
bowells were greatly moued towards this his flock:
and so hauing at last imbraced and conforted them all
with most sweet words, he with much ado tooke his
leaue, where at they bitterly wept, and lamented.

CHAP. V.

He fortelleth, and is Authour of a notable Victory, vvhich the Portugheses obtai-ned against the Barbarians.

*X*AVERIVS being thus glad to see the
Ternatians great deuotion, was againe presently stroken with sad newes of the per-
fidiousnes of the *Tolaneans*. *Tolum*, as we
sayd before, is a Towne belonging to one of the
Ilands of *Maurica*, hauing in it many Christians,
newly planted there by *Francis*; most of the inhabitāts
wherof, eyther through feare of one *Geliol*, a forraine
Tyrant, or else to curry fauour with him, had reuol-
ted

ted both from the King of Portugall , and the Chriſtiã faith ; & ouerthrowing the Church, had in deriſi-
on brooken the Croſſes and images of Saints ; ſeizing
alſo violently vpon the goods of the other faythfull &
pious Chriſtians . At this fact of theirs *Xauerius* being
much afflicted, left the ſame to God, who would iudg
his owne cauſe : but the iniury done agaynſt Heauen & Earth , armed them both with reuenge againſt
the Authors therof. And firſt God layd his heauy vengeance vpon them: for their ſoile which in former tymes had bin moſt fertile,became wholy barrain; their
corne alſo in their barnes conſumed away by an ac-
curſed putrefaction ; their waters of wholeſome vpon
a ſuddayne became bitter, and infectious , ſo as many of the people were taken away by famine and peſtilence .

The land offertile becometh barraine & the waters of wholeſome become vnwholſome.

And as they were thus ſcourged with direfull
wrath from heauen , the Portugheſes alſo came vpon
their backes with a terrible warre. For the Gouernor
of the *Moluca's* (*Francis* promiſing him that the warre
ſhould haue good ſucceſſe) ſent preſently a Nauy a-
gaynſt thoſe perfidious Rebels,together with a choice
band of Portugheſe ſouldiars. The chiefe Commaun-
der of the Nauy being encouraged by what *Xaue-*
rius had foretould , & through confidence in Gods diuine aſſiſtance , vndertooke the warre with great alacrity & diligence : notwithſtanding he thought it not
amiſſe before he ioyned battayle , to ſend Meſſengers
vnto them , and offer them pardon, if they would re-
clayme from their rebellion, and ſo ſaue their liues.
But after they had ſent backe their proud anſwere ,

the

the Portugheſes ſet on fire with reuenge, march on towards the enemy.

There was a Caſtle ſcituated vpon an high place no
leſſe fortifyed by art then nature, whereto alſo were
added other deceiptfull ſtratagems of the enemy. For
they being not ignorât of the war which the Portugeſes were to make vpő them, had about the wals thereof for a good cõpaſſe, ſtroken into the ground, certaine ſharpe ſtakes armed with foure pointed nayles, on
which the Portugheſes might be forced to runne if
they attempted to approach the Caſtle. Theſe engines
of theirs to defend theſelues, would not only haue defeated the Portugheſes comming theron, but haue alſo
broght great annoyance vnto thē, if *Fracis* his prayers
had not taken away the preſent danger, & opened the
entrance which was ſhut vp agaynſt them. The Portugheſes were not yet landed, when it appeared how
meruailous God himſelf did fight for them. The Sunne
about the tyme of midday being ouercaſt with a ſuddain cloud, made the day as darke as the night, whē
as in the toppe of a mountayne hard by, there brake
forth with horrible crackes & roaring, a filthy loathſome fire, which continued three daies & three nights.
Wherupon an huge great quantity of aſhes, & ſtones,
the like wherof was neuer ſeene before, being caſt vp
out of the earth, did not only couer the forſaid ſtakes,
but alſo made the ground leuell with the toppe of the
Caſtle.

And behould whilſt the Barbarians were aſtoniſhed at this vnexpected accident, there happened a-
nother thing which ſtrooke a greater terrour into thē.

For

[marginal note:] Prodigious wő-
ders giue
the Por-
tugheſes
the Vi-
ctory.

For at the very fame time a wonderfull ftrang earthquake ouerthrew an infinite number of houfes in the
Citty. Now when the *Tolanes* had endured thefe miferies, for fome dayes, the Portughefes came vpon the
with al their forces. But yet it cannot be properly called a battaile: for moft of the enemies were either oppreffed with the falling of the houfes, or elfe were fled
for feare; and the heapes of ftones which were caft
out of the Earth, carryed them vp eafily to fcale the
wals of the Caftles. And thus the Fort, Towne, and
whole Country were fubdued without any battaile at
all; and peace granted them who were conquered v-
pon certaine conditions, wherof the chiefe were, that
they fhould againe build vp the Church which they
had ouerthrowne, reftore the goods taken from the
Chriftian people, & finally imbrace againe the Chriftian religion, which they had once before receaued.

The Barbarians faw certainly, that this memorable victory was obteined more by diuine then huma-
neforce. But the Portughefes did abfolutly attribute
the miraculous burning of the mountaine, & the fuddain heaping together of the afhes & ftones to *Francis*
his merits, who like another *Moyfes* had obteined
diuine affiftance for them, whilft they fought againft
the enemyes of God; who, as he had fauoured the
warre, fo had he alfo affoarded fpeciall ayde therunto.

CHAP.

CHAP. VI.

He againe visiteth Amboynum, *and laboureth still amongst them.*

A prophecy.

HAVING in this time well increased, and setled Christian religion in *Ternate*, he sayled backe to *Amboynum*, with intention to returne thence into *India*, after his long absence frō those parts, & to visit the Society, wherof was he superiour, & which was now much increased by the arriuall of new supplyes from Europe. Now whilest the passengers were in the midst of their way discoursing merrily amongst themselues, *Francis* on a suddain stepping forth from the company wherein he was, with great vehemency and griefe of mynd cryed out: Good Iesu, what is this? they kill the man. Whereupon the rest being amazed at the suddaynes of the thing, ranne to *Xauerius*, and asked him what the matter was? Then he, being come againe to himselfe, dissembling the matter answered, that it was nothing, and so sate downe agayne amongst them in a familiar manner, behauing himselfe as though he had neither done, nor sayd any thing more then ordinary. But that which he cōcealed, within a litle while was after openly knowne. For as soone as they arriued at *Amboynum*, they found a Portughese who had byn slayne by certayne theeues, at the very instant when they heard *Xauerius* cry out in the ship.

There were in the Hauen at *Amboynum* foure

Por-

Portughefe fhippes of burthen . *Francis* therefore ftill
burning with charity , confidered ferioufly how he
might beft help both the inhabitants and fträgers, vntill he could get paffage into *India.* And fo eyther out
of loue of pouerty , or elfe becaufe he would be neere
the port, he maketh for himfelfe and his companion a
litle cottage of ftraw vpon the Sea fhore , & heerunto adioyneth a litle chappell of the fame workeman-
fhip , therein to heare Confeffions , and adminifter
the Sacrament of the holy Eucharift to the marriners
and fouldiers, giuing himfelfe wholy to fuch employments . Many alfo he made friends who were at deadly hatred amongft themfelues, but fpecially he helped
& ferued the ficke, both corporally and fpiritually. A-
mongft whome he found one who lay very ficke of a
vehemét feuer , whome he neuer left vntil he gaue vp
the ghoft, which he did euen in *Francis* his armes; who
gaue great thankes , and prayfe to God for his comming backe at that tyme to *Amboynum* for the fauing
of that poore foule, although he fhould gayne nothing
elfe thereby . Then making his circuit with great diligence ouer all the Chriftian villages, he baptized infants, & inftructed the rude & ignorant in the Chriftian precepts, with fruit anfwerable to his labour. He
moreouer imploied himfelfe inceffantly in preaching
to draw the people from vices , and incite them to
vertue, and good life. And how much beloued he was
of all , his departure well fhewed . Vpon the 20. day
after his arriuall thither, to preuent the lamentation
of the people at his departure which he forfaw would
happen, he made al things ready to take fhipping pri-

F f   uately

He buil-
deth
himfelfe
a cottage
vpon the
shore .

His con-
tinuall
attendã-
ce vpon
the ficke.

The *Am-
boynois*
loue to
Francis.

uately at midnight. But it was hard to deceiue louers, for they perceiuing what he intended, came running in the night to the hauen, where vpon a fuddayne was heard great crying out of men, women, children & feruants, bewayling and lamenting their forlone & defolate ftate, & making their moane, that fuch a man fhould in fuch a fort be taken from thē. *Xauerius* being moued at thefe their lamentations and mourning in the night tyme, with teares in his eyes cōforted them with all fweet words, and imbraced them one after another, who could hardly be pulled from him, they fticking as clofe to him as his owne bowels. At laft after much ado, intreating a certayne Prieft to employ euery day two houres in teaching thē the Catechifme, he tooke his leaue, commending ferioufly to their diligence the exercyfe of the Chriftian doctrine.

The time and tyde now vrged him to depart, & many Portughefe fhips being there ready, *Xauerius* was inuited into the *Admirall,* wherein were many of his friends and welwillers. But he, although he were earneftly and oftentimes requefted, conftantly refufed the fame. And when the maifter of the fhip asked him, why he would refufe fo kind an offer; he knowing, doubtleffe by diuine reuelation, what would happen, anfweared, that he was afrayd left fome mifchance might befall vnto that fhip in the way, and that God might punifh them for fome fecret finne of theirs. His feare was not without groūd · For the fame fhip being foone after by a cruell tempeft driuen vpon a rock, was in eminent danger to haue byn caft away: but yet was for that tyme miraculoufly deliuered (by the

prayers

A prefage of what would follow.

prayers perhaps of *Xauerius*) & held on her courſe, vntill meeting with another croſſe tempeſt, & being by
the violence thereof driuen vpon a vaſt quick-ſand,
ſtucke therin ſo faſt, that not only the ſhip, but all the
paſſengers in her, were accounted for loſt ; when as
notwithſtanding Gods Goodnes, which changeth the
courſe of things, ſupplied againe with help proportionably to the danger: for by force of the raging ſea ſhe
was at laſt driuen through the quick-ſand, & ſo eſcaped without much harme. But *Xauerius* who had pre-
ſaged the incommodities which would befall others,
hauing himſelfe a proſperous nauigation, came ſafe
without any ſtay, to the place he intended, & arriued
at *Malaca* in the yeare of our Lord 1547.

CHAP. VII.

He inſtructeth the Malacenſians *vvith all
the care he could: and by diuine reuelation he vnderſtandeth a Viſion vvhich
happened to* Durus *his Companion.*

AVERIVS therfore after long abſence
comming againe to viſit the *Malacenſians*
his ancient friends, he is by them very louingly entertained. But according to his old
cuſtome, refuſing to remaine with his friends, he taketh vp his lodging in the hoſpitall of the ſick . At the
ſame time there were three others of the Society newly arriued at *Malaca*, wherof two were Prieſts, *Iohn*

He lod-
geth in
an Hoſ-
pitall of
the ſick-

Beira,

Beira, and *Iohn Ribera,* whome he imbracinge with incredible ioy of mynd, retayned with him for a while. Then, after some good space of repose, he instructed them of the manners, and behauiour of the people of the *Moluca's,* and sent them thither to manure and cultiuate the vineyard which he had there lately

He inculcateth to the Neophites the comming of Christ.

planted. In the meane time he failed not himselfe to further the Christian cause, by seruing the sick, preaching to the people, composing of quarrels among the souldiars, hearing Confessions, & catechizing children, seruants, and ignorant people: especially he oftentimes instructed the Neophites in the Euangelicall history of the comming of our Lord & Sauiour Iesus Christ, that so the knowledge of so great a mystery might put out of their minds, the vayne and idle fables of their Gods.

Euening prayers for the dead and those that are in mortall sinne

Amongst other things, not forgetting his ancient custom no lesse pious then profitable, he tooke order that in the euening the people by their prayers might remember to assist the soules in purgatory, & such as were in mortall sin. For the City of *Malaca* at *Xauerius* request, had appointed a certayne mā, who carrying a lanterne in one hand, & a litle bell in the other, should go about the streets when it grew darke in the euening, & by ringing the bell, and calling vpon the people in a dolefull tune made of purpose, stirre vp their minds to the sayd deuotion. Which thing, as it stirred vp the vertuous to their duty, so it stroke a terrour of Gods indignatiō & wrath into the wicked. This practise being begun by *Francis* at *Malaca,* was soone spread ouer all the Citties and townes of *India,* the

the *Moluca's*, & the vtmoſt Eaſt, and is ſtill euen vnto this day, there in vſe, to the great good both of the liuing and the dead.

About the ſame tyme *Xauerius* gaue a notable example both of Euangelicall pouerty, and auſterity. *Iohn Durus* his Companion (as we ſayd before) thinking he was bound to prouide for *Francis* his neceſſities, had without his knowledge receiued of the Portugheſes ſome mony more freely then diſcreetly, vnder the colour of Almes. Which whē *Xauerius* vnderſtood (as he was no leſſe ſharp in reprehending then diligēt in obſeruing holy pouerty) he preſently baniſhed him for a time into an Iland neere by, lying right agaynſt the hauen of *Malaca*, which had in former tymes byn well ſtored with inhabitants, but was now left deſolate. *Durus* therefore liuing there, ſaw vpon a time in a certaine Church (whether awake or aſleep is vncertayne) the mother of God ſitting at the high Aultar vpon a cuſhion, vnder a Canopy richly adorned: with her he ſaw the child Ieſus, who endauoured to allure *Durus*, being much aſhamed of his fault, by ſweet meanes to come vnto his mother. She at firſt, as though ſhe had byn angry, turned from him, & put him away: then, when after he had humbly intreated, and beſeeched her to pardon him, ſhe at laſt receyued him; and admoniſhing him of certayne faults, ſhe left him ſuddaynly, and togeather with her child Ieſus mounted vp to heauen.

This viſion was altogether ſecret, no mortall man knowing thereof but *Durus* himſelfe, nor had he ſpoken thereof to any. Being therefore after a while

called

[marginal notes:]

A ſharpe puniſher of brech of pouerty.

He by reuelatiō knoweth things that be ſecret & farre of.

called backe to *Malaca*, and making his confeſſion to *Xauerius* as his cuſtome was , he ſayd nothing of the viſion . But *Francis* knowing it by diuine reuelation, asketh him, what that was which happened to him lately in a Church of the Iland where he was ? To me (quoth he ?) I remember nothing. The Father gently vrged him to tell , but *Durus* refuſed, & vtterly denied to haue ſeene any thing: & being in this māner oftentymes asked (ſo obſtinate he was to haue concealed the matter) forgetfull both of obedience & Religion, he ſtill anſweared from the purpoſe . Then *Francis* , whē he ſaw that he had to do with one of ſo obdurate a nature, began himſelf to recount euery thing in particular , as if he had byn preſent. Whereat *Durus* ſtood like one amazed , and being filled with an holy feare, declareth all the matter in order as it hapned ; and ſo at laſt the good Father receiued him agayne into his friendſhip . But this truth being wrunge out of *Durus* by diuine reuelation , made him more obſeruant heerafter vnto *Xauerius* , & eaſier in yelding to the truth . Who after *Francis*, his death declared all this vpon his oath , with a notable teſtimony of his incomparable ſanctity.

CHAP.

CHAP. VIII.

At Malaca *he procureth a Nauy to be set forth agaynst the* Acenians, *enemies of Christianity .*

AFTER this, there hapned another accidēt which made *Xauerius* name much spoken of in *Malaca.* The thing certainly is very remarkeable , by reason of diuers prophesies which hapned in the passage thereof, and therfore must be recounted at large, lest the breuity of the narration, should diminish the truth and euidency of the matter. From the Iland of *Somatra,* which (as we haue said) is scituated right ouer agaynst *Malaca,* a strong nauy of the King of the *Acenians* arriued there in the dead of the night. The Barbarians had in charge, some to inuade the Castle, & others to set fyre on the Portughese shippes which lay in the hauen . Therfore so soone as they were landed, and with all speed, they set vp ladders to the Castle to haue surprized the same at vnawares . But they deceyued not the Portugheses. For the garrison being instantly raysed by the watch, armed themselues , and with inuincible courage beat backe the enemy .

But now the businesse of their ships in the Hauen succeeded not so fortunately . For the Barbarians fell fiercely vpon the same at vnawares , and in the darke of the night, set on fire their principall
shippes.

fhippes, ftriking therewithall fuch a terrour into the Portughefe marriners that they ftood wholy amazed, like men without fenfe, not knowing what aduife, or courfe to take to help themfelues. In the meane fpace the Barbarians being out of danger, ftood looking on, and reioicing to fee the Chriftians Nauy on a flaming fire. And fo at laft with a moft clamorous fhout, and outcry they departed, infulting ouer the Portughefes, and Chriftians, as though they had gotten a notable victory.

An example of barbarous cruelty.

　　The Barbarians not content with this, hauing in their returne, met with certayne Chriftian fifher-mē vpon the fea, they manifefted vpon them a moft infolēt cruelty. For after they had cut of their nofes, eares, & heeles, they fent them to the Gouernour of *Malaca,* with a letter written with their bloud, wherein moft proudely, and infolently they prouoked him to battaile. When the fifher-men had giuen this letter to the Gouernour, he caufed it to be publickly read before the Souldiers, who were no leffe moued at the infolent brutifhnes of their enemies, then at the miferable fpectacle of their friends, who were thus mangled & disfigured by their wounds, and euery one had his hart full of pitty, and indignation.

　　Whilft they were in this perplexity and trouble of mind, *Xauerius* by chance commeth newly from faying maffe in the Church of the Hofpital, in the fuburbs where he lodged, according to his former cuftome. And euery one might fee, that the Barbarous *Acenians* had done this, out of their naturall hatred to Chriftian Religion, and in contempt of the Portughefes.

tugheses.The Gouernour therfore named *Simon Mcho,*
asked *Francis* his aduise, what he iudged fit to be done
vpon such an affront offered? He, by diuine instinct
(as afterwards appeared) tould him, that he thought
it best to send out some shippes presently after the e-
nemy,who was yet in sight, & by setting vpon them
of their owne accord, to quit themselues of this disgrace, to the end the Barbarians might be taught by
their owne harme, to abstaine from doing iniury to
others. And this he thought best to be done the rather,
because he saw that this publicke disgrace was not
offred so much to the Portugheses,and their King, as
to Christ himselfe,& to all Christians; and that by no
meanes it was to be indured, that the Portugheses,
Christians so renowned for their fortitude, should be
now accounted cowards,and made a laughing-stock
to their enemies. For who seeth not, quoth he, that
Christianity wil be ouerthrowne,if barbarous people
be suffered, not only to hate it, but also to vse it contemptibly? Wherfore he willed them to take courage
worthy of Christian souldiars,and with alacrity pursue the barbarous enemy,with all hope & confidence;
for although they were inferiour to them in forces,
yet their cause was better, and had also God to fight
for them, whose cause they mantayned.For certainly
he would not faile to assist them, whilst they behaued
them selues manfully in that pious conflict, and that
through his fauourable conduct they should remayne
victors.

    Xauerius counsell was approued of all that were
present, but they wanted shippes to put the same in
G g exe-

execution : for there were but only feauen left which had efcaped burning, and thefe alfo much impayred through tempeftuous weather at fea, & ftood in need of reparation before they could be fet forth for fuch an enterprize. Befids, they were not only out of order,

but wanted tackling and other furniture neceffary. As the Gouernour therfore was telling h m the want of fhippes: I efteeme it, quoth he, a matter of much importance , to be forward in the vndertaking of this great Bufines, in which not only the Kings, but God Almightyes Maiefty is interefled . And feeing in this fearefull enterprize you are amazed, not knowing what to refolue vpon, I defire with your good leaue, I may haue the charge of preparing the Nauy. Then turning to the foldiars : Brethren , quoth he, God certainly ftädeth for vs, in whofe name l warne you all before hand , that you fuffer neither feare, nor any

thing elfe whatfoeuer, to diuert you from hauing a part in this glorious action, to which he vndoubtedly calleth you. Behould heere I offer my felfe to go along with you to this noble and Chriftian combat, and to be your fellow , and companion in what danger foeuer may happen; that we may reuenge our felues vpon thefe Barbarians , Enemies of moft our Vertuous King , and Aduerfaryes of the Croffe of Chrift.

Thefe words fo inflamed the fouldiars harts, that al of them, being as it were fuddainly infpired by God ftroue to giue in their names to fight in fo religious a warre, nothing doubting but it would haue a profperous iffue, hauing *Xauerius* for the author , and furtherer

therer therof. And the Gouernour being glad to fee
fuch confent of the Captains & foldiars left al things
to *Francis* difcretion, who with no leffe prudence then
courage managed a bufines wch to all mens iudgmét
feemed moft ful of difficulty; as was to prepare a nauy
fo prefently vpon the loffe of fo many fhips, for that
the Armoury was wholy empty, & fmall help could
be expected from the publicke treafury. *Xauerius* therfore out of all the maifters of the fhips maketh choice
of feauen, excelling the reft both in efteeme & wealth.
He calleth them euery one by their names, and inter-
mingling gentle words with imbracements earneftly
requefteth them, that they would both for the honour
of their King, of Chrift our common Lord, and of
the Chriftian Name vndertake this bufines, how la-
bourfome or chargeable foeuer it feemed, & that they
would with al fpeed caufe feauen of thofe fhipps that
lay in the hauen to be fpeedily repayred, and they
fhould infallibly be repayed fhortly all their expences
with an 100. fould.

By feauē
rich mai-
fters of
fhippes
he fet-
teth
forth a
Nauy.

    The fhip-maifters were by thefe words fo fet on
fire, that euery one ftriuing who fhould make moft
haft, the nauy within foure dayes ftood ready in the
Port, well appointed of all things. One *Francis Saa* a
kinfman of *Mello* the Gouernour was made Generall
therof, to whome there were alfo affigned 180. Portughefe fouldiars. *Xauerius* was to go with them, but
that the *Malacenfians*, out of their great affection to
him, hindred it. For they came floeking to the Gouernour, and what by lamenting their fatherleffe & defolate ftate, what by protefting vnto him that they

would abandon the Citty, if *Francis* their only comfort and vphoulder fhould depart, they got at laft both the Gouernour of the Citty, and Generall of the fleet to intreat him (being himfelfe doubtfull what to do in this affaire, fince the people were of fuch different affections) to remaine at *Malaca*.

Precepts giuen to foldiers at their going to warre. *Xauerius* therfore calling togeather the Captaines and fouldiars into the Church, and making to them a comfortable exhortation, bad them be of good courage, and he for his part, becaufe he could not accompany them in perfon, would be prefent with them with his beft wifhes and prayers: and that they fhould fo difpofe themfelues both in mynd and affection, to efteeme nothing more pretious vnto them, then to dye for Chrift the fonne of God, who dyed vpon the Croffe for their fakes: That they fhould haue before their eyes that amiable and deuout fpectacle of their Sauiour, and imprinting it in their harts, fhould moft couragioufly take vpon them the battaile, and enter into combat with the Barbarians. Moreouer, in the midft of the battayle, they fhould cal vpon God imploring his diuine affiftance, and confidently hope that he will be ready to helpe thofe who fight for him.

Hauing faid this, he began to heare their Confeffions, and when he had reconcyled them, and armed them with the holy Eucharift, he animateth the againe to fet forward againft the Enemy, vnder God's conduct, not doubting of the victory. They all by diuine inftinct, of their owne accord, in prefence of God, & ftriuing at it were who fhould do beft, make

a folemne

a folemne protestation, that if occasion required it, they would fpend their liues for Christ in that quarrell. In refpect wherof, and for that they had thus cō fecrated themfelues to Christ, they were by *Xauerius* called, *The Army of Iefus Christ*, a Title very honourable. And thus full of good hope and courage, they were by the Cittizens accompanied to the Nauy.

CHAP. IX.

Hauing lost their Admirall, he foretelleth the comming of tvvo other ships vnto them, & ftirreth vp the flouthfull vvho drevv backe, to fight couragiously.

VT now, when they were all ready, and prepared for this warre, there fell out a difaftrous accident, to the end that *Francis* his vertue and fanctity might the better appeare, which did not a little hinder the bufineffe. The fhips were now afloat with their fayles & banners all difplaied, and their Ordinance playing in a triumphant manner, and the fhore thicke befet with the people of *Malaca* defiring to fee them depart; when behould on a fuddaine the Admirall, in view of the whole Citty, in the very hauen (by what chance no man knoweth) is funke, and ouerwhelmed in the fea, together with the loffe of all that was in her, except the marriners & fouldiars. Which accident was held

by

by all for a prodigious token of something else to follow. Wherupon the Cittizens fell a murmuring, that
it was certainly a manifest presage of Gods wrath hã-
ging ouer the Portugheses heads, if the fleete should
hould on her course against the enemy. Morouer they
cast forth bitter words against the Gouernour of the
Citty, and Generall of the fleete, as though they had
bin the authors of that disastrous warre: neither did
some spare *Xauerius* himselfe, saying; Who could euer
haue thought that the flower and strength of the Portughese garrison should be thus sent away to their certain destruction, seing that their enemies farre exceed
them, not only in number, but also in strength of
shipping and souldiars. Behould how God, hauing set
before our eyes the danger both of the General, and
whole Fleete, there wanteth nothing but plaine
words to tell vs, that this expedition is not pleasing
to him.

    Whereupon *Mello* being not able to endure this
extreme grudging, and exorbitant complaynts of
the people, sendeth presently a messenger vnto *Xarius* to intreat him he would please to come vnto him
with all speed. He finding *Francis* at Masse in the Hospitall Church, would haue instantly deliuered his
message vnto him. But being stayed by a signe which
Xauerius made, he expected vntill Masse was ended.
Then *Francis*, before he had spoken one word, Go,
quoth he, and tell the Gouernour that I will presently come to him, but byd him be of good courage, because God fauourably assisteth his seruants, at the instant when it is required. This he sayd to shew that he
              knew

*He by re-
uelation
know-
eth
things
absent.*

knew by reuelation all the bufineffe.

Francis then following the meffenger, findeth them all in feare & tumult. But he fhewing cherfulneffe & confidence in his countenance: What is the matter *Mello* (quoth he?) Doth fo little a thing difcourage thee? He is Omnipotent, whofe fatherly prouidence proteƈteth vs . Hauing fayd this , he imbraceth the Captaines & fouldiars ech one in particular, & partly by intreaty, partly by aduife, he ftill exhorteth them to go forward in fo glorious a feruice nor did he omit to put them in mind of the promife which they had lately made to Chrift , fo to ftirre them vp to the performance of their duty : wherat they were all fo filled with ioy, efpecially to fee fo great alacrity in *Xauerius,* that they feemed rather to behould hope it felfe, then caufe therof. The fouldiers being thus incited, hee turnes himfelfe againe to *Mello,* fhewing him their feruour and zeale in the bufines.

His cou-rage whē others are afraid

This was very grateful vnto the Gouernour who much fauoured *Francis* his defignement. But yet that nothing might be rafhly attempted , it was thought good to call the principall of the Citty to a counfaile & haue their opinions & confent herin. Their voyces were foone giuen (who would belieue it) concerning the euents of this warre, euery one iudging that expedition to be temerarious. For what difcretion were it (quoth they) to venter fix fhipps agaynft a nauy of 60. and leffe then 200. Portughefe fouldiars againft 5000. fighting Barbarians ? But now on the contrary part all the Captaines and chiefe of the foldiars, who were to vndergo the danger, cryed out, that by

A deli-beration held a-bout the warre a-gainft the Bar-barians.

all

The Por
tugheses
soldiars
renew
their
oath to
dye for
Chrift.

all meanes, that pious warre was inftantly to be followed, & that it were better for them to dye brauely
in the combat, if it fhould fo fall out, then to violate
the promife they had made to the King of Heauen.
And heerein they were fo refolute, that without more
ado they renewed their folemne oath to go vnto that
warre, and if need were, to fpend their liues for the
faith of Chrift.

Whereupon the others being all ftroken into an
amazement, *Francis* ryfeth vp ioyfully, and hauing
commended the noble courage both of the Captaines
and the fouldiars, did often inculcate this vnto them;
that they fhould be fure to put al the hope of the victory in God, for whom it was not hard to faue by many,

1. *Reg.* 14.

or by few; neither were there wanting euident fignes
of Gods diuine affiftance, wherby they might certainly belieue he ftood with them. And for one fhippe
which they had loft, there fhould that very day come
vnto them, two more for their comfort. Which pro-

A pro-
phecy.

phecy proued true. For that a litle before funne-fet
they efpyed two Portughefe fhips fayling by *Malaca.*
Thefe were priuate veffells belonging to one *Iames
Soarius* a famous merchãt of thofe parts, who to auoid
paying cuftome at *Malaca*, kept on his courfe directly for the *Moluca's*. But yet at *Xauerius* intreaty,
he put in at *Malaca*, and moreouer offered himfelf to
accompany the reft in that warre. Then were they all
by this accident, filled with a new ioy, & confidence.

CHAP.

CHAP. X.

The Portugheses, by Xauerius sollicitation obtayne a great victory against the Barbarians.

THE Captaynes therefore and souldiers of this Nauy much reioycing, vpon the 23 of Nouember in the yeare 1547. hoysed vp sayle, whilst euery one wished them a for-tunate voyage. They were only eight great ships in number, and not aboue 230. souldiers. Vpon the fourth day after their setting to sea, hauing had a pro-sperous wind, they arriued at the Promontory of *Cā-bilanum*, where they were commanded by *Simon Mello* the Gouernour, to seeke after the enemies fleet. Wherfore *Saa* the Admirall vsing all diligence that might be in searching for them, could not find to what coast they had retired; so as being wholy frustrate oftheir hope, they were constrayned to returne homewards agayne. Whilest, full of sadnes, they began to make backe for *Malaca*, behold vpon a suddayne there arose a cruell tempest, which enforced them to lye many dayes at ancker. And though this tempest hindred their returne, yet was it a meanes to obtayne the vi-ctory, the diuine Prouidence disposing of incommodi-ties themselues, to serue sometimes for good effects. Their victuals now growing short, so soone as the

(margin: Thepromontori Cambilanum.)

(margin: A tempest helped towards the victory.)

H h   violence

violence of the contrary wind was allayed, they sayled to the next towne of the Ethnickes, being their friends, to furnish themselues with new prouision: which when they had done, and hearing nothing of the Enemy, they held on their course homewards towards *Malaca*; yet they were not so much out of care, as out of hope to find the enemy. But hauing gone a little thence, they met by chance a fisher-man, who tould them, that the *Acenians* fleete, hauing spoiled the Country round about, lay not far off in a riuer, called *Perlen*, intending to intercept the Portughese Nauy, which (as was reported) was shortly expected from *Bengala*, to come vnto *Malaca*, hoping to make prey of the same, and to massacre all the Christians therein.

The Admiral hearing this vnexpected newes, much reioiceth, & to shew how glad he was put on straight a rich suite of apparell. And moreouer bestoweth vpō the souldiers all things most liberally to feast & make merry withall, and commandeth them all to be bountifully treated, and the Ordinance to be all discharged in token of his excessiue ioy; so that one would haue thought that there had byn rather a victory already gotten, then a battaile at hand: which though peraduenture was imprudently done, yet by the diuine prouidence it was to good effect. In the meane tyme the spies which he had sent priuately vp into the riuer with three boates, tooke some of the Enemies prisoners, by whome they vnderstood, that the Barbarias hauing heard the artillery of the Portughesesplay, had put their ships in order for battaile, & were comming

The cherfulnes of the Portugheses when the battaile was at hand.

Gods prouidēce turnes that to good which was ill carried.

ming

ming downe apace towards the fea , thinking that
the booty of the Portughefes from *Bengala* which they
expected, was now at hand .

The riuer *Perlen* being very large within the bankes, becometh almoſt like a fea where it breaketh into the mayne . For though the channell be deep , yet
runneth it neuer the flower by reafon of the breadth,
but glideth along violently like a torrent, not yelding
any foard to paffe ouer. *Saa* the Generall therfore making vfe of the Promótory, which runneth out by the
banke of the riuer, within the winding therof, where
the ſtreame hath leaſt force , fpeedily putteth his fleet
in order to fight . Thé earneſtly exhorting all the Por
tughefe Captaines and fouldiars , to call to mind that
day, wherin they had freely , before the Aultar of our
Lord, vowed to ſpend their liues for his Religion and
honour, and vpon which occafion they were intituled
the *Army of Iefus Chriſt*, encouraged them, & willed
them to imagine they faw *Xauerius*, the Authour of
that pious warre, praying for their fafety and victory.
He put them alfo in mind, not to forget what the
good Father had charged them to do; to wit, that behoulding Chriſt the fonne of God crucified for them,
they ſhould (neglecting their owne liues)couragiou-
fly vndertake the combat for his glory . That they
ſhould remember how they had twice bound themfelues by oath to Chriſt the King of Kings, and twice
of their owne accord vowed their liues for his fake.
That certainly they, who were to fight that religious
battaile for God, ſhould not want his diuine affiſtáce.
And that *Xauerius* Prophecy , promifing them an in-

*The Ri-
uer Per-
len.*

*The Por-
tughefe
Admi-
rall ex-
hortatió*

fallible

fallible victory, would proue true. The souldiars being with these words set on fire, cried out al together, that they were prepared to reder their liues for Chrift our Lord, for whose fake they had more then once vowed the same. And remembring *Xauerius* charge, they expected his affiftance, and promife in the battaile.

In the meane tyme, the enemies Nauy being set in battayle array, came downe the riuer with the streame, and the bankes and shores on both sydes sounded forth with horrible showtings, & confused noise of drummes. The first squadron was led by the Admiral of the Barbarians fleete, guarded on ech syde with foure Turkish galleys. Then followed six other Galleyes, with nine rankes of ships, and all abundantly appointed not only with great ordinace, but also with plenty of small shot. The admirall therfore of the Por-

tugheses, as soone as the first rancke of the enemy was discouered, maketh towards them presently at vnawares with three ships, commanding the rest to follow as they were ordred for the battaile. Whereupon the Barbarians, whether for want of skill, or rather by Gods ordinance, sayling on headlong with fury, discharged all their great shot agaynst the Portugheses before they could so much as reach them, so as the bullets fell all into the water, without doing any harme.

But the Portughese guner shooting a very great bullet out of the greatest Ordinance, stroke the Admira'l of the *Acenians* so flat, that presetly he sunke & drowned her. Which was not only a presage of a future victory but rather the conclusion of the combat it selfe. For

the

the Turkiſh Galleys ſtaying their courſe, left off the
fight, and began to help the Captaine, & other principall men ſwimming to ſaue themſelues; which cauſed both their owne, and the fleets whole ouerthrow. The Bar-
For the Turkes had placed their galleys ouerthwart barians
the riuer, & ſo had takē vp a good part of the ſame, to ſhips in-
receiue in thoſe that could ſwim vnto them, not once one with
thinking of the danger themſelues were in, God had another
ſo beſotted them. The ſix other Gallyes which follo- are ſhat-
wed the firſt ſquadron, comming downe with the tred.
ſtreame, ranne vpon the former that lay athwart, and
all the reſt of the nine rancks which came after, fell
againſt thoſe which went before, & became ſo intangled one with another, & ſo daſhed togeather, ech one
ſtriuing to get free from his fellow by force, that one
would haue thought there had byn a battayle among
themſelues.

The Portugheſes perceiuing manifeſtly that Gods The Por
hand was in this buſineſſe, fayled not to follow the tugheſes
victory which was thus offered them from heauen. ſet vpon
Wherefore preſently calling out alowd vpon the ſo- the Bar-
ueraigne name of *IESVS*, they began to grapple with barians
their enemyes, and on euery ſide to play vpon them fleet
with their ordināce, lying there ſo entāgled & hindred without
one by another that they were not able to ſtyr. Thrice any hurt
did they ſend out with all the violence they could, the at all to
ſhot of all their great ordināce vpon their ſhips, & no themſel-
one ſhot was made in vayne, nor was the Enemy able ues.
to reſiſt, or make any vſe at al of their owne artillery,
being ſo thruſt vp togeather; and this without any
loſſe to the Portugheſes that aſſaulted thē. Now with-

in a little while they had funke nine of the Enemies
ships, & battered many more to pieces, with no small
slaughter of the barbarians. Wherupon the rest were
put into so great a feare, that most of them, as well
rowers as souldiars throwing away their weapons de-
speratly cast theselues into the swift streame, thinking
saue their liues by swimming: but it vayne. For being carried away with the violence of the water, they
were all swallowed vp by the swift windings of the
streame, not so much as one remayning aliue to carry
newes of so great an ouerthrow.

The Portugheses hauing obtayned so noble a victory without so much as any drop of bloud shed on
their side, after they had giuen harty thankes to God,
whose present assistance they had found in this battaile, began to gather vp the spoyles of their enemies,
where the prey was not inferiour to their glory. For
they seized vpon the whole Nauy, and tooke all the
ships except those ten which were sunke. They also
tooke about 300. pieces of artillery, besides the great
abundance of armour, and all other pillage. And they
vnderstood by some of those whome they had before
taken prisoners, that there dyed in that conflict to the
nūber of 4000. barbarians. Among whome were many nobles of the King of *Acenians* Army, besids many
Turkes & Ianizaries that had ioyned themselues vnto him.

The report of this notable victory was presently
bruited all ouer that country; whereupon the King of
Perlen, who through feare of the *Acenians* had fled
into places of more security, being animated by this
ouer-

A slaugh-
ter of
the Bar-
barians.

An vn-
bloudy.
victory.

A great
prey.

The nū-
ber of
the Bar-
barians
slaine in
the fight

ouerthrow of his Enemies, began to take courage; and on the suddain setting vpon a certaine garrison of the *Acenians* which stood neere to the riuer *Perlen*, slew the guard thereof, destroyed it, and made pillage of all that he found therein. The memory of which benefit, although receyued from those that thought not of it, wrought so much with that Barbarous King that he presently came vnto the Generall of the Portugheses, and with great submission, and many humble thankes acknowledged him for the restorer of his liberty, & in recompence therof, of his owne accord, offereth himselfe Tributary to the King of Portugall. This was added to the victory, which was gotten by *Francis* sollicitatiō. This done, *Saa* the Generall of the Portughese fleet chose out from all the enemies nauy only 25. ships to carry along with him to *Malaca*, setting all the rest on fire as being eyther battered or otherwise not fit for seruice, & so returneth ioyfully loaden no lesse with pillage, then with glory.

The King of Perlen of his owne accord maketh himselfe tributary to the King of Portugall.

CHAP. XI.

Xauerius foretelleth to the Malacensians the obtayning of the forsayd victory, vvhereof he had byn the sollicitour.

Hirst these things were doing which was the space of six weekes, *Francis* shewed inuincible constancy in praying to God for the victory. He did not only by himselfe in
pri-

Francis his prayers for the victory.

priuate craue the fauourable assistance of the diuine
Gooodnes , but did publikely also incite the people to
do the same. For twice euery weeke, to wit , vpon
Sunday, and Friday , he preached to the people at *Malaca :* and his ordinary custome was at the end of his
Sermon, to intreate his audience to say with him one
Pater and *Aue* for the good successe of the Portughese
fleete agaynst the Barbarians . The people at first did
willingly as he requested them, for the space of 15. or
20. dayes , as long as there was hope of the victory.
But when , all that tyme , there came no newes of the
fleete, many of the Cittizens suspecting that their men
were ouerthrowne , gaue ouer , and left of that pious
practice.

**The Ma-
lacensians
griefe v-
pon the
false
newes of
the Por-
tugheses.
ouer-
throw.**

　　This sollicitude of the *Malacensians* was increased
by a rumour which the *Saracens* their neighbours ,
had diuulged abroad, without any ground , that the
Portugheses were ouerthrowne in battayle, and put
all to the sword by the *Acenians.* That which was
knowne to be true , made this false rumour to seeme
credible. For it was certayne that the enemyes were
stout warlike men, and their forces farre beyond the
Portugheses. The whole Citty therfore began to be
very heauy and afflicted : The matrones with aboundance of teares, bewayled the death of their husbands
their children , and kinsfolkes , & withall their owne
desolate and forelorne state . The Gouernour himselfe
of the Citty , because he was esteemed to be Authour
of this misfortune, durst not come abroad, or appeare
in sight of the people.

　　In this meane time *Francis,* according to his custome
prea-

preaching to the people, indeauored to take frō them
that vayne feare & griefe. Sometymes he inueighed
againſt certaine men who had gone about by witch-
craft, and ſorcery to know what was become of the
Fleete, earneſtly reprehending their ſuperſtition. At
other times he ſharpely rebuked the Cittizēs for their
forgetfulnes of Gods prouidence, and the ouermuch
ſolicitude for themſelues: Then againe, he rayſed thē
vp to hope. Finally he moſt earneſtly intreated them
all, to continue their prayers vnto God for the obtei-
ning of the victory, although he knew full well, that
thereby he incurred the ill will of many, who muttered, that the prayers which he required of them,
ought rather to be ſaid for the ſoules of thoſe that
were dead & ſlaine, then for the victory of the liuing.
But within a little after *Francis* his prophecy came to
be of credit.

    The day was now at hand, which was to be made
famous by that memorable victory. *Francis* therefore
vpon the very ſame day (which then hapned to be
Sunday) made a ſermon in the Church to the people,
and it was at the ſame houre when the Portugheſe
fleete was preparing for the fight. Being therefore
to conclude his Sermon, vpon the ſuddaine he turnes both himſelfe, & his ſpeach vnto the Crucifix, &
by diuine inſtinct, with great motion of body, breaking forth into a propheſy, he began by circūlocuti-
ons to deſcribe in words the firſt encounter of the
two Nauies, to the admiration and aſtoniſhment of
his auditours. Then with an inflamed looke & countenance, and aboundance of teares guſhing out at his

*He fore-
ſees and
foretol-
les the
victory
gotten
by the
Portu-
gheſe
fleet.*

eyes,

eyes, he cryed out aloud; *O Iesu, God of my hart, I humbly I beseech thee by the last torments of thy life, that thou wouldest not leaue them whome thou hast redeemed with thy pretious bloud.* Hauing vttered these, and other such like words which feare and confidence then suggested vnto him, and growing weake & faint with the violent agitation of his body, he leaned a while with his head vpon the Pulpit. Then by and by, as if he had awaked out of some extasy lifting vp his head he cryes out on a suddayne with a cheerfull & ioyfull countenance thus: O yee *Malacensians* cast off all sadnes & reioyce; for now at last our fleet hath ouerthrowne the enemy in battayle without any bloudshed on our part, hauing lost but three men only; so litle hath so noble a victory cost vs. And in a most triumphant maner will they presently returne home, loaden with spoyles and pillage of the enemy, together with many shippes which they haue taken from them; & forthwith (he appointed a certayne day) wil they be safe with vs. Come on therfore, and in thankesgiuing to God the Author of the victory, let vs say togeather once *Pater* and *Aue* for the same, and repeate it agayne for those few of ours that be slayne in the battayle.

A Prophesy.

Vpon this prediction of *Francis* the whole audience recited the prayers which he had requested, and in signe of approbation what he sayd became ioyfull, seeing the great cheerfulnesse of the worthy mans countenance who had thus rayfed them out of so heauy a sadnes. Hauing thus cheered vp the men with this hope, the same day in like maner he made a consolatory

latory fermō in another Church to the women a part
& fortould the very day, when certaine tydings fhould
be brought of the victory and fafety of their husbands
and friends. The euent wherof hapned in euery thing
as he had fpoken. For within two or three dayes after, there came a meffenger with the newes of the
victory. And prefently after the meffenger, followed
the Conquerours themfelues with an exceeding great
booty, and no fmall number of fhippes which they
had taken from the Enemy. Infinite therefore, was
the ioy which on a fuddaine furprized the *Malacenfiās*
when fo farre beyond all expectation they faw eight
fhippes to bring home 25. captiue.

The Ma-
lacenfiās
ioy for
the vi-
ctory.

As foone therfore as this victorious Nauy was arriued, the whole Citty (their late great feare being
now turned into exceffiue ioy) went out to fee, and
cōgratulate the fame. And *Francis* himfelfe to whome
a great part of that noble victory and triumph was
due, goeth amongft the firft; and as foone as the Generall was landed he imbraceth him, and the other
principall Captaines of the Nauy congratulating the
for their fortunate fucceffe. Then, in the heat of this
generall ioy and congratulation, when they inquired
more exactly after the time of the victory, they found
that not only the very day, but the battayle alfo did
iumpe aright with that which *Francis* had foretould.
Which was fo much the more to be admired, becaufe
the place where the battaile was fought, was diftant
from *Malaca* aboue 200. miles. From that time, *Francis*
was highly efteemed throughout all *Malaca*, no leffe
for the guift of prophecy, then for fanctity of life. The

8. Portu-
ghes
fhippes
driue a-
lōg with
them 25.
Barbari-
ans fhips
taken
captiue.

fame

fame whereof hauing fpread it felfe throughout thē
Eaſt, moued fome to come from the furtheſt parts of
the world, to fee him.

CHAP. XII.

A Iaponian *is by conference vvith* Xauerius, *conuerted to the faith of* Chriſt.

FTER he had fpent foure monethes or
thereabout in helping the Citty of *Malaca,*
hauing now gotten commodity of ſhipping, & being ready to returne into *India,*
there came from *Iaponia* vnto *Malaca*, a certaynē
Iaponian called *Anger*, a man of good account iñ
his owne Country, and of a ſingular wit. The cauſe
of his comming was, to feeke a remedy for cure of thē
wounds of his foule, cauſed by the intemperate heat
of his youthfull bloud. For hauing committed a heynous murder in *Iaponia,* & being narrowly fought for
to puniſhment, was forced, partly by the remorſe of
conſcience, and partly by his enemies who purſuēd
his life, to fly for ſanctuary vnto a Conuēt of thē *Bon-*
zies (who amongſt the *Iaponians* are accounted a kind
of Religious men) to feeke therby as well the quiet
of his conſcience, as a refuge for his fafety. But this
his hope fayled him in both ; which was finally thē
cauſe of his faluation. For when he found no comfort
nor yet fafety amongſt the *Bonzies,* he began to be a-
uerted from them, & to feeke for remedy elfewhere.

Bonzies
Prieſtsof
the Ia-
ponians.

It

It happened fitly, that certaine Portughese merchants had arriued in *Iaponia* for traffique ; amongſt whome *Alphonſus Vaſius* who was before acquainted with him, vnderſtanding the matter, for old acquaintance ſake offered him freely all the help he could affoard him, if he would put himſelfe out of danger, by eſcaping away priuately. He againe with harty thankes tould him, that he would make vſe of his liberality : whereupon *Vaſius* forecaſting with himſelf, that his owne ſhip was for the diſpatch of his buſines to make there ſome longer ſtay, commendeth him very effeđually by his letters to *Ferdinand Aluarez* a ſpeciall friend of his, being then ready to depart, out of another hauen, for *India.* And theſe letters of commendations he giueth to *Anger* himſelfe, who going to deliuer them in the night, miſtooke the merchant by reaſon there were two of the ſame Surname, and giueth them to one *George Aluarez* a maiſter of another ſhippe : which miſtake notwithſtanding proued well for him. For *George Aluarez* thinking that this occaſion of gayning a *Iaponians* friendſhip, was not to be neglected, diſſembled the miſtake, & in very courteous manner entertayned him, and carryed him along with him to *Malaca,* intending to preſent him to *Xauerius* his great friend there.

This *Aluarez* being a pious man, out of deſire he had to winne *Angers* affection, and alſo the better to diſpoſe him for the Chriſtian fayth, recounted to him oftentymes by the way many things of *Xauerius* eminent ſanctity, and worthy deeds, & of the inſtitutes of the Chriſtians. *Anger* therfore deſiring, much to

be

be acquainted both with *Xauerius*, and his manner of lyfe which he heard so highly commended, came to *Malaca* greatly longing to see, and heare him, whome by *Aluarez* report he admired as a diuine man : yet a certaine delay which happened much troubled him at first, as commonly it falleth out, but afterward inflamed his desire the more. *Anger* arriued at *Malaca* some monthes before *Francis* his returne from *Moluca*, and vnderstanding that he was absent, being disappointed of what he came for, resolued to retourne backe againe into *Iaponia*, being much grieued that he had taken so long a iorney in vaine. For *Moluca* is distant frō *Iaponia* about 800. leagues, lying in the mid-way, almost betweene *India*, and *Iaponia*.

Anger desireth to speake with *Xauerius*.

The distance of *Malaca* from *Iaponia*.

Taking therfore shipping at *Malaca*, after almost three months sayle, he was cast vpon the confines of *China*, some 500. leagues from *Malaca*. There he stayed a while intending to passe thence into *Iaponia*, distant from that place a most 800. miles. Departing therfore from *China* within six or seauen dayes he was come within sight of *Iaponia*, when vpon a suddain, a contrary wind, togeather with a cruell tempest hindred his going forward, & tossing him vp & downe for the space of foure dayes, draue him againe into the same heauen in *China*, where he had taken shipping. Whilst he remaineth there vncertaine & doubfull what to do, not without the infallible prouidēce of God, he meeteth with *Alphonsus Vasius*, the same man, who had bin the cause of his departure out of *Iaponia*. And by his persuasion, in the yeare 1548. he retourneth againe to *Malaca*, whither *Xauerius* was now

Gods Prouidence.

now come : At his very firſt landing he fortunately
lighteth vpon *George Aluarez* that brought him firſt
out of *Iaponia*, who being exceeding glad for his returne, bringeth him preſently to *Xauerius*, and told
him what he was, & what his buſines required. Then
Francis as it were preſaging, that he would be a meanes to opē a way into *Iaponia*, imbraced him louingly,
& ſhewed manifeſtly both by his words & contenãce,
the great comfort he tooke for his comming thither.

Xauerius
glad for
Angers
com-
ming.

Anger being not ignorant of the Portugheſe language, began to conferre with *Xauerius* about his buſines without an Interpreter ; whome he inſtructed
with ſuch diligence in the myſteries and precepts of
the Chriſtian faith, that he freed him from all ſcrupu-
lous anxiety of mind, and planted in his ſoule the ſeed
of a vertuous and happy life : whereof *Anger* gaue alwayes good teſtimony, that by *Xauerius* meanes he
had reaped moſt aboundant fruit both of his life, and
trauaile. And withall he affirmed, that the whole
courſe of his iorney, was certainly diſpoſed of by God
that he might at laſt imbrace that with greater deſire
which he had ſo long ſought to learne ; which mani-
feſted it ſelfe within a ſhort ſpace. For being continually preſent at the explication of the Catechiſme,
and noting downe in a little booke the articles of the
Creed, he ſo much profited in ſhort time, that he recited the whole by hart, in the midſt of the people, although he were a man of grown yeares : & moreouer
aſked many queſtions, and made many obiections,
with no leſſe prudence, then ſharpeneſſe of wit.

The *Iaponians* in their manner of writing differ
much

much from other natiõs : for beginning their lines a-
boue in the paper, they write directly downeward.

Which *Francis* perceyuing in *Angers* booke, & wondring at the strangeneſſe thereof, demaunded of
him, why they did not write according to our manner of *Europe*? Nay, quoth he, why doe not you rather
write as we do, who follow the dictamen of nature
which teacheth vs ſo to do. For as in a man the head
is higheſt, and the feete loweſt, ſo he ſhould alſo in
writing, bring his lines from aboue directly downeward. *Xauerius* therefore obſeruing both by *Angers*

words and actions, that he was of a notable wit, asked him agayne, whether the *Iaponians* would receyueth Ghoſpell, if it were brought vnto them? They
will not, quoth he, belieue preſently whatſoeuer is
tould them, but will examen both the religion it ſelfe
and the life of thoſe that preach it. And if by their
doctrine they can ſatisfy their demands, and do confirme alſo what they ſay by their owne liues, then no
doubt (being a Nation which is lead moſt by reaſon) when they ſee and approue the ſame, they that be
of yeares of diſcretion, will eaſily become Chriſtians.

Xauerius being greatly incouraged by theſe words
of his, & ſtirred vp alſo by the relation of ſome merchants who recounted wonderfull things of the good
diſpoſition of that nation, made a reſolution to preach the Goſpell vnto them. Vpon the eight day after
Anger came to *Malaca*, *Francis* (being himſelfe to viſit the neophytes of *Comorinum* by the way) ſent him
before to *Goa* with the forſaid *George Aluarez*, to remaine in the Colledge there, & to be better inſtructed

in

in the myſteryes and precepts of the Chriſtian faith.
Before *Xauerius* departed he was intreated by the Citty of *Malaca* to ſend thither two of the Society, who
might performe the ſame charitable offices in his abſence; which he could not deny them. And in the meane tyme he gaue order to a certaine vertuous Prieſt
of that Country, that he ſhould ſupply his place, by
inſtructing the Neophytes in the forenoone.

CHAP. XIII.

*Hauing eſcaped a tempeſt at ſea, he preſ-
cribeth precepts to thoſe of the Society of
Commorium.*

BEING to depart thence for *Commorinum*,
he intreated the Maiſter of the ſhip that
went to *Goa*, to tranſport into *India* certain
children (which he had brought from *Mo-
luca*) to be brought vp, and inſtructed in the Colledge
there. And as he was deliuering them into his charge,
vpon a ſuddain, by diuine inſpiration, he tould them
thrice, he was afraid leaſt that ſhippe ſhould meete
with ſome miſchance by the way. Neither were his
words herein fruſtrate. For as the ſhip was paſſing a-
long by the Iland of *Ceilanum*, ſhe fall vpon the quickſands, & ſtuck ſo faſt as that there was now no hope
to eſcape, when as the paſſengers all togeather calling vpon the B. Virgin Mary for ayde, ſhe is by the di-

A preſa-
ge.

K k   uine

uine goodnes on a fuddaine deliuered out of danger, and arriueth fafe at *Cocinum.*

The fhip likewife wherein *Xauerius* fayled, had as hard a iorney, but better fortune. For three dayes fhe was toffed with a moft terrible tépeft, in fuch fort that the marriners hauing throwne all the goods and merchandize ouer board, expected euery moment to be caft away themfelues. But *Francis* being not once moued at that which maketh others afraid, continued quietly to implore the help of all the celeftiall citizens one after another, and moft earneftly to call vpon the King and Queene of heauen. And being fecured by fuch potent interceffours, he found (as himfelfe declared) far more ioy in that tépeft, then he did afterward when he had efcaped the danger. For when all were in that extreme feare, & danger of their liues, he receiued fuch abundance of diuine confolation, that when others wept for forrow, he ouerflowed with teares of ioy : and moft earneftly befought God, that, although he fhould free him from that tempeft, yet if it were his diuine will, he was ready moft willingly to endure the like or greater, fo that he might therby adde any increafe to his glory. You would haue thought there had bin a combat between *Xauerius* patience, and the diuine liberality, he defiring moft bitter fufferances for Gods fake, and God agayne regaling him with moft aboundant comforts.

He was no fooner arriued in *India*, but prefently he began carefully to go about, to all the villages of the Chriftians in *Comorinum*, who being as it were the firft fruits of his labours, were moft deere vnto him.

He

His courage in daungerous tépefts.

Comforts in dangers.

He found there some of the Society , more then at his departure he had left . Wherfore making haſt to *Goa*, he committed all things to their prudence and truſt ; yet for the experience which he had of that nation, he left vnto them diuers inſtructions & documents: wherof theſe were the chiefe . 1 . That they ſhould go frō dore to dore &enquire for infants newly borne to baptize them , leaſt in ſo tender an age eyther through neglect of their Parents or want of Prieſts they might be in danger to looſe their ſaluatiō. 2. That they ſhould gather little children togeather , and inſtruct them withall diligence in the myſteries & precepts of the Chriſtian faith ; becauſe to inſtruct them in their youth & tender yeares, was a matter of very great importance for the leading of a good and vertuous life afterward. 3. That they ſhould vpon Sundayes and Holydayes cauſe all the people to come togeather to the Church , to pray and heare the word of God , wherof they ſhould warne the magiſtrates beforehand that they might therin giue others exāple of piety and deuotion . And reprehending of publike vices, they ſhould therby terrify their auditours from the like, laying before thē the paynes & tormēts both of this , & the next life . 4 . They ſhould furthermore inquire who were at ſtrife & debate amongſt themſelues, & ſhould call them togeather into the Church & there make them friends , the men vpon Sundaies , and the women on Saturdayes . And if therein any caſe of greater difficulty did occurre, they ſhould referre it to the Captayne of the Portugheſes. 5. That the almes which ſhould be giuen for the reliefe of the

Documents giuen to thoſe of the Society in Comorinum.

Kk 2   poore,

poore, fhould be fo diftributed amorgft the needy, as
that nothing thereof fhould remayne lying by them.
6. They fhould often vifit the ficke, and fay the Gofpell ouer them for help and comfort of their foules, as
the cuftome is. 7. That they fhould affift thofe that lay
a dying, and bury the dead. 8 That they fhould giue
charge vnto the men & women a part, that euery one
giue vp the number of their ficke vnto them; declaring alfo that they whofe names were not giuen vp, if
they happened to dye fhould be excluded from Chriftian buriall. 9. That they fhould haue no difcourfe
with the Portughefes, but of holy & pious matters, to
the end that vayne talke might not, as often tymes it
hapneth, take vp the place of their prieftly functions.
10. That they fhould vfe the Captayne of the Portughefes with all friendfhip and courtefy, & keep good
correfpondence and amity with him, whatfoeuer offence fhould happe. And the fame alfo they fhould do,
as much as might be poffible, with the other Portugefes, and fhould draw them by all meanes to frequent
the Sacraments of Confeffion, and the holy Eucharift. 11. That they fhould to their vtmoft, further the
Priefts of that country in matters of piety, and induce them to confeffe often, and dayly fay Maffe. 12.
That they fhould take great heed of reporting or writing any thing to any man, which might diminifh
the efteeme of the party, vnleffe it were to fuch an one
who might (if need required) be a meanes to remedy
the fame. 13. That he only fhould be acquainted with
the vices of the Priefts, who was able to cure them.
14. That they fhould neyther fpeake ill of the Neophites

The
good na-
me of
Priefts
is with
all care
to be
preferr-
ued.

tes to the Portugheses , nor of the Portugheses to the
Neophytes , but should commend them both to ech o-
ther , to the end that one might be desirous to imitate
the vertue of the other. 15. That they should neuer leaue
the place assigned them , although they were sent for
by any Prince or Noble man whatsoeuer, vnlesse they
had first licence granted them by the Father who was
Superiour of that Prouince ; and in such cases being
mindfull of holy Obedience should referre the matter
wholy vnto him. 16. Lastly , that they should endeauour by all meanes possible to gaine the affection of
all , because therein nothing is more forcible to win
mens minds euery way, then loue ; & therfore should
draw them as it were with the cords of *Adam* : and
should neuer punish any one, but with the aduise of
the Gouernour of the Country of *Commorinum.* These
were the documents of *Xauerius* : by which we may
see not only what he desired of his companions , but
what himselfe did also practice, seing that like a most
excellent Maister , he drew his patternes from his
owne actions .

All are to be praysed to on another .

Men are to be gouer-by loue

CHAP. XIIII.

Returning vnto Goa *, he establisheth matters in* India.

 AVING giuen these forsaid documents
vnto the Fathers in *Comerinū,* he ordaineth
F. Antony Criminalis of *Parma* Superiour of
the rest in that Coast , (who was afterwards

wards the firſt of the Society , that ſuffred Martyrdome in *India*) and about the end of February in the
yeare 1548. he ſayleth thēce to *Cocinum*; where hauing
gotten a litle leaſure, he writeth to *Portugall* and *Rome,*
deſiring to haue many more of theSociety ſent thither,
& among others inuiteth *Simon Rodriguez*, his ancient
collegue who had then the care of the Seminary at
*Conimbria,*to come & aſſiſt in the vineyard of the Eaſt.

  He aduiſed the King of Portugall alſo , to be
mindfull of his charge , and to prouide for the Garri-

Francis
his let-
ters to
the King
of Portu-
gall.

ſons of Portugheſes in *India* good preachers,out of a-
ny Religious Orders;and to giue ſtrict command vnto his Gouernours and Officers in *India* ,to help what
poſſibly they were able , towards the aduancement of
Chriſtian Religion ; & eſpecially to protect & cheriſh
the Neophites,ſince certainly there was no betterway
then that to augment the Chriſtian fayth . Moreouer
he humbly requeſted his Maieſty would be pleaſed to
take cōpaſſion of his own ſubiects, & in diuers places
to aſſigne habitation , and allowance for the bringing
vp of orphanes , both of the Portugheſes , and of that
country people. From *Cocinum, Xauerius* went by ſea
to *Cranganora,*which is a towne belonging to the Portugheſes , ſome 15. miles from *Cocinum* , and from
thence he came to *Goa,* in the beginning of March.

F. Nico-
las Lan-
celot Re-
ctour of
the Col-
ledge at
Goa.

  There were at that tyme many of the Society in the
Colledge of *Goa,*to wit,Father *Paul Camertes* who had
care of the Schollers ; Father *Francis Perez* their mayſter ; Father *Nicolas Lancelot* Rectour of the Colledge,
which cōſiſted partly of thoſe who came lately out of
Portugall , and partly of others that were receiued in
India

India: who, for the most part hauing neuer known *Xauerius*, but only by report, did much defire now to fee him. *Francis* therfore returning home from thefe farre Countryes, was as a common Father, receiued with incredible loue, & ioy of all the Society; he comming likewife in happy tyme for the comfort, & fpirituall good of *Cofmas Turrianus*, who (as we faid before) hauing in the Ifle of *Amboynum* beheld with admiration *Xauerius* rare fanctity, had defired to enter into the Society: and going thence to *Goa*, had now retyred himfelfe into the Colledge there, that by meanes of the fpirituall Exercyfe, he might learne of God what courfe of life was beft for him to vndertake. But whē at the end of thofe Exercyfes his mind was much perplexed with cares, and being vncertaine what to refolue vpon, fuddainly at the fight of *Francis,* as at the influence of fome fortunate Starre, his foule enioyed great repofe, and fo without further delay he entred into the Society.

Cofmas Turianus freed frō perplexity.

Now did the fruite of that Seminary begin to appeare. For befides the Priefts and Interpreters who had bin fent thence with no litle profit into the coaft of *Comorinum,* many fchollers who were well grown in learning & difcipline were fent abroad in miffions to the villages neere about, frō whence they brought many Ethnikes to *Goa* to be baptized. Wherat *Xauerius* much reioycing, efteemed it a thing of great importance, to be very exact, in the training vp of fchollers, from whome fo much fpirituall profit might arife. As he was thus bufied, he was giuē to vnderftād that *Iohn deCaftro* the viceroy of *India* was fomwhat auerfed frō

The fruite of the Seminary of Goa

the

He reco-
ciles the
Viceroy
to the So
ciety.

the Society through the fpeaches of fome maleuolent
perfons. Wherupon he refolued to go vnto him vpon
the firft occafion, and to giue him fatisfaction. But
there happened in the meane time an accident worthy
to be recounted, which manifefted his inflamed zeale
in meditation.

After-
noones
medita-
tion.

　　There was one *Andrew* an *Indian* borne, who was
a Scholler in the Colledge of *Goa*, and for that tyme
companion alfo vnto *Xauerius*, whofe cuftome ordinarily was to fpend fome tyme after dinner in meditating vpon heauenly things. He gaue therfore charge vnto *Andrew* to admonifh him as foone as the clocke had ftroken two, for that he was to go vnto the
Viceroy about a bufines of importance. *Andrew* did as
he was charged, and at the tyme appointed commeth to *Xauerius* chamber, where finding him fitting
with his contenance all inflamed, his eyes open, and
rapt in fuch fort, as he feemed to be abftracted from
his fenfes, called him oftentimes, but all in vayne;
and when he could not awake him eyther by calling,
or making a noyfe with his feete, or knocking at the

In medi-
tation of
diuine
matters
he is ab-
ftracted
from his
fenfes.

dore, he pulled him at laft by the clothes, wherewith
he awaked. In the meane tyme the clocke had ftroken foure. Wherefore *Xauerius* being admonifhed
went prefently to the Viceroies lodging: but the fame
feeling and feruour of fpirit made him that he could
not tell whither he went; fo as wandring vp and
downe the Citty, he fpent the reft of the day in meditation. And when the night came on, being admonifhed therof by his companion, he returned to himfelfe
agayne, and perceyuing to haue loft his way, turning
to

to his companion he fayd : Will, we well deale with
the Viceroy another day, for this day God hath taken
vp for himfelfe. The next day therfore, he went vnto
the Viceroy, & gaue him fatisfaction.

CHAP. XV.

*He reclaymeth two Portugheſes from a
lewd, vnto an honeſt life.*

FTER this, finding that an old friend of
his, was vnmeaſurably carryed away with
diſhoneſt loue towards his owne maides,
he went to him of ſet purpoſe about noone
and comming iuſt as he was going to dinner, inuites
himſelf to be his gueſt, & to dine with him. He ſtraight
perceyued *Xauerius* would proue vngratefull to his
taſt ; but hauing not the face to refuſe him, courteouſly bad him welcome, colouring his troubled
mind, with a feigned obſeruance towards him, and by
ſhewing outwardly a cheerfull contenāce. Dinner being ready they ſate downe togeather, and the faire
maydes his concubines wayted at the table. The man
was much aſhamed, becauſe none of his other ſeruāts
were at home, and ſuch a number of maydes might
bring him into ſuſpicion of incontiency. Now therfore when *Xauerius*, diſſembling as though he had obſerued no ſuch thing, ſpake nothing thereof at the table, his Hoſt, being taken in ſo open a fact, was afrayd
that after dinner he would haue reprehēded him. But

L l

To diffemble anothers finnes in tyme cōuenient doth more good then to reprehēd them.

Xauerius thanking him for his courtefy, and bidding farewell both to him and the maydes, went his way.

This diffembling the matter was of more force, towards the curing of his friends difeafe then his reprehenfion would haue byn. His Hoft being freed of this feare, and hauing paffed ouer fo great and manifeft a difgrace, & difhonour, without any reprehenfion; began afterwards more confidently to go vnto *Fra.cis*, and to inuite him freely to his houfe, yea oftentymes to bring byn home to be his gueft. *Xauerius* on the other fide vfing him very courteoufly, and allwayes faluting him kindly, asked oftentymes how thofe fifters of his did, without any further fpeach at all, thinking it inough to haue thus left a fting in his confcience by this his interrogation. Neyther was it in vayne. For within a few dayes after, his Hoft cometh to *S.Pauls* Church, & calling for *Xauerius* cafteth himfelfe proftrate at his feete: Father, quoth he, I am here ready to do what you command, for indeed that filence of yours hath ftroke my foule with fuch clamours, that being toffed vp and downe day and night it can take no reft. Wherefore I fhall be moft glad, if you will difpofe of all that is mine, to Gods glory, & the faluation of my foule. *Francis* feeing him thus ftroken by God, perfuadeth him to make firft a good confeffion of his finnes, then to put away his Concubins by beftowing them in honeft marriage, and laftly to betake himfelf to a good and vertuous life.

Xauerius filence cryeth out.

Neyther did *Xauerius* affift thefe only who were his friends and acquaintance, but ftrangers alfo whofe faluatiō feemed to be euen defperate. There was a certaine

taine Portughefe Sea-fouldiar, who defpayring of his faluation, had not bin at Confeffion for the fpace of 18. yeare, and was now ready to imbarke himfelfe for the fea to go with the Nauy to *Meca*, when as *Frācis* by chance had notice of him. Wherfore thirfting after his faluation, he prefently getteth into the fame fhip, and accompanyeth him in that nauigation. Then by fpeaking friendly vnto him, by fitting by him when he was at play, & by vfing all courtefy towards him, he fo wonne his affection, that of himfelfe he greatly reuerenced him, & much defired his company. Wherupon *Francis* thinking it now a very good time to put that in execution which he had refolued, fetteth vpon him vnawares. And falling with him into familiar fpeach of the danger of a Soldiars life, began to aske him in a friendly manner, how he was prouided for death, which this mortality could not efcape, & was haftned on alfo by a fouldiars life & conditiō; how long it was fince he was laft at Confeffion by which Gods wrath agaynft finne, the reuenger of Iniquity, is appeafed. At which words he fetching a deepe figh fayd, That he had now continued many yeares in the filth of finne without going to Confeffion; but it was rather another mans fault then his. For before the fetting forth of the laft fleete, he refolued to disburthen his confcience of the many and henyous finnes which he had committed; and hauing confeffed them to the Vicar, he refufed to giue him abfolution, fo as he had now no hope of faluation.

Then *Francis*, a fingular Phyfitian for the curing of forlorne foules, telleth him, that he wondred the

His zeale of foules

He by all courteous offices winneth a foldiar of very bad life to make his confeffion.

Vicar was fo feuere, if he had confeffed his finnes as
he ought to do. Then he biddeth him be of good comfort, promifing that he would willingly heare him, &
abfolue him, aduifing him to call to mynd all his fins
from his childhood, as farre forth as he could remember them, prefcribing him alfo an eafy and commodious method how to do it; which he, being now rayfed vp againe to hope, did willingly, and diligently
practice for many dayes togeather. And when he was
thus prepared, the opportunity alfo of a place was ready at hand; which was, that by the way the whole

He gi-
ueth his
penitent
a fmall
pennáce
intédiug
himfelfe
to fatis-
fy for
him.

fleet was inuited to make fome ftay at a towne as they
paffed. When therefore many went a land, *Francis*
alfo with his fouldiar went with them. And there in a
place remote from any company, he beganne to heare his Confeffion, who fhewed himfelf truly penitét
by his often fighes & teares, which many times interrupted his Confeffion. When he had ended, *Fran-*
cis abfolueth him, inioining him to fay for his pennáce
once *Pater* and *Aue*, and for the reft himfelfe promifed
to fatisfy his diuine Maiefty. Wherupon *Xauerius* leauing the fouldiar, withdrew into the next wood, and
there ftripping himfelfe naked, beate and fcourged his
backe extremely, with a whippe full of moft fharpe
prickes, and whereof he made no end, or meafure.

In the meane time the Soldiar hauing faid his pennance, and following the Fathers footefteppes, came
into the wood, and by the found of the lafhes, came
right vnto the place where *Francis* was a difciplining
himfelfe. As foone as he faw that horrible whip, & his
backe all torne, and begored with bloud, at the firft he
ftood

ſtood ſtill in amazement. Then with teares guſhing forth of his eyes, he leapeth vnto him, and caſteth himſelfe at *Xauerius* feete, nor would he riſe vntill he left off tormenting himſelfe for anothers ſinnes. Neither did this inuentiō of *Xauerius* proue vnprofitable. For this ſtrange ſight did ſo moue the ſoldiars hart, already mollified by Confeſſion, to the deſire of pennance, that he afterwards by voluntary mortification waſhed away the ſpottes of his former life, and ſatisfied for his offences by good workes. And *Xauerius* hauing thus compaſſed his deſire, and finding preſēt commodity of ſhipping, returneth backe againe to *Goa.*

CHAP. XVI.

Hauing diſtributed diuers Prouinces to others of the Society, himſelf determineth to go into Iaponia.

AVING ſetled all buſineſſes of the Colledge at *Goa,* & that there was at the ſame time a new ſupply of the Society come out of Portugall, he began to deuide & diſtribute them into diuers Miſſions. Wherfore he ſent *Nicolas Lancellot* to the towne of *Coulanum, Alphonſus Cyprian* to *Meliapora* the towne of *S. Thomas, Francis Perez* to *Malaca, Alphonſus à Caſtro* to *Moluca, Melchior Conſalues* to *Bazainum,* and laſtly *Gaſpar of Artois* to *Ormus* a Citty of ſpeciall trade and fame, ſcituated in

He prepareth in many places, houſes for the Society.

the

the mouth of the *Perſian* gulfe. *Xauerius* had indeed reſolued to haue gone himſelf to *Ormus*, to ſuppreſſe the
heynous vices which he vnderſtood the ſincke of Superſtition had nouriſhed in that place. But his iorney
into *Iaponia* changed this his determinatiõ, by ſending
thither the forſaid *Gaſpar*, a man of ſingular vertue &
ſanctity of life, and moſt like to himſelfe.

He ſent almoſt none of the Society where he him-ſelfe had not bin.

It was alwayes *Xauerius* practiſe, neuer (almoſt)
to command any of the Society to go where himſelfe
had not bin before. For he ordinarily firſt made tryall
of the place, to the end he might giue both documents
ſuitable thereunto, and alſo faithfully diſcharge his
promiſe made to the King of Portugall, of extending
the bounds of the Chriſtian faith. And whitherſoeuer
he ſent any of the Fathers to preach the Ghoſpell, he
alwayes aſſigned them a companion, and aſſiſtant of
the Society, giuing them (beſides particular inſtructions) certain generall documents, the ſumme whereof was : That before all things, they ſhould attend
vnto themſelues, & preferre nothing before the pure
and religious honour of God, and the ſaluation and

Inſtru-ctions giuen to the Soci-ety.

perfection of their owne ſoules. For being endued
with theſe ornaments, they would not only ſecurely
& eaſily help others in matters of ſaluatiõ, but would
alſo cheerfully and willingly apply themſelues to any
thing how hũble or abiect ſoeuer, without the which
the gouernment of Chriſtian affayres could not well
ſtand.

Now when he had ſent ſome of the Society into
almoſt all the countryes of the Eaſt, to manure and
cultiuate the tender plants of our Lords vineyard, he
began

began to thinke vpon greater matters . About this time *Anger* the *Iaponian* (who as we fayd before, had bin by *Xauerius* fent to *Goa*) being fufficiently inftructed in the myfteries of the Chriftian faith, was baptized by the Bifhop, togeather with two of his feruantes, & would needs be called (by the Name of the Colledge of *Goa*) *Paul of the Holy Faith*; of fuch force was the memory of that place, and the benefit which he had receiued therein. By him *Xauerius* vnderftood (which had bin alfo related vnto him by the Portughefes, who had byn there) that there were in *Iaponia* many Ilands, exceeding full of inhabitants of excellent good wits, & lay from *Goa* about 1300. leagues : and moreouer that the *Iaponefes* were addicted to the knowledge of diuine, and humane things. *Xauerius* therfore hauing had fome tryall of the *Iaponians* difpofitions in this man, and his feruants, began to be taken with fuch a defire of inftructing fo vnderftanding a People, that he determined, without delay to make a voyage thither.

Firft therfore he taketh order for the fufficient inftructing of thofe three *Iaponians* who were with him, both in the Portughefe language, and other literature, that they might ferue him for Interpreters. Then hauing fpent a fummer and winter in domefticall affaires at *Goa*, like a good and diligent Paftour by the way vifiteth the *Comorinenfian* and *Pifcarian* Coaft with all his flocke of Chriftians in thofe parts . There he is informed, that *Henry*, one of the Society, liued half difcontented in the next country of *Trauancoris*, for that he feemed to loofe his labour amongft the Neo phytes

Anger the *Iapo-nefe* is baptized

He by the way vifiteth the Comorinen fian Neophytes.

phytes of that place, who by reason of the persecution raysed by their new King, a deadly Enemy to Christians, fell oftentimes into Idolatry. *Xauerius* therfore by consolatory letters, full of fatherly affection, bad him be of good courage, telling him withall, that his profit was far greater, then he imagined. For although he should do nothing else, yet certainly there was no small number of infants, and children saued for being by him baptized, who otherwaies by vntimly death had byn euerlastingly lost. For put the case (quoth he) that there were but few of the elder sort saued, yet there is no doubt to be made of their saluation, who dyed in that innocency which they receiued in baptisme. And therefore he should beware least through the suggestion of the Deuil he might be drawne to go into some other Country, where he should not reape so good an haruest of soules. But now for those who laboured seriously in the vineyard of our *Lord, Francis* did not only comfort them himselfe, but somtimes also procured *Ignatius* to do the like, by his letters from *Rome*, fearing least their alacrity being oppressed by continual troubles and miseries, might be ouercharged by the labours which they tooke. And so, hauing in a certaine letter of his much praised *Henry Henriquez* a man of singular vertue, and exemplar life, who tooke great paines in the same Promontory, he commended him to *Ignatius*, desyring he would be pleased to write vnto him a letter consolatory.

Hauing thus setled matters in *Comorinum*, he returneth againe to *Goa*, to prouide for his *Iaponian* voyage. Wherupon presently he went into the kingdome of of *Cambaya*, to treat about certayne affayres for the *Moluca's*, with the Viceroy, who at that tyme was imployed in the war of *Cambaya*. By the way he came to *Bazain*, which is a towne belonging to the Portughefes, fcituated almoft in the midway betweene *Goa* and the riuer *Indus*. And going thence without any ftay into *Cambaia* he was very courteoufly entertained by the Viceroy, with whome hauing ended his bufineffe, he returned prefently agayne to *Goa*; where hauing made *Antony Gomez* Rectour of the Colledge, and appointed *Paul Camertes* to fupply his owne place, he prepareth himfelfe with all fpeed for his iourney into *Iaponia*.

It was no fooner bruited abroad, that *Francis* was to go into *Iaponia*, but prefently many of his friends came vnto him in all haft, to terrify him from fo dangerous a refolutiō, laying before his eyes the many and great dangers of fo long and vnknowne a voiage by fea, for that he was to go vnto the furtheft end of the world, *Iaponia* lying from *Goa* aboue 1300. leagues, and the way vnto it being but newly found out, was not as yet fufficiently knowne, for the auoiding of rockes and quickfands. Moreouer they declare vnto him the horrible ftormes and tempefts of that fea, in refpect whereof, the fury and rage of the reft of the Ocean, was but a fport, efpecially in the tyme of Autumne, when as thofe feas are toffed with a moft boifterous wind (called by the Inhabitants *Typhon*) and with fuch a fury and violence, as none can imagine but thofe who haue feen and proued it; by which alfo the greateft, and ftrongeft fhips being often loo-

The difficulties of the Iaponian nauigation.

The wind Typhon

Mm   fened

fened in their ioyntes, being not able to endure such
violent waues, become so broken and shattered, that
eyther swallowed vp in the billowes, or els dashed
agaynst, the rockes do miserably perish. And the very
name of the forsayd Wind, or rather Fury, striketh
such an horrour into the passengers, that euē the most
skillfull, and hardyest Pilots, and Marriners esteeme
this voyage into *Iaponia* to be no lesse dangerous then
toylsome, so farre doth the violent raging of that sea
passe all their art, and skill.

Moreouer, they tell him, that there be in diuers places many quicksands in the way, very hard to be difcouered, wherein their shippes, eyther by not being
acquainted with the tract, or else by drift of tempest
do sticke fast to their certayne destruction. Againe, all
those seas for the most part are much pestered with
most cruell pyrates. For besides the *Acenians,* who
being deadly enemies to the Portugheses, make continuall depredations in the gulfe of *Malaca* with great
fleetes ; there keepe also, about the Coast of *China,*
many nauies of most bloudy and desperate pyrates,
vsing no mercy to whomesoeuer they take. They
should also in those places meete with other nauies
of the King of *China,* which being appointed to pursue the pyrates, kept no more quarter with stragers
then with the pyrats themselues : in so much that one
cannot tell whether it be more dágerous to meet with
the pyrates themselues, or with those that pursue thē :
so that it was certaynely esteemed no bad fortune, if
but euery third shippe came safe into *Iaponia.*

Thefe, and such lyke things, though they were
indeed

(margin) A multi-tude of Pyrats.

indeed matters of no light moment, yet were they by
his friends greatly ex agerated, who for that they proceeded from very graue perfons , and skillfull of fuch
affaires, hoped they might auert *Xauerius* mynd from
that enterprize. But all in vaine: nor could they once
moue his noble courage , which contemned euen death , and vpheld it felfe with firme confidence in the
diuine prouidence. Whereupon they flying to their
laft refuge, began with teares moft earneftly to intreat
and befeech him, that he would not with certayne dāger of his life, thinke of going to thofe coūtries, which
Nature had fo locked vp from the fight of mortall mē:
and that hauing already fuffered miferyes inough , he
would now at length make an end of conuerting obfcure Nations , and haue compaffion , if not of his
owne, yet, of the common good.

But *Francis* thanking them for their fidelity , and
good will, tould them, that by Gods holy help & affiftance he feared none of thefe things; and wondred
they fhould thinke, that whither themfelues had gone
for gayne of trade and merchandize, he durft not vē-
ture to go for the glory of God , and faluation of foules . I haue affuredly (quoth he) fuch certayne fignes
and pledges of the diuine prouidence, that I thinke it
would be a great finne in me to feare any daunger ,
though neuer fo certayne and manifeft. For , by Gods
fpeciall goodnes , I haue paffed infinite tractes of the
Ocean , and haue compaffed round the Pɪomontory
of *Good hope*, and haue at laft arriued fafe hither to this
other world. I haue efcaped the fury of the *Trauan-*
corians , the treacheryes of the *Badages*, and the enco-

*Francis
fpeech to
his frieds
who dif-
fuaded
him frō
going in
to Iapo-
nia.*

«
«
«
«
«
«
«

» unter of Pyrates. Moreouer I haue trauayled ouer all
» *Malaca*, & the golden *Cherſoneſus*, the Ilands of *Moluca*,
» ſtanding almoſt in the vtmoſt partes of the world.
» Without any harme haue I gone to *Maurica*, and in-
» ſtructed and made ciuill that barbarous & ſauage na-
» tion, giuen wholy to ſpoyle, robberies, and murders.
» And hauing now had all theſe aſſurances and argu-
» ments of the diuine prouidence, do you thinke that I
» can eyther diſtruſt of Gods fatherly aſſiſtance, or giue
» ouer to amplify his glory, to which I haue wholy de-
» dicated & vowed my ſelf? Ought I to draw back for
» feare of any danger whatſoeuer? I will certaynely
» for no occaſion be wanting in what I haue vnderta-
» ken. Wherſoeuer I ſhall be, I will remember that I am
» expoſed to the view of the whole world, and do ſtäd
» in the ſight of God, and all the Court of heauen. Nei-
» ther was it my determination, when I paſſed ouer the
» ſea, to preach the Ghoſpell only in *India*, and other
» places adioyning, but alſo in the furtheſt parts of the
» Eaſt. I will tell you truly, I am aſhamed that I haue
» not yet brought Chriſtian Religion into thoſe coun-
» tryes, whither our merchants haue long ſince brought
» their vayñe, and petty commodityes. I will therefore
» with Gods grace, lay open at laſt a way into thoſe co-
» untries for the Ghoſpell, which Nature hath ſo farre
» ſeparated from our world: & to ſpend my life (if need
» require) in theſe imploiments, I account it not only an
» honour, but alſo a great bleſſing.

His friends being ouercome by this his incredible
conſtancy, and ſtroken into an amazement at his vndaunted courage, deſiſted wholy from their ſuite, and
praying

praying for his happy iourney they left him to his intended voyage, not without great forrow for his departure, and carefull follicitude for his fafety, in regard of the many dangers he was to vndergo.

CHAP. XVII.

At Malaca *he doth many things vvorthy of memory.*

XAVERIVS at his departure from *Goa*, left behind him in writing certayne profitable precepts vnto Father *Paul* that had byn lately Rector of the Colledge of *Goa*, whome now in his abfence he ordayned to fupply his place. The fumme whereof was : That being myndfull rather of Chriftian humility, then of the place & authority he had, he fhould carry a fatherly gouernment towards the reft of his companions, and fhould very carefully prouide for them in all their difcomodities, & difficultyes, and once a yeare to write vnto him into *Iaponia* of al things belonging to the Society, & of thofe that were thereof vnder his care & gouernment. Now when all the other Fathers defired to follow him into *Iaponia*, he comforted them with paternall words, by putting them in hope, that hauing opened a way into that Country, he might call them all thither : and in the meane tyme he would carry them along with him in his hart, and mynd.

Hauing therefore fetled all things in order & prouided

Fatherly gouerment.

uided for his iourney, in the yeare of our Lord 1548. and month of Aprill he imbarketh at *Goa*, togeather with *Paul of the holy Fayth* the *Iaponese*, *Cosmas Turrianus*, *Iohn Ferdinand*, and a few others of the Society. He was carryed in a goodly ship, pointed and barbed with iron, the Captayne whereof was one *Iames Noronia*. By his courteous behauiour he began to gayne both the Captaynes and the other passengers affectiõs hoping thereby to make way for the cure of their soules. Wherefore he would looke on whilst others plaid at Chesse, perswade those to play who seemed shamefast, and would many tymes also intermingle their game with witty and pleasant speaches. But *Noronia* the Captayne, who was not yet familiary acquainted with him, although he liked well of his courteous behauiour, yet in words he impeached the fame of his sanctity. For in discourse with his familiar friends, he would often cast forth certayne inconsiderate speaches; as that *Francis* seemed to be but as other men are, and that his sanctity was not answerable to the report therof. But within a while the spledor of his hidden vertue brake forth, and shewed it selfe. For when they were inforced to go a land to take in fresh water, *Xauerius* with certayne others went a land also; and whilest they prouided water, or else, as it often happned, recreated themselues by taking comfort and solace of the land, he withdrew himselfe into a desert, and solitary place neere by, there to conferre alone in prayer with almighty God.

Now the ship hauing receyued in those that went for water, was ready to hoyse vp sayle, when as *Noronia*

nia perceiued that *Xauerius* was wanting : Wherfore he presently sendeth out some to call him speedily to the shippe. They looking & calling him a great while by the shore side but all in vayne, find him at length in a priuate place at his prayers, wholy abstracted from his senses . Then the report thereof being spread through out all the Nauy , it caused such admiration both in *Noronia* and the rest , that turning their rash iudgment into reuerence towards him , they greatly honoured his singular sanctity, and courteous humanity. This occasio much furthered towards the curing of their soules , and restrayning their vices .

In his prayers he is abstracted from his senses.

Francis then arriuing, by the way, at *Cocinum*, wēt presently as his custome was , to lodge with the *Franciscans*, who was very friendly entertayned by them : Whither the chiefe of the Citty presently came to intreate of him, that some of the Society might be sent thither, to instruct as well the youth , as the whole Citty in vertue, & other discipline ; promising him a fit place, and all things necessary for those that should be sent . *Xauerius* being loath to reiect so iust and pious a request , leaueth the disposing of the whole businesse vnto *Peter Confaluus* the Bishops Vicar , making hast himselfe towards *Iaponia* , whither all his thoughts were now wholy bent. Afterwards hauing had for the space of more then 60. dayes a prosperous nauigation , vpon the last of May he arriueth at *Malaca* , and lodgeth with his owne Society , to their incredible ioy and consolation. At the same tyme *Alphonsus à Castro* of the same Society (who was afterwards slayne in *Moluca* by the Saracens, for defence Christian

He lodgeth with the Franciscans

ftian

ſtian Religion) ſung there the firſt High Maſſe with all ſolemnity , to the exceeding comfort of the Neophytes , who were greatly delighted to behold thoſe new ceremonies . And for the greater Celebrity therof, *Xauerius* made thereat a Sermon.

The Vicar of *Malaca* being out of his ſenſes recouereth them againe.

At the ſame tyme alſo the Vicar of *Malaca, Xauerius* ancient friend , lay very ſicke of a Feuer , no leſſe dangerous then vehement ; and his trouble of mind increaſed his corporall infirmity. As ſoone therefore as he vnderſtood of *Francis* his arriuall , being much diſtempered (as it hapneth) through the violence of his ſickneſſe, he calleth for his apparell, to go & ſalute his deareſt friend. But as he was pulling on his ſtockings he fell into a ſowne, and ſuncke downe in the armes of thoſe that were about him . *Francis* therfore being certifyed therof, cōmeth preſently vnto him, & findeth him fallen into a frenzy, and in ſome deſpayre both of mynd and body. Wherupon he voweth to ſay certayne Maſſes for this his friends ſafety . And his vow was very acceptable vnto God : for inſtantly he recouereth his ſenſes agayne , confeſſeth his ſinnes, & dyeth piouſly, and with great edification.

He cuaſeth a merchāt to leaue his connes.

Now whileſt *Xauerius* expecteth commodity of ſhipping into *Iaponia* , he imployeth himſelfe with no leſſe labour & profit amōgſt the citizens of *Malaca,* thē he had done vpon the Vicar. For he deliuered out of the Diuels iawes many lewd and deſperate men, who were extremely bewitched with harlots allurements. Amōgſt whome (that by one, a ſcātling may be made of the reſt) there was a cetayne Merchant , who kept at home with him ſeauen maydes to the ſhew, but indeed

deed were all Harlots. Which thing *Xauerius* vnderstanding, firſt diſſembled the matter, expecting a conuenient time. Afterwards meeting this miſerable man
vpon an Holy day (imitating therein our Sauiour
Chriſt who bad himſelfe to ſupper with *Zacchæus* the
Publican) tould him in a friendly manner, that he
would dine with him that day, if it were not incon-
uenient . The merchant , for feare his maydes might
be diſcouered, was at firſt extremely troubled , and
thought on all the meanes he could deuiſe how to ex-
cuſe the matter . But at laſt, moued through ſhame
leaſt he might ſeeme vnwilling to receiue ſuch a gueſt
into his houſe , he ſhewed himſelfe to be content .
And ſo framing both his countenance and ſpeach to a
courteous willingnes, carryeth *Xauerius* home to dinner , and cauſeth good cheere to be made. They ſate
downe , and his fayre mayds wayted at the table. The
merchant was indeed halfe aſhamed , that he had no
men to wayt , & that the mayds were conſtrayned to
ſerue; remayning alſo with an anxious & ſollicitous
mind , what the good Father might thinke thereof.
Which when *Francis* perceiued iudging it prudence to
free the man both of ſhame and feare, ſaid nothing
of what he intended. Wherupon preſently, as though
he had interpreted al things in the beſt ſenſe, he began
to commend the meate, and the maydes alſo who had
dreſſed the ſame, and made the ſauces to it , asking
them their names, and country, & how long they had
byn Chriſtians .

    The Merchant when he ſaw in him this mildnes
and ſimplicity, who (as he thought) ſuſpected no-

Prudéce in diſſembling matters.

thing by feeing fo many handfome maydes without
any men, began to take fome courage ; but when at
laft there was not fo much as a word fpoken that day
about that matter, fearing now no reprehenfiõ, he of
his owne accord inuiteth oftentymes *Xauerius* to fupper. *Francis* therefore obferuing this cunning of his,
diffembled all vntill he came to be throughly acquain·
ted with the man, and hauing found out his inclinatiõ
& which of thofe Concubines he loued beft; when he
faw a fit tyme for the purpofe, in a friendly manner as
his cuftome was : Why, quoth he, haue you fo many
maydes, feeing you haue no men ? If you will follow
my connfayle, you fhall do well to put away one or
two of them. And when, condefcending to *Francis*
his gentle inftance, he had put away one. *Xauerius* being by him inuited another day to fupper, by commending what he had done, drew him, without any
great difficulty, to put away another. In the meane
tyme he ceafed not priuately to vfe all the induftrious
meanes he could deuife to rid away his deereft miniõ,
that fo hauing weakened his loue to her, he might the
more eafily batter the chiefe hould, in which his In-
continency domineered. Some dayes after therfore,
being agayne inuited to fupper, he withdraweth from
him the third, and afterwards the fourth, and by litle
& litle all the feauen one after another : and finally
bringeth the merchant himfelfe, being now moued
thereto by diuine power, to cleanfe his foule of his
finnes by Confeffion, and to prouide honeft places for
the forfayd women ; vfing heerein no lefle difcretion
in curing a difeafe of many kinds, then in wholy taking

king away the caufes, and occafions thereof.

The fame courfe he tooke alfo not only in the Citty, but likewife in the fhip with men, who had no gouernment ouer their tongue. For if at any tyme he heard any one caft forth bafe or contumelious words, he diffembled for the prefent, making no fhew of being difpleafed thereat ; neyther would he ftraight-wayes reprehend the fame, but expect alwayes a fit tyme & occafion to admonifh the offenders, leaft his admonition might therby, as oftentymes it hapneth, rather increafe the fores of feftred wounds, then cure them. He being therefore a Phifitian very skillful in curing of fuch euils, to the end that his patients might quietly abide the applying of his remedy, he would firft gently infinuate himfelfe into his friend-fhip who was to be thus cured, then would he take him afide, and all alone reprehend him in fo fweet a manner, as a friend once tould, him that he wondred how fuch mild words proceeded frõ his mouth. And by this meanes he fo brought the matter about, that the offenders not only acknowledged their fault, but did fincerely amend it.

Prudéce in reprehending

Nn 2   **CHAP.**

CHAP. XVIII.

*Being carryed in a Pirats barke, he arriueth
at laſt in* Iaponia, *in deſpite both of the
Pilot, and the Deuill.*

W HILEST he was thus imployed at *Malaca* in the exerciſes of Chriſtian charity,
the tyme approached for his departure towards *Iaponia.* Wherupon, eyther through
want of a greater Portugheſe ſhip, or elſe to prouide
for the more ſecurity of his Neophites who were to
accompany him, he ventured to go with a Barbarian
Pyrate, ſo ſecure he eſteemed all things with thoſe
who rely wholy vpon God : For he was afrayd leaſt
the three *Iaponian* Neophytes, who went along with
him in that iourney, might be much ſcandalized at
the Portugheſes, if they ſhould perceiue them, being
Chriſtians, to offend in any thing. Wherefore meeting with an Ethnicke Pirate of *China*, who was not
without cauſe ſurnamed the *Robber*, he agreed with
him, that paſſing by *China*, he ſhould carry him, and
his companions directely into *Iaponia* . And taking
pledges for ſecurity (yet truſting more vpon the diuine aſſiſtance, then vpon the fidelity of that Barbar-
an) he aduentureth himſelf and his company in a litle Barke, which they call in their language *Iuncus* .

 He departed from *Malaca* in the month of Iune,
vpon

*The di-
uine pro-
uidence
fauou-
reth Xa-
uerius .*

vpon the Natiuity of *S. Iohn Baptiſt*, and had a reaſonable proſperous, and commodious nauigation, although his Pilot were neyther induſtrious, nor faythfull towards him. For he (as Ethnickes make no great conſciéce of their promiſe) hauing on a ſuddain changed his mind, was not willing to go into *Iaponia*; and therfore to trifle away the time, he ſtayd at euery Ilãd he met withall, without any reaſon or occaſion. *Xauerius* therfore being ſollicitous about his iorney, when he ſaw him of ſet purpoſe, by making delayes, looſe the tyme which was moſt conuenient for them, began to be afrayd leaſt the ſummer once paſt, he might be conſtrayned to ſtay all winter in ſome Hauen of *China.* Wherupon he earneſtly expoſtulated with the mayſter of the ſhip, put him in mynd of his pledges, and laſtly beſought and intreated him, that he would not breake his promiſe made vnto the Portugeſes. But when he could nothing preuayle with the Pyrate, although he was much grieued in mynd, yet he ſuppreſſed the ſame, caſting all vpon the diuine Prouidence, which he had alwayes found to be fauourable vnto him: notwithſtanding, the deteſtable Superſtition of the Pilot and marriners did mooue him much more, then their perfidiouſnes had done. For they had in the ſhip an Idol to which they very often offred execrable ſacrifices. They alſo oftentymes by caſting lotts asked aduiſe of the Deuill, and ſpecially whether they ſhould haue a proſperous iourney if they ſayled into *Iaponia. Xauerius* was indeed much incenſed heerat, & could in no caſe brooke that they ſhould thinke his voyage into *Iaponia* wᶜʰ he vndertooke for

Gods

gods fake fhould depend vpon the Deuils lot & pleafure ; yet relying wholy vpon the diuine Goodnes, he
contemned whatfoeuer the Deuill could act agaynft
him and fo by Gods all-ruling difpofition they driect
their courfe towards *Iaponia*. By the way there hapned two things worthy of note.

The firft was, that *Emanuel* a *Chinefe* one of *Xa-*
uerius company, being in a tempeft caft downe by the
extreme toffing of the fhip, fell headlong into the
pumpe which was by chance open; and the fall was
not without great danger of his life, for that he fell
both very high, and befides ftucke faft in the pumpe
with his head downeward. Euery one therefore thinking him to be dead, he was at laft with much adoe
drawen out, and a litle after by Gods help, and *Fran-*
cis his prayers came to life agayne. In the fall he receyued a wound in his head, but the feare therof was
more then the daunger, for within a few daies he was
perfectly cured.

One of *Francis* his companions falling into the pumpe is deliuered from death.

Not long after this there hapned another chance
with the like danger, but different in the effect. Whilft
Emanuel was in dreffing his wound by the furgeo, the
fhip being fuddaynly toffed, caft the Pylots daughter
ouer board into the fea, and being driuen on with a
violet wind, & a cruel tempeft that immediatly arofe,
there was found no meanes poffible to faue her crying
out for help. And fo in fight of her Father, and the reft
of the marriners the vnfortunate mayde is fwallowed
vp by the raging billowes. Vpon this mifchance there
arifeth a doleful cry, intermingled with a certain how-
ling out, and lamentation of the Barbarians, which
continued

The Pilots daughter is drowned.

continued all that day, and the next night. Now the
Deuill who had bin long since spitefully bent against
Xauerius, thinking that he could not haue a fitter occasion to wreake his malice vpon him, vsed many deceiptfull stratagemes against him in this busines. For
when they Infidels damaunded of the Idoll the reason
why the Pilots daughter was drowned; it was answered, that if Emanuell the Christian had dyed in the
pumpe, the maid should not haue bin cast away in the
sea. *Francis* presently perceiued that by this answere,
he & his company were aymed at, to make them odious both to the Pilot and the marriners : and withall
found himselfe to be oftentimes much tempted interiourly by that horrible beast. But calling vpon the
diuine assistance, he did not only defeate all the plotts
of this most cruell Enemy, but freed himselfe also frō
the imminent dangers, in which he was amongst
those Ethnickes.

The di-
uell ta-
keth oc-
casion of
treache-
ry.

    There was nothing which more cooled the mali-
ce of the Deuil, and the marriners agaynst him, then
his couragious mynd. Neyther did this combat
passe without some fruite vnto *Francis*. For by his
owne peril he experienced what horrible terrours the
Diuell striketh into others, when he is permitted, &
findeth opportunity Concerning which matter there
is extant a notable Epistle of *Xauerius* to the Society at
Goa, the contents whereof are : That there is no surer
way to defeate the vayne affrights of the Deuill, then
by wholy distrusting in our selues, & putting our cō-
fidence in God, with a couragious and vndaunted
hart, to contemne the feeble assaults, and threats of

His mag-
nanimity
against
the ter-
rours of
the deuil

The way
how to
ouer-
come the
affrights
of the
Deuill.

that

that Monſter ; and by depending vpon the diuine aſſiſtance, to keep our ſelues, with all the courage we can, from being afrayd . For in ſuch a caſe , and at ſuch a tyme nothing ought more to be feared, then diffidence and diſtruſt in God : ſeeing it is manifeſt, that our Enemy cannot , with all his forces, dovs any hurt, vnleiſe God permit him .

Xauerius hauing thus ouercome the Diuell, had now a new combat to fight with men. When they were arriued at *Cantonium* a hauen Towne of *China*, the Pilot and marriners conſulted againe with the Idoll by lottes, & receiuing no comfortable anſwere from the Diuell concerning their nauigation into *Iaponia* , caſt ancker, & reſolued to keep their winter there . Which *Xauerius* perceyuing, caſt about to help himſelfe. And firſt he humbly beſought the Pylot, to ſtand to his promiſſes ; then when intreatyes could do no good , falling from requeſts vnto threats, he layd before him the loſſe of his pledges , and the diſpleaſure of the Gouernor of *Malaca*, & the Portugeſes, to whome he had giuen his word : ſo as, at laſt the Pilot being ſomwhat moued with what was obieꝛted agaynſt him, he weighed ancker, and began to ſayle forward. But this conſtancy in him was no more then his fidelity. For a litle while after the perfidious Ethnicke fell agayne into his former humour of wintering in thoſe coaſts . Which perfidiouſneſſe of his, would infallibly haue hindred *Xauerius* iourney , had not the diuine Prouidence turned the Pilots courſe another way .

The ſhip now ſayled amaine with a proſperous gale towards *Cinceum* a hauen towne of *China*, where the
Pylor

Pylot intended to harbour all the winter, for that the
summer was now almoſt at an end; when as vpon the
ſuddaine they meete with a Pinnace which telleth the
that the port of *Cinceum* was much peſtred with Pyrates. The Pylot being greatly affrighted with this
newes, called his witts together, and began to thinke
what was beſt to be done. To go backe agayne to Ca-
tonium he could not, becauſe the wind was ful agaynſt
him, and withall lay very right for *Iaponia.* Wherfore
making his benefit of neceſſity, he reſolued to follow
the wind. And ſo in deſpite both of the Pilot, Marriners, & the Diuell himſelfe the ſhip was conſtrayned
to hould on her courſe into *Iaponia* : whither at laſt
he arriued vpon the very day of the Aſſumption of
our B. Lady, more by the fauour of God, and his Holy Mother, then of the wind or weather. Now when
as they could not well reach to other Hauens as they
deſired, they arriued with their ſhip at *Cangoxima*, a
Citty in the Kingdom of *Saxuma*, and the very Country of *Paul of the Holy Fayth.* There *Francis* together
with his companions, is very courteouſly entertayned
both by *Paules* friends, & the reſt of the inhabitants,
yea euen of the Magiſtrates theſelues : whoſe arriuall
being diuulged among the people, euery one, as it often hapneth, ran with admiration to behold the new
Prieſts that were come from *Portugall.*

O o   O F

OF THE LIFE OF
S. FRANCIS XAVIER.

The IIII. Booke.

He inquireth of the Manners, and Religions of the Iaponians.

CHAP. I.

A difcription of Iaponia.

APONIA is a Country of the vtmoſt Eaſt, and bordereth vpon the furtheſt part of *Aſia*. It conſiſteth altogeather of Ilandes, diuided by ſtrait and narrow armes of the ſea. Concerning the extent and bignes thereof (as much as can be obſerued by a Portugheſe skillfull in ſuch matters , who hath lately meaſured the ſame) we haue for certayne, that it is extended in length about 900. miles, and in forme not much vnlike to *Italy* , except that *Italy* ioyneth to the Continent

tinent, & is almoſt equall vnto it in greatnes. On the North, it lyeth towards the furtheſt part of *Scythia*, which we call *Tartary*; on the weſt it bendeth towards *China*, and on the Eaſt, it is oppoſite to *New Spayne*, being diſtant from thence leſſe then 500. miles. From *Goa* it is well neere 2000. leagues. It conteynes ſixty ſix Kingdomes; and which is very ſtrange, the whole Nation vſeth but one language, & that not hard to be learned. But all *Iaponia* (by reaſon of three Ilands bigger then the reſt) is diuided into three partes, which taking their names from the greater Ilands, haue many of the leſſer belonging vnto them.

That part which of all the reſt is the greateſt without compariſon, and furtheſt diſtant from *India*, is properly called *Iapon*, from whence the reſt of the country taketh its name. This Iland is in length 750. miles, but the breadeth is various, yet for the moſt part it is about 180 miles ouer. There be in it 53. Kingdomes; which certainly can be of no great extent: For euen to Lords, & Princes of ſeuerall Cittyes they giue the Title of King, of whome, many abound in wealth, eſpecially thoſe who haue the Dominion ouer many Kingdomes. Heerein is ſcituated *Meaco* which was anciently the head Citty of all *Iaponia*, but now of many Kingdomes only.

The next vnto *Iapon* in greatnes and wealth is *Xi*- The Iläd *mus*, which is ſayd to be 150. miles in length, and in *Ximus*. breadeth 70. This lying neereſt of all the other vnto *China*, and leſſe diſtant from *India*, is deuided into nine Kingdomes, whereof *Saxuma* is one, and where, as we ſayd before, *Xauerius* firſt arriued.

The

The third Iland lying betweene both thefe, is called
Xicus, or *Xieocus*, little more then halfe as great as
Ximus, and conteyneth only foure Kingdomes. This
whole country being altogether vnknown to former
ages, was difcouered by the Portugefes, who being by
tempeft of weather driuen thither, began by meanes
of traffique, to haue correfpondence with them, fome
ten yeares before *Xauerius* came thither. The Country
is very cold, vnpleafant to the eye, & in many places
mountanous and barrayne, yet for the moft part chã-
pion, enterlaced with many fayre riuers, & by nature
fertile, although they do not till the ground by reafon of their continuall warres; fo as it is more fit for
vines & oliues, if it were therwith planted : for want
whereof there be very few vineyards, and no oliues
at all, and yieldeth rather Rice, then Corne. Neyther do there want mines of gold, but skill to make it:
yet chiefly it excelleth in filuer mines, for which caufe
it is called *Argentaria*. Notwithftanding, for that the
Inhabitants are debarred from trafficque with the
Chinefes, in tymes paft it wanted many things which
now the Portughefes haue by their commercement
lately fupplyed, not without great profit to thefelues.
And although there be frequent Hauens in the whole
Country, yet the Iland *Ximus*, both becaufe it hath
more ftore of Port Townes, and lyeth moft commodious for the fhippes that come from *India*, is moft of
all frequented by the Portughefe merchants.

There was at that tyme one King who ruled o-
uer all *Iaponia*, called by the inhabitantes *Dayrus*;
whofe raygne, becaufe Kingly Maiefty was now
worne

worne out amongſt the Nobles, began to depend
vpon their pleaſures. The people of *Iaponia*, compared with the *Indians*, are white of complexion,
by nature moſt warlike, and in vertue and vpright-
neſſe doe farre exceed all other Nations which haue
byn found out of late. *Xauerius* therefore making his
abode at *Cangoxima* (which is the principall Citty of
Saxuma) before he would aduenture to ſet vpon the
Iaponians ſoules, thought beſt to ſeek out firſt all kind
of wayes & meanes how to do it, & chiefly to inquire
of their manners & religions. And hauing diligently
ſounded them all out, he found the matter for the
moſt part thus to ſtand : to wit, that the whole Nation
was of a very tractable diſpoſition, and for the moſt
part cannot endure any double dealing. They haue
no great ſtore of gold, riches, or wealth ; and therfore (as moſt commonly where there is leaſt money,
there alſo is leaſt ſeeking after it) their ſtudy is leaſt
about ſuch kind of things . Neyther do they account
any thing more diſhonourable, then to increaſe their
wealth & ſubſtance by trafficque, or any other art.
So as their manner of lyfe is vpheld by the direction
of pouerty, yet in ſuch ſort, that they hyde the ſame
with a neat and handſome adorning of their bodyes

They ſtand very much vpon their dignity and reputation, ſo that you would thinke them therin moſt
perfectly to reſemble the auncient Romans . They do
all for the moſt part, euen children, place their greateſt delight in martiall affayres, nor do they ordinarily, take content in any thing elſe. Notwithſtanding
(which is incredible to be ſpoken or heard) although

O o 3   they

they be of such couragious spirits, and so much giuen
to bearing of armes, yet they absteyne from all quarrels amóg themselues, reseruing the vse of their weapons for tyme of warre agaynst their enemies. For
the *Iaponians* haue such gouernement ouer themselues and their passions, that they seeme therein to be
of the sect of *Stoickes*. And to see a *Iaponese* brawling,
chafing, or wrangling one with another, is amongst
them accounted a monstrous thing. Wherfore the better to auoid all occasion of contentions, they neuer
deale about any businesse of importance or cótrouer-
sy by themselues, but by a third person. And this they
obserue, not only with strangers, but also with their
friends, and those of the same household with them;
wherby they conserue quiet of mynd in themselues,
and peace with others.

They take very great delight in hunting, in so
much that they eate no flesh which is not gotten by
that meanes. They can no more endure mutton, swi-
nes-flesh, beefe, or veale, then we can dogges, or horse-
flesh. They absteine from milke and cheese as we do
from raw bloud. They keep hennes and geese, not so
much to eate, as for their recreation & pleasure. They
do therefore seldome eate flesh, which when they
doe, is alwayes Venison. They feed for the most
part on fish, fruite, herbes, and rice : and by the
meanes of their temperate dyet they are very sound
and healthfull, liuing ordinarily vntill they be very
old, vnlesse they meete by chance with some violent
or vntimely death. At least, we may learne by this
their liuing so well vpon a little, that *Nature is content*
with

with few things, although fenfuality be neuer fatisfied.
Adulteries are with them moft feuerely punifhed .
They abfteine altogeather from dyce-playing , and
fuch like games, deeming that by thofe meanes, men
become defirous of others goods . They are alfo fo
farre from theft and robbery , that they iudg nothing
more vnworthy in a man : for which caufe they con-
demne felons to the gallowes, the moft difgracefull
of all punifhments amongft them.

They vfe cleanlineffe in their dyet , neatneffe in *The Ja-*
their attyre , and moft courteous ciuility in all their *ponians*
meetings , falutations, and conuerfation : wherein ciuility.
the men are not more exact, then the children; nor the
Nobility, then the Country people . You would belieue they were all trayned vp togeather to ciuill and
courtly behauiour in the fame Kings Court. But thefe
guifts of nature are obfcured by pride, a malady deeply rooted in this Nation . For they fo contemne other
nations in refpect of themfelues , that they are for the
moft part very arrogant and infolent in their carriage
towards ftrangers. This one thing only excepted they
want nothing , but the light of the Ghofpell, being of
themfelues a nation (if there be any in the world)
borne, and in a manner framed to al ciuility. For euen
the country people themfelues are very ingenious, &
defirous of learning; in fo much, that as euery thing
feemeth moft conformable to reafon, fo they do moft
willingly imbrace it. They are very attentiue to difcourfes, efpecially of God , and diuine matters . They
are moreouer commonly very good fchollers, & therfore fo much the more apt to receiue Chriftian difcipline.
                                                        Now

Now when *Xauerius* had vnderſtood theſe and
many other things (which for breuities ſake I omit)
of the diſpoſition & manners of the *Iaponians:* making
alſo iniquity after their Prieſts,& Religions,he found
things ſtanding almoſt in this manner; to wit, that
they account thoſe things moſt of all their Gods , by
whoſe meanes they receiue help . Some therefore do
worſhip the Sunne , others the Moone , and others
other Gods . There be alſo among them certayne Men
held for Gods , which they had from the *Chineſes:*
Amongſt whome are *Xacas,* and *Amidas* . But there
is no greater villanny, or impurity,then among their
Prieſts (whome they call *Bonzies,*)ſo that you may
eaſily know whoſe Miniſters they be . For hauing
brought in that heynous ſinne (which is not heere to
be named) of prepoſterous luſt, they haue caſt ſuch a
thicke miſt before the *Iaponians* eyes , that being not
able to diſcerne ſuch impurities , they commonly account that moſt deteſtable crime of al other, to be no
ſinne at all. Whereupon (both their kings , and ſubiects being alike infected with that abominable ſinne,
and running on headlong therin, as it were to armes)
their Cittyes euer ſince, vndoubtedly through Gods
wrathfull indignation,being continually in tumultes
and vprore,they are perpetually engaged in ciuill warres amongſt themſelues; wherby at laſt they may , by
Gods goodnes, open their eyes to fly from ſuch abominations . And in the meane tyme, that ſinne may not
want matter to worke on , the Nobility for the moſt
part, commit their children , like ſheepe to wolues ,
for their Education to the *Bonzies* . There be diuers

Con-

The *Ia-
ponians*
Gods.

Bonzies
Iaponian
Prieſts.

Conuents of them both men and women, called *Bon-zies*, & *Bonzieſſes*, and they haue alſo diſtinct habits, as amongſt our Religious men of *Europe*, the Deuil ther-in playing the ape with the Church of Chriſt. But al-though the *Bonzies* be not without good ground, eſtee-med to be giuen all alike to that beaſtly impurity, yet they are ſo cloaked, either with the reſpect of their Prieſthood, or elſe by the great opinion which is had of their abſtinence, that they are for all that, held in very great eſteeme, both with the Nobility and com-mon people: becauſe it is bruited abroad with more glory then truth, that they abſteine wholy from fleſh, fiſh, and wine, and liue only vpon hearbes, & ryce, & eate but once a day.

CHAP. II.

At Cangoxima *he conuerteth many to the Chriſtian faith.*

F R A N C I S hauing taken exact notice of theſe things, & iudging it fit (as the ſtate of ſuch buſines then required) that he ought firſt of all to preſcribe vnto himſelf a more ſtrict manner of lyfe, liued indeed more ſpa-ringly, and hardly then the *Bonzies* were reported to do; which was moſt certainly true, ſeing that he found in thoſe places not only want of things neceſ-ſary, but euen a quite different kind of dyet from that he was accuſtomed vnto; ſo as meere hunger and ne-

ceſſity

ceſſity did conſtrain him to change, as it were, his v-
ſuall manner of dyet, and euen his very taſt alſo. For
he kept himſelfe aliue with ryce inſteed of bread, and
for the moſt part, with fruit and hearbes inſteed of
meate, & this dreſſed after the *Iaponian* faſhiō. Which
new kind of frugality he moſt willingly imbraced,
for the vehement deſire he had of gayning ſoules to
God, like one, *Whoſe meate and drinke was to do the will
of him that ſent him.* And he was alwayes wont to ſay,
that he was much behoulding to *Iaponia*, becauſe that
euen then, when he was by the inhabitants inuited to
a Feaſt, he found none of thoſe daynties, wherwith
mortall men, being often deceiued, ſought more to
pleaſe their Senſuality, then to ſatisfy Nature, euen
to the ouerthrow rather of their forces, then to the
ſtrengthning therof: ſo as that vnuſuall dyet, and the
manner of dreſſing it, held him to greater temperāce
therein. Yet for all this, he was of no leſſe ability of
body then before. For he had his health no where better then in *Iaponia*; by which it is euident, that a ſpare
dyet doth not diminiſh, but increaſe ones health, and
forces.

But now he had much more to do, in acquainting
his tongue with their language, then his palate with
their dyet. For although the *Iaponian* language be not
of its owne nature very hard, yet haue the *Iaponians* by
their endeauours brought it to be exceeding difficile
to learne. There is not any language more copious
then theirs. For to expreſſe diuers conceits of things
in a different māner it hath wōderful ſtore of words,
all ſignifying the ſame thing; and in vſing thereof, it
hath

Francis
extreme
ſparing
diet in
Iaponia.

The *Ia-
ponian*
language

hath a certayne kind of Elegancy, and as it were, a fmacke proper to that country. They do not without great confideration, vfe any word which firft occurreth, but, as fome are more elegant, fome of a lower ftrayne, fo do they keep a proportion with the matter, and perfons to whome they are applyed. Nay, which is very ftráge, they fpeake far otherwife, then they write. The men vfe one kind of language, and the women another: and the letters which they fend one to another, are written with one kind of character, and their Bookes with another. By which copioufnes, and variety both of fpeaking and writing, much labour and tyme is required to learne their language. And no man of ciuility muft be ignorant in this kind. For if he do fwarue any thing from their manner of fpeach, they will laugh at him, as at an ignorant and rufticall fellow; no otherwife then we are accuftomed to do, when in fpeaking of latin, any one fhould make an odious iarring, in choice eares, by harfh and barbarous words.

Francis therefore thinking that it now ftood him vpon, to learne their language howfoeuer; when he had caufed *Paul* the *Iaponian* to fet downe the chiefe heads of the Chriftian doctrine in writing, he met with many rubs. For *Paul* being a man without learning, was no whit a better interpreter then a Mayfter. And although his endeauours were aboue his forces, yet he effected leffe then the matter required. For he interpreted thofe points fo ill, that there was no connexion in his fpeach. And he alfo wrote fo badly, that the *Iaponians*, who were euen learned, could hardly

read

read his writing without laughing. But *Xauerius* being of an vndaunted courage, which alwayes striued
agaynst difficulties, & making small account of mens
laughing at him when their saluation was in hand,
went perseuerantly stil on in the businesse. Wherefore dealing in the best in manner he could with the
people, he by the sanctity of his lyfe, and diuine feruour of spirit, wrought so efficaciously with the, that
he did more good by himselfe, then eyther by *Paul*, or
any other Interpreter. For at the nouelty of the thing,
and of the doctrine he taught, the inhabitants came
flocking about him by whole troupes, partly out of
desire to see stragers wholy different from them, both
in habit and behauiour; and partly also, to know
what Religion they had brought out of the other
world. But because for want of perfect language, they
could not well explicate their owne meaning, nor yet
resolue those who asked them questions, some scoffed
at them, others mocked at their strange habit and behauiour, & others pittyed them being strangers, deeming that such men comming out of another world
as farre as *Iaponia*, to bring thither a new Religion,
ought neyther to be fooles, nor to bring with them
matters of small moment: so as by this variety of iudgement many were moued with a desire to know the
new Religion they had brought, and receyued much
profit therby.

In the meane tyme *Paul* the *Iaponian* hauing setled
his affayres, began to be admired by his Countrymen,
because hauing trauayled ouer *India*, he recounted to
them many strange things, & neuer heard of amogst
them.

them. Going therefore to salute the Prince of *Saxuma* who remayned 15. miles from *Cangoxima,* he is by him courteously entertayned. After mutuall gratulations, the Prince asked him many questions concerning matters in *India,* & of the Portughefes wealth and manners. *Paul* hauing well fatisfyed him by his relation, of what he asked, taketh forth a curious table which he brought out of *India,* wherein was painted the Image of the B. Virgin Mary with the child *Iefus* fitting in his mothers lappe. And after he had tould the Prince diuers things of the Chriftians Religion, he fhewed him this picture, who forthwith bendeth downe his knees in veneration therof, & cōmandeth all that were prefent to do the like. But further then this veneration of the Picture, the Prince went not: yet his mother being in loue therewith, greatly defired to haue a patterne of it, but there was no painter found who could performe what the pious womā requefted. She had alfo afterwards a great defire to know the Chriftian Religion, & demanded to haue the principall points therof fet downe in the *Iaponian* language. *Paul* did fo indeed, but foone after fhe defifted from her good purpofe.

A King of *Iaponia* humbly adoreth the Image of our B. Lady.

Wherfore feeing his endeauours to haue no effect he returneth agayne to *Cangoxima,* and imployeth himfelfe with farre better fucceffe at home, then he had done abroad. For the deuout and laborious man, being as well moued by *Xauerius* example, as of his owne accord, fet himfelfe ferioufly to worke amongft his owne family and kindred, neuer leauing to teach and exhort them, day nor night; fometimes by one

Paul the *Iaponian* endeauours to propagate the Chriftiā fayth.

alone

alone, fometimes altogeather, vntill he had drawen
many of them to the Chriftian faith: fo as within a
fhort fpace his wife, daughter, and many of his kinf-
folkes both men and women, were inftructed in the
Catechifme, and baptized, the people no wayes mifli-
king what they had refolued vpon, and done.

The Ninxit or chiefe Prieft of the Bonzies.

But *Xauerius* vnderftanding for certaine, that the
peoples affections depended wholy vpon the authority of the *Bonzies*, and that if he could but once weake
the fame he fhould find all things eafy ; thought it expedient firft of all, to bend all his forces againft their
efteeme and credit amongft the people, as againft the
maine fort of fuperftition. Wherfore meeting vpon a
very fit occafion with the chiefe man of the *Bonzies*
(whome they call *Ninxit*, & who farre excelleth the
reft not only in yeares and dignity, but alfo in the o-
pinion of learning) he by his courteous behauiour infinuateth himfelfe into his familiarity. Then falling
from one difcourfe to another, by little & little he began to buckle with him about matters of Religion.
And not in vaine. For he found him prefently, not to
ftand conftantly to what he faid, as well concerning
the immortality of the foule, as in other points, but to
ftagger in his opinions, when he was preffed with the
truth ; fo as he had no great difficulty in ouercomming, and preffing downe the poore man. Yet the
Bonzy taking great content either in *Xauerius* prudēce
or els in the fweetnes of his conuerfation, held him in
great efteeme. Now the reft of the Bonzies following
their *Ninxits* example, defired alfo to conuerfe with
Xauerius, rather for oftentations fake, then for any
good

good will they bare vnto him. There was nothing
which they more admired in him, then the greatnesse
of his mind, who for Religions sake only, had by a
long and dangerous nauigation come from Portugall
through the vast Ocean, to those vtmost partes of the
world. They also with exceeding admiration and delight gaue eare to him, whilst he declared vnto them,
that there was an euerlasting Blessednes in Heauen,
layd vp for those who serue Christ with deuotion, &
sanctity of life.

Now the *Bonzies* being partly wonne by *Xauerius*
courtesy, and partly conuinced by his erudition, the
businesse seemed to be in a good forwardnesse. But because he could not deale with the people without an
Interpreter, his endeauors were indeed much hindred
through want of language. Wherfore being sollicitous how to procure the saluation of so many peri-
shing soules, he with all speed learneth the principles
of the *Iaponian* tongue, wherof he had before gotten
a tast. Then, that he might deale the more freely with
the people, he maketh meanes for accesse vnto the
King: wherin *Paul* the *Iaponian* stood him in great
steed. For he easily drew the *King* of *Saxuma*, who
much desired to haue friendship and commercement
with the Portugheses, to shew particular countenáce
vnto *Francis* and his companions, who were of great
authority with the Portugheses. *Francis* therfore being
admitted to the King, and finding him well disposed,
brought him without any great difficulty, to giue free
leaue vnto his subiects, to receiue the Christian Religion. This liberty was no sooner graunted, but presently

fently two of the *Bonzies*, and many other *Iaponians* vnited themfelues to the fayth of Chrift ; and within a few monthes fpace aboue an hundred Cittizens became Chriftians with the good liking of their friends and kinsfolkes: All whome *Xauerius* inftructed with a greater care & induftry, for that he had as yet no skill of the *Iaponian* characters, which (as wefayd before) are more difficile to learne, then the wordes themfelues. Wherefore hauing the chiefe points of the Chrinian fayth turned into the *Iaponian* language, but yet written in our European characters, he taught thê to the Neophites, reading them out of the writing it felf. He alfo fent diuers Neophytes into *India*, there to be brought vp in learning in the Colledge of *Goa*, that being afterwards furnifhed both with knowledge, & Chriftian behauiour, they might be more able to bring both admiration, and affiftance to their Country men.

CHAP. III.

He rayfeth a dead Mayd to lyfe : and cureth another of the Leaprousy.

FTER this, there happened a ftrange Euent, which augmented both the flocke of Chrift at *Cangoxima*, aud made *Francis* his name more famous alfo. There was in *Cangoxima* an honeft and fubftantiall Cittizen, yet no friend to Chriftian religion. He had a litle daughter

ter whome he loued moſt deerely, who by vntimely
death was ſuddainly taken away. Whereupon falling
out of wits with griefe, he ſayd, and did many things
vnbeſeeming a man of his ranke. Amõgſt others, there
came vnto him certaine Neophytes of his kindred &
friends, to condole with him, & to celebrate the funeralls of his daughter ; who being greatly moued with
the wofull caſe of their kinſman, aduiſe him with all
ſpeed to go vnto *Xauerius*, who was a holy man newly
come out of another world, and implore his ayde; for
certainly he would reſtore his daughter to life. There
was no great difficulty to perſwade the afflicted Father therto. Wherfore being ſet on with the deſire of
his daughters life, he runneth to *Xauerius* bedewed all
with teares, and declareth the matter vnto him, humbly beſeeching his help, who hauing loſt his child, was
now left all alone. *Francis* pittying his caſe, preſently
betaketh himſelfe to prayer, togeather with *Iohn Fernandez* his companion. And after a while he riſeth vp
cheerfully, & comforteth the man, willing him to be
of good courage, and telling him withall, that his
daughter was aliue. Vpon which words the Barbarian
began to be in choller, who had but euen now left
her certainly dead. Wherfore either thinking himſelf
to be accounted a lyar, or elſe that *Francis* diſdayned
to come vnto his houſe, he departed in a chafe. As he
was in the way homeward, one of his family meeteth him, and bringeth him tydings that the mayd
was aliue, and in good health. Wherupon the man,
feeling his ſorrow in an inſtant turned into ioy, haſt-
eth home with great deſire to ſee his daughter whome

Qq   he

he so dearely loued. When he entred into his house &
beheld her aliue and in health, he could hardly belieue
his owne eyes; and with teares trickling downe for
ioy, asked her by what meanes she was restored againe
to life? As soone, quoth she, as I was dead, there
stood ready at hand certaine cruel executioners, who
snatching me vp, went to cast me headlong into an
horrible pit of fire, but vpon the suddain there appeared two other singular men, by whose meanes I was
deliuered out of those executioners hands, & restored
to life againe. At this relation of the maid, the father
stood a while astonished through admiration. Then
perceiuing, manifestly, that it was done by *Xauerius*
help, he leadeth his daughter to him to giue him thankes. Assoone as she saw *Francis* & his companion, she
stood at first amazed, then turning to her father, she
cryeth out: Behould, Father, these be the two men
that rescued me from Hell. Then he with the mayd
falling downe at *Xauerius* feete, with aboundance of
teares gaue him humble thanks: who presently taking
them vp with ioy of hart, willeth them to giue thákes
to Christ the sonne of God, and Author of mans saluation.

    Neither was this great miracle done in vaine. For
this one mayds restoring to life, caused the saluation
of many others. And the Father, daughter, and all the
rest of that family presently became Christians. O-
thers also were, by this example, mooued to implore
Xauerius ayde, & desired to receaue the faith of Christ.
Amongst whome there was a certaine Leaper, borne
of good parentage, who had sent one to *Francis*, requesting

queſting him to come & cure him. But he receiuing the
meſſage excuſeth himſelfe in a courteous manner, by
reaſon of his ſo many other imployments; yet ſendeth
one of his companions to him, with inſtructions what
to do. When he came thither, he ſaluteth the ſick man
verylouingly, & asketh him three, times as *Xauerius* had
appointed, whether he would become a Chriſtiā? And
giuing a ſigne that he would, the other preſently maketh vpon him the ſigne of the Holy Croſſe. A wonderfull thing. He had no ſooner done, but the Croſſe
inſtantly wiped cleane away the leaproſy. Wherupon
the man was inſtructed in the Chriſtian faith, & a little after baptized. Theſe things being done in the view
of the whole Citty of *Cangoxima*, were ſtraight carried into *India*, and related to *Francis* his companions
there, not only by *Vincent Pereira* a Portugheſe merchant and *Xauerius* familiar friend, a man worthy of
all credit although in a matter of ſuch importance;
but by many others alſo.

CHAP. IIII.

*He receaueth newves of the Martyrdome
of Fa.* Antony Criminalis.

NOW whilſt *Xauerius* was reioycing at the
happy ſucceſſe of Chriſtian affayres in *Iaponia*, there came vnto him letters out of
India that did ſomewhat afflict him, by
which

which he vnderftood of the death of *Fa. Antony Crimi-*
nalis. This man, as we faid before, was by *Francis* made
fuperiour in the Promontory of *Comorinum,* & hauing
for the fpace of foure yeares, with great fruit of his
labours, managed the affayres of Chriftian Religion
in that Coaft, in the yeare 1549. a little before *Xaue-*
rius entred into *Iaponia*, obteined the crowne of Martyrdome, a reward due to his paynes. For when a great
band of the *Badages*, inflamed with hatred againft
Chriftian Religion, had from the bordring kingdome
of *Bifnaga*, broken into the coaft of *Comorinum*, fpoi-
ling & deftroying all before them, the Chriftians, in
fuch a fearefull tumult, prefently forfooke their villages, and houfes, and began to fly to the Portughefe
fhippes, which at that time lay there at anker.

Antony therfore being in a great throng of women and children, and troubled with many cares, incouraged thofe who were afraid to make haft away,
and withall affoarded his help and affiftance to others
that were weake, and cold not fly fo faft. In the meane
time the enemy approached, & he fearing leaft fome
of the Neophytes being intercepted by the Barbarians
might through payne of torments, be drawne from
the faith of Chrift, refolued like a good Paftour there
Ioan. 11. to fpend his life for his fheep, if need required. The
Portughefes inuited, and intreated him to come into
their fhippes to auoid the prefet danger; but he wholy
forgetting himfelfe, prouided more for the fafety of
thofe that were with him, then his owne, by ridding
out of the way thofe, efpecially women & children,
who by reafon of their weakeneffe, were moft in
danger

danger . Now whilst he freeth others from the cruelty
of the Barbarians , being himselfe stopped from recouering the shippes, for that the enemy had gotten betweene him & the shore, he fel into their hands. Then
all burning with the loue of God , and hauing his co
gitations fixed rather vpon Eternity, then vpon this
mortall life , kneeling downe vpon the ground, and
lifting vp his hands to heauen , offereth himselfe to
death with incredible courage and constancy . Nor
was the Barbarians cruelty, lesse then his valour. For
being thrust through the body with three launces, he
fell downe dead . And it is reported , that when they
were stripping him , as he lay thus grieuously wounded, he helped those cruell robbers to draw off his
owne cloathes, that he might not seeme to hold his
apparell faster then his life.

The Mar
tyrdome
of *Fa. An
tony Cri_
minalis.*

This newes, which could not otherwise choose ,
caused in *Xauerius* diuers affections . For as it grieued
him, that he was depriued of so notable a subiect ; so
was he greatly ioyed for the Fathers good fortune , in
receauing the reward of his labours , by so noble a
Crowne . So as honouring the memorable death of
this holy man both with teares , and prayses , he began to hope firmely, that the sterility of that field, being now watered with the bloud of this Martyr ,
would dayly yield more plenty of fruite. Neyther was
his hope heerein frustrate. For since that tyme the
Ghospell hath no where yielded a more plentiful haruest, then in the coast of *Comorinum,* so abundant hath
byn the increase of Neophytes in that coast, no lesse
eminent in piety , that in sweetnesse of manners .

CHAP.

CHAP. V.

The courſe of Chriſtian affayres being hindred at Cangoxima, *he goeth to preach the Ghoſpell at* Firandum, *&* Amangucium.

RANCIS hauing the like occaſion in the citty of *Cangoxima,* met with a farre different condition. For when he, thirſting after Martyrdome, had weakned & beaten downe the authority of the *Bonzies,* and that the forward ſpring of neophites begā to make now a glorious ſhew; behold vpon the ſuddaine a tempeſt was rayſed by the *Bonzies,* which brought great calamity to the Chriſtian cauſe, and which was more heauy to *Xauerius,* then euen death it ſelfe. Many were now by diuine inſtinct become Chriſtians; and many alſo by ſeeing the truth, were drawen to imbrace the fayth of Chriſt, when as the *Bonzies* (which thing *Francis* had long forſeene)hindred the courſe of the Ghoſpell. For when they perceaued, that by bringing in, and increaſe of Chriſtian Religion, the reſpect both to their Gods, and their owne authority came to be ſet at naught, they began in good earneſt to be all on fire with rage & anger. And ſo thruſt forward as well with madnes, as by the Deuill himſelfe, they come in great troopes to their king, telling him very reſolutely, and plainly: That he ſhould looke very warily

The Bonzies hinder the courſe the Goſpell.

ly

ly what he did, and fhould prouide both for his owne «
fafety and of the common good, whileft it was in his «
power. If he did permit his fubiects to entertayne «
ftrange Religions, their Countrey Gods would cer- «
taynly become a mocking ftocke euery where : and «
if they were once incenfed, what could he expect els, «
but that *Cangoxima*, and his whole kingdome would «
within a while be vtterly ouerthrowne? Did not he «
fee, that the Chriftian Religion was wholy repugnat «
to that of *Iaponia* ? & how it loft euery day fo much, as «
the Chriftian Religion gayned ? Neyther could he be «
ignorat that where ftrange ceremonies fhould be pre- «
ferred before thofe of their owne coutry, there would «
be caufed extreme forrow to the country Gods? And «
certaynely it was a leffe fault for the people to offend «
therein, then for the King to winke at others offences. «
The flower that Heauen was in punifhing, the more «
enraged would the wrath thereof be when it came. «
For no doubt but the firft founders of the *Iaponian* Re- «
ligion, would be reuenged of *Cangoxima* for fo great «
a difgrace, and that both he & his kingdome would be «
vtterly deftroyed for the impiety of a few. Wherefore «
if he had any refpect, or reuerence of his Country ce- «
remonies, or Gods, it were wifedome to looke ey- «
ther for their fauour, or ftand in feare of their anger. «

The King being ftroken with this fpeach of the
Bonzies, & being alfo out of hope of commercement
with the Portughefes, publifhed prefently an Edict
or Proclamation, prohibiting vnder payne of impri-
fonment & death, that all men fhould keep their Coutry Religion, & that heerafter none fhould become
Chriftians.

Chriſtians. But *Xauerius* hoping euery day, that times might grow better & calmer, tooke great care in looking to his yong flocke. And all the reſt of his tyme which he did not imploy therin, he was accuſtomed to beſtow vpon God, with whome he conuerſed more then with men, eſteeming ſuch diuine conferences to be, not only an incouragement to vertue, but a comfort alſo in the time of perſecution and labour. He therfore being a ſtranger in a Barbarous Citty, and which was wholy bent againſt him, endured with wonderfull quiet of mind, many and grieuous miſeries, as well of hungar and cold, as of other extreeme

The Kingdome of *Figua.*

difficulties. But hauing paſſed a whole yeare in theſe labours & incommodities, when he perceiued there was ſmall, or no hope left for increaſe of the Ghoſpell at *Cangoxima*, he reſolued to depart from thence to ſome other place. Wherfore bidding farewell to his Neophytes, he left the protection of them to *Paul of the holy Faith*: & togeather with *Coſmas Turianus*, and *Iohn Fernandez*, rayſed vp with new hopes, intended to paſſe into the kingdome of *Figua*, whither now the Portugheſes had reſorted for traffique.

It is incredible to be ſpoken what aboundance of teares the new Chriſtians ſhed vpon *Francis* his departure from them, for al did beare him extraordinary affection, as well for many other reſpects, as chiefly for his ſingular ſanctity of life. Wherfore weeping, & in lamentable manner, calling him *Maiſter*, *Guide*, and *Father*, they tooke at laſt their leaues, with infinite thankes for the great paynes he had taken, in ſhewing them the way to eternall ſaluation. There were well-neere

neere 800. Neophytes, ſo well inſtructed, that though they were within a few months after bereaued of *Paul* their maiſter, yet they perſeuered euery one of them in the Chriſtian faith ſeauen whole yeares, without any other guide, vntill ſome of the Society came thi-ther againe.

The kingdome of *Figua* is in that Iland of *Iaponia* which, as we ſayd, is called *Ximus*. In this King-dome there is a towne called *Firandum*, about 200. miles from *Cangoxima*, whither he repayed, and was courteouſly entertayned by the Portugheſes, and by their meanes alſo by the King himſelf; with whome remayning for ſome dayes, he brought well nigh an 100. of the Cittizens, to the faith of Chriſt. And al-though he repented not himſelfe of the paines which he had taken amongſt the *Portugheſes*, and thoſe of *Firandum* (for he had in few dayes made more Chriſti-ans in *Firandum*, then he had done in *Cangoxima* in many monthes) yet hauing greater matters in hand and committing the charge of the Neophytes to *Coſmas Turianus*, and taking *Iohn Fernandez* with him, he paſſeth ouer into the Iland of *Iapon*, intending to go to *Meaco*. But vnderſtanding by thoſe who were expe-rienced in thoſe parts, that *Amangucium*, a Towne of good note lay in his way, he preſently goeth thither, to ſound out, and try the diſpoſition and inclination of the King of that Country

Amangucium is a very ample, and famous ſea Towne, ſcituated in that part of *Iaponia*, which (as we ſaid) is properly called *Iapon*. For there the King of that Country hath his Royall ſeate; who being

The towne *Firandū*.

R r   very

very wealthy & potent, ſtriueth for the Empire with
the King of *Meaco* , who is accounted the greateſt
King of all the reſt. That towne of *Amangucium*, according to the faſhion of that country, is built of tym-
ber, conteyning in it to the number of 10000. families, and is diſtant from *Firandum* almoſt 300. miles.
As ſoone therfore as *Xauerius* came thither, he found
very many of the Nobility , and more of the vulgar
ſort, deſirous to know the Chriſtian Religion, wherof they had long ſince heard many things by report .
He therfore obſerued this order, that twice euery day
at the corners of ſtreetes, and in croſſe-wayes before
a great concourſe of people he explicated the Ghoſpel
of Chriſt out of a written paper , for he had not yet
gotten the *Iaponian* language perfectly ; yet all did not
with the like proſperous ſucceſſe giue eare vnto the
word of God : many did indeed hearken very willingly thereto, but more contemned the ſame; ſome alſo
laughed thereat in ſkornefull manner. In ſo much,

that when *Xauerius* went along in the ſteetes, a great
company of boyes, and baſer people followed, and
mocked him as though he had byn out of his wits, repeating alſo in a ſcoffing manner many words of the
ſacred myſteryes, and Chriſtian lawes which he had
read vnto him . All which things he bare patiently &
ioyfully, not conſidering ſo much the reproach, as the
cauſe thereof : ſo as he did much more good by his patient ſuffering , then by words . For the wiſer ſort of
his auditours, ſeeing playnly that he was no foole, admired at his ſingular patience, and quietneſſe of mynd
in the midſt of ſuch diſgracefull reproaches and con-
tumeli-

tumelious words, efpecially when they heard, that he
was come out of *Europe* into *Iaponia*, through fuch
huge and vaft feas, for no other end, but only out of
zeale to teach them a new Religion.

At laft, his ftrange vertue & fanctity of lyfe began
to be held in great admiration and reuerence, and to
manifeft it felfe not only by words, but by deeds alfo.
Whereupon many Noblemen defirous to know more
particularly, what Religion that was which he had
brought out of the other world, fent for him home to
their houfes, promifing of their owne accord, that
if he could yield good reafons of thofe ceremonies,
which he had introduced amongft them, they would
preferre them before thofe of their owne Country.
But this indeed was now a bufineffe, not confifting
in the wil, or any indeauour of ours, but in the mercy
of God. There were diuers others alfo who heard thefe
things, but moft of them attended therto, more with
their corporall eares, then with any interiour defire
they had to imbrace them. *Xauerius*, hauing thus fpent
fome dayes in the ftreetes, and in priuate houfes not
without fruit, was at laft fent for by the King himfelfe : who demaunded of him his Country, and the
caufe of his comming into *Iaponia*. He anfwered, that
he was a Spaniard borne, and came thither to preach
vnto them the law of God, out of the care, and zeale
which he had of their faluation. For that none could
be faued who did not acknowledge God the Creatour
of this vniuerfall World, and Iefus Chrift his only
Sonne the Sauiour of all Nations; and moreouer keep
his diuine lawes, and Precepts. Whereupon, being

Noble-men fed for him to their houfes.

R r 2 com-

He prea-
cheth
the Gof-
pell to
the King

commáded by the King to declare what that law was,
he willingly obeyed, & began to recite the fame out of
the booke which he had written. He was heard with
great attention, and admiration, for the fpace of an
hower or there about. But the barbarous King being
better difpofed to heare, then to performe thofe heauenly things, was careleffe of what was fayd.

Xauerius then applying himfelfe againe to his former function of preaching (as cuftome doth by little
and little qualify the moft vnruly difpofitions) found
the minds of the people more indifferently difpofed,

The Eth
nickes at
the hea-
ring of
Chrifts
torméts
fal a wee-
ping.

and began to reape more fruit of his labours. For that
now very many gaue willing eare to the admirable
paffages of our Sauiours life which he recounted. But
when he came to relate his bitter torments, and moft
vnworthy death, they could not conteine themfelues
from weping, the fame feeming, euen to the Barbarians harts, fo greatly to deferue compaffion. Thus
Mercy it felfe opened the way vnto Religion, & fome
began already to be Chriftians. But *Francis* thinking
it not worth his labour to remaine any longer in that
Citty, determined to go vnto *Meaco*, with intention
to demand of that King (who by reafon of the ampli-
tude of his Empire, is called the great King) permiffió

The
great
King of
Meaco.

to preach the Ghofpell. For he had vnderftood that
Meaco was the nobleft and chiefeft Citty of all *Iapon*,
and very famous as wel for the greatnes therof, as for
the fame of the Colledges (being alfo a prime Academy) & multitude of Conuéts therin; in fo much that
at his firft entrance into *Iaponia* he was in the mind to
haue gone directly thither. But God fauouring thofe

of

of *Cangoxima*, the ſhip, as we ſaid before, arriued thither firſt, where hopes of good ſucceſſe for the Chriſtian Cauſe, had longer deteyned him, then the fruit which he reaped therby. Being reſolued therfore to go vnto *Meaco*, he tooke with him for his companions *Iohn Fernandez* of the Society, and *Bernard* a Neophyte of *Iaponia*, a ſincere good man, & the firſt that became Chriſtian at *Cangoxima*.

CHAP. VI.

Of the great paynes vvhich he tooke in his iourney to Meaco.

THE Citty of *Meaco* ſtandeth almoſt in the midſt of the *Iland*, as it were the Nauil, of *Iapon*. It is diſtant from *Amangucium*, which is ſcituate in the firſt entrāce of the Iland, not aboue 150. miles, by a direct lyne. But the way of paſſing thither is much longer, by reaſon of the montaynes, and the many turnings & windings about thoſe narrow armes of the ſea. Thither did *Xauerius* direct his iorney in the yeare 1550. and month of October, at what tyme the weather is very could and bitter in *Iapon*. The way was then not only rough and craggy, but couered alſo with perpetuall ſnow, which the hard froſty winter had congealed togeather. Throughout the woods there hunge downe from the trees as it were certaine yſicles, like beames of congealed Snow, and Ice, threatning death and

deſtru-

deſtruction to all paſſengers who trauayled that way.
Beſides this, there was no ſmall daunger in reſpect
of the continuall ciuill warres, wherewith the whole
Country was then exceedingly peſtered; as alſo of
the great number of theeues wherewith thoſe woods
and wayes were ordinarily, yea daily haunted, and
infeſted.

Notwithſtanding all theſe, & many other vnſpeakable miſeries of the way, *Xauerius* hauing his mynd
wholy fixed vpon the Diuine Prouidence, and Saluation of Soules, vndertooke with incredible ioy, and
iubilation of hart, that ſo long and daungerous a iorney, entring into the ſame, euen in the moſt vnſeaſonable tyme of the yeare. And that he might the more
freely paſſe through ſo Barbarous a Countrey, and
ſauage a Nation; and withall to enioy the company,
and commodity of a Guide in ſo tedious, and vncouth a iourney, he maketh himſelf a ſeruant, and becommeth a Lacky to a certayne *Iaponian* Gentleman
of that Countrey, who by chance he met withall,
trauayling a horſebacke vpon buſineſſe to *Meaco*; accounting it an honourable thinge to ſerue a Barbarian, or Inſidell, euen in the baſeſt office, for Chriſt
his ſake.

Francis therefore, running a foote by his Maiſters ſide, ouer and aboue the burden of his owne
furniture for ſaying of Maſſe, and adminiſtring of
other Sacraments, he carryed at his backe his Mayſters implements and baggage, who rode on horſebacke, and euen diſdayned to carry his owne neceſſaries himſelf, when he found commodity of another

to

*Xauerius
maketh
himſelf
lacky
to one
that ri-
des on
horſe-
backe.*

to do it for him. Befides, the *Iaponian* when he was
to paffe through any theeuifh place, for feare of rob-
bing, fpurred on his horfe, more like one that were
running a race, then an ordinary trauayler by the
way; and this without any compaffion at all of his
Lacky, whome he faw, was not able to follow him
keeping on that pace, efpecially through fuch durty,
and vneuen way, and with fo heauy a burden on
his backe.

Therefore, for the moft part, he was forced
to trauayle barefoote, by reafon of the many and often flowes and plafhes of water he met withall, and
other little brookes that he was to paffe ouer. In fo
much that hauing his feete oftentymes greatly fwol-
len with fnow, and cold weather, he trauayled with
exceeding great payne; being alfo, partly through
running after his Mayfter, and partly through the
weight of both his burdens, that he carryed at his
backe, euen wholy fpent, and tyred out. Befides
being not able to take fure footing, by reafon of the
flyppineffe of the yce, and roughneffe of the way,
he receaued many a fore, and painefull fall.

The labours and miferies of his iourney to Meaco.

All which intollerable difficulties he not only o-
uercame with great quiet of mynd, but had with
withall his cogitations fo firmely fixed vpon God,
that euen at that very tyme he became wholy abftracted from his fenfes. For fuch was the force of his
heauenly contemplation, and fo greatly was he o-
uercome with the fweetnes thereof, that fcarfely
knowing what he did, he many tymes ran among the
brambles and bufhes, and ftrooke his feete agaynft
the

the ftones euen till the bloud came out, without any feeling or payne at all. Now at night he was commonly in as bad a plight as in the day. For oftentymes being all wet, and euen wholy fpent with cold and hungar, he came at night to his Inne, where there was no humane comfort to be had, nor any eafe for thefe his miferies. Wherof this may be a fufficient proofe, that during all that iorney, he eate nothing but only ryce (which himfelfe alfo begged as he trauailed) with no leife want of food then payne of body. Moreouer the infolency of the Country people, to thefe his miferies which he fuffred in the way, added fauce of the fame nature. For the *Iaponians* being of a proud and haughty fpirit, & feing him a ftranger, contemptible, vnexpert in their complements and behauiour, & one that contemned himfelfe, vfed him euen like a poore foole, or fotte : fo as in townes and villages where he was to paffe in boates, as alfo vpon the way, and in the Innes, he was the fubiect for euery one to play vpon. But all this he bare, not only patiently, but cheerfully alfo, reioycing with the Apoftle *to be for Chrift his fake reputed a foole, & the outcaft of all.* And hauing thus fpent two whole months vpon the way, after innumerable miferies paffed both by water and land, at laft through the goodnes of God he arriued fafe and found at *Meaco.*

Meaco is the royall Citty, and the greateft and moft famous of all *Iaponia.* This Citty when it flourifhed (if we will belieue what is reported therof) conteined well neere two hundred thoufand families; but hauing bin oftentimes deftroyed by warres, pillage & fire

Xauier is vfed like a foole.

fire it is now little more then halfe so great. The Circuit indeed of the walls, and the vastnes of the Citty do yet well shew to haue byn no lesse in forme times then that which hath byn sayd therof; but now when *Xauerius* came thither, it had only about one hundred thousand houses. There is in this Citty a very famous Academy, fiue principall Colledges of Schollers, and innumerable Conuents of men, and women: so as there seemed to be offered to *Xauerius* abundant matter to worke vpon. But so secret are the iudgments of God, that his hope wholy vanished away, & came to nothing.

As soone therefore as he came to *Meaco,* he expected some dayes at the Court, wayting for opportunity to come vnto the Kings presence, and to aske his licence to preach the Ghospell in his kingdome; but in vayne. For his ignorance of the *Iaponian* customes and behauiour, his vulgar, and worne-out apparell, and his Christian simplicity caused him to be derided, and wholy reiected by the Kings Guard. Finding therfore all passages vnto the King to be stopped in such sort, that he could not by any meanes get accesse vnto him; and vnderstanding that certayne Noblemen, who, by reason that the King of *Meaco's* Regall authority began to grow now out of date, had withdrawn themselues from his obedience, changing his determination, and leauing off all thought of obtayning the King Letters-Patents, began to try the *Meacensians* themselues how they stood affected towards the Christian Religion. But finding the whole Cittty in perplexity, and solicitous expectation, and

Xauerius is derided by the Kings guard.

S s   feare

feare of warres which were then cōming vpon them,
he loſt his tyme and labour in ſpeaking to them, who
had their eares, & mynds wholy bent another way.

He is
thowne
at with
ſtones.

    Moreouer, when he preached in the ſtreets to the
people that ſtood round about him (which had alſo
hapned to him in other townes) the boyes, and baſer
ſorte of people, threw old ſhoes, and ſtones alſo at
his head to driue him away; ſo far was obſtinate Superſtition from opening her eares, or vnderſtanding
to admit of wholeſome doctrine. But he went away,
*reioycing that he had byn held worthy to ſuffer reproach for
the name of I E S V S.* At laſt when he ſaw the Citty to
be both diſquieted in it ſelfe, & wholy auerted frō the
Ghoſpel, it much grieued him that after ſo lōg & pain-
full a iourney, he was to depart without doing any
good, hauing not ſo much as reaped one handfull out
of ſo large & ſpacious a field. But leauing all to Gods
diuine prouidence, he returneth agayne to *Amangucium*, comforting himſelfe with this conſideration,
That it is a great honour, not only to do, but alſo to
ſuffer for Chriſt.

CHAP.

CHAP. VII.

Hauing by Preſents obtayned the King of
Amangucium *his fauour, he conuerteth*
many to the Chriſtian Faith.

RETVRNING therfore to *Amangucium* with almoſt as much trauell and miſery, as he had gone from thence to *Meaco*, he determined preſently to go vnto the King, & to deliuer him certaine letters, and preſents from the Viceroy of *India*, and the Biſhop of *Goa*, which he had left at *Firandum*. He intended to haue preſented theſe guiſts to the King of *Meaco*, who was ſayd to be the greateſt of all *Iaponia*: but when he perceiued that he raigned now at other mens pleaſures, and that his authority was not ſo great as his Name, and withall, that the King of *Amangucium* was very potent and wealthy, changing his determination, he thought it beſt to preſent them vnto him; deeming it not amiſſe to gaine his fauour by guifts, who was by his authority beſt able to helpe the Chriſtian cauſe. So returning ſpeedily to *Firandum*, he bethinkes himſelfe of a new meanes to obteine acceſſe vnto the King, the which neceſſity had forced him vnto.

He had now learnt by experience, that the *Iaponians* (according to the common corruption of mortalls) eſteemed men by the outward ſhew, and orna-

ment

ment of their body, & that any one in poore cloathes was scarce accounted a man amongst them : as if the worth of man consisted rather in his outward attyre, then in his vertuous disposition . Wherefore laying aside his old worne coate ; he resolued to cloath himselfe in Court-like habit ; and by the splendour of his ornaments, so to feed the eyes of such as were carryed away, rather by the exteriour shew of things then by that which was truly good indeed, that afterwards he might bring them to conceiue the light of Truth. As soone therfore as he came backe againe to *Amangucium*, putting himselfe into rich apparell, and with two or three seruáts attending him, he went vnto the King. And the euent declared his prudence heerein. For being presently brought in to the King by his officers, he is by him receiued in a very friendly & courteous manner . Then making a short speach before hand, he deliuereth vnto the King, from the Viceroy of *India* , and Bishop of *Goa*, as pledges of their friendship, Letters, and certaine outlandish Presents, among which there was a Musicall Instrument , & a Watch, things very gratefull , and much esteemed in those places, not so much for the value, as for the rarity, and curiosity of the workemanship.

The King therfore being wonderfully glad for these letters & guiftes which the Portugheses had sent him, presents againe *Xauerius* very bountifully with a great quantity of siluer, & gold. But he remembring himselfe to be a Priest of God, & no merchant, giueth backe againe the things which were offred him , and withall earnestly requested the King, that he would

by

Marginal notes (left column):

By putting on rich apparell he procureth to speake with the King.

He presenteth his guifts to the King.

He refuseth the Kings guifts.

by his Royall Edict giue him leaue to publifh the diuine Law throughout his dominions, and his fubiects
to receiue the fame: for that nothing could be more
gratefull to his and the Portughefes defire, then that.
At which words the King being ftroken with admiration at his temperance, who defpifed that which o-
thers fought after with fo great dangers both by fea &
land, made no difficulty to fauour his Religion whofe
vertue he admired . Wherupon without any further
delay, he commandeth a Proclamation to be made
throughout all the ftreets of the Citty, that it was his
Royall pleafure , that the Chriftian Religion fhould
be propounded to his fubiects , and that whofoeuer
would, might become Chriftians: And that none
fhould either by deed or word offer any affront to the
Portughefe Priefts; neither fhould any of his fubiects
fuffer any detriment, or difgrace for hauing forfaken
his country Religion. Befides this alfo, the better to
enable *Xauerius* to performe that which was granted
vnto him, he gaue him for his dwelling place a certaine Conuent of the *Bonzies*, which then was voyd .

The
Kings E-
dict for
the
Chriftan
Religiō.

    This gayned both credit to *Xauerius*, and efteeme
to his Religion . For many defirous to know the new
Religion came flocking to heare him; nor was *Xauerius* wanting to giue them fatisfaction , hauing now
gotten fome pretty skill in their language. Twice
therefore euery day did he preach vnto the people, before a great affembly of the Cittizens . After he had
ended his fermon , he fpent fome tyme in conference
with his auditours about that which he had propounded vnto them out of the pulpit, eyther by anfwering

to

to their queſtions, or elſe by queſtioning them. Theſe
diſputes cōming one vpon the necke of another, held
out moſt commonly till it was very late in the night,
ſo that he had ſcarcely any leaſure to prouide for his
corporall neceſſities. And in all this buſineſſe nothing
hindred him ſo much, as his vnperfectneſſe in the *Iaponian* language. For oftentymes when any vnpro-
per word ſounded harſh to their nice and delicate eares, they laughed at his ignorant pronunciation. And
there wanted not ſome alſo, who did load him with
queſtions, for no other end, but to fynd out ſomething whereat to laugh.

But ſuch was the ſpirit which he ſpake with
all, ſuch the ſanctity of his lyfe and Religion, and ſo
farre excelling the lyfe and doctrine of the *Bonzies*,
that what he could not effect by words, he cleerly demonſtrated by deeds. Wherefore the *Iaponians* being
an ingenious nation, & much led by reaſon, ſaw now
well inough that the things he ſpake, had very good
ſenſe & connexion, howſoeuer he vttered them in bad
language. Many therefore came vnto him out of the
Couents both of *Bonzies* & *Bonzieſſes*; many alſo of the
Nobility, but much greater was the nūber of the vulgar ſort. The houſe was continually filled with people of all qualities, and many tymes it could not conteine the multitude which came thither. The queſtions which were diſputed to and fro, were ſo many &
diuerſe, that the foggy miſt of errour being diſperſed,
and the light of truth ſpreading abroad its glorious
beames, many perceiued by *Francis* his anſweres,
how vaine & falſe their ſuperſtitions were, and that
the

the diuine Law was true and folid : and this diligence of theirs to find out by examination the true Religion was feconded alfo on their part, with as great forwardneffe in receauing the fame.

Some dayes therfore being fpent in asking & anfwering Queftions, many became Chriftians, wherin thofe who had bin formerly the chiefe men, in obftinately ouerthwarting and contradicting *Xauerius* in his fermons and difputations, gaue the firft example; God turning their fpirit of contradiction into a mild & plyable difpofition. And heerin, Patience, and not Learning only, carried away the chiefe prize. For as *Fernandez, Xauerius* companion, was preaching to the people in the publike ftreet, a certaine *Iaponian* paffing by by chance, came to his fermon; who being an infolet rude fellow gathering his mouth full of fpitle, cafteth it forth, full into the preachers face, in fight of al the people: who bare that difgrace with fuch admirable patience, that he was not moued one whit therat, but only wept his face with a handkercher, and fo went on with his fermon. Wherupon one of the Affembly was fo moued by that example of Patience, that he verily belieued men endowed with fuch vertue, could not teach any Religion but that which was holy. And fo repayring to *Francis*, was inftructed, and the firft of all that was baptized.

Others afterwards followed his example. Amnogft whome, one *Laurentius Lusko* conceiued within his foule, fuch impreffions of diuine light, that quite abandoning all earthly things, he confecrated himfelfe wholy to Gods feruice, to the great good of *Iaponia*.

Fernãdez vertue at a certayne Iaponians infolency.

The force of patience to conuert Ethnickes.

Laurence Lufko a notable preacher

For

For being by *Xauerius* receiued into the Society, he became afterwards a notable Preacher, and brought
very many of his Country-men to the light of the
Ghofpell. After this many of good note were receiued
to the facred fountaine of Baptifme, who being therby bound to *Francis* in the higheft degree, endeauoured fo to gratify his loue, that they could neuer fatisfy themfelues therin. When he therfore asked them
about the *Iaponians* Sectes, and Religions, they difcouered all vnto him, and that with more freedome and
forwardneffe, then they were demaunded.

CHAP. VIII.

Hauing found out the Sects of the Iaponi-
ans, *he conuerteth many of them.*

The *Ia-*
ponian
fectes.

Y thefe men therfore, he got a farre more
exact knowledge, then before he had done
of the *Iaponians* Religions, & Ceremonies.
There were in all, amongft them, nine
principall Sectes, as well of men as women, wherof it was free for euery one to follow that Sect which
beft pleafed him : Whence it came oftentimes to paffe
that there were in the fame houfe almoft as many different opinions, as there were feuerall perfons, and all
at ftrife amogft themfelues, euery one endeauoring to
preferre their own fect before others. Among al thefe
Sects, there was not one which taught any thing co-
cerning the world, or the foules Creatio. And no meruayle

meruayle, fince they all togeather held, that they had no beginning . Yet they all agreed in this , that after this lyfe there be two places , one for the damned, the other for the bleſſed . But what manner of abyding place the bleſſed haue , or by whoſe power ſoules are thruſt downe into Hell, there was no mention at all amongſt them : only they ſpread abroad certayne old wiues tales, of the Authours of their Religion, among whome one *Xacas* and *Amidas* were eſteemed the prin-cipall Gods, who of their owne accord vnderwent moſt grieuous, and very long paynes, to ſaue the reſt.

Xacas & Amidas the Iapo-niš Gods

Of theſe Sectes , ſome of them conteyne 300. precepts , others fiue hundred ; yet they all hold that there be fiue points only neceſſary to ſaluation, wher-by is forbidden Murder, Eating of any liuing creature that is killed, Theft , Adultery & Lying, & the Drin-king of Wine . Theſe the *Bonzies,* & the *Bonzieſſes* vn-dertooke to ſatisfy for the people, who being hindred through the cares & affayres of the Citty , could not obſerue theſe lawes ; but yet vpon this conditiõ , that they ſhould allow them houſes to dwel in, yearely re-uenewes, & other maintenance ; & withal (forſooth) ſhould do them honour & reuerence . Wherupon the wealthier ſort of people, and the Nobility , that they might haue freer leaue to ſin, accepting of the condi-tions, gaue then readily whatſoeuer they demaunded, making no doubt but the *Bonzies* prayers would reſ-cue them , euen out of hell it ſelf. Beſids this, the *Bõ-zies* begge almes of all men , but giue to none.

The Bon-zies wic-kednes and aua-rice.

Now when *Xauerius* had found out theſe, & other ſuch like things, turning the *Iaponians* own practiſes as

T t   wea-

weapons againſt themſelues, he began in ſuch ſort to
deale with the *Bonzies* before the people, as that by
euident arguments and reaſons, he ouerthrew their
counterfaite fictions. But eſpecially he demonſtrated vnto them, that none could, by the *Bonzies* prayers, be freed from the torments of Hell, ſeeing that it
was certayne, they did not obſerue thoſe conditions
themſelues, which they had vndertaken to obſerue
for others. For it was manifeſtly knowen, that they
being now fallen frō their ancient diſcipline, vſed to
drinke wine, to eate fleſh priuately, and publikely to
Lye, and commit Adultery. Whereupon the people,
when they ſaw the *Bonzies* falſe dealing laid open before their face, began to be all-enraged, and to complayne, that they had by their treachery byn deceaued, and robbed of their goods. The truth whereof the *Bonzies* themſelues were driuen at laſt to con-
feſſe, ſaying ; that vnleſſe they had by their wits vpheld themſelues, they ſhould infallibly haue periſhed
with hunger. And ſo from this tyme forward, they
not only ſuffred many loſſes, but foule diſgraces alſo.

  Then *Xauerius* vnderſtanding by the relation of
of ſome *Iaponians* his friends, & by their ancient written Records, that *Xacas* and *Amidas* had liued full out
two thouſand yeares, and that *Xacas* had byn borne
eight thouſand tymes, and much other ſuch like ſtuffe
deſeruing rather to be laughed at, then recounted ;
he preſently with great inſtance ſet himſelfe to can-
uaſe out theſe idle fables, ſhewing that they were not
Gods, but diueliſh Monſters. Whereto when the *Bonzies* themſelues, the Sorcerers, & other aduerſaryes of
          God

*The Ia-
poniās fa-
bles of
Xacas &
Amidas.*

God (being vtterly vanquished) had nothing to say;
the Chriſtians were indeed very glad, and much cōfirmed in the fayth,and courſe which they had vndertaken : And the Ethnickes that were preſent,percei-
uing their Mayſters errours,began to ſtagger in their
owne Religion, and by litle and litle retyred themſelues to the ſtandard of Chriſt .

The *Bonzies* againe,vrged *Francis* with the authority of the *Chineſes*, from whome the *Iaponians* had
fetcht their Religion : and therfore that the *Iaponians*
would certainly neuer change their Religion, and ceremonies, vnleſſe the *Chineſes* firſt changed theirs.
Wherfore he ſhould goe, and carry the Ghoſpell thither firſt, and bring the *Chineſes* vnder the yoke of
Chriſt ; and when he had ſo done,then would *Iaponia*
alſo willingly imbrace the faith and Religion that he
taught. But theſe ſayings of the *Bonzies*, were litle or
no hindrance at all to *Xauerius* endeauours,who went
on neuer the ſlower with that which he had reſolued
vpon. The *Iaponians*, who had neuer heard any thing
at all of the Creation of the Sunne, Moone, Starres,
celeſtiall Globes, Land, Sea, Soules, & other things,
did not, for the moſt part, acknowledge any author
or maker of the world. When *Francis* therfore ſhewed
them that God was the Creatour of all things,and eſpecially of ſoules, they wondred very much that ſuch
a beginning of all things, had bin wholy hidden and
vnknowen,not only to the *Iaponians*, but alſo to the
Chineſes,from whence they had their Religion.At laſt
their admiration came to this, that looke how much
they reuerenced *Xauerius* & the ChriſtianReligion;ſo

*The Ia-
ponians
ignorāt
in aſtro-
logy .*

Tt 2   much

much they detefted the *Bonzies*, & the *Iaponian* Sectes.

By thefe difputations therfore *Xauerius* did fo vexe the whole generatió of the *Bonzies*, that they who before his comming, were continually iarring amongft themfelues about their owne Lawes, new leauing off that quarrell, there was no other fpeach among them, but of the law of God. And euery day there came many, who asked of *Francis* diuers queftions: as whether there were one beginning of good & bad things? And whether that, were good or bad, it felf? When he replyed, that there was but one beginning of all, and that good in the higheft degree; they alleadged againft him, the euill fpirits, enemies of mankind, who were certaynly knowne to be naught: If then God were good, why did he create fuch deteftable creatures as they were? Then *Xauerius* anfwered, that God had created them all good, who by their owne fault were become bad, and therfore were tormented eternally in Hell. But then they vrged him, why did God permit men, whome he had created to ferue him, to be deceyued by the Deuils? And why had he not created their affections rather inclined to vertue, then prone to vice? To which *Francis* demonftrated, that man was free by nature, & had diuine helps at hand, both to combat and get the victory, if he would make vfe therof: and withall fhewed, that al mankind was framed to honeft and vertuous carriage, but was by the finne of their Parents, and their owne faults growne depraued. Then they fly from mans fault to Gods feuerity, & aske him; Why he made that infernall prifon of Hell, the greateft of all euills? And why would

he

he neuer shew mercy to them that be condemned to e-
ternall torments ? *Xauerius* contrarywise declared vnto them , that such was the Maiesty of God , and so
great his benefits bestowed vpon all men , and euery
one in particular, that there could be no torment foūd
so great , which was not due to man for his abomina ·
ble wickednes ; who being a base worme of the earth,
durst violate the infinite power of Almighty God: yet
such againe was the diuine Mercy & Clemency , that
he alwayes punished lesse, then was deserued .

Thefe, & many other such things were heard with
exceeding good liking , so as they were all easily satisfied . But that which troubled thē most, that God
seemed neither bountifull nor indifferēt, who hauing
care of all other Countries besides *Iaponia* , had neuer
declared himselfe to the *Iaponians*, before *Francis* his
comming thither : Who likewise, had damned to the
paynes of Hell, all those who had not worshipped the
God they knew not ; and had permitted also their an-
cestours, who neuer enioyed that heauēly light,to be
carryed headlong thither ? Concerning this point
Francis made it cleare vnto thē , that the diuine Law,
which of all others is the most ancient , was imprin-
ted in the harts of men . For the *Iaponians* euen before
they had their lawes from the *Chinefes* , knew by the
light of reason that it was an heynous offence to kill
a man , to steale , forsweare , and other things which
were forbidden by the diuine law. Wherupon if any
one had committed any of these crimes, he was tormented with the worme of conscience , which tooke
as it were reuenge of that wickednesse . This (quoth
he)

he) we may vndoubtedly find to be true, in a folitary
man , who although he fhould be brought vp in the
wilderneffe , without any learning or knowledge of
humane law, would not for all that be ignorant of the
diuine law , concerning Man-flaughter, Theft, Periu-
ry, and other the like things. And if this were fo, euen
amongft barbarous nations, what fhould we thinke of
thofe , that were ciuill, and well trained vp ? Should
not they therfore be iuftly punifhed , who did violate
the diuine law, which was ingrafted in them by nature? which if they had obferued , they fhould infallibly haue bin illuminated with light from heauen .

After he had fatisfied them with this anfwere,
they began by little and little to put themfelues vnder
the wholfome yoke of Chrift . Wherupon within the
compaffe of two moneths, there were wel neere 500.
cittizens baptized , who bewailing the ftate of their
children , parents, kindred, and Anceftours , demanded ofté of *Xauerius*, whether there was yet any hope,
or meanes to deliuer them out of euerlafting mifery ?
But he with teares in his eyes affirming no , exhorted
them, that they who had the diuine light & faluation,
now offred them, fhould be fo much the more thanke-
full to God for it , and fhould mitigate the feeling of
others ruine, with the hope of their owne faluation: fo
that Patience might make that lighter, which they
could not auoid .

Then turning themfelues to other queftions, they
asked him of what figure the world was? what courfe
the funne and the ftarres held? from whence came the
blazing Comets, the winds, lightning, and thunder?
what

Margin note: 500. Iaponians baptized

what force that was which powred forth fnow, haile,
and fhowres of raine? Of all which, when *Xauerius*,
who was very skilfull in Aftrology, & natural Philofophy, had fully declared to thē the caufes, they being
wholy ignorant before of all fuch things, ftood wholy
amazed therat, admiring both his wit, and learning,
hauing neuer heard of the like. And when the report
hereof was fpread ouer all the Citty, it brought alfo
fuch efteeme to the Chriftian Law, that it was much
fpoken of, not only in publick, but alfo at home in priuate houfes. This thing alfo caufed no leffe domage to
the *Bonzies* families, then it did good to the Chriftian
caufe, by auerting the affections of many from their
country Superftitiōs: fo as fome were of opiniō, that
many *Bonzies* forfaking their manner of difcipline, &
their corporall maintenance failing them, many of
their Conuentes would heereby fall to decay, to the
great aduancement certainly of the Chriftian caufe.
And how much the *Bonzies* authority was weakened heereby, may euen appeare by this, in that there
was neuer a one amongft them all, though neuer fo
zealous, who was not detained in his former courfe,
rather out of neceffity, then for any affection he bare
vnto it.

There was in *Amangucium* a certaine Noble man
fo rich & wealthy, as few in that kind outwent him.
He, togeather with his wife, exceedingly fauoured
both *Xauerius* and the Ghofpell; but their too much
forwardneffe in former times did much abridge them
of their liberty afterward. For they had built many
houfes for the *Bonzies*, and endowed them with great
reuene-

reuenewes , to the end that *Amidas* , to whome they bare ſpecial deuotion & reuerēce, might be propitious vnto them for the attayning of eternall bliſſe . Where-upon they ſtood earneſtly vpon it , that they would neuer by changing their Religion vpō a ſuddain, looſe *Amidas* his fauour , which they had now purchaſed with ſuch expences , for ſo many yeares togeather ; & that if this were not, wᶜʰ lay heauy vpon their cōſciences, they would be otherwiſe aduiſed: ſhewing heer-in a double folly, who hauing once raſhly cōmitted an errour, had rather ſtill remaine plunged therein, then once to rayſe themſelues out . But that which they , out of a vaine reſpeƈt of their ancient inſtitute, would not do, to follow the glorious faith of Chriſt, was zea-louſly performed by many others , who were illumi-nated with the light of truth .

The *Bonzies* therfore, being not able to indure this ignominy, and diſgrace, began to be enraged agaynſt the Chriſtians , and in their Sermons to caſt out ma-ny impious wordes againſt God ; alſo to belch forth many reproches againſt *Xauerius* , which ſuited better with themſelues ; and withall to denounce vnto the *Iaponians* in a threatning manner , that as ſoone as *Iaponia* had receiued the faith of Chriſt , it ſhould be vt-terly deſtroyed . But theſe their reproachfull ſpeaches cauſed more hatred to themſelues, then cōtempt vnto *Xauerius* . For the *Iaponians* knowing for certaine that the *Bonzies* maledictions proceeded out of enuy and malice, begā not only to find fault therewith , but alſo to fauour the innocent , by turning their backbiting into *Xauerius* prayſe , and reſpeƈt towards his perſon.

In

In the meane time *Francis* making moſt diligent inquiry whether the *Iaponians* had had in times paſt any knowledge of Chriſt, & his Ghoſpell, found both by their writings, and teſtimony of the *Iaponians* thēſelues, that they had neuer ſo much as heard of the name of Chriſt before his comming: which thing (as good reaſon it ſhould) gaue the ſpurre to *Xauerius* feruent deſire, who was of himſelfe forward inough, in ſpreading abroad the Ghoſpell, being exceeding ioyfull that he was come thither for the aduancement of Religion : & that the ſound of the Goſpell which had bin heard in the furtheſt parts of the Land, might alſo now be preached in the vtmoſt Ilands thereof. Many therefore being thus brought into the fold of Chriſt, Chriſtianity began greatly to flouriſh, when as there hapned an accident which cauſed much furtherāce & honour thereunto. There is at *Bandua* in *Iaponia*, an Academy of very great note, both for the fame & nobility therof, as being frequented by more then 4000. ſtudēts. One of this Academy, a man of good eſteeme, and renowned for his wiſedome and learning, vpon a very memorable occaſion, became a Chriſtian.

The Japonians had receyued no knowledge of Chriſt & his Goſpell.

There were in that Academy a kind of *Bonzies* who gaue themſelues much to ſpeculatiō, pondering what would become of thē after this life, & other ſuch like things: wherof many through deep cōſideration, came atlaſt to be of opinion, that there was no meanes in the *Iaponians* Religion for the ſauing of their ſoules. For thus they diſcourſed with themſelues : That certainly there ought to be one beginning of all things, wherof in their Books & Records there was no mention at al,

The Academy of Bandua.

nor of the maker of this world. How therefore could they be faued who knew not their maker? But whilst others stood staggering betwixt shame and feare, this man, of whome we speake, ouercomming the one & the other, through desire of his saluation, was made a Christian. He was indeed of the mynd to haue vnited himselfe to the *Bonzies*; but as soone as by *Francis* his discourse he came to know their errours, thinking that he ought certainly to worship him that made both him, and the whole world, and whome the Christian Religion propounded vnto them to adore, changing his mind, he put himselfe vnder the triumphant standart of Christ.

The *Japonian* Neophites zeale.

This accident grieued the *Bonzies* no lesse, then it comforted the Neophytes. For when he for his learning, bare away the bell from the whole Citty where he dwelt, his authority gaue great aduantage to either part. Whereupon inciting others by his example to Baptisme, the Christian Common wealth began to be increased both in dignity and number. And this caused in the Neophytes such feruour of spirit, that euery one of them fell to dispute with the Ethnickes about matters of Religion: and when they had conuinced them, would lead them, as captiues to Baptisme, striuing in these their combats, and victories one with another. Whereat *Francis* took such content of mind, that it made him to haue no feeling of his labours.

Within the space of one yeare he baptizeth 3000.

Thus therfore was the Christian busines wonderfully increased at *Amangucium* (for within the compasse of one yeare there were baptized to the number of 3000.) and their piety equalized the increase of the flocke.

flocke. For they who in former tymes had fo often run
ouer their beades , by imploring the Authours of their
Sect; now turning fuperftition into true Religion, increafed wonderfully that deuotion of theirs . For in
faying the Beades of our Bleffed Lady, at the end of e-
uery *Aue Maria* (which is vfually faid vpon euery fmal
Bead) they always pronounced the wholefome na-
mes of *Iefus* and *Maria,* and withall endeauoured, as *Iaponian*
much as they could, to frame themfelues according to Beades.
Francis his fafhiõ , as being the only patterne they had
to imitate . And fo great was the progreffe in piety
which the *Amangucian* Neophytes made vnder *Xaue-*
rius their Maifter, that although , when he was called
away by other Kings who importuned him , they
were left almoft wholy deftitute both of maifters and
teachers, for the fpace of 25. yeares , in the midft of
Ethnickes : yet they held on moft laudably the fayd
Chriftian courfe which they had begun, being therin both guides, and maifters to themfelues.

CHAP. IX.

Going to the King of Bungo, at his inui-
tement , he is honourably receyued by
the Portughefes .

 O great was now *Xauerius* Name in *Iapo-*
nia , and fo great was the opinion of his
Sanctity , that it almoft exceeded all humane power : wherefore the *Iaponians* reuerenced

uerenced him as a diuine man. This fame of his Holines fpreading it felf farre & neere, had filled almoſt
all *Iaponia* with his renowne, and worthy acts. Whilſt
therefore he was imployed, efpecially at *Amangucium*
about the occafions whereof we fpake before, he
receyueth from the King of *Bungo* very courteous, &
refpectful letters to this tenour: That wheras by relation of a certaine Portugefe ſhip that was lately arriued in his Dominiōs, he had vnderſtood many things
of his fingular vertue ; and being greatly defirous to
impart an important bufineffe to his owne perfon, he
would be pleafed to repaire withal fpeed to *Bungo* &c.
At the very fame tyme alfo, one *Edward Gama* Gouernour of the Portughefe ſhips, had by his letters inuited *Francis* to a port Towne of *Bungo*, diſtāt 180. miles
from *Amangucium*. *Xauerius* therefore, conceauing
in ech place new hopes of happy fucceffe in his bufineffe, leauing *Cofmas Turrianus,* and *Iohn Fernandez*
to looke vnto the Neophytes at *Amangucium,* he prepareth himfelfe for this new iourney, and forthwith
fetteth forward oh his way, with two or three Neophytes in his company.

He had now gone almoſt 175. miles on foote,
when as *Gama* vnderſtood that he was comming on
his way, all wearied-out with trauailing a foot: wherfore he fpeedily fendeth out certaine Portughefes
with horfes to meete him; who hauing gone about a
mile, met with *Francis,* and his Neophytes. Thefe Neophytes were of noble Parentage in their owne country, and heertofore of great wealth ; but hauing had
all their goods taken from them by the King of *A-*
mangucium

Francis
is fent
for by
the King
of *Bungo*.

mangucium, becaufe they were become Chriftians, they went with *Xauerius* with intention to be brought vp at *Goa.* They rode vpon excellent horfes with good furniture, for fo *Xauerius* had commanded them. But he followed them on foote, loaden with his packe of Church-ftuffe, fo ardent was his loue to Humility, & the Croffe. This fight moued the Portughefes no leffe to admiration, then compaffion, that fo worthy a man, fhould in fuch fort fo debafe, and tyre out himfelfe. Prefently therfore they offer him a horfe, as alfo to take his packe to eafe him : but he by no meanes could be drawne to mount a horfe backe. Wherefore the Portughefes, although *Xauerius* were very vnwilling, and forbad them fo to do, went along with him on foote. This fpectacle was moft gratefull, & profitable vnto the Neophytes, who admired the ciuility and courtefy of the Chriftians. Thus they came vnto the Port of *Bungo*, which is called of the inhabitants, by the name of the Riuer, *Fingus.*

Xauerius loue of humility and the Croffe.

    Bungo is a Citty wherin the King keepeth his Court, ftanding in that part & Iland of *Iaponia*, which as we faid, is called *Ximus.* The King of *Bungo* was but a yong man, yet far furpaffing his age in grauity & wifedome. At that time he had only *Bungo* vnder his gouernment, being a King among the *Iaponians* more famous for prudence, then wealth. None was more fauourable to the Portughefes then he: For being greatly defirous of their friendfhip, he had long before fent letters with prefents to the King of *Portugall*, and the Viceroy of *India.*

Bungo the Royall Citty.

Xauerius is with all honour receiued by the Portughefes.

    As foone as newes was brought to the Portughefe

V u 3 fhips

ships that *Xauerius* was arriued , the men came all out
presently to meete him with great ioy & gratulation,
euery one endeauouring to honour so holy a man :
wherein they proceeded so farre , as to salute him one
after another in a triumphant máner , with foure vol-
ley of shot, from out their great Ordinance, being 18.
peeces in number. And the euent declared afterwards
that this was not done so much through the aboundance of humane affection, as by the diuine prouidéce. For that the thundring out of so many great shot ,
sounded to the *Iaponians* eares , as though there had
byn a battayle at sea . Whereupon the King , who
remayned in the Citty not farre from the Port , was
surprized with no small care, thinking that the Portugheses had byn at fight with Pirats . And therefore
with all speed he sendeth a principall Gentleman to
Gama the Gouernor, to demand of him what the matter was, that he might assist the Portugeses , if any occasion serued.

   Gama , after he had returned humble thankes to the
King , tould the Gentleman that all things were quiet
and ioyfull with the Portugheses ; and for that *Francis
Xauerius* an holy man, & much respected by the King
of Portugall their maister, was there arriued, they had
receyued him with that applause, and shew of good
will, as was fitting his deserts . At this the Gentleman stood amazed, & would hardly belieue that they
had affoarded such extraordinary honour to so poore
a beggar, whome he thought of no credit, by reason
of his beggary, and basenesse of attyre : For the *Bonzies* being afrayd, that if *Francis* (who was very famous

The Bon-
zies de-
fame Xa-
uerius.

mous for his fanctity of lyfe) came once to *Bungo*, he might there alfo leffen their credit, as he had done at *Amangucium*, had defamed him after an vnworthy manner, both with the King, and the people.

The Gentleman therefore ftood ftill as one great-ly aftonifhed, without once mouing, through admi-ration. But afterwards, when he faw *Xauerius* coun-tenance fhining out with worth, and fanctity in that old torne habit, he perceyued prefently the *Bonzies* crafty dealing. Whereupon returning with all fpeed he relateth to the King both what the Portughefes had anfwered him, and what himfelfe had alfo feene; and withall tould him, they had made as great a triumph for *Xauerius* arriual, as if a fhip had come into the port loaden with filuer; wherefore there could be no que-ftion, but al thofe things were falfe which the *Bonzies* (who were indeed fretted to the hart at his incom-parable vertue) had broached abroad of him. For that his very contenance was fo full of worth, that he was able to drawe the behoulders, to loue and reuerence him. The King greatly admiring heerat; Good reafon, quoth he, haue the Portughefes then, to reuerence and refpect him.

CHAP. X.

He is conducted to the Kings Court , in great pompe , by the Portugheses.

Resently vpon this relation, the King sendeth a yong Gentleman a kinsman of his to *Xauerius* with letters, in a most friendly & respectfull manner, earnestly requesting him, not to thinke it much to come vnto him the next day, pretending withall the great desire he had to be acquainted with the Christian Religion. The Princely youth therfore, cōmeth to the Portugheses, hauing in his company 30. Noblemen, besides his Tutour. Who as soone as he beheld *Francis*, although in poore attire, yet most venerable both in countenance and corporall presence, and much honoured by the Portugheses, was amazed. Wherupon, after he had deliuered the Kings letters to him, looking vpon his Tutour; Certainly, quoth he, this Nation cānot but haue a most excellent God, whose secrets are wholy hidden from vs, seeing that his pleasure was, that the Portughese shipps should doe homage to so poore a man; giuing all to vnderstand by that solemne triumph of theirs, what a gratefull iewell Pouerty was in the sight of Heauen, which is commonly so basely esteemed, & contemned by mortall men. The next day *Gama* calling to counsayle the merchants, & the other Portugheses, concluded with the generall

The Japonians admire at the loue of pouerty.

consent

confent of all the reft, that it would make much for the aduácement of the Chriftian caufe, if perhaps that firft encoûter of *Francis* with the Ethnicke King did carry fome fhew of Maiefty, by fetting the fame out with all the preparation that might be; as well to preuent the *Bonzies* flaunders and culumniations, that there might be no hindrance to the current of the Gofpell; as alfo that *Xauerius* high efteeme might be able to traple vnderfoote that authority, which a moft proud generation had vfurped through falfehood and lying. For certayne it was, that how much he fhould feeme to be efteemed by the Portughefes, fo much the more alfo would the *Iaponians* account of him.

The Portughefes preuent the *Bonzies* calū- niations.

But now, when all the reft agreed to the Gouernours propofition, *Francis* only, who could not endure to heare of fuch honour, as holding faft his Euágelicall fimplicity, was of a contrary opinion: yet being conuinced not fo much by reafons, as by the vnanimóus confent of the Portughefes, he was forced at laft to condefcend vnto them. Whereupon the Portughefes putting on euery one the moft coftly apparell they had, fet forward with *Xauerius* towards the Royall Citty, with fuch folemne preparation, as is worthy to be obferued. They were carryed in fmall boates, hauing their fayles all of filke, bedecked & fet out with glittering banners. Befides this, there went a long with them Trumpets and Cornets, anfwering one the other by turnes, with notes declaring their feftiuall ioy. At this vnufuall fpectacle the inhabitants flocked by troopes from all parts there about, in fo much as the bankes vpon the riuer fide where they

He is a- gainft his will condu- cted with gre- at pôpe to the King of *Bungo.*

were

were to paſſe, were all ſo thronged with people who came to behold this ſolemnity, that the Kings Officers were conſtrayned to keep backe the multitude, and to make place for the Portugheſes landing. There was alſo one of the Nobility ſent by the King, ready with a coſtly Litter wherein to carry *Xauerius*; but he very courteouſly giuing the King thankes for his honourable offer, would not accept thereof; and ſo ſending backe the Litter, came on foote to the Court with very many of the Nobility of *Iaponia* attending him.

Amongſt all thoſe that accompanied him, the Portugheſe trayne far ſurpaſſed the reſt in brauery. They were 30. in number, all gorgeouſly attyred, hauing chaynes of gold about their neckes, and euery one his man following him in a rich Liuery. *Francis* alſo (the Portugheſes hauing forced him therunto) had ſet himſelfe forth better in his apparell then ordinary, intending afterwards to reſume againe his old habit. For he had put on a very fayre gowne, ouer which he wore a fine linnen Surpliſſe, and about his necke there hung a Prieſts ſtole of green ſilke grogran down to his knees, with a fringe of gold, ſuch as Prieſts did ordinarily vſe to weare. *Gama* the Gouernour, as though he had bin his Steward, wēt before him with a long wand in his hand: Then fiue of the choyſeſt yongmen of the whole company followed *Francis*, attending as it were vpon his perſon; whereof one carryed his Breuiary in a litle bagge of ſilke, another his Veluet Pantofles, another his ſtaffe made of a *Bengalian* Reed, which had a typpe of gold at the top, another
ther

ther his Hat , and the laſt an Image of the Bleſſed Virgin mother of God, vnder a Canopy of crimſon Damask. The reſt of the Portugheſes marched after,in a foure ſquare ranke.

This was the Portugheſes owne inuention , not ſo much approued by *Xauerius*, as winked at , becauſe he could not hinder it . They went in this pompe to the Court through nine of the principall ſtreets of the Citty,with ſuch concourſe of the inhabitants who flocked to ſee them, that the very houſes were ſtucke, and euen couered with the people.

CHAP. XI.

The King of Bungo *vſeth* Francis *vvith honourable reſpect , although the* Bonzies *vvere agaynſt it.*

FTER this, when *Francis* was come into the Pallace,he findeth at the entrance or vtter Court thereof , 600 . Souldiars of the Guard , all well appointed ; and by and by in a large Gallery he meeteth with many more of the Kings Attendance . Heere , thoſe fiue Portugheſe yongmen, whereof we ſpake before , bowing downe their knees , offered to *Xauerius* with great reuerence that which euery one carryed ; wherat the *Iaponians* were ſo ſtroke with admiration , that preſently they muttered out theſe, and the like words : Let the

Bon-

Bonzies now be gone with a mifchiefe , and neuer heerafter haue the face to appeare in the fight of men, idle companions as they were. For certainly this man is not fuch a one , as they haue defcribed vnto vs and the King , but rather indeed one, as we may thinke, fent hither by God himfelfe , to curbe the flaunders of malicious tongues.

A child of feaué yeares of a rare wit. From this Gallery there opened a fayre and fpa-Hall ful of Noblemen, where a Child of feauen yeares of age(but of a rare wit, as might eafily be perceaued) being led by a Venerable old man, meeteth with *Xauerius*, and faluteth him according to the Country fa-fhion , telling him, that his fortunate arriuall at the Court would be as deare, and pleafing to the King, as a feafonable fhowre of rayne , is to a thirfty field of corne in the fummer tyme. Wherefore he willed him to enter with ioy,& to know that he was as welcome to the good , as odious to the bad . To whome, when *Francis* had courteoufly faluted , and kindly returned anfwere : O Father (quoth the Child agayne) happy are you , who are come out of another world into forrayne countryes , defiring to carry hence no other merchandize but the ignominy of Pouerty! O infinite goodnes of the God, whome you ferue! O hidden wifedome of his, who is comforted with the Want & Pouerty of his Priefts ! Behould our *Bonzies* do fo abhorre the difgrace of Pouerty , that confpiring all together , they auouch openly , that the way to heauen is ftopped, and rampierd vp agaynft poore people . Heere *Francis* replyed, that he was in good hope , that God, the moft mercifull Lord of Heauen and Earth, would

would at laſt driue away the cloude of errous, which
bad blinded the *Bonzies* vnderſtandings , and beſtow
vpon them the light of truth; and that they would alſo, when they ſaw that heauenly ſplendour once ariſe,
forſake their peruerſe and ignorant opinions.

Then the Child diſcourſing a while vpon very
weighty matters far beyond his age , brought *Francis*
and the Portugheſes into a further Hall , where the
Noblemens ſonnes ſate all together. Who as ſoone as
they ſaw *Xauerius* enter , roſe vp preſently euery one,
and bowing their heades thrice downe to the ground,
according to the Country faſhion , make reuerence
vnto him. Then two of them, made a ſpeach in the
name of all the reſt, which I will heere ſet downe in
briefe, wherby it may appeare what kind of eloquence
the *Iaponians* are delighted in. Thus therefore they
are ſayd to haue ſpoken. Your happy comming, Sacred Prieſt, will be as gratefull to the King, as the
ſmile of the ſweeteſt infant is to the mother when ſhe
giueth it the pappe to ſuck. And what wōder? ſeeing
that the very walles , which heere you behold, reioycing as it were at your preſence, command vs to celebrate your comming with great loue and affection: &
this for the honour and glory of that God, of whome
as the report goeth, you haue declared certayne ſtrange things at *Amangucium*.

After this, they paſſed into another ſpacious Gallery leading into an inward Hall, where *Ficharondono*
the Kings Brother remayned with the chiefe of the
Nobility. As ſoone as he ſaw *Francis*, he receiued him
courteouſly with the reſt, & after mutuall ſalutations

The Noblemens children make reuerence to Xauerius.

What kind of eloquence the Japonians haue.

be-

betweene ech other, he tould him, that the Court neuer faw a more ioyfull day; and with good reafon, fince the King accounted himfelf more happy, by the arriual of fo worthy a mã, then if he were Lord of the 33. Treafuries of *China:* for fo many there are fayd to be. At laft *Xauerius* being brought by *Ficharondono* into the inmoft Hall, which for richeneffe of furniture furpaffed all the reft, he there findeth the King himfelfe, who expected his comming. The fame of his worthy actes had long before this caufed in the King a great admiratiõ, but now vpon his meeting he conceyued a much greater efteeme of him, fo farre did *Francis* his prefence furpaffe the imagination (how great foeuer it were) which the King had conceyued of him in his owne vnderftanding. For his maiefticall and venerable afpect which Nature, and Age had now beftowed vpon him, was alfo much graced by the fplendour of his fanctity, which euen dazeled the eyes almoft of all that beheld it.

The King of Bungo ftanding vp expecteth Francis his comming.

The King therefore feeing *Xauerius*, came on a litle towards him, and receyued him, both in a refpectfull and courteous manner. And when *Francis* according to the cuftome was kneeling downe, he prefently forbad him, by lifting him vp by the hand. And forthwith making himfelfe reuerence vnto *Xauerius*, by thrice inclining of his head as the coũtry fafhion was, caufed him to fit downe, on the fame feate by him. After thefe falutations, & gratulations paft on both fides, the King looking vpon *Ficharondono* his brother, and the other Noblemen, began with a lowd voyce that all might heare, to fpeake in this manner: O that it

Xauerius maiefticall countenance.

it were lawfull for vs to demaund of God, the maker The
and Lord of Heauen and earth, his secret iudgments, King of
and to aske what the cause hath byn, why he hath ey- *Bungo* his
ther suffered vs to lye so long buried in such darknes, testimo-
or else bestowed such light and wisedome vpon these ny of the
men who come out of another world? For we all ma- Christian
nifestly see, that whatsoeuer they say, although it be fayth.
agaynst our Religion, is confirmed which such solid
reasons, that we are not able to contradict it, if we
will follow the light of reason, or vnlesse we be wholy voyd of all vnderstanding. Contrariwise we see
our *Bonzies* to keep a stammering, when they are to
explicate any difficultyes of our Religion, and to be
so variable and inconstant, as neuer to stand fast to
what they say; in so much that if they be now of one
mynd and opinion, presently they wilbe of another.
Wherby it sufficiently appeareth, that their doctrine
and Religion is nothing els but a rabble of confusion
and vncertainties; so that one cannot with any dis-
cretion hazard therein the euerlasting saluation of his
soule.

At this speach of the Kings, a certayne *Bonzy* nobly borne, called *Faciandono*, being by chance present
and finding himselfe touched to the quicke, rose vp &
answered the King very boldly and freely : That the
cause of Religion was not of that nature that it might
be determined by him, who was ignorant of the do- A *Bonzies*
ctrine therein conteined ; Wherfore if he Maiesty had arrogan-
any doubt in his mind, he had those present there who cy.
could easily resolue him. And euen he himselfe would
vndertake not only to ridde him of his scruple, but also

so to make whatsoeuer he doubted of, more cleare vnto him then the sunne that shines : whereby all might plainly see, that those things which the *Bonzies* taught were both true; and that they also well deserued the stipéd which was payd them for their learning. Then the King smiling : Goe to (quoth he) incomparable Doctour, declare at last these secret and hidden mysteryes of your Religion, we will with silence giue eare vnto you . *Faciandono* then, looking about him

» with great grauity : First, quoth he, it is impiety to
» call the *Bonzies* sanctity into question; for all do know
» well inough that they lead a lyfe which is holy, gra-
» cious, and acceptable in the sight of Heauen it selfe.
» For they are men who do religiously obserue chastity,
» abstayne from fresh-fish, teach and instruct young
» youth, giue Bills of Exchange to those that lye a dy-
» ing for the taking vp of mony in heauen, and ryse in
» the night to pray for the sinnes of the people. And be-
» sides this, they are great friends to the sunne, starres,
» and celestiall Gods, with whome they haue often dif-
» coufes in the night tyme, and whome they do also
» many tymes imbrace, after a most sweete and louely
» manner.

The *Bonzies* fooleries.

The Kings temper.

The *Bonzy* hauing stuft his Preface with these & such like fooleries, anger so boyled in his proud and passionate hart, that he began, without feare or shame to inueigh intemperatly agaynst the King himselfe. Whereupon he gaue a signe, twice or thrice to his brother, to cause the *Bonzy* to hould his peace. Who being commaunded so to do, and the King firmely fixing his eye vpon him, tould him, that indeed he

ga-

gathered by his manners a sufficient tryall of the *Bon-zies* sanctity; and withall auerred, that he was so well edifyed, by the intemperancy & temerity of his ton-gue, that he durst sweare, Hell had more right to his person, then he to Heauen. Heerupon the *Bonzy* ad-ding intollerable pride to his former violent humour, cryed out aloud, That the tyme would come when *Faciandono* should be exalted so farre aboue all mortals that neyther the King of *Bungo*, nor any other should be able to aspire to his throne. The King at these his wordes began to be moued, yet withall laughed at his arrogancy, looking vpon *Xauerius*, who aduised his Maiesty not to trouble himselfe, but to expect vntill the *Bonzies* fury were past. But the King commanded *Faciandono* to be gone, and warned him withall, that henceforward when he spake of God, he should not be so vaine glorious before men: In the meane time, he wished him to keep hand ouer his passions, and come againe to himselfe before he returned to the Court. The *Bonzy* therfore, being set on fire with this disgrace in respect of the assembly of Nobles who were present cryeth out alowd; *Fyre from heauen consume the King, who dares do these things against the Prelates of the Gods;* and so in a fretting and chafing manner flingeth vpõ a suddain out of the Presence, leauing the King & No-bles greatly moued with indignation at his vnciuill behauiour.

The pride & intéperate tongue of a *Bon-gy*.

The King then ready to sit downe to table, inui-teth *Xauerius* to dinner. But he alledging that he was not acquainted with the *Iaponian* daynties, courte-ously refuseth: and withall making due reuerence to the

The King in-uiteth *Xauerius* to dinner

Y y

the King, befeecheth God, for whofe fake he did him
that honour, to beftow vpon him fufficient diuine
light & grace, that he might ferue him in this life with
fanctity, and purity of hart, and in the next enioy him
for all eternity. At laft the King, at *Francis* intreaty,
giueth him leaue to depart, and withall earneftly requefteth him that he would now and then vifit him,
and teach him the myfteries of the Chriftian faith.
Xauerius promifed he would. And then the King prefently with a cheerfull and friendly countenance of-

The King gi-ueth to *Xauerius* from his owne ta-ble.

freth him with his owne hands, a difh of meate which
ftood before him, defiring him to take it; who, to comply with the King, accepted of the fame. Then the Gouernour with the reft of the Portughefes, who ftood
about *Xauerius*, fell downe vpon their knees all togeather, giuing the King humble thanks for the great honour he had done vnto the Father, & themfelues, euen
againft the *Bonzies* wills.

CHAP. XII.

Xauerius *inftructeth the King and people in the mifteries of the Chriftian faith, & curbeth the audacity of the* Bonzies.

RANCIS remained 46· dayes in this
royall Citty of *Bungo*, imploying himfelfe
with al poffible diligence in the inftructiõ
of the Inhabitants. Yet his principall care

was

was to make deep impreſſion of the myſteries,& ob-
ſeruances of the Chriſtian faith in the Kings mind.
For which cauſe he became ſo inward with the King,
that there was then no comming for any *Bonzy* to
his preſence. For that he beganne to be much aſhamed of the foule enormities, which he had committed, through the doctrine of the *Bonzies*. Wherfore by
Xauerius perſwaſion he firſt abandoned many vicious
habits in his owne perſon, rid his Pallace of all vnlawfull loues and pleaſures, and began liberally to
relieue, & ſuſteine the neceſſities of the poore, contrary to the doctrine which the *Bonzies* taught. Then
turning his thoughts to the reformatiō of his people,
by litle and litle he enacted many and ſeuere lawes a-
gaynſt the murdering of infants (an vſuall practice in
thoſe places) and other haynous crimes, and enormi
ties, which hauing byn brought in by the *Bonzies* were
now growne to a cuſtome. He reuerenced *Xauerius*, as
one that came from Heauen, & ſent vnto him by the
fauour of celeſtiall powers. Him only he admired, ſaying many tymes, that he ſaw in his face, as in a glaſſe,
to his great confuſion, all the hainous offences, wherwith, by the *Bonzies* incitemēt, he had defiled his own
ſoule; ſo as he was now vpon the point to be made a
Chriſtian.

The
King by
Xauerius
perſuaſi-
on refor-
meth
both his
owne &
his ſub-
iects mā-
ners.

Yet *Francis* did not ſo imploy himſelfe about the
King, as that he neglected thereby the people. For being wholy vnmyndfull of himſelfe, he ſpent ſo much
of the day in preaching to them in the market-place,
that the Portugheſes could ſcarce get from him one
houre after ſun-ſet, to confer about pious matters,

and

and another before day to heare their Confessions.

Wherefore when some of his familiar friends complayned, that he came home late; he earneſtly requeſted them, that they would neuer at any tyme expect for him at dinner, nor in the day tyme euer thinke him aliue, for if they did otherwiſe, they would cauſe vnto him much trouble. For the dainties whereon he fed with chiefeſt delight, were the good of ſoules: neyther did he eſteeme any cheere better then the ſaluation of one only *Iaponian*, by vniting him to the flocke of Chriſt. And to this pious auarice of his, the diuine Prouidence was not a litle indulgent.

There came flocking to him an infinity of people, not of the vulgar ſorte only, but alſo of the Nobility, and many of the *Bonzies* themſelues: whereof one of a very Noble Family became Chriſtiã, with no ſmall good vnto the Chriſtian cauſe. He was called

Saquaygirano, the chiefe of the *Bonzies*, a man of great note both for his learning, and Nobility of birth: who entring into diſputation with *Xauerius*, & being ouercome by reaſons, & inſpired by the diuine goodnes, yielded himſelfe captiue to the truth. Wherfore, not thinking vpon any thing els then the truth which was offered him from Heauen, he publikely in the midſt of the market place, before an infinite aſſembly of people falleth downe vpon his knees, and lifting vp his hands and eyes to heauen, with teares falling from his cheekes, cryeth out with the lowdeſt voyce he could. Behold, O Ieſu Chriſt, eternall Sonne of Almighty God, I yield, and dedicate my ſelfe wholy vnto thee. And what I haue conceyued in my hart, I

heere

heere freely professe with my mouth. Do not thou, I «
beseech, thee who of thyne own accord hast called me, «
repell me now , when I come vnto thee. Then with «
weeping eyes looking vpon the multitude who stood «
round about him he added . And yee, O Cittizens , I «
intreate & beseech you,that you will both your selues «
pardon me,and desire also othersto do the like,for my «
so often setting to sale those things vnto you for true , «
which now I vnderstand to be false . «

This Confession of that famous *Bonzy* wonder-
fully moued the affections of that Country people, & 500. *Ia-*
was an example to many of imbracing the Christian *ponians*
Religion . For it is well knowen , that *Xauerius* him- wonne
selfe often affirmed to the Portugheses , with whome in one
he there liued, that if he would, he could haue bapti- day.
zed more then 500. *Iaponians* in one day . But (which
was very rare in such feruour of spirit) he was more
prudent, then forward in the making vp of the mat- *Xauerius*
ter ; and also very circumspect,that nothing might prudence
be done rashly, or in passion,which might giue aduantage to the *Bonzies* fury, beeing now ready to burst
forth . For that, being mortall enemies to the Christian cause , they were long since, incensed against
Xauerius and his friends , and had persuaded the people , that seeing they would needs cast away themselues, they should damaund of *Francis* a great summe of
mony in recompence , for changing their Religion ,
that they might not perish for nothing . Which plot Pouerty
of the *Bonzies* had this drift,that the vulgar sort taking a disgra-
notice of *Xauerius* pouerty , might haue lesse esteeme ce amōg
of his sanctity : so great a disgrace was pouerty a- *nians.*
the *Iapo-*

môgſt the *Iaponians.* Yet little or nothing did they preuaile by this calumniation againſt the knowne & tryed
truth, but rather like water caſt vpon hoat burning
coales, it made *Xauerius* zeale flame out with greater
force & vehemency . Whereupon the enraged *Bonzies*
being put to the plunge, not knowing what to do, left
nothing vnattempted, which might ſeeme for their
purpoſe. But whê they perceaued their endeauours not
to correſpond to their deſirs, they reſolued to try their
very vttermoſt.

They had now oftentimes by entring into diſputation with *Francis*, byn ſo foyled, & euen driuen out
of the field, that they durſt not open their mouth before him. Therefore they falſly ſlaundred him behind
his backe, but in vayne. For that the threats which
they had denounced, of the Heauens Wrath, agaynſt
the people, were now accounted idle. Wherefore ſeeing their ancient authority, to be worne out in the
eſtimation of the Cittizens, turning their paſſion into
fury, they began to waxe mad indeed . And firſt they
heaped vpon *Xauerius* all the reproaches and maledictions they could deuiſe, calling him in ſcorne, *A foule
ſtinking dogge; the moſt beggarly fellow aliue ; and a deuou-
rer of dead mens carkaſſes* . Then they caſt forth threatning words againſt him, and his company, that they
would make them repent it, vnleſſe they preſently
deſiſted from their enterpriſe. At laſt their paſſion &
fury went ſo farre, that they plotted to make a tumult
in the market-place, and therein vpon a ſuddain, to
kill both *Francis* and the Portugheſes. Yet were not
theſe things kept ſo ſecret, but that *Xauerius* and the
Por-

Portughefes had notice thereof. But he accounted it
the greateft fauour which God had beftowed vpon
him, to be threatned by his enemies: taking heed withall that he might not vnaduifedly prouoke thofe who
had no ftay ouer their owne enraged paffions. As for
the Portughefes, they hauing the Kinges guard to fecure them, contemned the vayne threats, and plottes
of fuch mad-brayne fellowes. Wherupon the *Bonzies*
feeing violence would not ferue the turne, they bent
their defignes another way.

C H A P. XIII.

*In a difputation before the King, he ouer-
commeth the moft learned of the Bonzies.*

HERE was a certayne *Bonzy* called *Ficarondono,* the only efteemed man for learning among them, & who carryed the bell
away from al the reft. For he had for thirty
yeares togeather, taught their profoundeft & deepeft
fciences in the moft famous Vniuerfity of *Iaponia.* He
was at that time Prefident of a Conuent of *Bonzies*
fome 40. miles diftant. The *Bonzies* therfore of *Bungo*
perfwaded him, without much difficulty, to difpute
with *Francis,* thinking it would be a great honour, if
(as to him it feemed eafy) he could in the prefence of
the King confute that ftrange Prieft, who, as al knew,
had already beaten downe the reft of the *Bonzies.* He
hafteth therfore with all fpeed to the Royall Citty,

with

with fix or feauen other famous Doctours in his company. It fell out very opportunely, that at the fame time *Xauerius*, & the Portughefes were gone to Court to take their leaue of the King, being the next day to depart. And whilft they were rendring his Maiefty thankes, and requefting his paffe-port for their iourney, newes was fuddainly brought vnto the King, that *Ficarondono* was arriued with a cōpany of choice *Bonzies*. The King (as might be noted by his countenance) was not very ioyfull at this newes, fearing leaft *Xauerius*, & the truth might be beaten downe by his great learning. *Xauerius* therefore, feeing the King troubled, & doubtful whatto refolue vpon, trufting in the goodnes of his Caufe, humbly intreated his Maiefty to let *Ficarōdono*, that pillar of the *Bonzian* race, be brought in, knowing for certayne, that although learning could do much, yet Truth could do more. Wherupon, the King being at laft content, the *Bonzy* was admitted.

After he had made due reuerence according to the vfuall cuftome, when the King demaunded the

The pride of a *Bonzy*.

caufe of his comming to Court, he anfwered: That he came to fee a ftrange Prieft, who was fayd to be come out of another world, and to know what manner of man he was, and the newes he had brought thence. This he thundred out with fuch boldneffe and arrogācy, that one might eafily defcry what a moft proud and diuelifh mayfter he ferued. And prefently fixing his eyes vpon *Xauerius* (who courteoufly faluted him) and making an end of his ceremonious complements (whereof the *Bonzies* are very liberall) with a looke,

euen

euen aboue the *Bonzian* ſtrayne, he demaundeth of him, if he knew him? and when *Xauerius* told him No, becauſe he had neuer ſeene him before, he turned to his companions, and ſayd: I perceiue, we ſhall haue no great difficulty with this fellow, who knowes not *Ficarondon* by his lookes. Fixing then his eye vpon *Francis*: Doſt thou, quoth he, remember what merchandize thou ſoldeſt me at *Finorama*? He tould him he had nothing to anſwere to that, whereof he was wholy ignorant, for he had neuer byn eyther a Merchant, or ſeene *Finorama*, or ſpoken with him before that tyme; how therefore could it hang together, that he had ſold him wares at *Finorama*? The Bonzie affirmed for certayne that it was ſo, and he could not chooſe but remember it, vnleſſe he were very forgetfull. *Xauerius* therefore requeſted him, that becauſe his memory fayled him in that point, he would help him out therein. Then very confidently, and ſetting on it ſuch a face as bewrayed his inward pride: Call thy ſelfe, quoth he, to remembrance with me: It is now 1500. yeares agoe ſince thou ſoldeſt to me at *Finorama* an 100. balles of raw ſilkes, in the vtterance whereof I became a great gayner.

The Bonzies Pythagoreā fooleries concerning the tranſmigration of ſoules

Hereupon *Xauerius* looking vpon him both grauely & pleaſantly: And I pray, quoth he, how old are you? The Bonzy anſwered that he was one and fifty. Then quoth *Francis*, how can it be, that you haue beene a merchant 1500. yeares ago, who before one and fifty were not borne? vnleſſe perchance you played the merchant before you were borne. And I vnderſtand, quoth *Xauerius*, you all agree, that this Country of

Iaponia began to be inhabited ; not aboue 600. yeares since: how therfore doth this hould togeather , that you were a Merchant 1500 . yeares ago at *Finorama* , which at that time was nothing but a meere wildernesse and solitude ? See then , quoth the *Bonzy* , how much better we know things past , then you do what is present. Thou shalt therfore know , (becaufe hitherto thou haft bin ignorant of it) that neither the World , nor Mankind , hath either had any beginning , or shall haue any end. And fo , mens foules being immortall , go fucceffiuely out of one body into another, both of men and women, according to the coniunction of the Moone , with the Sunne , and the starres, who frame and fashion the Bodies tender limmes . Wherfore foules which haue good memories (fuch as myne is) do eafily remember all whatfoeuer they did in their life time , when they were vnited to other bodies , which is not fo with forgetfull foules, as it feemeth yours is .

Xauerius hauing heard this foolery, & being very learned both in Philofophy and Diuinity , found no difficulty , by folid arguments, to confute thefe Pythagoricall and Platonicall dreames . Firft therefore he fheweth, that the World was not from all eternity , but was made at a certayne tyme, feeing that it neyther was of it felfe, nor could be equall or coeternall with the maker thereof. And that it was made, and adorned with men, and other liuing creatures by God , the Parent and Authour of all things . When he had proued this by many arguments, it was eafy for him to fhew, that the foules of men , had alfo a beginning, and

He conuinceth the Pythagoricall fables .

and were not before the bodies, which they do infor-
me; but being by God infused into bodyes aptly orga-
nized for them , did make vse of the corporall senses,
for the gaining of arts & sciences. For who is so blind
that seeth not, that Soules would willingly , if they
could choose, with losse & domage of so great a good,
be creeping into new and mortall bodies ? And that
they would not , vnlesse it were by constraint, yield
themselues prisoners to their bodyes , to be partakers of all their miseries ? Wherfore hath God, as euen
reason it selfe teacheth vs , who is a most iust Iudge,
appointed for mortall men after this life, eyther eternall rewards, or torments, according to their deserts ;
since we playnly see, this equity is not vsed amongst
them whilest they liue in this world?

When *Francis* made these things cleere and manifest, by euident arguments, most fit similitudes and e-
xamples, the King indeed & Noble men agreed vnto
him, declaring by their fauourable acclamations, that
what he sayd, was very coherent , and most conformable to reason . But the *Bonzie* , although in the iudgement of all he had the foile giuen him, would not
for all this, through the pride & obstinacy which was
rooted in his hart , giue ouer , least he should seeme to
grant his aduersary the victory , if he should acknowledge himselfe ouerthrowne . Going therefore from
the Controuersy concerning the world and soules, he
began to inueigh bitterly agaynst *Xauerius*, for that he
seuerely censured preposterous lust to be a most heynous offence , notwithstanding it was cleere & euident,. that the same was allowed by the lawes of *Ia-*

Z z 2   *ponia ,*

ponia, which neuerthelesse punished murders, adulteries, and thefts most rigorously. To which *Xauerius* (after he had euidently demonstrated, that, that abominable kind of lust, was most repugnant both to nature, reason, propagation of mankind, and honest behauiour) answered, that it was no wonder the makers of the *Iaponian* Lawes, being themselues blinded with the very same vice, saw not the fowlenesse therof; or if they did, yet would they not by any Law restrayne the liberty therof in others, which they would haue to be common to themselues. But grant it be so (quoth he) that no Law of the *Iaponians* did forbid it, yet certayne it was, that the law of Nature, engrauen in the harts of men, and Reason it selfe (if it were not depraued by euill custome) did wholly forbid it. For proofe wherof, this is a most impregnable argument, that in these kind of enormities specially, the doers therof seeke out darke holes, and corners, and vse all meanes that none may see, or know it. Besides this, if any one be knowen to be branded therwith, it is the very first thing that is cast in his teeth, when one intends to do him a disgrace, if he be once knowne to haue committed the same.

　　Heere now *Ficarondono's* obstinacy being in the iudgment of euery one conuinced, gaue way to the truth. Yet he, because reasons failed him, held on his combat with spitefull clamours, & that in a more froward then obstinate manner. In so much, that the violent course into which this arrogant fellow did at last run, moued both the King and his Nobles, who began to cry all out vpon him, and that if he came to fight,

The peeuish pertinacy of a Bonzie.

fight, he fhould get packing into the kingdome of *Amangucium*, which then was vp in armes, & there he fhould not want matter of combat ; for that heere all peace and quietnes was defired ; But if he came to difpute, he fhould abftaine from paffion and obftinacy, and fhould imitate the forreyne Prieft with whome he difputed, for that his temper & modefty in difputing ought to giue him example. At this the *Bonzy* (as he was naturally much inclined to chollar) being carryed on by the intemperance of his tongue began to curfe the King and his Nobles, as though he had bin mad, or drunke. Wherupon the King, incenfed and ftyrred vp to indignation , commanded him prefently to be thruft out of the Pallace , folemnely protefting withall , that were it not for reuerence to his Priefthood, he would haue commanded his necke to be broken.

CHAP. XIV.

Francis *his conftancy vvhilft the* Bonzies *be vp in tumult* .

THIS fo publick a difgrace (as they termed it) wherwith the Name of the *Bonzies* was for euer branded , droue them prefently into a tumult, and vprore. Wherupon the dores of all the Temples in the Royall Citty were fhut, and an Interdict put vpon the people, & Nobility ; fo as now the bufineffe was come vnto a com

motion

motion amongſt the vulgar , when as the King by his
prudent diſſembling the matter , did eaſily allay both
the tumult of the one , and ſedition of the other .

In this meane time , the Portugeſes partly fearing
the vprore of the common people , and partly the
Bonzies rage, had with-drawne themſelues into the
Hauen , counſayling *Xauerius* alſo to giue way vnto
the time,& quit himſelf of the preſent danger . But he
alleadging , that the Cathecumens would be therby
left ſuccourleſſe and deſolate, vtterly refuſed . Wherupon the Portugheſes being in great care and ſollicitude leaſt they ſhould leaue ſo worthy a man , in the
hands of Barbarians,thought it very expedient , that
Gama himſelf ſhould go backe into the Citty, to draw
him thence, before any miſchance hapned vnto him ;
and in the meane tyme, they would expeĉt him in the
Road , vntill he returned backe with *Xauerius* . *Gama*
therfore haſtning to the Citty in a little boate , findeth *Francis* in a pooreCottage,inſtruĉting one of that
Country , who was preparing himſelfe for baptiſme,
and ſheweth him the charge which the Portugheſes
had giuen him to fetch him away ; ſometimes alleadging reaſons for the ſame,then againe intreating him
that he would auoyd the preſent ſtorme of perſecution,which was comming vpon him from the *Bonzies* .

But *Xauerius* being endowed not only with an vndaunted courage againſt dangers, but deſirous alſo to
encounter euen with death it ſelfe for Chriſt his ſake:
O how fortunate(quoth he)would he be if any one of
vs ſhould chance to ſuffer that which you are ſo much
afrayd of ! I for my part know well inough,that I am
not

not worthy of so great an honour : yet if the diuine «
bounty pleafe to beftow fuch a fauour vpon me , al- «
though not deferuing it, God forbid I fhould refufe «
it. Wherfore in that you aduife me fo earneftly , to «
prouide for my felfe , by flying away, I thanke you, & «
acknowledge my felfe much obliged to you for your «
great loue : but I neither may , nor can in confcience «
do as you counfaile me. For what greater calamity cā «
befall thofe, whome we haue lately begotten vnto «
Chrift, then being forfaken by their Father to be ex- «
pofed to the rage and fury of the *Bonzies* ? And what «
can be more gratefull to the *Bonzies*, then for him to «
giue backe to their threats , who neuer fhruncke at «
their arguments ? and by difgracefully flying away , «
to loofe the honour of the victory already gotten a- «
gainft them, and to leaue the fpoyle behind vs?As for «
my felfe I will neuer , by Gods grace , fuffer that my «
feare may be an incouragement to the wicked attépts «
of Chrift enemies . For we haue to deale with thofe »
who be terrified by our confidence,and confirmed in «
their prefumption when they perceiue vs once to be «
afrayd . Goe too, therfore, fince now you know what «
my abfolute determination & refolution is , returne «
backe to your Companions, who expect you. I fee «
well how much you are bound to affift them in their «
merchandize ; but I know withall what obligation I «
haue to fo bountifull and mercyfull a God, who for «
my fake & other mens faluation, hath fuffred death, «
yea the death of the Croffe.

This he fpake with weeping eyes, and with fuch
forcible words , and fo inward a feeling , that *Gama*

not daring to reply one word to the contrary , like a man wholy amazed, returned backe vnto the ſhips. When therefore he had related to the Portugheſes, how all had paſſed betweene him and *Francis* , he tould them plainely , that ſince he was bound by the agreement he had made with them to carry their merchandize to *Cantona*, an hauen towne of the *Chineſes*, he would there leaue them his ſhip , to do with it as they pleaſed : But for himſelfe he was abſolutely and fully reſolued to come backe agayne to *Bungo*, and eyther to defend *Xauerius*, or els to dye with him . This incomparable fidelity of the *Gouernour* , wrought very affectually in the pious mynds of the Portugheſes. Whereupon , when they had all togeather commended his reſolution , they alſo offer themſelues to accompany him in ſo glorious an aduenture , ſtriuing withall who ſhould be moſt forward therin ; ſo as preſently they returned backe agayne with their ſhips into the hauen, intending there expect the euent of the buſineſſe . This newes greatly comforted both *Xauerius* and the *Cathecumens* , and withall tormented, and euen brake the *Bonzies* harts , being a people very audacious where they ſee others fearefull ; and very cowards, when they perceyue them reſolute .

By the Gouernours meanes the Portugheſes vndergo the danger with *Xauerius*.

CHAP.

CHAP. XV.

Xauerius *getteth a nevv victory ouer the Chiefe of the* Bonzies.

THE *Bonzies* therefore, falling from open violence to priuate plottes, came togeather in great troupes to the King, making earnest suite vnto him, that he wouldcōmand the disputation betweene *Ficarondono* & *Francis* concerning Religion which had byn broken of, to be againe renewed. The King at first was no wayes incli ned therto, but yet vpon certaine conditions he at last condescended; To wit, that the busines might be carryed without clamours, & falling into chollar; That for deciding of matters which might occurre in any cōtrouersy, there should be appointed certaine arbitratours, not any of the *Bonzies*, but of other indifferent & moderat men, whose office should be to iudge, what was granted and confirmed on eyther part, and to see that the arguments were made according to the rule of reason; That the disputation ended, the said arbitratours, and the other Auditours should giue their sentence of euery article of Religion disputed, and that which was confirmed by the greater part of voyces, should be held for certaine & ratified; And lastly that the *Bonzies* should neyther by themselnes, nor others hinder any frō being Christians that desired the same. These conditiōs were not so much approued, as acce-

The Cōditions of the disputation.

pted

ted off by the *Bonzies*, becaufe they could not indeed refufe them. The next day therfore, commeth *Ficarondono* to the Court with aboue 3000 other *Bonzies* in his company: fo as one would haue thought he had bin going into the field with an army. But the King out of his prudence, admitted only foure of al that nūber, alleaging the danger of a tumult, and the difgrace alfo which might come therof vnto the *Bonzies*, for whome it could not be any credit, if it fhould be fpread abroad, that 3000. *Bonzies* had difputed with one only forreine Prieft. Neither were the Portūghefes failing in their affections towards *Francis*. For being aduertifed of this his new combat with the *Bonzies*, they came againe vnto the Citty in a brauer mãner thē before; in fo much that the pompe they came in, and the fingular reuerence which they vfed towards *Xauerius*, did greatly amaze the *Bonzies*.

The Portughefes new affections to *Xauerius*.

When the company was affembled, the King firſt asketh of *Ficarondono*, what reafon he could alledge, why a new Religion brought out of another world might not be diuulged in that Royall Citty? To whome the Bonzy, being now taught by the late difgrace he had fuffred, to vfe more temper, anfwered calmely; that the reafon was eafy to be giuen, becaufe there was nothing more hurtfull then that, to their ancient Religion, to the Common-wealth, and to the whole order of the *Bonzies*, who both had, & alwayes did ferue the Gods after a holy & pure mãner: wherof there were extant moſt certayne approbations, and teftimonies of the Kings of *Iaponia*; fo that it were impiety in they *Iaponefes*, to feeke to faue their
foules

ſoules by other meanes, then had byn vſed by their forefathers, & predeceſſours for ſo many ages.

Then *Francis* being by the King willed to anſwere vnto this, deſired that there might be ſome order, & method obſerued in this diſputation. Wherfore he re-queſted the King, that ſeeing the *Bonzies* were come of their owne accord to oppugne him, he would be pleaſed to command *Ficarondono* to declare in parti-cular, whatſoeuer either he, or the other *Bonzies* mi-ſliked of that which he taught, that ſo he might an-ſwere vnto them all. And moreouer he intreated, for the auoiding of contention, that that might be ratifi-ed, and held for good, which his Maieſty, with the greater part of the arbitratours, ſhould agree vpon, touching matters in the preſent cōtrouerſy. The King granted *Francis* his requeſt, and commanded that all matters ſhould be ſo carryed. To which the *Bonzy* alſo agreed.

Then *Ficarondono* demaundes of him, why he, be-ing a Prieſt of a ſtrange Coūtry, inueighed againſt the *Iaponians* moſt ſacred Gods? Becauſe (quoth he) I iudge them vnworthy of ſo glorious, and diuine a Title; which the rule of right reaſon hath made pro-per only to him, who by nature is Eternall, and Im-mortall; and being the Author of all things, made both heauen and earth, wherof he is ſole Lord and gouernour. For ſuch is the infinite power & maieſty of God, that hardly can the wit of man, by imaginatiō or thought cōprehend it. Wherfore theſe few things which heere we ſee with our eyes, the motions of the celeſtiall globes, and ſtarres; the certaine and fixed

courſes

courſes of times ; corne , fruite, and other things pro-
claime him to be the only true and proper God , who
gouerneth & ruleth this world, which himſelf made.
As for *Xacas*, *Amidas*, *Giron*, and others whome you
hold for Gods, looke but into your owne Chronicles
and Monuments , and you will find them to haue bin
men, very rich , and potent indeed , but yet mortall
as we are .

    This anſwere which *Xauerius* gaue, cauſed in the
Iudges a ſoft whiſpering among themſelues, wherby
they declared that it pleaſed them well . Wherupon
when the *Bonzy* was ready to oppoſe him , the King
bad him go to ſomething elſe , for that was already
iudged for good by the Arbitrators , whoſe ſentence
they were to ſtand vnto . He therfore demandeth of

The Bon-
zies bills
of Ex-
change.

Francis, Why he diſallowed of the *Bonzies* bills of Exchange , wherby the dead were prouided of mony in
heauen, ſpecially ſeeing by that meanes they who departed out of this lyfe, became rich in heauen on a
ſuddaine, who otherwiſe would haue remained poore
and beggarly ?

    To this *Xauerius* replyed, that their riches who
went to heauen , conſiſted not in the *Bonzies* Bils, but
in the Merit of good workes. And thoſe workes were
good which proceeded from right reaſon , and true
Religion , being without queſtion gratefull, and acceptable to that Eternall God , who giueth rewards
to euery one according to their merit . As for Religion there was none true & pure, but that of the Chriſtians, whereby, ſincerely and piouſly the true God is
worſhipſhed ; the which is alſo called *Chriſtian* , becauſe

cauſe Chriſt the ſonne of God deliuered it vnto men.
For Chriſt, quoth he, being made Man for mans ſake
brought downe that excellent doctrine from heauen,
who being alſo glorious in miracles, repleniſhed the
harts of men with heauenly precepts; and laſtly for
mans ſaluation ſuffred death, waſhing away their ſinnes with his owne bloud. Whoſoeuer therfore being
baptized according to the Chriſtian rites, do truly &
ſincerely obſerue the commandments of Chriſt in this
mortal life, ſhall at laſt be admitted into heauen, to an
euerlaſting life, abounding with all happines.

Neither is the Chriſtian Religion ſo niggard, and
pinching as the *Bonzies* is, it ſhutting out neyther
poore people nor women from heauen, ſo that they
liue and dye as Chriſtians ought to do; and yet the
Bonzies either out of niggardneſſe, or ſuperſtitiō will
not affoard them any entrance into bliſſe: wherby it
is eaſily ſeene, that the *Bonzies* courſe of life, aymeth
rather at their owne profit and commodity, then at
truth of Religion; and that they reſpect their owne
gaine more, then the honour of God, or ſaluation of
ſoules. For ſeeing God, who is Lord of Heauen and
earth, hath created women as well as men, poore as
well as rich; he will without partiality, haue them
alſo to be ſaued and bleſſed, if they leade a good, and
vertuous life.

The *Bon-
zies* ſhut
out of
heauen
poore
people
and wo-
men.

Heere now the King, and the other arbitratours
approued the diſcourſe of *Francis* for very good; whereat the *Bonzies* were extremely grieued and aſhamed,
it galling them to the hart, to depart the field with
the loſſe of the victory, by the iudgement both of

King

King and his Nobility. For with this, the difputation ended; notwithftanding that their obftinacy in defending what they had once fayd, was not yet ouercome.

After this other *Bonzies*, gallant fellowes both for learning and eloquence, that they might not feeme wholly vanquifhed, fet againe a frefh vpon *Xauerius*. As he was therfore fpeaking to the people, they beganne to preffe him with very many, and different queftions. This bufineffe lafted for aboue fiue dayes; all which time the King was neuer abfent, either to benefit himfelfe by the difputations, or elfe by his authority to defend *Francis*, of whome he had vndertaken the protection; hauing not the patience to fee the *Bonzies*, with more obftinacy then truth, impugne his anfweres, which were very cleare, and according to reafon : fo as when the *Bonzies* ran crying out, and rufhing togeather in throngs vpon *Xauerius*, he caufed them to be kept backe, telling them aloud, that if any one would try whether a Religion were according to reafon, he fhould not himfelfe be void of reafon, as they all feemed to be. And with this, rifing vp, he tooke *Francis* by the hand, and with his Nobles following him, led him to his lodging, which was not indeed more gracefull and glorious for *Xauerius*, and the Chriftian Religion, then difgracefull & ignominious for the *Bonzies*, who vpon this their new ignominy, heaped vp alfo new rage in their fpitefull minds. Wherfore like men out of their wits with fury they fell openly a roaring out, and with lowd voices to wifh, that Thunder from heauen would confume

the

the King to aſhes, ſeeing he made leſſe account of his
Anceſtours Religion, confirmed by authority of ſo
many Kings, then of a ſtrange, and infamous ſect; &
had a more ſleight eſteeme of the *Bonzies* authority,
then of a ſtinking, roguiſh, and baſe fellow.

CHAP. XVI.

He procureth the Kings of Amangucium *and* Bungo *to fauour Chriſtianity.*

N the meane time whilſt *Francis* was glad
to ſee matters fal thus out happily (God
almighty ſeaſoning his ſweet meate with
ſoure ſauce) he commeth to vnderſtand
how variouſly things had bin carried at *Amangucium*
ſince his departure thence. *Coſmas Turianus* had al that
while imployed himſelf there with no leſſe fortunate
ſucceſſe in refuting the *Bonzies*, then in inſtructing
the Neophytes, when as a ciuill warre breaking forth
vpon a ſuddain, diſturbed all. For that a certaine
potent Prince ſetting vpon his King at vnawares,
with a great army of ſouldiars, had driuen him out
of his kingdome; who being not ignorant that his life
was ſought for, & that he might not fall aliue into the
hands of his enemy, being his owne ſubiect, had
deſperatly killed himſelfe. Vpon this, the Citty became all in a tumult, and all things were turned vp
ſide downe, whilſt the ſouldiars without any reſtraint
had

had practised their cruelty vpon all that stood in their way, without respect eyther of quality, age, or person, wasting also in a furious manner, euen the very houses themselues.

In the middest of these so many slaughters and deuastations by fire, the malicious *Bonzies* intended to haue oppressed the Christians and their Instructors, if the diuine Prouidence had not with present ayde protected thē. For presently vpon the newes of the Kings death, that dismall warre soone was turned into a ioyfull peace, by meanes of the chiefe Nobility of the Kingdome, who conspiring all togeather, sent forthwith Embassadours to *Ficarondono* the King of *Bungo* his Brother, to demaund him for their King. Wherefore *Xauerius* hoping for a fit opportunity to obtayne the new Kings fauour, towards the Neophytes at *Amangucium,* went straight vnto the King of *Bungo*, & requested him to commend vnto his brother, the Fathers of the Society, and the Christians that liued at *Amangucium.*

The King did very carefully what *Francis* requested, and the new King of *Amangucium* also made vnto him a liberall promise of what he desired, which heafterward faythfully performed. Moreouer the King of *Bungo*, that his deeds might adde force to his words, began presently himselfe to practise that in his owne Kingdome which he persuaded his Brother to do in his, by fauouring of the Neophytes, and appointing a certayne house for such of the Society as should come at any tyme to *Bungo*: Yet himselfe durst not imbrace the Christian Fayth, which he so much appro-

The King of *Bungo* giueth an house to the Society of IESVS.

approued and fauoured, for fearing he might be thruſt out of his Kingdome by ſedition . Wherefore *Francis* hauing done his endeauour, although in vaine, to draw him to the fayth of Chriſt , when he ſaw that he loſt but his labour therein , and that the buſineſſe was not yet ripe , turneth his thoughts another way .

Now when *Xauerius* was to depart , the King with teares in his eyes , looking vpon the Portugheſes that accompanyed him ; I do , quoth he , in all ſincerity, much enuy you, in this your Companion , of whome I being depriued , cannot refrayne from teares ; and the more , becauſe I feare that this is the laſt tyme I ſhall euer ſee him . Then *Xauerius* giuing the King humble thankes for theſe tokens of his good will towards him , told him that he would certaynly, if God ſpared his lyfe and gaue him leaue, returne vnto him agayne ere long; by which promiſe he put the King into ſome comfort. Then entring into ſpeach with his Maieſty about the Chriſtian Religion , he put him in mynd of thoſe things which he thought moſt profitable for him , aduiſing him ſeriouſly to remember that he was a mortall man, and therefore ſhould deeply conſider with himſelfe , how many foule crimes and offences would cry vengeance agaynſt him after his death, vnleſſe he purged himſelfe therof whilſt he liued: And that he ſhould for certayne know , that whoſoeuer dyed out of the Chriſtian fayth , was infallibly to be tormeted euerlaſtingly in Hel: but they who were Chriſtians, and liued as they ought, ſhould by the help & grace of Chriſt, enioy euerlaſting bliſſe in heauen . Theſe words of *Francis*, ſo ſtroke the King

The King weeping at Xauerius departure.

Francis his exhortatiõ to the King.

Bbb   vnto

vnto the hart, that in the presence of them, he agayne
brake forth into aboundance of teares.

Xauerius now humbly bidding his Maiesty fare-
wel, departeth from him at last with much a do. Then
comforting the Catechumens with hope of his speedy
returne, or else to send one in his place, he departed also
the Citty, ful of hope and confidence, for that he left
the King, & a good part of the people well affected
to the Christian fayth. Besides, he had much confidence, that so great a Kings fauour might be a singular defece to the Christia cause in those places. Neyther was he mistaken therein. For euer since the King
of *Bungo* entred into amity with the Portugheses, and
tooke vpon him to protect the Christian Religion, he
hath alwayes proceeded with very much fauour and
friendship towards the; assigning also a comodious
place for *Francis* his companions, that were after sent
thither, and by his letters of Commendations, opening the way for them, to enter into the familiarity
and fauour of his neigbour Kings. Besides this, he
furthered also the propagation of the Ghospell, and
fauoured those of the Society, in the greatest muta-
bility of times that might be, with extraordinary benefit both to himselfe & all *Iaponia*. For by his meanes
although an Ethnicke, Christianity came afterwards
to be exceedingly increased. And he by the goodnesse
of Christ, who rewarding in due time al these fauours
of his did not only add foure other kingdomes to that
which was left him by his Father, but was also made
a Christian about the 30. yeare after *Francis* his death,
as hauing no small reference vnto his merits. For that
the

The
King of
Bungo
his desire
to pro-
tect and
propa-
gate the
Christiā
Religiō.

the King when he was baptized, eyther out of respect
which he bare vnto *Xauerius*, or for that he attributed
that benefit vnto his merits, would needs be called
Francis.

This moſt prudent Kings example, was by many
of the Nobility, and ſome Princes alſo followed : yet
he went beyond them all, no leſſe in piety then in dignity. For God Almighty hath granted this our age
the fauour, as to ſee an Embaſſadour ſent from him
to *Gregory* the XIII. ſupreme Paſtour of his Church;
when as certaine yong Noble men of the bloud Royal
were ſolemnely ſent to Rome, from the Chriſtian
Princes of *Iaponia*, to acknowledge the Biſhop of
Rome for the chiefe Prelate of Gods Church, and Father to all Nations : Who comming out of another
world, & returning againe into their Country, were
honoured greatly as they deſerued, not only in *Rome*,
but alſo throughout *Italy* and *Spayne*. For which way
ſoeuer they wēt they became a moſt pleaſant ſpectacle
vnto all; the like wherof had neuer bin ſeene or heard
in the memory of man. So as they were euery where
receiued not only with great concourſe, & admiratiō
of the people, but with applauſe, congratulations, &
other tokens of exceſſiue ioy; that euen the memory
of *Xauerius*, who firſt of all brought the Ghoſpel into
Iaponia, might alſo ſeeme heerin to triumph.

Yet was there one thing which did not a little
trouble *Xauerius* mind, for that he had wrought ſo
ſmall good amongſt the Nobility of *Iaponia* (whoſe
authority euer beareth great ſway among the people)
and that neuer a one of them had receiued his whol-

*When
the King
of Bungy
was bap-
tiſed he
would
be called
Françis.*

Bbb 2 ſome

some counsayles. That which most hindred this businesse, was the great authority of the *Chinefes*, from whome the *Iaponians* had receaued their Religion; which the *Bonzies* of *Bungo*, and *Amangucium* commonly vsed for their starting hole, when they were ouerpressed by *Xaucrius*, saying: If the Christian Religion were true, why did not the *Chinefes* approue of it? Moreouer the King of *Bungo* his example was no small blocke in their way, who being very famous both for prudence and learning, seemed in his iudgment to disallow therof all that tyme, because he did not imbrace it. When *Francis* therfore saw that the *Iaponians* could not be won to submit their vnderstanding to the true Faith, vnlesse the superstition of the *Chinefes* were first ouerthrowne, he resolued to lay his battery to the principall Fort it selfe, with great hope and confidence, that if he could once draw the *Chinefes* to the standart of Christ, the *Iaponians* would easily follow their example.

Why he determinedto go into *China*.

O F

OF THE LIFE OF

S. FRANCIS XAVIER.

The V. Booke.

Intending to paſſe into China, *he determineth firſt to returne into* India.

CHAP. I.

THE Confines of *China*, are diſtant from *Iaponia*, where the ſea is narroweſt, not aboue 200. miles. This kingdome in the continent is far the greateſt & peaceableſt of all the Eaſt. It is a Countrey inferiour to none for number of goodly, & wealthy Cittyes and Townes, repleniſhed not only with ſtore and plenty of people and all other things, but alſo with excellent wits, and liberall ſciences. It is ruled by one ſole Monarch, whoſe

The deſcription & manners of the Chineſes.

Bbb 3

whofe becke all do obay. And certayne it is, that there
is not any Prince in the whole world, who hath eyther his fubiects, or officers more at command, then he.
The King himfelf attendeth rather to moderation in
his gouernement, then Power, ruling wholy by the
aduife of the Senate, & according to the lawes of the
Kingdome. You would thinke it to be rather a Com-
monwealth then a Kingdome, fo great a fway doth
counfayle and equity beare therein.

The people of the Country in fauour, are like to the
Iaponians, white of complexion, and ingenious : but
not fo much giuen to warre. As for the *Bonzies* the
Priefts of their Gods, they are of litle or no reputation
and efteeme amongft the, for that the opinion of their
fanctity is long fince worne out of date. There is
almoft no Nation more apt then they to receyue the
Chriftian Religion, were it not that Luxury, and the
craft of the Diuel did hinder the fame. For by Sathans
meanes, who is there, euen afrayd of himfelfe, the
whole country is fo kept, & as it were locked vp, that

Thecou- it affoardeth no entrance at all to Preachers of the
try of Ghofpell; it being enacted by the moft ancient Lawes
China of the Realme, that all ftrangers whatfoeuer be exclu-
fhut vp ded, excepting only the Embaffadours of Princes. In
againft fo much, that it is a death for any one to come thither
Chrifts without commaund from the King.
Ghofpel

Xauerius vnderftanding this, began to thinke how
he might worke himfelfe in amongft them. And
it came to his mynd, to returne agayne into *India*,
there to deale with the Viceroy, and Bifhop of *Goa*,
concerning the fending of an Embaffage to the King
of

of the *China*, and so he going as companion to the Embaſſadour, when he had gotten entrance, might bring in the Ghoſpell amongſt the *Chineſes*. And becauſe ſo many People, and Prouinces were gouerned by the command of one King, it ſeemed as an euident token frõ God, that the propagation of Religiõ there would be the more eaſy. Wherefore he was not out of hope but that (as it had in tymes paſt happened in the Roman Empire) Religion begining with the King himſelfe, who was head of the whole Country, it might be conueyed to all the reſt of the Prouinces of *China*, as members of the ſame Kingdome.

He had now remayned two whol yeares in *Iaponia*, and had not only vnited many to the flocke of Chriſt in the chiefe kingdomes therof, but procured places alſo of abode for thoſe of the ſociety, when as he begã to thinke of returning into *India*. Beſides the cauſe wherof we now ſpake, of procuring an Embaſſage to be ſent into *China*, the ſollicitude & care of his owne Society inuited him alſo home ; not that he was ſo much troubled for the great diſtance of place from them, or for any longing deſyre he had to ſee them, but that he deemed, he ought not ſo to employ himſelfe in gaining of Ethinckes to Chriſt, as wholy to abandon the flocke & company which was committed to his charge, both by Chriſt, and *Ignatius*. For although he often vnderſtood by letters from *India* whatſoeuer was done by thoſe of the ſociety there: yet he remembred well the Prouerbe that ſayth, The fore part of the head is better then the hinder; & that vigilant paſtours ought to viſit their flockes, with

their

His care of the Society.

their owne eyes, rather then with other mens. He therfore determined, hauing now bin long abfent, to vifit the Society in *India*, wherof he was Superiour, & to fend fome thence into *Iaponia* ; and after hauing fetled all things there, and procured the forfaid Embaffage, to go prefently into *China*.

CHAP. II.

Going into China *, he recouereth, by his prayers, a Cocke-boate vvhich vvas carryed avvay by the violence of a tempeft.*

EING therfore inuited to *China* by the opportunity of a Portughefe fhip, which was going thither, he, togeather with the King of *Bungo* his Embaffadour, who wét with prefents to the Viceroy of *India* , imbarketh in the moneth of Nouember, & yeare of our Lord 1551. He tooke with him out of *Iaponia*, *Matthew* and *Bernard* two of that Country, whome he had there baptized, intéding afterwards to fend them to *Rome*, that others might behold them, as a patterne of the *Iaponian* Nation; and they likewife benefit themfelues, by feeing the dignity & Maiefty of the Church of Chrift: that fo, hauing byn eye witneffes of the glory, and riches of that Church, efpecially at *Rome*, they might, returning home agayne, caufe the *Iaponians* to conceiue

ceyue a worthy esteeme of the Christian Religion,
by relating vnto them what themselues had seene.

Departing therefore from *Iaponia* with a prosperous wynd, they found this their nauigation afterwards very various, & remarkable for miracles. The
seauenth day, after they had put to sea, there arose v-
pon a suddaine a cruell tempest, which by mayne force & violence carryed away their ship into a sea wholy vnknowne to the marriners. And as they wandred
vp and downe amongst the billowes, without once
knowing where they were, or whither they wet, they
were so tossed with crosse-waues, that they were in
imminent daunger to be cast away. For the sky was
ouercast with such thicke and mysty clowdes, that
they were wholy depriued of the light of the sunne, &
so remayned in darknes for the space of fiue whole
dayes. At which tyme, not only *Francis* his sanctity,
but also his care and sollicitude manifested it selfe He
incited the rest to assist the marriners in their offices,
not more by words, then by his owne example. He
was behind none in labouring, both night and day.
He comforted the afflicted, and put them that were
out of hart, in hope to escape. One would haue sayd
he had byn the Captayne, or rather Gouernour of the
ship.

Francis imploy-
eth him-
selfe to
help the
ship be-
ing in
danger.

But when the wind was enraged with greater fury,
and tossed the waues higher and higher, the Maister
of the ship fearing (which after hapned indeed) that
some soddain puffe of wind might violetly rend away
the Cock-boate frō the ship, caused it to be fast bound
thereto with cable ropes. As they were now labou-

C c c   ring

ring about it (being fifteene men in number, besides
two Saracens) they were presently ouercast with
a mist as darke as pitch. And not long after, their ca-
bles burst asunder with the violence of the tempest,
and the boate, with the men, was carryed away with
such swiftnesse and vehemency, that almost in an instant it was out of all their sights. Wherupon the Mayster lamenting their case, making accompt they were
all but lost men, vnlesse the Cocke-boate could be
recouered, directed his course that way, which he
thought the boat was carryed. But the waues growing rougher & rougher, and the ship compassed round
as it were with mountaynes of water, was vpon the
suddayne driuen vnder the waues, ready to sinke.
Whereupon *Xauerius* stirred vp by the clamours of
the marriners and passengers who called vpon our
B. Lady, commeth running out of the Maysters ca-
bin, where he was at his prayers, and there findeth
the passengers & marriners cast one vpon another on
a heap, expecting nothing but their certayne casting
away. He therefore not caring so much for himselfe,
as for his companions, cryeth out: O Iesu Christ, God
of my hart I beseech thee by those fiue wounds which
the Loue of vs gaue thee vpon the Crosse, help these
thy seruants, whome thou hast redeemed with thy
precious bloud. A wonderfull thing. The ship on a
suddayne mounted vp aboue the waues, and got out
of present daunger, euery one acknowledging Gods
most liberal, and helping hand therein.

When they had thus escaped their owne perill, all
their care was for their neighbours: and euery one
who

He deli-
uereth
out of
danger
the ship
almost
cast a-
way.

who had kindred, or friends in the loft boate, began greatly to lament their misfortune. After they had thus a while bewayled their friends, they fall to pitty themfelues. For they were toffed vp and downe in an vnknowne fea, where neuertheleffe together with the Cock-boate, they had loft almoft all hope of fauing themfelues. *Xauerius* therefore, feeing them all weeping, and halfe dead through feare, biddeth them take courage, and telleth them withall, that within three dayes the daughter would agayne come to her mother, fignifying thereby that the Boate fhould returne agayne vnto the fhippe. They generally gaue no great credit to the matter, yet they were not altogeather out of hope. The next day in the morning as foone as it was light, *Francis* commeth forth amongft them with a cheerfull countenance, and faluting the Mayfter of the fhip after a courteous manner, willeth him to command one to clime vp the Maft, to efpy whether the Cocke boate were in fight or no. Wherupon an ancient and expert marriner, called *Peter*, anfwered in a gibing manner, that they fhould then recouer their Cock-boate, when they had loft their fhip. To whome *Francis* replyed: why, Peter, thinkeft thou any thing hard for God to do? I for my part am not out of hope, but that by the goodneffe of God, & our B. Lady of *Malaca* her help, to whome I haue vowed three Maffes, the boate with thofe poore wretches in her, will fhortly be fafe with vs againe.

A prediction of the boates returne to the fhip.

Then when he who had afcended the Maft fayd, that it could not yet be feene, *Fracis* fhut himfelfe clofe vp in a Cabine, and there with teares fpent a good

part

part of the day in prayer, and at laſt commeth out telling them good newes, that they ſhould preſently ſee
the boat returne home againe : and forthwith intreateth the Maiſter to ſtrike ſayle, and to ſtay for the
boate, for certainly all that were in her, eſpecially
the two Saracens, ſhould by Gods and his B. Mothers
help be ſaued. The maiſter of the ſhip refuſed his requeſt, and the others cryed out vpon it, both becauſe
it was in vaine then to expect the boate, and alſo becauſe they could not do it, without manifeſt perill
of their ſhip. For euen ſtill they thought they ſaw before their eyes the danger which they had ſo lately eſcaped. But the Maiſter, being at laſt wearyed out
with *Francis* intreaties, cauſeth the ſmall ſayle which
then was only vſed, to be let downe. Hauing thus
ſtayed his courſe for a good ſpace, and the boate not
yet appearing, and the ſhip alſo ſeeming to be in
ſome danger becauſe the ſea was ſtill very rough and
the wynd boiſterous, he commandeth the ſayle to be
hoyſed vp againe. But *Xauerius* ſtill vrged him, and
intreated the marriners to expect yet a while, confidently aſſuring them that the boat would come preſently without any danger to their ſhip. But when the
marriners, who were out of all hope, and moued alſo
with the preſent danger they were in, would notwithſtanding haue hoyſed vp the ſaile, the Father
runneth vnto them, and laying his hand faſt vpon
the yard, beſought them by the pretious death, and
woundes of our Sauiour, that they would be pleaſed
to expect yet a little longer. With much ado they
obeyed; and he ſet himſelfe againe to pray.

In

In the meane time *Antony Dias* was at his requeſt gone vp to the toppe of the Maſt, who looking all about, tould them he could yet ſee nothing; and therefore intreateth *Xauerius* to giue him leaue to come downe: but he, on the other ſide, wiſhed him to ſtay there ſtill a while. And as he prayed earneſtly with his hands lifted vp to heauē, he biddeth the Maiſter and the reſt to be of good courage. Now all this while the ſhip (being as it were warranted by *Francis* from any preſent danger) was toſſed with mighty waues, and floated vp and downe the ſea without any harme at all. And hauing in this manner expected almoſt three houres, and the matter held for deſperate by ſome, behold vpon a ſuddaine *Dias* cryeth out that the boate was in ſight, and comming towards them. Then they being all exceedingly comforted, began to giue thankes to God, and to *Francis Xauier*. As ſoone as the boate came within all their ſights, preſently they turne the ſhip croſſe-wiſe to receiue her, and ſhe, God certainly guiding her, cōmeth directly vpon the ſhip. As ſhe approached neerer vnto them, the marriners, now leaping for ioy, went about, as the cuſtome is, to caſt out a rope vnto her: but *Xauerius* tould them that there was no need ſo to do, for ſhe of her owne ſelfe would come cloſe to the ſhip ſide. And ſo it came to paſſe indeed; all the company being aſtoniſhed at the miracle. At laſt ſhe came ſo right vnto the ſide, that the poore men might be cōmodiouſly taken vp. Beſids this, although ſhe were in the midſt of the waues, yet remained ſhe firme without any to hold her, vntil ſhe was againe faſt bound vnto the ſhip.

The boate of her ſelfe cometh to the ſhip ſide.

Ccc 3   Beſides

Besides this so euident a miracle, another strange &
almost incredible thing is recouted by *Fernand Men-
dez Pinto*, a graue and vertuous Portughese, who was
companion vnto *Francis* in that voyage out of *Iaponia*
into *China*, & partaker also of all these dangers; which
was, That after the men were taken vp safe into the
ship, & the marriners would haue thrust of the boate

*Francis
being in
the ship
was
seene
at the
same
time also
in the
boate.*

wᶜʰ was now empty & fast tyed therto, they all cried
out vnto them that they should first help forth *Xauerius*
who was stil in the boat. When the marriners replyed
that *Xauerius* was well & safe in the ship, & had neuer
byn in the boat, they affirmed constantly one after
another, that all the while they were tossed by the té-
pest, & driuen vp and downe in the sea, *Xauerius* was
seene comforting them, & putting them in hope to escape euen vntil the boat came backe. Then they began
to vnderstand, that *Francis* whilest he prayed for their
deliuery appeared also vnto them (as it is recounted
of *S. Nicolas* Bishop of *Myra*) by whose prayers it was
manifest they had byn saued from shipwracke. This

*He fore-
tels a
calme
sea.*

thing was much spoken of by all the passengers, and
marriners. But *Xauerius* affirmed, that it was Gods
handy-worke and not his, and willeth the Mayster of
the ship, with all speed to make ready all his sayles,
for that presently the tempest would cease, and they
should haue faire weather. This proued also very true,
for the marriners had scarce put in order their sayles, when vpon the suddaine, the storme wholy ceased, and the ship sayled on with a prosperous gale.

Now this regayning of the Cock-Boate, made also
much for gayning of the two Saracens soules, who
had

had byn in all the danger . For they being moued by
so euident a miracle, were by *Xauerius* without great
difficulty conuerted to the fayth of Christ ; and being
by him instructed and baptized , were, next to God ,
bound vnto him for the saluation both of their bodies
and soules. The ship then hauing afterwards a prosperous voyage, came safe to *Cinceum*, an hauen Towne of
China, whither she was bound.

CHAP. III.

*He maketh the Port of the Chineses , and
his voyage to Malaca, very famous by
his Prophesies .*

A S soone as *Francis* was landed, he met very
fitly with *Iames Perera* his ancient & great
friend, a man of note both for Nobility of
birth and riches , who was shortly to returne into *India* . When they had saluted ech other
with great signes of ioy & affection , *Francis* acquainting him with his determination, of coming to speach
with the King of *China*, asked his aduise therin. Wherupon he being a prudent man , and experienced in
such matters, thought his best course would be to
procure the Embassage which he spake of, and also
Presents from the Viceroy of *India* to the sayd King
of *China*. And to second his aduise with his helping
hand , he offered cordially for that purpose not only
his owne endeauours, but his ship also , and all he
had besides; so much did the loue of *Xauerius* togeather

*Iames
Pererias
notable
bounty.*

together with aduancement of Chriftian Religion in *China* moue him. And truly his deedes proued greater then his words : for he fent with *Xauerius* to *Goa*, a man of purpofe to conduct him, & furnifhed him with 30. thoufand Crownes for that voyage. *Francis* giuing him many thankes prayed God to requite him, and promifed alfo, that his King fhould do the like.

　　From thence he paffed to *Machao* a very famous Mart Towne of the *Chinefes*, where finding a yong mayd, who through pouerty and want had expofed her Chaftity to be abufed, he prefently began to beg money to make her vp a dowry. He therfore going to one *Peter Vellius* an ancient acquaintance of his, and a wel monied merchãt, & finding him playing at cheffe in another mans houfe, openeth the matter briefly vnto him, and withall intreateth to borrow fome gold of him to be payd agayne an hundred for one in heauen . *Vellius* being fomewhat troubled at *Xauerius* vnfeafonable comming vnto him, tould him that it was then no tyme to talke of fuch things, for that he was not at his owne houfe where his money was. *Francis* vrged againe in a very friendly mannner, faying, that to one who was to dye, no time was amiffe to do good deeds in . At which words *Vellius* being moued, gaue him the key of his cheft where his mony was (for *Xauerius* knew wel his houfe & where to find any thing) bidding him take as much as he would. *Francis* went and tooke out 300. crownes, and prefently bringeth him backe the key, telling him withall how much he had taken. Then, quoth he, Father, you haue committed an errour, and your modefty hath done me an
iniu-

Peter
Vellius
his great
liberali-
ty.

iniury, hauing taken farre leſſe then I intended you
ſhould . For by deliuering you my key , I meant you
ſhould haue taken the halfe that was in the cheſt
(which I thinke are 30000 crownes of gold) & haue
equally deuided it betweene vs ; but alas , what a
ſmall ſumme haue you taken thence , for your ſelfe ?

Francis admiring hereat, perceiued that *Vellius* ſpake
ſincerely frō his hart, & that his words were not more
complementall then true. Wherupon he replyed : Go
forward *Vellius,* quoth he, ſtil in this thy liberality, for
thy noble & reall Hart teſtified by theſe effects, is gratefull and acceptable to God ; in whoſe name therfore
I promiſe , that God ſhall neuer fayle thee , and that
thou ſhalt alſo by reuelation from him, foreknow the
laſt day of thy lyfe . Wherein God neyther deceyued
Francis , nor he the merchant . From that tyme forward *Vellius* became quite another man , and was very much addicted to bounty and piety . Some yeares
after , being forewarned from heauen of the tyme of
his departure out of this lyfe , he began to caſt vp his
accoumpts, and to ſetle his houſehold affayres, diſtri-
buting a great part of his ſubſtance among the poore ,
and made himſelfe ready for that laſt combat, now
whilſt he was ſtrong and luſty .

When his laſt day was come , he went vnto the
Church, & cauſed the Prieſt to ſing a ſolemne maſſe of
Requiem for *Peter Vellius ,* at which himſelfe was preſent, reckoning himſelfe euen then for dead. Then going to euery one of his friends, he biddeth them farewell , for he was to take a long iourney . When they
asked him, whither he meant to go? To heauen, quoth

A nota-
ble Pro-
phecy.

D d d h e,

he, I truſt. Wherupon they thought he had but ieſted
being alwayes a merry and pleaſant man. But he per-
ſiſted with many aſſeuerations that indeed he went to
heauen. Then they thought verily he was diſtracted,
or crazed in the braine, wherein they were abſolutly
confirmed when they heard it reported, that *Peter Vel-*
lius hauing gotten a Maſſe ſayd for his ſoule, had ſhut
himſelf vp in his houſe, & there expected deaths comming. They therfore came vnto his houſe by troupes,
& endeauoured one after another to draw him from
that melancholy cogitation. But he, carrying himſelfe
with a cheerfull contenance, ſhewed manifeſtly, that
he had no griefe of mynd, and withall very ioyfully
openeth to his friends *Xauerius* his prediction, and the
euent thereof. At laſt, when he had tould them the
whole matter, he intreated that they would euen that
very day, keep the funeralls of *Peter Vellius* who was
preſently to dye. It ſo fell out indeed: for being well
ſtroken in yeares, he was preſently taken away by
ſuddayn death; and the very ſame day his friends accompanied his Corpes to Church, being greatly aſtoniſhed and amazed, partly at his departuie, and partly
at *Xauerius* prediction.

In the meane tyme, as *Francis* was going to imbarke
himſelfe in *Perera's* ſhip, turning vpon a ſuddayne to
thoſe that accompanied him, who were many in nūber: Let vs, quoth he, pray to God for the Citty of *Ma-*
laca, which is preſſed by the Enemy that beſiegeth it,
& if any one can affoad any help to it in this diſtreſſe,
let them make haſt, leaſt they come to late when all is
loſt. This fearefull ſaying wrought much in them all,

A dou-
ble Pro-
phecy.

eyther

either by reafon of the *Malacenfians* danger, or els for the
miraculous prophecy it felfe : for *Malaca* was diftant
from thence 900. leagues, or thereabout. Through this
fpeach of *Francis* they all fell together to their praiers.
Nor was it in vayne. For whilft the marriners were
preparing for this their iourney , *Iames Perera* aforefaid, being much moued by what *Xauerius* had fpoken
made prouifion both of armour and fouldiars to affift
the befieged. Whome when *Xauerius* perceyued to be
in fuch care, through feare of danger wherein the *Ma-*
lacenfians were : Away *Iames*, quoth he, with this feare
and preparation for warre, and giue God thankes togeather with vs ; For now *Malaca* is by the diuine
Goodnes freed from the fiege : wherby all might perceaue that the *Malacenfians* were fuccoured by the
prayers which were lately made for them vnto God.

Now *Xauerius* imbarking in *Perera* his fhippe ,
they arriued vpon the fortith day after their departure frō *Iaponia*, at *Sincapura* a hauen Towne 120. mi
les diftant from *Malaca* , and where they remayned
fome few dayes. From thence *Xauerius* leaft any thing
might peraduenture hinder his iourney at *Malaca* ,
wrote letters to the Society there, aduertifing them of
his returne, & warning them to prouide him with all
fpeed of all things neceffary for his voyage into *India* ,
for that he was in very great haft. The chiefe feafon
for commodious paffage into *India* was now a good
while paft , when they departed from *Sincapura* towards *Malaca* , intending from thence to paffe into *India*. Wherfore *Perera* was very anxious, doubting
that there was not at that tyme of the yeare any fhip

The Ha-
uen Sin-
capura.

A Prophecy.

to be gotten at *Malaca*, to transport *Francis* vnto *Goa.* Then *Xauerius :* Iames, quoth he, be not afrayd, but caft away this care : For *Anthony Perera* hath now ftayed for vs a good while, with a fhippe ready for our iorney. The euent fhewed prefently after, that what he faid was true.

As foone therfore as they came to *Malaca*, they find *Anthony*, who had now three dayes expected the comming of *Xauerius* with a fhip fraught, and ready to fet forth. And withall, they vnderftood that *Malaca* had byn lately ftraitly befieged by thofe of *Iaua*, a barbarous people that border vpon them ; and that it was freed from the fiege, & danger, at the very fame time that *Francis* had foretold. As foone as it was reported abroad that *Xauerius* was returned out of *Iaponia* to *Malaca*, prefently there came vnto him great

At *Malaca* he is receiued with great ioy & gratulation of all.

concourfe of al forts to congratulate with him for his fafe returne. For when he departed for *Iaponia* he had comitted himfelf to fo long & dangerous a nauigatio euen againft their wils, to their great griefe, and forrow. But as foone as newes was brought that he was fafely returned agayne at *Malaca*, the whole Citty prefently making a proceffion to the Church of the Society, gaue there publike thankes to Almighty God, demonftrating thereby the great affection which they bare vnto him. Wherfore his fafe returne, togeather with the good newes of the conuerfions he had made in *Iaponia*, brought aboundance of ioy vnto the whole Citty.

CHAP.

CHAP. IIII.

At Goa *he cureth one that vvas ready to dye : and taketh account of vvhat the Society had done, since his departure.*

RANCIS hauing stayed at *Malaca* some few dayes for the comfort of the Society which there resided, imbarketh himselfe in the shippe, which had now byn there a good while ready, and with a prosperous gale arriueth at *Cocinum,* where he is receiued with the generall ioy and gratulation of all the Citty. Now at the very same time that *Francis* arriued at *Cocinum,* there were shippes ready bound for *Goa.* Wherfore making vse of the benefit which was at had, he presently with all speed maketh hast thither. As soone as he was landed, he went as his custome was to the hospitall of the sicke before he would go to his owne house of the Society. After he had in a sweet manner comforted the sick he went vnto the Colledge, being earnestly expected there by all his Society. Where after he had most louingly & tenderly saluted & imbraced them all one after another, that he might not seeme more courteous vnto externes, then to those of his owne family, he asketh whether there was any sick in the house? To whome it was answered, that there was only one. Wherupon he goeth presently vnto him, before he

As soone as he came to Goa he visiteth the sicke

D d d 3   went

went to his owne chamber.

　　The Patient at that prefent lay in great extremity, and was watched day and night by fome of the Society who had care of his foule. All things were now prepared for his buriall, yet the fickeman himfelfe, although he was then euen ready to giue vp the ghoft, was not out of all hope of life, faying oftentimes with a broken and dying voice, that if *Xarius* would come before he were dead (for he was euery day expected)he fhould certainly by his merits & prayers recouer his health, although euen then defpayred of. *Francis* failed not to anfwere to the ficke mans hope, and affoone as he entred the chamber, he faluteth him as he lay euen a dying, reciteth the Ghofpell ouer him, and deliuers him from death; fo as being inftantly eafed of his paynes, not long after perfectly recouered his health. One would haue thought that God had fo difpofed the matter, that both the fick man fhould expect the comming of *Xauerius*, and *Xauerius* make haft on his iorney to come to him.

　　After this, incredible ioy was conceyued not only by thofe of the Society, but alfo by the principall of the Citty for *Francis* his fafe returne, who greatly longed to heare how matters went in *Iaponia*. *Xauerius* found alfo in *Goa* that Chriftianity, & the Society had there much increafed in his abfence. For the Portugefes hauing bin very carefully inftructed both by the *Francifcans*,*Dominicans*, and thofe alfo of the Society, after their vices were once rooted out, liued very ciuilly and pioufly, euen amidft the greateft liberty and affluence of al things. For although they were warlike

and

He recouers one of the Society ready to dye.

The Francifcans & Dominicans induftry.

and martiall men, yet they lead a life void, and free not only from quarrelling, wrangling, and iniuries, but euen from thofe pleafures alfo, which are lawfully granted vnto men; in fo much that it was held for a monftrous thing for any one to keepe a Concubine: fo farre did the force of heauenly myfteries reftraine the liberty of Souldiars . For many times in the yeare, and as often alfo as they were to be fent vpon any feruice, they armed themfelues with the Sacraments of Confeffion and Communion . One would haue thought they had bin rather religions men, then fouldiars .

    Fa. Paul Camertes alfo (*Francis* his Vicar) hauing inftituted an Hofpitall at *Goa* for the poore, did himfelfe begge almes about the Citty for the maintenance therof, with no leffe incouragement to pious people, then comfort to the poore themfelues. Befides this, *Fa. Anthony Gomez* by the Viceroyes and Bifhops command hauing byn fent to *Malauaria*, had inftructed in the myfteries and precepts of the Chriftian faith, the King of *Tanoris*, (who had bin lately conuerted and baptized priuatly by *Vincentius* a Francifcan Friar) and brought him at laft (being much afrayd of the fpeeches of men) to prefer religion before feare, profeffing himfelfe a Chriftian publikely euen in the Citty of *Goa*. Where being intertayned by the Bifhop and Viceroy with all honour and folemnity, he became an example to many Kings and Princes, and to his owne fubiects alfo, to make the fame tryall of the Chriftian Faith .

    Thofe alfo of the Society, whome *Xauerius* had

The King of *Tanoris* baptized

had fent abroad into diuers other places, had ech of
them wrought great fruit by labouring in our Lords
vineyard. For in the Promontory of *Comorinū*, which
as we fayd before, had byn manured by *Fa. Anthony
Criminalis*, & watered with his deareft bloud, was to
be feene a moft plentiful harueft of foules, there being

In the
Promō-
tory of
Comorinū
there are
numbred
400000
Chriftiās
numbred 400. thoufand Chriftians. So that there
may be a queftion whether his life, or death caufed
more increafe to the Chriftian caufe. But at *Ormus*,
that moft fayre and rich Citty (as we faid) feated in
the mouth of the *Perfian* gulfe, *Gafpar Barzæus* the low
Country mā had moft nobly carryed on the bufineffe.
For that Citty, being the very fincke of Ethinckes,
Saracens, and Iewes, had now publikely giuen full
fcope to all abufes, being growne euen degenerate, &
wholy ignorant of their owne country cuftomes and
ceremonies. Wherefore *Gafpar* being fent thither by
Xauerius order, had in a fhort fpace greatly correced
and reformed their corrupt & wicked manners, fhewing himfelfe a fchollar not vnworthy of fuch a maifter; whofe worthy acts being by others already recoū-
ted, I will only mention one in this place, whereby
a coniecture may be made of the reft.

There was at *Ormus* a moft ample and famous
Temple dedicated to *Mahomet*, wherein he was fer-

A memo
rable
fact of
Father
*Gafpar
Barzæus*
ued by the Saracens with the greateft folemnity and
deuotion that might be. *Gafpar* could not endure to fee
the honour due to Chrift, giuen to that wicked Apo-
ftata from the Chriftian Religion. Wherfore inflamed with diuine zeale he performed a noble act, worthy of all memory. For leading with him a troupe of
children

children with great croſſes in their hands and ſinging
a loud, he ſetteth vpon the Temple, in the open day
time; and himſelfe carying alſo a Croſſe, firſt of al ru-
ſheth into the midſt of the chaunting Saracens, and in
the ſight of thoſe Barbarians, who ſtood amazed at
the ſtrang accidēt, planteth at leaſure ſix great Croſſes
faſt in the pauement of the Temple. One would haue
thought the fury of that franticke people, to haue
bin with-held by diuine power from doing any out-
rage vpon him, who was moued by God to performe
that noble act. The which was afterward made more
euident by the euent of the thing it ſelfe. For that the
ſight therof did ſo diſcourage and terrify the Saracēs
that they forſooke the Temple euer after, and ran a-
way like men diſtracted, as the Deuills are wont to
do when the ſigne of the Croſſe is made againſt them.
Gaſpar at firſt, by *Francis* his appointment, remayned
in the hoſpitall. But afterwards when the Citty of
Ormus had receaued euident triall both of his, & his
companions vertue, they built a proper Houſe and
Church for the Society. Both which, the Society for
certayne reaſons, thinking good afterwards to leaue,
yielded them vp freely to the *Dominicans* (who with
much prayſe & fruit laboured in that vineyard of our
Sauiour) for the reſpect they bare vnto that moſt holy
Family.

The force of the Croſſe.

The Dominicans commended.

    With no leſſe labour did *Fa. Cyprian* liue in *Meli-
apora* the Towne of *S. Thomas*, who after he came
thither, ſo moued the townes-men by his preaching
and exemplar life, that of themſelues they freely gaue
to the Society a place for their perpetuall habitation.

E e e

Cyprian

Cyprian therefore aſſiſted by the diuine goodnes, did therin many and worthy things, but amongſt others, this one was very remarkeable. A certaine Marriner hauing taken away a Chriſtian woman by force from her husband, put her into a ſhip, not without the Mayſters knowledge, to carry her away. Wherof *Cyprian* being aduertiſed, when he could not by any meanes hinder ſuch an abominable faƈt, pronounced this prophecy out of the pulpit. Certaine perſos haue carryed away another mans wife, but it ſhall not be long before they be puniſhed, according to deſert, for their ſinne agaynſt God and man. For the ſhip whereinto the woman is conueyed ſhall periſh; amd wheras he that hath committed this faƈt, hath now but one eye, and ſtammereth with his tongue, ſhall ere long looſe his other eye, and ſpeach alſo. All this fell out as he foretould. For within few dayes after the ſhip was caſt away; whereupon the Mayſter thereof, being enraged agaynſt the ſayd marriner, pulled out his other eye. And he lykewiſe, by his loud crying out in the ſhipwracke, became of a ſtammerer, wholy ſpeachleſſe.

Cyprians notable vertue.

Moreouer *Fa. Nicolas Lancelot* at *Colanum*, *Baltazar Gage* at *Bazain*, *Francis Perez* at *Malaca*, *Iohn Beira* in *Moluca* and *Maurica*, & others of the Society, ſome in one place, ſome in another, by the help of our Lord imployed their labours not without great profit, in confirming the Neophytes, and gayning of Ethnickes to Chriſt. And all of them carryed themſelues with ſuch wonderfull ſanƈtity of lyfe, euen amidſt ſo great want of humane aſſiſtance and hardnes of all things,

things, that with eafe they obtained, or eftablifhed places of Refidence for the Society. About the fame time
alfo *Gaſpar Conſalues* procured a Refidéce for the Society at *Tanaa* a towne diftãt from *Bazain* 17.miles, where
the Townes-men being inftructed by the fame Fathér
in Chriftian piety, became good husband-men, & of
a vertuous life. And many of their children were trained vp according to ech ones capacity & propenfion,
fome to learning, and others to diuers handycrafts; fo
as, they were taught at once, both to behaue themfelues vertuoufly, & alfo to get their liuing for the maintenance of their lyfe.

At this place there came vnto Fa. *Gaſpar*, from
the furtheft part of *India* for religion fake, a certayne
Indian who was very aged, and almoft withered vp
with leaneffe of body; yet of fuch comportmēt both
in habit & countenance, that he refembled one of the
ancient Hermits. He being in a fhort fpace inftructed
in the precepts of the Chriftian Fayth, when one day
he beheld, drawne in a Table, the Child Iefus in his
mothers lap, began prefently with great veneratiõ to
take vp the diuine babe into his armes, & forthwith,
as he was in that fort imbracing the picture, being
like another *Simeon*, admonifhed that the tyme of his
death was at hand, vrged and inftantly befought the
Father that he might, without delay, be made a Chriftian, for that his laft day and death was at hand. He
was therfore forthwith baptized, and the next morning at breake of day he departed this life in peace,
after he had imbraced the Sauiour of the world.

Xauerius being certified how matters went in all

*An Jndiã like ano-
ther Si-
meon dy-
eth after
he had
imbra-
ced
Chrift.*

E e e 2   places,

places , and of the difficulties alſo which many of his ſubiects were in , he ſent vnto euery place according to the condition & neceſſity therof, not only ſupplies, but rules and precepts alſo for their further direction; which not to interrupt the order of this our Hiſtory we haue thought good heere to omit, intending afterward to ſet them downe in their proper places .

In the meane time whilſt euery one greatly reioyced for the good newes he had brought out of *Iaponia*, with a ſpeciall feeling; only he, who had bin the Author therof , ſtill burning with an vnſatiable deſire of the good of ſoules and glory of God , thought the conuerſion of *Iaponia* but a matter of ſmall moment , in compariſon of thoſe other things, which he hoped, and intended to compaſſe . For he had now a good while , fixed his cogitations vpon *China* . That was the Countrey , ſo repleniſhed with townes and inhabitants, yea the Court it ſelfe of the moſt ample kingdome of the world , which his intentions aymed at , as the complete and finall end of his trauailes , and a thing whereon the ſaluation of all the Eaſt did ſpecially depend.

CHAP.

CHAP. V.

Hauing procured the Embassage before spoken of, he goeth himselfe to China.

SCARSE was he come to *Goa*, when as the care he had of *China* ranne so continually in his mind, that he began with all diligence to set forward the businesse, making account, that how long the matter was differred, so long was the saluation of the *Chineses* delayed. He therfore out of hand dealeth with *Alphonsus Noronia* the Viceroy of *India*, and *Iohn Alboquercius* Bishop of *Goa* about the sending of an Embassage vnto *China*. The person appointed heerto was *Iames Perera* a man of singular piety, & by *Xauerius* the only desired, and one who was no way failing in that which was expected from him. For out of the desire he had to aduance Religion, he so tooke the businesse to hart, that in setting out his Embassage, and prouiding of Presents, he spent the greatest part of all his wealth. *The piety and liberality of Iames Perera.*

In the dispatch of this businesse *Xauerius* carryed all things with extraordinary speed. For within the compasse of a moneth, he had gotten ready not only the Patents, Letters, and Presents from the Viceroy, and Bishop for the Embassage, but also all other things that were necessary for so hard a voyage. Wherin he was much furthered by the prompt liberality of the Viceroy, a very pious man, & *Xauerius* speciall friend,

who

who gaue him both an Embaſſadour according to his deſire, and prouided all things neceſſary for that iorney, not with more care then ſpeed, & beſides commended earneſtly the whole buſineſſe by his letters vnto *Aluares Thardus* Gouernour of *Malaca*.

Now though *Xauerius* were daily imployed in this buſines of *China*, yet was he not vnmindful of his charge at home in *India*; ſetting in order all ſuch things as were neceſſary for the Society, in thoſe and other places round about. Wherfore he calleth *Gaſpar* the low country man from *Ormus*, and ordayneth him his Vicar, and Rectour of the Colledge of *Goa*, leauing with him moſt prudent and wholſome precepts for his direction. At the ſame time he ſent alſo a Prieſt, with a Coadiutor to aſſiſt him, vnto *Diu* (a Fort in the Portugheſes dominion ſtanding vpõ the mouth of the riuer *Indus*)& diuers others vnto other places, giuing to euery one inſtructions fit for the place, wherunto they were ſent.

Gaſpar the low countryman Frãcis his vicar.

The Towne Diu.

In this meane time *Mathew* one of the two *Iaponians* chanced to dy at *Goa*. Wherfore *Bernard* was his other companion was ſent to *Rome* in cõpany of *Andrew Fernãdes* whom *Xauerius* ſent vnto the King of Portugal, and to Rome alſo to *Ignatius* Founder of the Society, to bring backe with him ſome ſtore of the Society, and ſuch as were moſt fit for the *Iaponian* harueſt, and expedition of *China*. *Xauerius* writing at the ſame time vnto the King of Portugall, declared what his drift was, in going into *China*, in theſe words: We are only three of the Society who go into *China* with *Iames Perera* the Embaſſadour, with intention to redeeme the

The ſumme of Francis his letters to the King of Portugall.

Por-

Portugheſes who remayne there in captiuity, and to «
make a league of friendſhip betwene the King of *Chi-* «
na and them; & moreouer to wage warre againſt the «
Deuils, & thoſe who worſhip them. We will therfore «
in the name of the King of Hauen, denounce firſt vn- «
to the King of *China* himſelfe, then vnto the people, «
that they do not hereafter worſhip the Deuil, but God «
the creatour of mankind, & Ieſus Chriſt who redee- «
med and ſaued them. This may ſeeme indeed a bold «
attempt among ſo barbarous a people, and with ſo «
mighty a King, as to reprehend their errours, and «
preach vnto thē another law. But then we are againe «
greatly encouraged, that this deſire of ours cōmeth aſ- «
ſuredly from God, who hath ſo repleniſhed vs with «
firme hope and confidence heerin, that depending «
wholy vpon his goodnes, we ſhall not need to doubt «
of his omnipotent power, which by infinite degrees «
ſurpaſſeth that of the King of *China*.

Beſides this, he writeth alſo many other things in
the ſame Epiſtle to the King of Portugall, wherby
did euidently appeare his great courage of mind, accompanied with the like humility; as alſo his ſingular
feruour and zeale for the aduancement of the Chriſtian Faith, euen with the manifeſt danger of his
owne life. But, becauſe thoſe things belong not properly to this preſent Hiſtory, we will heere paſſe them
ouer in ſilence, reſeruing the ſame to a Volume a
part, wherein we haue made a collection of allmoſt
all *Xauerius* his Epiſtles., that haue come vnto our
hands.

Francis being now ready to depart from *Goa*, to the
end

end he might ftirre vp in thofe of the Society a great loue to Humility and Obedience, he called togeather all the Fathers and Brothers, and like a rare maifter of Obedience, very efficacioufly exhorted them all to the practife of thofe Vertues, & finally confirmed by this notable deed of his, what he had commended

An exá-ple of Chriftiá humility vnto them in words. For hauing conftituted *F. Gafpar* aforefaid Superiour ouer all the Society in *India*, and ouer himfelfe alfo, he fell downe at his feete, and after an vnufuall manner, not heard of before, promifed entyre Obedience vnto him; ftriking thereby no leffe admiratió into the reft of the Fathers prefent, then into *Gafpar* himfelf. Wherupon all the reft with weeping eyes through the tender feeling they had therof, proftrate themfelues in like manner, and promife one by one to performe the fame; no one refufing to imitate the example which *Xauerius* their Maifter had giuen them. Then, becaufe that being perhaps the laft time he was to fee them, all bedewed with mutuall teares, he imbraceth euery one; & out of all thofe who earneftly defired to follow him, he chofe only foure, not fo much to take them with him into *China*, as to fend them for a fupply into *Iaponia*.

He departed therefore from *Goa* vpon the 15. day of Aprill in the yeare 1552. leauing behind him many good wifhes, both to himfelfe, and his iourney. As foone as the fhip was come into the mayne Ocean, there arofe a vehement tempeft, which put her into extreme danger. When the ftorme was moft violent, and euery one (efpecially *Iames Perera*, who was a skilfull Pilot) affrighted with the imminent danger they were

were in, *Xauerius* remayned without any feare at all.
And looking vpon *Perera*, who ſtood as one benum-
med with feare: Take courage *Iames*, quoth he, the
Diuine Prouidence protecteth vs. Would to God the
other ſhip which put out of the Hauen togeather with
vs, fared as wel, the ſignes of whoſe calamity we ſhall
ſhortly behould. As for the ſhippe wherein we are
carryed, in a docke was ſhe built, and in a docke ſhall
ſhe be taken aſunder agayne. This triple Prophecy
was verifyed by the euent thereof. For preſently the
wind began to fall, and the ſtorme to ceaſe. Then by
the planckes, veſſels, and bodyes which floated vp &
downe the ſea, they manifeſtly perceyued that the o-
ther ſhip was caſt away. And laſtly, that very ſhip
wherin they ſayled, being thirty yeares after brought
into the Docke, to be taken aſunder and mended,
verifyed the whole Prophecy of *Xauerius*.

A triple Prophecy.

About the eight day after their departure from *Goa*
they arriued at *Cocinum*. There, when he had with
much ioy & côfort, viſited thoſe of the Society in that
place, being informed of the neceſſity of others that
liued in *Comorinum*, and *Colanum*, he wrote backe in
all haſt to *Gaſpar* his Vicar, to ſuccour them as ſoone
as might be, and whatſoeuer he ſhould do in that kind
to certify him therof by writing with the firſt opportunity, not doubting but that he would vſe the more
ſpeed and diligence therin, ſince he was preſently to
giue an accompt therof.

Hauing ſtayed a few dayes at *Cocinum*, he ſayled
to *Malaca* the ſame moneth, and about the midſt of
their courſe, a vehement tempeſt put both the paſ-

F f f   ſengers

fengers & marriners into great feare. The confideration of the prefent danger had now ftroken them all with a difmall terrour, when as *Xauerius*, whilft others bewailed their owne, & their friends diftreffe commeth forth amongft them with a cheerfull countenance, willeth them to take courage, and put away all feare. Then going vp to the Poope of the fhip, he hangeth in the fea a little Reliquary, tyed by a cord, and hauing withall made his prayers vnto God, returneth againe into his cabbin to heare Confeffions. A ftrange thing. Vpon a fuddayne the winds ceafe, the tempeft is allayed, and they fayle on forward with fayre weather. When they had giuen thanks to God for this their preferuation, their feare as comonly it hapneth, was turned into ouer much fecurity. But *Xauerius* aduifing the maifter to looke vnto himfelf, told him, that he was very much afrayd, leaft in the fame iorney other difficulties no leffe dangerous then the former, were hanging ouer their heades. And iuft fo, it came to paffe. For the fhip running twice againft the rockes, was almoft caft away, which perhaps would haue fo happened, if *Xauerius* prayers had not preuented the danger.

Neither did he in this iorney, foretell their owne dager only, but the calamity alfo of others, though in a more hidden manner. He was at that time farre diftant from *Malaca*, nor had any man come lately fro thence, when vpon the fuddain he earneftly intreated the paffengers, to make feruent prayer to God for the Citty of *Malaca*, which was, as he feared, at that time infected with grieuous fickneffe. The euent pro-

A tepeft by Xauerius is calmed through Gods helpe.

proued this to be a diuine preſage. For aſſoone as they
ariued at *Malaca* they find it almoſt vnpeopled throgh
a grieuous plague, which happened among them by
reaſõ of the great wants they had endured in the late
ſiege. And firſt of all, it had ſpread itſelfe amongſt
the Cittizens, afterwards it made as great hauoke a-
mongſt the Country people, & ſtrangers; and was at
laſt by litle and little crept into the Nauy, which was
then lately come from Portugall. And although in
the very ſame ſhippe wherein *Xaucrius* came, this plague had made an end of fourty men; yet by Gods
goodnes, it had not once touched any of his companions.

CHAP. VI.

He Excommunicateth the Gouernour of Malaca.

AVERIVS was more friendly entertained at *Malaca* by the Cittizens, conſidering the calamities wherwith they were
oppreſſed, then by the Gouernour himſelf.
As ſoone therfore as he was come to the Reſidence of
the Society, being not ignorant of the combat he was
ſhortly to vndergo, he earneſtly intreated all his cõ-
panions, by their ſerious prayers, to commend to God
his iourney into *China*, greatly fearing that the e-
nemy of mankind would by all poſſible meanes ſeeke
to hinder the ſame by his miniſters. Which feare

Fff 2   of

of his was not, indeed, without good ground. For the Gouernor of *Malaca* hauing no difpofition in him worthy of a Portughefe, began to enuy *Iames Perera's* glory, to whome he had long before borne a grudg; well forefeeing that not only great gaynes, but much honour alfo, would redound to an Embaffadour that fhould be fent from the Viceroy of *India* into *China*. Wherefore by a deuice, and help alfo of fome of the chiefe of the Citty, vnder colour of a fiege that was feared might happen to *Malaca*, he refolued to hinder *Perera* his Embaffage.

Francis, who had his mind wholy fixed vpon his iourney perceauing this, began by all māner of fweet meanes, to draw the Gouernour from his refolution. But emulation which had blinded his mind, ftopt alfo his eares. For neither the Bifhop of *Goa* his Letters, nor the Viceroyes Patents, nor all the allegations, or intreaties of friends could any whit mooue him, fo obftinate he was. *Xauerius* therfore who had lately followed a fuite of his with the Viceroy, & procured him money by way of reward, commeth vnto him with great humility, and firft requefteth him for friendfhip fake; then befeecheth him for Chrifts fake who was their common Lord and Father, that he would permit him to go into *China* with the Embaffadour, whome the Viceroy had appointed; & that he would not be any hindrāce or obftacle to the fetting forward of Chrifts Ghofpell; laftly that he would not comply with the diuell whofe defire was to hinder the fame, nor offer any fuch iniury to the Bloud, and Name of Chrift.

But

But the Gouernour, who through his infatiable pride & auarice, had already, in conceyt, made himfelfe fure of the Embaffage, fhewed himfelfe no leffe vngratefull towards men, then impious to God. For hauing loft all feeling of humanity, neither *Francis* his authority, nor the late courtefy he had done him, nor Religion it felfe, which was obiected vnto him, could once moue him a iote. Then *Francis* ioining threats to intreatyes, began ferioufly to aduife him, that he fhould beware he did not incurre the difpleafure and indignation of the Viceroy of *India*, the King of Portugall, and of God himfelfe; feeing that in this one bufineffe, he fhould violate the authority & maiefty of them all togeather. But he for all this remayned obftinate, and fhifted off all, in a moft contemptible manner.

Xauerius therfore, when he perceyued the fenfeleffe man neyther to refpect his King, nor feare God, being alfo vncertaine what to determine of, was conftrained by neceffity, to vfe the beft meanes he could deuife. He had indeed before that tyme, neuer carryed himfelfe publikely for Legate Apoftolicall: but now feeing that neyther his words, nor intreatyes would ferue the turne with that obftinate fellow, he thought beft to take vpon him for a while the perfon, which for humilityes fake he had fo long layd afyde, & terrify him, by threatning againft him prefent reuenge from heauen. He therfore produced the Popes Breue which he had fo long kept clofe, wherin was denounced Excommunication expreffy againft all fuch, as durft any way prefume to hynder the aduancement of Chriftiã Religion.   F ff 3

Now *Francis* his moderation was neuer more admired, then at this time. For though he were much
moued to fee fo great an iniury offered rather vnto
God, then to himfelfe; and though he could not obteine that which was iuft: yet neuertheleffe he kept
himfelfe in all quiet of mind, and did fo moderate his
grief, & held fo mighty a hand ouer his paffions, that
euen at the very time, when he was by the Gouernour vfed moft infolently, he fhewed no leffe temper
& mildnes in his words, then authority in his deeds.
For fo fweet was his behauiour vnto all forts of perfons, and fo wifely did he produce the forfaid Breue,
that he defired not to wound, but to terrify with the
fame. Yet if mildnes would not ferue, he determined
to vfe feuerity: and fo at laft when he had tryed all o-
ther meanes, being conftrained therunto by neceffity,
he pronounced the fentence. In the execution wherof notwithftanding he fhewed no leffe prudence, then
moderation. For to the end the bufineffe might be
carryed without tumult, or vproare, he thought it
beft to deale by a third perfon, as the *Iaponians* vfe to
do; thereby to auoyd meeting with the Gouernour
whome he knew had no ftay ouer his owne paffions.

He therfore went vnto *Iohn Soarius* the Vicar of
Malaca, and relating to him all the matter, intreated
him to vndertake the bufineffe. Now when the Vicar
had taken vpon him to performe it carefully, as wel
to fatisfy his duty therin, as for friendfhip fake, *Fracis*
giueth vnto him a fupplication, as a teftimony, no
leffe of his moderation in this bufines, then his authority; which fupplication we haue thought good to
insert

Francis notable modera-tio when he was iniured.

His mo-deration in exco-munica-ting.

He dea-leth with the Go-uernour by a third per-fon, as the Iapo-nians vfe to do.

infert into this Hiftory, wherby it may more euidently appeare what tranquility of mind and moderatiõ
Xauerius held, when he was moft intemperately abufed. This therfore is the tenour therof.

    Pope *Paul* the III. at the inftance of our gracious "
King, fent me into the Eaft for the cõuerfion of Eth- "
nickes, that to the vttermoft of my power I might la- "
labour in dilating the Gofpell of Chrift, and drawing "
men to the knowledge & worfhip of him who made "
the world, according to whofe image and likeneffe "
they were created. And that I might performe this "
bufineffe the more exactly, and with more ample au- "
thority, his fayd Holines hath alfo made & cõftituted "
me Legate Apoftolicall, in teftimony whereof he fent "
vnto the King of Portugall, his Letters Pontificall, "
together with a Breue, that if he iudged it expedient "
(becaufe indeed he fēt me hither at the Kings requeft) "
he might by thofe helpes, fet forth and ftrengthen my "
authority. Whereupon his Maiefty, when I came vn- "
to him at *Lifbone*, whither he had called me, deliue- "
red me with his owne hands the fayd Breue, in tefti- "
mony of my Apoftolicall Legation, and togeather "
with it, his owne Letters Royall. "

    Thefe, at my firft arriuall in *India*, I prefented vn- "
to *Alboquertius* Bifhop of *Goa*, who did both acknow- "
ledge and approue the fame. Wherefore he thinking "
alfo that there might be much good done concerning "
matters of Chriftian Religion in *China*, hath fent me "
thither with this intention, that I might lay open to "
thofe people the true Religion, then the which there "
is no other way to faluation. That this is fo, you may ".
                know

know by his owne letters to the King of *China,* which I haue purpofely fent you, that you may therein ma-nifeftly fee what his Lordfhips opinion, and defire is concerning my voyage into *China.* The Viceroy of *India* alfo thinking that it was much for Gods glory, for me to haue fafe entrance into the bounds of *China* hath fent with me *Iames Perera* vpon an Embaffage vnto the King of *China.* This is teftifyed by the fame Viceroyes commands, and letters to *Iames* himfelfe. And *Francis Aluarez* keeper of the Caftle of *Goa,* who is alfo the Kings Procuratour, and Attourney Gene-rall caufed all things to be difpatched as the Viceroy had commanded. Yet the Gouernour of *Malaca* is not afraid to hinder this our iorney, fo acceptable to God, fo beneficiall to men, and vndertaken by fuch, and fo great authority; and withall to withftand the Ghofpell of Chrift.

Therfore I earneftly intreat and befeech you, in the name of God, & of the Bifhop of *Goa* whofe au-thority you beare, that, for as much as in this place you reprefent the perfon of the Bifhop, you will care-fully declare vnto the Gouernour of this Citty, his Holines Decrees which begin thus: *Qui verò de cætero;* (wherby all thofe who hinder his Holineffe Legates are excommunicated) and to requeft him for Gods fake, that he will not hinder our faid iorney, vnder-taken by the Viceroyes and Bifhops authority. If he wil not defift, then prefently denounce vnto him that he is excommunicated, not by the Bifhop of *Goa's,* or by yours, or my authority, but by the fupreme po-wer, and authority of thofe holy Bifhops, who firft
made

made thofe Decrees and Canons. Wherfore you fhall «
intreate him in my behalfe, by the death, & pretious «
wounds of our Sauiour Iefus Chrift, that he will not «
caft himfelfe headlong into fuch grieuous Ecclefiafti- «
call cenfures. For God will certainly lay farre greater «
punifhments vpon him, then he doth imagine. «

Then I do befeech you, to fend me back this very «
fupplicatió, togeather with the Gouernours anfwere, «
to the end I may teftify to the Bifhop, that my negli- «
gence hath not bin the caufe, why I haue not gone «
forwards on my iorney into *China*, which I vnder- «
tooke by his aduife and counfayle. Alfo I moft ear- «
neftly befeech you, that you wil difpatch this with all «
fpeed that poffibly may be, for the fit feafon for na- «
uigation into *China* paffeth away. If you do this, you «
fhall at once, do both God great feruice, & me a fpe- «
ciall fauour. Neither can I be brought to belieue that «
the Gouernor is fo obftinate or hard-harted, but that "
he will difmiffe vs prefently, as foone as he is made "
acquainted with his Holineffe decrees.

The Vicar therfore moued by this fupplication &
intreaties of *Francis*, goeth to the Gouernour, and declareth vnto him plainly, that he is forthwith excommunicated by his Holines authority, vnleffe he defift
from hindring of *Xauerius* endeauours, & withal intreateth him by the death and paffion of our Bleffed
Sauiour not to commit any thing which might caufe
vnto him fo deadly a wound, together with no fmall
difgrace. And withal, that he would beware how he
intangled himfelf in fo heinous & vnexpiable a crime
for which certainly, God would take a more feuere

accompt

accoumpt of him, then he could imagine. But the
poore Gouernour harbouring a world of difordinate
affections within his breft, could not be perfuaded to
heare what was fayd vnto him. For neyther his Holineffe authority, nor the threatning of excõmunica-
tion could once induce the miferable man to giue o-
uer what his madneffe had begun; fo farre is Enuy
from thinking any thing vnlawfull. Wherby it manifeftly appeared that it was not fo much the cbftina-
cy of the Gouernour, as of the Diuell himfelfe, who
was afrayd of the kingdome of *China*, and his owne
ample domination therein. At laft, with much ado it
was obtained of him, to permit *Francis* to go forwards
into *China*, but for *Perera* the Embaffadour, he could
by no meane be drawen vnto it. Thus was the whole
Embaffage, and *Xauerius* defigne brought to nothing,
as afterward appeared by the effect, through the default of one paffionate man.

The Em
baffage
into *Chi-
na* hin-
dred.

Then *Francis* being indeed greatly moued at fuch
impudent audacity, thought it high tyme to giue an
example of his feuerity, that none might thence forward dare to attempt any fuch thing heerafter. Wherfore he giueth order, that the Gouernour, with all his
minifters and officers by name, according to courfe,
fhould be declared excommunicated by Apoftolicall
authority, not that his intention was to inflict any
new woūd vpon them, but that they might acknowledge the wound which they had before receyued. For
Xauerius himfelfe is reported to haue fayd, That he for
his part would neuer counfayle any one to lay fo fore
a wound as Excommunication is, vpon another; yet

he

he would by all meanes caufe their wounds to be laid *Xauerius*
open, to the view of all, who for their contumacy opinion
were wounded by Apoftolicall Decrees, to the end of exco-
munica-
that others might by their punifhment be warned frō ted per-
the like folly, and themfelues, at leaft through fhame fons.
might feeke a fpeedy remedy for fo loathfome a fore.

But *Xauerius* receiued no fmall wound in this cō-
bat. For it is certaine that of all the many & vnfpea-
kable vexations and troubles which he fuffered all
his whole life after, nothing euer hapned more bitter
vnto him, then that fo important a iourney fhould be
hindred by one, who ought to haue hin a chiefe furtherer therof. Wherfore being grieued not fo much
for himfelfe, as for the Gouernour, who by his owne
fault had caft himfelf into that danger, he is faid with A grie-
a fighing hart to haue cryed out in this manner : In- uous
fallibly that violatour both of humane and diuine law prophe-
will ere long pay deerely for his vnfatiable defire of cy.
money & honour ; not only in money, and honour,
but in body, if not (which God forbid) in foule alfo.

Then looking vpon the Church which ftood ouer
againft him, he caft himfelfe downe vpon his knees,
and with his hands lifted vp to heauen, began to pray
to God for him ; & with his eyes all gufhing out with He by
teares, cryed out: I therfore befeech, and earneftly his pray-
intreat thee, O Iefu Chrift, God of my hart, by thofe ers obtey
neth of
moft bitter torments of thy death, that thou wilt be- God pā-
hold thofe thy pretious wounds, which continually nance
thou fheweft vnto thy heauenly Father for vs, and for the
vouchfafe alfo to apply the benefit therof to this mi- Gouernour of
ferable wretch; that being taught by his owne mifery *Malaca,*

Ggg 2   he

he may at laft come to himfelfe againe. Neither were
his prayers, nor prophecy in vaine. For not long after,
whē he had againft al iuftice done many other things,
and with the fame impudency, and audacioufneffe
contemned the Viceroyes command, wherwith he
had contemned *Xauerius* authority, he by the watch-
full wrath of Gods indignation, was punifhed according to the height of his arrogancy. So as by the Viceroyes order, and command the obftinate wretch
was caft into fetters, being accufed to haue gone a-
bout to reuolt from his King; and forthwith, bound
as he was, was carryed to *Goa* to the Viceroy, & from
thence fent into Portugall to the King; where being
defpoyled of all the goods which he had vniuftly gotten, branded with ignominy, condemned to perpetuall imprifonement, and his body couered all ouer
with a moft loathfome leaproufy, he ended his dayes
in fuch mifery, that the King feemed not fo much to
reuenge the tranfgreffion of his Command, as God
the violating of his diuine Maiefty. At laft this wretch
being euen tyred out with calamities, opened his eyes,
and by wholfome pennance, wafhed away the ftaynes
of his former finfull life.

CHAP.

CHAP. VII.

The designe of going vvith the Embassa-dour into China *being broken of,* Xaue-rius *notvvithstanding setteth forvvard thither.*

N O W although *Xauerius* his designe were broken of, yet was he not a whit discouraged; but knowing his combat was not so much with men, as with the common Enemy of mankind, he thought he was bound to make all resistance he could, not to giue ground therby vnto the Diuell. He was not ignorant that in the kingdome of *China* there were very many prisons full of prisoners; and that all strangers who presumed to enter in thither, without publicke warrant, were condemned to perpetuall imprisonmēt. These things which would haue bin a terror vnto others were an encouragement to him. For that, burning both with the loue of Christ and men, he bequeathed himselfe vnto perpetuall imprisonemnt, that he might first preach the Ghospell vnto those that were in captiuity, and afterwards by them to others. And he conceyued such an hope within himselfe, that if he could but once bring any of the prisoners to imbrace the fayth of Christ, they would afterwards, when they were set at liberty, bring their owne family to the same fayth; and might also, if it

His desire to propagate the faith.

Ggg 3   were

were Gods bleſſed will, procure his freedome alſo, ſo to propagate the Chriſtian Religion.

Now though *Xauerius* in reſpeᶜᵗ of the peruerſity of men, found no humane aſſiſtance in ſo hard and difficult a buſineſſe; yet for all this, placing a firme confidence in the diuine Goodnes, he reſolued to go forward into *China,* and try what he could do alone; hoping at leaſt, that if he could not himſelfe enter into the kingdome, he might yet open a way therinto for others of the Society, and leaue an example to them that ſhould come after him, of what himſelfe intended and deſired to haue done. He therefore ſendeth three of his cōpanions, to wit *Baltazar Gage*, *Edward Silua*, and *Peter Alcaceua* into *Iaponia*, & departeth himſelfe

He ſhaketh of the duſt of his ſhooes.

from *Malaca* with one companion only, & a *Chineſe* for his Interpreter. And at the gate of the Towne ſhaking off the duſt from his feete (as Chriſt had commanded his Diſciples to do) he denounceth to that Citty, wrath from heauen, and many other miſeries. And as he had denounced, ſo it fell out. For ſhortly

A denouncing of calamities.

after, the Citty was ſo waſted, and exhauſted with warre, famine, and plague, that being before of great reſort, it was almoſt left vnpeopled.

Now *Xauerius* although he were not ignorant that *Perera* the Embaſſadour was much afflicᵗed by reaſon his Embaſſage was thus hindred, and for the great expences alſo which he had byn at, in ſetting forth the ſame; yet for al that, he could not be induced to ſpeak with him at his departure, leaſt by imbracing one another, both their griefes might be increaſed, as ordinarily it hapneth. Wherefore hauing a greater feeling
ling

ling of *Perera's* griefe then his owne, he writeth vnto
him from out the ſhip, a moſt friendly letter, aſſuring
him, that the contumely togeather with the dommage
which he had incurred, would one day turne both to
his great gayne, & honour. Which fel out accordingly. For that by the King of *Portugall* (to whome
Francis had moſt earneſtly commended him) he was
afterward rayſed, to great wealth and dignity.

    Xauerius leauing *Perera* the Embaſſadour behind
him, imbarked himſelfe for *China* in a ſhip of his, by
his permiſſion, whereby the very ſhip it ſelfe might
put him in mind both of the loue to his deereſt friend
and of the benefit he had receyued from him . Now a
little before his going away, the Vicar commeth to
him abcard, & intreated him that he would ſalute the
Gouernour before his departure from *Malaca* , leaſt
he might giue occaſion to the people to thinke he was
not in charity with him, if he went away without due
ſalutations. But *Francis* inflamed rather with the zeale
of Gods honour, then with any anger, whereto notwithſtāding he was iuſtly prouoked: Shal I, quoth he,
go to ſalute one that is caſt out of the Communion of
the faythfull ? Aſſuredly I ſhall neuer heerafter either
ſee him, or he me in this life, nor after death alſo, but
then, when I ſhal accuſe him in the valley, of *Ioſaphat*
before the ſupreme Iudge, for that, being blinded by
his moſt wicked and baſe couetouſnes, he hath hindred ſo great an harueſt of ſoules. As for the rumours
& ſpeaches of mē, I do not any whit feare them, ſeing
it is manifeſt that he is excommunicated , & therfore
all men ought to fly his company, and conuerſation ,
                                which

[marginal note:] He auoideth by all meanes ſpeaking with an excommunicated perſon.

which I defire may be made knowne to all, by my authority, and example. Nay rather, quoth he, it may be feared, leaft by my faluting an Excommunicate perfon, the Cenfure wherwith the Pope hath bound him, and the paine of the excommunication fhould be extenuated: and fo I might perhaps be caufe, that others by my example, would conuerfe with him without any fcruple. Wherfore I pray yow let him alone with his owne bufines, for he fhall certainly neuer haue me his friend, as long as he hath God his enemy.

When he had difmiffed the Vicar with this an fwere, who was not able to make any reply therto, he putteth to fea in the moneth of Iuly, making all the haft he could from *Malaca*. But comming to make fome ftay at the ftraits of *Sincapura*, being not vnmindfull of his friends, he againe comforted *Iames Perera* the Embaffador, who remained ftill at *Malaca* afflicted for this late accident, with a letter full not only of affection, but piety alfo, earneftly befeeching him to cure the wound which he had receiued, with difcretion and prudence, and from thenceforward, by vniting his foule to God more feruently, by the Sacraments of Confeffion and Communion, to feeke thereby fecure meanes of confolation, and to conforme himfelfe wholy to the diuine will. For there was no doubt, but that difgrace & griefe would one day turne vnto his honour, and comfort. Then betaking himfelfe againe to fea, his two Companions fell into a long and dangerous fickneffe, in the tending and curing wherof, *Francis* his charity and patience

Comforts in fadnes and miferies are to be obtained of God by the Sacraments.

ence was continually employed, to the end that the Louer of the Croſſe, might neuer be without his Croſſe. And ſo hauing a proſperous nauigation, he came to *China* the third moneth, after his departure from *Malaca*.

CHAP. VIII·

He endeauoureth, though all in vaine, to open a paſſage into China.

THE Country of *China* is the furtheſt part of Aſia, inferiour to no one Regiõ therof in largeneſſe of extent, nor number of citties and Townes. For it is ſaid, to be in length aboue 400. leagues, and in breadth 300. And the Cittyes therin are ſo fraught with inhabitants, that the multitude being more then they can hould, the very riuers themſelues are couered ouer with ſhips, and inhabited like Townes. Towards the Eaſt & South it is compaſſed with the Ocean. On the North ſide it is diuided from thoſe *Scythians* of *Aſia*, whome we call *Tartarians*, with a moſt vaſt, and almoſt endleſſe wall. The Weſt ſide therof lyeth towards the furtheſt part of *India*.

The description of *China*.

The *Chineſes* themſelues being a people more inclyned to peace then warre, liue al vnder the obediéce of one King. There be no petty Kings, nor Princes among them as in other Kingdomes; but one King only ruleth ouer them all. He appointeth Gouernours

The cuſtomes of the *Chineſes*.

ouer

ouer euery Prouince, and is alwaies by them informed of the moſt important affayres of euery place. Theſe Gouernours are not brought vp in the Court, but in Academyes : For by their Lawes, thoſe that be of the Kings bloud and alliance, haue neuer any thing to do with the gouernment of the Kingdome. Out of theſe Academies are choſen men, famous both for eloquence, and knowledge in the Lawes, and theſe are made Gouernours ouer Cittyes and Prouinces, but yet neuer of their owne Prouince, or Citty. They ordinarily eſteeme ſo baſely of their Gods, that when either their prayers do not take effect, or any ill fortune befalleth them, they whippe, and beate their Houſhold Gods, like ſlaues. One would thinke there were no Gods among them, but their owne magiſtrates, of whoſe power they ſtand in great feare, by reaſon of their extraordinary ſeuerity. There be indeed many other things, and thoſe not of common note, recounted of the manners and cuſtomes of the *Chineſes,* which becauſe they make nothing to our preſent purpoſe I willingly heere paſſe ouer. Yet I can hardly ſay, whether that cuſtome of theirs be more inhumane, or imprudent, whereby contrary to other Nations which haue entercourſe with one another, they debarre all ſtrangers from comming into their Country, vnder payne of death.

The Iland Sanciana.   There is adioyning to the ſea coaſt of *China,* an Iland called *Sanciana,* a deſert place, and without any tillage, lying about 70. miles from the Continent. In this Iland the Portugheſes, and *Chineſes* meeting togeather for traffique ſake, had ſleightly built themſel-

ues

ues certayne cottages of straw, and boughes to serue
them for their present vse. *Xauerius* therfore tending
to this place for his traffique also, as they sayled along
by the coast of the Iland, the mayster began to doubt,
whether he were not already past the Port of *Cunianū*
or no, whither he had directed his course to land. Yet
thinking he was still short thereof, sayled forward
with good speed, when as *Francis* (seeing him in that
doubt) telleth him that he was already past the *Port*.
Whereat not knowing what to thinke, he presently
stroke sayle, for that *Xauerius* had yet neuer deceyued
him in any thing he affirmed: so as deeming, that he
ought to giue more credit to *Xauerius* then to himself,
casteth ancker, and causeth the Cock-boate to be let
downe into the sea, wherin he sent certaine marriners
with all speed to make enquiry of the truth. Within
a few houres after, they returned backe together with
certain Portugeses in their boat who remained in the
Iland, certifying them that they were past the Port of
Cunianū, as *Xauerius* had affirmed. At which newes the
marriners being all stroken into admiration, cryed
out and sayd, that certaynly *Xauerius* had it reuealed
to him from heauen. Then weighing ancker, and turning their course backe agayne, they sayled towards
the Port.

As soone as it was bruited amongst the inhabitants of the Iland, that *Francis Xauerius* (for his name
was also famous in those places) was coming thither,
presently all the Portugheses runne with ioy to the
shore side to meete him. When he was landed, after
they had courteously saluted ech other, they conten-

ded

ded amongſt themſelues who ſhould haue ſo worthy a
man for his gueſt. But *Xauerius* ſoone decided the có-
trouerſy, without wrong to any, and lodged with
George Aluarez his ancient and deere friend. Then he
deſired the Portugheſes in generall, that they would
build him vp a litle Chappel of ſtraw, and boughes,
with the leaſt expence they could; wherin he might
ſay Maſſe, adminiſter the Sacraments, & inſtruct children, and ſeruants in their Catechiſme, according to
his cuſtome. They condeſcended moſt willingly to
what he required, and very diligently ſet vpon the
buſineſſe; ſo that within two dayes there was built a
chappell for him, vpon a hill, which runneth downe
with equall deſcent vnto the Port.

   Xauerius therefore, as his ancient cuſtome was,
began preſently to exerciſe therin his ſacred functions
with all diligence, by comforting ſometymes thoſe
that were ſicke in the ſhips, and at other tymes relieuing the poore with almes which himſelfe would beg
of the richer ſort. Sometymes alſo would he diſpute
with the *Chineſe* merchants concerning their owne, &
the Chriſtians Religion. And in theſe labours & exerciſes he ſpent two moneths & a halfe with extraordinary feruour of ſpirit: which made him alſo renowned, euen amongſt the *Chineſes* themſelues, no leſſe
for wiſedom then for ſanctimony of lyfe. In the meane
tyme he inquired of the *Portugheſes* & *Chineſes* if there
could be any meanes poſſibly found, to bring in the
Ghoſpell into *China*. They both anſwered that it was
a very hard matter, & full of danger, ſeeing that by
ſpecial cómand of the King himſelf, al entrances into
                                                  the

The *Chi-
neſes* ex-
clude
ſtrangers

the Kingdome were kept with a moſt ſtrict watch, & al ſtrangers debarred frō acceſſe thither vnder paine of death, no leſſe to the commers themſelues, then to the bringers of them in. Moreouer, it was not lawfull for any forreyner to touch vpon the Continent, without expreſſe command of ſome of the Gouernours: neyther durſt the *Chineſes* aske leaue of them, by reaſon of their rigorous gouernement : nor were the Portugheſes able to do it, being excluded no leſſe then other ſtrangers. Wherefore there was neyther *Portugheſe* nor *Chineſe* to be found, who durſt vndergo ſo manifeſt a dāger as death, or certayne captiuity.

But *Francis*, as he was of an vndaunted courage euē in thoſe attempts which ordinarily ſtrike terrour into others, was notwithſtāding greatly inflamed through the continuall good ſucceſſe of his indeauours, to encounter with this danger. Wherfore, ſeing there was no other way to compaſſe the buſines, he reſolued to aduenture euen vpon the dangers themſelues, and to contriue by one meanes or other, to be conueyed ſecretly into ſome Citty of *China*, that ſo he might haue acceſſe vnto the Gouernour, & deale his buſines with him himſelfe. This deuiſe of *Xauerius* was generally diſliked of by all the Portugheſes, as ouer bold and temerarious. Wherfore there wanted not ſome who out of their friendſhip and familiarity with him, endeauoured al they could to terrify him frō that deſigne, diſſuading him not to caſt himſelf wilfully into ſo manifeſt a danger, either of death, or perpetuall ſeruitude. For the Gouernours (whome the Inhabitants call *Lutij*, and the Portugheſes *Mandarino's*) were ſo

Francis his inuincible courage in time of dāger.

The Magiſtrates of China's cruelty towards ſtrangers

H h h 3   ſeuere,

feuere, or rather harſh, and cruell in keeping their
Lawes, that euen for the leaſt fault, they do without
any difference of perſons beate to death, as well Inhabitants, as Forreiners. Of which cruelty they had
lately had a domeſticall example of certaine Portugheſes, who hauing the yeare before, bin by a tempeſt driuen vpon the ſhore of *China*, had found the
Chineſes diſpoſitions farre more cruell then the waues
of the Ocean, where they lay vntill that day in priſon
and miſery, cruelly rent, and torne with ſtripes, without any hope of deliuery. What reaſon therfore could
Xauerius haue to leaue of labouring amongſt other
nations, with certaine and ſecure hope of great good
which might be done, & to hazard his owne liberty,
only to intrude, by force, the Ghoſpell vpon a nation
fierce & cruel? and this which the Portugeſes ſaid, was
alſo confirmed by the general conſent of the *Chineſes*.

His zea-
le of ſou-
les.

But *Francis* being vndaunted at theſe things (ſo
much doth the force of diuine loue ouercome all humane feare) replied: That he deſired nothing more
from the bottome of his hart, then euen with his
owne death to bring the *Chineſes* to euerlaſting ſaluation. For do you not know (quoth he) being euen
taught by experience, that feare giues way to hope,
where the rewards are greater then the dangers ? can
you make any queſtion, but that the Citties of *China*,
if they ſhould once receiue the ſeed of the Ghoſpell,
would yield moſt plentifull fruit, by reaſon of their
moſt exaƈt manner of diſcipline, and gouernement?
And as it is doubtful whether my endeauor may haue
proſperous ſucceſſe or no; ſo is it certayne that my
ſer-

feruice will be gratefull to God. For fetters, torméts, ɛ
and death it felfe for Chrifts fake, ought to be to me ɛ
as a beatitude, and immortality.

He had now put his friends to filence with thefe
and the like fpeaches, when as being much troubled
with cares, he was taken fomewhat fuddainly with
an ague which held him 15. dayes, but by Gods fauourable affiftance foone cured ; yet in fuch māner as
that the fame feemed the forerunner of his death,
which was fo neere at hand. As foone as he was recouered, he returned prefently to his former exercyfes, hating nothing more then idleneffe, and reft.

CHAP. IX.

He agreeth vvith a Chinefe, *to carry him
priuately to* Cantona.

Otwithftanding all that could be alleaged
againft his going, he neuertheles diligétly
fought how he might be tranfported into
China. And firft hē began by all the art he
could inuent, to try the Portughefes, and afterwards
the *Chinefes*, propounding many wayes vnto them,
how they might conceale the bufineffe, & intreating
them to pleafure him in fo reafonable a requeft. But
they, being abfolutly refolued to take heed of themfelues, could not be wonne therto by any meanes or
intreaties, fince Feare had wholy fhut vp their eares a-
gainft the fame, being not willing to expofe their fortunes

tunes, and liues to fo manifeft a danger.

Francis therfore being not only depriued of all help, but alfo not knowing what to refolue vpon, had many different cogitations in his mind. And that no mortification might be wanting vnto him, both his companions lay very ficke. Befides, *Anthony of the holy Faith*, a *Chinefe* borne, and Schollar of the Colledge of *Goa*, whome he had brought with him from *India* for his Interpreter, hauing through want of vfe almoft forgotten the *Chinefe* language, could now ftād him in little fteed, efpecially feing he was wholy ignorant, and vnskilfull of that ciuill, and gentile language, which the Gouernours there are wont to vfe. But *Xauerius* hauing an inuincible hart & courage, & thinking with himfelfe that he was bound to leaue nothing vnattempted, perfifted neuerthelefe to follow on the bufines very hard, hoping that yet at laft he might, through Gods affiftance, ouercome the difficulty.

In the meane time there fell out no fmall accident which fet on fire, and inflamed his hope & defire. For he vnderftood that he King of *China* at that very tyme had fent abroad Embaffadours vnto all places round about, to make diligent inquiry after the Lawes, and Cuftomes of other Kingdomes. Wherefore there was great hope that it would be a gratefull and comfortable thing vnto his Maiefty, to vnderftand alfo of the Chriftians Lawes, & manner of lyfe. There were alfo fome of the *Chinefes*, men of good worth, and *Fracis* his familiar friends, who did earneftly perfuade him to go to *China*, thinking very wel of the Chriftian Religion,

ligion, by the fanctity of his life; perfuading themfelues that there was conteyned in thofe Bookes which
he carryed with him, fome excellent Law, and far better then theirs. Heerupon *Xauerius* being more ftirred
vp then before, vnto this noble enterprize, thought
verily that God had thus difpofed the *Chinefes*, & their
Kings mind, to the end the Ghofpell might at laft,
receaue entrance into that Kingdome, and fpread it
felfe ouer thofe moft populous Citties. Wherfore ful
of hope and confidence in God, he determined to try
all manner of wayes to haften on the matter. For he
doubted not, but that either without much danger,
and with great aduancement to the Chriftian caufe,
he fhould get acceffe vnto the King; or els if any hard The loue
mifhap fhould fall vnto him, he would efteeme it for of the
an extraordinary gayne. For to be tormented, and Croffe.
flaine for Chrift (which feemed was the greateft danger that could befall him) he thought it indeed, the
greateft benefit, that God could euer beftow vpon
him.

But all thefe difficulties giuing way at laft vnto
his Conftancy, as commonly it happeneth, within a
little while there was another who offred himfelfe for
his interpreter. Then finding out a merchant of *China*
who feemed a couragious man, he folliciteth & draweth him on by hopes and promifes, to vndertake that
hardy enterprize. And when as nothing could be
effected without prefent money, he beggeth of the
Portughefe merchants, and for a certaine quantity of
Pepper, to the valew of about 300. crownes, agreeth
with the merchant to carry him, with his interpreter

and his bookes very secretly in the night, and to set
him a land in *China* neere to the Port of *Cantona*. This
Cantona is a famous port Towne standing in the Continent, about 80. miles from *Sanciana* . The merchant therfore to keep the matter secret, least he shold
venture his life vpon the fidelity of his marriners,
of whome he was not secure, had thought to haue v-
sed his owne children, and the most trusty of his seruants for that purpose, and to transport *Xauerius* in
the night in a small vessell. Moreouer he had of his
owne accord promised to harbour him in his howse
and keepe him secret for the space of two or three
daies, till he might by some meanes or other declare to
the Gouernour of *Cantona* the cause of his comming
into *China* .

Now there were in this businesse two dangers obiected vnto *Xauerius* by his friends. The one, least the
merchāt hauing fraudulently taken the money should
breake his promise, & to conceale the matter, might
either expose him vpon some desart Iland, or els cast
him ouer board into the Sea . The other was, that
(though the Barbarian should keep his word, and set
him a shore neere the Port of *Cantona*) the Gouernour
of the Citty finding he had gotten in thither, being a
stranger, against the Kings Edict, without any publike warrant, might to make him an example vnto
others, cruelly whippe & murder him, or els cast him
into perpetuall prison . Against these obiections, *Xa-*
uerius opposed farre greater dangers which they were
not aduised of. First, said he, it was rather to be feared
least his owne diffidence, more truly then his warineffe,

neſſe, might be iniurious to the Goodnes and Prouidence of God, if the fearefulneſſe of mortall men ſhould cauſe him to leaue off that, which he had vndertaken by diuine inſtinct, and motion. Secondly (quoth he) I ſhould proue my ſelfe an vnworthy Diſciple of Chriſt,if I did not heare him, denouncing vnto me:*Who ſo looſeth his life for me, ſhall find it.*Wherfore ſeeing that the daungers of the body were farre lighter then thoſe of the ſoule, he thought it more ſecure to breake through thoſe, which might put his lyfe in hazard, then to hazard the ſaluation of his ſoule; ſeeing that to go to the *Chineſes,* and to ſubdew them to the faith of Chriſt (maugre the enuy of thoſe that went about to hinder it) carryed not, by Gods grace, more difficulty with it, then Glory.

*Math.*10.

At the ſame time alſo there hapned another ſtráge accident. *Peter Gerra* a chiefe Maiſter of a ſhip was going for *Iaponia* ; and now the Port which he meant to go vnto was in ſight, when as vpon a ſuddaine the wind wholy ceaſing,there followed ſuch a calme, that for two or three dayes the ſhip could make no way. Wherfore being troubled, and diſcontented in mind he thought to bend his courſe towards *China,* when as he ſaw *Xauerius* comming from *China* towards him in a litle boat (for the great ſhip ſeemed not to be farre of) and ſaluting him in a friendly manner, biddeth him be of good cheere, & ſpeedily make ready his full ſayle,for that he ſhould by Gods grace haue a proſperous wind. This prediction fayled not. For they had ſcarce hoyſed vp ſayle, when by a Weſterne gale they were carryed into the hauen. And to ſhew manifeſtly

that

this was a miracle wrought by *Xauerius* from the hand of God, they were no sooner come into the hauen, but the wind turned againe Southwest, which would certaynly haue driuen them into *China*, had they not already gayned the Port.

In the meane tyme whilst *Francis* expected the returne of the merchant, with whome he had agreed to carry him into *China*, he wrote many letters as wel to thofe of the Society, as to other friends. And first he wrote to *Fa. Gaspar* Rector of the Colledge at *Goa*, that he should with all speed procure the Bishop (so far was he from affuming any thing to himfelfe, although he were Legate Apostolicall) folemnely to declare all thofe of *Malaca* excommunicated by the Popes authority, who had hindred his iourney into *China*, to the end, that the wound being agayne renewed, might put thofe wretches in mind, to feeke at laft for fome remedy. He wrote alfo to *Francis Percz* Superiour at *Malaca*, that feeing the Gouernour had hindred his voyage into *China*, he should, togeather with all the reft of the Society there, depart from thence with the firft occafion into *India*. Neither did he forget his deere friend *Iames Perera*, but eafed his griefe now the third tyme by fending him confolatory letters, wherof this one claufe manifeftly declared his notable courage : I would to God (quoth he) we might one day meete one another in the K. of *China's* Court although I hope, if I can get into *China*, that you shall find me there, either made a flaue, or elfe a prifoner in the goale of *Cantona*, or the Kings Caftle.

CHAP.

CHAP. X.

His transporting into China *being differ-red, he fortelleth his owne death.*

VT now, *Xauerius* thinking vpon the con-uersion of *China*, and of obteyning there a crowne of Martyrdome, behold new and greater difficultyes are still cast in his way. For whilst with much ioy, for the hope lately concey-ued, he prepareth himselfe to his iourney, his new Interpreter, eyther through the secret dealing vnder hand of the Portugheses, or else through feare of tor-ments which he might likely vndergo, on a suddaine changeth his mynd : so as, regarding more the Feare which was represented vnto him, then the faythfull promise he had made to *Xauerius*, suddainly forsaketh him who had not the least feare of any such thing. Yet *Xauerius* constacy was no whit daunted with this vn-expected disaster ; but determined notwithstanding, to set forward with his old Interpreter, although, as we sayd, he were nothing fit, by reason of his discon-tinuance from exercise of the *Chinese* language.

Presently therefore, the Portughese Merchants not more sollicitous for *Xauerius* case, then for their owne, came all flocking vnto him of purpose, and compassing him round about, besought him most ernestly, that now at last he would desist from that so desperate an enterprize ; & if he had no feeling of his

owne

owne danger, that yet at least he would take some cō-
passion of his neyghbours, for that theron depended
not only his, but also all the Portughefes liues. Becaufe
the Gouernours of *China*, if they were once exasperaⴰ
ted by so bold an attempt, would not perhaps rest cō-
tent with the punishment of one, but might also call
all the other Portughefes to account for the same; and
therefore he ought not, togeather with his owne,
draw the fortunes, and liues of all his friends into the
same danger. But if he were absolutely determined,
and resolutely bent to try his fortune in this kind, that
yet at least he would expect a more cōmodious tyme,
and that the Portughese ships might first retyre from
that place, therby to free themselues from danger.

Xauerius
humani-
ty to-
wards
the Por-
tughefes
Vpon these their speaches *Xauerius* willeth them
to be of good courage, for if any dāger should happen
vnto them, himselfe being a base & miserable wretch
worth nothing, would vndergo it alone: wherefore
he was willing to atttempt nothing more vntill they
had made themselues secure. And so, whilst the Portughefes hasten to be gone, *Francis* also made himselfe
ready for his iourney. Yet certaynly, it was not the
will of God, that he should euer enter into *China*. And
that no difficulty heerein might be wanting, the *Chi-*
nese merchant aforesayd with whome he had contracted for his transport, deceyued him also. For whether by some accident that hapned in the meane time,
or out of feare of punishment, or by the instinct of
the Diuell, he wholy fayled in his promise. So as *Frā-*
cis hauing a long tyme expected him, but all in vayne,
was at last forced to cast of al hope of being transported

ted thither. When therefore he found as little fidelity in his merchant, as he had before done in his Interpreter, not knowing what to refolue vpon, and being
deftitute, both of all hope, and humane affiftance, he
had recourfe vnto the diuine; and with his wonted,
and vndaunted courage he began to thinke of new
meanes how to tranfport himfelfe into *China*, not i-
magining that he was fo foone to be tranfported into
heauen.

Whilft things ftood in this manner, there happened a new occafion, which began to put him againe
in good hope, but proued nothing to the purpofe, as
it afterward fell out. For he vnderftood that the King
of *Sion* (which is a Kingdome neere to *Malaca*) had
determined to fend an Embaffage the next yeare vnto
the King of *China*. Wherefore being glad of this good
newes, which he hoped would be for his purpofe, he
refolued, that if the *Chinefe* merchant came not to him
backe in tyme, he would take fhip for *Sion*, and there
endeauour that he might be tranfported into *China*
with the faid Kings Embaffadour. But now the tyme
approached when he was not, as he thought, to begin his trauayles and labours, but to make an end of
them. For whilft he fought for new helpes if his old
fhould fayle him, and thought of his tranfport into
the Kingdome of *Sion*, he was vnexpectedly called
to the celeftiall *Sion*.

He had now earneftly commended his ficke companion (that he might not be a burden or hindrance
to him in his iourney into *China*) to the Portughefes
who were to returne into *India*, to go along with
them

them , himſelfe with *Anthony of the holy Fayth* , and another ſeruant remayning ſtill in *Sanciana* . After the Portugheſe ſhips were gone, *Francis* (as the property of hope is neuer to giue ouer) ſtill expecting the *Chineſe* merchant, employed himſelfe with neuertheleſſe diligence in his accuſtomed exerciſes of Charity , to gayne thereby , by Gods holy aſſiſtance , the victory ouer Sathan, who as he perceyued , vſed all the ſtratagemes he could to defeate his endeauours. But God whoſe counſayles are vnſearchable , & wayes incomprehenſible had otherwiſe determined of the buſines : and being content with *Francis* his endeauour, reſerued the glory of conuerting the *Chineſes* , vnto others who were to come after.

God being therefore greatly delighted with the inflamed hart and deſyre, which *Xauerius* had both to labour , and ſuffer , pleaſed to beſtow vpon him rather the reward of all his trauayles formerly taken for his ſake (which were both many and great) then to open the way for him to new . And ſo vpon the very ſame day , which was appointed for his paſſing ouer into *China* , he fell into a ſicknes , whereof ſoone after he dyed. His diſeaſe was cauſed by the inhumanity of his Hoſt. For when the ſhips departed towards *India, Francis* his Hoſt alſo changing his mynd, and violating the right of Hoſpitality , being eyther taken with ſome toy the head, or prickt forward with deſire to be gone, departed in all haſt, without euer taking his leaue of *Xauerius* his old friend and gueſt ; no not expecting a ſhip which himſelfe had lately bought in another Iſand of *China*. For *Francis* according to

Francis being left by his hoſt falleth ſicke.

his

his cuſtome going to ſay Maſſe was accompanied with his ſaid Hoſt, who leauing that ſacred myſtery wherat he was preſent, and forſaking his gueſt, departed the Iland more like a fugitiue, then a friend.

Xauerius, as ſoone as he had done Maſſe, and made his accuſtomed recollection, & ſayd the prayer for the dead, looking about, perceyued that his Hoſt was abſent, and inquiring what was become of him, anſwere was made, that he was ſhipt in all haſt with the reſt for *Malaca.* Then *Xauerius*: Verily, quoth he, I am afrayd that his conſcience being guilty of ſome heinous ſinne ſuffereth him not to reſt in quiet through the wrath of God towards him. For what meaneth this ouerhaſty ſpeed? Behould the ſhip which he hath lately procured to be bought, is hourly looked for, yet is he loath to expect her. But let him go in Gods name to *Malaca*, from whence he ſhal neuer depart, for there the wretch will ſoone end his dayes. Of theſe two Prophecies the one was preſently verified, and the other not long after. For they who were preſent were ſcarcly come out of Church, when the ſhip he had bought vpon a ſuddayne appeared in ſight; wherat they were all ſtroken into admiration, and eſteemed *Xauerius* as a man ſent from God. And his Hoſt (as was afterward verifyed) a few dayes after his ariuall at *Malaca*, going into the forreſt to prouide himſelfe of wood was murdered there by theeues, and ſo made a miſerable end, for that he had byn the cauſe of *Francis* his vntimely death.

But *Xauerius* knowing he was not long to liue, fortold the ſame to ſome familiar friends, yet after a

A double Prophecy.

manner

manner no leſſe profitable, then admirable . As he
was one day in an aſſemby of *Portugheſes* : Let vs ſee
(ſayd he) how many we are heere, for within a yeare
moſt of vs ſhall dye. This Prophecy was more true,
then ioyfull . For of ſeauen who were then preſent,
fiue dyed that very yeare , whereof *Xauerius* himſelfe
was one, who certaynely both foreſaw and foretould
that his owne death was at hand . For that about
the ſame tyme alſo , he by diuine inſtinct, no doubt ,
forgetting all humane things, began to haue a great
deſire to ſee God, which was no ſmall token of the
beatitude wherunto he was now approaching. Wherupon he wrote in a certayne Epiſtle, That although
he had vntill that tyme deſired to haue lyfe graunted
him for the ſeruice of Chriſt, and the propagation of
his Ghoſpell; yet now thoſe liuely ſparkes were grow-
en but cold in him, through a burning deſire he had of
ſeeing , and inioyning the diuine Maieſty .

CHAP.   XI.

He endeth his life in a moſt holy manner.

Xauerius
liues by
begging.
THE ſuddayne, and vnfriendly departure
of *Xauerius* Hoſt, conſtrained him to begge
his victuals. And ſo much the more did
his pouerty afflict him , by how much the
more ſcarſe all things were made, by reaſon of the
ſtrict watch which the *Manderino's* made, who permitted no man to tranſport any victualls out of *Chi-*
na

na. Which incommodity he moſt patiently indured, hauing his mynd fixed more vpon Euangelicall pouerty, then vpon his owne neceſſity : wherefore he thought good, not to ſeek out any new Hoſt, but heerafter to prouide his victualls by begging. But now although his mynd, being wholy deſirous to ſuffer, did valiantly encounter with ſo great difficultyes, & diſcommodities of all things ; yet his body could not chooſe but be much broken therby, being euen worne out, as well with age and continuall labours, as with his late ſicknes alſo, whereof he was not as yet perfectly recouered. Beſides this, he was greatly afflicted in mynd, through the care and ſollicitude which his deſire of going into *China* cauſed in him.

Being therefore ſicke, not in body only but alſo in mynd, & earneſtly wiſhing his ſoule might by death be freed of all her anxietyes, about the twelfth of Nouember he fell agayne into his former ſicknes. He had ſcarefly made an end of ſaying Maſſe for the dead, when as a mortall feuer came vpon him, to open him the way to lyfe eternall. Wherfore, ſicke as he was, he withdrew himſelfe into the ſame ſhip which brought him thither, partly to viſit the ſicke therein as his cuſtome was, and partly alſo to take vp his lodging there among them: yet ſome few daies after, his ſicknes grew ſo violent, that being not able to endure the toſſing of the ſhip, he was conſtrained to go agayne to land. A Portugheſe Merchant therefore ſeeing ſuch a man as he, ſo pittifully tormeted with an hoat burning feuer, and lying abroad in the open ayre moued to compaſſion towards him, inuiteth him pre-

He agayⁿ nefalleth into his former ſicknes.

ſent-

He is en-
tertained
by a Por
tughese
in a cot-
tage.

sently in a courteous manner to take a lodging with him; and bringing him home to his house (which stood alone vpon a litle hill, being indeed more truly a cottage then an house) vsed him very liberally, considering the want of all things at that present. And taking a great care of his health, he intreated him to suffer himselfe to be let bloud. *Xaucrius*, although he knew well inough what kind of Phisitians that desert Iland could affoard, sayd notwithstanding, that for all things which belonged to the cure of his body, he would most willingly put himselfe into the Phisitians hands. And this he performed with all alacrity and resignation seeking all occasions whereby to exercise his obedience.

He prom
ptly o-
beyeth
the Phy-
sitian.

He therfore was let bloud, not without great paine, and conuulsion of his nerues. After which there followed in him a certayne loathing of all meates, although indeed there was not any meate to be gotten in the Iland fit for a sick person, except a few almonds which were sent vnto him by a Portughese Mayster of a ship, and that also too late: For he did now so much loath al kind of food, that he could not take any thing at all. In the meane time, perceauing that his last day was neere at hand, he caused all such things as he had brought with him vnto the cottage to be carryed backe agayne into the ship, to the end they might not be lost. Hauing now passed two whole dayes without receauing any sustenance at all, as his sicknesse more and more increased, so also did his patience & vertue more and more shew it selfe.

The grie
uous pai-
nes of
his sick-
nes.

His loa-
thing of
his meate

He had now layne fifteene daies in that poore shelter

ter

ter of Cottage expofed to the wind and weather, and
in the cold of winter, not only deftitute of all humane
help and affiftance, but tormented alfo with the vehemency of his burning, and mortall feuer; yet bare
he all thefe difcommodityes, and the violence of his
ficknefe alfo, with fuch a quietnes of mynd, and admirable patience as cannot be expreffed. He was neuer
heard to fpeake fo much as one word, either by way of
complaint for the payne of his infirmity, or to aske
any thing of any that were about him, as men are
wont to do in tyme of great ficknefe. Nay contrariwife, all his fpeaches and geftures were fuch, that
it fufficiently appeared, he accounted his infirmity
to be a very great benefit, beftowed vpon him from
God, as a fubiect wherupon to exercife himfelf in folid
vertue, & to deferue an euerlafting crowne of glory.

His excel
lent pa-
tience.

One thing only there was which did a litle grieue
him, to wit, that he fhould dye a naturall, and ordinary death in his bed, and be depriued of the crowne
of Martyrdome, which he had fo vehemently defired,
efpecially feeing that he was at that time, as it were v-
pon the point to obtaine the fame. But being not ignorant that the Glory of Martyrdom was a free guift of
God, the which was oftentymes denyed to thofe who
defired it, & giuen to others that thought leaft on it;
he conformed his will to the difpofition of the diuine
Prouidence, quietting his mind by thinking himfelfe
vnworthy of fo great an honour.

Now, the violence of his infirmity growing more
& more vehement, fully declared the fanctity which
was fo deeply ingrafted in him. For, as we fee, moft

Kkk 3   com-

commonly in others, when they are tormented with payne, then their corrupt nature moſt of all maniſeſteth it ſelfe; but in *Francis* contrarywiſe, there appeared at this tyme a true and ſolid piety. For that he vſed the ſelfe ſame actions almoſt, when he lay euen a dying, that he was wont to do, whē he was in health, ſometymes caſting his eyes to heauen, and ſpeaking to Chriſt our Sauiour with a ioyfull & cheerful countenance, as though he had byn viſibly preſent: at other times reciting certaine Verſes out of the Pſalmes, with great feeling of deuotion; repeating very often theſe words, & the like: *Ieſu Sonne of Dauid, haue mercy on me.* And, *Thou O God take pitty on my ſinnes.* *Mary Mother of God, remember me &c.* Wherein he ſpent two whole dayes.

He departteh this lyfe.   The laſt houre of his lyfe was now come: Wherfore holding a Crucifix in his hands, and fixing his eyes ſtedfaſtly thereupon, he fetcheth many a feeble ſigh, and often cryeth out, O *Ieſu God of my hart*: perpetually mingling his prayers with his teares, vntill both voice, and lyfe did fayle him. And thus combatting moſt valiantly, both with his infirmity, and with death it ſelfe vntill the laſt gaſpe, vpon the ſecond day of December (being the Feaſt of *S. Bibiana* the Virgin)calling inceſſantly vpon the ſweet Names of *Ieſus* and *Maria*, with all content and quietnes of ſpirit, he reſted in our Lord, and rendred vp his ſoule to heauen, there to accompany thoſe, whome in his life he alwayes bare in hart, and at his death were neuer abſent from his mouth.

     After he was departed, there ſtill appeared ſuch a cheer-

cheerfulnes & sweetnes in his coūtenance, that the beauty of his body was an euident demonstration of the
beatitude of his soule. He died about the 55. yeare of
his age, ten yeares after his arriuall in *India*, & in the
yeare of our Lord 1552. A man without all question,
admirable both for true vertue, & incredible courage
of mind, and aboue all, for the feruent desire he had
to conuert Ethinckes to the Ghospell of Christ. He
neuer refused any labour, or danger whatsoeuer for
Gods cause; yea not contenting himself with the saluation of all *India*, & other Nations bordering theron,
he comprehended the whole East within the bosome
of that Charity, which esteemed the whole world to
litle for him, to do good in. Wherfore hauing planted
the Ghospell of Christ, and the Society also, throughout the whole East, almost at the very tyme when he
was thinking how to get into the hauen of *Cantona*, he
transcended the waues of this mortality, & arriued at
the hauen of eternal blisse, there to set vpon the *Chineses* by his forcible praiers in the sight of God. And there
is no doubt, but that he who is now Blessed in heauen,
hath by his contiuual praiers vnto God opened a way
into *China*, not only for the Society of IESVS, but
also for the Portughese merchants, and the Christian
Religion. For a litle after *Francis* his death, there was
a generall leaue graunted to the Portugheses to resort
vnto the Port of *Cantona*, and there to make their a-
boad for traffiques sake, it being the generall opinion,
that *Xauerius* had by his prayers opened that way into *China*, which was before so straitly barred vp on
euery side. And about 30. yeares after this agayne,
when

When he
was dead
he ope-
ned a-
way into
China.

when as the *Chineses* kept not so narrow a watch v-
pon their coaftes, as before they were wont to do,
some Fathers of the Society of *Iesus*, emulating therin
Xauerius his vertue, got entrance at laft into *China*, &
there by Gods fauourable affiftance, layd the founda-
tions of Chriftian Religion.

CHAP. XII.

His body is buried in quicke Lime.

The Por
tugheses
feeling
of *Xaue-
rius*
death.

AS foone as it was knowen, that *Francis* was
departed this lyfe (for his feuer being more
dangerous then it feemed, had deceyued all
men but himfelf) the Portugefes that were
left in the Ilãd being as it were ftrocke dead with that
dolefull newes came running prefently to his Body, as
if they had haftned to their Fathers funerall. Al places
about the cottage were filled with cryes & lamentations: then followed a difmall filence, with an earneft
longing to fee his body. Which affoone as they beheld
to be as it were the picture of his foule, & to reprefent
to them the eternal felicity which he inioyed, they fell
agayne vnto their former weeping, fince they could
neyther fatisfy their harts, nor eyes, with fo louing
and moft amiable a fpectacle.

Xauerius was of a well fet, and ftrong body, tall of
ftature, though not much aboue the ordinary pitch,
fayre of complexion, and of a gracefull afpect. His
countenance was exceeding cheerfull, and liuely:

his

his eyes grey, and quicke ; his nofe of a moderate fize, his beard and haire naturally blacke, but now turned gray with age and cares ; his habit poore & ordinary, but yet neat and decent. His vpper garment (accor-ding as the Prieftes of *India* vfe to weare) reached downe vnto his ankles, fo that it ferued alfo for a gowne. Thofe therefore, who thus beheld him, cal-led to mynd his exceeding courtefy, and fingular be-nignity vnto all men ; his courage & magnanimity of hart, giuing way to no dangers, or difficultyes what-foeuer; his perpetuall contépt of death, the very name wherof ftriketh fuch terrour into others ; his infinite defire to aduance Gods Glory and Religion ; his Hu-mility equall to his magnanimity; but fpecially his Piety, and fanctimony of life, tranfcending farre the higheft ftrayne of other men.

They therfore made dolefull complaints, becaufe that fweetneffe of behauiour, that example of forti-tude, that charity towards their ficke was taken from them ; becaufe Religion had loft fuch an excellent ad-uancer thereof ; becaufe the world was depriued of fuch an vpholder ; and finaly becaufe that new Starre was now vpon a fuddaine fet, which gaue light to the *Indians,* who before had laine in almoft perpetual dar-kneffe, and which had driuen away the foggy myft of the Eaft, by the radiant beames of Chrifts Ghofpel. Where was now one to be found, to carry on the Chriftian Religion to the furtheft part of the world ? Who fhould heerafter cure the Portughefes both cor-porall & fpirituall difeafes ? Who fhould fucceed *Xa-uerius* roome and place ? In the meane tyme, whilft the

L l l

Portugheſes compaſſing his body, feed both their eyes and thoughts with the moſt comfortable ſight and remembrance of their deareſt father, and ouerwhelmed with teares, wholy vnmindfull of themſelues bewayled ſo great a loſſe, *Anthony* the Intepreter who had attended vpon *Francis* all the tyme of his ſickneſſe, and at his death, ranne vnto the ſhip for *Francis* his Prieſtly habit, which was kept therein. When the Portugheſes who were aboard vnderſtood of *Xauerius* departure, they alſo with ſtreams of teares guſhing from their eyes, brake forth into lamentations and ſighes, being ſtrucken, not ſo much for their owne preſent griefe, as for the ſorrow which they knew it would cauſe in *Perera* their mayſter, who remayned at *Malaca*.

He is pur into the ornaméts of a Prieſt.

The Interpreter therefore returning backe with *Francis* his apparell, and accompanied with the marriners weeping, cloathed his body in Prieſtly garments as the manner is; and by aduiſe of the Portugheſes determined to put him into a woodden coffin, as the *Chineſes* are accuſtomed to doe: which, as the euent afterward declared, was done certaynly more by diuine, then humane prouidence, to the end that thoſe things which miraculouſly happened to his holy body, might be made the more manifeſt. Being therefore put in a woodden cheſt, and his funeralls celebrated with the greateſt ſolemnity that could be, in ſo great penury of all things, it was carryed forth by all the company to be buryed in the very ſhore of the Hauen. Hauing there prepared a Graue, and ſetled the Coffin therein, it came into their mynds, by diuine inſtinct,

ſtinct, to put vnto the body quick lyme, to eate away the fleſh, that the bones might be afterward tranſported into *India* .

Opening therfore the Coffin agayne, they couered the whole body with lime, to the end the fleſh might the ſooner be conſumed, and ſo cloſing it vp, they carefully buried it in the ſame place. Then they heape togeather certayne great ſtones vpon the graue , to ſerue as a marke to find it out by, if any of the Society ſhould chance to ſeeke after the ſame ; and ſo depart with many teares, ful of exceeding griefe and ſorrow, for the loſſe of ſo worthy a man.

vnſleckt
Lime is
put into
the Cof-
fin.

C H A P. XIII.

His body being found vvhole and incor-
rupt, is carryed to Malaca, *and there a-*
gayne interred.

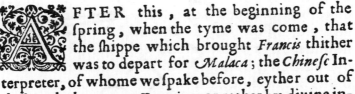

A FTER this , at the beginning of the ſpring, when the tyme was come , that the ſhippe which brought *Francis* thither was to depart for *Malaca* ; the *Chineſe* Interpreter, of whome we ſpake before, eyther out of the loue he bare vnto *Xauerius*, or rather by diuine inſtinct goeth to the Mayſter of the ſhip , and ſighing ſayth : What! ſhall we heere leaue *Xauerius*, who came with vs as farre as *India* , in a deſert Iland of the *Chi-neſes*,amongſt the barbarous people ? O what a man

LIl 2 was

was he ! Did we not our felues behold his Heroicall fanctity, both in life and death, with thefe our eyes, which all pofterity fhall admire? Why fhould not we rather carry his facred Body into *India*, to remayne there, where it may be honoured., then leaue it heere, where it wilbe contemned? I would (quoth the maifter) with all my hart carry his body with me into *India*, if the flefh were confumed from the bones, that he might eafily be tranfported. Wherefore I will prefently fend exprefly one to view the fame, and if the hope be anfwerable to my defire, I will carry it along as you requeft, not for your fake more, then for my owne. For I am not ignorant, what great fauour I fhall reape thereby of my Mayfter *Iames Perera*, who will certaynly receiue no fmall content, and comfort alfo, to haue *Xauerius* with him dead, whome in his life tyme he fo deerly loued.

Wherefore he difpatched prefently a trufty perfon to open both the graue and coffin, & if his body were confumed with the lime, to bring it away with him vnto the fhip. The meffenger haftning to the graue, *Francis* diggeth vp & openeth the Coffin, & putting the lime *his body* afide from of the body, a wonderful thing to be fpoke, *is found* he findeth it fo wholy entiere, & incorrupt as if it had *entier 4.* byn but newly buryed. No ill fent or fauour, rather a *monthes* moft fweet and odoriferous fmell did iffue from it; no *after.* putrefaction was there found at all, no not fo much as of the nofe, which vfeth firft to be corrupted. The colour as frefh as if he had byn aliue; his garments no whit confumed or hurt; his flefh was fayre and foft; nor had the very colour, which dependeth of the lyfe,

fo

fo much as once forfaken his vifage, fo that he durſt ſcarcely touch him with his hands, for that he feemed euen to be yet aliue.

Being therefore wholy aſtoniſhed at the ſtrange-neſſe of the thing, he prefently acknowledged Gods fauourable handy-worke therein, and by the integri-ty of his body, he moſt highly valueth that of foule. His admiration alfo fo much the more increaſed, be-caufe he knew *Xauerius* to be by nature, not hoat and dry, but cold and moyſte : and that it was now alfo the fourth moneth that he had layne thus buryed in quicke lime. Fearing therefore leſt he might be heer-in deceaued, he cut a little piece of fleſh from off his thigh, and carryeth it vnto the maiſter of the ſhip, re-lating at large what he had feene and found : and the piece of fleſh which he had brought, gaue credit to the miracle. Wherupon prefently the maiſter, mar-riners, and paſſengers being ſtroken into admiration, began to withall ſpeed to run vnto the graue, and fin-ding euery thing as was related, fome of the company who had bin either niggard, in giuing to *Xauerius* things neceſſary for his fuſtenance, when he was li-uing; or els had ſpoken fomwhat difgracefully of him after his death, began to powre forth aboundance of teares, & to beat themfelues vpon the face with their fiſts, for ſhame and forrow of their fault. Others gaue prayfe to God, who tooke fuch care, euen of his fer-uants dead corps.

This done, the Maiſter of the ſhip commanded the body to be prefently carryed aboard, as it lay in the Coffin, intending to make more certaine tryall

therof

thereof himfelfe, that fo the miracle might be publifhed to others. And hauing throughly fearched the
body, and found it found and incorrupt, with great
reuerence he putteth in the lyme againe into the Coffin as before, and hoyfing vp fayle departed from
Sanciana in the month of *March* with a very profperous wynd towards *Malaca*, where he foone arriued;
fo as one would haue thought the winds themfelues
had obeyed *Francis*. They fent their little boat before
to *Malaca* to carry newes, that *Xauerias* body was foûd
intier and incorrupt, & was comming towards them.
At which tidings the *Malacenfians* being ftirred vp
with deuotion, and defirous to make fatisfaction for
their former iniury done vnto him, refolued to receiue
his dead corps with all the honour & reuerence that
they could, whome whilft he liued, they had caft out
with no fmall difgrace.

The *Ma-*
lacenfians
zeale in
recea-
uing *Xa-*
uerius
body.

Then they began to cal to mynd, and feemed euen
to behould with their eyes the feruour, and countenance wherewith *Xauerius* was wont to preach vnto
the people, and wherwith he fought to draw men frô
their euill life, to feeke their faluation; to cure their
fick and poffeffed perfons; & laftly to foretell things
far abfent, and to come. Wherfore turning their contumacy into reuerence towards him, they all fetled
themfelues with great ioy to folemnize the funeralls
of fo worthy a man. But *Iames Perera* who had all
that tyme remayned in *Malaca*, outwent all the reft
in his loue to *Francis*, and which he fhewed alfo by his
deeds. For he mitigating the griefe which he had conceiued for his friends loffe, by the comming of his body

dy, prefently prouideth with extraordinary diligence an aboūdance of torches, & all other things neceffary for the funerall pompe. In this meane tyme the fhippe was come into the hauen, and they had put the Coffin into a Church neere by , there expecting vntill the Citty came forth to meete them.

Now, as foone as it was knowne in the Citty that *Xaucrius* Body was landed, all the people prefently thronged out of the gates to meete it, partly to fee, and partly to touch the fame with their beades. The Vicar alfo of the Citty with his Clergy came thither in Proceffion, who opening there the coffin before the people findeth the body entiere & frefh, without any the leaft corruption whatfoeuer, breathing out a moft fweet and pleafant fauour. Heerupon the people that were prefent with great admiration began to extoll Gods diuine power, to kiffe the facred reliques, and touch them with their beades, efpecially *Iames Perera*, who hauing heerby his long forrow changed into a fuddayne, & exceffiue ioy, celebrated the arriuall of his dead friend with the greateft affection of hart that poffibly he could. And that Gods approbation might adde more credit to humane iudgements, a certaine fick man by touching of the body was inftantly reftored to his health.

Xaucrius funerals at Malaca.

A fickman is healed by touching his body.

The next day therfore in the morning the whole Clergy of the Citty together with al the people come againe in proceffiō to meet the body with burning tapers & torches in theirs hands, as alfo with extraordinary feeling of ioy & deuotion. There was not at that time any of the Society remayning in *Malaca*, for they

were

were all departed lately thence, by *Francis* his expreſſe
order. Yet the Citty thought good to haue his body
carryed into the Church, which had formerly belonged to the Society, wherby they might haue *Xauerius* in the meane tyme as a pledge of their returne.
Wherfore with a moſt ſolemne proceſſion, & aboundance of lights the coffin was coueyed to the Church
aforſaid. And there after they had with all ſolemnity
ſung maſſe, the body being ſeparated from the lyme,
was put into a new Coffin, and buried in a moſt eminent place of the ſame Church, cauſing all that were
preſent to burſt forth agayne into new teares partly
through ioy of the late miracle, & partly alſo through
the griefe which the want of ſuch a man had cauſed
in them: and preſently there followeth one miracle
vpon another.

　　The ſhortneſſe of the new Coffin, had conſtrayned thoſe who put him therinto, ſo to bend & ſtray-
ten the Body as that there preſently iſſued freſh bloud
from out his ſhoulders, breathing forth a moſt ſweet
& odoriferous ſauour. Which the behoulders perceauing, and attentiuely conſidering, were driuen into
admiration at the ſtrangeneſſe of the miracle, in that
a body which had bin now fiue monthes without a
ſoule (ſo rare & perſeuerant was the miracle) ſhould
ſtill retayne not only the fleſh, moyſture and colour,
but alſo euen bloud it ſelfe, and that ſo ſweet as it ſeemed to be the odour, not of his bloud, but of his ſanctity. Wherfore thinking good to keep it without
a Coffin, it was taken forth againe, and by the *Malacenſians* not only honourably interred, but preſerued
alſo

(marginal note:) Bloud floweth out of *Xauerius* dead body the 5. month after.

alſo, as a pledg of the diuine Clemency towards them. Wherin they were not fruſtrate of their hope.

At the ſame time, there was through God heauy wrath towards thē, a moſt contagious ſicknes ſpread ouer all the Citty, which hauing almoſt vnpeopled a great part therof, had put them all into a wonderful feare. Wherfore being much perplexed, and through remorſe of conſcience, calling to mind the prediction which *Xauerius* had pronounced agaynſt them for the wronge they had done vnto him, they verily thought there was no other cauſe of Gods indignation againſt them but that. But this peſtilence wholy ceaſing vpon the very day that his funerals were kept, ſhewed ſufficiently that God was now pacified agayne, by the merits of *Xauerius*, by whoſe interceſſion the ſicknes was remitted.

CHAP. XIIII.

His Body is tranſlated from Malaca *into* India.

FTER this, vpon the 13. of Auguſt *Iohn Beira* a Prieſt of the Society of Ieſus going with ſome other Companions to *Moluca*, tooke *Malaca* in his way. He for the reuerence and deuotion which he bare vnto *Xauerius*, hauing heard by report that his body was incorrupted, greatly deſired to viſit & behould the ſame. Wherfore going priuatly into the Church with his companions

Mmm   in

Francis his body intier the 9. month after his death. in the night, and opening the Sepulcher, he findeth *Francis* like one aliue, no leſſe intier and incorrupt in the ground, then he was before in the lime, it being now nine monthes after his death. Wherfore ioyntly giuing prayſe to God, who is admirable in his Saints, with great veneration, and many teares, they kiſſe and adore his ſacred body.

The veile died with freſh bloud. Neither was there wanting, at the ſame time a new miracle. For they perceiued that the veile wherwith his face was couered, was, by reaſon of the heauines of the earth which was throwne vpon him, beſprinkled as it were with freſh bloud. Wherefore *Beira* being moued by the euidency of the miracle, bethinketh with himſelf of doing greater honour to *Xarius*. And conferring the matter with *Iames Perera*, they iudged it conuenient, that his body ſhould be taken vp, and kept in the Sacriſty of the Church; and *Perera* himſelfe procureth a new Coffin to be made and lined within, with rich Damaske, and couered on the out-ſide with cloath of gould. *Beira* hauing thus incloſed *Xauerius* in his new Coffin, departed to *Moluca*, and leaueth *Emanuel Tabera* one of the Society at *Malaca*, with order to tranſport that rich and precious Treaſure, with the firſt opportunity vnto *Goa*.

In the meane *Iohn Mendoza*, a noble and wealthy Portugeſe-merchant had a ſhip newly arriued at *Malaca* fraught with *Chineſe* merchandize. His factour hauing vnladen the wares kept them in the Citty expecting a fit ſeaſon to tranſport them to *Goa*. But when the time for nauigation came, he could not get

a ſhip,

a ſhip, for that there was but only one in the Hauen, & that not fit for ſea, as being old, & halfe rotten, & her keele ſpecially ſo very weake, that ſhe was ready to fall aſunder: So as the ſea men and marriners gaue their opinion abſolutly of her, that ſhe would not be able to brooke the ſeas, but ſtraight grow looſe in her ioynts and leake, and ſo be quickly caſt away. Wherfore the factour being ſad, knew not what to do. But when he vnderſtood, that *Xauerius* holy *Body* was to be tranſported vnto *Goa,* he ventured in her, not only all his merchandize, but his perſon and life alſo, hauing aſſured confidence in God, that by the merits of *Xauerius,* of whoſe admirable vertue he had had ſufficient experience, the ſhip would arriue ſafe.

In the meane time *Peter Alcaceua* of the Society of Ieſus being ſent by *Coſmas Turrianus,* was come vnto *Malaca,* to bring away thoſe ſacred Reliques vnto *Goa.* Wherfore he, togeather with *Tabera,* conuey the holy ſhrine into the ſhip, to the exceeding ioy, both of the marriners, and paſſengers, as thinking themſelues ſtrongly armed therby againſt al tempeſts. There was a chamber in the ſhip prepared of purpoſe for the ſacred Body, richly hung with ſilke, wherin the ſhrine was placed, togeather with ſtore of excellēt perfumes and waxen tapers. All which dutifull ſeruices, *Xauerius* did aboundantly requite. For when they were in the midſt of their courſe, the ſhip running vpon certayne vnknowne rockes, ſtuck ſo faſt amongſt them that ſhe could be haled neither forward, nor backward, but remayned immoueable, as if ſhe had bin faſt nayled therto.

At

At length, after the Marriners had laboured for many houres to get her loofe but al in vayne, they begā to defpayre. Wherfore hauing no hope in humane they implored the diuine affiſtance. And prefently they came to Father *Alcaceua* intreating him earneſtly to fet forth *Xauerius* Body. He without any difficulty yieldeth to their requeſt, that they might all togeather call vpon the Saint for help. There was no delay made, and fo all with burning tapers in their hands fell downe vpon their knees, and in moſt fuppliant wife, and with may teares began to call vpon *Xauerius*, befeeching his ayde in this their diſtreſſe. And not in vaine. For as they were thus ſeriouſly imploring his help, the Rock vpon a fuddaine leauing its faſt hold, the ſhip got loofe, and gaue withall a great cracke; then by little and little wynding her felfe frō out the ſhallowes, held on her courfe with a profperous gale. At other times alfo, being in manifeſt danger of caſting away, ſhe efcaped miraculouſly, by the paſſengers & marriners calling vpon *Xauerius*, whofe holy Body was there prefent, and fo at laſt arriued fafe at *Cocinum*. Where as foone as it was knowne that *Francis* his body was comming thither whole and incorrupt, the whole Citty was fo ſtirred vp with the ſtrangeneſſe of the thing, that yow might prefently fee the hauen full of people, and many alfo making haſt in fmal boates to meet the ſhip, therby to fatisfy their longing eyes. Then climing vp vnto the decke, they came into the chamber where the body lay, and there one after another, touch, and kiſſe his facred reliques, admiring to behould the body intiere and found,

Thezeale which the *Coçinenſians* ſhewed in going to viſit *Xauerius* body.

found, and extolling the diuine Bounty of Almighty God, who had shewed it selfe so admirable, euen in the dead corps of holy men.

The ship hauing made some few dayes stay at *Cocinum*, departeth thence for *Goa*, yet stayed a little by the way at a towne of *India* called *Baticala*, some 80. miles from *Goa*, with no smal benefit to the inhabitants of that place. For there, by *Francis* his merits a principall Portughese woman was deliuered of a great sicknes, & many other miracles wrought besides which we shall afterwards set downe in their proper place. But now, for that the wynd was ful against the they were forced to stay their course at *Baticala* for a tyme. Wherfore the gouernour of that place taking a small gally maketh hast to *Goa* before, and there declareth the whole busines vnto those of the Society. Their desire, as often it hapneth, was by that delay & expectation more inflamed; nor could they satisfy themselues to make any longer stay.

Wherefore *Melchior Nūnius* Rectour of the Colledge went vnto the Viceroy, and easily obtained of him, a light barke to fetch away the sacred shrine with all speed. The barke belonged to one *Alphonsus Noronia*, a vertuous man, and one that alwayes much esteemed of *Xauerius*, who lent the same far more willingly then it was demaunded, & moreouer imployed his owne indeauours carefully therein. But the mayster of the ship, who had brought *Xauerius* body from *Malaca*, opposed himselfe, and earnestly requested, that, seeing his ship was not now farre from *Goa*, she might not be despoyled of so sure and safe a guard. Yet

the

the great defire they had to fee their Father *Xauerius*, ouerfwayed his iuft requeft.

Melchior therfore leauing many of the Colledge behind who defired to accompany him, with certaine of the principall Fathers, and a company of Orphane Children taketh boat, & with al the fpeed that might be hafteth to the fhip. And when he was arriued, he forthwith went aboard, and entring into the chamber where the fhrine was kept, findeth *Xauerius* body wholy found and vncorrupt, retayning ftill the felfe fame countenance which he had yet liuing; fo that he feemed to be but newly dead, or rather ftill aliue. Wherefore fhedding teares for ioy, after he had a while contemplated his holy vifage, as an euident token of his heauenly felicity, he fweetly kiffeth his facred hands and feete, with extraordinary feeling of deuotion; and the like alfo did all the reft, euery one ftriuing who fhould be moft forward therein.

In the meane while, the Maifter had commanded his fhip to be fet out with many flagges, and tapeftry hangings, and the great Ordinance to be all couered with filke.. As foone as the Body was brought aboue the hatches, the Orphane Children that were come frō *Goa*, with garlands made of flowers on their heads, & boughes in their hands began very deuoutly to fing the Canticle *Benedictus Dominus Deus Ifrael &c.* wherat neyther themfelues, nor the reft that were prefent could abftayne from weeping. Whileft they fung in that manner the Body was let downe into the Barke, & gently placed in the poope: & prefently the great fhip taking her leaue of *Xauerius*, fent forth a mighty peale

Honour giuen to Xauerius by the mariners &others.

peale of Ordinance, which renewed againe the ioy &
teares of al that were preſēt, whilſt they called to mind
how good God was, who would euen in the midſt of
the ſea honour his humble ſeruant with ſo great ma-
gnificence. Then the forſaid ſhip, hauing deliuered vp
the body, & being lightned alſo of all her merchādize,
to perform as it were her laſt duty to *Xauerius*, in the very ſame place, and at a calme ſea, ſinketh downe of her
ſelfe vnder the water, and is drowned; to ſhew therby
that hitherto by his holy aſſiſtance ſhe had paſſed ſafe,
through both waues and rockes.

This done, the Barke arriued in the ſame euening
at a Church of our B. Lady called *Rebandaria*, about
a mile and halfe from *Goa*, ſeated in the mouth of
the riuer, which runneth along by the Iland of *Goa*.
There Fa. *Melchior*, greatly deſiring once more, to
behould and cōtemplate *Xauerius* Body at leaſure, did
at midnight, all the doores being faſt ſhut, take vp the
ſame in his Prieſtly ornaments, as he lay, from out
the ſhrine, it being then 16. monthes after his death,
& findeth him to haue the very ſame face, countenance, and feature of Body, as he had whilſt he liued; together with his fleſh full of moyſture, his ſkinne freſh
and flexible, and his colour ſo liuely, that one would
haue taken him to haue byn rather aſleepe then dead.

Francis his body is intier 16. monthes after his death.

He had vpon his body a garment of fine linnen
which he had carryed with him in his iourney, intending to cloath himſelfe therwith, according to the worſe
Country faſhion, when he came vnto the King of
China. This, becauſe he had neuer vſed it in his life,
they made to ſerue him for a ſhirt when he was dead:

Francis his ſhirt alſo no-thing the worſe after ſo many monthes buriall.

the

the which , notwithstanding that his dead Body was
wrapped therein , the space of so many moneths, and
also that it had byn often couered ouerwith lime, and
earth, seemed so neat and cleane, that one would haue
thought it had bin newly put on, & preserued rather
then any way impayred by the Body .

Hereupon *Fa. Melchior*, after he had rendred due
thankes & prayses to the diuine maiesty, remembring
what an incitement to vertue *S. Paul* the Hermits
coate of Palme-tree was vnto *S. Anthony*, and how
Elias his cloake had byn beneficiall to *Elizeus*, felt in
himselfe a vehement desire to be made possessour of
Xauerius shirt. Wherfore taking it of from his body, he
kept it most carefully , either as a memory of *Xauerius*
himselfe, or as an ornament for his owne vse . For
that he going afterward into *Iaponia*, carried the same
with him thither , intending to cloath himselfe therwith, when he went to speake with any King , or No-
bleman of that Country, to the end that by *Francis* his
merits and intercession for them ; he might not only
delight their eyes, but also winne their harts to God.
And the euent proued afterward answerable to his
desired deuotion .

CHAP.

CHAP. XV.

His Funerall is kept at Goa, *vvith all so-lemnity.*

IN the meane time, the Viceroy (who was then at *Goa*) being certified ouer night of the cōming of *Xauerius* body, for the great veneration which he bare vnto him, was exceeding ioyfull, & presently commāded a solemne Pompe, and preparation to me made ready againſt the next day. But the Fathers of the Society, whome *Melchior* had left at home againſt their wils, were so ouercome with ioy, that hauing their harts wholy poſſeſſed with deſire to see their deereſt Father, could not sleepe, nor take any reſt all that night. Neither was there any one among them either so could in ſpi-rit, or weake of body, that did not watch the whole night, so great poſſeſſion had the loue of *Xauerius* gotten in all their harts. Wherefore all that night, they buſied themſelues to adorne their Church with greene boughes, Tapeſtryes, Carpets, and other or-naments, intending to receiue their moſt deſired Fa-ther with the beſt preparation they could deuiſe. Now it chanced, that this day fell out vpon the Frydaynext before the Holy weeke : yet they thought good to adorne the Church, and Aultars in the moſt ſumptu-ous manner they could, and with the rich ornaments which they commonly vſed vpon the greateſt Feaſts

of

of the yeare . For they deemed , that this holy Man , whose funerall God would haue celebrated with sollemne pompe , ought to be receiued rather in ornaments of ioy , then in dolefull and mourning blacke.

This funeral then was kept vpon the 15. of March in the yeare 1554. Vpon which day early in the morning , *Iames Perera* who was come from *Malaca* thither , embarketh himselfe with a traine of choice friends in a galley, and all with white torches in their hands, goe to meete his deerest Father , and Friend *Xauerius* . Presently after him there followed six little boates , wherein there were to the number of fifty persons , all ardent louers of *Xauerius* , and admirers of his vertues . Euery one had a great torch lighted in his hand, and his page a lesser taper . As soone as they were come to the Church where the holy body was kept , they all togeather prostrate themselues vpon the ground , and with teares adore the sacred reliques . But yet *Perera* went beyond them all in piety , who had alwayes borne so speciall an affection to *Xauerius.* Then there followed other small vessels one after another, to the number of twelue of *Portugheses, Chineses* , and *Malacensians* , all men of very good account , and in equipage accordingly , both for apparell and lights : Who when they had , with all the rest, performed their deuotions vnto the Body , retyred themselues , ech one to his Boate .

Now, when it was well in the day , the shrine adorned with cloath of Gold, was placed in the Poope of a small Barke al beset with burning tapers of waxe; the Fathers of the Society in their white surplisses , &
the

the Orphane children with garlands on their heads, compaſſing the ſame round about & ſinging of hymnes and pſalmes, and ſo conueyed it to *Goa.* There followed this little Barke, in a long row, to the number of about twenty other little boates, all beſet with burning torches & tapers likewiſe, the more to grace the ſolemnity of the funerall pompe. The Sea ſeemed all on a fire with lightes, the ſhores reſounded with ſuch melodious muſicke, that it cauſed moſt that were preſent, through their great feeling of deuotion, to ſhed aboundance of teares. But when the Barke thus gliſtering with the ſplendour of ſo many tapers appeared within ſight of the Citty, wherby they vnderſtood the Body was at hand, the people were ſo greatly moued thereat, that they ſeemed to leape, and triumph for ioy. For although the Fathers, not vnmindfull of their humble modeſty, had dealt already, and that earneſtly, with the Viceroy and Biſhop, that *Xauerius* might not be receiued as a Saint, but as the ſeruant of God, vntill his Holineſſe ſhould otherwyſe determine thereof: yet by the Viceroyes order and command, the bells of all the Churches began to ring forth peales of ioy and melody. At the hearing whereof the whole Citty began to runne forth, to meete the Body, ſo as the ſhores, walls of the towne, windowes, Garrets, & toppes of houſes, from whence they might diſcouer the comming of the Barke, were all beſet, and filled with people. And the neerer the Barke drew vnto them, the more did the multitude, & their deſire to ſee it, increaſe. Yea many out of feruor and zeale leapt one after another into the water, ſtriuing who should first touch the holy shrine.

In this meane tyme the Viceroy, and all the Nobility, with a great number of chiefe Cittizens, stood
expecting the Barke at the Hauen, with burning tapers in their hands, and the Chanons of the High
Church, with all the other Priests in white surplisses
came with their Crosses in Procession wise, to meet
the same. Thither also came the Sodality of *Mercy*
with their banners, and ensignes all glittering with
gold and siluer. After them followed a very sump-
tuous Beere, couered ouer with cloth of Gold, whereon those of the Sodality had determined to carry the
Shrine aloft, that so it might make the more glorious
shew.

A great concourse to Xauerius bo dy. As soone therfore as the Shrine was brought aland by
those of the Society, the people made such a presse out
of desire to touch and kisse the same, that very many
were thereby throwne downe one vpon another. And
because those who came last, would not make way
for the first to retyre, they were so thronged vp together on a heape, that many were in danger to haue bin
pressed, and stifled to death, if great prudence had not
byn vsed to auoyd the danger. The Viceroy therefore
was forced to send this Guard to put back the throng,
and to make way for the Procession, that was ready
to begin.

His land funerall. Now, when the multitude with much adoe
was forced backe, the Procession set forward, & was
performed with all the pompe that might be. After
which there followed the Shrine placed vpō the Beere
most sumptuously adorned, and carryed by certayne
Fathers

Fathers on high vpon their shoulders, togeather with two other empty-Beeres, borne on each side one, and richly furnished like the other. After the Body followed the Viceroy, and his Court, togeather with all the Nobility, and whole City, with such aboundance of torches and tapers, that the streets seemed to be on fire, and this with such applause of extraordinary ioy in all sorts, that one would haue thought it had rather byn a triumph, then a funerall. The Shrine or Coffin glittered all with gold, the way was al strowed with greene boughes, and odoriferous flowers; The windowes and walls of all the houses were adorned with costly hangings and tapistry; besides the many sweet perfumes, set euery where about; on both sides, There were moreouer hung about the Beere diuers Censars of siluer, in which were cast continually many sweet and fragrant odours.

Francis therefore in this triumphall manner, returning from his *China*-voiage, was at last brought into the Church of the Society at *Goa*, giuing vs therby to vnderstād with what honour his soule no doubt is now glorified in heauen, whose Body being dead, throgh the sanctity of his soule, did notwithstanding so triumph heere on earth.

CHAP.

CHAP. XVI.

The great Concourse of people to behould his Holy Body .

AS foone as they came to the Church of the Society, a folemne Maſſe was ſung . And to auoyd the great preſſe of people, the Beere was placed within the Cancells of the Altar. It was told the people that when Maſſe was ended, the Coffin ſhould be opened , and that all who would , might fee the Body . Whereupon the multitude made ſo great a throng that they brake downe the rayles of the Cancells. But the Coffin being ſhut, was kept ſafe by nothing more, then by the preſſe of people , hindring one another . Then the Rectour of the Colledge , fearing the violence of the pious people, earneſtly intreated the Viceroy that he would be pleaſed to retyre vnto his houſe with the Nobility ,for that the people would then certaynly follow his exãple ; and that when afterwards the chappell was voyded & the preſſe of people gone, they might themſelues the more commodiouſly fee the body .

An incredible cõcourſe to Xauerius body.

The Viceroy therfore yelding to his requeſt, withdraweth himſelfe , and all the Nobility followeth him . But the people remayned ſtill immoueable, vrging , and requiring to haue the Body ſhewed vnto them : for vnleſſe they had their deſire, they ſayd they would not ſtirre a foote. And by ſtanding out thus

ftifly, they obteined at laſt their demand. For when as
no delay would ſerue the turne, F. *Melchior* was forced
at length to giue way vnto the tyme, and putting the
preſſe of people a litle backe, vntill the Cancels were
agayne ſet vp and faſtned, *Xauerius* body was ſhewed
to them in his Prieſtly robes, as he was brought thither. Which when the multitude beheld, they were
ſo deſirous to ſee it neerer hand, that ruſhing on with
great violence they agayne brak downe the Cancels.
Wherupon the Fathers through a ſuddayne feare preſently ſhut the Coffin agayne, that there might no
violence be offered therunto, & would by no meanes
open it any more. So as the people being out of hope
to ſee it agayne, and weary with expecting, they that
ſtood neereſt, & had ſeene it though a far of, at length
retyred, and told the reſt what they had ſeene. They
being ſet on fire by what they ſayd, neuer left vrging
vntill the Cancels were agayne ſet vp, and the Body
alſo ſhewed them.

  The ſame day in the euening *Anthony Perera* a
Portugheſe, arriued at *Goa* with preſents, and letters
frō the King of *Bungo* to the Viceroy of *India*. He was
ſent thither by the King to procure *Xauerius* returne
agayne into *Iaponia*, although it were now too late.
The contents of the Kings letters, were theſe : That
Francis Xauerius had oftentymes diſcourſed before him
of God the Creatour and redeemer of the world, and
that his words had taken faſt hold within his hart,
& the inmoſt bowels of his ſoule. Wherefore he was
now fully determined and reſolued to be baptized by
Francis his owne hands, although it were with the hazard

zard of loofing his kingdome . *Xauerius* had indeed at
his departure promifed him, that he would fhortly returne vnto him , if God fpared his lyfe . But becaufe
his returne was not fo fpeedy as he had hoped , he
thought good to fend one expreffely vnto *Goa* , who
might certify him of the caufe of his fo long delay .
Wherefore he intreated the Viceroy , to fend *Xaue-*
rius vnto him with the firft opportunity : whofe comming would certaynely be both a great incitement to
the Chriftian Religion , & alfo a pledge of the Portughefes friendfhip vnto his perfon. When the Viceroy
had perufed the Kings letters , he eafily perfuaded Fa.
Melchior Nunius (who was one of the chiefe Fathers
of the Society in *India*) to go himfelfe with all fpeed
vnto the King of *Bungo.*

    In this meane tyme *Xauerius* Body was expofed at
Goa , not only to the view, but alfo to the admiration
of all the behoulders . But the great defire of the people was not fatisfied by feing him, but rather more inflamed : Yea the felfe fame perfons did oftentymes returne agayne to looke vpon him , & others came flocking almoft euery moment to behould him . The Fathers therefore through neceffity , were conftrayned
to change their determination . And fo to fatisfy the
longing defire of fuch an infinite multitude , the body was expofed three dayes in a Chappell well fenced
with ftrong Cancells to the full view of all, and euery
one that would might looke vpon it at their leafure :
So as there came from all parts an infinity of people
to behold, & touch the fame with their beades, which
they performed with aboundance of teares and much
                                                    inward

inward feeling of deuotion.

Now whilſt ſome became doubtful of the incorruption of his body, the ſame was made therby not only
more certayne, but more glorious alſo. For ſeeing
the miracle did ſurpaſſe all humane beliefe, there were
not wanting ſome, yea Religious perſons, & men of
good authority, who gaue out, that *Francis* his body
being bowelled, was by art, & certayne precious em-
balmings kept thus liuely. The Viceroy therefore,
to examine the truth of the thing, commaunded *Coſ-*
mas Saraina, a Phyſitian of great fame and experience
to try, and looke into the Body. But he beginning
to launce the belly with an inſtrument, when he perceyued freſh bloud to iſſue thence, being aſtoniſhed
at the miracle, gaue ouer his deſigne. Then putting his
finger into the hole he had made, he findeth his bowels intiere & ſound, without any ſigne of balme, or
other preſeruatiue applied; which he cōfirmed by publicke teſtimony vpon his oath. Wherfore the matter
being throughly examined, and diuulged abroad, *Xa-*
uerius Body began to be greatly honoured & reuerenced, not more by others, then by thoſe who had byn
authours of the falſe rumour aforeſayd, euery one
kiſſing his feete and hands, and touching them with
their beades. And ſo great was the opinion of *Xaue-*
uerius ſanctity, that euery one did ſtriue to get, yea
purloyne ſome ſmall particle of his body, or garments: in ſo much that all the care and vigilancy the
Fathers could vſe to looke vnto it, did hardly hinder
the violence of the deuout pepole.

In the meane tyme *Xauerius* prayſes were ſpread

By order from the Viceroy a Phyſitian examineth the integrity of his body.

Ooo   all

all abroad, & his worthy actes, prophecyes, and miracles were blazed far and neere, not only by those who had themselues byn eye-witnesses thereof, but by others also, who had heard the same from credible authours; so as all *India* sounded forth his sanctity, as it were with one mouth. And likewise for the confirmatiō of the former miracles there were many others added anew. For that many who went to behould that sacred spectacle, affirmed vpon their oath, that there came thither many persons who hauing eyther lost the vse of some of their lymmes, or otherwise sick of some disease, were by touching *Francis* his body healed, & returned home sound, and in perfect health.

Now, when these three dayes were past, although the people had not yet their fill of behoulding & contemplating the sacred Body, the shrine was for a time placed in a Sepulcher, which they had prepared for the purpose, vpon the right hand of the high Aultar, vntil a fayrer monument were erected and adorned, fitting the dignity of so worthy a man, according to the Fathers desires, and deuotion of the Cittizens of *Goa*, if the King of *Portugall*, as they hoped, would procure his Canonization from the Pope.

The Bishops Vicar againe examineth the matter. About the tenth day after his buriall, *Doctour Antony Ribera* the Bishops Vicar, and Inquisitour Generall, determined, in respect of his charge and office, to examine the matter with his owne eyes, and see whether those things were true which had byn diuulged abroad of *Francis* his incorruption. Wherefore opening the Sepulcher about Midday himselfe, with many lighted torches attending, throughly felt, and
vie-

viewed the whole body all ouer. And finding nothing which was not entiere, he gaue teftimony therof vnder his hand and feale to all pofterity. This caufed the reuerence, and deuotion to *Xauerius* dayly to increafe . There were allmoft none, who came not with veneration to his fepulcher; many brought thither flowers and garlands, and the number of white wax tapers to burne continually before it, were exceeding great . And this deuotion of the people towards his feruant was by God himfelfe approued alfo. For there is euident proofe, that a wax Candle of a cubit long only, being lighted before the Sepulcher did burne perpetually for the fpace of 18. whole daies, and nights togeather.

The King of Portugall being moued by thefe relations, gaue order prefently to the Viceroy of *India,* to make exact inquiry of *Xauerius* worthy facts, and miracles, & to fet them carefully downe in writing, the which he afterward fent to *Rome* to his Embaffadour, that he might deale with his Holines about his Canonization. But this moft Excellent Kings pious endeauours were hindred by his vntimely death. The Fathers therefore hauing finifhed their new Church at *Goa,* and diffolued the old, remoued *Xauerius* Body into a priuate Chappell within their houfe, where to this day his memory and name is honoured, vntill his Holineffe fhall graunt (if it pleafe God) that folemne Honour and Veneration, may be publikly exhibited vnto him .

The King of Portugall maketh meanes to haue Françis Canonized .

OF

OF THE LIFE OF

S. FRANCIS XAVIER.

THE VI. BOOKE.

*By the King of Portugall his command,
Francis his deeds, and miracles are committed to vvriting.*

CHAP. I.

 LTHOVGH the guifts and fa-
uours, which the Goodnes of God
had already heaped vpon *Francis*,
shined forth at sundry times in al the
parts of his life, as we haue demon-
strated before: yet will it not be a-
misse heere to propound those things to be maturely
côsidered, which haue byn touched by the way, and
as it were in an obscure manner; that so by vnfoul-
ding

ding the chiefe heads of matters, we may at once behould all whatsoeuer appertaineth thereunto. And to
the end, we may first of all speake of such passages,
which ordinarily cause most admiration, and are e-
steemed both by good, and bad-willers ; many things,
not only through the whole course of his lyfe, but
much more at the very tyme of his funeralls, haue by
diuine power happened vnto *Xauerius,* which no natural cause can any way excuse frō being miraculous.
Wherefore we will heere, in a more exact manner,
treate of these signes, and testimonies of his sanctity;
& will cite for euery thing such authors & witnesses,
whose authority, and fidelity camnot iustly be called
into question.

Iohn the third King of Portugall, by whome, as
we haue sayd before, *Xauerius* was sent into *India,* whē
he had vnderstood, & made tryall of his sanctity, honoured him no lesse dead, thē aliue. For as soone as the
newes of his death was brought vnto him, moued, as
indeed he had reason, for the losse of so worthy a man,
he was inwardly grieued at the blow which the whole East had receyued thereby, then the which there
could not perhaps an heauier haue byn giuen by the
wrathfull hand of God. When his griefe was something ouerpast (as his owne singular piety and prudence admonished him) he sought a remedy for the
same, from that source which had caused it. For hauing vnderstood, of the many miraculous thinges,
which had byn wrought by *Francis,* as well aliue as
dead, and being inflamed with deuotion towards the
blessed man, out of his feruour to Religion, he giueth

order by Letters Patents vnto *Francis Barret* his Viceroy of *India*, to make all diligent inquiry after his il-
luſtrious aƈtes and miracles, and to ſend them to him
with expedition, for that he determined to preſent the
ſame to his Holineſſe, that he might according to the
cuſtome of Holy Church, if he thought it expedient,
decree a publike honour and reuerence to be exhibited vnto him, who was famous both for ſanƈtity, and
miracles.

But to the end this Religious Kings opinion of
Xauerius vertues may be knowne, and teſtifyed to all
the world, we iudge it not amiſſe heere to ſet downe
a Copy of his Letters Royall. Friend Viceroy, I the
King, ſend you harty greeting. *Francis Xauerius* lyfe
and labours haue byn ſo profitable by their exemplar
edification, that we iudge it will be moſt acceptable vnto God, to haue them brought to light, to the
honour, and glory of his Diuine Maieſty. Wherefore, being publiſhed abroad, to the end they may
receaue that full authority and credit, as it is meet
they ſhould; We giue you all charge, and commiſſion
that wherſoeuer throughout *India* it ſhall be thought
that good and ſubſtantiall witneſſes of theſe matters
may be found (I meane of ſuch as haue liued and conuerſed with him) you will procure with the greateſt
diligence you can, publicke inſtruments, & teſtimo-
nialls to be iuridicially made thereof, and vnder the
witneſſes oathes, both of his life, & behauiour, as well
of all thinges which he hath worthily performed for
the ſaluation, & example of mortall men; as of thoſe
things alſo which he hath miraculouſly wrought, either

**The
King of
Portu-
gal let-
ters to
the Vice-
roy of
India.**

ther aliue or dead . Thefe inftruments, togeather with "
all the teftimonialls and authorities, fubfcribed with "
your owne hand , and figned with your feale, you fhal "
fend ouer vnto vs three fundry wayes . This if you "
carefully , and fpeedily performe, you fhall receaue "
great thankes from vs . From *Lisbone* this 27. of "
March 1556.

   As foone therfore , as the Viceroy had receaued
thefe letters, he, by fit perfons expreffely ordained for
that purpofe , prefently commanded exact inquiry to
be made of fuch things accordingly , not only at *Goa*
the Metropolitan Citty of *India* , but in euery part of
that Country ; and alfo at *Malaca* , and in all places
where it was knowne *Xaucrius* had euer bin . Wherupon very many things were found by the teftimony
of vndoubted witneffes which *Francis* had both in his
life and after his death , eyther performed with great
profit, or elfe wrought miraculoufly by diuine power.
Of which the Viceroy hauing caufed publicke inftruments to be made , fubfcribed & figned the fame with
his owne hand and feale , and fent them fpeedily vn-
tо the King his Lord and Mayfter .

   The matter now was come thus farre , that the
King had fent the Inftruments aforefayd to *Rome*, and
dealt by his Embaffadour with his Holineffe, for the
proceeding therein to his Canonization , when as his
vntimely death brake of that his pious determination.
An authenticall Copy of all which inftruments, iuridically fealed & figned by the Viceroy, we haue at this
prefent in our hands, from whence, for the moft part,
we haue taken thofe things which we haue hitherto

                  men-

*The Vi-
ceroyes
Inquifi-
tioh af-
ter Xaue-
rius acts.*

mentioned, and fhall heerafter alfo recount. And for that we haue in thefe our former Bookes comprized moft of them already; we will therefore in this laft, relate only thofe which we haue of fet purpofe referued vnto this place, as not feeming good for diuers reafons, to haue put them downe before.

CHAP. II.

Hovv Xauerius *foretelleth things future, and abfent, and feeth mens invvard Thoughts.*

XAVERIVS was indeed remarkable for many worthy fauours which God Almighty had beftowed vpon him; yet for nothing more, then for his manifold guift of Prophecy. Whereof many vndoubted fignes are clerly to be feene, throughout the whole paffage of his lyfe. But thefe which heere enfue are of moft particular note.

One *Cofmas Ioannes* Procuratour of the King, had bought in *India* a Diamond of extraordinary bigneffe for 8000. crownes, which would be worth foure times as much in Portugall. This Iewell he had deliuered vnto one *Ferdinand Aluarez* at his departure for Portugall, to be carryed vnto the King his Mayfter. At the fame tyme *Francis* commeth to *Goa,* and out of familiarity with *Cofmas* asked him how his trafficque went forward? He recounteth all vnto him, and in

particu-

particuler concerning the said diamond, which he had
sent vnto the King, hoping all things went very prosperoußy with him. Then *Xauerius* asked him againe in
what ship he had sent so precious a Iewell? And when
he had told him the name of the Ship; I would to God
quoth *Francis*, you had not sent it in that ship. Why,
quoth *Cosmas*, is it, because she was almost cast away
this last yeare by a contrary tempest? No, quoth *Francis*, for she is to vndergo a greater danger. Vpon this
speach he began to intreat *Xauerius* earnestly, that he
would not giue ouer praying to God for that ship, seeing that he had vpon his owne hazard sent the Diamond vnto the King. And being thus pensiue for his
Iewell, newes was brought vnto him, that the ship
hauing one of her chiefe planckes rent away, by the
violence of a tempest, was euen at the point to haue
byn drowned; but that by the prayers of *Xauerius* she
miraculously escaped, & was safely arriued in Portugall.

The day also before *Francis* put to sea from *Malaca* towards *China* (as they of the Society who were
then present, haue recounted) lying after an vnusual
maner vpon his bed, all along vpon his belly, like one
betweene sleep and awake, he continued a great while in the same posture without euer mouing, wholy
alienated from his senses. Whereat those of the Society that were by chance present, being astonished at
so strange a posture, durst not, for the great reuerence
which they bare him, eyther awake, or speake vnto
him. Wherefore turning their admiration into care,
they with solicitous and perplexed mynds expected

He being at Mala- ca fore- seeth a danger which the Soci- ety vn- derwent in Por- tugall.

Ppp   the

the euent of the thing. At laſt awaking as it were out of a deepe ſleepe, and like one that had eſcaped ſome great trouble, called vpon a certaine perſon by name who was then in Portugall, & oftentimes cryed, *God pardon thee &c.* ſo as for the preſent (except himſelfe only who knew it) none could imagine what that his complaint meant. But ſoone after letters comming out of Portugall it was knowne that at the very ſame time, through the fault of him, whome *Xauerius* had ſo often called vpon by name, in that Extaſy, the Society had in Portugall ſuffered a great detriment, which notwithſtanding through Gods goodnes and *Xauerius* prayers, turned to their benefit. Whereby it plainly appeared that God had ſhewed him what hapned at that very time in Portugall, that by his prayers he might auert the danger which was imminent to the Society there.

Moreouer *Xauerius*, being at *Malaca*, did not only tell of things that were abſent and farre off, but foretold alſo thinges to come, and thoſe as well dolefull, as ioyfull. I paſſe ouer with ſilence the deuaſtations of the Country, the beſieging of the Citty, the grieuous contagions amongſt the inhabitants, & other miſeries, which either in his publicke ſermons, or priuate conferences he foretold ſo long before vnto the *Malacenſians*, euen in the very ſame manner that afterward they fel out. Let vs cal againe to mind that memorable victory acheiued againſt thoſe Barbarous *Acenians* ; that Prophecy glorious by ſo many predictions of *Xauerius*, and enobled by ſo many tokens of the diuine prouidence. How many & diuers alſo alfo were his predictions at *Amboynum*, and the *Moluca's*? What notable prophecies were thofe of the Victory againft the *Tolanians*; of the returning againe of the Cock-boate, which had bin carryed away with the tempeft? But all thefe we haue related before, excepting this which followeth.

When in his voyage to *China*, as he was fayling to *Malaca*, the great iron-barbed Ship wherin he went being on a fuddain toffed with a cruel tempeft amõg the Ilands of *Sumatra* by which they paffed, was in eminêt danger to be caft away. Now as they were all euen in defpayre, beholding prefent death reprefented before their eyes, *Francis* commeth to *Iames Sofa* the mayfter of the fhip, and biddeth him, and the reft that were prefent, be of good courage, for that very day in the euening the tempeft fhould ceafe, and the fhip ariue fafe at the Hauen. And fo it fell out, iuft as he had foretould. For before funne-fet, the wind which was in the South ceafed, the fea grew calme, and they arriued at their defired Port. *A Pro-phecy of fayre weather in the feare of fhipwracke.*

Moreouer he did oftentimes foretell to many, not only their fafe arriuall, but their deaths alfo which were neere at hand. For to fay nothing of *Iohn Araufius* his death, which he plainly foretould, as he was one day at *Malaca* in familiar conference with *Antony Sofa*, & falling into fpeach of the Gouernour of the Citty, he tould him playnly, that although he were then in very good health, yet he would within a little after dye. And his death following the next moneth, proued what he had foretould to be true. Then agayne when he was going for *China*, he out of friendfhip ad- *He fore-tels the fpeedy death of thé that were in good health.*

uifed

Iames Perera a wealthy merchant, in whose ship he wēt to substitute another factour ouer his wares, because he whom he had appointed should not arriue thither. And the euent was answerable to the Prophecy; for the Factour dyed by the way, before the came to *China*.

Being also at another tyme bound for the *Moluca's*, and he setting out in one ship, and *Iohn Galuano* a merchant in another, *Xauerius* being carryed away by the violence of a tempest, soone arriued at the port he desired; Where whilst *Galuano* the merchant was earnestly expected, *Francis* vpon a suddain, as he was preaching to the people exhorted them to pray to God for *Galuano* his soule, who was then dead. And three dayes after *Galuano's* merchandize being found cast vp vpon the shore, testifyed the ship-wrack, and death of their mayster.

This Prophecy of his is also admirable, which the euent of late hath proued very true. There was in *India* a ship so weakened with age and tempests, that all were of opinion if she went to sea, she would be shaken asunder by the stormy weather, before she could arriue within sight of the Hauen. Wherupon *Xauerius* (for he chanced to be then present) moued by diuine instinct, Bee of good courage, quoth he, for this ship will not be cast away in this iourney, but at last indeed shall perish, yet without losse to any man. Credit was giuen to this prediction, and the euent fell out accordingly. For presently the Merchants nothing doubting of what *Xauerius* had by diuine reuelation fortould as well cōcerning that ship, as of many other things

A prophecy of a ship to perish in the haué.

things, ſtroue exceedingly to lade their goods in her, aſſuring themſelues, as indeed it hapned, that they might conueigh their merchandize to and fro therin without danger of ſhip-wrack, or other loſſe. Nor were they any whit deceaued. For the ſame ſhip, although very old and rotten, remayned alwayes ſafe in many iorneyes and tempeſts, vntil the yeare 1583. with was almoſt 30. yeares after *Xauerius* death. And at laſt, as ſhe lay empty in the hauen, falling to pieces of her ſelfe, was there made an end of, without dommage vnto any mã; giuing therby teſtimony to *Francis* his prediction, no leſſe whilſt ſhe remayned ſound, then when ſhe decayed.

Neyther did he only foretell things to come and farre abſent, but pierced euen into the harts of men, & knew their very cogitations and ſinnes. And although this be ſufficiently demonſtrated before in its proper place by the knowledge he had by diuine reuelatiõ of the priuate reſolution which *Iohn Durus* had made of running away: yet theſe things, which now we are to ſet downe, will make them much more manifeſt.

There is in *India* a towne called *Bazain,* which lyeth with equall diſtance almoſt, betweene *Goa* and the riuer *Indus. Xauerius* going thither, about the tyme he went into *Iaponia*, to ſpeake with the Viceroy who remayned at *Cambaya*; behould a certayne *Malaſenſian,* that bare very great affection vnto him, offered to imbrace him. *Francis* hauing formerly reduced this man from a lewd to a ciuil life, that he might heereafter looke better to the good of his ſoule, had commanded him, vpon iuſt cauſes, to returne backe a-

gaine

gaine into Portugall, and there to frequent the Sacrament of Confession. But he, although at first had
promised to do them both, had indeed performed neither; and moreouer had not only cast off all thought
of returning into Portugall, but had now also passed
ouer the third yeare without Confession. As soone
therfore as *Xauerius* beheld him, and withall by diuine
reuelation saw the inward wounds of his Consciece,
refusing vtterly his imbracement: Away (quoth he)
get you hence; is this your stading to the promise you
made me? Behould with shame (to say nothing els)
since you tooke leaue of me to sayle into *India*, you
haue neuer byn at Confession. I will certaynly neyther speake vnto you, nor acknowledge you for my
friend, vntill you haue by Confession purged your
soule of your filthy sinnes. Whereupon the man (his
conscience accusing him, both of differing his Confession, and of his heynous offences) being stroken
with these words, easily perceiued that *Xauerius* knew
what he obiected to him, by diuine reuelation, for
speaking humanely he could neuer haue knowne it.
Wherefore accusing himselfe and acknowledging his
fault, he presently by Confession washeth away the
spots of his soule, which he well saw were so abominable in *Francis* his sight.

　　Hauing also asked another friend of his at *Cocinum* how he did, and he answered, well: Well indeed,
quoth *Xauerius*, in body, but not in soule. Vpon these
words, the man who was at the same tyme plotting
I know not what villany, and wickednesse in his
hart, pricked in conscience, confessed playnely, that

*By diui-
ne light
he seeth
his friēds
sinnes &
how lōg
he had
abstained
from cō-
fession.*

*He seeth
that his
friend
was in
his hart
plotting
a great
sinne.*

Francis

Francis could better iudge, how he did, that he himfelf, and fo confeffeth his finnes entierely vnto him ;
and leauing off quite his wicked determination , recouereth agayne his foules health, which *Xauerius* had
perceyued was wanting in him.

Moreouer the day before he departed this life, ca- He being
fting a fterne looke vpon one of thofe who attéded on ready to
him when he lay fick, cryed out thrice with a pitty- dy fore-
ful voice, *Wo be to thee.* Which lamentable denunciatió deftru-
of his, was not in vayne . For fhortly after the party ction of
hauing bin a long while intangled in difhoneft loues, one that
was vpon the fuddaine flaine , and dyed miferably . nied him
So that *Xauerius* thrice crying out, might feeme to haue
denounced vnto him a triple mifery, to wit the woúd
of his confcience, his bodily death, & the deftruction
of his foule.

CHAP. III.

In his life time, he vvorketh miracles of all kinds .

MOREOVER *Xauerius* vertue hath fhewed it felfe moft admirable in almoft all
kind of miracles, wherof we will recount
in this place fome few, contenting our felues to haue touched the reft briefly in other places. As
concerning Deuils , he did not only ouercome them
oftentimes in fingle combat, when at *Meliapora* in *S.*
Thomas his Church he contemned their frights and
threates

threates , although he were cruelly beaten by them ; and againe in his nauigation into *Iaponia*, when as with an inuincible fortitude of mind he preuailad a-gainst their deceipts, and subtilities : But oftentimes also both in the coast of *Comorinum*, *Malaca*, and in o-ther places, he cast them out of possest bodies , partly by himself, & partly by the Neophytes whome he sent vnto them.

And this vertue of his was no lesse seene in curing of diseases, then in casting out Deuils by diuine po-wer . For to passe ouer with silence , many whome he freed both from feuers and other diseases in the fore-sayd coast of *Comorinum* (as we haue before demon-strated) as well by himselfe, as by the children whose help he vsed in teaching there the Catechisme ; going one day to visit *Michael Fernandez* who was exceeding-ly tormented with the Stone in the Iland *Ceilanum*, he willed him to take courage , and to put great confi-dence in God , telling him withall, that he would the next day say Masse for him, and did not doubt but by Gods grace he should recouer his strength both of bo-dy and mynd , sooner then he could haue expected . And euen so it fell out, iust as he foretould.

He mira-
culously
cureth
the stone

He likewise helped those who were ready to dye, and eyther through the defect of nature, or else by some casuality wanted their senses, or members . For it is sufficiently knowne, that at *Amangucium* he resto-red a lame man to his former strength ; two others that were dumbe to their speach ; and two lykewise deafe vnto their hearing. Many also that were brought vnto him being ready to dye, he presently restored to
their

their corporall health, being out of all hope of reco-uery, by making only the figne of the Croffe, and ca-fting of Holy water vpon them. At *Goa* alfo (as we fhewed before) in his returne from *Iaponia*, vifiting one of the Society, who was giuen ouer by all, and reciting the Gofpell ouer him, he deliuered him euen out of the iawes of death.

Neyther did he deliuer only fuch as were ready to dye, but reftored alfo thofe that were allready dead to lyfe agayne. For it is euidently knowne, that there were three dead perfons reftored to lyfe by him, in the coaft of *Comorinum*. But that is very ftrange, which is recounted of him in another kind. There was a cer-tayne Portughefe merchant (whome we will not na-me for his credit fake) very induftrious, & practicall in many things, who at *Francis* his firft comming into *Iaponia*, had contracted great familiarity with him; but returning backe fome years after into *India*, liued there more warily then honeftly. To him therfore *Xa-uerius* on a tyme appeared (whether he were then a farre off, or already dead is vncertayne) denouncing vnto him that God would fpeedily be reueuged of him. And when the other ftraight confeffed, that he had By mira-culoufly indeed well deferued no leffe: Thou haft, quoth he, reprehe-truly deferued it, who haft committed fuch a detefta-ding a ble finne; and withall named a certayne heynous of- very wic fence, which no mortall creature knew, but he him- ked man felfe. Whereupon the merchant being put in mind of he makes this fecret finne of his, was prefently ftrucken to the him be-hart, and with admiration cryeth out: Certainly, Fa- Francif-ther, this hath him reuealed to you by God. Goe to cifcan.

there-

Qqq

therfore, fince you haue feene the fore, prefcribe alfo the cure, and fhew me, who haue gone aftray, the fure path fo faluation. Thou fhalt then (quoth he) enter into the Order of S. *Francis*, which rule if thou diligently obferue, thou fhalt be certainly faued. For I perceiue thou art, as it were borne, and made for that Order aboue all other. He prefently obeyed his wholfome counfayle, as though he had byn commanded by a voyce from heauen; & afterwards, much reioycing at the happy euent, related the whole matter to others.

Xauerius moreouer wrought very many miracles of other kinds. There is a Towne ftanding beyond *Malaca* called *Semorra*, by which there runneth a broad and deepe Riuer. They who dwell vpon the Banke therof, being fet on by the inftigation of the Diuell, threw many ftones, and darts at *Francis*; who being eagerly preffed, and purfued by thofe Barbarians, remoued without difficulty a huge beame that lay ouertwhart the banke, and hindred his way from flying, & thereby efcaped and faued himfelfe; whereupon the Barbarians being aftonifhed, and amazed at fo miraculous a thing, were terrifyed from purfuing him any further; for they playnely faw, that that beame could not be ftyrred without the ftrength of many men, & therfore that *Xauerius* had remoued the fame by diuine, not humane power.

This which followeth was euer fcarcely heard of. At *Amanzucium* in *Iaponia* he preached dayly to the *Bonzies* and other Ethnickes, the Chriftian Religion. After his Sermon the inhabitans (being a Nation no leffe vehement, then infolent agaynft ftrangers) afked

ked of him very maliciouſly, onevpon another, many
queſtions, concerning that which he had preached.
Xauerius therefore, when he was vrged thus by ſo many at once, with diuers & ſundry queſtions, often ſa-
tisfyed them all (which is very admirable to be recounted) with one anſwere, as though he had anſwered euery one apart. This was teſtifyed by one *Bernard*
a Laponian, a man of ſincere vertue and credit, who
was preſent himſelfe at thoſe diſputations and interrogations, and had, together with many others, more
then once obſerued the ſame.

No leſſe authenticall, and wonderfull is that
which is recounted to haue happened in a certayne
Towne of *India* called *Coramandela*. *Xauerius* being
there by chance, a poore man, who had newly ſuffered ſhipwracke, came vnto him, beſeeching him to
beſtow ſome almes vpon him, to relieue his miſery.
Francis, although he had not where withall to ſhew
his Charity, could not for all that, find in his hart to
ſend the poore wretch away, without ſomthing. Therfore, not thinking of his owne pouerty, he put his
hand into his pocket, but found there nothing at all.
Yet would he not deſiſt from his determination, but
began to haue recourſe to him, who is Lord of all riches. Wherefore lifting vp his eyes to heauen, he biddeth the poore man put his confidence in the diuine
liberality. And God neyther fruſtrated *Xauerius* hope,
nor he the poore mans. For putting his hand agayne
into his pocket, he brought it out full of fayre pieces
of gold (which the inhabitants call *Fano'es*) and preſently gaue them all, ſince God had thus affoarded

them,

them, vnto the poore man, putting his whole confidence in the endlesse Treasure of diuine hope.

A Portughese Souldiar also, playing at dyce had lost 600. Crownes; wherfore being sad, & not knowing what to do, or courſe to take, he maketh his moane to *Francis*. He iudging it meete to apply a playſter fit for the poiſon of the diſeaſe, demaundeth of him a

He vſeth ſtrange meanes to make a gameſter at dice deteſt that play.

Dye, and hauing ſhaked it in his hand, giueth it him backe, and biddeth him go play againe to recouer his loſſe. Neither was he therin deceiued. For on a ſuddain the fortune of the game began to chãge, & the ſouldiar hauing good lucke, ſoone recouered all againe. When he had got his owne againe, he would haue played on ſtil, but *Xauerius* forbad him, nor did the ſouldiar contradiᶜt him, but remembring the benefit he had receiued, promptly obeyed his wholſome commãuds : and promiſed furthermore of his owne accord, that he would neuer after play at Dyce. And he was indeed as good as his word. For from that time forward, he could neuer indure to handle Dyce, ſuch an auerſion he had to that game, by *Francis* his meanes.

It was an ordinary practiſe with *Xauerius*, that

The oyle veſſell which was emptyed was miraeulouſly filled agayne.

in his voyages by ſea, whatſoeuer he brought aboard into the ſhippe for his owne vſe, or prouiſion, he would ſtrayght diſtribute it all amongſt the poore paſſengers, and marriners, and liue himſelfe by begging. Wherefore on a tyme, giuing out his oyle freely to them that asked of him, his veſſel was within a little ſpace wholy empty : Notwithſtanding another comming afterward to demand a litle therof, *Xauerius* bad that ſome ſhould be giuen vnto him. His

Com-

Companion told him, there was no more oyle left, and that the bottle was now spent, for he had turned vp the bottome, and shaken it, & could not wring so much as one droppe thereout. Go yet, quoth *Francis*, for all that, & looke againe. He doth as he was willed, and by and by he bringeth word, that the bottle was now full againe, notwithstāding he had but a little before left it empty. But *Xauerius* taking no notice of the miracle, as his custome was; Giue therfore, quoth he, liberally to him that asketh.

Moreouer, lighting by chance vpon a child which was sick, and very full of vlcers; and moued to compassion towards him, he made at first a little stand, & then taking him vp in his armes, and hugging him in his bosome, he began to repeate these words, *God make thee whole*; which he had scarce pronounced twice or thrice, when as he restored the child whole & sound to his mother. This was witnessed by *Vincent Perera* a mayster of a ship, & *Xauerius* familiar friend (whome we haue named in another place) and recounted to those of the Society in *India*. But of this kind we haue in his lyfe set downe innumerable examples although we referred these vnto this place, because the tymes wherein they were done, were not then sufficiently knowne vnto vs.

He by his prayers cureth a childfull of vlcers.

This also is very admirable which hapned in the Iland of *Sanciana*. *Xauerius* as he stood baptizing a number of *Saracens*, who were men of extraordinary great stature of body, seemed vnto the Portugheses, who beheld the thing a far off, to be much taller then they. Which caused in them such admiration that they

ap-

approched neerer to fee whether he did not baptize
out of fome pulpit or high place. But comming clofe
vnto him, they find him ftanding vpon euen ground.
Then indeed they perceiued that his greatnes of mind
had added fo much to his body, that he feemed to furpaffe the ordinary pitch of the talleft men.

Neyther is this a fmall argument of his vertue and
fanctity, that whereas the *Sanciana* fea, which in former times had bin very dangerous, & fubiect to often
fhippewracks, by reafon of a certaine furious wind
called *Typhon*, *Francis* by celebrating the facred myfteries of the maffe there, hath as it were fo fanctified the
Iland, and made the fea fo calme & temperate, that the
raging *Typhon* doth very feldom bring any great incō-
brance to the fhips that fayle therein. So great was the
force eyther of *Xauerius* fanctity, or the vertue of the
Holy Maffe.

CHAP. IIII.

Miracles vvrought by him after his death.

VT now *Xauerius* life was not more glorious nor remarkeable by fuch like fignes of
fanctity, then his death. For God, who is
admirable in his Saints, adorned *Francis* his
Body after his death with many illuftrious miracles,
which whilft he liued had bin a Temple of the Holy
Ghoft. For (as we faid before) his dead corps being
digged vp after it had layne three moneths in quicke
lime, was found wholy entiere, breathing forth a
moft pleafant and fragrant odour, which was no
doubt

doubt a perpetuall, and manifold miracle, seing it reteined the same integrity, and fragrant odour, after he bad bin interred six months at *Malaca* in the groūd without a Coffin. This diuine vertue which was imparted to his body, redounded likewise euen to his garments, and preserued them wholy incorrupt, & found from all putrefaction.

Moreouer (which is very admirable) fiue moneths after his death, when he was interred at *Malaca*, he bled a fresh, the signes whereof remayned liuely to be seene, vntill his Funerall at *Goa*, being 16. moneths after his decease. Wherupon not only the Cittizēs of *Goa*, but almost all *India* being stirred vp no lesse by the report of the integrity of his body, then by his eminent sanctity, came flocking thither to his buriall; which indeed, as before we haue shewed, seemed rather a triumph then a Funerall, the multitude wherof from all places was so great, as the like was neuer seene or heard; so that they were constrained, as before we haue said, to leaue the Body exposed for three whole dayes to the view of the people, to giue them satisfaction. And besides this, they were all so taken with deuotion to his holy Body, that euery one did striue to touch the same with their beades, and to get away, euen by stealth, some Relique thereof.

Lastly, this miracle of his Body hath (as after we shall declare) bin honoured by God himselfe with so many, and euident signes, that all men, yea euen the maleuolous, haue bin satisfyed therby concerning the Beatitude of his soule. And these things which we haue recounted of *Francis* his body, haue bin so testy-
fyed

fied, that there were as many witnesses therof, as were people at that time in the Citty of *Goa*, that is to fay, almost all *India*. But least perhaps such wonderfull fauours of Almighty God, might seeme to some more admirable, then credible, both humane and diuine Prouidence hath so concurred in this busines, that these priuate testimonyes haue byn confirmed by publick Records. For *Ambrose Ribera* the Inquisitour, and Vicar Generall of the Bishop of *Goa*, when the fame of that great miracle was spread ouer *India*, iudging it to be a matter which belonged to his office, togeather with certaine most skillfull Physitians went to visit *Xauerius* body, before it was buryed, to try whether the fame were wholy intiere and incorrupt, as was reported, or no. He therfore hauing with his owne eyes throughly beheld the integrity of the fame surpassing all humane faith, and then by making inquiry therof, as the King of Portugall had commanded, hauing found out his incomparable sanctity, confirmed the truth with a most worthy testimony, which I haue thought good heere to insert, in the selfe same words wherein he gaue it. I D. *Ambrose Ribera*, Inquisitour, Vicar Generall, and Assistant of the Bishop of *Goa*, and *India*, do testify, that *Francis Xauerius* for the space of nine whole yeares (for so many haue I byn resident in this place) hath gone vp & downe to the townes and villages of *India*, *Malaca*, the *Moluca's*, *Iaponia*, and other farre remote places of the Barbarians, preaching and teaching the mysteries & precepts of the Christian faith, as well to the Portugheses, as to other People, and Nations; and hath in the same places

The Inquisitors and Vicars testimony of Xauerius sanctity.

places couerted an exceeding great number of Ethnickes to the Chriſtian Religion, building euery where
Churches ; and for the effecting thereof hath endured very many great miſeries, and labours, euen to
his dying day. And that his body hauing bin brought
to *Goa*, and there receiued with all ſolemnity, was
by the whole Clergy and Citty conueyed to the Colledg of *S. Paul*, and there buryed . But for that there
was a certayne rumour ſpread abroad, of the integrity of his Body, which ſeemed to ſurpaſſe the forces
of Nature, and to be euidently a diuine Miracle ,
ſince a Body that had byn dead ſo long, and layne
buryed an eleuen monethes before, to wit, three in
China, and eight at *Malaca* (as the Viceroy of *India*
Alphonſus Noronia, and my ſelfe haue proued by
vndoubted witneſſes) ſhould remayne the ſpace of
16. moneths free, and entiere from all corruption;
I thought it belonged vnto my office, to examine
and make tryall of the ſame. Wherefore I went into
the Church where he lay, cauſed the Coffin to be opened, looked vpon his body with lighted torches about
an houre before midday; and I felt, and handled, for
a good while, his armes & legges, his knees & thighs
& the greateſt part of his body (ſo that by thoſe parts
which lay open a coniecture might be eaſily made of
that which was not ſeene) and found the Body entiere, & wholy free from all kind of corruption, with
the fleſh altogether freſh, and ſolid, euen reteyning
the naturall moyſture and colour. Moreouer I ſaw in
his left thigh, a litle aboue the knee, as it were a woūd
from whence there had byn a little piece of fleſh taken

*His teſti-
mony
alſo of
them te-
grity of
his body*

» about the biggnes of a fingar. And another wound
» alfo in the belly, whereinto I putting my fingars,
» found all entiere and incorrupt, and without any
» kind of ill fmell. And moreouer, I layd my mouth to
» his month, and felt, and looked vpon his face all ouer
» with the greateft diligence I could. Whereupon after
» examination made of all thefe things, as I found them,
» I commanded my Notary to fet them downe in wri-
» ting. In teftimony whereof I haue heerunto fet my
» owne hand and feale, the firft of December 1556.

The Viceroyes Phifitian alfo, one of excellent
skill, hauing by his Lords command, throughly examined the body, gaue no leffe euident a teftimony of
the integrity thereof, which was this: I *Cofmas Sa-*

An ex- *raina* Phyfitian to *Alphonfus Noronia* Viceroy of *In-*
cellent *dia*, do teftify, that when *Francis Xauerius* body was
Phifitiās brought to *Goa*, I looked very diligently vpon it, and
teftimo- felt it all ouer, efpecially the belly, which vfeth to be
ny of moft fubiect to corruption, and I found his entrayles
the inte- wholy found, & folide; notwithftanding it was ma-
grity of nifeft, that there had neyther balme, oyle, or any o-
hisbody
» ther thing agaynft putrefaction byn applyed thereto.
» Afterwards when by my aduife one of the Society of
» I E s v s did put his fingar into a wound, which was
» open in his left fide, clofe to his hart, there iffued out
» bloud, and water togeather, to which I fmelling,
» found no kind of bad fauour at all. I alfo found his
» thighes, and the other parts of his body entiere, with
» the flefh fo folid, and naturall, that it could not by art
» of Phyficke be in that manner preferued. For the bo-
» dy had byn now dead almoft a yeare & a halfe, & had

layne

layne well neere a yeare, in the Sepulcher. Thefe « things according to the charge which is giuen me in « this bufineffe, I do teftify vpon my oath. Giuen at « *Goa* the 18. of Nouemb. 1556.

And thefe humane teftimonyes were alfo confirmed by diuine. For about the fame tyme, there were many miracles wrought, to teftify as well *Xauerius* fanctity, as the happines of his foule in heauen. *Iohn Mendoza* his fhip, which brought *Xauerius* body back into *India* miraculoufly efcaped many great dangers, efpecially in the Iland of *Ceilanum*. From thence when it came to *Baticala* a towne in *India*, *Mary Sarra* a Portughefe woman of good note, and wyfe to the Kings Solicitour there, lay very fick of a dangerous infirmity, who being certifyed of the coming of *Xauerius* body caufed herfelf prefently to be carryed to it, where fhe imploring the holy mans affiftance with no leffe confidence then deuotion, was forthwith by *Xauerius* interceffion, & the diuine goodnes cured, & recouered her health. She alfo hauing obtayned by earneft intreaty a litle piece of the girdle, wherwith he was girt, enclofed it in a filuer reliquary, and wore it about her necke, eyther as a remembrance of him, or as a preferuatiue agaynft fickneffe. And heerein her deuotion fayled her not. For her litle fonne who had byn then grieuoufly afflicted for the fpace of fix moneths with an ague, was cured by applying the fayd reliquary vnto him; the which alfo recouered him afterwards, of an Apoplexy wherewith he was greatly vexed. It being alfo hung about the necke of a woma-feruant, who was very dangeroufly in trauayle, caufed her an

A fick woman bydoing reuerece to Fraci his body is cured.

Xauerius girdle cureth many & great difeafes.

eafy

eafy deliuery. Moreouer it cured a ficke man of a feuer. And from two children, who were grieuoufly ficke of the Pox, it tooke away both the ficknefle, and the markes thereof. All this the follicitous woman of *Baticala* related vpon her oath.

It is furthermore euidently knowen, that many ficke were at *Goa* recouered by touching *Francis* his body. Amongft whome one was a woman-feruant, who in the time of labour, being out of her fenfes, & in extreme danger of death (for the child being dead in her wombe, and lying ouerthwart, fhe could by no meanes be deliuered) was vpon a fuddain preferued, & deliuered of the dead child, by applying vnto her certayne hayres of *Xauerius*, which were religioufly kept in a reliquary. This, her maifter *Anthony Saa* teftified vp his oath; who alfo furthermore affirmed, that there was in his houfe a another woman of that Country, who being alfo in labour of Childbirth, and brought to fuch extremity, that there was no hope of her life, was by the meanes of the fame Reliquary applyed vnto her, deliuered prefently, and quit of the danger.

A Gétle man recouereth his fight by applying *Francis* his hâds to his eyes.

It is alfo certainly knowen, that many others haue with diuers reliques of his cured fundry difeafes. This following is worthy of note. *Antony Rodriguez* a man of no fmall ranke, had through a long rheume fo loft the fight of his eyes, that he could not fo much as fee thofe with whome he fpake, although they were clofe by him. He therfore being out of hope to find any help by art of Phyficke, hauing tryed all kind of medicines, but in vaine, caufed himfelf to be carryed

to

to *Xauerius* Sepulcher, and intreating the Fathes to open the Shrine, put *Xauerius* hands to his eyes, and presently began to see, finding that thick dimnesse to be driuen away; and shortly after he fully recouered his sight. This also he himselfe affirmed vpon his oath.

No lesse memorable was that which hapned to *Baltazar Dias* a Priest. He being tormented with the Squinancy in his throat, could not swallow downe any thing at all: wherefore dispayring of all humane help, he had recourse to diuine; & intreating the Fathers of the Society to lend him the Key of the Shrin wherin *Xauerius* Body was kept, toucheth his thoate therewith, and the rheume on such a suddayne went so away, that the Key seemed by *Xauerius* fauourable assistance, to haue opened an entrance into his throate.

The key of his shrine driueth away the rheume.

But this is farre more glorious. A certaine woman of good note, named *Ioane*, hauing byn tormented with a long sicknes, was now brought to the point of death at the very time that *Xauerius* body was brought to *Goa*, being watched day & night for her departure. Wherupon being stirred vp by the solemne ringing of the bells, and also by the fame of his sanctity and miracles, she earnestly besought *Christopher Perera* her husband, and others that were present, to permit her to be carryed to *Xauerius* funerall. They affirmed plainly, it could not possibly be done, without manifest danger of her life, and would by no meanes yield thereunto. Yet the woman lost not the fruite of her deuotion. For from that time forward she began to be

A principal woman desiring to visit Xauerius, is recouered of a great sicknes.

better

better, and euery day more & more amending, within a while after perfectly recouered; so powerfull was the desire, not only of touching, but euen of seeing his body, in restoring health to the sicke.

It is also recounted, and that by assured testimonies, that a certaine whip made of little cords, wherwith *Xauerius* was wont to discipline himselfe, being kept with great deuotion by a certaine *Neophyte*, restored diuers sick persons to their health, and wrought many other wonderfull things. For which cause *Xauerius* name both was, and is, not only glorious, but also greatly reuerenced in *India*, and throughout the whole East; all the people thereof ordinarily, imploring his protection and patronage. And as often as any ship passeth by the Iland of *Sanciana*, where, as we said, *Xauerius* was first buried, the Marriners and passengers haue got a custome to call vpon *Francis*, as a Saint raigning amongst the blessed in heauen.

Francis his discipline restoreth many to their health.

Neither was *India*, or the whole East able to comprehend the vertue, and glorious Name of *Xauerius* within their owne bounds, but passing ouer the Ocean, it penetrated into *Europe*. There is in Portugall a Citty called *Ebora*, a place of speciall note, wherin there is a Colledge of the Society of Iesvs, built by *Henry* the Cardinall, who was afterward King; a worke well beseeming both the bounteous liberality of so worthy a Prince, & the magnificéce of the Citty also. In this Colledge, at the same time that newes was brought of the death and miracles of *Xauerius*(as we haue byn informed by one of good credit, whilst we were writing things of the same nature) two of the

the principall Fathers, *Leo Henriquez* the Rectour of the Colledge, and *Andrew Capreda* the Ghoftly Father, very worthy and venerable man, were fore oppreffed with a burning feuer; who vpon the report of the wonderfull effects which had bin wrought by *Xauerius*, conceiued both of them great hope of recouering their health. *Leo* therfore caufed the *Indian* letters wherein was written *Xauerius* happy departure out of this lyfe, & his funerall made glorious by the miracles which had happened therein, to be brought, & read vnto him. As foone as they were read, he prefently as it were, moued by diuine inftinct, and ftirred vp with admiration of *Xauerius* vertues, rayfeth himfelfe vpon his elbow in his bed, and lifting vp his hands & eyes to heauen, calleth vpon him with no leffe deuotion then confidence againft the violence of his feuer, befeeching that he would be no leffe fauourable to his owne, the he had byn to ftrangers. And his confidence & fupplication were neyther in vayne. For his health followed vpon this prayer, & he prefently felt his feuer, to be as it were driuen away, by Gods diuine hād, and his former ftrength to be agayne reftored vnto him. Whereupon crying out aloud with ioy, and teares in his eyes, he giueth humble thankes to God, and extolleth *Francis* his miraculous vertue, to the aftonifhment of all that were prefent. So as inftantly finding himfelfe to be wholy found and lufty, he leapeth out of his bed, and runneth with all ioy, and alacrity to *Capreda* his ficke Companion. *Capreda* knowing how extreme ficke *Leo* was but a little before, began to be amazed, and to aske him what the

Two Fathers in Europe recouer their health by calling vpon Francis.

matter

matter was? Whereupon *Leo* declared vnto him, not more in words, then by effect, what soueraigne help he had receiued from *Xauerius* in the curing of his sicknes, and withall counsayled him to do the lyke, and without doubt he should in the same occasion find the lyke help from him. *Capreda*, without more ado followeth his aduise, stirreth vp himselfe to confidence, & calleth vpon *Xauerius* : nor is he frustrated of his hope, but freed from his feuer, sooner then any one could haue expected. Thus was the Societyes ioy redoubled, by this double miracle, & *Francis* his sanctity more euidently demonstrated. One of these Fathers, wherof we now speake, to wit *Leo Henriquez*, is yet liuing in Portugall, as a glorious witnes of *Xauerius* approued vertue. The report whereof, afterwards as soone as it was spread abroad, caused many not only of the Society, but euen strangers also to admire his power, and reuerence his sanctity.

　There was (to say nothing of lesser matters) still liuing in *Paris*, euen when we write these thinges, a certayne honest and deuout person, venerable no lesse in respect of vertue, then age. This man was wont to make this relation; to wit, that when newes was first brought of *Francis Xauerius* death, whome he had neuer knowne but by report, and heare-say only, he felt himselfe wonderfully stirred vp with reuerence & veneration towards him. Whereupon his wife being at the same tyme sicke, and in danger of death by reason of her labour in child-birth, yea & giuen ouer by the Physitians, he recounted to her certayne passages of *Xauerius* sanctity and vertue, and withall persua-

ded

ded her earneftly to implore that holy mans affiftance, and no doubt he would help & cure her. She gaue
diligent eare vnto her husbands counfayle, and forthwith hauing called vpon *Xauerius* for help, fhe was eafily and fafe deliuered of her child . And thus were
both the mother, & the child by *Xauerius* merits freed
from prefent danger of death.

Nor was *Xauerius* natiue foyle euen at this tyme
without all knowledge of her Childs great fanctity .
For it is euidently knowne that his death was by certaine prodigious fignes forefhewed in the fame place
where he had receiued life . There is in the Caftle *Xauerium*, being the manfion houfe wherin *Xauerius* was
borne, a Chappell wherin is to be feene a Crucifix of
exceeding great deuotion, and very much efteemed
in thofe parts . There hapned at this tyme a prodigious accident, miraculous both for fight , & the euent
therof . For certaine it is, that this Image, or Crucifix
of our Sauiour, being made of wood, did manifeftly
fweate, as often as *Xauerius* had any great fuffrance in
India, which they of the Caftle found out, by the letters which he himfelfe had fent from thence, by calcu-
lation of the times. But vpon the very yeare wherin
Xauerius departed this life, it fweat bloud euery friday
after, for a whole yeare togeather, and made an end
of fweating vpon a Friday alfo . Which many fo interpreted, as if it had portended *Francis* his death, after many long and painefull labours vndertaken for
Chrift his fake, who had continually carryed in his
body the mortification of the Croffe.

Sff   CHAP.

CHAP. V.

Xauerius *his feruent loue to Prayer*.

THESE admirable things, which (as we haue before declared) haue as well byn wrought by *Xauerius* diuine power, as other wayes hapned vnto him miraculoufly, were certaine fignes and teftimonies, of the extraordinary vertues and guiftes, which the diuine Goodnes had with a moft liberall hand, heaped vp togeather in his foule. For he was not more glorious in miracles, then in heauenly Vertues, fome wherof we will fet forth to publicke view; which, although he vfed all art and diligence to conceale, did notwithftanding difcouer themfelues of their owne accord. And thefe I fhall recount more willingly then the former, in refpect, they are not bare tokens alone, but liuely examples alfo of his rare fanctity. And wheras thofe other ferue only for admiratiõ, thefe are brought within the compaffe of imitation.

Wherfore to begin with that vertue which is the fource & fountaine of the reft, it is to be obferued that *Xauerius* was extraordinarily addicted vnto Prayer, Meditation, and Contemplation of heauenly things. For although he had his mind perpetually fixed vpon God, and diuine matters; yet did he affigne vnto himfelfe euery day, a fet and determinate time, which, by withdrawing himfelfe from al exteriour affayres,

he

he imployed in meditating vpon celeſtiall things. But the meditation wherin he chiefly exerciſed himſelfe, was vpon the life and death of our Sauiour: knowing very well, that he might there behould, and imitate moſt excellent and exemplar patternes of all kind, li-uely repreſented in that noble maiſter-piece.

This moſt wholſome, and fruitfull manner of meditation (as being indeed the principall modell of a Chriſtian life, and a ſingular incitement to diuine Charity) he moſt diligently obſerued himſelfe, and commended the ſame alſo vnto others, imploying all his faculties heerein, with no leſſe conſtancy of mind, then feruour of ſpirit. The which did neuer more diſ-couer it ſelfe, then whilſt he laboured amongſt the ſick in the Hoſpitalls. For when his other continuall labours would not affoard him any part of the day free for that purpoſe, he hauing his mind more vpon prayer then vpon ſleepe, did alwayes vſe to take ſome howers from his corporall reſt, that his ſoule might not be defrauded of her heauenly food, and repaſt ; ſuch poſſeſſion had the ſweetnes of his diſcourſing with the diuine Maieſty taken of his hart. He ordina-rily ſlept but two, or at the moſt, three houres of the night, and that in ſuch ſort alſo, as his very ſleepe was not without prayer. For oftentimes in his ſleepe he brake forth into theſe words: *O good Ieſu, O my Crea-tour*, & other the like; ſo as one would haue thought him to haue bin praying, and not ſleeping.

His night prayer.

It is moreouer certainly knowne, that he did not ſo much as breake off this cuſtome of prayer, euen in his greateſt imployments in the Promontory of *Como-*

rinum ; for he held his meditation to be the most important affayre which he had in hand . At *Meliapora* also , when he lodged neere to *S. Thomas* his Church , as we haue before declared , rising in the night tyme, he went often into the Church , & could not eyther by the speeches of men , or strypes and other molestations of the Diuells be affrighted , or debarred from discoursing with God ; with whome he often spent the whole night almost in prayer.

Lykewise at *Malaca*, when he remayned there in a chamber made of Mattes , certayne persons moued with the opinion of his sanctity , did oftentymes by stealth , as themselues did afterwards reporte , looke through the chinckes and slifters of the Mattes , to espy what *Francis* was a doing in the night tyme ; and they found him alwayes (though he had byn but immediately before , long kneeling at a Crucifix) liuely perseuerant in prayer , both in spirit and body , vntill sleepe seizing vpon him , constrayned him by force to yield a while vnto necessity of nature ; & then laying himselfe downe vpon the ground , and resting his head vpon a hard stone insteed of a pillow , he in that máner refreshed his body fora while , euē worne out with continuall toyle and labour day and night ; so as one would haue thought him to haue vsed sleepe as a medicine ; and whilst he tooke his rest, to loue nothing lesse then rest.

But he , well knowing that God giueth more fauourable audience to those who pray in places which be more religiously honoured , whensoeuer he could find opportunity , he alwayes vsed to make his prayer

with

with much more feeling in the Church ; and therefore he would commonly take vp his lodging next to
the Church, that he might go thither secretly in the
night, for that purpose. And those of the Society at
Malaca obserued, that like another *Samuell* he was
wont often to lye vpon the bare ground in the Vestry
vntill the dead of the night, and then would steale into the Church, and there fall to his prayers vpon his
his knees, before the high Aultar, in presence of the
Blessed Sacrament : and when his knees were weary,
he would eyther lay himselfe along vpon the steps of
the Aultar, or else leane vpon his hands, and still go
on with his exercise, vntill eyther sleepe constrayned
him to giue ouer, or else the light of the morning
came vpon him. And when he could not haue the
commodity of a Church, he notwithstanding held on
this exercise of prayer, in some other place.

As often as opportunity serued he prayed in the Church.

A certayne Priest in whose house *Xauerius* lodged
related, that he vsed oftentymes to pray late in the
night, & somtimes to sit vpon a litle stoole (eyther because such a seate was more commodious, or else because
he could kneele no longer, being wholy tired out with
kneeling) and so go on with his deuotions. Moreouer
many Cittizens of *Malaca* of good account haue giuen testimony, that *Francis* when he was in familiar
conuersation with them, would oftentimes withdraw
himself priuately from their company ; & after much
& long inquiry made, they should find him eyther in
some vncouth wood, or desert and forlorne place,
deuoutly at his prayers, or else a disciplining himselfe
there ; who not to interrupt his deuotions would le-

He goeth into solitary places to pray.

aue

aue him thereunto, & diſſemble the matter as though they had perceiued nothing.

And in this feruour of prayer, *Xauerius* was no leſſe conſtant by ſea, then by land, wherof ſo many demõ-ſtrations in his often nauigations are extant, which we haue already ſet downe, that to ſeeke out more ex-amples therof, would not only be ſuperfluous, but a troubleſome labour alſo. For though he were conuer-ſant in many & differēt places, & with ſundry perſõs, yet he remayned alwayes like himſelfe, and kept as it were, one faſhon and method throughout the whole courſe of his life. Notwithſtanding we will not con-ceale that which properly belonged to the ſea. For there be certaine and euident proofes, that whilſt he was a ſhip-board, he did vſually ſit vp watching in prayer from midnight, vntill breake of day; and in the midſt of any tempeſt, or whatſoeuer danger, he called on God with a moſt patient and quiet ſoule. In ſo much that the marriners and paſſengers acknow-ledged both themſelues, and their ſhip to haue bin ve-ry often ſaued by *Francis* his prayers.

His pray er in the ſhip.

Moreouer, he was always feruent and inflamed in his prayers, & moſt commonly ouerflowing with heauenly ioyes: the which was ſeene and knowne by many, & moſt euident arguments. For to ſay nothing of thoſe extraordinary contents which he receiued from God, amidſt his exceſſiue labours in *Comorinũ*, and *Maurica*, wherof we haue already ſpoken in their proper places; at *Goa* he was obſerued by the Fathers there to walke oftentymes in the dead of the night in the garden, with his eyes fixed vpon heauen, & to

His fer-uour in prayer.

be

be wholy carryed away with contemplation, and loue
of God: so that one would haue thought for certayne
that his soule, as being abstracted from his senses, had *He puls*
byn departed out of his body. And afterwards when *his clo-*
he came agayne to himselfe, opening his Cassocke *aths frō*
from his inflamed breast as his custom was, he would *being in-*
oftentymes repeate these words: *It is inough O Lord*, *flamed*
it is inough, & this in such a tune, as manifestly decla- *by the*
red, that so aboundant was the heauenly ioy which *force of*
ouerwhelmed him, that humane Nature was scarse *prayer.*
able to beare it.

At *Goa* also, as he was conuersing familiarly with
the other Fathers, there came vpon him oftentimes
such excessiue ioy of spirit, that it constrayned him
to with-draw himselfe from the sight of men, because he could by no meanes conceale the aboundan- *The ar-*
ce of Consolation which he felt. And euen in humane *dour &*
affayres, there appeared in him such a diuine semblan- *splēdour*
ce of heauenly Ioy, that they who conuersed with *of his*
him, being often stroken with a reuerent respect to- *counte-*
wards him, could not forbeare behoulding and admi- *nance:*
ring him, as if he had byn a second Moyses.

Lastly, in his iourney to *Meaco*, wherein, as we
sayd before, he suffered extreme miseryes and incom-
brances, being notwithstanding as it were almost in
a continuall rapt through the excessiue comfort and
consolation, which his soule receaued in meditating
vpon celestiall obiectes, and with that sweet conuersation with God; he often stroke his legges, and feete
agaynst stubbs and stones, yea hurt and bruised them
sore, without euer feeling therof; going forward with
such

such ioy & iubily of hart, that he euen seemed to participate of the happinesse of the Blessed in heauen, rather then to meditate vpon their lyfe. And verily it is an admirable thing to consider that there could be in him, such a combination of contemplation, & action togeather. For it is incredible (as we haue byn certaynely informed) that he, being a man perpetually imployed in so weighty affayres, & cōtinuall trauayles, and nauigations most hard and difficile, and being also of so affable & pleasant a conuersation; should notwithstanding, be endowed with so extraordinary a guift of diuine contemplation, and comforted so aboundantly by the holy Ghost, and with continuall ouerflowing of diuine streames into his soule. For certaynly this diuine man, wheresoeuer he was, or whatsoeuer he did, kept alwayes his habitation with himselfe, and with God. Wherupon it followed, that euen from his very exteriour imployments, and conuersation amidst aboundance of people, he came alwayes to mentall prayer & meditation with his soule so fresh and rectifyed, that presently he could cast, and as it were, euen embosome himselfe into the most sweet conference with his heauenly Spouse. In so much, as one would haue thought him to haue alwaies bin kept in a most strayte solitude, he had his soule so firmely fixed vpō God, euen amidst his greatest imployments.

No lesse was the feeling of deuotion which he found, nor the diligence which he vsed, in Vocall Prayer, as they call it, and in reciting the Psalmes, and Hymnes. For he had gotten a custome, which with great care he alwayes obserued, to recite the diuine

A great combination of contēplation & action togeather.

uine

uine office & Canonical Houres very diligently & deuoutly. First therfore following the aduise of *Ecclesiasticus. Before Prayer prepare thy soule, and be not as a man that tempteth God*, he prepared himselfe with a recollected care, the better to stirre vp attention, and deuotion in his mind; and before euery Houre he vsed to recite the Hymne *Veni Creator*, to implore therby the assistance of the holy Ghost. Which Hymne he alwayes pronounced with such feruour of spirit, that his hart seemed euen to burst out of his breast, & his forces to faint. And very certaine it is, that being many times interrupted therin by some that came & spake vnto him, he againe repeated the same from the beginning, with such feruour, as if he had not byn interrupted at all.

This singular deuotion of his, in this kind, was caused by the liberty of those times. There had byn lately, for the more ease and commodity of such men as had great imploiments, a new Breuiary set forth of three Lessons only (called of the *Holy Crosse*) the which was also granted vnto *Francis* at the first, by reason of his weighty affayres. Yet he, although he were cōtinually imployed, would notwithstanding neuer make vse of that Grant, but alwayes sayd the old Breuiary of nine Lessons, although it were a great deale longer, to the end he might haue therby more tyme to conferre with God, in whose conuersation he tooke incomparable content.

But aboue all, his feruour of deuotion shewed it selfe in celebrating the diuine mystery of the sacred Masse, especially in the tyme of Consecration, and

He recīteth his diuine office withgreat preparation & attentiō of mind.

Eccles.18.

He preīfers the longer Breuiary before the shorter.

Xauerius feruour in saying Masse.

Ttt   Consum-

Confummation of the Holy Eucharift. For at thofe
tymes he vfed fo to weepe for ioy, that his face & bo-
fome were all bedewed with teares. There alfo appeared both in his pronunciation, countenance, and all
the geftures of his body, fuch a feeling of heauenly deuotion, that it euen redounded to the ftanders by;
and ftrooke them into fuch a pious admiration, that
they oftentymes forgot themfelues. Moreouer, there
wanted not fome, who affirmed, that whileft he was
at Maffe, they faw him eleuated and lifted vp a little
from the ground. He had befides this, a cuftome in his
Maffe, before all other things, to begge moft earneftly of our Sauiour Chrift, the Conuerfion of Ethnickes
by that precious death which he had fuffered on the
Croffe for their fakes; and for this end, he oftenty-

Xauerius prayer for the conuerfion of Infidels.

mes alfo added a prayer of his owne making which
was this: Eternal God maker of all things, remember
that the foules of Infidels were created by thee, and
man made to thine owne image and likeneffe. Behold
O Lord, how to thy difgrace Hell is fillled with them.
Call to mind, how Iefus thy bleffed Sonne dyed a moft
bitter death for their faluation. Doe not, I befeech
thee, O Lord, any more permit thy Sonne to be contemned by Infidels; but being pacifyed by the praiers
of Holy Men, & of the Church the moft facred fpoufe of thy Sonne, remember thy mercy; and forgetting their Idolatry and Infidelity, make them alfo at
laft to acknowledge Iefus-Chrift our Lord, whome
thou haft fent; who is our Saluation, and Refurrecti-
on, by whome we are faued and deliuered, and to
whome be all honour, and glory for euer. Amen.

Now

Now after Maſſe, when he had giuen thankes to God, he was alwayes accuſtomed to recite a certaine prayer for the Dead, that euen then, when he offered Sacrifice for the liuing, he might alſo giue ſome refreſhment to the ſoules departed. His deuotion alſo in adminiſtring the moſt ſacred Body of Chriſt, was no leſſe remarkeable then in the conſecration thereof. He had this cuſtome peculiar to himſelfe, that where it could commodiouſly be done, he would giue the holy Communion to the people vpon his knees. The euent whereof declared how pleaſing a thing it was to God. For *Coſmus Saraina* (the Phyſitian afore named) and many other perſons of good account, haue openly teſtifyed, that they oftentymes ſaw *Xauerius*, as he was in the Church at *Goa* communicating the people vpon his knees, rayſed vp miraculouſly, more then a cubit aboue the ground; ſo as one would haue thought, that God had then exalted his Humility.

Moreouer, he was extraordinarily deuout vnto the moſt *B. Trinity*. For he vſed to adore, and to name the ſame with the greateſt and religious reſpect that could be. He bare likewiſe a moſt ſingular affectiō to Chriſt the worker of mans Saluation: and was alſo ſpecially deuoted to the B. V. Mary, the Mother of God, & the moſt benigne Patroneſſe of mankind: wherupon he had gotten ſuch an habituall deuotion, by continuall practice therof, that when he lay vpon his death bed, he oftentimes implored the help of the moſt *B. Trinity*, of our Sauiour Ieſus Chriſt, and of the *B. V. Mary*, that ſo he might at his death call often vpon them, to whome in his life he had alwayes car-

Marginal notes:
After maſſe prayer for the dead.

He adminiſtreth the holy Euchariſt vpon his knees.

He by diuine power is eleuated from the ground.

His deuotion to the moſt B. Trinity and the B. Virgin.

Ttt 2   ried

ried such extraordinary deuotion.

His deuotion to S. Michaell the Archangel. Next vnto these, he was singularly deuoted to *S. Michael* the Archangell, Prince of the Court of Heauen, and Patrone of the Holy Church. Then he reuerenced the Congregation of all the Blessed & Faithfull, and of the Church the Spoule of Christ, whose assistance he often implored. Also in all his imployments, iourneys, miseries and dangers he very often implored the help and patronage of his Angell Guardian, and of the Archangells and Patrones of those places, where he made his abode, or whither he went.

CHAP. VI.

His purity of Hart, and Chastity.

THIS excellent Deuotion which *Francis* had in Prayer, was, by the like Purity of his soule, enflamed to behold God. The which is not only manifested by the purity, and innocency of his life, but approued also by the assured testimonys of such as côuersed familiarly with him; who haue solemnely auerred, that they neuer obserued any thing in him, which might be displeasing, or giue the least offence to any. This also is a further argument therof, for that he did oftentimes euery day examine his Conscience with very great rigour and diligence, & seriously exhorted others also to doe the like, a thing whereon he esteemed the perfection of lyfe chiefly to depend.

He examineth his conscience oftentymes euery day.

He vsed also to confesse euery day, when he could haue

haue a ghostly Father. And this purity of his soule was
much graced by the perpetuall sanctity of his body. It
is well knowne that he preserued the flower of Virgi-
ginall Chastity, euen till his dying day. This the Vicar of *Meliapora* testifyed publikly, that he found it to
be certayne by the often conference he had with him
in that place; & many others also who vsed to heare
his Confession, haue affirmed, that they gathered no
lesse from out of himselfe. He bare indeed a most singular affection vnto Chastity; & as great was the hatred which he bare to the contrary vice, in so much
that hauing a detestation to the least staynes which
might be in that kind, he could not without horrour
heare it once named, as we may easily coniecture by
that which now I am to recount.

Whilst he remained at *Lisbone* in Portugall, expecting to go into *India*, he lodged in the same chamber
with *Simon Rodriquez*. Being once vpon a suddayne
in the dead of the night, as he lay in his bed, awaked
out of his sleepe, he became so vnsually moued, that
there gushed out a great deale of bloud from his nose.
Wherof when *Simon* oftetimes asked him afterwards
the cause, he kept it close, and would by no meanes
speake of it, as long as he was in Portugall. Yet at last,
whe he was vpon his departure, & ready to take shipping for *India*, he tooke *Rodriquez* aside into a priuate
place of the ship, and said: Now *Simon*, quoth he, it is
time to declare vnto you that which you haue so often
in vayne demaunded of me: for this (as I suppose)
is the last tyme, that I shall euer see you in this lyfe.
You shall therefore know, that there was that night

an

an impure thought prefented to me in a dreame, the which, I endeauouring all I could to reiect, caufed me to fhed that bloud at my nofe.

And thefe fignes, and humane teftimonies were no leffe confirmed by the integrity of his Body, after his death, then by the fentence, and approbation of God himfelfe. Which fingular benefit of the diuine goodnes, among many other, we muft acknowledge as granted to his extraordinary Virginall Chaftity. **His vaines in matter of chafti-** And he, to preferue this fo fingular and heauenly a treafure, was not more chaft then wary. For albeit the holy Man being very much giuen to the contempla- tion of heauenly things, and fenced with the fhield of more then vfuall temperance, could eafily extinguifh the fiery darts of the moft malicious Enemy; yet he was as fearefull, & wary in this kind, as if he had bin much fubiect to fuch a Vice. He neuer therfore fpake with any woman, vpon what neceffary occafion foe- uer, but openly, where they might be both feene, & alfo with witneffes by; thinking there was not com- monly fo much profit, as danger, in womens con- uerfation.

CHAP.

CHAP. VII.

His Loue of the Croſſe, and Euangelicall Pouerty.

NO leſſe exact alſo, was *Xauerius* in the auſterity of his life, as a chiefe meanes for the conſeruing of Chaſtity. For he to tame his wanton youth (as we haue ſaid before) did oftentimes (yea and for a long time togeather) begird his naked fleſh with certaine litle cords, which cauſed him intolerable paine; & moreouer, throghout his whole life, he greatly afflicted his body, both by frequent faſts, and very ſore diſciplines. His food was euer very ſlender, & ſuch as might be eaſily made ready to eate, which he alſo either begged himſelfe, or elſe, was brought vnto him by way of Almes. But when he tooke his repaſt abroad with others, following the example of our Sauiour, he vſed to eate indifferently, of whatſoeuer was ſet before him; wherby he auoided all troubleſomnes to thoſe who entertayned him; and by hiding his ſingular abſtinence, recompenſed alſo the dainty fare to which he had bin inuited with the hardnes of his owne priuate diet afterward. And the meaſure in his meate and drinke, was meerely the neceſſity of nature, not any delight he tooke therin.

The ſlendernes of his food.

His cuſtome was to eate only once a day, and that ordinarily, of one only ſort of meate, which did

He eates but once a day.

not

not so much please his taft, as sufteine nature . Whatsoeuer meate he got when he was busily imployed ,
with that he contented himselfe. He very rarely tasted
either flesh or wine , vnlesse it were among strangers ,
and at other mens Tables. He neuer eate his fill, euen
of bread , although he had it lying by him. In his iorney to *Meaco* which was very long, tedious , and troublefome , he liued only vpon a little Rice parched on
the fire . And all the time of his abode in *Iaponia,* he so
accuftomed himself to the *Iaponians* vnfauoury meates
& to extraordinary fpare dyet, that when he returned
againe to *Goa ,* he had loft all taft of his Country vi-
ands , to which he had bin formerly vfed .

He abftey ned wholy from wine for many yea-
He abftei ned from wine. res , yea euen vntill his old , and fickly age ; and then
his ftrength being greatly decayed through continu-
all labours, he was conftrained to vfe a little wine, yet
well mingled with water . Wherefore when *Alphonsus Sofa* the Viceroy of *India* fent vnto him , whilft he
remayned in the Promontory of *Comorinum,* two veffells of excellent wine for a prefent, he without euer
tafting thereof, diftributed it all amongft the poore.

Moreouer, he was so farre from taking any delight
in the foftnes of his bed , that whatfoeuer place feemed fit to lye downe vpon , that ferued him alwayes
for his Couch: yea the bare ground very often (which
was vfuall with him in the Promontory of *Comorinum,* the *Moluca's ,* and *Iaponia*) was the place where he
tooke his repofe . When he was at fea , he lay eyther
vpon the hard plankes , or els vpon fome Cable-
rope rolled vp togeather . And if at any tyme he had
the

the commodity of a bed, yet would he seldome, or neuer make vse therof, but lend it freely vnto thofe who were fickly and weake. And in the coaft of *Comorinum* alfo, that he might the more freely lye vpon the bare ground, he gaue away vnto the ficke, a fayre Bed and Pillow, which the Viceroy of *India* had fent vnto him. In his trauailes by land, although oftentimes he might haue had a horfe to ride, yet he went moft comonly on foot; & this euen in *Iaponia*, where for euery ftep he went, he was exceedingly troubled with ftones, fnow, ice, & torrents of water in his way.

But nothing was more obferued in him, then his bridling of all difordinate appetites and affections, & wholy ouercoming of himfelfe, which is the hardeft and moft glorious kind of victory of all others. This appeareth euidently by that, which hapned at *Venice*, where whilft he ferued in the Hofpitall called *Of the Incurable*, as we haue before related, he continually ouercame himfelfe, in tending one fo full of vlcers, that it caufed a great horrour vnto him. He alfo oftentimes admonifhed thofe of the Society that they fhould accuftome to conquer and ouercome themfelues firft in fmall things, to the end they might afterwards obtayne the victory in greater combats. And himfelfe following this rule, which he prefcribed to others, had all his paffions and affections euermore fo bridled, and reftrained within his owne dominion & power, that he continually inioyed moft full tranquility and repofe of mind, and withall a moft fweet and amiable countenance. And if at any time he were forced to reprehend any one for his fault, he fo tempe-

He mortifyeth his affections & ouercometh himfelfe.

He ouercometh himfelfe in fmall matters.

He kept alwaies the fame countenance.

V u u   red

red feuerity with mildnes, that hauing once rebuked him, he prefently, as it were, vnmasked himfelfe, and returned againe to his former fweetnes & affability.

Moreouer, he efteemed more of this interiour moderation, then of exteriour mortification. For well knowing that al paffionate and vnruly motions of the mind ought euer to be fuppreffed, he accounted the affliction of the body to ayme principally at this, that the exteriour mortification might help the interiour. Wherfore he moft of all commended thofe kinds of mortificatio, wherby the interiour motions might be reftrained, and vertue and piety quickned, and encouraged. He fo dominiered alfo ouer the paffion of anger, as if he had neuer known how to be angry at al.

But his extraordinary Mildnes was euery where very remarkeable, & efpecially at *Malaca*, where he had that fore combat with the fenfeleffe infolency of the Gouernour of the *Citty*. For when the Gouernour (as we haue declared before) by his moft iniurious intercepting of the Embaffage into *China*, had both obftinately and impudently hindered his worthy endeauours, & the aduancemet of the Ghofpel; *Xauerius* notwithftanding carryed himfelfe fo mild therein, that being at laft forced to denounce his Holines Excommunication agaynft that temerarious and madbraine fellow, although himfelfe were Legate Apoftolicall, yet he oftentimes fent the Bifhops Vicar vnto him, in moft fuppliant manner; fo as one would haue thought, that he had rather done, then receiued the iniury; or that he intreated, rather to auoid the blow himfelfe, then to haue threatned it to another.

Moreouer

The mortification of affections.

The dominion he had ouer his anger.

Moreouer in the greateſt reproaches, ſufferances, & vexations that could be offered, he neuer complained of any man, but prayed to the diuine Maieſty for thoſe who cauſed him the ſame, and that he would vouchſafe, rather to receyue them to mercy, then to exercyſe his diuine iuſtice vpon them. Wherefore at the ſelfe ſame time when he was by the Gouernour of *Malaca's* officers, without cauſe, moſt iniurious1y & diſgracefully treated, he notwithſtanding ſaid Maſſe dayly for that outragious Man, praying to God, that though he had begun to fall, he might not yet be vtterly ouerthrowen. *He prayeth for his enemies.*

The loue of voluntary Pouerty alſo, which ſhined in him, was not inferiour to the moderation of his mind. For through long and ſerious meditation vpon the pouerty of Chriſt Ieſus, *who when he was rich, became poore for vs*, he bare ſo ſpeciall an affection vnto Euangelicall Pouerty, that he dayly found by experience, the Riches of Pouerty to be ſuch, that they not only diſcharged and freed the mind from all troubleſome care, but enriched it alſo moſt aboundantly with celeſtiall treaſures, and cauſed him who had nothing, not to be in want of any thing. Wherfore he alwayes for the moſt part, liued by begging, euen in the Colledge at *Goa* it ſelfe, where all things were at hand without ſeeking for : neither alſo, when he trauailed as well by land, as by ſea, had he any care at all of any Viaticum, or prouiſion of victuals. *His loue to Euangelicall pouerty.*

Of this his extraordinary Pouerty his whole life affoardeth vs notable examples. For to ſay nothing of ſuch as be of leſſe note, let vs call to memory his de-

parture

parture out of Portugal towards *India*, how he would carry nothing with him but a forry mantle, to vſe in the Promontory of *Good Hope* (a place much peſtred with the extreme vnſeaſonable colds of the Antartick Pole) and a few bookes for his neceſſary vſe, although the Kings Officers by expreſſe order from his Maieſty vrged him earneſtly to the contrary. And in the ſhip itſelfe he could not by any intreaty, either of principall perſons therein, or of the Viceroy himſelfe be drawne from begging his victuals, and other neceſſaries. For he chooſe rather for Chriſt his ſake, to aske of the Souldiars in the Nauy, not only victuals, but ſhooes alſo, ſhirts, and other things neceſſary, thē to haue them freely giuen him by the Viceroy, or his followers; ſuch ſweetnes found he in Euangelicall pouerty. His iorney alſo into *Comorinū*, was not much vnlike to that into *India*, contenting himſelfe with only a payre of bootes.

Moreouer, his apparell and habit was of the vulgar ſort. He went in an old caſſocke from *Rome* into Portugall, and ſo on forwards into *India*. In *India* it ſelfe he refuſed euen a decent, and ciuil habit which was offred him, & made choice of a caſſock of courſe linnen cloth, without a cloake, fearing leaſt, as oftentimes it hapneth, ſome pride of mind might follow vpon ſuch gayneſſe of apparel. His gowne being now worne out and torne, his friends offered him a new one : but he wraping himſelf vp in his pouerty, would neuer ſuffer his old one to be taken from him for a new. Wherupon ſome, in the dead time of the night when he was aſleep, ſent one to take away his old

He prefers his old gowne before a new one.

old ragged gowne, and to lay a new one in the place.
He riſing before day put on the new gowne he found,
inſteed of his old, and went abroad therein, neuer
dreaming how charitably his friends had deceaued
him. Now, this new gowne was of a farre different
faſhion from his old one. Wherupon being the ſame
day at ſupper with *Francis Paiua*, & others of his friéds
who were acquainted with the matter, they as it were
wondering, began to aske him in ieſt, what kind of
habit that was? And when he perceiued by looking
vpon it, and feeling it, that it was a new one, and that
be was therewith deceiued, he ſmiling ſayd; Indeed
this ſtrang habit is more fit for others, then for me.
Wherefore by his earneſt intreaty he preuayled at laſt
ſo much with them, that they reſtored to him his old
gowne, which they had taken away, and receaued
the new one backe againe. He therfore with his old
gowne indured the extreme hard weather of *Iaponia*,
although oftentimes he euen ſhiuered, and trembled
for cold. Afterwards alſo he returned out of *Iaponia*
to *Goa* triumphant, as it were, ouer braue and gay apparell, with glorious enſignes of Pouerty, to wit, with
an old hat, a ragged ſhirt, a torne gowne, & that alſo
patched in diuers places.

But if we deſire to know, how willingly he imbraced all the incommodities which pouerty brought
along with it, and how he was wont to reioyce in the
extreame want of all things, as in the midſt of heauély delights; we may eaſily gather it out of a certaine
letter which he ſent from *Maurica* to thoſe of the Society at *Rome*; where deſcribing that Country, after

he had fayd, that it wanted all commodities both of victuals, and other neceffaries for the maintenance of life, he affirmeth that he neuer receiued from God greater and truer content. In his letters alfo which he wrote out of *Iaponia* to the Society at *Goa* he fpeaketh thus : I befeech you, deereft Brethren, to helpe me to giue God thankes for fo great a benefit. We are now by Gods fingular goodnes arriued in *Iaponia*, where there is extreme want of all things ; which I indeed efteeme as one of the greateft fauours of the diuine Prouidence. For in other places, plenty of victuals & commodities doth moft commonly inuite the people to fatiate, and fill their vnbridled fenfual appetits. And fo their foules being not acquainted with Euangelical pouerty, are extremely oppreffed through the want of heauenly graces and delights. And many times alfo their bodyes being tormented with difeafes, and other incommodities, indure no fmall, nor fhort punifh-ment for their intemperance.

CHAP. VIII.

His Obedience, and Humility.

THIS abandoning of the vfe of other things was not more exact in him, then the for-faking of his owne Free-will, and proper Iudgment, wherin the chiefeft prayfe of Obedience confifteth. Which vertue being the prin-cipall ornament that the *Society* of IESVS hath, fhewed

it

it selfe most of all in *Francis*, euen at the first, when he was by *Ignatius* sent into *India*. It was well knowen, that the Nauigation into *India* was no lesse dangerous then long and tedious. And the Society at that time, whatsoeuer state it had, was not gouerned by any cōmand which *Ignatius* had ouer it, but only by his authority. Notwithstanding *Francis* forgetting all things besides Obedience, did more promptly obey then he was commanded; and without any delay prepared himselfe, euen against the next day, for that long, & almost endlesse iorney: so that God may seeme to haue opened the vtmost parts of the East to his incomparable alacrity, by this his prompt Obedience.

In *Portugall* also, and in *India*, it is incredible to say, how willingly and exactly he performed whatsoeuer *Ignatius* by letters commanded him; and gaue him therin such satisfactiō (since he was one who exacted to haue all things squared out by the rule of Obedience) that none excelled in that point more then he, shewing himself therby a schollar, worthy indeed of such a maister. For he had such an esteeme of *Ignatius* his Sanctity, that he reuerenced him as a most holy man, sent from God: in so much, that whensoeuer he did name *Ignatius* either in his discourse, or letters, he alwayes gaue him the title of *Blessed*, or *Holy*. And in a reliquary Case that he wore about his necke, he kept inclosed *Ignatius* his Name, written with his owne hand (cutting it from the subscription of a letter which he had sent him) togeather with other holy reliques, and the forme of his owne profession. And when he commanded any thing, to any of

How much he esteemed Ignatius.

the

the Society, he was wont to say: This I command you, for the Reuerence, and Obedience you owe vnto our Holy Father *Ignatius.*

Ignatius his opinion of Xauerius obediēce

No leſſe was the confidence which *Ignatius* had in *Francis* his modeſty, and obedience. Whereof this may ſeeme an euident argument, in that he was allwayes very free in commanding him diuers things, how hard ſoeuer they were, neuer doubting but that he would preſently execute whatſoeuer he ſhould cōmaūnd. And when *Ignatius* foreſaw *the depoſition of his Tabernacle was at hand*, and iudginge it expedient that *Francis*, as the chiefe vpholder of the Society, ſhould be called backe to *Rome*, he wrote vnto him in ſuch ſort, that whē he had ſet down the reaſons which moued him to that determination, by adding in a Poſtſcript thereof apart, one ſingle Charaċter only, to wit the letter, I, he ſeemed to ſignify thereby that he ſo confided in *Francis* his obedience, that he did not doubt, but he would returne backe to *Rome*, euen from the furtheſt part of the world, and where he was then planting, and ſetting forward the Ghoſpell of Chriſt, with the greateſt ſpeed that might be, although he had giuen him no one reaſon for this his returne, being inuited by one ſole letter, by which he was cōmaūded to *goe*. And certainly *Ignatius* would neither haue bin deceiued in his opinion he had of *Francis*, nor of his moſt prompt obediēce. For without doubt, that only letter, I, *Goe*, would haue ſpoken ſo forcibly in his hart, that he would without delay, haue euen ſeemed to fly from the furtheſt part of the Eaſt, had he not already bin flowne to heauē, there to

receyreceiue the reward of all his labours, before *Ignatius* letters could come vnto him.

And as *Francis*, throughout the whole courfe of his life was moft eminent in this zeale of Obedience; fo defired he alfo, all thofe of the Society to haue a fpeciall regard vnto the fame Vertue. Wherefore, he oftentymes inculcated vnto them, in his Admonitions both by words and letters, That without true, and generous Obedience, that is, prompt and cheerfull, no man could be the true and naturall difciple, and fonne of the Society: and whofoeuer wanted that vertue, could not continue long in that, Order with profit, or ioy of mind. Wherfore he alwayes gaue this precept to his fubiects, that by harty, and fincere Obedience, they fhould wholy conforme themfelues to the iudgment of the fuperiour of the Society, & of the Church; hauing their eyes fixed, not only vpon their Command, but euen vpon their leaft figne, or becke. For it was far more fecure to be gouerned, then to gouerne, & to obey then command. Wherfore inciting *Fa. Paul Camertes* Rector of the Colledge of *Goa* (charging him to be ruled by *Iames Borban* a *Francifcan*, who had care of the fame Colledge) to the practife of Obedience, he wrote vnto him, that if he were in his place, nothing would be more gratefull vnto him, then to obey him who had command ouer him. For one cannot take any more certaine and fecure courfe, to come directly and without erring to the iorneys end which he intends, then by following his guide who is skilfull in the way. And contrariwife, nothing is more dangerous, then to liue according to ones owne wil,

Commḗdation of obediēce

Interiour humility.

X x x   and

and to flight the precepts of Superiours.

Extradinarily alfo was *Xauerius* Reuerence, and Obedience vnto Bifhops , and their Vicars . For that honoring God in them , he defired to exercife his fun-ctions by their authority,& left himfelfe in al things, wholy to their difpofall & determination; & the fame he commanded others of the Society alfo to do , fay-ing oftentimes, that thofe of the Society ought to giue example of true Obedience towards all Ecclefiafti-call perfons and Prelates . And whofoeuer tooke not true content , in the Societyes kind of gouernment , which confifteth chiefly in Obedience, him he iudged to be of a quite differēt fpirit from the Society. Neither did he thinke it expediēt, to expect vntil that man had committed fome thing againft the honour of the So-ciety, whome he forfaw, by that his beginning, would one day furely do it ; but before any ignominy happe-ned , he would difmiffe him ; and thereby effect the fooner, what the other intended , and by his example make his companions more wary in the fame kind.

Xauerius Obedience to Bifhops and their Vicars.

The fame Obedience alfo he required of thofe of the Society vnto Ecclefiaftical Prelates, and that they fhould not preach vnto the people, nor exercyfe the functions of the Society, without licence firft granted by them, or their Vicars : nor that they fhould at any tyme exercife , or do any thing , whereby the fayd Prelats might be iuftly offended , or be auerted from them, though neuer fo iuft caufe or occafion were gi-uen them . And if at any time it fell out otherwife,he alwayes tooke it very ill.Wherfore whē two certayne Vicars did by their letters complaine vnto *Francis* , of

Obedience to-wards Ecclefia-fticall Prelats.

two

two Fathers who aboad within their diſtriᵭs, he preſently wrote vnto them, that they ſhould forthwith go to the *Vicars*, & humbly kiſſing their hands, ſhould aske them pardon, and from thence-forward, in token of the great reſpeᵭ they ought vnto them, they ſhould go euery weeke once to ſalute them. This, & ſuch like Humility & ſubmiſſion, he ſayd, was neceſſary, both to beate downe the Deuill, the ring-leader of Pride, and to gaine the Prelates of the Church, by ſpeciall obſeruance, to be fauourable and courteous vnto them, that ſo they might be the better able to aduance the Chriſtian cauſe.

But aboue all other things there ſhined in *Xauerius* a moſt profounded humility, the mother of Obediéce, and the gayner of good will both with God and man, wherof we find in his life many admirable teſtimonies. For in his iorney into *Portugall*, as before we haue ſayd, he looked very diligently to the companies horſes, and perpetually both at home and abroad in the Hoſpitalls of the ſicke, with the greateſt affeᵭion that could be, he tooke vpon him all the baſeſt offices therof. And when he came to *Goa*, although he were Legate Apoſtolicall, yet he fell downe at the Biſhops feet, and deliuered vp to him the Kings Letters, and the Popes Breue, which he would not vſe otherwiſe, then might ſeeme fitting vnto him. Which modeſty of his ſo gayned the Biſhops good will, that he did not more reuerence *Xauerius* authority, then admire his Humility. But *Francis* had the Prelates of the Church in ſuch ſpeciall veneration and reuerence, that he exhibited vnto them, euen diuine honour almoſt, as

*Humili-
ty.*

*Xauerius
Reueré-
ce to the
Prelates.
of the
Church.*

X x x 2   repre-

reprefenting the perfon of God himfelfe ; vfing with very great reuerence, both to kiffe their hands, and fometymes alfo, to caft himfelfe proftrate at their feete.

Moreouer (fuch was his fingular Humility) he not only bare thefe great refpects and fubmiffions to Prelates and their Vicars, but alfo to priuate Priefts and Clergy men, carrying himfelfe rather as a feruant to them all, then as Legate Apoftolicall. Yet his exteriour Humility (which is a token of the interiour) was not the only marke his affections chiefly leuelled at, but rather the interiour it felfe, which confifteth in the knowledge, and contempt of ones felfe. For when in refpect of his fingular fanctity, he was held for no leffe then an Apoftolicall Man, yet he efteemed himfelf to be the moft wicked of all mortall men, as may be gathered out of many of his letters.

Wherefore being a true Contemner of himfelfe, he no leffe detefted prayfe and honour (the allurements to pride & arrogancy) then others do hate difgrace and difhonour. For he fo neglected both honour it felf, & thofe that gaue it to him, that all might playnely fee, he bare moft cordiall affection to that ancient Simplicity, which in former tymes was neuer acquainted with flattery or ambition. Wherefore he alwayes vfed great diligence to keep fuch thinges fecret which he had done worthy of prayfe or commendation ; and if at any tyme he were for the good of others conftrayned to make them knowne, he did it in fuch fort, as you would haue thought they had

His hatred of honour.

Concealing of heauenly guifts.

belon.

belonged to some other & not to himself. And so writing to those of the Society out of the Promontory of
Comorinū of things which he himself had there done,
he attributeth the health which many sicke persons
had recouered, by his meanes, vnto certayne Neo-
phyte-children, whose help he had vsed therein, although it were neuer so litle.

Writing also of the heauenly Ioyes, which God,
in the same Promontory, had bestowed vpon them
who labour for his sake, he recounted what had hap-
ued to himselfe, as appertayning to a third person,
without any equiuocation at all. Nor was there any
thing in him which more declared his singular modesty, then a certaine remarkeable blush, which straight
arose in his face when he heard himselfe praysed, as a
manifest demonstration of his interiour Humility;
which we may see sufficiently declared by this one e-
xample. At his returne out of the coast of *Comorinum*
to *Goa*, when *Iames Borban* asked him, whether that
were true which was reported of him, to wit, that he
had restored a dead man to lyfe ; he was so wholy
confounded, and out of countenance through shame-
fastnesse, that *Borban* taking great compassion of him
could not find in his hart to vrge him any further in
that point.

A remar-
kable
blush in
Xauerius
at his
owne
prayses.

Moreouer, he was so farre from affecting titles of
Dignity, that for the space of ten yeares (for so long
he liued in those Countryes) there was none, but the
Bishop of *Goa* only, who knew that he was Legate A-
postolicall, so carefully he concealed the matter. Neither did he euer discouer his authority vnto others,

His fly-
ing titles
of ho-
nour.

vntill

vntill he was driuen therunto by necessity, to curbe the insolent audaciousnesse of the Gouernour of *Malaca*; wherin notwithstáding he so moderated his authority, that it seemed to be rather Humility, then power. And (for as much, *as out of the aboundance of the hart the mouth speaketh*) in all the Exhortations almost which he made to those of the Society, he insisted most cōmonly vpon the perfect rooting out of Pride and selfe esteeme from their minds. And he was wont to say, that looke how much any one was in the iudgement, and estimation of God; so much, & no more, ought euery one to deeme of himselfe, although the whole world should otherwise esteeme of him. Wherfore he admonished them neuer to extoll themselues for the good opinion which other men had of them; and that ballancing themselues in their owne knowledge they should humble themselues, and consider that they were far otherwise in their owne conscience, and in the iudgement of God, from that which they seemed vnto men. For they who want the knowledge of themselues, are soone puffed vp by the prayses of men, thinking themselues to be such indeed as men esteeme them; as though they were able to deceaue both God and men.

His exhortations to true humility.

This also he was wont oftentymes to say with inward griefe of hart: O arrogácy, the poyson of Christian vertue! How much hast thou, doest thou, and wilt thou hurt the world! How contrary art thou, to the institute and perfection of the Society of IESVS! What a deadly enemy art thou to the pious, & wholesome endeauours of those that be of that profession!

For

For he affirmed, that none could be a true Child of the the Society of I E s v s , or imploy himfelfe faythfully for God , who did not contemne himfelfe, and thinke lowly and humbly both of himfelfe , and of all his a-ctions. Wherefore, as he could by no meanes away with fuch as too much efteemed themfelues, who ey-ther vnder the colour of Humility , or for the Nobili-ty of their Anceftours , defired to be honoured : fo he bare an extraordinary affection to fuch as were truly humble, & contemned both themfelues, and whatfo-euer els was theirs , although they were perfons of ne-uer fo meane condition .

CHAP. IX.

His Magnanimity of Mind, and Confidence in God.

THIS Humility of *Francis* did not , for all that , caufe in him fo abiect a mynd , that he durft not ayme at high matters , or af-pire to any noble enterprize ; but putting his whole confidence in God , and accounting no-thing to be eyther hard , or difficile to the magnani-mity of his mynd , he attempted euen the greateft things. For whenfoeuer the Honour of God required it , he gaue way to no difficulty , nor daunger : fo as, he ordinarily attempted nothing , which he did not effect, or bring to fome good paffe. This indeed is pro-per to the feruants of God, to be humble and abiect in

their

their owne fight, but moſt couragious and conſtant in the affayres of God.

This magnanimity of mynd, and ſlighting of all difficultyes & dangers, appeared manifeſtly through-out the whole courſe of *Xauerius* lyfe. And indeed it oftentymes ſo farre ſurpaſſed the vſuall ſtraine of or-dinary Fortitude, that it might haue bin accounted te-merity; if it had not depended rather vpon diuine, thē humane aſſiſtāce. For in his iorney to *Trauancoris*, when he paſſed through the midſt of his enemies, he ſeemed to thruſt himſelfe into manifeſt danger. But far more euident was that perill, when he attempted to in-ſtruct the inhabitants of *Maurica*, a Nation extraor-dinary fierce and cruell, hauing no other defence a-gaynſt thoſe barbarous and ſauage people, but his confidence in God. He alſo aduentured to paſſe in a Pyrates ſhip into *Iaponia* the furtheſt part of the Eaſt, without any feare of danger, although his deereſt fri-ends, and ſuch as were moſt expert therein, preſented before his eyes how many & extreme difficulties there were. Concerning which thing he wrote himſelf vn-to the Prouinciall of Portugall in theſe words.

All my well-willers and friends are amazed, that
» I am not afrayd to vndertake ſo long, and dangerous
» a iorney. They lay before me many dangers of tēpeſts,
» quickſands, and Pyrates. But I am no leſſe amazed
» at them, that they haue ſo little confidence in God,
» in whoſe hands and power, all thoſe things are pla-
» ced. I for my part, knowing for certaine that al things
» are gouerned according to God Almighties beck and
» commandment, do feare nothing elſe, but God himſelfe

selfe, leaft he fhould punifh me according to the de- «
ferts of my negligence, and floth in his feruice, and «
of the obferuance of my Religion. But as for other «
terrours, dangers, miferies, and croffes, I do not at «
all weigh them. For I feare only God, the maker and «
moderatour of all things, becaufe other things how «
hurtfull foeuer they be, cannot annoy vs, but on- «
ly fo farre forth as God permits them.

It is wonderfull alfo, what Confidence he repo-
fed in the diuine affiftance. So as hauing only God for
his guide, through fo many dangers both by fea and
land, through fo many Nations different in language
and manners, he penetrated to the furtheft parts
of the Eaft, and by his often paffing ouer the Ocean
he inftructed thofe fauadge, and barbarous Nations
in the myfteries of the Chriftian faith, and brought
them at laft to a ciuill life. And indeed his Confidence
in God did neuer fayle, but alwayes freed him from
the dangers, both of enemies, tempefts, and other *He is af-*
calamities. For to pretermit with filence other things *faulted*
wherof we haue already fpoken in their proper pla- *by the*
ces, in paffing ouer the *Iaponian* feas, when as the Bar- *Barbari-*
barians bent all their fury agaynft him, he by diuine *ans.*
Affiftance, efcaped all their machinations, without *He fuffe-*
any hurt or danger at all. He alfo in the fea of *Mo-* *reth fhip-*
luca fuffered fhipwrack thrice; and once alfo he mi- *wracke*
raculoufly efcaped by lying vpon a plancke after fhip- *thrice.*
wracke toffed vp & downe the fea, without any hurt *He is de-*
at all, for the fpace of two or three dayes. More- *liuered*
ouer he auoyded the fury of the *Saracens* who were *from ma-*
fet in armes againft him, by lying fecret for many *ny dan-*
gers.

Y y y   daies

dayes togeather in a wood hard by. Alſo he did not only defeate the ſtrategems which his enemies had plotted againſt him by the force of armes, but diſcouered
their ſecret inuentiõs alſo, when as they ſought to poiſon him. And beſides all this, he very often eſcaped
the incurſions of Pyrates by ſea, as likewiſe of theeues
by land.

His loue   Agayne, being wholy inflamed with the loue of
of the   God, he did not only contemne difficultyes and dan-
Croſſe.   gers, but ſeemed alſo to imbrace them willingly.
Wherfore as deſirous to ſuffer in the very midſt of incommodities & dangers, he earneſtly beſought God,
not to free him from them, vnleſſe it were to vndergo
greater, for the glory of his diuine Maieſty. And the
diuine Goodnes, correſponding ſweetly to the magnanimity of his mind, heaped vpon him ſtore of ſuf-
ferings, and merits, with no leſſe approbation in the
ſight of Heauen, then ioy & comfort to himſelfe. He
likewiſe in that moſt hard and difficile expedition into *China* ſhewed no leſſe courage. For notwithſtanding (as we haue ſayd before) that no ſtranger could
enter the bounds of that Countrey, without certayne
danger of his lyfe or liberty (the ſame penalty being
deſigned as well for the ſtranger that entreth in, as for
him that bringeth him;) yet hauing an admirable cõ-
fidence in God, who had moued him to that reſolution, and to the vndertaking of that iourney, he determined to commit his lyfe to the truſt of a *Chineſe*
merchant, which was no leſſe doubtfull and dangerous, then the entrance it ſelfe into *China*. Concerning which, he wrote himſelf to *Francis Peren* at *Ma-*
                                                    laca

laca to this tenour.

In this bufines, my friends bring two dagers againſt
me, the one leaſt the merchant hauing already receyued his money, may breake his promiſe, and eyther
leaue me in ſome deſert Iland, or elſe caſt me headlong
into the ſea, that ſo his bargayne of paſſing me ouer
may not come to light. The other is (ſuppoſing he
ſtand to his promiſſe)leaſt the Gouernour of the Citty may make me (being a ſtranger) an example to o-
thers of comming into *China* agaynſt the Kings Edict
without publicke warrant, & eyther put me to death
by torments, or elſe caſt me into perpetuall priſon.
Againſt theſe dangers, I obiect others farre greater,
which themſelues do not perceyue. And the firſt is,
leaſt we diſtruſt the diuine Goodnes and Prouidence: For we come hither for Gods only Cauſe, to preach to theſe Countryes his ſacred Law, and his ſonne
Chriſt Ieſus the Redeemer of mankind, whereof God
himſelfe, who gaue me this mind, is my witneſſe.
So as now to caſt off our hope, and confidence in
his Diuine Prouidence and power, for the dangers
we are ſaid to be ſubiect vnto in labouring for his cauſe, ought certaynly to be eſteemed a far greater danger, then whatſoeuer the enemyes of God, and Men,
are euer able to bring vpon me. Eſpecially ſeeing,
that neither the Diuels themſelues, nor their miniſters
can hurt vs at all, but only by the permiſſion and will
of God.

What can we ſay to this? That if God do approue and further our endeauours, we ſhall by his fauour
not only be deliuered from dangers, but alſo follow

the

the admonition of our Sauiour Chriſt, who ſayeth: *He that ſhall looeſe his lyfe in this world for me, ſhall find it.* Wherefore for as much as we hould theſe dangers of the ſoule farre greater thē thoſe of the body, we eſtee-
» me it far better, and more ſecure, to breake through
» thoſe of this lyfe, rather then to hazard the ſaluation
x of our ſoule. I am fully reſolued, God willing, to
» go into *China*, in deſpite of all his enemies. For, *if*
» *God be with vs, who ſhalbe againſt vs?* We do, without all
» doubt, go vpon great danger, although there were
» nothing elſe but perpetuall ſeruitude: But this conſi-
» deration comforteth me, that it is much better, to
» ſerue in captiuity for Gods cauſe, then to enioy liberty
» by running away frō the Croſſe &c. In which words
he doth indeed ſufficiently ſhew an vndaunted courage againſt all dangers. And how much *Xauerius*
contemnēd all the miſeries of this world, appeared
alſo by another letter of his to *Iames Perera*, whereof
we haue inſerted a clauſe in its proper place.

This greatnes of *Xauerius* mynd was not leſſe a-
gainſt the inſolency of Chriſtians, then againſt the
threates and terrours of the Barbarians. The Gouernour of the coaſt of *Comorinum* being a Portugheſe, &
potent, through his couetouſneſſe, had held the Neophytes in cruell ſubiection. Which when *Francis* vnderſtood, he threatned, that vnleſſe he carryed himſelfe moſt mildly towards the Chriſtians there, he
would by letters complaine vnto the King of Portugall of his inſolencies and Tyranny. Likewiſe he cauſed his companion to declare to a certayne Portugheſe
Captaine, who treated the new Chriſtians iniuriou-

ſly,

fly, that vnleſſe he ceaſed frō his cruelty, he would be far more ſauage then *Herod*, becauſe *Herod* ſlew only the bodies of the Innocents, but he alſo ſlew their ſoules: and this would certainly be the effect therof, that if through his inſolécies the Fathers ſhould leaue that Coaſt, the little infants would dye without Baptiſme.

The Gouernour alſo of *Malaca*, who, as we ſayd before, moſt iniuriouſly, and obſtinately hindred his iorney into *China*, was by *Xauerius*; who turned at laſt his patience into ſeuerity, excommunicated, and the ſentence publiſhed formally in the Churches; to the end others, through feare to incurre the like ignominy, might carry themſelues, as their duty required.

But nothing more declared the incredible greatnes of his mind, then a certaine infinite deſire (as we may call it) which he had to preach the Ghoſpell throughout the whole world. For not contenting himſelfe with the vaſt Countryes of *India*, he extended his deſires, and endeauours to *Malaca*, the *Ilands* of the *Moluca's*, *Maurica*, *Iaponia*, *China*, and in fine to all the Eaſt; intending certainly, to haue extended them afterwards to all the parts of the world, if his life had bin anſwereable to his feruour of ſpirit. For he with ſuch ſpeed trauailed ouer the vtmoſt parts of the Eaſt, that the huge vaſtneſſe of *Aſia*, ſeemed too ſmall a circuite for his couragious mind.

Yyy3 CHAP.

CHAP. X.

His Charity, to God, and his Neighbours.

THIS fo great Fortitude of mind in *Xauerius* was matched with the like Charity both to God & men. For throughout the whole courfe of his life, there is to be found no one vertue more eminent, then his defire of increafing the Honour of God, and fauing of foules. And no wonder; for he was fo greatly inflamed with fuch fpeciall loue of hauing cleane abandoned the world, that he became now wholy wrapt in the perpetuall contemplation of celeftiall things. Hence it was, that his foule being rayfed to God, the fupreme goodnes, and to the loue of his moft bountifull Creatour and Redeemer, held continually moft fweet difcourfes with his diuine Maiefty; nay euen then, when he was moft ferioufly imployed in conuerfing amongft men. Hence proceeded that inflamed loue to Iefus Chrift his benigne Lord & Sauiour, repeating fo ofté in moft fweet manner, that moft comfortable & wholfome Name. Hence alfo arofe in him that burning defire of Martyrdome, which finding no entertainmét among the Turkes, went on to the furtheft parts of the Earth thirfting after the glory thereof, by a thoufand meanes, amongft thofe fauage and barbarous people, & amidft euident danger of peftilent difeafes, fhipwrackes, and Pyrats; fo that Martyrdome it felfe fled rather

ther

ther from him, then he from Martyrdome.

This boundleſſe charity of *Francis* towards God,
had enkindled in his ſoule the like loue to men, which
neuer ſuffred him eyther to reſt, or to be weary. This
it was, which made him euery where as it were a ſlaue
to the ſicke, impriſoned, and wretched perſons, and
to feare no contagious or infectious diſeaſe, euen whē
the bodyes lay dead round about him. This it was
which pricked him forward to inſtruct barbarous &
ſauage Nations, euen with euident hazard of his owne
life, & kept him amongſt them as long as was needfull, although he were extremely oppreſſed with wāt
of all things. In fine it was this, which cauſing him to
ſleight the raging billowes of the ſtormy Ocean, the
incurſions of Pyrates, and inconueniences of an endleſſe Nauigation, drew him to the furtheſt part of the
world, to make the *Iaponians* alſo members of the
Church, who had no knowledge at all of the Goſpell:
ſo as hauing paſſed ſo many ſeas, & inſtructed almoſt
all the ſea coaſting Countrys of the Eaſt in the fayth
of Chriſt, he was now come euen to the furtheſt end
of the world. The ſame charity to ſaue mens ſoules, ſet
him on ſtill with no leſſe manifeſt danger of his owne
life, to attẽpt to get entrance into *China*, which was ſo
mured vp, both with rigorous lawes, & ſtrict watch;
ſo as the inſatiable zeale which he had of ſoules, ſuffered nothing to ſeeme impoſſible, nothing terrible
vnto *Xauerius.*

But now, after he had brought ſo many Nations
and people to the fayth of Chriſt, it grieued him extremely to be with-held from entring into *China*, and
hauing

hauing determined with himfelfe the conuerfion of the whole world, be forced now to make as it were a ftand at the begining almoft of his endeauours. And no doubt, if he had liued vntill he had difpatched his expedition into *China*, and had come backe agayne to *Rome*, whither he was fent for by *Ignatius*, he would haue byn a moft potent meanes, to haue reduced alfo thofe forlorne partes of the Wefterne Church. For in what office foeuer he fhould haue byn placed, either of the Generall, or of the Generalls Affiftant, he would neuer haue giuen ouer fending Religious men, of the Society, to cure the wefterne Nations, infeaed with Herefy, vntill either there had byn none left who needed fuch cure, or elfe his owne lyfe had left him.

He ferueth his neyghbours forgetting his owne meate and drinke.

It is incredible to fay, how exceeding zealous he was for the faluation of foules. For at *Malaca*, and elfe where in the Eaft, he imployed himfelfe continually in hearing Confeffions, in making reconciliation betweene thofe that were at variance & debate among thefelues, & in helping the ficke, wherein he fo forgot himfelfe, that oftentymes he paffed two or three daies without eating or drinking any thing; in fo much that one would haue thought he had byn fed which fuch exercyfes, & feruices done to God. And no meruayle, for the zeale & defire he had to help his neyghbours, & to propagate the Chriftian Religion, was fo engrafted in him, that it feemed almoft naturall. To this all his forces were bent; in this he was wholy imploied; this was his only defire; in this he tooke his greateft ioy, to vnite as many as poffibly he could, to the flock of Chrift. Neither was his care greater in gathering new

fheep

sheepe vnto that sacred fold, then in attending those diligently, whome he had already brought thither. For he gaue them such godly precepts & instructions that they scarce needed any other Pastor to help them.

Eudonicus Fraes of the Society of IESVS, a man both of great prudence and piety, gaue vp this relation: That when himselfe first of al trauailed ouer the Iland of *Iapon*, he came by chance to a castle there scituate in a corner of the Iland, where he met with three of the habitants of that country, who asked him what was become of *Francis Xauerius*? At which suddaine question, he at the first stood a little astonished, then pawsing a while vpon the matter, he found that *Xauerius* had sometimes bin there amongst them, and had conuerted many of the inhabitants to the faith of Christ; had also built them a Church, and so diligently instructed the Neophytes, that Christian discipline continued stil amongst them, without any other Maister. For *Xauerius* being to depart from *Iaponia*, had prouided for them for time to come, & giuen them written in their owne language the life of Christ, and a briefe Summe of the Ecclesiasticall history, as also the Roman Kalendar, with a table of the moueable feasts, a forme also for the inuocation of the Saints, which we call the Litanies, the Seauen Psalmes, togeather with the forme and manner of Baptisme, aduising thē to assemble themselues all togeather vpon holy Dayes and there to read something of the life of Christ, and out of the holy Scripture; to obserue the Festiuall dayes, to inuocate the intercession of the Saints, and to recite the seauen Psalmes. Moreouer he ordayned

Zzz   that

that the clarke of their chiefe Guide fhould baptize the little infantes, vnleffe fome neceffity otherwife diffuaded. And the Neophytes hauing kept thefe precepts which *Francis* had giuen them in memory, were fo throughly inftructed in matters of Chriftian Religion that they came not farre fhort of thofe of Europe, Wherupon *Froes* concluded, that he had no more to fay, but that by *Xauerius* example, Religion ought fo to be fowen, and planted euery where, that it might be able to vphold it felfe by its owne proper forces.

And although *Xauerius*, as much as in him lay, ceafed not at any tyme, to aduance his Neophytes by thofe of the Society: yet his Charity was not fo imployed in helping of whole Cittyes & Nations, as that he neglected particular perfons, how peruerfe and obftinate foeuer they were. At his departure frō the Iland of *Ternate*, of an exceeding great number of Chriftians that inhabited therin, he left only two, whome he could not draw to forfake their cōcubins. Wherfore when he came backe to *Amboynum* (compaffion fucceeding in place of indignation) he wrote *His zeale* vnto a certaine *Ternatian*, a friend of his, intreating *of foules* him to falute thofe two perfons in his name, in the moft friendly manner he could deuife, and fignify vnto them, that if they would at laft refolue to arife out of the fincke of finne, he would prefently make all haft thither, & in the meane time he would not ceafe to pray to God our cōmon Father for their faluation.

At *Malaca* alfo, as he preached vnto the people, *He con-* there was oftentimes prefent at his fermons a certaine *uerteth* Iew, a man of fufficient learning, but (as the proper- *a Iew.*

ty

ty of that nation is) moſt obſtinate; and who ſcoffed no leſſe at *Xauerius*, then at the truth it ſelfe. He being intangled both in vices and errours, ſtifly oppoſed the Ghoſpell , and his authority kept back many other Iewes from the faith of Chriſt. *Francis* therfore treating this man ſweetly by all kind of obſequiouſneſſe , and vſing to ſuppe with him in a friendly manner , ſo wrought with him at laſt, that being quite altered frō what he was , became of an obſtinate Iew, a vertuous and deuout Chriſtian . And this Charity of his to his Neyghbours , was not more forcible thē induſtrious .

There ſtandeth betweene *Goa* and *Cocinum* a for- treſſe belonging to the Portugheſes called *Canonora*, much frequented by reaſon of a good hauen in that place . *Xauerius* comming thither endeauoured by the way to draw a certaine perſon to make his Confeſſiō , but in vayne; wherupon he deſiſted for a while frō his intreaty, that when the other thought himſelf ſecure, he might at vnawares more forcibly ſet vpon him. For being preſſed hard therto, as one moſt obſtinatly bent he had paſſionatly ſworne neuer to yield therein to *Francis*. Therfore as ſoone as they came to land *Xaue-rius* reſolued to try all the remedies he could deuiſe a-gainſt ſo deſperate a diſeaſe , & ſo faygning as though his mind were ſet on other matters, got this obſtinate man into a wood , in a courteous manner vnder pre-tence of recreation, beſet (according to the Nature of that Country) with many Palme-trees . As ſoone as they came into a priuy place where none could ſee them, *Xauerius* ſuddainely caſting of his clothes, and baring his backe , falleth downe vpon his knees ,

His wō-derfull induſtri-ouſneſſe in mo-uing ſuch as were obſti-nate in ſinne .

& prefently (the other standing amazed, & expecting to fee the iffue of fo fuddaine an alteration) pulleth out a very sharpe difcipline full of iron pricks , and beating his owne backe extremely, before the others face, cryeth out, that he willingly fuffred that torment for his fake thereby to turne away Gods indignatiō from him . In the meane time the Wood runge againe with the mighty stripes of the difcipline, and he that stood looking on , in that amazement, like one out of himfelfe, was all befprinkled with *Xauerius* his bloud. Wherfore turning his admiration , into compaffion of hart, he instantly cafteth himfelfe at *Xauerius* feete , and befeecheth him , to leaue off reuenging anothers fault vpon his owne backe , for now he was ready to purge himfelfe of his finnes by Confeffion . *Xauerius* being glad he had thus wonne the victory , prefently apparelleth himfelfe , & hearing his Confeffion, bringeth that wretched man , backe againe into the right way , and hope of faluation.

But now his Prudence & induftry was farre more feene in curing the difeafes of the Citty of *Malaca*, which was almoft brought therby vnto a defperate ftate. For when he perceiued the *Malacenfians* minds to be fo inueterate, and drowned in the corruption of all wickedneffe , that they would by no meanes heare of remedy, he, being an exquifite Phyfitian of foules , found out a new & foueraigne antidote wherby to cure them . Wherfore fetting vpon them in a fecret and couert manner, he vfed to infinuate himfelfe into the company of the fouldiars when they were at their wanton fportes , comming oftentimes vpon
them

them as they were at play, seeming as though he tooke
delight in their game and conuersation; and if any
one vpon his presence, or otherwise through shame-
fastnesse, absteyned from playing, he in a sweet,
and friendly manner would exhort him to be merry
for he also loued the like pastime; and that souldiars
ought not to liue like Monkes : and if it were vsed
without offence to God, it was better to play, and be
merry, then to speake ill of other men, or to commit
any other wickednesse . Then hauing wonne their
affections by this his gentle behauiour, he would by
all manner of obsequiousnesse insinuate himselfe into
the greatest familiarity with them that was possible,
that so he might find out their secret inclinations, &
thereby take some occasion to apply fit remedies to
their diseases .

He be-
comes all
to gayne
all to
Christ.

Now, for others who were intangled with dishonest loue, and kept Concubines, he would oftentymes himselfe appoint certayne daies to dine or suppe
with them, where sitting at table, and by bringing in
some familiar discourse, as commending of the dishes
of meate which were serued in, and inquiring of the
mayd-seruant, that had so well seasoned the same,
requesting his Host oftentymes to send for her, & then
to comend her for her diligence & skill in Cookery, &
the like; he opened to himself away for his future designes. If he found one that would not willingly admit
him to his table, he at vnawars would earnestly intreate him, that he might see his house, & being brought
in, did often wyn the mans affection by his sweet,
conuersation, & then concealing his determination he

left

left no corner of the houfe which he did nor fearch into, as if he had hunted after fome wild game : where if
by chance he light vpō his hofts Concubine, he inquired what that woman was, & to whome fhe belonged;
making as though he liked all well that he faw, yet ftill
watching for an occafion wherin to effect his bufines.
Finally , he became in fuch fort euen all to all , that
among fouldiars he feemed a fouldiar, & among merchants a merchant. Wherefore not only the Portughefes, but alfo their Concubines themfelues by reafon of
his fingular affability , defired greatly to haue him
come to their houfes and table, neuer fo much as once
dreaming of what he aymed at.

But *Xuerius* as foone as he had gotten himfelfe inward with them , he would begin couertly to apply
his cure to their feftred foules. If he met with any that
had a beautifull and handfome mayd with whome
he was in loue , he would commend her vnto him, &
tell him that indeed for her extraordinary beauty , &
good difpofition fhe deferued to be an honeft woman,
and was worthy to be marryed to fome man of good
account. Then would he aske his Hoft, that if he loued
her, why did he, to both their difhonours , and vtter
ouerthrow , rather keepe her as his Concubine , then
honeftly and religioufly to take her to his wife ? Thus
turning the caufe of the difeafe to the cure therof , he
tooke away finne , & brought honourable wedlocke
into place therof . But if the woman were deformed,
he would demand whether he were wel in his wits or
no, who could fet his affections vpon fo ill fauoured a
Creature, & for whome all the Portughefes talked of
him,

him , and laughed him to ſcorne? Or why did he not rather ſeeke a wiſe fit for him ? For that would certainly be a great honour to him , as it had bin to others, whome he would then name.

But now, with others that could not ſo freely marry, by reaſon that they were intágled with many Concubines at once, he tooke another courſe. Firſt he would aske them, why they kept in their houſe ſo many maydes, who ſerued almoſt for no other vſe but to ouerthrow their ſoule, and conſume their ſubſtance, beſides the often diſquiet of the houſe by their chiding and brawling. And if they either could not , or would not put them all away, he aduiſed them ſeriouſly to rid themſelues of ſome one of them . Then comming againe vnto them after ſome dayes ſpace, he in a friendly manner would importune them, to diſmiſſe the ſecond, & ſo one after another al but one, for they ſhould be both leſſe hatefull to God, & the ſooner obtaine pardon , if they kept but one woman, then if they kept many . At laſt, vpon ſome new occaſion, he would vrge them againe either to put that one away , or elſe to marry her, whome they ſtill kept vnlawfully, that ſo at length they might appeaſe the diuine wrath incenſed againſt them . And thus by little and little he reclaimed thoſe loſt ſoules (by taking away from them all enticements to ſinne) to a ciuill and vertuous life.

Xauerius had perpetually this property & cuſtome to ſeeke moſt of al to be familiar with thoſe who were moſt wicked , thinking that where the ſicknes was moſt grieuous, there was greateſt need of a Phyſitian, and

and antidote: neither would he euer giue them ouer
vntill he had restored them to their soules health. This
also was another chiefe care of his, that all men by his
owne and the Societyes examples, might be inflamed
to vertue and deuotion, and none offended by them.
Neither did he vse to inculcate any thing more often

Rom. 1. and seriously to those of the Society who were sent in
mission to any place, then, *That they should prouide for
good things before God, and men.* And besides this he
oftentymes also put them in mynd by letters, of those
precepts which he had giuen them at their departure.

But if any one had at any time giuen offence, he
How gre was so afflicted in mind therfore, that he might well
atly he a- haue said with the Apostle, *Who is scandalized, and I not*
uoyded *burned?* Wherfore he gaue strict charge by letters, to
to scan- *Fa. Gaspar* the Rectour of the Colledge at *Goa*, that
dalize o- whosoeuer of the Society should giue publick scandal
thers. he should by all meanes dismisse him; and being once
2. Cor. 11 dismissed neuer to receiue him againe vpon any ter-
mes; iudging it a heauier lesse for the Society to be depriued of its good Name, then of any member therof;
imitating heerin that sentence of the Apostle, appro-
1. Cor.5.6 ued by dayly experience: *A little leauen corrupteth the
whole past.* And where the offence was giuen, there he
iudged it conuenient, that satisfactiō should be made,
therby to take away all scandall from such, as had receiued it.

The care   Neyther did he thinke it fit that satitfaction should
he had be giuen only to those who were offended, but to those
to edify also who were otherwayes offensiue vnto them. At
his neigh *Corinum* therefore, when as he vnderstod, that a cer-
bours. tayne

tayne Sodality, who had granted a Church to the Society, was displeased with the sayd Fathers, *Xauerius* casting himself prostrate on the groūd, before a great assembly of worthy personages, layd the keys of the Church at their feete, and by that Humility wholy pacifyed their offended minds. For he was alwaies wont to say, that he preferred the good name of the Society before all the riches and wealth of the world ; seeing God did commonly bestow better, and more durable riches vpon pious men, who made not so much account of their owne commodities ; as of the common estimation of their Religion ; then vpon those, who enioyed their owne rights and commodities, with the losse and dommage of their good Name. Wherefore in his letters which he wrote to those of the Society, he was alwaies wont to adde, that he had rather haue a litle fruite without offence, then a great deale with the offence of any. For that a little seed of soules sowen without offence, would like corne increase, and continue without weeds ; whereas neuer so great a Crop, once ouer-growne with displeasures, as with weeds, consumeth and wasteth away to nothing. And all this he obserued in himselfe with far more care & diligence, then he commāded it to others, manifesting himselfe indeed better by his examples, then by his commands.

Aaaa   CHAP.

CHAP. XI.

His svveetnesse of Behauiour, and Conuersation, ioyned vvith Grauity.

MOREOVER to procure the saluation of soules his sweetnes of Conuersation accompanyed with extraordinary Grauity was of special force; which two Vertues being different in shew, were yet so combined togeather in him, as neyther of them detracting from the others force, he was both very graue, and also incomparably sweet in his conuersation. For as we sayd before, there playnely appeared in *Xauerius* Countenance, Gesture, Speach, and Conuersation, a most incredible sweetnesse, which being engrafted in him by nature, and augmented by Grace, could easily draw, and conserue also, the affection of any one.

He was wondrous cheerfull in his countenance, tractable in his discourse, and most sweet in his conuersation and behauiour. His lookes were so gracious and pleasant, that they gaue great comfort to the sick, and ioy to all those that were in health: And oftentymes, many of the Society came to visit him, for no other cause, then that receiuing comfort from his heauenly aspect, they might by the remembrance of his extraordinary alacrity, and admirable feruour, be the more enflamed towards the pursuite of a blessed life. For so often as they could get but an essay of this his alacrity,

Xauerius lookes pleasant to the beholders.

alacrity, or euen but a breathing only of fo couragious an hart, they neuer came away fad or heauy from him. Againe, the fingular fweetneffe of his countenance and fpeach, drew vnto him as wel the bad as the good, great and little, and got fuch firme hold ouer the affections of their harts, that he was able to drawe them which way he pleafed : fo as he neuer demaunded any thing of any one, how great, or hard foeuer, which he did not at laft obteyne.

His ordinary difcourfe alfo, he was wont to feafon with great dexterity, and to intermingle with wonderfull variety, that it might not caufe any tedioufneffe in the hearer. He was very skilfull both in Aftrology and Philofophy, & therfore alwayes when he trauailed by the way, to relieue the wearifomneffe of the iorney, he would oftentimes bring in difcourfe of the motions of the celeftiall Globes, & the Planets. Alfo the Eclipfe of the Sunne and Moone, he would foretell long before it hapned. Againe, he would declare the caufes of thofe things which we behould to be admirable, both in the heauens, and the world; what the caufe, or origen of Hayle, Froft, Snow, and Rayne was; whence clowdes, myftes, winds, and thunder proceeded; what that was which caufed the fwelling, and raging of the feas. Many other things alfo, he would adde of the fame kind; which as they were very admirable, fo were they delightfull to the hearers; and in the end of all, he would referre them to the honour, and feare of God.

Of thefe things therfore, he difcourfed fo learnedly and pleafantly amongft the *Iaponians*, who are wholy

ignorant

ignorant of such matters, that they were wont vsually to say, that in *Xauerius* company one might trauaile all *Iaponia* ouer without being once a weary; and this delight of his discourse carryed his companinons along in such sort, that he ordinarily wonne them both to himselfe, and to God. Yea this sweetnes of his Conuersation was tempered with so weighty a Grauity, that in the height of his most pleasant discourses what he sayd, or did, breathed forth a most sweet odour of sanctity. Wherof al men had now gotten such an opinion, that although he conuersed often, & very familiarly, euen with the most vitious, yet the same was neuer any staine to his reputation; since the constant fame of his sanctity defended him, not only from euill tongues, but also from the least suspicion of euill it self.

Moreouer, *Xauerius* had this property, that his familiarity did not any whit diminish, but rather increase a most reuerend & religious respect of all sorts of people towards him: in so much as one would haue said, that his sanctity, like a pretious stone, grew daily brighter and brighter, by continuall vse and exercise. *Consaluus Fernandez* a Maister of a shipp, and a man of good account, was very conuersant & familiar with *Xauerius*, in that he oftentymes went in his ship, and lodged also in his house at *Goa*; yet he bare such reuerence and respect vnto him, that whensoeuer he came vnto his house, he with his whole family, would go out to meete him, and casting themselues prostrate on the ground, did alwayes receiue him in that manner. And although *Consaluus* were oftentimes intreated

by

by *Francis*, not to vse that respect vnto him, yet he would neuer refraine therefrom, such possession had the Reuerence of his holy person taken of his hart.

Iames Perera also, who was so great and familiar with *Xauerius* as no man more, was wont to say, that he could neuer stād before him with his head couered although *Xauerius* himselfe intreated the same; protesting, that whensoeuer he spake vnto him, he vsed to be taken with such reuerend and religious a respect towards him, that he seemed to behould God in his person. Yet as occasion required, *Francis* wanted not Seuerity also, the sting of Grauity, which we shall heere recount by an example, or two. A certayne deuout Matron of good esteeme, was wont alwayes to to confesse to *Francis* when he was at hand. This woman (as herselfe afterward recounted to a Religious man) *Xauerius* sharply reprehended, becaufe she had vpon occasion cast her eye vpon an handsome, proper man, and well attyred: Hast thou, quoth he, looked vpon a mā? Thou deseruest that God should not looke on thee. Which words so stroke her chast and pious heart, that she could neuer after throghout her whole life, endure to looke any man in the face.

He was also, aboue all other things, a most seuere reuenger of obstinacy. In the Promontory of *Comorinum* vnderstanding that a certaine Neophyte had blessed an Idoll, he was so greatly moued with the indignity of such an abominatiō, that he presently caused the house to bet on fire, to the end the seuerity of the punishment might make others afrayd to commit the like offence. And when as, many persons of worth

requested him to mitigate the penalty, he only permitted, that the dwellers might carry out their household stuffe, but the house it selfe which was the receptacle of that sacrilegious Monster, he would by all
meanes haue consumed, euen to the ground.

CHAP. XII.

*His Prudence, and the Precepts he gaue
to the Rectour of the Colledge of* Goa;
and to Gaspar *the* Lovv-*countryman.*

OREOVER, Prudence, the Modera-
tresse of other Vertues, shined not a little
in *Xauerius*, as wel in his dexterous gaining
and conuerting of soules (which euident-
ly appeared throughout his whole lyfe) as in his pro-
pagating also of Religion, & gouernment of those of
the Society committed to his charge. For he knowing
well, that nothing so much hindred the Christiã faith,
as the bad examples, and vices of euill Christians, he
would not set vpon Ethnicks to instruct them in matters of fayth, vntill he had reclaymed the ancient
Christians from their vicious and sinnefull life. And
those Neophites also, which he had broght vntoChrist
with infinite labour and patience, he first of all instructed them himselfe with the greatest diligence that
could be, before he committed them to others of the
Society for their further education in vertue. And as
for

for thofe of the Society ; he neuer fent them vnto any place, where himfelf had not firft bene, and laboured. Thofe alfo whome he fent, he armed with certayne wholefome and proper inftructions agaynft inconue-niences that might happen, vntill they were well ac-quainted, and experienced in thofe thinges which himfelfe had learned by long practife, and diuine in-ftinct.

Now, concerning *Francis* his Prudence, being no leffe-profitable a Maiftreffe vnto others, then to thofe of the Society, it fhewed it felfe moft of all in thofe Precepts, and Inftructions wherof I haue before fpoken; although I deeme it worth my labour to fet downe a good part of the againe, fince they may be of as great force to teach vs knowledge and prudence, as they were to make him admirable. Hauing therfore conftituted *Fa. Paul* Rectour of the Colledge of *Goa*, at his departure he left him thefe admirable enfuing inftructions.

Firft of all, I pray and befeech you, for the loue you beare to God, and for the obferuance you owe vnto our holy Father *Ignatius*, that you will louingly and courteoufly receiue, and treate the whole Society of I e s v s, and al the Fathers, and Brothers therof, co-ming either out of Portugal, or already difperfed ouer *India*. I for my part haue indeed fuch an opinion of all thofe of the Society, that (for fo much as I can gheffe) I do not thinke they haue need of a Rectour. Notwith-ftanding that others may neither want a fubiect of o-bedience, and that all things may be kept in right & due order, I haue thought good, that there fhould be

His o-pinion of the vertue of the Soci-ety.

fome

” fome one, to whome the reft, in my abfence, may be
” obedient. Wherfore confiding in your Humility, Pru-
” dence, and Wifedome, I haue iudged it expedient,
” that you fhould be made Superiour ouer all thofe of
” the Society in *India*; fo as all of our Order in, & out of
” *Goa* fhall obey you, vntill it be otherwife ordayned.
” *Antony Gomez* fhall be Prefident of the Colledge of
” *Goa*, and fhall gather vp the rents, and difburfe them
” vpon neceffary occafions, as fhall be thought fitting.
” In thefe things I haue giuen him ful power; wherfore
” you fhall not therin interpofe your authority. If you
” find him to do otherwife then well, you fhall direct
” him by your counfayle, rather then by command.

Againe, I earneftly pray and befeech you, for the
” obedience which you owe to Father *Ignatius*, that

**His care
of con-
cord.**

there may be nothing done, which may at any time,
fow difcord betweene you & *Antony Gomez*, or affo-
” ard fubiect of talke, either to thofe of the houfe, or to
” others abroad. And on the other fide, to indeauour all
” you can, that you may alwayes carry the bufineffe to-
” geather betweene you, with all concord, both in wills
” and actions. If at any time thofe of the Society in *Co-
” morinum*, or others that labour in the vineyard of
” Chrift, fhall require of you any thing belonging to
” the faluation of foules, you fhall with all fpeed, and li-
” berally prouide them therof. And when you write to
” thofe poore wretches, who are fo greatly oppreffed,
” take heed you write not any thing harfhly which may
” offend them.

” Moreouer, to fuch as labour couragioufly for Gods
” caufe, you fhall readily, and liberally adminifter fuch
    things

things as be neceſſary, but eſpecially to thoſe of *Como-* ''
rinum and *Malaca*, who carrying a moſt heauy croſſe, ''
beare the burden and heate of the day. You ſhall ther- ''
fore both carefully & ſpeedily furniſh them, not only ''
with ſpiritual, but with corporall ſupplyes alſo requi- ''
ſite for their ſoules: and if any of them come vnto *Goa* ''
to retire themſelues, you ſhall receiue, and cheriſh thē ''
as beſeemeth both your ſelfe and them . And this I ''
charge and command you , in Gods & Father *Ignatius* ''
name. ''

Moreouer, I beſeech you, deere Brother , that you ''
will dayly go on forward in the way of vertue , and ''
become a patterne and example therein vnto all men ''
as hitherto you haue bin . Write to me alſo often in- ''
to *Iaponia* , wherby I may know how all things goe ''
with you, and with thoſe of your Family, & eſpecially ''
how you and *Antony Gomez* , and the reſt of the So- ''
ciety do loue & agree togeather ; and of the number, ''
quality, & ſufficiency of thoſe Fathers, both in natural ''
and ſupernaturall talents , who ſhall heereafter come ''
vnto you out of *Portugall.* This you ſhall not fayle to ''
do euery yeare twice , to wit, in the moneths of April ''
and September. ''

You ſhall likewiſe take care, that ſome others of ''
the Houſe alſo (to eaſe you of labour) do certify me ''
by writing of ſuch things , concerning the Fathers & ''
Brothers throughout *India* , which you thinke I de- ''
ſire to know. And if any thing require ſecrecy , you ''
ſhall write it with your owne hand in a poſtſcript. ''
Laſtly, I earneſtly requeſt of you, that you will make ''
much of theſe precepts , and read them ouer euery

,, weeke once, and withall being mindfull of me that
,, you will both by your selfe continually pray to God
,, for me , and incite others to do the like .

Other like precepts he also gaue to *F. Gaspar* the
Low-country man when he was to goe to *Ormus*, & to
other Fathers who went to labour in *India*, as follow :

Attend principally to your selfe , being very carefull
,, both of Gods honour and your owne Saluation . For
,, assuredly if you be vpheld with these two props, you
,, will both affoard more help to others , & be also your
,, selfe the better prepared for humble and religious ex-
,, ercyses . You shall therfore instruct the Portughese
,, children, and bondslaues , and other ignorant persons
,, in the Christian precepts ; and this charge you shall
,, not commit to any other, since it is a thing of so great
,, importance , for the saluation of soules, and gaining
,, of good will . You shall diligently visit the poore, and
,, sicke in the hospitall , and by telling them that sick-
,, nes is most commonly a punishment of sinne, you shal
,, gently incite them to examine their conscience , and
,, confesse their sinnes. Then, when you haue leasurely
,, heard their confessions, and refreshed them with hea-
,, uenly food , it will be conuenient to commend them
,, to the Prefect of the Hospitall, and to help them with
,, such things, as they shall want.

It is likewise fit, that you goe oftentimes vnto the
,, Prisons , to visit the prisoners , and to exhort them
,, to make a generall Confession of their life . For a-
,, mongst those kind of men you shall find many, that
,, neuer made a true Confession. You shall commend all
,, to the Sodality of *Mercy*, that no iniury may be done

Precepts giuen to Gaspar.

Care of the Catechisme

Workes of mercy

to

to any one ; & for fuch as be in extreme neceffity, you "
fhall alfo begge meanes to affift them, therby to re- "
lieue them in their mifery. You fhall likewife prouide "
for the Sodality of *Mercy*, fo farre as you fhall be able. "
Wherfore when any money is to be reftored, and is "
vncertaine to whome, I thinke abfolutely that you "
had beft giue it to the faid Sodality of *Mercy*. For al- "
though there want not poore, for the relieuing of Almes
whofe neceffities thofe helps may well be imployed ; ought to
notwithftanding the deceipt and cunning of beggars buted to
vfeth oftentimes to caufe fome note of infamy in this the poo-
bufineffe ; by whofe impoftures others may fooner be re by ex-
deceiued, then thofe of the Sodality of *Mercy*, who by fons.
long experience, haue learned prudently to beware "
of fuch cofenage. Wherfore it is beft to leaue that bu- "
fineffe wholy to them of the Sodality, who may di- "
ftribute the Almes, according to the quantity thereof, "
amongft fuch as are knowen to be truly in want. "

  This you ought to do, for many and weighty "
reafons. Firft, becaufe if you diftribute the money to "
the poore your felfe, many will certainly aske of you "
fome reliefe, efpecially for their bodies, which they "
would affuredly neuer do, if they faw that you vfed "
only to help the neceffities of the foule. Secondly to "
auoid the fufpitions, & rumours of thofe that fhould "
giue you fuch money to be diftributed amongft the "
poore. For (as men are apt to belieue the worft) it is "
to be feared, leaft that exacting of money may carry "
with it fome fufpition of auarice ; as though you in- "
tended to turne the money, begd vnder colour of re- "
lieuing the poore, to your owne vfe & benefit. Wher- "

„ fore it is better to giue ouer that charge to others, of
„ whome there can be no fufpition. Yet if at any time
„ occafion moueth you to the contrary, you may do as
„ may be moft for the glory of God, and the good of
„ foules.

„   Yow fhall alfo fo carry your felfe before thofe with
With   whome you conuerfe, although they be you friends,
friends   and familiar acquaintance, as if they were one day
we muft to be your enemies. This confideration will eafily re-
liue as if ftraine your behauiour from growing diffolute throgh
they   liberty, and keep you backe from giuing offence to a-
wereto   ny, through too much friendfhip and familiarity: and
be our   fuch kind of warineffe wil alfo make them afhamed to
enemies. breake friendfhip with you without caufe. This wa-
„ rineffe, I fay, keepes not only others from being in-
„ folent with vs, but alfo maintayneth piety in our fel-
„ ues. For if you be prefent with your felfe, you will
„ both enioy God the more, and haue the better know-
„ ledge of your felf; wheras certainly the want of know-
„ ledge, and forgetfulneffe of ones felfe, is the mother
„ of many Monfters of vices, which make vs loofe our
„ friends, and infteed thereof procure vs enemies; fo
„ as they who are not ignorant of our fafhions, do a-
„ ryfe with more bitternes and vehemency againft vs.

Reuerē-   Towards the Bifhops Vicar you fhal alwayes car-
ce to-   ry your felfe with extraordinary reuerence and obe-
wards   dience. Wherfore fo foone as you come to any towne
the Bi-   where he refideth, you fhal prefently go, & caft your
fhops   felfe at his feete, and alfo kiffe his hand, as the cu-
Vicar.   ftome is. Then you fhall aske of him leaue to preach,
„ heare confeffions, and to exercyfe other offices of piety.

ty. And no offence whatsoeuer shal at any time with-
draw you from him, but shall rather inflame you by
all kind of complying with him, to gaine him sweetly vnto you, that being at last wrought by pious considerations he may become better, & more plyable.

You must also seeke & maintaine friendship with
other Priests, that they may also be the more efficaciously drawne to the same wholsome considerations.
Moreouer, to the Gouernours of Townes you shall
be very obseruant, and seeke to gaine their good wils
by all seruiceable and familiar endeauours, so farre as
may be possible. Neither shall you incurre their dis-
pleasure, or hatred for any cause although it be iust.
But if any one of them shall chance to commit any
great offence; first hauing entred into some fit discourse, you shall in a friendly & sweet manner shew vnto
him, how much you are grieued for the infamy, wherwith his dignity and reputation is stained. Then with
the like sweetnes and humility, you shall in such sort
declare the rumours which be spread abroad of him,
that of himselfe he may acknowledge, and amend his
fault. And this must be done when there is hope, that
your admonition will take good and prosperous effect. Otherwise it is better to let it all alone, then to
labour in vaine, and to gaine nothing (as they say)
but ill will for your paynes.

Vpon Sundayes & Holydayes in the after-noone,
hauing called togeather the men & mayd seruants of
the Portugheses, as also their free-men and children
into the Church, with a little bell; besides the heades
of the Christian fayth, you shal teach vnto them also

A manner how to admonish Prin ces.

a method

,, a method how to pray, anh how to haue care of their
,, foules. And to ignorant perfons, the practife of this
,, method fhall be for fome time inioyned them for their
,, pennance after they haue made their Confeffion, that
,, being by litle and litle exercifed therein, they may at
,, length get a wholfome cuftome therof. I know by ex-
,, perience that this hath bin the faluation of many. The
,, fame methode fhall be written in a table, and fet vp in
,, the Church, that they, who will vfe it, may write
,, it out.

A man-
ner how
to take
away
fuites in
law.

Some tyme and labour muft be alfo imployed in
making peace betweene enemies, & reconciling fuch
as are at variance among themfelues. In taking away
alfo of controuerfies and fuites in law, you fhall infift
much vpon this point, that ordinarily there is more
fpent in the fuite, then the thing about which they
ftriue, is worth. And for that this practife will proue
vngratefull and odious to Lawyers and Notaries, they
are therefore fpecially to be gayned alfo, and by fit
confiderations brought to conforme themfelues to iuftice & equity. For if we rightly confider the matter,
we fhall find them to be the chiefe authours, and a-
bettors of all Controuerfies, and fuites in law, as turning to their owne gayne.

Away to
conuert
fuch as
be very
vicious.

If you meete with any that be fo intangled with
fraudes, vnlawfull lufts, and hatreds, that they doe
not only vfe no meanes to free themfelues of thofe vices, but reiect all neceffary remedyes alfo: there muft
be all care taken both by humane and diuine meanes,
that their foules, although they be already as it were
paft hope, may at laft be cured. Wherfore vnleffe they
be

be wholly fenfelefle, you are to propound vnto them «
the loue & reuerence which they owe to Chrift their «
God & Sauiour : and to ftrike into them an horrour of «
Death & Hell that hangeth ouer their heads . If nei- «
ther the loue of God, nor feare of Hell wil moue them «
they muft be terrified with thofe moft bitter tormēts, «
which euen in this lyfe the wrath of God inflicteth v- «
pon wicked men. Wherfore it wilbe then a fit time, to «
threaten againft them , the grieuous & long ficknes of «
this life, ouerthrowes of temporall ftates & goods, the «
priuation and want of children, the reproachfull dif- «
honefty of wyues, dangers both by fea and land , fud- «
dayne and difaftrous chances, and other fuch like mi- «
feries , wherewith God is wont to take reuenge of «
foule finnes and enormityes, fuch efpecially as by long «
continuance of tyme haue taken deepe roote in man . «
For we dayly fee that many are moued much more «
through the feare of fuch wordly miferies and incom- From
modityes, then by the terrour of euerlafting tormēts. whence
The caufe of which infenfibility , or rather madnefle, obftina-
is eyther the forgetfulnes of the diuine Maiefty , toge- cy pro-
ther with the great neglect of their owne confcience ; ceedeth
or the flendernes of fupernaturall beliefe in fuch moft and hay-
lewd and wicked perfons , who like fenfuall beaftes, nous of-
meafure out all things according to what they behold «
with their eyes , & tread vpon with their feete; who- «
ly vnmyndfull of the ioyes of heauen, and of the laft «
combat, whereon their euerlafting weale or woe de- «
pendeth; that is , whether they fhall be bleffed, or mi- «
ferable for all eternity . «

Some alfo fhall you find, who fticking faft in the «
finke

" finke of finne, will notwithftanding feeke to haue
" friendfhip & familiarity with you; not that they may
" be drawen out therof, but that they may fo efcape the
" reprehenfion which they deferue, and gaine a good
" opinion alfo from others by keeping company with

Preachers are to refufe prefents.

you. Wherefore I aduife you, to be prefent with
your felfe: and if at any tyme fuch lyke perfons inuite
you eyther to their houfes, or fend you Prefents, take
" heed your liberty be not fo reftrayned by their guifts,
" that you dare not reprehend them, euen fharply when
" they offend. Therefore if they inuite you to dinner,
" you fhall not (indeed) refufe to go; but yet require
" them agayne, by inuiting them likewife to the holy

Whenin-uitation to dinner is to be accepted of.

Sacrament of Confeffion. And if you fhall perceyue
that you do no good at all with them, but wholy loofe
your labour, then you fhall tell them playnely, that
vnleffe they leaue fuch courfes, you will from that
tyme difclayme from hauing any friendfhip, or con-
" uerfation with them.
" Notwithftanding what I fay of receiuing Prefents

What prefents are to be receyued

from any one, I do not meane fmall & feldome gifts,
as fruite, and fuch like, which being fent backe, do oftentymes much offend thofe that fend them: But I
meane great & precious Prefents, which may chance
" to take you, if you take them. If at any tyme there
" be a great quantity of victuals fent vnto you, it fhall
" be diftributed amongft the poore in the Hofpitall of
" ficke, or in the prifons, and other places; that all men
" may fee the greateft part, euen of fuch things, to be di-
" uided amongft the needy, and that you keepe hardly
" any for your felfe. This Charity wil giue better example

ple of your abstinence, then if you should refuse to ""
receiue such Presents, specially when they who send ""
them, account it a dishonour to haue them sent backe ""
againe. ""

Now, when you intend to correct any one for their The
bad demeanours you shal not do any thing therin vn- manner
till you haue throughly found out his most inward howe to
disposition. Wherfore I seriously aduise you, first to "" correct.
search out and examine whether he, by reason that ""
he is intangled with some vice, or trouble of mind, ""
do neglect the good of his soule. If you find him to ""
be of a quiet disposition, and ready to receaue admo ""
nition, then you may diligently aduise him of such ""
things, as you shall thinke good. If you perceiue him ""
to be moued with anger, or any other trouble, you ""
must then forbeare to admonish him, and endeauour ""
gently to pacify his distempred mind by certaine in- ""
ward insinuations, & sweetnesse of speach. Then you ""
shall bring him to haue a consideration and care of his ""
saluation, trying him at the first with lighter admoni ""
tions, and if they succeed well, then to set vpon him ""
with sharper. And at last when you haue wholy wóne ""
him vnto you, & that he commit himselfe intierly to ""
your direction, you shall prescribe him certaine rules ""
to obserue, and plainly, and openly declare vnto him Are reme-
all such things as shall be necessary for the good of his dy how
soule. And the only remedy to ease his trouble of mind to pa-
or qualify his anger, is, by speaking prudently vnto cify an-
him, to extenuate & make lesse the cause of his griefe ease trou
or anger: As if he be moued with passion, to impute ble of
the iniury rather to want of consideration, then to mind.

C c c c   any

,, any malice, or ill will which the other had; or to tell
,, him, that God permitteth it for the punishment of his
,, former sinnes; or that perhaps himselfe had heereto-
,, fore comitted something against his Parents, knisfol-
,, kes, friends, or other innocent persons, for which his
,, diuine Maiesty did now iustly, and duely punish him.

,,   These things, or such like, which are of force to
,, extinguish passions of anger, must be inculcated vnto
,, him. And this rule which I haue giuen against Anger,
,, may be also applyed to other vnbridled motions of the
,, mind. This likewise you shall vrge vnto him, that al-
,, though he then seemeth to haue some iust cause to be
,, moued, yet if he will recollect himselfe a little, & by
,, calling backe his thoughts to the truth it self, & more
,, narrowly and attentiuely consider of the matter, he
,, shall infallibly find, that, that which so much trou-
,, bleth him, is nothing at all. And so at last with a cheer-
,, full and ioyfull looke, you shal wipe away al his trou-
,, ble of mind, and in a friendly and careful manner ad-
,, uise him, what is needfull to do, according to the
,, condition of the party, and the promptitude of his
,, will.

Endea-
uour
must be
vsed that
they
who are
instru-
cted by
one
must ope
to him
their tep
tations.

You shall also endeauour what you can, to cause
them whome you instruct in the way of vertue, to o-
pen vnto you all their temptations, and the thoughts
which assault their mind. For this is an especiall help
for those who are ignorant in this kind of combat,
or at leastwise not sufficiently experienced or practised therin, to arriue to the perfection of vertue. But
if you carry your selfe with more Seuerity, then
Benignity towards them (seeing that Seuerity often
excludeth

excludeth Confidence) they wil eafily conceale from
you how they are affaulted by the Deuill, thinking it
eafier to fuffer the Deuils affaults, then their Inftru-
ctors harfhneffe: and fo, being depriued of all neceffary help, & expofed to the darts of their moft cruell enemy, wil be fo long affaulted, and oppreffed, vntill at laft being ouercome with vexations, they yield
themfelues as prifoners.

If you fhall perceyue any to be tempted, eyther
with pride, carnall concupifcence, or any other vice,
your beft courfe perhaps wilbe, by giuing them fome
time to deliberate, to wifh them to bethinke themfelues vpon fome remedy againft thofe vices. Which
that it may fucceed according to their defire, you fhal
firft open them the way to inuent fome fuch remedy;
then you fhall will them to confider ferioufly, what
courfe themfelues would take, to perfwade fick perfons, prifoners, or others to auoid fuch like vices; and
fo the fame medicine which they would giue to others
they may apply to themfelues. For if they be commu-
nicated to others, they will both profit them, and they
will alfo of themfelues be incited to thofe things,
which they perfwade vnto others. This rule may alfo
ferue for others, who by reafon of fome impediment,
cannot be abfolued. For it is good to demand of the,
that if they fhould go about to reclaime another from
the fame vice whereto themfelues are fubiect, what
courfe they would in fine take? & fo at laft perfwade
them to make vfe of that counfayle and remedy themfelues, which they would giue vnto others vpon the
like occafion.

Mildnes
is necef-
fary in
one that
inftruct-
eth o-
thers.
"
"
"
A way
how to
correct
vices.
"
"
"
"
"
"
"
"
"
"
"
"
"
"
"
"
"
"
"

Cccc2   This

» This alſo muſt be looked vnto, that in exerciſing
» thoſe that be brought vp according to our Inſtitute,
» and in inioyning them imployments of vertue, there
» be a meane obſerued, ſo as euery mans burden be al-
» lotted him proportionably to his forces. For if they
A meane be greater then he can commodiouſly carry, they wil
in the not ſtirre vp vertue, but rather keep it downe in him.
exercyſe And ſo being diſcouraged & tyred out, he wil refuſe
ofvertue to take the burden which is to be impoſed vpon him,
» and perhaps ſhake of that alſo, which he hath already
» vndertaken.

The And for as much as the King of Portugall hath out
King of of his free bounty giuen order, that we ſhall be euery
Portu- where prouided of all things neceſſary, I iudge it fit,
gall his that you make vſe of his liberality, rather then of any
liberali- other. For aſſuredly, he that receyueth thinges from
ty. another, looſeth his owne freedome, eſpecially ſeeing
» that bounty impoſeth a neceſſity of being obſequious
» for the benefit receaued; and that liberty which is ſold
» for a benefit, is ſo ſeruile, that although it be bold
» ſometymes to aduenture vpon ſomething, yet the effi-
» cacy therof is of farre leſſe weight, then it would be,
» if it had the full diſpoſing of it ſelfe. To which you
» may alſo adde, that if he, who beſtoweth any thing
» vpon you, commit a ſin, you cannot reprehend him
» freely. For who will haue ſo bold a face, as to preſu-
» me to barke at him that feeds him?

CHAP.

CHAP. XIII.

Precepts giuen by Xauerius *to* Iohn Brauius, *and others of the Society.*

A S soone as you rise out of your bed in the
morning, you shall obserue this rule: For
halfe an houre at least, to meditate something of the life of Christ; and this order
you shall keepe therin, to begin with his Natiuity, &
then going on with your meditation, by little & little
to runne through all the other noble passages of his
life, vntill you come to his glorious Ascension into
heauen. And for euery day, there shall be particular
points assigned, in the very same manner, as is pres-
cribed in the little Booke of *Spirituall Exercises:* so that
you may euery moneth run ouer the whole life of our
Sauiour Christ in your Meditations.

    Moreouer, I would aduise you euery day when you
haue ended your meditation, to renew your vowes
of Pouerty, Chastity, & Obedience; then the which,
for such persons as are consecrated to God, there is
scarce any more safe defence against the assaults of
our deadly enemy the Deuill. Wherfore you shall
hould this in highest esteeme, dayly to arme your selfe
with those wholsome weapons. And in the After-
noone, when you haue taken your corporal refection,
you shall againe imploy almost as much more time in
the repetition of your morning meditation, which

Margin notes:
Manner of medi-tating.

Vowes dayly to be rene-wed.

Cccc3   you

„ you fhall alfo in the like manner , conclude with the
„ like renouation of your vowes, as before .

A māner how to examine ones cōfcience.

Moreouer, at night after fupper , before you go to bed, you fhal betake your felfe to the examen of your Confcience ; fo as taking an account of all that you haue thought , fayd , or done that day, you fhall eafily „ fee , if there be any thing wherin you haue offended „ God, or your Neighbour : and this you fhall performe „ in as exact a manner, as though you were prefently to „ make your confeffion. Then you fhal demand of God „ pardon for all your offence, purpofing from your hart „ to amend your life. And laft of al, hauing fayd the ac- „ cuftomed prayers of *Pater Nofter*, and *Aue Maria*, you „ fhall for a little while, thinke what courfe you may

Care of amendment.

beft take for the fpeedy amendment of thofe your de- fects.

The next day therfore in the morning whilft you „ arife , and apparell your felfe, you fhall call to mind „ your late offences of the day before, and hauing hum- „ bly implored the affiftance of the diuine Maiefty, that „ you may not offend in any thing that day (and fpe- „ cially not to fall into thofe ordinary & viuall faults) „ you fhall beginne your meditation , in the manner „ we fpake of before . And this you fhall do euery day . „ But if throgh negligence you omit any of thefe faid „ things, making a confcience therof, you fhal acknow-

Victory ouer o-nes felfe.

ledge your fault as the cuftome is , and that openly before your companions , that you haue neglected „ thofe things which were prefcribed you.

„ You fhall moreouer in all things , wherof you „ perceiue your inordinate defire, or corrupt nature to haue

haue an horrour, couragiously ouercome your selfe,
knowing that our chiefe care ought to be of Christiā
humility. For without lowly submission of mind, &
true Humility, you will not be able to profit either
your selfe or others; nor will you be gratefull to God
and his Saints, nor yet worthy to be long indured of
the Society of Iesus, as being no way able to brooke
haughty spirits, who commonly follow their owne
wils, and iudgments. Wherfore you shall diligently
vpon all occasions indeauour to obey your Superiour,
and that without any excuse, or vnwillingnesse, no
other wise then if Father *Ignatius* himselfe should command you. To him you shall declare the temptations
which the Deuill suggesteth vnto you, of what kind
soeuer they be, that being armed by his aduise & assistance, you may the more easily auoyd the assaults of
that most cruell Tyrant. For humility in discouering
the Aduersaryes temptations and assaults, obteyneth
no lesse ayde & assistance, then fauour at Gods hands.
Wherfore it doth not only defeate his most crafty
plottes for the present, but also weakeneth his forces
and indeauours for the time to come. For perceauing
that his subtilties are once discouered, by little & little
he looseth his hope of the victory, and is discouraged
also from setting vpon vs.

These admonitions he gaue to *Brauius*, remayning
at *Malaca*; & these also which follow vnto others whē
they went to *Cocinum*. Aboue all things (as much as
shall lye in you) you shall gayne the loue of the Citty,
but especially of Religious persons, & of those of the
Sodality of the B. V. Mary. Let therefore both your

words

Marginal notes: Humility and obedièce necessaris for those of the Society. " " " " " Temptations are to be discouered. " " " " " " " " " "

,, words and deeds manifest that you desire nothing
,, more then to deserue well of all, and to aduance both
,, those of the Citty, and of the Sodality also, in piety.

Courte-
ousnes
in salu-
tations
& visits.
Courteousnesse in going to salute those of the Sodality, will easily gaine them to assist you in your difficultyes. If you shall stand in need of any thing, for reliefe of the poore, you shall request it chiefly of them,
,, but in such sort, that you teach the poore to acknow-
,, ledge them to be the authours of that bounty. This
,, course also you shall take with the poore, that when
,, they lay open vnto you their corporal necessities, you

What
course is
to be ta-
ken with
the
poore.
shall in likesort lay open to them the necessity of their
soules, which they themselues do not perhaps perceaue: and after you haue taken care of their soules, then
you shall also, if you can, assist them in their corporall necessities.

,, In your conuersation and discourse with others,
,, you must take heed least a kind of too much grauity
,, in you, yield suspicion of arrogancy, which looketh
,, to be reuerenced: but rather carry your selues with a
,, cheerfull countenance, and alwayes shew affability

Too
much
grauity
is to be
auoided.
in your speach. Your chiefe care shall be to behaue
your selues humbly, and modestly in all things. Yow
shall therefore beare great respect not only to the Prelates of the Church, but to Priests also, and all others.
,, It is also very necessary to make them partakers of
,, such things, as shalbe by you laudably performed, to-
,, geather with the prayse therof, that they may become
,, fauourers, and Patrons of those workes wherof they
,, reape the fruite.
,, In your Sermons also, you shall gently recall your
Au-

your auditours from the errours, and vices wherein they liue. But such as be hard-harted and obstinate, are now and then to be terrifyed with the seuerity and rigour of the diuine iustice; as contrarywise, such as shew themselues tractable are to be comforted and animated by propounding to them the clemency and mercy of God. Moreouer such as are obstinate, and stick fast in the sincke of heynous sinnes, must be vrged with threathes from heauen, yet in such sort, as they may not loose all hope in the diuine Mercy, but that their hartes may be sometymes cheered vp by remembrance thereof.

By all meanes procure, that the good name of the Society may be spread abroad by you, farre and neere. For the which there is no vertue of more importance, then true and sincere submission of mynd. Remember how those Enlargers of our Society in the very heate of many, and great vexations, exercised themselues very carefully in all kind of vertues; and so shall you be partakers of their merits and glory, if you imitate their industrious labours in aduauncing the Societies good estimation. You must also remember that to gayne authority with the people in sacred affayres, and such things as belong to the good of soules, is the guift of God; which is bestowed *gratis* vpon pious and vertuous persons (but is ordinarily denied vnto the crafty and subtile, and to such as seeke after it by humane meanes) to this end without doubt, that peruerse men may not thinke contemptibly of diuine guifts; which they would doe, if they were dispensed equally, as well to the arrogant, as to the humble.

Diuers wayes to deale with diuers persons.

Authority with the people is a guift of God.

Dddd You

,,   You muſt therfore earneſtly beſeech of God, that
,, he would be pleaſed in euery thing to declare, and lay
,, open vnto you the impediments , which , through
,, your imprudency , you caſt in the way before the di-
,, uine indeauours , by reaſon wherof he doth not by
,, you impart his guifts to the people; wherby you do,
,, without doubt, deſerue that he ſhould not giue you
,, that authority , and eſteeme, which is neceſſary for
,, ſuch a buſineſſe . This certainly muſt be taken heed
,, of, with the greateſt diligence that can be poſſible .

In exa-
mine of
our con
ſcience
we muſt
looke
into our
offices &
charges.
,, Wherfore in your examen of conſcience , you ſhall
with a very inward care, take an eſpeciall account of
your ſelues, whether you haue done any thing amiſſe,
either in preaching , hearing confeſſions , or in your
conuerſation and diſcourſe; and ſhall take ioy in amē-
ding thoſe faults which you perceiue in your ſelues, &
in purging your ſoules of all bad affections . For certainly the further you remoue your ſelues from vices,
,, the neerer you approach vnto celeſtiall guifts.

Popular
applauſe
is by no
meanes
to be
ſought.
,,   Do not therfore admire, much leſſe imitate thoſe
,, who inuent new wayes to pleaſe the people , hunting
therby after popular eſteeme, and prayſe. For ſuch
kind of perſons attend rather to their owne , then to
Gods glory , & are more ſollicitous about their owne
commodities, then of the ſaluation of ſoules . Wherfore their courſe is very vnſtable, & ſubiect to ruine ,
,, which being puffed vp with a blind deſire of glory,
,, ſetteth it ſelf forth with oſtentation to the people, be-
,, ing in the meane while hatefull to God. You muſt al-
,, ſo by all meanes endeauour , to haue both a feeling in
,, your meditations of thoſe things, which I ſhal ſuggeſt
                                                vnto

vnto you, and alſo to put them carefully into execution . And if by diuine inſtinct, there happen to be a-
ny ſuch feelings or motions in your ſoules, you ſhall
for memory ſake, ſet them downe in writing, & expreſſe them afterwards in your actions : and thus by
practiſing thoſe things wheron you haue meditated,
vertue (being as it were nouriſhed with good feeding)
will ariſe to a greater grouth . For it is wonderfull to
thinke what difference is betweene that guſt and feeling thoſe holy men had, who haue left vs their wry-
tings concerning this ſubiect, & that which we now
haue, who only read, or heare their writings read. For
thoſe things which they meditated vpon, and conceiued in their mind, gaue them great incitements to
vertue; wheras for the moſt part, they do not make in
vs, any great impreſſions .

Things medita-ted are to be put in execu-tion.

Wherfore I do ſeriouſly aduiſe & exhort you, that
euery one be carefull to keepe in writing, and diligently to looke ouer thoſe feelings, and motions of
piety which he ſhall receiue from God . The which,
that God may dayly more and more increaſe, you
muſt endeauour to roote your ſelues euery day deeper
and deper in humility . You ſhall alſo ſeeke out ſome
faythfull friends and admonitours, who may tell you
in a friendly, and free manner, if you fayle in any
thing that is appointed you, that ſo you may by others
come to the knowledge of your owne faults, & amend
that which you your ſelues doe not ſee, becauſe euery
one is more quick-ſighted ordinarily to behould anothers imperfections, then their owne.

Things medita-ted are to be loo-ked ouer

Fayth-full ad-moni-tours are to be ſought after.

Theſe, and the like admonitions did *Xauerius* giue,

partly

partly to Superiours of the Society , and partly to o-
thers. But those are very singular which at his departure towards *China* he left vnto *Gaspar* his vicar Which
notwithstanding , as well as others (to auoyd the tedi-
ousnesse of repeating the same things) we do heere of
purpose omit , reseruing them for another place. For
seeing that the same precepts are accommodated for
the instruction of diuers sorts of persons , we haue
thought good to distribute them into certayne Chap-
ters , that euery one may benefit himselfe , by that
which he shall perceyue to be fittest for him.

CHAP. XIV.

VVhat kind of Gouernours , and Superi-
ours he required in the Society.

Care of
ones
selfe.

AVERIVS required, that Superiours in
the Society, should be such, as himselfe
was. He vsed therfore so say, that aboue all
things , they ought first to haue a care to
looke vnto themselues, before they tooke vpon them
to help others. For that man could neither haue any
care of another, who had none of himselfe; nor looke
vnto other mens saluation , who was negligent of
his owne. Wherfore he said, that it was not for euery
one to be a Superiour. For the person of a Gouernour
could in no wise be vndertaken , and endured by the
vulgar sort, and such as were imperfect, without infinite danger to himselfe.

It is not
for eue-
ry one to
gouerne.

Moreouer

Moreouer he serioufly admonifhed thofe that were fuperiours that they fhould not fuffer themfelues to be intangled with other publicke affayres , efpecially fuch as belonged to the Common-wealth, deeming them a great diftraction and hindrance to their proper and domefticall charges For no man, who is a fouldiar of Chrift vfeth to intangle himfelfe in fecular bufineffe. Wherefore their chiefe care fhould be , to performe well and daily their owne office, and alfo to affift , & looke to thofe who were committed to their charge. And when they had performed that with care & diligence, if they had any tyme to fpare they might employ it vpon others : whereto he applyed that fentence of our Sauiour Chrift , *Thefe things you ought to doe , and not to omit thofe .* This principall Precept therfore he gaue to *Gafpar* his Vicar.

Your firft and chiefe care muft be rather concerning your felfe, then thofe who are vnder your charge . *For he that is bad to himfelfe, to whome will he be good ?* Let your owne faluation , I fay , and theirs who are of your houfe-hold be more deare vnto you , then others, becaufe we muft chiefly giue an account to God of our felues , and for thofe alfo that be committed to our charge. And they who omit their owne domefticall affayres , and bufy themfelues about others , do erre no leffe, then they who being vnmindfull both of God and themfelues, feeke to pleafe and content men. Wherfore you fhall firft take care of your owne Houfehould , and afterwards of others , if you haue any leafure. As for your manner of helping them , the more generall it is, the more profitable it will be ; fuch

Ciuill bufineffes to be avoyded 2. Tim 2.

Superiours firft care muft be of their owne. Mash. 23.

Ecclef. 14

are

❧ are the exercifes of often preaching , explication of
❧ the Catechifme , and hearing Confeffions.

Superi-ors muft excell in humility & other vertues. He would alfo haue Superiours to go before others,
no leffe in humble fubmiffion of mind , temperance ,
charity , and prudence, then in power and authority;
& with a fatherly affection to beare as well with their
fubiects weakeneffe and imbecility , as to eafe them
of vexations , & troubles. This likewife he much infi-
fted vpon, that they fhould alwayes defire to be loued
rather then feared , and endeauour in all they could,
to be as a louing Father vnto them all, by which meanes it would eafily come to paffe , that themfelues
fhould be fure to imploy their admonitions with profit, for the reformation of bad habits , and the other
could not choofe but take all fuch things in good part
alfo . Wherefore in their gouernement, they fhould
vfe rather lenity & gentlenes, then authority and command, left they fhould feed their flocke as *dominiering*
ouer the Clergy, which *S. Peter* forbiddeth . And this

Arrogāt perfons are to be kept downe. courfe they fhould hold , efpecially with the quiet &
humble. Now for fuch as were turbulent , arrogant ,
and immoderate prayfers of themfelues , they ought
to be fharpely reprehended for their abufes , and punifhed alfo if need were, that the rod of difcipline might
bring vnder , the haughtines of fuch difpofitions . In
which kind he gaue to *Gafpar* certayne precepts in
thefe words .

❧ To the Fathers , and Brethren , who be commit-
❧ ted to your charge, carry your felfe rather gently and
❧ with moderation , then feuerely and with too much
❧ grauity , vnleffe any one chance to abufe your benignity;

"gnity; for then to prouide for his good, you muſt take "vpon you ſome ſeuerity; the which, if you perceyue "any one to be puffed vp with arrogancy and pride, "will be to good purpoſe to beate downe, and abate his "ill-diſtempered ſpirits. For as it is expedient to beare "with thoſe who fall, out of ſome inconſideration "or forgetfulneſſe; ſo lykewiſe it is neceſſary to repreſſe "and keepe thoſe vnder, who through arrogancy be-"come inſolent and contumacious. And by no meanes "muſt you giue any one cauſe to thinke, that you being "his Rectour, and ouercome by his inſolency and ſtub-"bornes, do giue therby way vnto his abuſes. For there "can no greater miſchiefe euer happen to ſtubborne "natures, then if you wincke at them by treating them "timorouſly & gently in their errours and obſtinacies, "ſeeing, the giuing way to ſuch perſons, cauſeth them "to take more ſtomake, & putteth them oftentimes in "hope to do what they liſt, without any to correct, or "puniſh them.

　　Neither would he haue the Rulers and Superiors of the Society to be ouer haſty, or too facile in recei-uing any into their company without choice, but out of many to chooſe few, & thoſe fit members, becauſe there is farre greater ſtrength in a choice band of men then in an infinite multitude of the vulgar ſort. And ſuch indeed, were wiſhed to be admitted into the So-ciety, who ſeeme to be borne, and framed as it were, for that courſe of life, and vpon whoſe vertue one might aſſuredly rely both at home, and abroad. But for ſuch as ſhould come vnto the Society inforced ra-ther by ſome difficulty or neceſſity, then out of deuo-
　　　　　　　　　　　　　　　　　tion,

Choice is to be made of ſuch as are to be admit-ted into the So-ciety.

tion, or defire to ferue God; to fuch the Society fhould
in no cafe giue way. And this opinion was fo groun-
ded in *Xauerius* mynd, that he had rather haue feruants, either hyred for wages, or procured by fome o-
ther meanes, then to admit fuch into the Society, as
were not fit, for the manage of domefticall affayres.
Wherfore he gaue *Gafpar* this charge.

"   Do not eafily, and without choice receiue many
" into the Society, but a few, and fuch as may be fit. For
" both the nature of the Society requireth it, and a few
" extraordinary fpirits are more profitable, then a thou-
" fand of the vulgar fort. Such therefore as are weake,
" dull, and of no fpirit you fhall not admit, as very vnfit
" members for the Society, which requireth men that
" be induftrious, generous, and indowed with extra-
" ordinary vertue, and who performing great matters
" are contented with a little. And as for fuch to whome
a pious and vertuous difpofition had giuen a fufficiét

How the
vertue
of thofe
that
were to
be admit
ted was
to be
tryed.

commendation, and were iudged fit men for the Society, thofe he would haue to be long, and well exer-
cyfed and tryed, vntill their vertue were fufficiently
made knowen, by many and great proofes. He commaunded alfo, that their Vertue fhould be tryed rather
by ouercóming themfelues, and fuppreffing the turbulent motions and appetits of their mind, then by
any fhew of deuotion, by teares, fighes, or rigorous
mortification of the body. Wherfore he gaue order

A man-
ner of
mortifi-
cation.

fo to mortify their members, which were vpon the
earth, that the fame might ferue to caft off the old má
and put on the new. And therfore he prefcribed this
method, leaft by giuing way to new inuentions, the
                                        vnwonted-

vnwontednesse of the thing might displease the eyes
& minds of the behoulders. Concerning which matter he giueth this command to *Gaspar.*

  Those whome you shall admit into the Society, I «
thinke it better to exercyse them in the ouercomming «
of their vnbridled passions and affections, then in cor- «
porall mortifications, and such like new inuentions. «
But if any exteriour mortification be applyed to re- «
straine the inward motions of the mind, let it be al- «
waies such, as may not cause laughter in the behol- «
ders, but be approued; As for example, continuall «
seruing of the sick in the Hospitals, begging of money «
& other almes for the relieuing of poore prisoners, & «
the like. It much auaileth some also to Humility, to «
declare publikely to their companions, the manner, «
functions, and imployments of their former life be- «
fore their entrance into the Society, and other such «
like things which may help to humility. But in this «
kind, there is great respect of persons to be had, and «
much consideration also of what euery ones conditi- «
on, and vertue can beare. For vnlesse this heed be ta- «
ken, there may arise more harme then good therof.

  Xauerius iudged it likewise fit, that Nouices should
be accustomed to declare themselues to their Instructors, and to lay open vnto them all their temptations
inclinations, and passions, as likewise their feelings
of deuotion, their diuine consolations, and voluntary pennances; that so they may infallibly defeat all
the machinations of the enemy, who most of all as-
saulteth there, where his deceit is least feared, by manifesting the same to those who are experienced in
      E e e e   such

ſuch kind of matters : And if by chance they ſhall

haue erred in any thing, they may thereby agayne be
brought into the right way. Moreouer he required
that Superiours ſhould take great heed, that they did
not inconſideratly admit all to receyue holy Orders,
but ſuch only of whoſe fidelity, and vertue they had
had long triall, and whoſe prudence, & learning was
at leaſt ordinary. For Prieſts of the Society, to liue according to their inſtitute, cannot without great danger want theſe helpes. Whereupon he giueth *Gaſpar*
this admonition.

You ſhall iudge none fit for Prieſthood, vnleſſe
» he haue the commendation of long, and throughly-
» tryed Vertue : becauſe the Society requireth Prieſts
» of approued Vertue and learning, for the perfor-
» mance of the funƈtions of their Inſtitute. This our
» experience hath taught vs to be true : for they that
» haue not byn ſuch, we know to haue byn rather an
» hindrance, then an help vnto the Society.

And before all others, he would haue thoſe that
be abſent, labouring in our Lords vineyard far from
the company of their Brethren, to be eſpecially prouided for of all commodities, becauſe they (as he
was wont to ſay) were workemen, who indeed did
beare the burthen of the day, and the heate. For
which cauſe he ſayd, that both their corporall and ſpirituall neceſſityes ought carefully to be conſidered &
relieued. And that it was alſo good, to aske oftentymes of ſuch men of credit as came thence, how they
behaued themſelues, and oftentymes lykewiſe, to
giue them comfort by letters ; but neuer to write any
thing

thing sharpely vnto them, or of that nature which
might either cause them trouble, or put the out of hope
of effecting what they haue vndertaken, for that they
commonly suffer vexations inough where they be; &
therefore it was good to absteine from all seuerity, &
not to heape affliction vpon the afflicted. Moreouer
he forbad they should be often changed (vnles necessity
did perchance vrge vnto it) especially by such Superiours,
as had not yet sufficient knowledge of the
places, countryes, and imployments wherein they liued.
For there was danger least the changing of the
labourer should bring some disturbance to their fruitfull,
and profitable workes.

Frequēt changes to be auoided.

He would also, that the Rectours and Superiours
should haue great care, that the Societies good name
might be spread abroad, and that all offence might be
euery where auoyded, although it were with some
detriment in their temporall meanes, for *better indeed
is a good name, then store of riches*. Wherfore he seriously
exhorted them, that attending more to the edification
of Vertue, then of Colledges, they should cause their
Houses to be built in such sort, that they might not
so much carry a glorious shew, as serue them for necessity,
and commodity of habitation. If any thing
belonging to their temporall meanes, should cause
them much trouble, as the exacting of rents or money
due vnto them, they should commit that businesse,
being no lesse odious then necessary, to some hyred
Attourney, rather then to one of their owne Company.
Likewise, he most earnestly intreated the Superiours
of the Society, to gaine the good will of the

Scandall by all meanes to be auoided. Prou. 22.

The building of howses.

Superiours

Superiours of all other Religious Orders & families,
as also of Clergy men and Priests, and to liue with the
in the greatest vnity and friendship that could be. To
which end they should sometimes go to visite, and salute them, as well to gaine, as to conserue their good
will, or otherwayes to shew their vnion, and amity
with them.

Other Religious men to be woone.

CHAP. XV

VVhat kind of men Xauerius *vvished, should be in the Society.*

AVERIVS required, that those of the
Society should be humble obedient, moderate, and conquerers of themselues in all
things which are repugnant to our corrupt nature. For without these vertues none of the
Society could either be gratefull & acceptable to God,
profitable to himselfe and others, or euer liue with a
quiet and contented mind in the Society. All therfore
ought to exercyse themselues very diligently, and for
a long space in the knowledge of themselues, that by
plucking vp disordinate appetites, as weeds by the
rootes, they might lay a deep foundation of true humility and solide vertue. For as he who in meditating
vpon the most bitter death and torments of Christ,
by feeling a pious enflamed griefe in himselfe, can
easily enkindle in another the same sorrow of hart; so
he that hath conquered and beaten downe the disor-

dinate

dinate motions of his owne mind, can without difficulty, reftraine, and bridle the fame alfo in others.

Moreouer he faid, that none ought to efteeme much
of himfelfe becaufe he had byn long of the Society.
For the worth of thofe that be in the Society, was not
to be meafured by the length of the time, but by the
greatneffe of their vertue. Seing that they ought rather to be afhamed, then to boaft of themfelues, who
hauing bin fo long in the fchoole of Vertue, haue
made fo fmall progreffe therin, *Alwayes learning, and* 2. Tim. 3.
neuer arriuing to the knowledge of truth. He likewife forbad them to make any account of the efteeme which
other men had of the, leaft perhaps a difguized fayre
gloffe of things might breed in them pride & haugh-
tineffe of mind, the moft certaine and greateft plague,
and poifon which can befall the Society. But contra-
rywife he willed them to turne their confideration
to the knowledge of their owne weakeneffe, and efpecially to ponder oftentymes the difference between
the iudgments of mens and the iudgment of God, and
there indeed to lay the foundation of their Humility.
For he that attentiuely confidereth, what a different
iudgement God, *Who is the fearcher of harts,* frameth
of men, from that which men themfelues do, who
behould only exteriour actions; will vndoubtedly de-
preffe himfelfe to the loweft ranke that may be in
Gods fight, & repute all humane prayfes (as ayming
far amiffe from the truth) for nothing els but croffes, Confi-
and fcornes of men. Yet we muft not for all this, dence in
through confideration of our owne weakeneffe, loofe God.
courage in the war-fare and feruice of Chrift: but we

are

are rather to endeauour, as well by diſtruſting our owne forces, as by repoſing our confidence in the diuine aſſiſtance, to take hart in all thinges, ſince we muſt imploy our ſelues in great matters for his ſake, who alwaies is ready to put therto his helping hand.

The way alſo to arriue to the perfection of vertue which he ſhewed them, was this. That euery one ſhould in the firſt place haue a care of himſelfe, and twice euery day (if it could be)or at leaſt once, to examine his owne conſcience: vſing the greateſt endeauour he could by all meanes to amend thoſe defects which he perceyued in himſelfe; and that he ſhould moreouer make the greateſt eſteeme that might be of his daily meditation, and neuer ſuffer any day to paſſe ouer, without affoarding his ſoule ſome ſuch kind of repaſt. And this meditation he would haue to be alwayes made with ſerious ponderation vpon the lyfe, paſſion & death of Chriſt our Sauiour, as being a ſubiect of perfect vertue, and peculiarly proper to the Society of IESVS. He counſayled them lykewiſe after meditation ended, agaynſt the incurſions and aſſaults of the diuell, euery day to renew their vowes, & to declare al the temptations of the enemy of what ſort ſoeuer, together with their bad inclinatiõs, as wel as their deſires of vertue, to their Ghoſtly Fathers, Superiours, and other ſpirituall Directours, who were able both to counſayle and aſſiſt them. For ſuch is the force of this humble ſubmiſſion, that it doth not only obteyne more light and help from God in the tyme of combat, but fruſtrateth alſo the moſt importune Aduerſary, who perceyuing his plot to be diſcouered,

uered, his affaults defeated, and his defignes broken off, becometh affuredly more remiffe in his batteries, and at laft flyeth away with loffe of the victory, ouer whome he had before triumphed.

He alfo required blind, and fimple Obedience in thofe of the Society, that leauing their owne iudgmēt and opinion, they fhould in all things (excepting fuch as were contrary to the diuine Law) obey with-out any reply, or demurring vpon the matter. That they fhonld not demaund of their Superiours fuch things as they defired after an odious, and importune manner, or by any inuention wreft their commād to their owne wils; but that euery one fhould freely direct his iudgment and opinion to that of his Superiour, and leaue himfelf wholy therin to the iudgment of thofe that reprefent the perfon of God; houlding this for certaine, that in all things which they command, God will fo infpire them, as may be moft for his diuine honour, and their profit. For, quoth he, they that fhould do otherwife, would oftentimes fall into great troubles, vexations, and miferies. Which inconueniences, thofe who are pernicioufly blinded with errour might thinke proceeded from the Croffe of our Lord, or from the Obedience; when as indeed they were the fruites which fprung from their owne peruerfe iudgement, and felfe will. Wherefore they fhould alwaies make choyce rather to obey their command; efpecially feeing that it is alwayes fecure to be ruled by another, but often daungerous to gouerne ones felfe. For although one may fometymes rule himfelfe well, yet there be very few, as being deceyued

ued with a certayne blind loue of themſelues, who do not moſt commonly the contrary.

He furthermore commanded them, that if at any time they were imployed in humble & abiect offices, Humble offices are to be imbraced. they ſhould carefully, and ſeriouſly performe them, and draw out of them the greateſt profit of humility which they could, fully perſuading themſelues, that they could not at that tyme do any thing more gratefull, and acceptable to God, in whoſe name they were commanded : remembring alſo themſelues, that ſmaller exerciſes were entrances alwayes vnto greater; & that he who was not quicke in the loweſt, vſed not to be excellent in the higheſt : whereas contrarywiſe he that went with alacrity about little thinges, would eaſily find courage in matters of more importance. For as our Sauiour Chriſt ſayth ; *He that is* Luc 16. *faythfull in the leaſt, is ſo alſo in the greateſt.*

Moreouer he prudently admoniſhed them, not to forſake, or neglect the place or ſtation which was aſſigned them by their Superior, although they might be in hope to do more good ſomewhere elſe. For it was infallibly a deceipt of the infernall enemy to ſuggeſt vayne flouriſhes of the future and vncertayne fruit that might be reaped in other places, thereby to draw vs from the preſent, & aſſured good which we do in the place aſſigned vs ; that ſo, whileſt we are diſtracted with wauering cares, he may make a mocking ſtocke of vs, and ſend vs away without any fruit at all : Seeing, that as long as you remayne in this vncertainty what to reſolue vpon, you are not well able eyther to labour in another place where you are not,

or

or in that where you are, becaufe you mynd is fome-
where elfe. For confirmation of this wholefome precept he vfeth that common fentence of the Apoftle: *Gal . 10.*
While we haue tyme, let vs do good. Wherefore he wifhed
fuch to be confident, that if what they defired was
pleafing to God, he would vndoubtedly moue their
Superiour to fend them thither where it fhould be moft
for his diuine honour.

He was alfo wont to fay, that they were indeed
grieuoufly miftaken, who defired to be honoured for
the vertue, and notable deeds of their predeceffours,
from whome they themfelues were become degenerate; imitating therein thofe, who adorning themfelues with other folkes apparell, fought to be honoured
and efteemed for great perfons. It were indeed better
for them by following their anceftours foote-fteps, to
emulate their vertue and worth, then degenerating
from them, to boaft of others goods, as if they were
their owne.

Moreouer, this aduite of his was not more prudēt
then profitable. He charged thofe that were ftill in
trayning vp at home in regular difcipline, that they
fhould not be ouer defirous to go into the field to
fight before their tyme, nor truft too much vpon their
owne forces, although they fhould fee thefelues fub-
ie&t to no great fault: For certayne it is, that young
beginners are many tymes guarded, not fo much by
their owne vertue, as by the place where they liue,
which eafily defendeth them from the affaults of their
enemies, and allurements to finne. Wherefore in the
time of their Nouice-fhip they fhould carefully arme

We muft not go to help others before our tyme.

F f f f

them.

themfelues with folid vertue, that afterwards they
might liue fafely in the midft of their enemies darts.

CHAP. XVI.

VVhat manner of Preachers he required in the Society.

Prea-
chers
ought to
preach
not thé-
felues
but
Chrift.

HE oftentimes admonifhed the Preachers of the Society, not to preach themfelues, but Chrift crucified; that is to fay, that they fhould, not by handling fubtile queftions and arguments farre from the reach, & vnderftanding of the vulgar fort, make a flourifh of their owne learning and wit, therby to get efteeme, and applaufe of the people: but their Sermons fhould for the moft part be of moral matters, fuch as were plaine and fuitable to the capacity of their vulgar audience; which being modeftly, religioufly, and prudently explicated, would certainly preuaile not a little towards the curing of mens foules. This therfore fhould be their ayme, by laying before their Auditours, the foulenefe of finne, and the greatnefe of the offence againft the diuine Maiefty, togeather with the wrath which from heauen is threatned againft fuch enormities, to draw them to forrow of hart, and repentance. But it will not be amiffe to heare what inftructions he himfelfe giueth vnto *Gafpar.*

　　The chiefeft office of a Preacher, fayth he, is to caufe in his auditour great feeling of his finnes, and to terrify him from future crimes and enormities,

by

by layi ng before him the infallible, and neuer ending «
tormēts of the damned. To difcouer alfo the deceiptes «
and treacheries of Sathan ; and in fine to treate of fuch «
things , as may be rather vnderftood, then admired,e- «
uen by the vulgar fort . Wherfore in his Sermons he «
was not to cite too many teftimonies out of holy «
fcripture, nor to handle fuch things as were doubtful, «
& in controuerfy among Doctours ; but fuch as were Teftimo-
certayne , plaine, and fit to draw men to the amend- nies out
ment of their liues , and good deportement in their of fcrip
behauiour . He fhould therfore much infift vpon re- ture
prehending of vices, making grieuous complaints for ought
the iniuries which are done to our Sauiour Chrift,ea- not to
gerly threatning reuenge from heauen, and euerla- be too
fting torments , which are prepared in hell for lewd , « much v-
and wicked perfons, togeather with the imminent « fed.
terrours of death , which oftentimes feizeth vpon mē «
when they leaft expect it. «

Certaine points alfo were to be propounded by «
way of colloquy either of a penitent finner with God, «
or of God all-enraged with a finnefull man . But all «
meanes muft be vfed , that by the feruour of their fpe «
ach , the auditours may at laft open the eyes of their «
harts , to behould the wounds of their foules , & cure «
them by meanes of the Sacraments . And thus his Ser- «
mons will in the end proue profitable , and fruitfull; «
notwithftanding he is to take great heed , that he do «
not let fall any inconfiderate words , which may re- «
prehend, or touch any one in particuler either prefent «
or abfent,efpecially if they be Prelates or Magiftrates. «
For if fuch perfons fhall chance to offend , it will be «

,, better and more secure to admonish ech of them pri-
,, uately, and difcreetly at home in his owne houfe, or
,, in confeffion. For to reprehend them publickly is no
,, way conuenient:fo apt are men, when they are tould
,, of their faults, to be rather exafperated therat, then to
,, amend the fame ; efpecially Gouernours and Magi-
,, ftrates, whofe authority certainly feemeth much im-
,, peached , when they are reprehended before their
,, owne fubiects; becaufe great Honours caufe ordina-
,, rily great fpirits , which may not eafily be reprehen-
,, ded.

'A man-
ner how
admo-
nifh gre-
at men.

If any fuch perfon be admonifhed in priuate, this
courfe fhall be taken , to do the fame more earneftly,
or gently according as you are acquainted with him;
for that which is accounted freedome amongft fami-
,, liar friends , may feeme oftentymes too much bold-
,, neffe with ftrangers : & the rigour alfo of the repre-
,, henfion it felfe, muft be tempered with cheerfulneffe
,, of countenance, and mildneffe of fpeach. Wherefore
,, let al fterne looks & harfhneffe of words be layd afide,
,, & let there be intermingled imbracements fuitable to
,, that purpofe (if the ftate of the perfon will allow it)
,, with frequent fignes of humility , that being woone
,, therby, he may with a more contented mynd receaue
,, that foueraigne antidote of your admonition . For if
,, the reprehenfion , which of it felfe is allwayes bitter
,, inough, fhould be prefented vnto fuch men in a harfh
,, or crabbed manner, perfons of great fpirits being not
,, able to brooke the affront, will certaynely contemne
,, and reiect your wholfome admonifhment ; & moreo-
,, uer will caft of all refpect vnto vs , and vpon the fuddayne

dayne become our enemies, who before were friends. "
And these things are to be vnderstood of principall "
persons, and such as are placed in gouernement, and "
authority. "

Moreouer, he required often and frequent sermõs, A prea-
supposing that out of that common fountayne, there chers
might flow many and particular benefits. Wherefore pruden-
he would not haue a Sermon omitted without good quire out
cause, nor preachers to be busied in other affayres. the vices
Concerning which subiect, as also about the diligent and be-
endeauours of a Preacher, he giueth to F. *Gaspar* this of the
diuine instruction. You shall, sayth he, neuer prefer people.
a priuate good, before a common. Wherefore prea- "
ching must not be omitted for the hearing of Confes- "
sions, nor the instruction of Children or ignorant "
people be put of for priuate exercises of charity. If you "
come into a Towne which you do not know, your "
chiefe care shallbe, to inquire of some persons of e- "
steeme and credit, about the vices vnto which the in- "
habitants are addicted, and what vniust contracts be "
among them. Agaynst which your sermons shall in- "
deed be carryed on with a certayne feruour, that such "
vices, and corruptions may, by reprehending after- "
wards more sharpely in Confession, be wholy taken "
away. For the chiefe meanes to help soules is to know "
the disposition and behauiour of the poople in gene- "
rall, and the diseases (as much as may be) of euery "
one in particular, to wit, who disagree amongst them- "
selues, who beare emnity to one another, what de- "
ceipts, what iniustice in matters of equity, what per- "
fidiousnesse of witnesses, what corruption of Iudges "

and

» and iudgements there be among them. Thefe thinges
» therefore muft be inquired after, of prudent and expe-
» rienced perfons, and all carefull confideration be vfed
» to find out, what courfe ought beft to be taken for
» the curing thereof.

» You fhall moreouer by all meanes poffible, draw
» your penitéts to lay open their whole foule vnto you,
» for you will find no other way better, wherby to
» help thofe with whome you conuerfe, in matters con-
» cerning their faluation, then if you can throughly
» found out their inclinations and conditions, and all
» fuch things as hinder them in the way of vertue. This
» indeed ought to be their chiefe ftudy, who imploy
» themfelues for the gaining of foules. This in fine, is
» the true reading in liuing bookes, which will teach
» you, what you cannot find in dead papers. For the
» things which are deliuered in writing vfe not alwayes
» to be fo good for practife, as thofe which are taught
» in liuing bookes, who are the perfons with whome
» you be conuerfant in the fame affayres. Thefe bookes
» affuredly will eafily teach vs a prudent method, both
» how to conuerfe warily amongft men, and to preach
» alfo with profit vnto the people. Notwithftanding I
» fpeake not thefe things in fuch fort, as that I would
» not haue the worthy monuments of holy and learned
» men to be read, but to giue you this rule; That you
» fhould gather doctrine frō thence to confirme therby
» fuch cures of vices, which you haue drawen out of
» thofe liuing bookes; for fo much as both the examples
» and fentences of holy men, as alfo the teftimonies of
» facred Writ, are of great force to giue credit to any
thing

thing you teach.

Moreouer, in your conuersation and difcourfe, there muft rather appeare a cherfulneffe & fweetneffe of countenance, then fadneffe and feuerity. For if you carry your felfe with heauineffe, & too much grauity many will be terryfied with your lookes, and will affuredly auoid your company: and what then is to be expected of fuch, but that they become a prey ready for the wolfe to deuoure, feing the Paftour hath frighted them away. They be certainly the cords of *Adam*, wherwith men muft be drawne, whome gentleneffe allureth, and feuerity driueth away. Wherfore it is beft to endeauour to carry your felfe mild and affable to all. Let your reprehenfions in any cafe be gentle, & mollified with the fpirit of lenity: and let there be very great heed taken, leaft any harfhneffe in your behauiour make your conuerfation troublefome, and odious to others.

Cheerfulnes of countenance.

Againe, he gaue this inftruction to Preachers, that they fhould both thinke humbly of themfelues, and alfo carry themfelues fo in the Pulpit, that their very countenance and fpeech might eafily fhew their humility of mind. Whatfoeuer good they fayd, or did, they fhould attribute it to God the Author of al goodneffe, & acknowledging only to be their owne whatfoeuer fhould be ill, or done amiffe. In fo much, fayd he, as they ought fometimes to examine their owne Sermons, and if they found to haue committed any errour in their preaching, & hindred either the glory of God, or the profit of the people, they might humbly aske God pardon for the fame. For that a principall

pall profit which may be drawen out of holy sermons confisteth in the amendment of such faults. In which kind there is extant a notable admonition of *Xauerius* to *Gaspar* his Vicar, who was an excellent Preacher.

    The principall thing, fayth he, as well in other
,, things, as in the office of preaching, is to referre to
,, God, whatfoeuer good arifeth therof. For it is vn-
,, doubtedly he who both giueth to the people a feeling
,, of deuotion to heare the word of God, and to you
,, to preach it. Remember therfore, that you haue not
,, receiued that very guift, fo much through any merit
,, of your owne, as by the prayers of the Society, which
,, often moft inftantly befeecheth the diuine Maiefty to
,, beftow his guiftes vpon thofe that be members ther-
,, of : bearing alfo in memory, that whatfoeuer you fhall
,, vtter in your Sermon which is good or pious, is not
,, your owne, but Gods who fpeaketh in you. Exercife
,, therfore that diuine talent with all care & diligence
,, whereof you are one day to render an account. Attri-
,, bute nothing to your felfe but only defects, flouthful-
,, neffe, pride, and ingratitude both to God, to the peo-
,, ple, and to the Society, who haue by their prayers
,, obteined that guift of God for you. Wherfore you
,, fhall humbly againe, and againe, defire of God, that
,, he will cleerly manifeft vnto you, wherin you haue
,, hindred his diuine grace, as that he hath not effected
,, thofe things which he would, whilft your vnworthi-
,, neffe was an obftacle to greater matters. And laftly
,, you fhall from your hart caft your felfe proftrate be-
,, fore God, the examiner of harts and reines, and ear-
,, neftly befeech him, that you may not in your fermos
or

or difcourfes giue offence to any one.

This confideration is the nurfe of true and perfect The
humility. For the knowledge of ones-felfe, that is to grounds
fay, a perfect vnderstanding of ones owne weakeneffe lity:
confidered, breedeth, nourifheth, & increafeth Chri- "
ftian humility and vertue. I would haue you by all "
meanes to remember this, and deeply to ponder the "
fame, That there be many Preachers now tormented "
in hell, who were more copious, and eloquent then "
you are, and haue alfo conuerted more from a lewed "
and wicked to an honeft and veruous lyfe: and who "
(which is euen a prodigious thing) hauing byn the "
caufe of many others faluation, haue notwithftãding "
moft miferably perifhed themfelues. And why fo? Vn- "
doubtedly for this reafon principally, becaufe becom- "
ming infolent through pride & arrogãcy they did not "
referre the diuine guifts which God had beftowed v- "
pon them vnto him, but attributed them vnto thefel- "
ues. So as hunting greedily after popular applaufe, & "
puffed vp with a vaine opinion of thefelues, they were "
by an infatiable defire of pride & glory, eleuated to a "
moft dangerous precipice, frõ whence they fell down "
headlong to their euerlafting deftruction. Let euery "
one therfore call his wits togeather, and looke wel to "
himfelfe. For if we will atrentiuely diue into the truth "
of this doctrine, we fhall eafily fee, that we haue no- "
thing at all in our felues wherin to glory, vnleffe we "
do perchance defire to be honored for our imbecillity, "
imperfections, for fuch be the flowers, or rather weeds "
indeed, which our garden affoardeth, and are truly & "
properly our owne. For if in our good workes there "

be

  be any fault or blemiſh, it cōmeth from our ſelues, but
all the worth proceedeth from God, who ſometimes
euen from our weakenes produceth good effeȼs, making vſe of poore and abieȼ men for the performance
of glorious deſignes ; as well to declare his owne infinite power and goodnes, as alſo to humiliate and re-
,, preſſe our arrogancy of ſpirit. Take heed therfore that
,, you do not contemne your companions and brethren
,, as though your burden, or labour were more then
,, theirs : But rather perſwade your ſelfe, that by their
,, deuout prayers, the diuine Goodnes is moued to af-
,, foard you greater forces, for the due performance of
,, your charge, ſo as you owe much more to them, then
,, they to you. This conſideration aſſuredly, will not
,, only repreſſe all haughtineſſe of mind in you, ſo that
,, you ſhall not deſpiſe any one how humble or abieȼ
,, ſoeuer; but will alſo ſtirre vp ſuch flames of charity
,, in your hart, that you will beare a fatherly affection
,, vnto all.

  Moreouer, he ſeriouſly aduiſed ſuch as were preachers, to procure vnto themſelues certayne truſty
friends, eyther of the ſame place where they liued, or
otherwiſe, that were prudent and vertuous perſons,
who might freely admoniſh them of what was amiſſe
in their ſermons, that ſo they might more eaſily come
to know the ſame, and amend it. That they ſhould
alſo giue themſelues to prayer, and meditation of
ſuch things which they were to propound vnto the
people in their ſermons; and endeauour by all meanes
if it were poſſible, to get a taſt themſelues firſt, by ſome
inward feeling, of the force of thoſe thinges which
            they

they intended to fpeake of. For there is great difference betweene him who with feruour of fpirit thun-
dereth out thofe things which he hath before medita-
ted vpon, and him that barely, and coldly produceth
that which he hath learned by hart. He would moreouer haue them to confirme their words by deeds, and
alwayes to fecond their Sermons with the exercifes
of charity and mercy. Wherefore they fhould be carefull to ferue the ficke in the Hofpitals, vifit reftrayned
perfons in prifon, prouide for the neceffity of fuch as
were in want, & diligétly employ themfelues in other
offices of Chriftian charity & humility. For certainly
fuch offices were much holpen by fermons, & fermós
agayne by fuch offices. They fhould alfo fometymes
condefcend to Paftours & Vicars, when they intreated
them to preach to the people in their Churches. Furthermore what kind of people foeuer they fhould vndertake to inftruct in their Sermós, they fhould beare a
fpeciall loue vnto them, & very carfully looke to the
fpirituall good, and commodity of their Auditours.

He charged them likewife, by all meanes to auoid
contentions & ftrife with other Preachers, efpecially
with the Bifhops Vicars, although there might happen many, great, and iuft caufes of the fame. For by
fuch falling out there commonly aryfeth not only offence to God and the people, but alfo great diftur-
bance to the contenders themfelues, and hindrance to
the diuine feruice For indeed the good name and reputation of the Society ought not to depend vpon có-
tending about their dignity, but vpon labouring for
the augmentation of the diuine glory. Wherefore our

Contentions with other Preachers to be auoided.

con-

contention with others muſt not be with detraction
and pride, but with gentleneſſe and humble ſubmiſſion, bending all our forces to beware that our emulation about dignityes, make vs not odious, and
hatefull to others. If perchance, there ſhould aryſe a-
ny controuerſy which could find no end, the matter
muſt rather be handled by priuate diſputation before
Eccleſiaſticall Prelates, then publikely, with ſcandal
to the people. Concerning which ſubiect he gaue to
Gaſpar his Vicar, this no leſſe profitable, then prudent
inſtruction.

,, With all Religious perſons, and Prieſts your ſtrife
,, ſhall be in courteſy, & humility. If any offence chan-
,, ce to ariſe, you ſhall by your humility appeaſe their
,, anger, whether it be iuſt or no, yea although you may
,, ſeeme vnto your ſelfe to be innocent. And you ſhall
Away to require no greater reuenge, then to ſuppreſſe the iniu-
reuenge ry with ſilence, where right can haue no place. But
an iniu- if any of them ſhould any time ſwarue from their du-
ry. ty, you ſhall be hartily ſory for him, who vnleſſe he
,, amend himſelfe, ſhall ſooner or later pay for it deerer
,, then one can eaſily imagine. Wherefore taking com-
,, paſſion of the poore mans caſe, you ſhall continually
,, pray to God for him. Nor ſhall you make only a con-
,, ſcience of reuenging your ſelf either by deed or word,
,, but alſo to permit the leaſt anger or diſquiet of mynd
,, remayne with you. For both anger and reuenge are
,, alike to be auoyded, ſeeing they do both ſpring from
,, the ſame roote. God certaynly beſtoweth many, and
,, great fauours vpon thoſe who do for Chriſt his ſake
,, patiently ſuffer the troubles which happen vnto the:
and

and seuerely reuengeth also, though sometymes it be "
long first, the iniury which thereby is done vnto him, "
and brandeth commonly at last the aduersaryes ende "
auours, with the marke they deserue. But God will "
by no meanes take reuenge on you, if you go about, "
eyther by deed, word, or thought to be reuenged on "
your selfe. "

    If there should (which God forbid) any dissensi   Away to
on arise betweene you and other Religious men, you   compose
shall looke carefully that it be suppressed, and take   discords
heed that you do not by any signes of auersion giue "
notice therof, either to the Gouernour, or others of "
the Citty. For it is not to be thought how greatly "
wordly persons are scandalized, when they see reli- "
gious men, and such are consecrated to the diuine ser- "
uice to be at discord amongst themselues. Wherfore "
if any controuersy chance to aryse among you, you "
shall both take the Bishop for arbitratour, who by his "
authority may compose the mater without offence to "
any; and you shall also request the Bishop in my name "
that if at any time the enemy shal sow debate between "
brethren, he as a father will make peace amongst you; "
and as the author of concord take away whatsoeuer "
difference may be betweene you, that the matter may "
not come to the Magistrates, or publicke Tribunall. "
Remember likewise, that if the other part shall at any "
time speake ill of you, you are not to defend your sel- "
ues by speaking ill of them againe; but restraining "
both your speech and anger, you shall (as I sayd) haue "
recourse vnto the Bishop, who by comparing the mat- "
ter with equity, may take away all matter of conten- "

tion.

» tion. And since you know , that the dignity and esti-
» mation of the Society consisteth not in the opinion
» of men , but in the grace and protection of the diuine
» Maiesty , you shall haue a very speciall care , not so to
» defend the Honour of the Society , as thereby to in-
» curre the offence both of God and men .

Lastly , he aduised such as were Preachers , that
if any , especially men of note, who were plunged in
publick enormities , did desire their company and familiarity, in such sort as notwithstanding they would
not aryse out of that sinke of sinne ; they should declare vnto them , that such friendship and familiarity
had only this end, to reclaime those that were our
friends and familiar acquaintance, to seeke the good
& saluation of their owne soules ; seeing we vse only
to conuerse with them so farre forth , as our conuersation may help them towards their saluation . He
furthermore added, that Preachers , wheresoeuer they
had that which was necessary to maintaine life, ought
not to take any thing of others , because guiftes did
hinder their freedome: but if any small things were
sent vnto them , as signes of good will , rather then as
guiftes , they were not to be refused , least they might
seeme to reiect the friendship of those who sent them.

CHAP.

CHAP. XVII.

VVhat manner of Confessours Xauerius *required in the Society.*

MOREOVER he serioufly exhorted such as were Ghoftly Fathers, that in hearing Confeffions (hauing firft an inflamed defire of curing foules) they fhould midly & gently receiue such as came vnto them, wherby the lenity of such fpirituall Phifitians might draw them without delay to difcouer all the foares of their confcience. Wherefore they fhould not (efpecially at the begining of Confeffion) make any fhew of grauity, or feuerity, but rather of fweetneffe and mildneffe. To which effect he gaue to F. *Gafpar* at this fetting forth towards *Ormus*, this inftruction.

A Ghoftly Father muft haue mildnes in hearing Confeffions,

" You muft take very great heed, leaft in hearing
" of Confeffiōs, feare may be an obftacle of freedom to
" men in difclofing their fins, if you hearken vnto them
" with a feuere eare: but muft rather feeke with fweet-
" neffe, to adde courage to the fearefull, by extolling
" the diuine clemency, & by compaffionating of them,
" vntill they haue freely vngorged themfelues of all the
" poyfon of their finnes. And in this kind there muft be
" great warineffe vfed. For there want not fome, who
" through fhamefaftneffe commit greater offences by
" concealing their finnes, then they had before to con-
" feffe, turning therby the wholefome remedy of Con-

feffion

,, feffion to their owne deftruction . Wherefore againft
,, fuch peftilent bafhfulneffe , all meanes & endeauours
,, poffible muft be vfed. And to get out their finnes from
,, fuch perfons , there is no better way , then to fhew
,, them , that we haue heard farre more grieuous , and
,, fowle finnes of others , and withall fomewhat to exte-
,, nuate by certaine fit words , thofe very fins which they
,, fhall with feare and much ado confeffe , that fo taking
,, hart they may more confidently lay open all the other
,, offences of their lyfe . And to get them confeffe free-
,, ly , this may be as the laft remedy (although it muft
,, be feldome , and warily vfed) to open vnto them in a
,, generall manner , the offences of your owne former
,, lyfe . For how good a meanes this is , tyme and expe-
,, rience will teach you .

How great finners are to be vfed .

This courfe he prefcribed againft fuch as were fearefull and bafhfull ; and that other againft fuch as were inthralled in crimes , and abominations of long continuance. And vntill the penitent had fo declared all his finnes , whilft perhaps he ftandeth wauering be-twixt hope and feare , they fhould encourage him , by putting him in mind of the diuine clemency & mercy , and namely they fhould produce fome for an example who hauing byn notorious for their abominable wic-kedneffe , were afterwards receyued into Gods fa-uor , of which company he fhould alfo make one , if he would but confeffe his finnes with the lyke fincerity and forrow of hart. At laft, when the Confeffour had throughly examined all the foares , and wounds of the penitents confcience , then he fhould liuely prefent be-fore him the heynoufneffe and fouleneffe thereof , and

by

by terrifying his staggering spirit, with the indignation of God hanging ouer his head, & the punishments
which miraculously haue byn inflicted vpon great
sinners, draw him to a detestation, and sorrow for his
sins ; differring also his absolution, if it were thought
conuenient, vntill another tyme .

But now, to such as were obstinate, & hard-harted
he would haue to be propounded not only the euerlasting torments of the damned in hell, but also the punishments which haue bin inflicted vpon the like offe-
ders in this life, and especially vpon such, and such
as themselues had knowne, who had receyued grieuous and bitter torments for their sinnes and wickednesse, to the end they might be a warning vnto others
lyke vnto themselues. For he sayd, that he had learned
by experience, that such kind of persons are sooner
mooued by the present detriment which they may suffer, eyther in their body or goods, then by the future
torments of their soules, which seeme to be absent, &
a farre off.

*How to
moue ob
stinate
persons ;*

If there should at any tyme come to Confession,
rich and wealthy merchants, Magistrates, or Gouernours of a loose lyfe, he iudged it fitting before all
other things, seriously to admonish them, that making
diligent inquiry into their former lyfe for the space of
two or three dayes, they should (if they distrusted their
memory) note down their sins in writing, & humbly
craue of God with great feeling, sorrow and contri-
tion for the same. Then, at the beginning of their Cō-
fession they were to aske of them an account of such
offices and charges whereof they had the care ; of the

affayres

affayres wherein they were imployed ; how diligently they did , or had carryed themſelues therein. For by
theſe interrogations they might more eaſily find, whether there were any thing to be reſtored , then if they
were demaunded in generall , whether they ought to
make reſtitution to any one? becauſe to ſuch interrogations, they vſe cõmonly to giue a negatiue anſwere ,
either out of auarice, or elſe through ignorance of the
thing. Now, when they haue heard their Confeſſions,
they muſt apply certaine admonitions , and remedies
for the cure of their ſoules; nor muſt they be abſolued
preſently after their confeſſion,but rather when they
haue reſtored thoſe things they ought . Wherfore of
ſuch perſons he giueth *F. Gaſpar* this inſtruction.

They ſhal not preſently be abſolued as ſoone as they
haue made their Confeſſion , but two or three dayes
ſhall be giuen them to prepare their hart by certayne
meditations , that in the meane time they may waſh
away the ſpots of their ſinnes by teares and voluntary
pennance. If they owe any thing to any one, let thẽ
make reſtitution; if they haue any grudge againſt any,
let them put it away , and be made friends with their
enemies; let them alſo be freed from libidinous cuſtomes,and all other vices wherwith they were intangled . Theſe things ought rather to go before abſolution, then to follow it. For ſuch kind of men when
they are at confeſſion, promiſe that they will do all
things ; but after abſolution is giuen them , as care-
leſſe of their promiſe , they do nothing. Wherefore
all diligence is to be vſed , to cauſe them to performe
before they be abſolued what they ought to do after.

Moreo-

Moreouer, concerning the meanes how to confirme such as are staggering in their fayth, these documents he gaue to the same *Gaspar*. You shall fynd some also (and I would to God they were not many) who " are very weake concerning their beliefe of the Sacraments , especially that of the Holy Eucharist , ey- " ther because they haue now byn depriued of the fruit " thereof, or by reason of the great conuersation which " they haue with the Ethnickes , or else because the im- " pure life of some Priests maketh the vulgar and igno- " rant sort not to esteeme so highly of this Sacrament. " With these therefore you shall deale in this manner: " First you shall get out of them their suspicions and " doubtes , then you shall confirme them in their fayth, " by instructing them so, that they may belieue for cer- " tayne that the true body of Christ is conteyned in that " mystery . Neyther is there any more present remedy " for the curing of this malady , then a pious and dili- " gent frequenting of the sacred Eucharist it selfe . "

But now because for the most part, in conuersing Familia-
with women there is more danger then profit , he se- rity with
riously aduised such as were Ghostly Fathers, that in women
hearing their confessions , in discoursing , and con- is dange-
uersing with them , and in reconciling them to their rous.
husbands , they should be very wary, and attentiue to
auoyd not only all offence and sinne , but also the suspicions & rumours of the people. Concerning which
he left to *F. Gaspar* his Vicar very notable and wholesome instructions , which I thought good to insert in
this place.

You shall not (sayth he) speake with women of
what

» what condition ſoeuer, vnleſſe it be by day-light, and
» in publicke; that is, in the Chnrch. And you ſhall
» neuer go home vnto them, vnleſſe it be vpon ſome vr-
» gent occaſion, as to heare the confeſſion of one that
» is ſicke. And then alſo you ſhall take great care, that
» her husband, or ſome other kinſman, or at leaſt ſome
» honeſt neighbour be by. If you haue occaſion to ſpea-
» ke with ſome Virgin or widdow, you ſhall go to their
» houſe accompanyed by men of approued integrity of
» lyfe, in whoſe company there may be, not only no
» ſcandall, but alſo no ſuſpicion. Yet theſe viſits of wo-
» men ſhall be both very ſeldome, and alſo not at all but
» vpon neceſſary occaſions. For it is a ticklisħ piece of
» buſineſſe, where ſmal profit is made with a great deale
» of perill. And foraſmuch as women (for ſuch is the
» inconſtancy, and leuity of their diſpoſition) do for
» the moſt part, cauſe to their ghoſtly Fathers a great
» deale of trouble, this warineſſe is principally to be
» held with them. You ſhall with more diligence labour
» about the inſtruction of Chriſtian men, then of their
» wyues. For ſeeing that men are more conſtant by na-
» ture, and the ordering of the houſe dependeth vpon
» them, it is certaynly better, & more profitable to im-
» ploy ones labour vpon thē. For as the wiſeman truely
» ſayth : *Such as the Gouernour of the Citty is, ſuch alſo are*
*Eccleſ.*10 *they that dwell in it :* and withall many ſcandalls and
» ſpeaches are auoyded, which vſe to ariſe vpon famili-
» arity with women.

» If there happen any debate betwixt man and wife,
» to take away al controuerſy, & to appeaſe their mind,
» you ſhall firſt of all procure, that ech of them, diſpoſed

fed therunto by fit meditations, do make a good con- «
feſſion of their former life; and as you ſhall ſee it fit- «
ting, you may differ to abſolue them for a while, that «
they may come againe better prepared for the amend «
ment of their liues, and eſtabliſhing of concord be- «
twixt themſelues. If the women tell you, that if they «
might abſteine from the company of their husbands, «
they ſhould be much more diligent in the ſeruice of «
God, do not by any meanes belieue them. For beſides, «
that ſuch feminine feruour groweth eaſily cold, it can ‟
hardly euer be vndertakē without grieuous offence to ‟
their husbands. Take heed how you lay the fault vpō ‟
the huſband in the preſence of his wife, although he The
be certainly in the fault; but ſuppreſſing the matter busbāds
with ſilence for the preſent, you ſhall afterward be- part
tweē him & you alone draw him to purify his whole ther be
life by Confeſſion. And when he is at Confeſſion, takē thē
then you ſhall reprehend him in the moſt modeſt mā- thewiues
ner that you can, and aduiſe him to looke carefully to ‟
the peace of his howſe. But by all meanes you muſt ‟
haue a care of this (being a buſineſſe very apt to breed ‟
ſuſpitions.) that you neuer by taking the wiues part, ‟
ſeeme to take againſt her husband. Wherfore he muſt ‟
firſt by little and little, in a friendly manner be admo- ‟
niſhed, to acknowledge his owne fault, and at laſt ‟
you ſhal gently and louingly giue him abſolution. For ‟
the Indians affections are moued by loue, but violen- ‟
ce ouerthroweth them..

    You ſhall therfore (as I ſayd a little before) take ‟
heed of accuſing the husband in the hearing of his ‟
wife. For as the nature of women is to be a little im- ‟

,, pudent & malepart, they will eafily caft their husbâds
,, in the teeth with their faults, efpecially if they be iud-
,, ged guilty by Priefts themfelues. Wherfore it is better
,, by diffembling the matter, to lay before the wiues,
,, the refpect which they owe vnto their husbands, and
,, to fhew them alfo, that they, for the contempt which
,, they haue oftentimes had of their husbands, haue de-
,, ferued indeed to be feuerely chaftifed. If therfore there
,, happen to them any trouble from their husbâds, they
,, ought to beare it humbly and patiently, and to be o-
,, bedient vnto them. Do not eafily giue credit to either
,, of them when they complayne of one another, (for
,, oftentimes they are both deceiued themfelues, and de-
,, ceiue others alfo) but you fhall with the greateft indif-
,, ferency that may be, heare them both, & not condéne
,, eyther of them before you haue examined the matter.
,, This I fay, that you may the better, and more eafily
,, make accord between them, and auoyd fufpicion your
,, felfe. But if at any time you cannot make any reconci-
,, liatiô between them, you fhall refer the whole bufines
,, to the Bifhop, or the Vicar General, but in fuch fort, as
,, not to wrong either of the partyes that are at varian-
,, ce, which you cannot but do, if you feeme to fauour
,, one more then another. You muft vndoubtedly vfe
,, great prudence to giue no offence at all in this bad
,, world. And the euents of things, which are carryed
,, heere, muft be alwaies forecaft; for our aduerfary the
,, Diuell doth not ceafe, *but roameth about feeking whome to*
,, *deuoure*. And it argueth great want of prudence, not
,, to forefee the inconueniences that may arife of actions
,, which be vndertaken with neuer fo good intention.

Moreouer

Moreouer he would not haue Ghoſtly Fathers to take mony vnder pretence either of reſtitution , or almes , but according to the intention of the giuer, procure it to be laid out in pious vſes , or els giuen to the Sodality of *Mercy* : for ſo that Sodality might the better prouide for the neceſſity of the poore , and they alſo for the conſeruation of the Societies reputation . If any come to confeſſion not ſo much to cure their ſoules , as to ſeeke ſome reliefe for their bodyes , ſuch would he haue to be admoniſhed of the vſe of that holy Sacrament , ſhewing them that the ſufferances of the ſoule , are more intollerable then thoſe of the body : and at laſt (if it be iudged expedient) to commend them to the Sodality of *Mercy.*

In like manner, he aduiſed ſuch as heard côfeſſions not to make too much haſt with their penitents , but to vſe all diligence about them , and that they ſhould rather deſire to heare a few côfeſſions well made, then many haſtily poſted ouer . For how could they els carefully apply remedies to their ſoares, vnleſſe they cured them by leaſure? for there is no doubt but one confeſſion well made , is better then many paſſed ſleightly ouer , eſpecially ſeing Côfeſſion prepareth the way to the holy Sacrament of the Euchariſt . Laſtly he aduiſed them , that they ſhould take ſome tyme to looke into the Confeſſions which they had heard , and attentiuely conſider whether they had done any thing amiſſe therin , & to ſatisfy for the ſame in their owne Confeſſion , and after to amend the fault ; ſeing ſuch diligence is a great help for the well diſcharging of a Ghoſtly Fathers duty.

CHAP.

CHAP. XVIII.

VVhat kind of persons Xauerius requi-
red for the instruction of soules.

AV ERIVS required, that those of the
Society who were to labour in the con-
uersion of Ethnickes, and instruction of
Neophites, should be not only of the most
choyce that could be gotten, but such also as were
most addicted therunto; so that they should preferre
nothing, how specious soeuer, before so noble an im-
ployment, since there was nothing more gratefull to
God, or beneficiall to mankind. Neither did he so
greatly exhort vnto this enterprize only, but layd
himselfe also for foundation therof, expressing more
in deeds, then he willed in words. For as we haue before declared, he neuer made more account of any
thing then of the conuersion & instruction of Ethnickes. Insomuch, as those of the Society who came vnto
him out of *India* or *Portugall*, he so called them to be
his compartners in this diuine function, that where
he found any of most emineut talents, he would commit this charge vnto thé as a reward of their labours;
following therein the example of the Apostles, *Who*
Act. 18. *when they heard, that* Samaria *had receyued the word of*
God, sent vnto them Peter *and* Iohn, who were the chiefe
of the Apostles. Wherefore he held it fit, that such as
were chosen to this Apostolicall function, should be
men

me n extraordinary, and of tryed fidelity, vertue, cō-
ftan cy, and fanctity of lyfe. But becaufe fuch imploi-
men t required fuch men, as alfo for that he had found
by e xperience, that fuch charges were expofed to
moft grieuous temprations of the Diuell, vexations,
and miferies, therfore in thefe labourers of our Lords
vineyard he required prudence and fanctity, rather
then knowledge and learning; well knowing that
Vertue was abfolutely neceffary for the ouercōming
of fo many and great difficulties, and that Sanctity
was of more importance then learning, for the conuerfion of Ethnicks. But where vertue and learning
were beautifully combined togeather, fuch, he faid,
were indeed fingular, and perfect preachers of the
Ghofpell, and fpecially fit for *Iaponia*, and other fuch
places, where the Barbarians, being a fharpe-witted
people, do by their fubtile interrogations make found
tryall of the Chriftian Religion.

He required moreouer, in all fuch as laboured a-
mongft Ethnickes, a propenfion, and defire to learne
their ftrange language, fince without that knowledge
there could be fmall profit made in gayning the Barbarians to the Chriftian faith, or in the inftructing
of new Chriftians. For which caufe the Apoftles,
before they began to teach the Gentils, were miraculoufly endowed with the guift of all tongues. And
his chiefe defire was, that all fhould be inflamed with
ardent zeale of fauing foules, fo as neuer to omit any
occafiō in that kind, but prefently to lay hold therof,
and follow it clofe. He likewife charged them to infift
thoroughly vpon the faluation and inftruction of the

Iiii   Neophy-

Neophytes, to teach Children their Catechifme, and
aboue all things to baptize children and infants, fo as
none, if it were poffible, might euer dye without Baptifme, the only fafeguard of that tender age. He alfo
exhorted them, that by gayning the affection of the
Neophytes, they might be loued & refpected by them
euen as their parents. For loue naturally taketh all
things in good part; and to one that loueth nothing is
hard.

  Furthermore in the inftructing of new Chriftiás
they fhould fhew no leffe fortitude then perfeuerance
as well by enduring their vices, as bearing with their
weakeneffe; and as good husbandmen expect with
our Sauiour, the harueft of the feed they had fowen, &
the fruites of their labours though it were long firft,

Pfal. 125. knowing, *that they who fow in teares, shall reape in ioy.*
And if they found the Chriftians at firft not to be fuch
as they defired, they fhould carry themfelues towards
them as good parents do towards vntoward children,
putting their confidence in God, who in due tyme
bringeth forth fuch fruit in men, as is to be hoped for
& wifhed. Wherfore they fhould attend vnto them diligently, fince God our common Parent, although we
infinitely offend him, doth not ceafe to beftow his benefits vpon vs. Yet would he not haue too much time
fpent with the ancient Chriftiás, leaft the new fhould
be defrauded. But if in ciuility their conuerfation
could not be auoided, they fhould at leaftwayes bring
in difcourfes of heauenly matters, and of things per-
taining to the good of their foules, that fo they being
plyed continually with fuch pious admonitions, they
             might.

might either grow better; or elſe being wearyed out therewith, might ſuffer vs to buſy our ſelues with helping the Neophytes.

He likewiſe eſteemed more of a little fruit with approbation of the people, then of a great deale with offence, though neuer ſo ſmall of any, becauſe a little fruit reaped with example of vertue, was both of lōg continuance, and always receiued new increaſe; wheras oftentymes a great deale, with offence vnto the people, did by little and little dry vp, and wither away. Hetherfore charged them to behaue théſelues mildly & humbly towards all, *hauing* (as the Apoſtle ſayth) *peace with all men*, and by all meanes to auoid contentions, eſpecially with Religious men & Prieſts, and to be mindfull always of Gentleneſſe and Affability, that ſo they might gaine all to Chriſt. He vſed alſo to ſay, that what good ſoeuer was not gained by vertue, could not any way be gotten, but by vertue. Wherfore they ſhould take great heed, that they did not, according to the practiſe of the world, ſeeke (or ſeeme to ſeeke) after dignityes and honours; neither by words or deeds endeauour to get the fauour rather of men, then of God, ſince the high authority, which alwayes accompanieth Vertue was a guift not of men but of God. And it often cōmeth to paſſe, that whilſt by humane fauour (neglecting the diuine) men ſeeke to purchaſe authority, and euen ſweat agayne to get it, they by the great prouidence of God, wholy looſe it; to this end no doubt, that they may not haue ſo baſe an eſteeme of things diuine. For they who in procuring the ſame haue more regard to humane fauour

then

then diuine do manifeſtly ſhew, they do not reſpect
the diuine honour, ſo much as their owne ; and that
ſuch ſacrilegious ambitions wil turne at laſt vnto their
owne confuſion and deſtruction. Euery one therfore
ought firſt to haue a ſpeciall care of his owne ſoule &
then to help other mens . For he that neglecteth his
owne, will hardly haue a care of anothers ſaluation :
neither can he well be mindfull of another , who is
forgetfull of himſelfe. Wheras contrariwyſe, he that
hath care of his owne good, will alſo haue a care of his
neighbours . Wherfore no day ſhould paſſe without
meditation of diuine matters and perfect examination
of their conſcience, obſeruing wherin they had fayled in the diuine ſeruice, or in their owne duety ; and
withall conſider with themſelues, how many things
God, through their default, had ceaſed rather effect,
then what he had performed by them: ſince the one
was an incitement to humility and perfect vertue, the
other to pride and folly , challenging thereby Gods
workes vnto our ſelues; then the which a more deadly
plague may not be found among religious perſons.

Now, foraſmuch as he eſteemed the education of
children to be a mayne & principall mayſter-piece, he
ordayned, that they ſhould deliuer the Chriſtian doctrine to whole troupes of children togeather , neuer
omitting ſo fruitful an employment, nor committing
it to others . They ſhould neuer exaſperate or prouoke
Epheſ.6. any child to anger , but *forbeare threates* (as they A-
poſtle aduiſeth) to the end that ſo tender an age might
with the more alacrity imbrace their wholeſome inſtructions. Towards magiſtrates, and Eccleſiaſticall
Prelates

Prelates they fhould carry themfelues with all moderation and humility, and vpon no occafion whatfoeuer maintayne iarres or quarrels agaynft them, allthough they fhould by neuer fo great iniuries be prouoked. For Magiftrates are fooner woone by others
fuffering, then by withftáding their authority. Wherfore they fhould communicate vnto them, as to the
Patrons of their endeauours and labours, part of their
fruit, and gayne, attributing vnto them (next after
God) all the good they had receyued: fo as by this
meanes they who labored in the Vineyard of our Lord
fhould haue more helpers and defenders of their labours, or at leaft, fewer aduerfaries. He lykewife aduifed them to employ themfelues no leffe frequently,
then willingly in the exercife of charity & humility,
by helping the ficke of the Hofpital, and prifoners the
Goales, both with charitable attendance, as alfo with
almes which they fhould gather for them; but fo,
as their help might profit them both corporally and
fpiritually For by fuch exercyfes of Charity we fhall
haue our owne foules inflamed with diuine loue, and
others alfo wilbe ftirred vp to the lyke deeds, and the
feruants of God get credit, and authority towards the
aduancement of the Chriftian caufe. But efpecially,
they fhould neuer make account of ill rumours made
agaynft them without caufe, which do often ouerthrow, and weaken the endeauours of thofe that be
fearefull. Concerning this, there is extant as notable inftruction, which he gaue to Fa. *Gafpar*, in thefe
words.

If, when at any time you go about a good worke, &

» ill difpofed perfons giue out flaunderous reports a-
» gainft you, you fhall not be moued therewith; but be
» fure that none perceiue you are by fuch mens words,
» hindred from the feruice of God. For they who are a-
» frayd of falfe rumors, in fuch a cafe, are more truly
» Souldiars of the world, then of Chrift. Laftly, I would
» haue you greatly to efteeme of this; That remem-
» bring your felf to be a member of the Society of Iᴇsᴠs,
» you would in all your words and actions, carry your
» felfe worthy of fuch an Head and Body. By which
admonitions it might eafily appeare, how diligently
and ferioufly *Xauerius* both by examples and precepts
trayned vp thofe of the Society to the higheft perfection of prudence and fanctity; as alfo how conformable *Ignatius* and he, were in all their iudgments and o-
pinions, notwithftanding that at the very fame time
they were almoft infinitely diftant the one from the
other, *Ignatius* being fuperiour of the Society in *Italy*,
& he in *India*. But without doubt, one & the fame fpirit dictated the fame things vnto them both, fafhio-
ning the Society in ech place, to a certaine forme
of difcipline, and infpiring them both with diuine
wifedome alike.

Xauerius prudence was not more feene, in giuing
his inftructions, then in his gouernement. For wherfoeuer he refided, he would alwayes be certified by the
locall fuperiours of the Society how all things paffed,
prouiding remedies for all difficulties, no otherwife
then if himfelfe had bin prefent. For at his departure
into *Iaponia* he gaue order, that they fhould at certaine
times write vnto him, & acquaint him what number
there

there were of the Society, as alfo with their qualities, & tallents both of vertue, learning, & arts, yea with their inclinatiós alfo, & to what they were moft addicted, as well by nature as by difpofition; what zeale of foules appeared in ech of them, what fruit euery one reaped, with what griefes or afflictions ech one was oppreffed, tryed, and afflicted. And laftly fo great was his care euen in the fmalleft thinges, that he would be certified of the meaneft houfhould feruant, as alfo what debts were owing, and the like: and fo accordingly he difpofed of ech perfon, and thing in particular by letters, as was requifite. And not contenting himfelf with hauing giuē order what was to be done, he charged alfo the Superiours, to fignify vnto him with all fpeed, whether euery one had carefully performed his commands or no, to the end that his command to them might fet an edge vpon their cares, for the better difcharging of their office.

Moreouer, although in his trauailes throughout the vtmoft Eafterne parts, he bent all his forces for the conuerfion of thofe barbarous Nations, notwithftanding in his returne back, through almoft infinite tracts of the Ocean, he at times vifited thofe of the Society which were committed to his truft, deuiding his care according to his double charge, that he might fo affift ftrangers, as not to be wanting to his owne. Certainly, by his fingular induftry and vertue, he fo contriued all things, that if you confider, how much he aduaunced the Chriftian Religion, he may feeme to haue had no time to think of the Society: & againe if you turne your confideration to the care which he

had

had of the Society, you will thinke, he neither did,
nor could poſſiblyhaue had tyme to performe, any
thing els.

FINIS.

Gentle Reader,

THE faults which haue eſcaped in prin-
ting(by reaſon of imploying ſtrangers
heerin,not skillfull of our Language) I hope
are not very many, nor yet ſuch,as may not
eaſily be corrected,by thy iudicious Reading